MANNERS *and* CUSTOMS *of* MANKIND

MANNERS *and* CUSTOMS *of* MANKIND

An Entirely New Pictorial Work of Great Educational Value
Describing the Most Fascinating Side of Human Life

Edited by

J. A. HAMMERTON

Over Fifteen Hundred Photographic Illustrations from All Over the World—and Twenty-Seven Plates In Color

Volume One

LONDON
THE AMALGAMATED PRESS, LTD.

PUBLISHED IN THE UNITED STATES OF AMERICA BY
WM. H. WISE & CO., NEW YORK

Printed in the U. S. A.

CONTENTS OF VOLUME I

CONTENTS

COLOR PLATES—VOLUME I

MANNERS AND CUSTOMS OF MANKIND

Editorial Foreword

NOT only for its intrinsic fascination, but as an essential part of our education, is the study of human manners and customs worthy of consideration. "The proper study of mankind is man," and the more we know about the habits of life, the customs and observances of other races, the better able are we to appreciate their points of view, to understand their mentality, and to regard them sympathetically as our fellow creatures.

AT most universities there are chairs or lectureships for Anthropology, Ethnology or Ethnography, all doing invaluable work in furthering the proper study of mankind. But these studies provide rather the material for a science yet to be developed than a definite science in being, and among their most eminent exponents agreement of opinion is not yet conspicuous. This condition, however, only enhances the interest of our present survey and is accountable for the richness of our pictorial documentation. For it is always in times of inquiring activity and not of general agreement that instructive data are forthcoming.

WITH unexampled thoroughness of expert examination in association with a collection of actual photographs unrivalled in extent and in perfection of detail, all living types of the world's inhabitants were reviewed in our widely known work *Peoples of All Nations*. But since its publication fresh material illustrative of the manners and customs of the world's races has been rapidly accumulating. To give shape and permanence to this instructive and unhackneyed material is one of the objects of the present entirely new and original work.

NOTHING that appeared in *Peoples of All Nations*, literary or pictorial, finds a place in MANNERS AND CUSTOMS OF MANKIND, which is quite distinct in character and treatment from the earlier work, to which it may be accepted as complementary. Here we are not concerned primarily with the description or illustration of the diverse types of mankind, their costumes and individual peculiarities. We survey the whole world, civilized and savage, concentrating our attention upon the customs and beliefs of social humanity, and seek by comparative study to relate to each other the habits and observances of the most diverse peoples in widely distant regions of the world.

THE methods of comparative anthropology are essentially modern. The era of detached and unrelated studies of tribes and races is past. It crowded our museums with miscellaneous collections of savage handicrafts, weapons of war and the chase, masks and ornaments, which were mere curiosities as individual items, and meaningless until brought into relationship with other "native" objects from other parts of the world. MANNERS AND CUSTOMS OF MANKIND has therefore been planned on the lines of modern ethnological study. First and last our interest concentrates on the existing customs of living races, the historic and the traditional being only incidental to our studies. Although many of our chapters may seem to be detached and individual, it will be found, as the reader pursues his studies of our pages, that all fit into a large and homogeneous scheme. The classified subject index at the end of the work will make this apparent at a glance.

NO such work could have been produced before the war. The necessary photographic illustrations did not exist until within the last eight or ten years. And need we say that without the pictorial appeal no effort at so large and comprehensive a treatment of the subject could ever hope for success. Most of our beautiful and instructive illustrations are reproduced direct from photographs taken by field anthropologists and explorers within the last five years.

UNLIKE most of the large works of general information and specialised instruction published under the same editorship, MANNERS AND CUSTOMS OF MANKIND does not make its appeal with a long list of expert contributors. It has been thought that a work more closely knit and homogeneous would result from the judicious collaboration of various expert writers instead of their acting as isolated contributors. Where each contributor is responsible for his own signed work and at liberty to urge his own personal views the editor is necessarily limited in his efforts to attain unity of the whole, but the plan here followed permits of several writers co-operating even on a single chapter, and the greater editorial freedom in revision makes for a desirable uniformity of treatment.

IT is also worth noting that we are probably preserving here the last records of numerous customs which are dying out. Although dead religions could be named by the score, it has been said, with truth, that no man ever saw a religion die. But many men must have seen ancient customs, or even religious rites, die out. It is astonishing, however, to know that the native practices described in 1900 by Skeat in his "Malay Magic" have so largely disappeared that the investigator in the same field to-day would encounter the greatest difficulty in finding natives capable of demonstrating them: many of the practices having now passed out of native memory.

CHANGE is the watchword in every manifestation of life on this planet, and only by means of the written and pictorial record is it possible to save from oblivion much valuable knowledge of the mind and actions of Man. MANNERS AND CUSTOMS OF MANKIND is offered especially to that large public typified by "the general reader" as an instructive and entertaining work for young and old, and for those who are scientifically interested as teachers or students it furnishes an inexhaustible mine of literary and pictorial matter to which in their specialised studies they will have continual recourse.

J. A. HAMMERTON

G.P.A

Keystone and Sport & General Press Agency

RACIAL INDIVIDUALITY CONCEALED BY SARTORIAL MONOTONY

Mass production and easy distribution of articles of clothing are leading to the universal adoption of European dress. Here are shown a Cantonese bride and bridegroom as attired for their wedding at Boston and, beside them, three members of the Japanese Diet wearing Western evening dress for a banquet at Kyoto. Mustapha Kemal Pasha (top left) advertises his Westernising policy in Turkey by requiring like attire at social functions, and even in the negro republic of Liberia the women flock to buy the latest European fashionable wear that reaches Monrovia.

Introductory Chapter

ON THE VARIETY OF HUMAN MANNERS AND CUSTOMS

by R. R. Marett, D.Sc., LL.D.

In this chapter Dr. Marett sets forth the methods practised and the objects kept in view by modern anthropologists, among whom, as Reader in Social Anthropology at the University of Oxford, he occupies an eminent place. Lucid and complete, its brevity notwithstanding, the chapter furnishes an admirable introduction to this work as a whole, deftly suggesting its great educational value.

SOLITARY confinement agrees with no man. Why, then, remain a prisoner when it is possible to range the wide world with a free intelligence and an open heart? Anthropology is the higher gossipry. It means literally 'talking about people'; and there can be no harm in such a practice so long as it simply bespeaks a friendly interest in one's neighbours. Over and above the sheer intellectual fun of surveying humanity at large, there is unlimited moral gain to be got in the enlarged consciousness of the fact that man is of one kind—that as a species we are near enough to each other in our type of mind to share all the thoughts and feelings most worth having. Moreover, whereas a good deal of our morality involves the disagreeable necessity of holding oneself in, the development of kindliness on a world-wide scale simply requires that we should let ourselves go. There is a latent power of sympathy in us all in virtue of our mating and herding instincts: and to quicken it into full activity is the secret of human happiness, since in no other way can self-realization be achieved in so positive and ample a form.

There must, however, be method in our study of the diverse ways of mankind. Thus it is no use to trudge through endless galleries if one does not know how to look at pictures. To see a picture as a coloured board or canvas is not enough, since it must be apprehended and appreciated for what it truly is, namely, a creation of mind, the outward expression of the artist's inward yearning for beauty. So, too, then, the mere surface-view of human manners and customs can yield nothing illuminating, and many a globe-trotting sightseer comes back no wiser than he went away. Strange customs must be interpreted in terms of their underlying motives; though if this is done thoroughly most of the strangeness will be found to disappear in the process. Difficult as it may be to part with settled convictions about the general unreasonableness of foreign ways, a little reflection will make it plain that all human beings are striving, each after his own fashion, not only to live but to live well. Living however, is an experimental affair, and of the numberless experiments that make up the history of our race a great many were bound to prove unsuccessful. Yet the worst failures leave no record; so that we can reckon on having to do with at least partial successes, whichever way we look among known peoples, including even the most backward in culture. The humblest of them has hit upon a good thing or two, and so has managed to keep in the running.

Making due allowance, then, for the particular conditions, the judicious observer will always find something to admire—nay, more to admire than to blame—in any and every attempt of man to be master

Photopress

DIM INTIMATIONS OF IMMORTALITY

Grotesque as these crude animal forms appear, they have an intrinsic significance that cannot be overestimated. The Baluba tribe of the Belgian Congo believe them to be the abode of the spirits of the dead and keep them supplied with food and drink, thus demonstrating their participation in a belief in an after-life for which parallels are found in all primitive faiths

of his own fate. There is a magnificent hopefulness to be discerned in all the strivings of this importunate creature, who as he emerges out of the mirk of the far past is already scheming to work wonders—to confer immortality on his dead, to command fertility of nature, and so on. No facts are so hard that he does not seek to trick them into conformity with his visionary demands. Sole adventurer among the animals, he is ever ready to treat the unfamiliar as a manifestation of the divine, and is justified in so doing by the fresh access of vitality which a richer experience brings in its train. It is his prerogative to convert mere cosmic process into a progress. He can affirm and will into being certain values which, though revealed gradually and always in response to much groping in the dark, are for him the most real thing in life—far more real than the passive conditions that must be overcome and transformed before his dream can come true.

This, then, is the only way in which to take an intelligent interest in human history—not to regard it as a cinematograph show, a moving pageant of diverting antics, but as the progressive triumph of spirit over matter. Slowly and painfully, but none the less surely, mankind has been fulfilling a creative mission in evolving out of a welter of blind instincts a 'kingdom of ends'—an organized life-scheme centred on a supreme good comprising truth, beauty and righteousness, the three in one. No one can afford to be sceptical about this inner meaning attaching to the human struggle for real existence; for, if he denies the good—denies, that is to say, our common interest in the making of it—he deserves to be eliminated. Luckily, however, there has always been plenty of good fighting material in the host of mankind; and never is one more aware of this sterling quality of our race than when contemplating the first beginnings of culture. Every little savage group that keeps its flag flying in the face of the grimmest odds is a forlorn hope entitled to the greatest respect; because at first all is confusion, and it is only by degrees that a battle array is established by forming up on some brave handful that, although unsupported, have managed to make a stand.

Hence, to do full justice to the anthropological outlook—in other words, to consider human history universally and in its true perspective—one must concentrate attention on that evolutionary inspiration—that divine urge for advancement—which lends its sole intrinsic significance to all our actions, and converts what would otherwise be an empty

PALAEOLITHIC MACHINE STILL IN USE TODAY

What has been described as the first machine invented by man of which remains exist was the spear-thrower. Like the wommera of the Australian aborigine it had a notch to receive the spear butt, and it trebled the effective range of a spear. Australian aborigines used it also to make fire, working the edge with a sawing action over the face of a soft wood shield

spectacle into an absorbing drama. At the same time, though this task of building up a moral universe is mightily serious at bottom, life has likewise its lighter side; and, human nature being what it is, it almost looks as if too much earnestness might sometimes defeat its own purpose. Play serves as a preparation for work with the young of many an animal kind. Man has, however, immensely extended the sphere of his recreative activities until they intermingle with every interest of his adult life. There is a curious indirectness about the process whereby the higher culture has been in large part achieved. Many an unpractical pursuit yields solid advantage in the long run. In fact, all work and no play makes not only a dull boy but a stupid man. Human progress has all along owed more to the liberal than to the material arts; in other words, the best way of looking after the body is to cultivate a soul. Science, fine art and even religion, with its symbolic procedure, transport the mind away from the plane of the actual, in the first instance; so that when it has to come down to earth again it feels dissatisfied, and tries change after change in the hope of bringing the existent into closer resemblance with the ideal.

R. St. Barbe Baker

AN EARLY INVENTION OF PRIME UTILITY

Dug-outs go back at least to neolithic times, and even amongst primitive peoples show a high level of craftsmanship. In Southern Nigeria the tree after it has been hollowed is smeared with wet clay and a fire is lighted underneath while it is opened with a series of levers. This is highly skilled work, but the usefulness of the canoe depends largely on its proper execution.

THUS it is not in the direction of the economic life that one must look for most of the extraordinary variety and colour displayed by human institutions as one surveys them in their vast range round about the world and up and down the ages. No doubt there have been devised in more or less direct relation to the food-quest a large number of appliances which are a credit to human intelligence, such as among hunting weapons the boomerang and the spear-thrower, the blow-pipe and the bow. Again, take fire-making—that decisive achievement of man which raised him once for all head and shoulders above the rest of living nature; or the domestication of animals and plants; or the smelting of metals; or inventions so useful in their several ways as the canoe, the cooking-pot, the wheeled vehicle and the plough. Such clearly defined milestones along the highway of nascent civilization imply a tireless application of human ingenuity through long ages to the problem how to make the world a more comfortable place to live in.

Even here, however, where it seems a question of adapting means to ends of obvious utility, one wonders—and in default of definite information about these early victories over the environment one must continue to wonder—how much of the experimentation that led up to these fruitful results was initiated in a spirit of pure play. The poet goes too far when he suggests that 'idle hands' can only work mischief; for both manipulatively and mentally that fondness for fidgeting which we share with the monkeys can stand us in good stead, seeing that, unlike them, we have the good sense to follow up and perpetuate any novel experience that takes our fancy.

MAN, then, in addition to utilitarian instincts that probably could do no more for him than keep him alive at the animal level, has an itch for the superflous. Overbrained as he is, he has mental energy to spare, and can sport with trifles at no risk of vital ineffectiveness. Nay, since the liberation of pent-up energy is pleasant in itself, he is grateful to such relaxations in proportion as they afford him internal peace. Moreover, this discharge on to the play-object is not only soothing but at the same time stimulating, because of the self-revelation involved in bringing latent feelings out into the open. Now, when this happens in real life the agent is too busy with the affair in hand to dwell on the accompanying mental state. In play, however, which is but the mimicry of real life, the thing done hardly matters, and a corresponding mood can be appreciated for its own sake. The appetite for experience grows by thus savouring it consciously.

So we find the typical savage to be a mystic—the very opposite of the modern business man, who must have 'real values' to deal with. An Australian greybeard will wander about the country for days carrying in his hand one of the sacred bull-roarers and 'singing' the grass so that it may be persuaded to grow. No doubt he means it very seriously, but in any case the operation is purely symbolic, and, whatever its influence on the grass, has likewise the more immediate and verifiable effect of making the operator feel 'full of virtue'—a spiritual condition so prized for its uplifting quality that the older men, we are told, are wont to make the acquisition of such experiences the chief interest of their lives. Whereas, however, a trained intellect can enjoy its inner resources in the form of more or less articulate conceptions, the undeveloped mind of the savage must perforce regale itself with crude emotions shot through with but the vaguest thoughts and mostly excited and sustained by vivid sense-impressions. To obtain this thrill of self-awareness the primitive man has recourse to movements, sounds and sights designed expressly to work him up to the pitch required. The whirling dance, the throbbing drum, the grotesque mask are so many stimulants which appeal to him as much for their quantitative as for their qualitative results. Indeed, his sentiment about all such means of stirring up his faculties would probably agree with that of the boatswain in Treasure Island as to choice of wine: 'so it's strong, and plenty of it, what's the odds?'

It remains to note that this characteristically human habit of clarifying and enlarging conscious experience by exercising it in leisure moments on toys and shams is largely social in its origin. It is true that a negative way of inducing ecstatic conditions favourable to the development of a certain kind of self centered personality is to withdraw from the crowd and its distractions; and of this or any other form of voluntary abstinence it can at least be said that it helps to give the will control over the passions. But such aloofness is not congenial to the temperament of the ordinary man, and least of all to that of the ordinary savage, in whom herd feeling amounts to an obsession. His chosen method, therefore, of intensifying his inner man is the positive one of mutual excitation by means of what the Greeks knew as the 'chorus'—the collective ceremony or dance. The result is, no doubt, to produce what is usually known as a group-consciousness; but it must not be forgotten that this exists only in so far as it is individually shared. Because a large part of our education has been acquired in class, it does not follow that we have no right to claim it as our very own. Indeed, all culture is traditional, that is, a social inheritance, as it first comes to us, though we may hope to pass it on to others a little different and better for having been transmitted by way of our minds. Hence a savage cannot be denied to have a private soul because fellow-feeling forms the core of it. Nay, just because this is so, the civilized observer is apt to regard primitive ceremonies as devoid of meaning, not realizing that so long as they engender the sense of fellowship little more is asked of them by the participators, who, after all, are principally concerned in the matter.

When it is a question of a more or less definitely religious rite of the primitive pattern, we should be wrong in assuming any consistent doctrine to underlie the performance. The general nature of the blessing sought may be indicated to some extent by the occasion, as when rain is wanted, or a disease has to be banished, or a marriage must be solemnised, or the dead man laid to rest. But the rich medley of forms that has come down from the past as appropriate to each recurrent situation is, as it were, repeated by rote and without any attempt to make sense of the separate elements of the mystery. It is a common fallacy to suppose that the savage has forgotten what it would be truer to say that he never tried to understand. A play of images sufficiently forcible to arouse by diffused suggestion a conviction that the tribal luck is taking a turn in the required direction is the sum of his theology; and yet the fact remains that a symbolism so gross and mixed can help the primitive man to feel more confident of himself—to enjoy the inward assurance that he is in touch with sources and powers of grace that can make him rise superior to the circumstances and chances of this mortal life.

As regards the persistency with which the human mind clings to any well-tried device for stirring the emotions through the imagination, much is to be learnt from folk lore, a branch of anthropology which has sometimes been defined as the study of survivals. Now it is true that the folk, by which is meant the relatively uncultured and, in particular, unlettered portion of a civilized community, is itself on the way to extinction; so that its customs are necessarily taking the same downward path. Nevertheless, along most of the European countryside and even in parts of America—among the French Canadians, for instance, or the mountain-people of Kentucky—there are remains of an old-world tradition propagated by imitation and word of mouth on which, however secretly, the majority depend for a good deal that gives their life its flavour. Some of it, indeed, can have no other function than to keep alive feelings unworthy of an enlightened society—the fear of witchcraft, for example, and kindred superstitions. Many folk customs, on the other hand, are and have always been quite healthy in their moral tone, and in essence are diversions, providing, as it were, relief from the common round with its

H. A. Bernatzik

CHORIC EXPRESSION OF TRIBAL LAMENTATION: AN AFRICAN DEATH DANCE

Among ordinary savages herd feeling amounts to an obsession, and it is in the mutual excitation of the collective ceremony or dance that they find most easily satisfaction of their own individual crude emotions. Tribal dances serve many purposes, religious, bellicose and social, and study of them richly repays the anthropologist. Here we see a death dance of the Tonga branch of the Shilluk tribe, one detail of which—the carrying of the spear head downwards—has its parallel among civilized peoples in the bearing of arms reversed at military funerals.

soul-destroying because all-too-absorbing insistence on the needs of physical existence. Whereas a misguided puritanism once dealt hardly with maypoles and the like, it might as well have declared that Milton's poetry was pernicious fooling, because it sought a wider horizon by mounting on the wings of fancy.

The same kill-joy attitude towards many a perfectly harmless institution of the savage is to be noticed to-day among ourselves, who profess to be engaged in improving his condition and, on the whole, may be taken to mean what we say. Clearly, if he loses more spiritually than he gains materially, we shall have failed in our mission. Our only chance, however, of making a new and better man of him is to leave his highest values intact, so that by preserving this foundation we can build solidly upward bit by bit. Our first duty as educators, then, is to leave him a play-world of his own. It is certain that in the past he has found himself chiefly in and through his ceremonial life. Let not his future be rendered as drab as that of many a drudge of civilization by cutting him off his spiritual holidays, which he has a right to spend just how he himself chooses.

Let it be agreed, then, that spiritually it takes all sorts, as the saying is, to make a world. Difference is not incompatible with unity, but, on the contrary, a diversity of elements yields the richer harmony. On the economic plane we are gradually moving towards a relative uniformity of conditions. The time has gone by when each people had to make what it could of the material resources nearest to hand. Widened communications have facilitated the distribution of the means of life until there prevail common standards of comfort such as are bound to provoke a no less universal demand for their satisfaction. Even the differentiation of habits imposed by climate has been largely counteracted in the modern world by ingenious protection of the body; so that, in its physical aspect, human life throughout the globe is threatened with a certain stupefying sameness. All the more reason, then, is there to give free scope to our natural variability on the side of the spirit.

In this direction there are always discoveries to be made, new worlds to conquer. Whether in science, or in art, or in religion, which at its best should comprise all the higher interests of life, the mind is not merely exploring experience but is literally creating it. Here lies the true work of man: having secured his modest place in the sun, to devote all the rest of his superabundant energy to accommodating himself

H. A. Barentzik

G.P.A.

SYMBOLISM THAT STIMULATES THE GROWTH OF THE NATIVE SOUL

To the unintelligent onlooker many of the customs of savage races may appear merely as so many diverting antics, but they lose much of their oddity if the motive underlying them is discerned. Even the grotesque tricks of such fantastic creatures as these masked and tailed medicine men of a Congo tribe are pathetic efforts at communication with the divine; and there is ritual significance in the Shilluk doctor's care (top) to provide a hole in the ground into which the blood he has drawn from his patient's scalp may flow.

Topical Press Agency

OLD PAGAN CUSTOMS THAT STILL SURVIVE IN ENGLAND

In the west of England at the New Year the people go round the orchards and wassail the apple trees. A solemn incantation is addressed to the trees to make them fruitful, guns are fired to drive away evil spirits, and toast soaked in cider is hung on the trees to propitiate the robins. Another widespread custom is that of choosing a May Queen. At Rushton (top) the ceremony includes carrying her in procession to the village well, where a thanksgiving service is held. Frowned upon at one time as essentially pagan, such customs now receive clerical support.

Keystone

MODERN SYMPATHY WITH PAGAN LIFE: MISSIONARY IMPERSONATES A MEDICINE MAN

Missionaries have always had exceptional opportunities for studying the customs of the people among whom they worked. At one time there was a tendency to interfere somewhat drastically with practices that offended the susceptibilities of civilized races, but a wiser policy is now pursued, and save where they are positively baneful, tribal customs are interfered with as little as possible. A missionary is here shown giving an impersonation at a Congo exhibition in London of a Congo medicine man conducting a ceremony

within that region of inner light where he can live so much more spaciously.

The upshot of such considerations would seem to be that we should be tolerant of variety in human affairs and suffer strangers gladly. Behaviour, however odd it may seem, must be judged by its intention. First impressions of the meaning of a kindly act are often misleading, as when by way of salutation a savage sheds tears, or offers to rub noses, or actually spits in one's face. Given tact and a sense of humour it is always possible to adapt oneself to the local code of correct manners; and it is a mark of inhumanity to refuse to do so. Or, again, it is sheer impertinence to want to interfere with customs in dress, even if some primitive fashion-plates subordinate concealment to emphasis, as, indeed, do some of our own. Indeed, as regards all matters of taste, one can heartily endorse Kipling's assertion that

'There are nine and sixty ways of constructing tribal lays.
And every single one of them is right.'

They are right, that is to say, for others, if not for us: essays not to be denied the right of publication because they may or may not find many readers. Any number of vehicles of expression will serve to convey the same message, and it is indifferent which of them is used so long as the meaning comes through with sufficient clearness. Just as one can learn to think in more than one language, and by so doing become all the more competent to distinguish sense from sound, so acquaintance with different cultural conventions helps the mind to detach essential values from their casual context and to measure them by the sole value of their intrinsic worth.

At this point, however, one will be reminded that there is an evolutionary process—that even of ideals it is true that only the fittest survive. Granting this, one may at the same time insist that the evolutionary principle be interpreted correctly. Thus, the so-called 'unilinear' version of it is quite out of date. We human beings are not advancing in one long line up a beaten track. Rather we are thrown out like skirmishers along a wide front, making for an unspecified objective, but obeying a general order to go forward. In these circumstances it is hard to say which part of the line is ahead of the rest, since rapid movement will not make up for loss of direction. In practice we look back over our shoulders to count the dead, and decide that the least dangerous track will lead us farthest. Meanwhile, it cannot be said that it is reserved for the big battalions to make real progress, since imposing civilizations in the past have been overwhelmed in sudden and wholesale disaster.

To assume, then, that we are culturally and even racially the dominants destined to lead the species to final victory is decidedly premature. Certain it is that mechanical aids will not compensate in the long run for lack of morale, which perhaps is not our most conspicuous asset. Have we solved the marriage problem ? Do we know how to educate the young ? Can we produce intelligent government, or a noble art ? Does our religion concentrate on essentials ? That we can propound such questions to ourselves in a spirit of sincere self-criticism is perhaps the most hopeful sign of the times. But such recognition of the need of putting our own house in order carries with it an obligation to be chary in passing moral judgement on our neighbours, even when from our position in the line they seem to be hanging back. We have seen reason to concede them a right to their own manners. How far, then, can we extend the same privilege to their morals ?

Hard saying though it may be, it looks as if it might be better for all, including ourselves, to treat ethics as an experimental science and, within limits necessary for the common safety, to allow and even encourage a diversity of moral institutions. Indeed on grounds of policy only the British Empire has to treat on a more or less equal footing distinct and even rival religions, systems of law, and so on. While policy approves, need conscience protest ? Surely if it be allowed that morality, or religion, or law, or any other scheme of values evolves or has a history at all, then it follows that alternative possibilities should be thrashed out if the selective process is to be thorough. As we are prepared to advise our neighbours, so let us be ready to take a hint from them on occasions. Even the so-called savage—a word which originally had the innocent meaning of 'wood lander'—is not a mere Caliban, but can sometimes provide so edifying an example of the simple life that sympathetic observers such as Alfred Russel Wallace are set wondering whether it is possible to be both civilized and good. Even when primitive ways appear at first sight less edifying than shocking, as, for example, when we come across customs of courtship and marriage highly offensive to our taste it is well to look carefully into the facts, when we may well be led to view the matter in a new light. Thus, we are horrified to hear of a savage buying his wife. When it turns out, however, that by means of what is misnamed the bride-price he is simply purchasing the right to enrol the woman's children in his own clan, the practice seems reasonable enough ; and one is perhaps led on to take to heart the old-world view that the end of marriage is to have a family.

So much, then, by way of introduction to a series of pictures that show our race engaged in some of their most striking and characteristic attempts to transcend the level of brute existence—to snatch a grace from their life by investing it with meaning as the pursuit of a spiritual good. To realize how much steadfast trial and bewildering error went to the discoveries embodied in each custom here reported is beyond the reach of any imagination. Yet everyone can at least study the human record with a proud sense of the pluck and determination that have carried mankind along from strength to strength, eternally dissatisfied, eternally hopeful.

H. A. Bernatzik

PRIMITIVE NOTION OF PERSONAL ADORNMENT

Puritans who profess to be shocked by the scanty costume of savage tribes should remember that dress designed to display and emphasise, rather than to conceal, physical charms is not a monopoly of uncivilized peoples, but may be observed in any European capital.

Mondiale

DEAD WINTER'S LAST JOURNEY BEFORE THE COMING OF LIFE-GIVING SPRING

At Helpa, in Slovakia, one of the ceremonies connected with the coming of spring goes by the name of 'burying Death.' Here Death stands not for death as it comes to mortals, but for winter, the season of decay and death in the fields. A dummy is made and dressed up as winter, and this is carried aloft in procession through the district, so that all who run may see winter's last journey and know that spring is at hand. The funeral procession accomplished, the effigy is 'buried' by being thrown into a river. The processionists and peasants then dance to welcome spring, nature's glad season of life. As a general rule a girl of the district is chosen to take the part of spring.

SURVIVING CUSTOMS OF SPRINGTIDE

We deal here with a few only of the more typical springtide customs still surviving among the races of the world. Other chapters examine closely related customs, as, for example, those on British folk-dances and on Lenten observances and Holy Week; but the most important further studies touching springtide customs will be found in our chapters on May Day and the Carnival.

In this mechanical age man has tried to systematise even the seasons. Thanks to the ingenious Mr. Willett we have, since 1916, begun our summer in the middle of spring. Ignoring the divisions of the tropical year, according to which summer starts in the present year at nine o'clock on June 22, we shall gallantly put our clocks forward an hour on Sunday, April 19, and pretend that the summer has come. Among springtide customs this putting on of the clocks may be regarded as the very latest innovation. The system has been adopted from us by both France and Belgium.

Under this arrangement, whereby spring may begin officially as early as two o'clock on March 21, the season is shorn of its full complement of days. In the country, however, all almanacs are still held suspect, and the rural labourer, in spite of the wireless in his cottage, will maintain that spring has not arrived until he can cover nine daisies with his boot. Even in our cities the calendar is ignored, and the old habit of regarding spring as the natural beginning of the year can still be traced in the fact that the financial year ends in March and not on December 31. The Old Slavs still begin their New Year in March.

In the western world the Great War played havoc with ancient customs, but so deep-rooted in the past is the mind of man that many of them still survive. And they all have a common origin. In the primitive days of the world man was early impressed by his economic surroundings. If in the hunting age there were no animals he could pursue, he must die; if in the pastoral age the harvest failed, then he would suffer. He was entirely dependent upon the powers of nature. To secure that those powers should continue and operate, he endowed an animal, or a sheaf of corn, or another man, with these powers to preserve them and carry them on from one spring to another.

Inevitably this rite, so simple in its origin, became elaborated. The being who embodied the creative spirit of nature was treated as human. He must decay and die, and in the process the incarnate spirit might be lost—with disastrous consequences. It therefore became the custom to detach the divine life by the simple process of killing its incarnate embodiment and transferring the vernal force to a vigorous successor. A striking instance of this custom, according to Frazer, is to be found in a rite of Ancient Rome surviving at the sanctuary of Diana Nemorensis on the northern shore of Lake Nemi. The priest of this sanctuary was known as the King of the Wood—the incarnation of vernal life—and led a harassing and unpleasant existence, because anybody who could kill him assumed at once his powers and authority

Christianity, unable to destroy this rite, robbed it of its bloodthirsty aspect. The representative of the spirit of spring was no longer killed in order to promote and quicken the growth of vegetation, but was simply subjected to a form of physical violence. Here is an illustration of how the myth and the rite survive. At Schluckenau, in Bohemia, at Shrovetide the Wild Man is dressed up in the bark of trees—bark being essential to the life of a tree—and, pursued by a crowd, is driven down a narrow lane. Across this lane a rope is drawn, over which he trips. As soon as he is down he is assailed by the crowd, who burst the bladders of blood he carries beneath his clothing. The spilling of the blood on the ground completes the rite for that day. The following day a straw man, made up to

Karl Dornach

MASKS TO GREET THE SPRING

These grotesque figures are villagers of Imst, in Tirol, taking part in one of the festivals that are so common in many parts of Austria in early spring. Masks such as they are wearing are a striking feature of the paraphernalia of these festivals.

Mondiale

PAGAN RITES OF SPRING THAT LINGER ON IN CHRISTIAN EUROPE

In several Austrian villages, especially in Tirol, the first days of spring are ushered in with festivals, which, pagan in their origin, have in their passage down the centuries shed little of their pagan colour. Those taking part dress up in quaint costumes and elaborate masks, and parade the streets with much dancing and merriment, carrying out a personification of winter and bringing in one of spring, the latter a young girl tricked out in gay finery. The upper photograph shows a group of masked dancers at Imst. in Tirol, the lower a festival parade at Telfs.

look like the Wild Man, is placed in a litter and taken to a pool, into which it is thrown. This custom is known as 'Burying the Carnival.'

A similar custom prevails in the Pilsen district of Bohemia and with local variations elsewhere. At Lerida, in Catalonia, the Funeral of Carnival used, until recently, to be attended by a grand procession of infantry and cavalry. The effigy in this case is known as His Grace Pau Pi. At the place of interment all lights are extinguished, and immediately certain members of the crowd, dressed as the devil and his angels, dart from the press seize the remains and fly with them, hotly pursued by the mob. The body having been rescued from the Satanic clutches, is duly laid in a grave and the rite closes. In Provence, on Ash Wednesday, an effigy called Caramantran is brought in procession to the principal square, tried, sentenced to death, and, after being stoned, is thrown into the sea or river. In the Ardennes, too, on Ash Wednesday, the Carnival is burned and buried, a young man sometimes taking the place of the effigy and going through a form of execution by being fired at with blank cartridges. This latter practice, however, was stopped when a young man was accidentally killed by a wad from a blank cartridge

SPRING IN HER PRIDE UNTOUCHED BY WINTER'S FATE

Springtide customs vary widely, but in many places it is the practice, before the genial season can be fitly welcomed, to dispose of winter in a more or less violent manner—for instance, by burning. In the part of the procession depicted here of a spring festival at Zürich, spring, in the person of a young damsel, is being carried shoulder-high, while the fate of winter is the flames

In the neighbourhood of Tübingen, on Shrove Tuesday, a straw man called the Shrovetide Bear is made up. He is dressed in a pair of old trousers, and a fresh black pudding or two squirts filled with blood are inserted in his neck. After a trial he is laid in a coffin, and on Ash Wednesday is buried in the churchyard. Among some of the Saxons in Transylvania the Carnival is hanged. In Swabia and in the Hartz mountains the resurrection of the pretended dead person is ritually suggested.

A variation of the 'Burying of Carnival' is the ceremony known as 'Carrying out Death.' It is always followed by a rite suggesting the bringing in of summer, spring, or life. Death goes, and spring comes. In Poland, near Gross-Strehlitz, the effigy is called Goik, and is carried on horseback to the nearest water and there thrown in. In Upper Silesia the effigy, known by the name of Marzana, is made in the house where the last death occurred, and is duly burnt or drowned in mid-Lent. In some districts in Silesia it is the practice to throw the ill-omened figure over the boundary of the next village, the inhabitants of which are on the look-out to prevent the outrage.

In certain German villages of Moravia the straw man is hoisted on a pole and carried

Mondiale

KNEES BEND AND HANDS JOIN HANDS IN MAZY DANCE

Though it is by no means always a sign of joy, dancing very often forms an important part of the gay ceremonies used for welcoming spring. Some of the dances performed on such occasions are purely natural, while others reach the limit of complicated formations. The photograph shows a party of Swedes going through the evolutions of one of these intricate dances.

E N.A

CELEBRATING WINTER'S DEATH WITH A BIG BLAZE

The spring ceremony of 'burning winter' is common throughout Germany and Switzerland, and is seen to particular advantage in the Black Forest and at Zürich. An effigy of winter, made of wool or some other inflammable material, is placed on a funeral pyre and ceremoniously burnt. The festival takes place on the second Monday after Easter, and is known as the Fest des Sechselautens. It gets its name from the fact that clocks, which during the winter have struck the vesper hour at five o'clock, now for the first time strike it at six.

by the lads and lasses into the open fields. During the procession they sing a song telling how they are carrying Death away and bringing dear summer into the house, and with summer, the May and the flowers. On reaching an appointed place they dance in a circle round the effigy, and then suddenly rush at it and tear it to pieces with their hands. Lastly the pieces are thrown together in a heap, the pole is broken, and fire is set to the whole. In some parts of Lusatia women alone are concerned in 'carrying out Death,' and suffer no male to meddle with it. After the effigy has been torn to pieces they take the shirt with which it has been draped and hang it on a tree which they have cut down. This last piece of ritual symbolises the revivification in a new form of the destroyed effigy—just as the King of the Wood, having been killed, transferred his virtues to his assailant.

THE Death, in these springtime ceremonies which are to be met with in Transylvania and Moravia, is really the principle of life. The ascription of life-giving virtue to the figure of Death is put beyond a doubt by the custom observed in Spachendorf, among other places, of taking pieces of the straw effigy and placing them in the fields to make the crops grow, or in the manger to make the cattle thrive. Further reference will be made to the prevalence of this myth in our chapter dealing with May-day ceremonies.

Throughout the world we find that the springtide customs invariably include the idea of this struggle between the forces of deadening winter and awakening spring. The struggle is pictured in different ways at different times, but it is now in Europe merely a dramatic performance. Among the central Esquimaux of North America, however, the rite is kept up as a magical ceremony. In the Kanagra district of India there is a custom observed by young girls in spring, closely resembling the European spring ceremony. It is called the Rali Ka mela, or the fair of Rali, the Rali being a small, painted, earthen image of Siva, or Parvati. The celebration, confined to young girls, lasts through most of March into the middle of April. On an appointed morning all the young girls of the village take small baskets of dub grass and flowers, which they throw into a heap. Round this heap they stand in a circle and sing. This goes on every day for ten days till the heap of grass and

Col. F. D. Fayrer

Mondiale

UNVEILED WOMEN AND DRESSED-UP DOLLS IN INDIAN FESTIVAL OF THE YOUTH OF THE YEAR

The festival of the dolls, which takes place in early spring in Udaipur, Rajputana, is the only Indian festival in which women may take part It is also one of the rare occasions when the Maharana (a sacred person to the Hindus) is seen in public. From morning until night the women gather in the streets and line the banks of Lake Pichola, on which stands His Highness's palace. Almost every woman carries a doll (bottom). After riding through the town on an elephant the Maharana is rowed round the lake in the state barge (top), and then returns to seclusion

G. Krull

SPRINGTIDE PROCESSION IN BRITTANY FOR THE BLESSING OF THE FIELDS

In few places do we find tradition kept so green as in Brittany, that land of folk song and story and age-old customs. The Breton is passionately devoted to his little shut-in corner of the world, and is strongly opposed to change. Although large areas of Brittany are unfit for cultivation, the well-watered valleys are amazingly fertile. Here we see a procession of devout Bretons winding like a great snake through the sun-illumined landscape. They are taking part in the time-honoured ceremony of blessing the fields, to the end that they may be fruitful.

flowers has reached a fair height. Then they cut in the jungle two branches, each with three prongs at one end, and place them prongs downward over the heap of flowers so as to make two tripods or pyramids. On the single uppermost point of these branches they get an image-maker to construct two clay images, one to represent Siva, and one Parvati. The girls then divide themselves into two parties—one for Siva and one for Parvati, and marry the images in the usual way, leaving out no part of the ceremony. At the next Sankrant they all go together to the riverside, throw the images into a deep pool, and weep over the place as though they were performing funeral obsequies. The object of the ceremony is said to be to secure a good husband.

The marriage of these Indian deities in spring corresponds to the European ceremonies we have noticed. The throwing of the images into the water and the mourning for them are the equivalents of the European customs of throwing the dead spirit of vegetation under the name of Death into the water and lamenting over it. Again in India, as often in Europe, the rite is performed exclusively by females. In Central Australia the natives regularly practise magical ceremonies for the purpose of awakening the dormant energies of nature at the approach of what may be called the Australian spring.

To produce the rain which can alone turn their deserts into a verdant landscape, the natives go through a curious ceremony reminiscent of the performance given by the priests of Baal. First they build a special hut. Two men are then bound tightly by the arm and with a sharp flint they are cut until the blood flows freely. Handfuls of down intended to represent the clouds are thrown on the blood, which signifies rain, or the vernal spirit. In Russia, where such rites have been stamped out by the Soviet Government, there were endless variations of a similar ceremony

One of the most interesting of these spring festivities of productiveness and rejuvenation is the Festival of the Dolls at Udaipur. Though the State is perhaps the most orthodox in India the primitive customs, as in Christian Europe, cut right across the religious tradition. The women who for the rest of the year are purdah and are kept in strict seclusion, on this day in early spring throng the streets from early morning to nightfall. They gather on the banks of the beautiful lake Pichola, whose waters reflect the

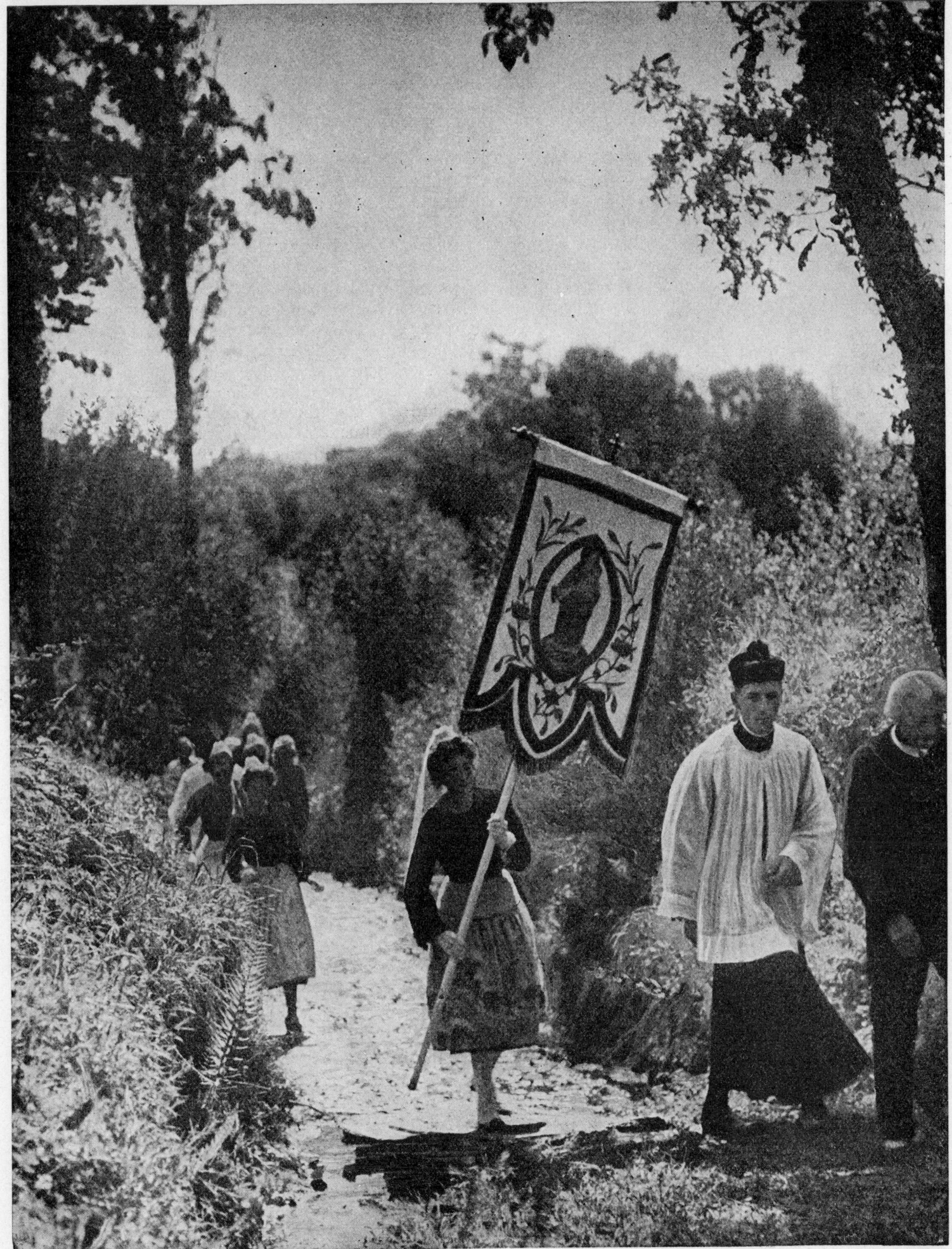

G. Krull

WHERE MUD AND WATER ARE NO STUMBLING BLOCKS TO PIETY

No difficulties or discomforts can daunt the Breton when he is set upon carrying cut a duty. If part of the route of a religious procession happens to be under water, that is no reason, to his thinking, for altering the route. The procession has always passed that way, therefore it is unthinkable that it should go any other way. Whether ankle-deep in mud or water, or on firm ground, the procession continues its accustomed course, for the fields have been blessed by the priests in the spring from time immemorial.

architectural wonders of the palace of the Maharana. Almost every woman carries a doll of some kind, from a rag one to the most elaborately dressed toy. The great moment of the festival is when the Maharana embarks in his state barge. It is the only occasion on which his subjects see him at a recognizable distance during the year, for the Maharana, claiming descent from the Roman Caesars, is of such high degree that he lives his life in almost perfect seclusion. Guarded by nobles of high rank, with brilliantly equipped officials clearing a way through the town, His Highness, on a gaily caparisoned elephant, approaches the lake side, where the women with their dolls are collected.

THE spirit of spring, typified by the Tree Spirit and the Corn Spirit, is also represented in springtide customs by the ox. At Great Bassam, in New Guinea, two oxen are slain annually to procure a good harvest. If the sacrifice is to be effectual it is necessary that the oxen should weep All the women in the village sit in front of the beasts chanting ' The ox will weep; yes, he will weep.' From time to time one of the women walks round the beasts, throwing manioc meal or palm wine upon them, especially into their eyes. When tears roll down from the eyes of the oxen the people dance, singing, ' The ox weeps, the ox weeps.' Then two men seize the tails of the beasts and cut them off with one blow. The oxen are afterwards killed and their flesh eaten by the chiefs.

In China, also, the ox figures in the springtide ceremonies. On the first day in spring, usually on the 3rd and 4th of February, which is also the beginning of the Chinese New Year, the governor or prefect of the city goes in procession to the east gate of the city and sacrifices to the Divine Husbandman, who is represented with a bull's head on the body of a man. A large effigy of a cow or buffalo has been prepared for the occasion and stands outside of the east gate with agricultural implements beside it. The figure is made of differently coloured pieces of paper pasted on a framework either by a blind man or according to the directions of a necromancer. The colours of the paper prognosticate the character of the coming year ; if red prevails there will be many fires; if white there will be floods and rains; and so with the other colours. The mandarins walk slowly round the ox, beating it severely at each step with rods of various hues. It is filled with five kinds of grain, which pour forth when the effigy is broken by the blows of the rods. The paper fragments are then set on fire and a scramble takes place for the burning fragments, because the people believe that whoever gets one will be fortunate throughout the year. A live buffalo is then killed and its flesh is divided among the mandarins. According to one account the effigy of the ox is made of clay, and after being beaten by the governor is stoned by the people till they break it in pieces, ' from which they expect an abundant

Topical

FOOTBALL WITH GOALS A QUARTER OF A MILE APART

From time immemorial a special game of football has been played on Shrove Tuesday at Alnwick, in Northumberland. The hale (goal) posts are a quarter of a mile apart, and are decked with evergreens. The game is played on pasture land between townsmen of the parishes of St. Michael and St. Paul, with a ball provided by the Duke of Northumberland. Hundreds take part. After the game proper is over the ball is kicked off and becomes the property of the player who takes it over certain boundaries, of which one is the river Aln.

A TIME-HONOURED BALL GAME WITH WATER MILLS FOR GOALS

Every Shrove Tuesday a game of football takes place at Ashbourne, in Derbyshire, a custom which can be traced back for six centuries. It is played between the Up-towners and the Down-towners—the 'Uppies' and the 'Downies'—and lasts from noon till dusk. The distance between the goals is three miles, and the goals themselves are water mills. The ball is made of stout hide stuffed with cork shavings. Some of the players, who in all number at least five hundred, are here seen tussling for the ball in the brook.

year.' Here the Corn Spirit appears to be plainly represented by the corn-filled ox, whose fragments may be supposed to bring fertility with them.

In our own country within the memory of people still living are to be found traces of this myth. The Grass King, the King of the May, Jack o' the Green—these were all so many incarnations of the spirit of spring in vegetation. Cocks were frequently used as embodiments of this Life Spirit, and were brutally done to death at Shrovetide. Absurd as it may seem, it is more than probable that the Christian Church, in its attempt to abolish this cruelty, was responsible for one of the most ridiculous innovations at Court. The cock might embody the vital forces of nature, but it was also the bird which called Peter to repentance. During Lent, therefore, an officer called the King's Cock Crower crowed the hour each night within the precincts of the palace—much to the annoyance of George II, it is said, who thought he was being made fun of.

Less than a hundred years ago in the List of Appointments in the Lord Steward's Department of the Royal Household you will find that of 'Cock and Cryer to Scotland Yard.'

TIME, and the efforts of the Christian Church to adapt deep-rooted pagan customs to its own ritual, have so blurred the line which distinguishes the primitive cult observances from religious ceremonies that it is often difficult to disentangle the one from the other. Throughout the season of Epiphany, the period preceding Lent, and the days of approach to Easter, springtide customs merge with ecclesiastical ceremonial. Again and again through the sacred vestments of the priest there peep, as it were, the old habits of a long-lost race of men, seeking in the darkness of their ignorance for the face of God. We can only note some of the old customs which it is difficult to place in either category.

The most universal is the eating of pancakes on Shrove Tuesday, a custom which must be very ancient, because Shakespeare speaks of being 'fit as a pancake for Shrove Tuesday.' The now well-known ritual of the 'throwing the pancake' in Westminster School is another interesting survival of this old custom. According to the regulations, at 11 a.m. a verger of the Abbey, in his gown, and bearing a silver baton, emerges from the college kitchen followed by the cook of the school, in his white apron, jacket and cap, carrying a pancake. On arriving at the schoolroom door the cook announces himself 'The Cook'; and having entered the schoolroom he advances to the bar which separates the upper school from the lower one, twirls the pancake in the pan, and then tosses it over the bar into the upper school, among a crowd of boys who scramble for the

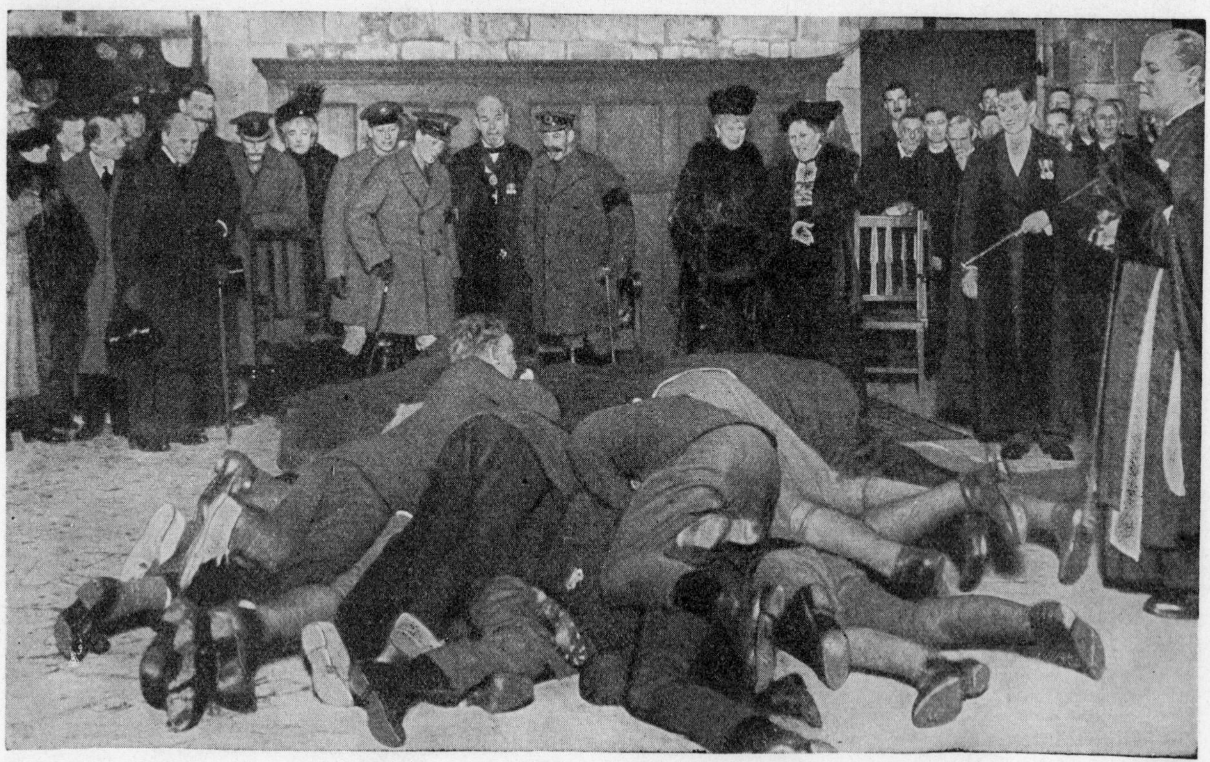

Topical

SCHOOLBOYS STRUGGLING FOR THE LION'S SHARE

A well-known Shrove Tuesday custom at Westminster school is tossing the pancake. At eleven o'clock in the morning one of the Abbey vergers emerges from the school kitchen followed by the cook, who carries a pan containing a single pancake. Having entered the schoolroom, the cook tosses the pancake over the beam in the roof. The pancake is then scrambled for by twenty boys, and the boy who secures it, or who gets the largest piece, is awarded a guinea. King George V and Queen Mary are here seen watching the scramble.

pancake. The one who gets it unbroken and carries it to the Deanery demands the honorarium of a guinea —sometimes two guineas—from the Abbey Funds. The cook receives two guineas for his performance.

Of all the strange Shrovetide customs which survive in England the strangest and most interesting are the traditional games of football still played in Derbyshire, Northumberland and Scotland. In his classic work on the 'History of Rugby Football' the Rev. Frank Marshall not only gives a description of these games in detail, but claims that 'the Romans, who occupied this island during the first four centuries of the Christian era, played at a game called Harpastum (introduced from Greece and deriving its origin in all probability from remote times), which presented the special features of carrying the ball and the scrummage, found in no other modern game of football, save the Rugby game; that it can be traced back to Roman times when a game of football was played in Britain, and that as far as can be gathered from tradition all games then played were characterised by much carrying and little kicking of the ball. It can also be concluded that the game of ball—passing under the various names of "football," "hurling," "camp-ball," and the like—has always been a popular sport with the low orders of society, and though such games have differed from each other they all concurred in being "carrying games."'

Whether there is any foundation for giving Rugby football a classic origin or not, the fact remains that on Shrove Tuesday an ancient form of football game is played in several places in England and Scotland. The games that used to be celebrated at Chester and Derby—the latter was supposed to commemorate the defeat of a Roman cohort—have been for some years in abeyance. These football revels still take place at Ashbourne in Derbyshire between the Up-towners and Down-towners—at Alnwick, where the porter of the Castle throws out a football to be struggled for by the young men of the neighbourhood—at Hawick, where it is now played between the parishes of St Michael's and St Paul's, the rival factions being divided into East and West, and he who 'hales' it beyond a particular point at the end of a town receiving a reward in cash—and at Chester-le-Street in Durham, where the struggle for the ball, beginning in the main street, ends in the burn.

At no season of the year so much as with the approach of spring do the ancient aspirations of Man show themselves in his descendants. With the coming of spring a shadowy familiar takes his place by our sides, and we catch a glimpse, amidst the fret and fever of modern life, of the lineaments of that 'King of the Wood' who embodied the vernal principle of nature.

TABLE MANNERS, PRIMITIVE AND POLISHED

PROBABLY no common practice is more diversified than the familiar one of eating in company, for what Europeans consider as correct and decent may by other races be looked upon as wrong or indelicate. Similarly, few social observances provide more opportunities for offending the stranger than the etiquette of the table The ceremonial aspects of food and its preparation are dealt with in other chapters

IN the matter of its meals, modern society is tending to become increasingly cosmopolitan. This is apparent not only in the dishes composing the meal, for which the material and method of preparation come from far and wide, but also in the elaborated service and equipment of the table. It is producing a common standard of manners which overrides racial and local peculiarities. In addition, although it has a ritual of its own in the proper management of table appointments, it is gradually eliminating observances which, as survivals, preserved a memory of the character of the common meal as a ceremonial occasion and something more than the mere opportunity for providing sustenance for the body. Many of these observances, if they occur at all, are now reserved for formal occasions, or are found among societies which pride themselves on their reverence for tradition, such as the colleges of our universities

Notwithstanding the weakening of ritual on ordinary occasions, the urge to express a common sentiment, or to give form to a common purpose through a meal eaten in company with others, is still a potent factor in the organization of modern society. A dinner, or lunch, or, more rarely in these days, a breakfast is still a usual method of initiating an enterprise and marking its successful conclusion, or of celebrating a memorable occasion, whether in the life of an individual or an organization. Even while admitting the obvious fact that such reunions now have for their aim the promotion of fellowship or merely of conviviality, it must be remembered that this method of attaining the feeling of solidarity essential to the well-being and continuance of an association, however restricted or extended it may be, has a long pedigree in the history of social and religious ritual. Club dinners and Freemasons' banquets have their counterparts in ancient Greece and Rome and far beyond, while their prototypes may be found in the feasts for the dead or the sacrificial ritual of some of the simplest forms of primitive society.

GOOD manners have their foundation in a respect for the feelings of others. Above all is this true of the table ; but as to what will give rise to feelings of disgust there will be considerable variation according to circumstances. Readers of Dickens will recall a particularly disgusting and, as the author calls it, 'juicy' instance on a Mississippi steamer which annoyed Martin Chuzzlewit, but passed without remark by other passengers. Physical relief of a feeling of repletion after a meal which would nauseate us is taken as a compliment in the East and among primitive peoples. The Macedonian or Moroccan host, for instance, would regard it almost as an insult if his guest failed to express gratification at his entertainment by eructation after the meal. Among the ancients, we know that the Romans actually made special provision to enable guests to eat more than nature intended. Pliny tells us, in describing his villa, of the *vomitorium* to which the guests were expected to retire between the courses of the long, and too ample, Roman dinner. Often, by tickling the throat with a feather, they rid themselves of the earlier courses and returned to the table to resume their gorging. In Egypt representations of the

E.N.A.

WIELDING THE 'NIMBLE ONES'

For the inexperienced user of chopsticks any implements less suitable for conveying food to the mouth it is difficult to imagine According to Chinese records they have been used for four thousand years. The Chinese call them the 'nimble ones.'

BEER-DRINKING IN COMPANY IN GERMANY

The Bockbier festival in Berlin is a well-known instance of convivial drinking. The restaurants are filled with light-hearted customers, who celebrate the occasion with uproarious merriment. The beer is served in earthenware jugs, and white radishes are eaten to stimulate thirst. The festival, though so popular in Berlin, is actually a people's festa imported from Bavaria

banquets of the Pharaohs show that not only did the ladies of the court indulge in wine to the point of intoxication, but that maids were specially detailed to administer to the needs of those whose digestions were not equal to their indulgence.

That fingers were made before forks is an aphorism that is borne out by the development of table implements. Among primitive meat-eating peoples, each man roasts for himself on wooden spits or skewers the slices of meat that have been hacked from the carcase with spears. The spit, or skewer, serves as both dish and fork for the meat, from which pieces are bitten or torn.

In the East, and in the Moslem world generally, food is taken with the right hand from a common dish or bowl. On more formal occasions and among the better classes the meal is served on a small and low table, usually of ebony or some dark wood ornamented with mother-of-pearl. Around this the guests gather, sitting on the floor with one knee raised, or seated upon low divans. The host, if of high rank, may himself be seated on a divan, but more usually takes his place with his guests on the floor. When the meal has been served, he himself must be the first to begin to eat. In accordance with Moslem principles, the women of the household were not present. This tradition, however, is now breaking down, and since the Young Turk movement, women in Turkey have taken a consistently increasing part in social intercourse.

Each guest, or diner, is supplied with a piece of bread, which serves, if required, as a plate, just as a manchet of bread served our ancestors even to Tudor times. A piece of crust, doubled, is sometimes used to catch and lift a piece of meat from the bowl, much in the manner employed by a skilled user of the Chinese chopsticks. To Europeans, who are careful to avoid allowing the food of another to come into contact with their hands, it seems strange that the host should take from the dish a choice morsel which he offers in his hand to a favoured guest whom he wishes to honour. In Persia he may even place it in his mouth.

This seals the bond implied in the common meal. In East Africa, in the blood-brotherhood ceremony of the Nandi, each of the two participants, at one stage of the ceremony, places a morsel of bread, soaked in the blood of a sacrificed goat, in the mouth of the other.

H. A. Bernatzik

ISLAM'S RITE OF THE COFFEE CUP IN EASTERN EUROPE

Among the Mahomedans to drink coffee with anybody is regarded as a sacred rite of hospitality, a token of peace. The berries are roasted over a charcoal fire, and the coffee is allowed to boil three times and is thickly sugared. The cups are very small. Here we see a party of young Albanian villagers at coffee with their diminutive cups.

American Colony and E N.A.

E N.A

OPEN-AIR EATING HOUSES, SOPHISTICATED AND SIMPLE

The practice of eating and drinking out of doors is conditioned not only by climate but also by racial tendencies. The Continental European rather enjoys the publicity of such meals, whereas the Englishman prefers greater privacy. The lower photograph shows an open-air restaurant in Montmartre. The proprietor of the primitive outdoor restaurant in Jerusalem (top left) is roasting meat on iron spits over a charcoal fire The pilgrims in Sinkiang, China (top right), help themselves, with their fingers, to pilau out of the great bowl in which it is cooked.

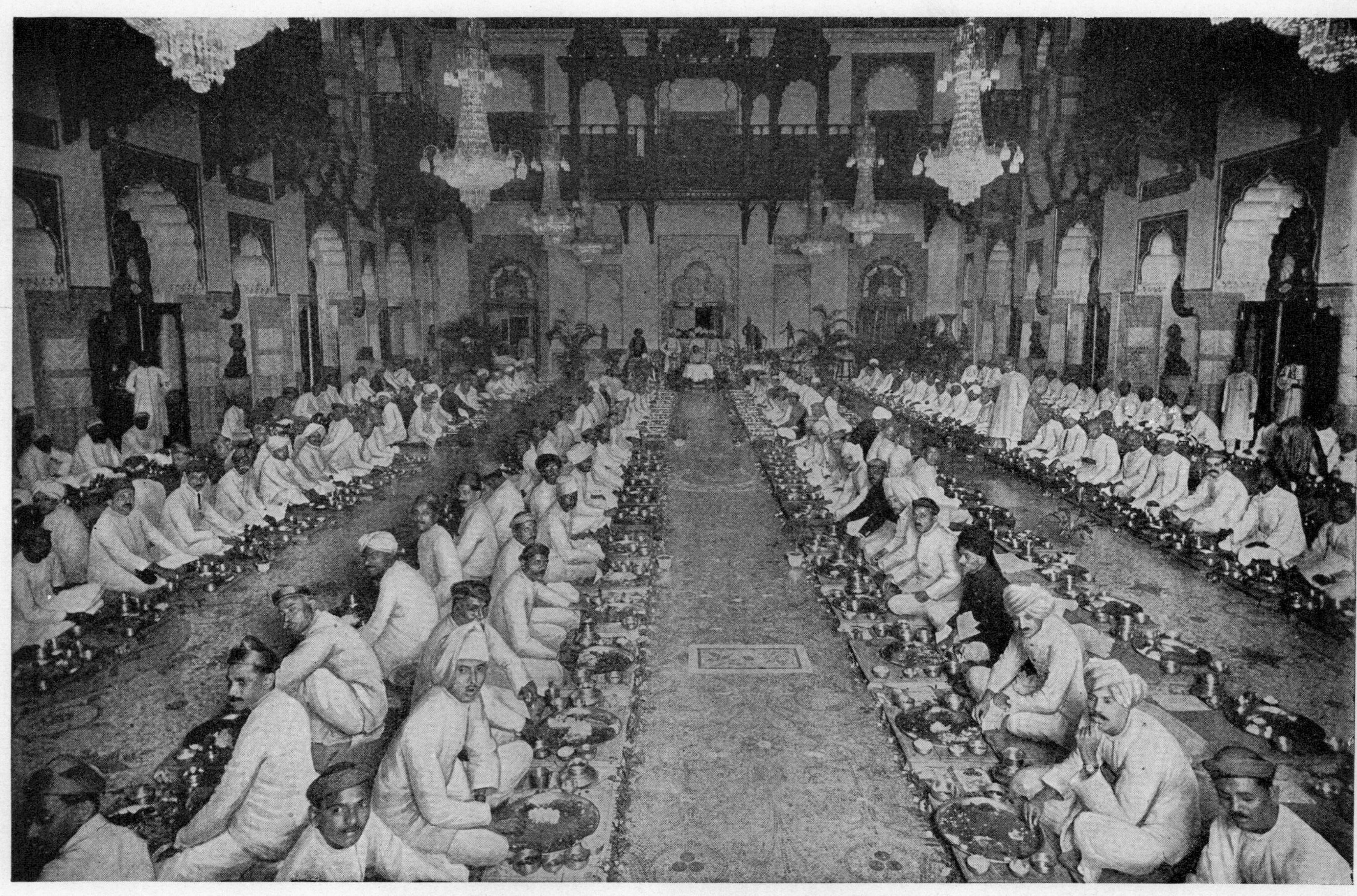

DINING ON THE FLOOR: AN ORIENTAL POTENTATE'S BANQUET

In many parts of the East it is usual to sit on the floor at meals. Sometimes the host, particularly if he is of high rank, has a higher seat, but as often as not he joins his guests on the floor. The photograph shows a state banquet in true Oriental style. It was taken at a dinner given by the Gaekwar of Baroda to the leading men of the city to celebrate the fiftieth year of his accession. The guests are seen sitting on the floor in long lines, each with a dish on a low tray before him and many supplementary bowls, while the host occupies a chair of state at the end of the hall A curious feature is the back-to-back arrangement of the rows

Owing to the practice in the East of using no table implements, cooked meats are usually served in the form of stews, ragouts, curries and so forth, while roast joints are commonly of some especially tender meat —lamb or chicken. Joints, however, are sometimes divided with the two hands, though some pride themselves on their skill in using one hand only for this purpose. It is possible that our Saxon and Scandinavian ancestors' predilection for roast joints may be responsible for the greater use of the knife in northern Europe. Even in France at one time, and within living memory, it was the custom in the more exclusive circles of society to employ the knife only at the beginning of each course. The whole of the food on the plate was cut immediately it was placed before the diner, the knife was then laid on a rest provided for the purpose, and the fork only used in eating.

The custom of eating with the fingers is, of course, still followed in England in the eating of olives, asparagus, green corn and the like, but now it is exotic; for this mode of eating has been imported with the food.

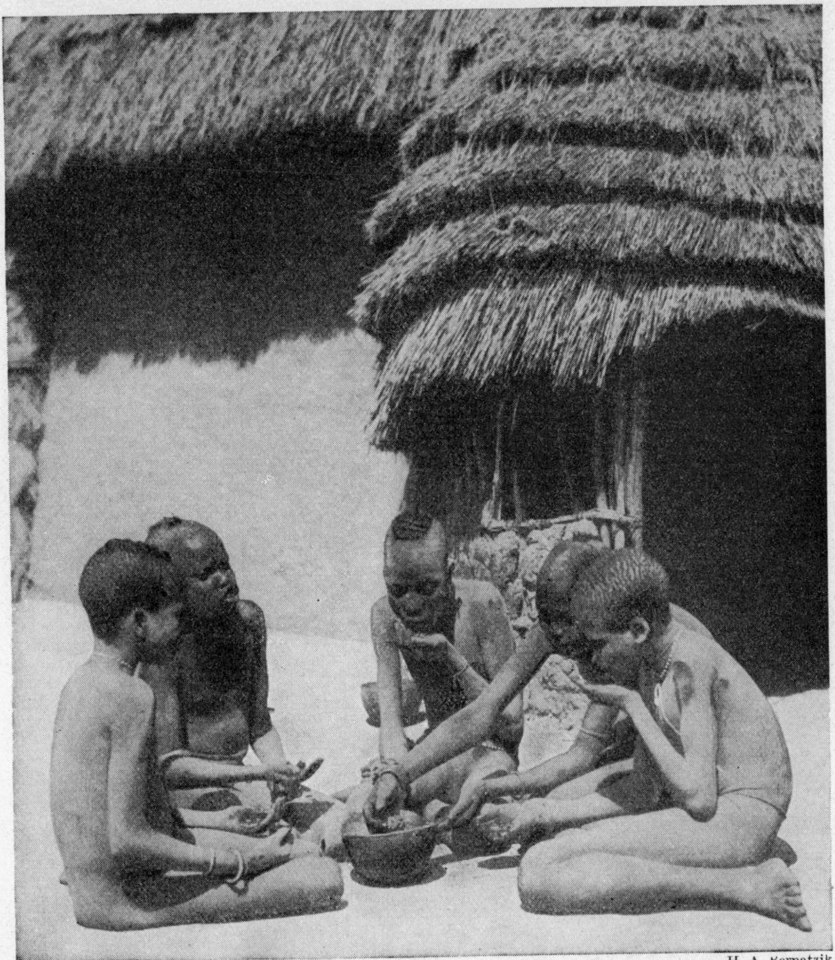

H. A. Bernatzik

A MEAL WITHOUT MANNERS IN THE SUDAN

Eating from a common bowl or dish is a widespread custom. These dusky Shilluk youngsters use no ceremony at their meal. Tables, chairs, and eating implements they have none. They simply sit round a bowl of food and dip their hands into it. The Shilluk are Nilotic negro cattle and sheep breeders of the grasslands of the Upper Nile Province of the Sudan.

An interesting concomitant of the meal from the point of view of cultural distribution is the cocktail habit. The cocktail as now compounded in Europe is an introduction from America which has grown enormously in popularity since the war. The habit of the *apéritif*, however, first came to us from France, where probably it had been introduced from the East.

Wine, though forbidden the followers of the Prophet, was not entirely eschewed by them. In place of being served during the meal, however, it was offered the guests before it. In the near and middle East raki (spirit) is offered. In Russia, which has drawn much from the Moslem through the Caucasus, vodka and fish, dried or smoked and in various forms, are given to the guest before dinner. In fact, spirit with a relish of some sort appears to serve as a ceremonial form of hospitality. In Albania a guest admitted to the patriarchal house, not a matter of easy achievement, was required to accept hospitality in the form of a goblet of raki and a lump of goat's milk cheese, which it was polite, as well as expedient, to take in alternate mouthfuls. In Constantinople, when the English meal of afternoon tea was introduced among the Greek-speaking population, more or less as a compliment to foreign visitors, it was not uncommon to find *doussiko*, or *mastik*, a highly spirituous liquor, and dried fish offered before the visitor left the house, as an earnest of a hospitality not too readily offered, just as among the Arabs salt was a symbol and a pledge of friendship.

Interesting as is the study of the component parts of a modern meal, its full significance becomes apparent only after consideration of its more formal aspects. It is remarkable how, from this point of view, primitive custom throws light upon many of the practices of the more advanced societies.

Owing to the magical and spiritual influences which are believed to be specially powerful in relation to food and the act of eating, primitive man is reluctant to eat in the presence of others. Hence, if occasion arises, among many peoples it is customary to turn the back while eating. Traces of this custom appear to survive in both Scotland and Ireland, especially in the presence of persons of higher rank.

E.N.A.

E.N.A.

FEASTS PREPARED WITH CEREMONY AND ENJOYED IN FORCED HASTE

Among the Fiji Islanders a kava feast (top) is an important occasion, and is attended with much ceremony. The natives squat round a large bowl, from which the kava is ladled into the shells of coconuts. Kava is made from the roots of a variety of the pepper plant. The liquor produces a dreamy, melancholy intoxication, and its consumption is associated with much ceremony. Below, Sudan natives inspecting a hippopotamus they have captured with a view to cutting it up forthwith into joints. Some parts are eaten without avoidable delay, else they become tainted

E.N.A

ELEGANCE AND DECORUM IN THE LAND OF THE CHRYSANTHEMUM

A family lunch party in a non-westernised household in Japan is a model of elegant decorum. Apart from the tiny charcoal stove, which is regarded as an essential, a Japanese house is virtually bare of furniture. There are no tables or chairs. Everything unnecessary is eliminated. In the room where the meal is taken the most conspicuous objects are the rice bowl—for rice is the principal food—and the teapot. The lunchers sit sedately on the floor with little trays in front of them. Like the Chinese and the Koreans, the Japanese use chopsticks.

As a rule only those of the same totem, social group, or in India of the same caste, will eat together. This is one of the reasons why in so many parts of the world the women of the family do not eat with the man, even though the eating of a common meal by husband and wife may have constituted an important, or even the sole, feature in the marriage ceremony. In the Solomon Islands the women are rigorously excluded from the ceremonial feasts offered to the spirits of the dead, and are not even allowed to take part in the long preparatory storing up of food for the occasion.

The concept of eating as a group activity common to individuals united by a spiritual bond is clearly brought out in the ceremony of sacrifice, to which only members of the spiritual group are admitted. The reason for such restriction is abundantly clear when the sacrifice is in honour of the ancestors of the group. The same ideas underlie the whole conception of primitive hospitality. It is by no means a question of promiscuous entertainment, but involves admission to the group. It is for this reason that we find that so many travellers who have won the confidence of primitive peoples have been admitted to the tribe either by initiation or by the ceremony of blood-brotherhood. The proverbial hospitality of the Arab is based on the concept of the host and guest having eaten salt together. The spiritual or magical idea implicated in the salt has imposed upon the host the protection of the stranger who sojourns in his tent, and loyalty to his host on the part of the guest The magical and social significance of the salt also serves to explain the medieval custom of 'sitting below the salt.' Those who sat above the salt either were, or were regarded as, members of the family, while those who sat below were retainers merely. In the same way the custom of taking wine with a fellow diner, a custom now almost obsolete except in certain colleges and similar associations tenacious of old traditions, is an expression of an assumption into the group analogous to the ceremonial of the blood-brotherhood.

It would be possible to multiply instances of the details in which the formal elements in the table customs of more advanced races point to the sacrificial feast of the primitive group as their prototype. Among these we may even include the table itself as the sacrificial altar, sometimes no more than a strewing of leaves or a mound of sand. upon which the victim was laid. It will suffice here to point to the grace before meat, which among the ancient Romans was an offering to the gods of the household and in ancient Greece a libation to Zeus. It enshrines a memory of the invocation by the head of the primitive group when calling upon the ancestors or the totemic spirit to join them in the feast and render the meal innocuous for their eating.

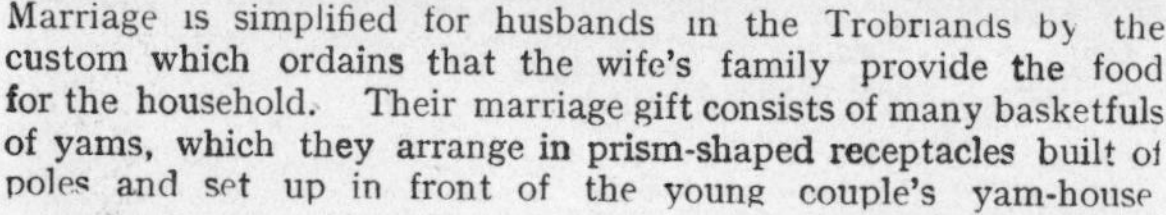

Marriage is simplified for husbands in the Trobriands by the custom which ordains that the wife's family provide the food for the household. Their marriage gift consists of many basketfuls of yams, which they arrange in prism-shaped receptacles built of poles and set up in front of the young couple's yam-house

Prof. B. Malinowski, 'Sexual Life of Savages in N.W. Melanesia.'

MELANESIAN PREPARATIONS FOR MARRIAGE AND MATERNITY

When a young married woman is definitely assured that she is to become a mother for the first time her relatives provide her with a long cloak of white fibre (top right) impregnated with magic, and this she has to wear until the birth of the child or until the garment is worn out. The woman is then bathed and ceremonially invested with the cloak, into which beneficent magic formulae are breathed (bottom left). Two relatives then carry her to her father's house, carefully guarding her from contact with the earth

THE SEXUAL LIFE OF SAVAGES

THIS section is necessarily intertwined with Courtship and Marriage, and particularly so in the present chapter, devoted to a study of Professor Malinowski's famous work, The Sexual Life of Savages (Routledge & Sons, Ltd.). It is here shown that when savages follow practices repellent or ridiculous to the civilized they may do so from reasons which to them are convincing

WE are so accustomed to the patriarchal system, the rule of families by fathers, the subordination of wives to husbands, that most of us find it difficult to consider any other system possible. All the civilizations of which we have record have been based on the supremacy of man as husband and father. Yet almost all the primitive societies we know about—those which we call 'uncivilized'—appear at some time or other to have taken the opposite line, to have made the mother the most important person in the family and to have traced descent, not through the male, but through the female line. This is commonly known as matriarchy, the rule of mothers, though it is more exact to call it the matrilineal plan.

In some out-of-the-way corners of the earth this plan is still in force. It has been studied in recent years with more care than was ever expended on it before. The old way of studying the manners and customs of those whom we describe as 'savages' was to collect their legends and, as far as possible, their history, to probe into their ideas about the origin of life, the possibility of a future state, methods of government, and so on. Collections of their tools and household possessions, their costumes and weapons, their rough manufactures and their attempts at decoration, were displayed in museums. This did not carry us very far towards acquaintance with their actual existence, their real beliefs, their standards of conduct. Since ethnographers have taken to spending long periods among such primitive peoples as still exist, since what is called 'field-work' has been in operation, our knowledge of uncivilized societies has been very widely extended.

Living among such peoples, speaking their language, gaining their confidence, observing how they live, students of ethnology have added very valuable contributions to that science—if it can be called, as yet, a science. Since it is concerned with groups of human beings (races, peoples, nations, tribes and so on), and since human beings vary so much and are continually changing, some authorities contend that it can never be strictly scientific. However this may be, there is no question about the interest and the value of the work of ethnographers—those who describe the existence of out-of-the-way communities and so provide materials for a science of ethnology, if there is to be one. Such books, for instance, as those of Prof. Bronislaw Malinowski, who holds the chair of Anthropology at London University, have enlarged greatly our comprehension of the ways of life and the states of feeling common among savages. This author spent four years in one of the islands of British New Guinea among the Melanesian aborigines; the volumes in which he related his experiences gave him a world reputation.

In one book he has described 'the sexual life' of the islanders, intending that term to cover (in addition to love and marriage, family life, birth customs, divorce and morality) art and culture, magic, witchcraft, and spells, all these being pretty closely connected with the sex appeal and sex consciousness. In that island lying to the north of Australia the matrilineal system is still strictly adhered to—that is to say, descent, kinship and all social relationships are legally recognized through mothers alone. Fathers are not even the legal guardians of their children; that office is entrusted to the children's uncle, their mother's brother. It is suggested that the belief on which this system rests—the belief that men have nothing whatever to do with the production of babies—is still common among these New Guinea natives. How the babies come they do not clearly know. They give explanations which are very much like the story of the gooseberry bush and the little boy or girl found under it which is told to very young inquirers after knowledge in our own country.

ONE is that spirits bring the babies in plaited coconut baskets or on wooden platters and cause them to enter the bodies of the women who are to be their mothers. These spirits appear in dreams and announce their errand. Sometimes they are spirits of relations who have passed into 'Tuma' (paradise). A native phrased it thus: 'My wife dreamed her mother came to her, she saw the face of her mother in her dream. She woke up and said: "There is a child for me."' In due course the child appeared, and neither of them saw any other explanation of its appearance than this! Another version of the mystery is that spirit babies float about in the sea and enter the bodies of women while they bathe. Those who do not wish for children abstain from bathing when the water near shore is thick after a storm with scum, pieces of wood, leaves and small branches of trees; they are afraid that the spirit babies might be hiding among these. A man who claimed to have seen one of them described it as 'looking like a mouse.' Others declare that they are perfect children in every detail, but far smaller than when they are born as earth children.

Husbands being thus treated as having no part in the formation of families, one might suppose they would take little interest in their children. Actually they are devoted to them, they do as much nursing and give the little ones as much attention as do their

WEAVING CHARMS AND SPELLS OF BEAUTY MAGIC

Magic plays an essential part in the making of the fibre garments for an expectant mother. They are spread upon a mat and strewn over with the creamy white leaves of a certain white lily cut into strips. The robe makers kneel round the bundle and thrust their faces right into the fibre material, breathing into it a magic formula to impart whiteness and beauty to the wearer.

wives. Thus, there grows up a mutual affection between children and the 'stranger' in the house (that is what he is called) who holds them so often in his arms, washes, feeds and lovingly fondles them. Not less surprising is it that a likeness between father and child is considered natural and proper, while it is regarded as an offence against right feeling and good manners to remark on a child's resemblance to its mother or to any of her relations. No insult could be more outrageous than to say that a man is like his sister. Prof. Malinowski got into trouble once for detecting a similarity of feature in two brothers. What the reason for this taboo is he could not discover.

ONE result of the matrilineal system is that men do not have to support their households. Their wives' families make them handsome allowances—in the shape of yams, which are the islanders' staple food.

So long as the household exists, this tribute must be kept up. It may be supplemented by work on the husband's part and by the wife, but they are relieved by it from any anxiety about their living expenses.

Women do a good deal of work—especially in the gardens, where most of the food is grown. They do the cooking as well as the gathering of the fruit and the shell-fish on which they usually live. For a man to cook (except on expeditions when no women are taken or on certain ceremonial occasions) is thought disgraceful. 'He-cook' is a term of abuse. Nor will any man demean himself by carrying a load on his head. Women do this as a matter of course, but men bear burdens only on their shoulders.

In most respects women are the equals of men. They inherit rank, they are magicians, they can practise sorcery and lay on spells. Girl babies are given just the same welcome as boy babies, which is not so among tribes that are frequently at war. In no way is the woman at any age subject to the humours or under the domination of the man. The one terrible right which husbands do possess is to kill their wives if they discover them to have been unfaithful. But this right is seldom exercised. As a rule, the affair is somehow arranged in a more or less friendly way. Marriages of real affection seem to be about as large (or as small) a proportion of the whole number as in civilized communities. The one thing that husbands and wives must not on any account do, however fond they may be of one another, is to betray any feeling of fondness in public. Kissing is unknown, so there is no temptation towards that. Biting and scratching, common forms of endearment, can hardly be indulged in when lovers are among other people. But the prejudice against endearment goes farther than that. When a married couple go out, they do not even walk side by side. One walks behind the other. As for holding hands, caressing, or even looking at each other with love in their glances—that is never done. They often talk quite cheerfully, and even chaff one another, when others are present. but there is a restraint upon their tongues, and any allusion to sex would be an unpardonable breach of decorum.

FOR although in many ways their habits differ from ours, the islanders have a code of morals; their standard of decent behaviour is quite as rigid as our own. Trial marriage seems to the people of Europe and America a dangerous, distasteful, and even a disastrous experiment. On the other hand, we see no harm in an engaged couple lunching or dining together. Among these New Guinea folk young men and young women make many experiments before they settle down to family life. They do this openly, it is part of the regular routine of existence, no one thinks of finding anything undesirable in it. But if an unmarried boy and girl were to share a meal, the islanders' sense of propriety would be shocked, their moral susceptibility would be outraged. This taboo is connected, no doubt, with a general disinclination to eat in company, which must have originated in the fear of being poisoned. Even in their homes these savages prefer to take away their portion of a dish and eat it in solitary fashion. In a strange village they will not eat at all.

Again, it is common enough in some European countries, in England and in America, to see young men and women with their arms around each other, sometimes kissing in public places, sometimes going even further than that. For the boys and girls of New Guinea who are living together as an experiment to indulge in any such behaviour would bring down upon them not only the disapproval but the anger of the community. 'Living together' is not quite exact. They continue to live during the day with their parents, working and taking their meals at home. They meet only at night and part again in the morning. No legal obligation is incurred. Very seldom are children born of these temporary unions, though every one who was questioned about this denied that any measures were taken to prevent it. Often many such 'trials' are made before the parties to them decide to marry. They wait until they find a partner with whom they feel sure of living happily in a home of their own. None remain unmarried unless they are deformed, diseased, or exceptionally unpleasing. The reason for this is that only married persons can be full members of the community. Neither men nor women can have households of their own until they are husbands or wives. Apart from that, the girls, as a rule, want children and the men desire the tribute which will be paid to them by the families of their wives.

Although to European eyes these islanders are anything but attractive in feature and expression, they have a positive hatred of what they consider ugliness and a delight in what is beautiful according to their standards. There are many magic rites among them for increasing good looks; more effective than these are their frequent ceremonial cleansings, in which they first wash all over and then anoint themselves with coconut oil, which makes their brown skins shine. Wreaths of flowers are worn and chaplets made from the leaves of sweet-smelling shrubs. Personal attraction is the strongest factor in their love affairs. If young men cannot succeed in awakening a response to their advances, they have recourse to love potions or spells, which often have the desired result simply because the girls are made to understand that they have made complete conquests of their suitors.

Marriage, when it comes, is attended by no ceremony except the exchange of presents. The parents of the prospective bride signify their consent by asking the young man for a small gift. Then one day, instead of returning in the morning to the house of her parents, the girl goes with her 'boy' to the house of his parents. There she takes her meals and all day she goes about with him. The village knows from this that they have decided to take one another for good or ill as life-companions. Henceforward they are looked on as man and wife. There is more exchanging of presents, and the girl's family must now begin to provide their handsome contribution towards the young folks' housekeeping. But no other sanction to marriage is required other than mutual agreement.

When the first child is known to be on the way, elaborate preparations in the way of clothing are made—not for the baby, which for a long time will wear nothing at all, but for the expectant mother. With careful adherence to tradition a cloak of fibre known as the 'pregnancy dress' is got ready. By incantation it is given magical qualities. Then a day is appointed for putting it on. All the women assemble on seashore or river-bank or by the village water-hole. A number of them carry the young wife into the water and a vigorous game of splashing follows. Back on land, she is rubbed with coconut husk fibre and with coconut oil. Her cheeks are stroked with a mother-of-pearl shell to make them resemble its smoothness and delicacy. Her hair is combed and flowers are fastened in it. At last the cloak is put on. It is not discarded until the fibre has worn away and become ragged.

RITUAL BATHING BEFORE A HAPPY EVENT

At dawn of the day of her investiture in the maternity fibre cloak the prospective mother is ceremonially bathed. Female relatives line up in two rows in the sea and, crossing hands, form a living bridge on which she walks dry foot to a point where she is allowed to jump into the water. She is then playfully ducked and drenched, thoroughly washed and carried ashore to undergo a ritual anointment, dressing and adornment.

Marriage being so simple, divorce, when it happens, is equally so. If the husband desires it, he sends his wife to her mother's dwelling or, if her mother is not living, to that of her legal guardian (uncle) or other near maternal relative. If the wife wishes for a dissolution of the union, she goes of her own free will. Should one or other wish to avoid divorce, gifts are sent as a peace-offering ; if these are accepted, the marriage is not dissolved ; husband and wife return to their home. Refusal to accept presents means that they must separate. Each then looks out for a fresh partner. They are freed from all ties, and can start making experiments again. When a divorced wife remarries, her new husband has to give her old one a present. After that, he begins to receive the regular gift of yams which constitutes his wife's dowry. The children always remain with their mother, as a natural consequence of the notion that she alone was responsible for bringing them into the world.

KEEPING VIGIL AGAINST SORCERERS AND DISEASE

Shortly before and for a month after the birth of a child a Melanesian mother spends most of her time on a raised bedstead under which a small fire is kept burning. The natives consider such baking and smoking to be very good for the health, and also a prophylactic against black magic. No men are allowed in this house during this period, but it is not a matter of serious taboo.

Oddly at variance with that view are the indignities and even suffering which are inflicted on widows. They are compelled to go through a long period of ceremonial mourning, watched all the time by the dead husband's relatives, who are ready to complain at once of any attempt to escape performance of any traditional rite. To begin with, the poor woman's head is shaved and she is made to look in all ways as unattractive as possible. Her body is smeared with black grease, she must twist a dirty black cloth about her, no ornaments are permitted, and none of the scented blossoms which take the place of European perfume in bottles. The object of this is to make widows unpleasing to men, so that they may not dishonour their late husbands by securing others too quickly. That, at any rate, is the islanders' explanation, but there is probably more in it than this. Taken in connexion with other funeral customs, it seems to be derived probably from some ancient ritual of which, it may be, the origin has long been forgotten. For it is not only the widow whose hair is cut off and whose body is greased. All the neighbours who are not related to the dead man must subject themselves to the same disagreeable treatment. Not his relatives, as one would expect ; they go about as usual. No sign of mourning is worn by members of the dead man's family or clan, though they may take part in the shrieking and howling which for days, and even weeks, are kept up as tributes of respect, if not of inconsolable grief.

Twice the corpse is buried and dug up again before it is left at peace. The first time it is examined carefully for any indications that death was caused by magic. The second time a number of bones are taken from it, to be treasured as keepsakes (widows are supposed to wear the jawbones of their husbands hung round their necks). Until the final committal of the body to the earth the widow must keep watch over the grave.

After the last burial the poor woman's most trying ordeal begins. She goes into a small wicker cage in a dark corner of her dwelling, and there she remains for months, never coming out for any purpose, never speaking above a whisper, never feeding herself even, but relying upon others to put food into her mouth. Widows of men who rank high undergo this misery for as long as two years. What it means is doubtful, but in all likelihood it was instituted in far-off times as a means of propitiating the spirit of the departed, which might take vengeance on the living if they failed to show it proper respect.

In this, as in other matters of myth and tradition these New Guinea savages have not worked up their ideas into any system. It is only their ' taboos ' and their ceremonial rites which are fixed. So long as these are observed thought is free—on the subject of sex as on everything else.

WEDDINGS WITHOUT THE BRIDE

ACCUSTOMED as we are to regard the bride as the central figure of a wedding, there are some countries in which she does not appear. Even where the matriarchate obtains and woman is an important personage, the bride is often absent from the marriage ceremony itself. Other aspects of marriage are noted in our chapter on The Various Forms of Marriage.

MARRIAGE by proxy is much more common than might be at first expected, and the farce of stealing the bride, a relic of days when the strong-arm man forayed wide afield in search of plunder and women, survives in quite peaceful wedding ceremonies in many parts of the world—even in Europe. It must be realized that marriage in earlier times was an unceremonious affair, and that the multifarious festivities and customs, now differing so greatly amongst races and tribes, have grown up in later times, the ceremonies developing under natural and religious influences. The bridal veil is preserved still amongst civilized people, and is a very important feature of marriage ritual in the East and elsewhere. This, as well as the custom of the bride-to-be hiding from the groom, possibly originates in the primitive idea that it is dangerous to the bride if her husband's eyes fall on her.

Hiding from the groom has become exaggerated in the Hindu purdah and the Mahomedan veiling of womenfolk. In New Britain the bride stays alone for five days in the hut of her prospective husband. Certain South African tribes have a marriage custom which necessitates the seclusion of the bride in a hut apart, from which she is taken to another hut some days later, before being handed over to the husband. Bedouin tribes incorporate hiding and stealing the bride in pre-marriage ceremonies. The girl must run away into the hills the night before the wedding, and the groom goes in search of her. When he has found her he must stay the night with her in the hills, and this constitutes the marriage.

To trace the origins of the mimic warfare which is so important a feature in the marriage customs of many lands it would be necessary to dig right down to the birth of humanity, and then to follow the history of woman's gradual 'emancipation' through the ages. In all early primitive communities man was the stronger and more masterful animal, woman generally the merest chattel, or beast of burden. Slowly, as the household became a settled feature of life, woman's sphere became more important. The man, a hunter, was attracted to the hearth, where cooked meats were available, and with the rise of religions woman's position as a mother was recognized.

IN certain cases this recognition developed till mother-right and the matriarchate became the social system, and even to-day in many backward communities there is no recognition of paternal rights. In the rise of the woman in history to a position of equality it is to be noted that there was also a mental and physical improvement. Amongst primitives, however, man is generally the finer specimen of humanity, and if we look at man's nearer relations, the male gorilla is nearly twice as large as the female. It was therefore perhaps natural that the finer animal should steal his female companions and maintain them in a form of slavery to him.

Keystone

PURE GOLD A BRIDE'S FIT CORONAL

Elaborate head-dresses are worn by brides of the Minangkabau race, a mountain people of Sumatra. The ornamentation of the bride's crown—here seen in profile to show the method of attachment to the head—is of pure gold collected locally for the occasion.

The innumerable customs which have grown up round and about marriage constitute a subject of vast extent. It is a very widespread custom that not only the preliminaries of marriage, but the ceremony itself shall be performed in the absence of the bride, and that the proposal of marriage and arrangement of the contract shall be carried out not by the bride and bridegroom, but by their friends and sponsors, or parents. In Egypt the marriage contract is arranged between the bridegroom and the bride's deputy, these two joining hands, which are ceremonially covered with a cloth. It is the sponsors and not the two principals amongst the Karens who offer the ceremonial

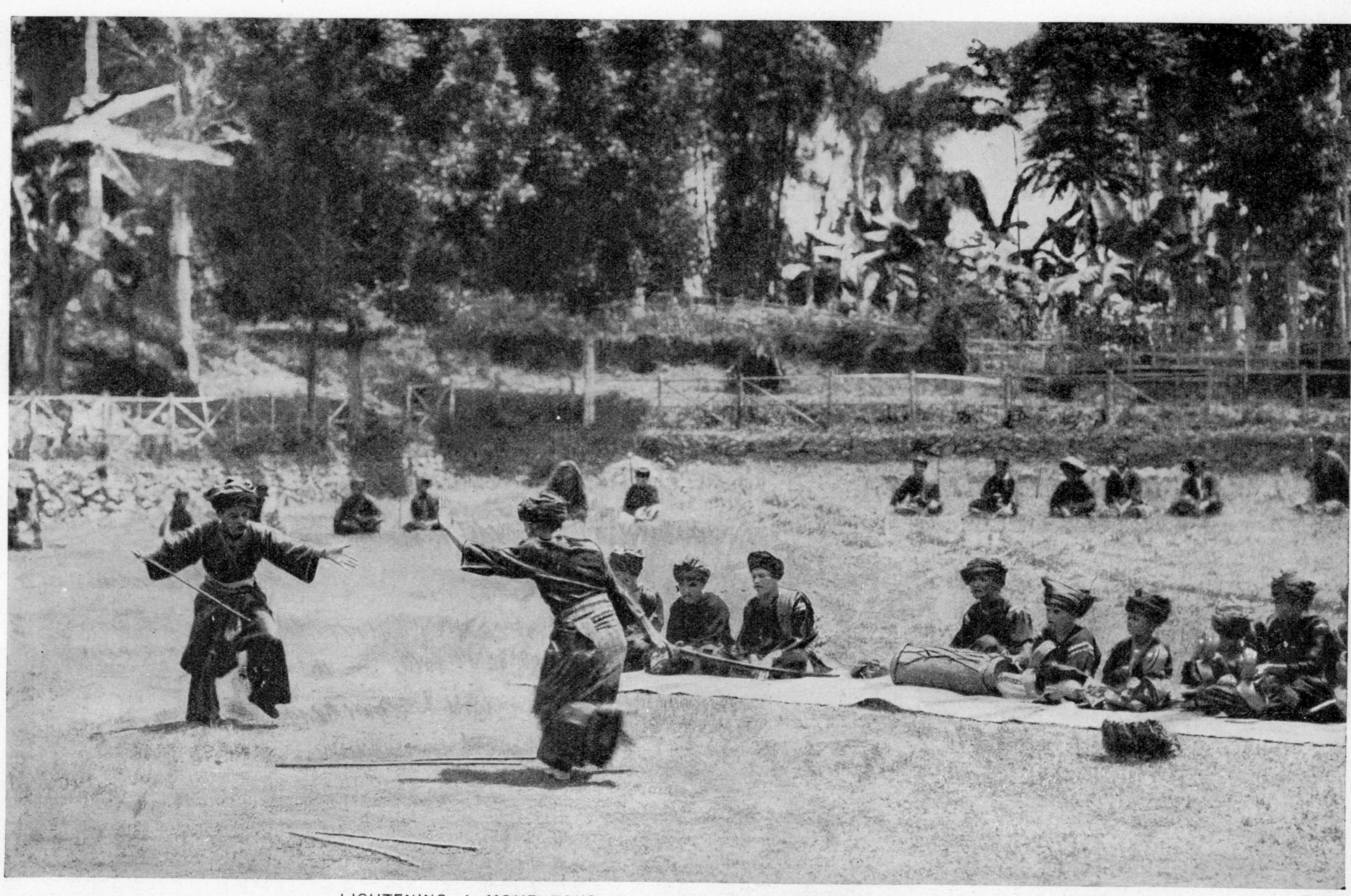

Keystone

LIGHTENING A MOMENTOUS DUTY WITH MUSIC AND FEATS OF SKILL

In the country of the Minangkabau, high in the Sumatran highlands, the matriarchal system prevails, according to which the mother, not the father, is the source of authority. Among the people of this lofty region weddings are conducted with great ceremony, a strange feature being the absence of the bride from nearly every part of the proceedings. The first step is taken by the maternal uncles of the bride-to-be, who call a meeting of the panghulus or clan chieftains for the purpose of deciding upon the prospective bridegroom. The panghulus are here seen seated in a semicircle on their stones of office watching a foot-boxing match, which is being performed as part of the ceremonies. The group immediately behind the boxers is the orchestra.

G.P.A.

MARRYING THE BRIDEGROOM AT A BRIDELESS WEDDING

Wedding ceremonies among the Minangkabau lose something of their central significance in Western eyes in the absence of the bride. At only one stage of the proceedings does she appear, and then not at the actual marriage rite, which is shown in the photograph. The functionary known as the wali marries the bridegroom, who wears on his head the traditional buffalo's horn. The word Minangkabau means 'victory of the buffalo.' In far-off days, so runs the legend, a Sumatran buffalo met a buffalo of Java in single combat and defeated it

cup to each other, and drink from it, thus confirming the marriage. And again in Persia marriage by proxy is the general rule. Here the groom never sees his bride till the marriage is consummated, and in Ceylon, where an astrologer first casts a horoscope, the groom, if his horoscope is unfavourable, is represented by his infant brother, who is then married to the bride. Both bride and bridegroom have a representative in the South Celebes, and the bride does not appear at the wedding, being represented by her deputy. She, meanwhile, is hidden away in an inner room, and the groom, after the ceremony, leaves his sword behind to represent him and goes home. Three days later he comes to reclaim his sword. A very strange ceremony is the marriage to the mango tree amongst the Kumis. First the groom is married and embraces the tree, and then the bride is also married in a similar way—afterwards she is brought to her home in a basket.

In the Malay countries there are two forms of marriage, but it must be remembered that the customs and ceremonies have been considerably qualified by the practice of Islam. The Moslem religion prevails, and has had an important influence on all the festivities. In the south-western division on the western seaboard matrilineal descent prevails and the family consists of the mother and her children. This follows the matriarchate of the Minangkabau of the highlands of Sumatra, and the marriage ceremonies and various rights of the parties are somewhat similar. In this wide and little known area of the great island an ancient Malay people descendant from the old empire of the 'Victorious Buffalo,' preserve a matriarchal social state in a pure form. The father is a nonentity. He is permitted to visit his wife in the evenings when he cares to, and is then made welcome. But he lives, as he has done all his life, at his mother's home, and works for his mother's family, while his wife lives with her mother, and the mother's brother takes on the duties of father to any children of the marriage. The oldest centre of these interesting people is in the Padang highlands, where the settlements are a collection of a few very large and well-built family houses with buffalo-horn gables, richly carved and painted. In these houses all the descendants of the mother or grandmother live, and sometimes there is a great-grandmother who is really the head of the house. Descent, of course, as to name and heritage, is on the mother's side.

Keystone

A SIGNIFICANT INTERLUDE: THE BRIDEGROOM RECEIVING THE TJERANO, A SYMBOLICAL CASKET

One of the most important parts of the elaborate wedding ceremonies of the Minangkabau of the Sumatran highlands is the handing over of the tjerano. This is a box containing lime and betel nuts, and its transfer from the possession of the bride to the care of the bridegroom is a symbolical act of the highest significance. When the bridegroom and his retinue are about to pass the bride's home the procession is stopped and halts in front of the entrance to the house. With all due ceremony the casket is given into the hands of the bridegroom, and, this part of the proceedings having been successfully accomplished, the bridegroom and his party are free to continue their progress.

It can be easily realized that in such circumstances the laws and ceremonies take a different course, and may have a different significance from events of a similar nature in modern patriarchal communities. Marriage, for instance, though the woman is here the important personage, is celebrated without her assistance. There are long preliminaries conducted by deputies and heads of families, with some assistance of the proposed husband, and eventually he has to pass a test before the wali as to his fitness to become the husband of the girl chosen ; this after the bride's family have arranged the contract to their satisfaction, of course. When the man expresses his desire to wed he informs his parents, indicating the girl chosen, who must be of another village from his own. The maternal uncles meet and then call a gathering of the Panghulus, or clan chieftains, when, with much ceremony on a broad open greensward, the preliminaries are decided. The Panghulus seat themselves in a wide circle on stones set at intervals and are entertained by an orchestra and players, wrestling and story-telling. There follows the betrothal ceremony, at which the bride-to-be is not, however, asked for her consent, but subsequently the lover makes a series of presentations to her. Meanwhile the girl takes the utmost pains to keep out of her lover's way, and to accomplish this she is said to be as 'watchful as a tiger.' No communication whatever may pass between the pair.

On the day of the wedding ceremony the houses of both parents are decorated, and at the same time a special dais, or platform, is erected at the bridegroom's house on which he dons all his wedding finery before going to meet his bride. After four days of celebrating and feasting the bride is dressed up in all her ornaments and awaits the coming of the groom, also on a raised dais. This dais is piled up with pillows, the number indicating the rank of the parties. The procession sets out with the women leading, the groom being carried on his friends' shoulders. On arrival at the bride's house there is sometimes a mimic conflict before he enters to await the priest.

The actual ceremony, at which passages of the Koran are recited, is between the priest and the groom in the absence of the bride, and having successfully passed a sharp interrogation the husband is led to the bridal chamber and seated on the left-hand side of the bride. Both the bride and the bridegroom display their utmost finery on this occasion, the ornaments in both cases being of pure gold, and collected from friends all over the district for use at the ceremonies. After everything is settled the husband goes back to his mother, and even if the

Keystone

THE SOLE OCCASION WHEN A SUMATRAN BRIDE APPEARS AT HER OWN MARRIAGE

The only part of the wedding ceremonies among the Minangkabau of Sumatra in which the bride herself appears in person is the announcing of the marriage by the wali. What we should consider to be the most important stage of the proceedings, namely, the actual marriage rite, is performed at the temple or mosque—for the Minangkabau are Mahomedans—in the presence of the bridegroom, but not of the bride. The photo shows the wali announcing the marriage to the bride and bridegroom, who are wearing their symbolical wedding head-dresses

Keystone

HOUSES THAT GROW, GABLE BY GABLE, AS THE DAUGHTERS MARRY

After a Minangkabau wedding the couple do not set up house together, but proceed to their old homes, the bride going back to her mother's house, the family house (below), where her husband becomes a visitor. These family houses are picturesque buildings, and sometimes cover a very large area. Whenever additional accommodation is needed a fresh gable is thrust out, with the result that a house containing married daughters may in time become a veritable congeries of buffalo-horn gables. The upper photograph shows the bridal pair after the wedding.

C. P. Skrine

KIRGHIZ WEDDING WITH NEITHER BRIDE NOR BRIDEGROOM

In this wedding group in Central Asia those wearing turbans are women. The rugs in the foreground are for the bridal tent. Among the Kirghiz of this region, when the bride-price has been settled the bride's parents invite the neighbours to a feast. This, together with the announcement of the marriage, is the sole marriage ceremony. Neither bride nor bridegroom is present at the feast. For several months afterwards the bride lives with her parents, busying herself with her new tent. When this is finished the bridegroom carries off bride and tent.

marriage be blessed with children he acquires no more power in his wife's household. As the family expands so the house is increased by adding another gabled portion, and the number of gables of a house is an indication of the number of inhabitants.

UP amongst the Khasis, another people with matriarchal laws, living in Assam the marriage customs differ somewhat. The most remarkable feature is that usually the husband goes to live with his wife at his mother-in-law's house. As long as the wife lives in her mother's house all her earnings are taken by her parent to go towards the upkeep of the family. In some cases the husband only goes to visit his wife after dark, and the ancestral property is vested in the mother. Still, the father here is of some importance despite the matriarchate, though the mother's elder brother is the head of the house. When a boy of from 17 to 25 years decides on the girl he wishes to marry he mentions the name of the girl to his parents, who make the necessary arrangements with the girl's parents. An auspicious day for the wedding ceremony is chosen by divination from broken eggs and the entrails of fowls. The day selected, both parties dress up in their best and the groom visits the bride's house and is handed over to her, taking a seat beside her. Both then recite the marriage contract. Two or three days later the bride goes to the groom's mother's house, and afterwards they visit each other at their respective homes at will.

In the remoter valleys of the Kashgar Mountains in Chinese Central Asia the marriage customs are in some ways different from those which obtain in the more accessible places, and quite the reverse of the customs of the Turkis of the plains. Girls amongst the Kirghiz of the mountains are at a premium ; the would-be husband has to pay a heavy bride-price, and the amount leads to long preliminary haggling. When the payment, chiefly in yaks and sheep, has been completed, the bride's people invite all the neighbours to a feast at which the marriage is announced. But the bride and bridegroom do not attend this ceremony ; they remain alone and apart in their home tents. This feast and announcement constitute the marriage—there is no other ceremony. The bridegroom must not take his wife straight away to his tent. She continues to live with her parents for a period of two to five months, during which time she is occupied with her people in making and preparing the furnishings for the new aquoi, or felt tent. The bridegroom continues to live with his parents and visits his wife secretly every week. When the new aquoi is finished the bridegroom takes it and the bride to his own place, the wife and the parents making a brief pretence of resistance.

Marriage customs of a similar nature are common throughout the East. They differ in various respects according to the origin and the religious influences of the people, while the most divergent ideas of betrothal and marriage will be found amongst peoples living almost side by side.

KRISHNA AS IMPERSONATED BY A JAVANESE ACTOR IN THE WAJANG WONG

For the material of its drama the Javanese Wajang Wong relies mainly upon the two great Hindu epics, the Mahabharata and the Ramayana. In the former are chronicled the exploits of Krishna, usually regarded as the eighth incarnation of Vishnu the Preserver. The calm dignity proper to the divine nature of Krishna's personality is admirably represented by this actor to whom the part was entrusted in 1926, the latest occasion on which the Wajang Wong was celebrated in Java.

ANIMAL DANCES OF THE EAST

FOR the information about the Wajang Wong in this chapter, and the remarkable pictures in black and colour, we are indebted to Mynheer Tassilo Adam, one-time Ethnographer to the Government of the Dutch Indies. Although, as mentioned here, animals figure largely in the Devil Dances of Tibet, these are more strictly ritual performances, and as such form the subject of a later chapter in this work.

IN that enchanted garden men call Java the exploits of the lotus-born Vishnu and his satellites of the Hindu Pantheon are featured on many a crumbling façade of the ancient temples, which, scattered far and wide over the country, recall the era when Moslem Java once embraced the Hindu Faith. But the ancient mythology of Hindustan is not only preserved architecturally; it is also lavishly besprinkled with local legend, the subject-matter for the drama of Java's national theatre—the Wajang.

The Wajang is usually played with puppets who cast their shadows on a screen; but in the more elaborate presentations the part of the puppets is often taken by men, and this kind of Wajang is called the Wajang Wong (Shadow Men). A feature of the Wajang Wong is naturally the imitation of the shadow-puppets, and thus the action of their play is calculated to produce, by slow movements of the dance order, that impression. The actors are silent, and the story is explained by the Dalang showman or Greek Chorus, to the accompaniment of the 'gamellan,' a native Javanese musical instrument, and the rebab,' the Persian viol Since the subject matter of the Wajang is invariably that of ancient Hindu mythology—two favourite presentations being the epic poems of the Ramayana and the Mahabharata—it is of a religious character, and the actors, influenced no doubt by the character of the parts they play, by their silence, by the plaintive melody of the 'gamellan,' the long-drawn notes of the 'rebab,' and the rhythmic character of their dance, frequently fall into a trance-like state analogous to that achieved by the dancing dervishes of the Sudan.

Animals play an important part in the mythological stories of the East, and are closely identified with the culture-heroes whose exploits form the subject-matter of innumerable dramatic representations all over the Orient. Dances which form an integral part of Oriental drama often figure the animals of local legend and ancient mythology.

The Hindu trinity is composed of Brahma, the creator, Vishnu, the preserver, and Siva, the destroyer. The cow is sacred to Brahma and Vishnu; to sacrifice a bull to Siva is the duty of every devout Hindu. Vishnu, in the ancient mythology, is represented by a series of incarnations, many of which take an animal form; he is sometimes fish, tortoise or boar, and, in one case, lion-headed. Of the Ramayana, which is perhaps the favourite drama of the Javanese Wajang, Valmiki, its poet author says:

As long as mountain ranges stand
And rivers flow upon the earth,
So long will this Ramayana
Survive upon the lips of men

JAVANESE EPIC HEROES IN CASQUE AND HELM

Great beauty of line distinguishes the head-dresses worn by all the human characters in the mythological and religious epic dramas of the Javanese. Infinite care is bestowed upon every detail of the production, and the process of making-up alone occupies the company for something like three hours

SIMPLE DEVICES SATISFY DEVOUT IMAGINATION IN THE GREAT ANIMAL DANCE OF JAVA

While most of the animals figuring in the Wajang Wong are elaborate products of the property maker's art, convention is satisfied with a much simpler presentation of the horse. Small ' hobby horses ' made of plaited bamboo suffice for the purpose of the drama, no doubt because they lend themselves more easily to the evolutions of the dance. How seriously the actors take their work in these arduous performances is suggested by the expression, at once alert and grave, of this Knight mounted on a steed that among more sophisticated people would serve as a child's toy.

REPRESENTATIVE FIGURES FROM THE JAVANESE CORPS DE BALLET

All the designs for the costumes in the Wajang Wong are stereotyped, and the garments are made from costly materials exquisitely woven in various colours. The cost of providing them, as indeed the cost of the entire production, is borne entirely by the prince giving the entertainment, and the honour of being allowed to participate in the ceremony is deemed full recompense for their services by the actors, who receive no remuneration of any kind. The performance is almost entirely pantomimic, only sporadic dialogue being spoken by the actors themselves.

Sport & General

CHINESE DEVIL DANCERS IN ANIMAL MASKS

Tibet is the original home of the Devil Dance, a celebration inaugurating the New Year. From Tibet it spread to China, and for many years was performed in the Lama Temple at Peking. It has now been suppressed as superstitious by the Nationalist Government.

Though this prophecy was made about 500 B.C. it was a singularly true one, for the story of the Ramayana is perhaps the most popular epic in the Oriental repertoire, and in various forms it is found in countries as far apart as India and Siam.

Rama, heir to the throne of Ayodhya in India, goes into voluntary exile in the forests of Dadanka. Here he encounters and vanquishes numerous monsters, amongst others a giant in the form of a tiger. He incurs, through these pursuits, the enmity of the demon king Ravana, who, assuming the shape of a golden deer with silver spots, steals Sita, Rama's bride, and carries her to his island home of Lanka (Ceylon). Rama enlists the aid of the monkey-god Hanuman, the reddish-gold one, who with the aid of a regiment of monkeys builds a bridge from India to Ceylon, and enables Rama to cross with his army, defeat Ravana and regain Sita. Rama, who is divine, is regarded as the seventh incarnation of Vishnu.

Krishna, whose exploits are chronicled in the Mahabharata, portrayals of which share an equal popularity in the Javanese Wajang with the Ramayana, is usually regarded as the eighth incarnation of Vishnu, and is therefore also divine. The legends of the Ramayana and the Mahabharata are more or less complementary to one another ; the same stories of animals being repeated in the Mahabharata in a slightly different form. The legends finally close with the death of Krishna, whom the hunter Jara shoots by mistake.

Of the fabulous monsters which appear in these two epics, a prominent place must be given to the Garuda birds, Lords of the Air, who offer timely help to Rama when Ravana steals his bride. But, like most of the animals in the Hindu mythology, the

Illustrations Bureau

PREPARING FOR A TOTEMIC DANCE IN CENTRAL AUSTRALIA

It is among the Australian aborigines that animal dances persist in their simplest form, the participators—who are exclusively men—representing the totem animal venerated as the ancestor of their group. Four members of the Emu totem of Central Australia are seen here preparing for the performance. Two on the left, painted, befeathered, and wearing exaggerated head-dresses, are holding the sacred churingas, rudely carved wooden representations of an emu's head and neck. The others wear huge rosettes made of feathers and down symbolising the bird.

J. L. P. Gaskin

TIGER DANCE OF INDIAN SUNNITES AT THE MOHARRAM FESTIVAL

Mahomedans of the Sunni sect trace the descent of the Khalifate from Hussein, son of Mahomet's daughter Fatima, whose martyrdom, together with that of Hasan, is commemorated at the Moharram festival. In India the festival has become one of rejoicing rather than of mourning, and the popular celebrations include a dance in which men made up to represent tigers and led on chains caper about on all fours. The allusion is to the lion that legend says watched over the corpse of Hussein; lion and tiger being interchangeable animals in India.

Garudas have also a place in the Hindu cosmogony, and are usually represented as the enemies of the elephant, who, connected with the pluvial god Indras, would naturally give way to the sun-birds (the Garudas). Birds have a very special place in Hindu mythology, and to them is attributed great wisdom; Krishna does not fail to hold mystic communion with them, and in Java they take the form of the Ritualistic Fowl, whom the populace hold in some dread. The lord of the serpents, who is Sesha in India, and is closely connected with Vishnu, becomes in Java Prince Prabu Wisamuka; the crocodile and rhinoceros also make their appearance. Bears in the Hindu cosmogony are connected with the constellation of the Great Bear; the King of the Bears also takes part in the expedition to Lanka with Rama. These stories of ancient Hindustan are not confined to Java alone, and the fable of Hanumat is enacted in the Malay Wayang, a feature of which is the monkey dance, while versions of the Ramayana and the Mahabharata can be seen in Siam and Cambodia to-day.

In India animal dances or mythological representations of fabulous animals are not restricted to Hindu legendary lore. Amongst the Moslems of the Sunni sect in the Central Provinces at the feast of the Moharram, the first month of the Mahomedan year, men and boys, usually of the lower classes, paint and dress themselves as tigers and go about on all fours led by keepers, imitating the antics of the tiger. Here it seems likely that the tiger represents the mythical lion (the lion and the tiger are interchangeable animals in India) which is said to have watched over the body of Hussein, son of the Lady Fatima (daughter of Mahomet) at the time of his death, and from whom the Sunni sect trace the descent ot the Khalifate. A man in tiger form appears on the tomb of Hussein in the drama of his murder at Karbala, Persia, which is enacted at the Moharram

The Lion dance of Tibet is based upon the mythological lion of the Himalaya snows who brings good fortune wherever he appears. The lion is represented as about the size of an ox; its head and shoulders are formed by a framework of wood which a man manipulates from the interior, while another occupies the hindquarters. The lion is introduced by a harlequin or clown, and proceeds to prance and kick in a life-like fashion. In the Tibetan mystery-plays there is a dance of the Red-Tiger Devil, a deity of pre-Buddhist Tibet. The original motive of the dance was to expel the old year with its demons of bad luck, and to propitiate the new year and its guardian spirits with human sacrifices, and, probably, formerly with cannibalism. In China the advent of the New Year is always the occasion of a great festival, and throughout the first days of the year processions representing scenes of ancient history are formed which traverse the streets, and are always headed by large brightly-coloured paper dragons carried by men whose bodies are partly concealed within the mask. Masked devil dancers abound among the Taoist and Buddhist priesthood of China, and the masks are often representations of animals or animal-devils.

Though legendary lore has been and still is largely responsible for the dramatic representation of animals, there are yet other kinds of animal dances to be considered.

THE aboriginal Australians divide mankind into groups or totems, in which the totem animal is often considered as the ancestor of the group and is treated with great reverence. In ceremonies connected with the initiation of young men as full members of the totem, dances in which the men represent themselves as the totem animal often take place. These dances, which are for men only, are invariably held at night, and are not to be confused with the corrobboree, in which the women are allowed to participate. In the light of the flickering campfire the sacred churingas, slabs of wood on which totemic designs are carved, are brought from their sacred hiding-place. The bull-roarers set up their deafening racket, and the men of the Emu totem, daubed with paint and tricked out in feathers, wearing an immense superstructure, made of down, feathers and twigs, to represent the head and neck of the bird, circle slowly round the fire, throwing their arms about and moving their heads to resemble the birds when feeding. The exact significance of these totemic dances which the aboriginal takes so seriously has never been definitely ascertained; but it is possibly connected with a powerful belief in the infallibility of the totemic ancestor to provide the means of existence or to avenge injuries done to the group, or simply to impress the young men to whom the full rights of manhood have been given, but who have not, as yet, witnessed the sacred ceremonies.

ANOTHER kind of animal dance is the hornbill dance of the Kayans of Borneo, which is simply a comical imitation of the movements of the bird, in fact a kind of buffoonery which delights the bystander. Sometimes local legend inaugurates a new species of dance, and in Yap of the Caroline Islands there is a dance to represent the iguana, who is famous, or infamous, as Galuf, the hen-roost robber. The natives usually stand up in a line striking up a lively chant with a trampling accompaniment which goes faster and faster as the dancers warm to their work. The dancers alternately face front and flank, swaying backwards and forwards in unison, and marking off the cadences with a measured stamping. The movements are supposed to represent, by means of twists and turns and violent convulsions of limbs, the stealthy and serpentine crawl of the iguana prowling on its marauding errand. In Lau of the Fiji Islands the boys often dance the snake dance, which consists of a party of boys imitating the action and movements of a snake.

Amongst the peoples of Asiatic Siberia the dance assumes the character of pantomimic drama. The Yukaghir, who may be described as a nomadic people, have a singularly graceful and vivacious mimic dance called the 'dance of the long-necked one'—the swan. Girls and youths form a circle and revolve from right to left round a couple representing a male swan making love to a female. The male circles the female, lifting alternately the right and then the left arm (that is, in the mimicry, the wing), while the female tries to evade his approaches. At the same time the dancing couples imitate the mating calls of the swan.

THE Chukchee, who are chiefly remarkable for the fact that they have domesticated the reindeer, often dance in pairs, to the sound of music, imitating the young deer in spring. The children perform a dance called the raven dance, which consists of hopping round on one leg pretending to search the ground for something to peck at, while from time to time the raven's croak is imitated. The Koryaks another primitive hunting people of Eastern Siberia, perform similar dramatic dances in which seals are imitated. A row of Koryak men faces a row of women, and the men and women produce in turn guttural rattling sounds, tramp on one spot, bend and unbend their knees, and sway their bodies to and fro. The primitive inhabitants of the Aleutian islands, the land bridge from America to Asia, have pantomimic dances which are accompanied by songs; in one of these pantomimes a hunter shoots a beautiful bird which is suddenly transformed into a beautiful woman, with whom he at once falls in love. It would be impossible to leave these Eastern Asiatic peoples without some mention of the Shamans or priests. Shamanistic dances very often feature animals; for instance, the Buriats sometimes perform a pantomime of the taming of a horse in which the young people take the part of various common animals and the shaman that of the bear, ox, wolf, pig, or porcupine.

It is obvious that among the hunters of the Asiatic North, to whom the close observation of the habits of animals is a means of livelihood, dances in imitation of the habitual sports of the chase were fairly common. Animal dances of the East are usually included in pantomimic dramas, and are superficially little different from the animal antics of our pantomimes from Dick Whittington's cat to Mother Goose. As in the East, our animal figures are the subject of legendary lore, as in the East, the successful imitator must study the habits of the animal closely, as in the East, our animals are often figures of fun; the difference lies in the underlying religious motive of the dance and the trance-like state the dancer attains; superficially this is a difference of little import: fundamentally it is all-important.

GREATLY ENVIED WOMEN: THE ONLY FEMALE DANCERS IN THE WAJANG WONG

Since the eighteenth century human actors have been substituted for the cleverly manipulated marionettes previously employed to cast the shadows on the screen in the Javanese Wajang, or shadow dances. One noteworthy feature of these revised entertainments is that there is only one play in which women are allowed to take part. This is the Wajang Wong of the Prince Mangku Negoro, in which, as shown here, female dancers represent a pagan goddess and her waiting women. In all the others the female parts are taken by boys and young men, as was the practice of the Elizabethan drama in England. Their exclusion is attributable to the ritual character of the dances, but is further justified by the enormous physical strain imposed upon the performers. Some of the individual dances last as long as an hour and a half, and the whole series of performances occupies four days of sixteen hours each—from six in the morning until ten o'clock at night. Photographs in pages 49 to 52 by Tassilo Adam.

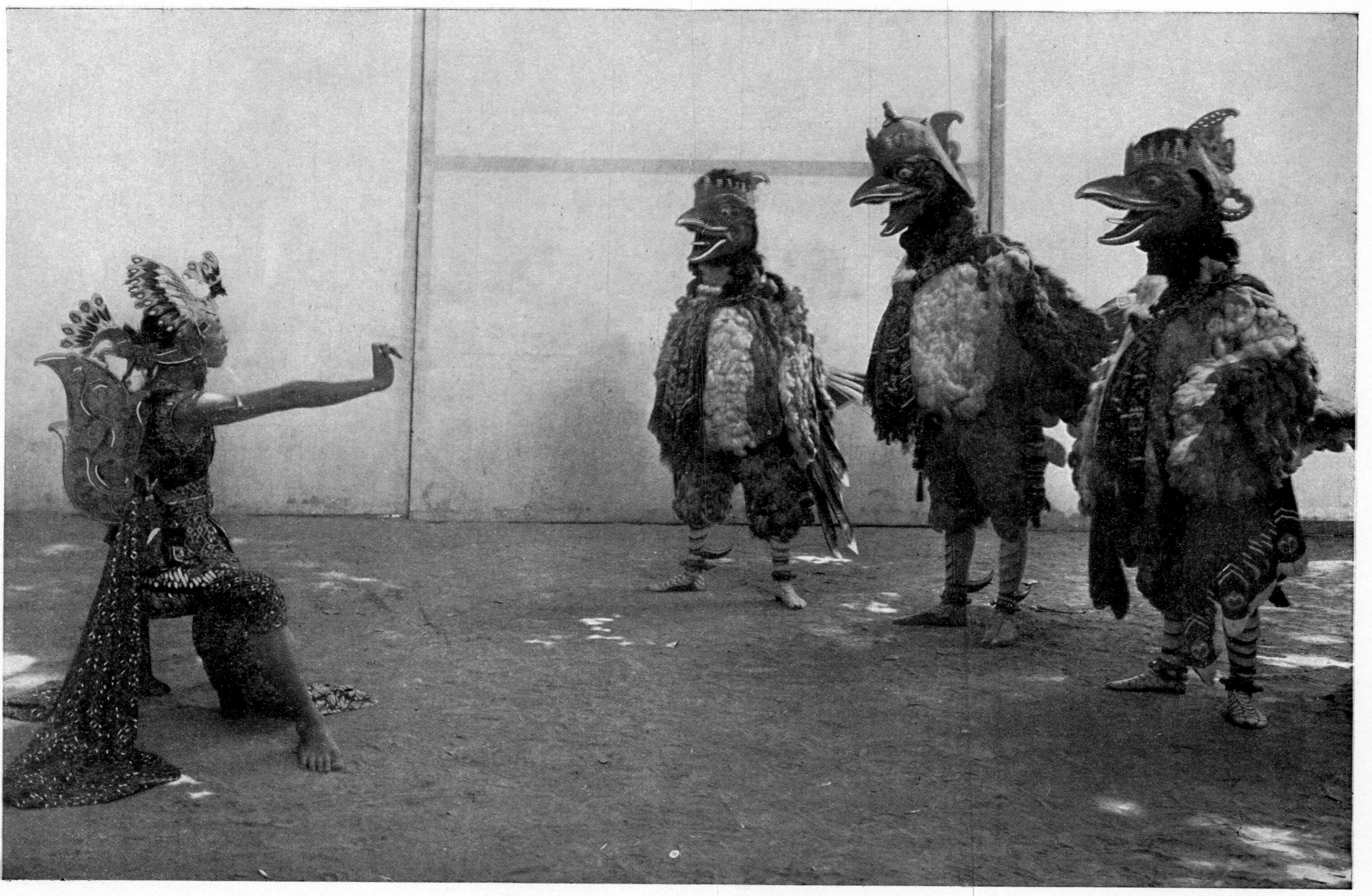

KRISHNA WITH THE GARUDAS, THE RITUALISTIC HUMAN BIRDS OF THE JAVANESE

Birds occupy an important place in Hindu mythology and are credited with great wisdom. In the Ramayana they figure as the Garudas, Lords of the Air, who come to the aid of Rama when Ravana the demon king abducts his bride Sita. In Java as the Ritualistic Fowl they are regarded with reverential awe, and they appear in one of the most striking scenes in the Wajang Wong, where Krishna holds mystical communion with them, addressing them much as S. Francis of Assisi is reputed to have addressed the birds. Special care is devoted to the construction of their costumes, which are adorned with feathers of the barnyard fowl imposed in life-like fashion on vestments so exquisitely woven and dyed as to be indistinguishable from real feathers of the birds. One dress alone took the plumage of four hundred hens.

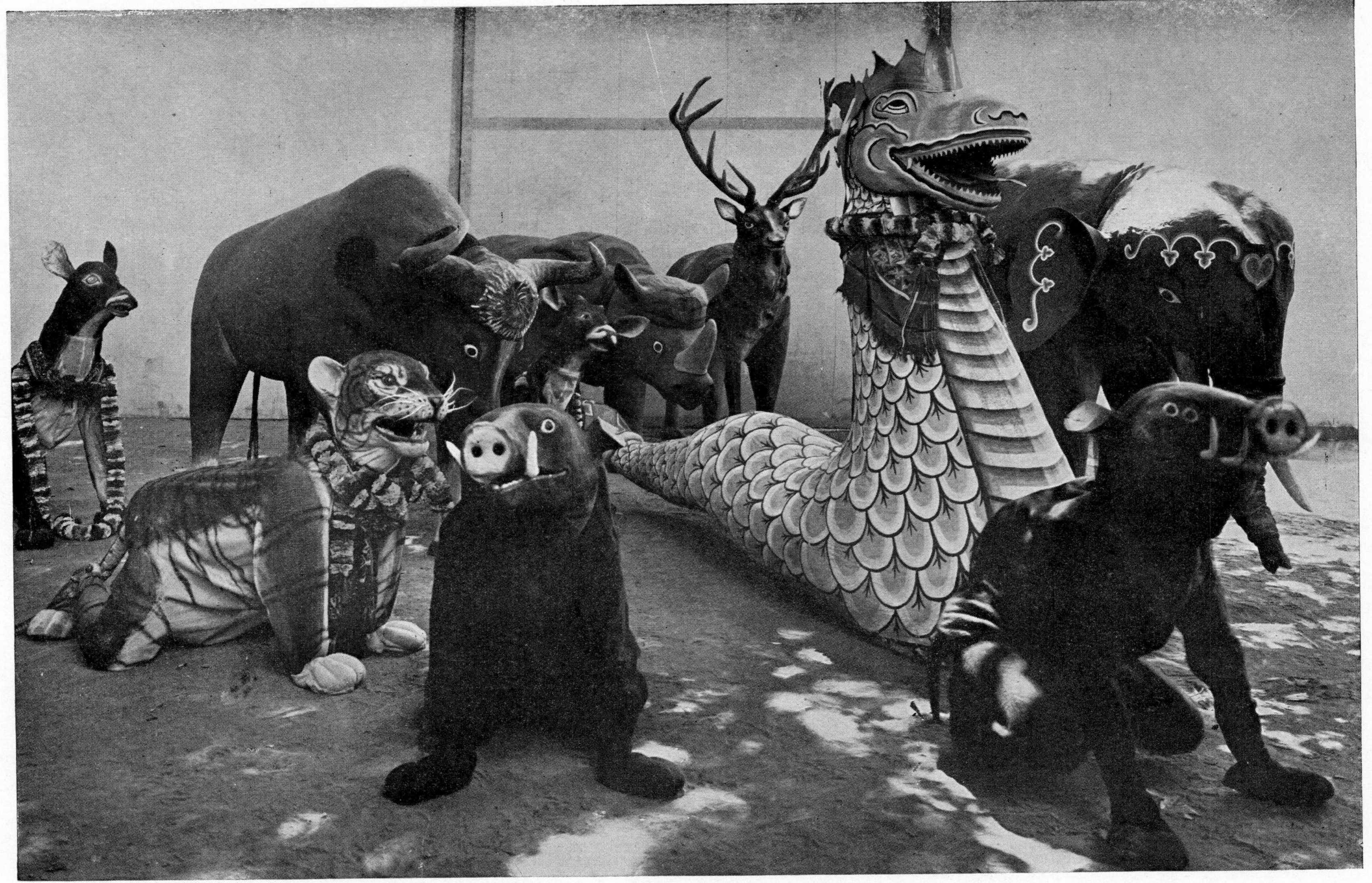

MEN IN MYTHOLOGICAL BEAST FORM ASSEMBLED FOR HINDU RITUAL DANCE

These are some of the many animals that figure in the Javanese stage representations of the legends of Hindu mythology. Most prominent among them is the Serpent Prince, Prabu Wisamuka, lord of all reptiles, whose effigy combines the characteristics of both serpent and crocodile, having the flexible darting tongue of the former and the latter's ridge-toothed gaping jaws, both of which are practicable and are moved by the actor concealed within the frame. One of the most poignant scenes in the play shows the critical meeting between the serpent prince and Siva the Destroyer. Another powerfully dramatic scene shows the mortal combat between the elephant and a pagan god. The menagerie includes a number of monkeys, which play a large part in one particular dance under the leadership of Hanuman, the famous White Monkey of Hindu legend.

MASTERPIECES OF THE JAVANESE PROPERTY MAKER'S AND ANIMAL ACTORS' SKILL

All the property jungle beasts, farmyard animals and birds of the air appearing in the Wajang Wong were modelled in the theatre studio of the Sultan's palace by the artist-in-ordinary to the court. They are wrought in the baroque Javanese style of art and reproduced in the identical colours of the originals. All the performers in the Wajang Wong, the marvellous ritual dances in animal form which date back several centuries, are subject to almost military discipline and are much more strictly trained than an ordinary corps de ballet. Absolute physical fitness is indeed essential to the performers representing the animal characters, since they have to endure the weight and heat of their burdensome costumes for so many hours at a time. Preparations for the most recent production of these ritual dances—given in honour of the silver wedding of the Queen of Holland—took a year and a half to complete, during which time the entire company of 350 dancers practised and rehearsed every day except Friday—the Sabbath day.

DRIVING OUT THE DEVILS OF DISEASE

EVERY country and social group has its own original methods of combating the evils that attack the body. Here we consider those savage peoples who, attributing disease to devils, spirits and other supernormal agencies, attempt to drive them away by magical processes. The more systematised magic of the medicine man and the wider subject of native leechcraft are dealt with separately.

AMONG primitive peoples, and indeed among many at a comparatively advanced stage of civilization, the conception that death and disease are due to natural causes lies beyond the bounds of their comprehension. As contact between the white man and the savage, particularly at the early stages of intercourse, usually leads to a high mortality among the latter, their fear of the supernatural agencies which they regard as the cause of the calamity has frequently involved travellers and employers of native labour in serious difficulties. In the earlier half of the last century, when missionary effort was extending to Savage Island, the natives would not allow a Samoan teacher to land because, they said, 'the foreign wood would cause disease,' alluding to the spirit they attributed to his boat, which they expected to be hostile to them, as they attributed spirits to their own canoes. Similarly in South Africa, at the beginning of this century great difficulty was experienced in obtaining labour for the mines owing to the high rate of mortality, which had convinced the natives that if they were employed there they would be particularly exposed to the fatal attacks of witches.

The means employed by backward peoples to meet the attacks of disease and its fatal results are devised to accord with their conception of its supernatural origin. Broadly speaking, two theories of disease are current among primitive peoples. On the one hand it may be held to arise from something which is introduced magically into the body; on the other it may be thought to be due to something which has been drawn out by magic means. Hence, although among many peoples who are at this stage of thought herbs and substances used as drugs may be administered medicinally—not a few of these have real medicinal value, and some are to be found in our own pharmacopoeia—it is their employment as an element in magic that is the efficient factor, and it is the magical formula or the performance of the ritual that in their conception is the curative agent. When the various methods of primitive healing are examined it is found that, generally speaking, they involve a species of magical conflict in which the spirit of disease is driven out, overcome by superior power, or otherwise defeated.

AT the earliest stage of primitive thought of which we have direct evidence, namely that of the Australian aboriginal, it might appear at first sight as if the idea of the magical origin of disease had hardly attained a spiritual level. The aborigine, living in a world in which every one of the objects with which he comes into contact has a spiritual entity, does not discriminate between material and spiritual. But although disease, it is believed, is caused by the projection of a stone, a quartz crystal, a bone or some other material object into the body of the victim, it is sometimes specifically stated that only the spirits of these things enter the body. As, however, their real existence is demonstrated to the patient, perhaps they are to be regarded as materialising there in the spiritualistic sense.

The occurrence of quartz crystals among the objects which cause disease is peculiarly interesting and important. They are among the most prized objects of the Australian medicine man's dilly-bag; and it is by the introduction of quartz crystals into his body, as revealed to him in a dream, that frequently the medicine man acquires his powers. Consequently when the disease is caused by or through the intervention of a medicine man, the quartz crystal is the agent he generally employs.

AT this stage magic is not the monopoly of the medicine man; any individual may work magic. The following is the method of causing illness employed by members of the Dieri tribe. Any man who has an enemy procures a stick or a bone—if a human bone, so much the better—about a foot long and pointed at one end. To the other end is attached porcupine grass resin, to which adheres, if he has been able to procure it, hair of the victim or something which has been in close association with him. If twine is attached to the stick, it is afterwards burnt in a fire. Retiring to the bush or scrub, the man points the bone several times over his shoulder in the direction in which his enemy may be supposed to be. The man will then fall ill and, unless cured by more powerful magic, will die.

Various methods of performing the 'pointing bone' ceremony are found. Some are considerably elaborated and require two men for their performance, with various accessories such as lengths of string to convey the blood of the victim to the bone—this giving the operator power to control the victim—emu feathers, fat and the like. In all, the essential feature is the same, the passing of the material object carrying the disease, whatever it may be, into the body of the victim from the point of the bone.

The Australian medicine man's method of treatment of a patient where the pointing bone method has been used—it is not employed by all the tribes—was to utter incantations over him as he lay on the ground, to massage the body, squeezing hard and sometimes causing intense pain, and then to apply

From Sir Baldwin Spencer, 'Wanderings in Wild Australia,' Macmillan & Co.

be inherited by her daughter. It wears a grass petticoat like that of a woman except that it is shorter, and produces diseases by inserting a sliver of bone or fragment of coral in the victim's body.

The belief in the expulsion or extraction of disease in material form from the body and the methods by which the Australian medicine man performed that operation are of wide distribution. Primitive medical practice consists mainly in rubbing, massage and the real or fictitious withdrawal from the body of foreign substances by cupping or suction Among the Mafulu of New Guinea the medicine man, or in this case woman, removes a snake from the stomach of the patient.

his mouth to the body of the patient. Sucking hard, he drew from the body into his mouth the cause of the trouble, exhibiting it to the spectators as a piece of bone, a stone, a quartz crystal, a rag or piece of twine. Various elaborations were practised in different parts and among different tribes, but essentially the methods were identical.

It was sometimes recognized, as has been mentioned, that it was not a material object that had entered the body. In north-west Australia, disease was caused by evil spirits sent by neighbouring and ill-disposed tribes. These the medicine man drew out of the body into his mouth by suction, then carrying them a short distance away in his hands, he carefully buried them. He then returned and inserted a good spirit into the body of the patient.

Francis Birtles

'SINGING' OVER THE SICK

The Australian aborigines believe disease to be due to magical substances gaining entrance into the body. Above, a group of medicine men, having 'sung' over the invalid, are consulting concerning the source of the evil magic. In the lower photograph a native woman occupies herself first with domestic remedies, and after encasing her sick child in mud, she has placed upon it a newly killed turtle to promote warmth. Next, the medicine man will be called in.

Further stages in the full development of the idea that disease is caused by a spirit may be seen in New Guinea and Melanesia. In the New Hebrides, for instance, disease is sent by means of an arrow, to the shaft of which charmed material has been attached. In Papua a 'sending' is regarded as an emanation from an individual, while at Gelaria the 'sending' has assumed a form. It resembles a shadow which dwells in a woman, and is sent from her body. At her death it may either go with her spirit, or it may

A bark cloth is rubbed up and down the front of the patient's body, and then the woman makes a gesture as if removing and wrapping up a snake. It is unnecessary to multiply instances.

There is, however, a ceremony among the Huichol Indians of Mexico which it is worth while to describe more at length. The medicine man first rubs his hands several times as if washing them, then stretches his fingers quickly one after another so that the joints crack. This he does to imitate the crackling of fire.

E.N.A

BRUSHING OUT THE EVIL SPIRITS OF ILLNESS WITH LEAVES

Among some peoples disease is regarded as being caused by a spirit that dwells either within the body or else upon the skin of the victim. Until this spirit has been removed the patient cannot get well. In instances where the skin is thought to be the abiding place of the spirit of disease, recourse is had to such methods as fumigation, beating, washing, and various forms of massage. In the photograph a Papuan sorcerer is charming away illness by gentle massage, that is, by brushing the patient with leaves supposed to possess magic curative properties.

He next breathes on his hands and, holding them together, spits on them. He then holds them out towards the south, north, west and east, and also towards the ground. He places his mouth on that part of the patient's body which is the seat of the pain. Making a kind of gargling noise, he sucks out the disease in the form of a grain of corn or small stone, afterwards coughing. The grain of corn is then burned or thrown on the ground for the wind to carry away. He then breathes on the affected part, making passes as if to sweep the disease away. A similar ceremony was performed in ancient Mexico, but there the priests used a mixture of aromatic herbs, previously masticated by them, with which they first rubbed the patient.

This very interesting ceremony combines the material and spiritual conceptions of healing. The invocation to the four quarters of the heavens in the raising of the hands may be compared with the belief in Anglo-Saxon leechdom that diseases were sent by winds from the four cardinal points; in the appropriate charm the leech blows away the diseases as if they clung to the exterior of the body. The use of masticated aromatic herbs and the spitting of the Huichol medicine man recall the importance of spitting and the spittle, with or without the accompaniment of chewed areca nut, betel or some herb, as a purificatory agent in healing ceremonies. The efficacy of spittle survives in higher civilizations in the custom of spitting when an offensive object is mentioned.

With purification we pass from the material to the more purely spiritual conception of the causation of disease. The object of ceremonial purification is to cleanse the person by driving away spiritual influences, usually through the operation of material agents such as fire, smoke, water and the like. Disease is here conceived as due to an indwelling spirit or ghost. The latter may be either the ghost of a member of the family or an ancestor or it may be that of a foreigner. It is for this reason that primitive peoples are hostile to strangers, fearing that the ghosts or spirits they bring with them may cause disease. At one time great difficulty was experienced in recruiting

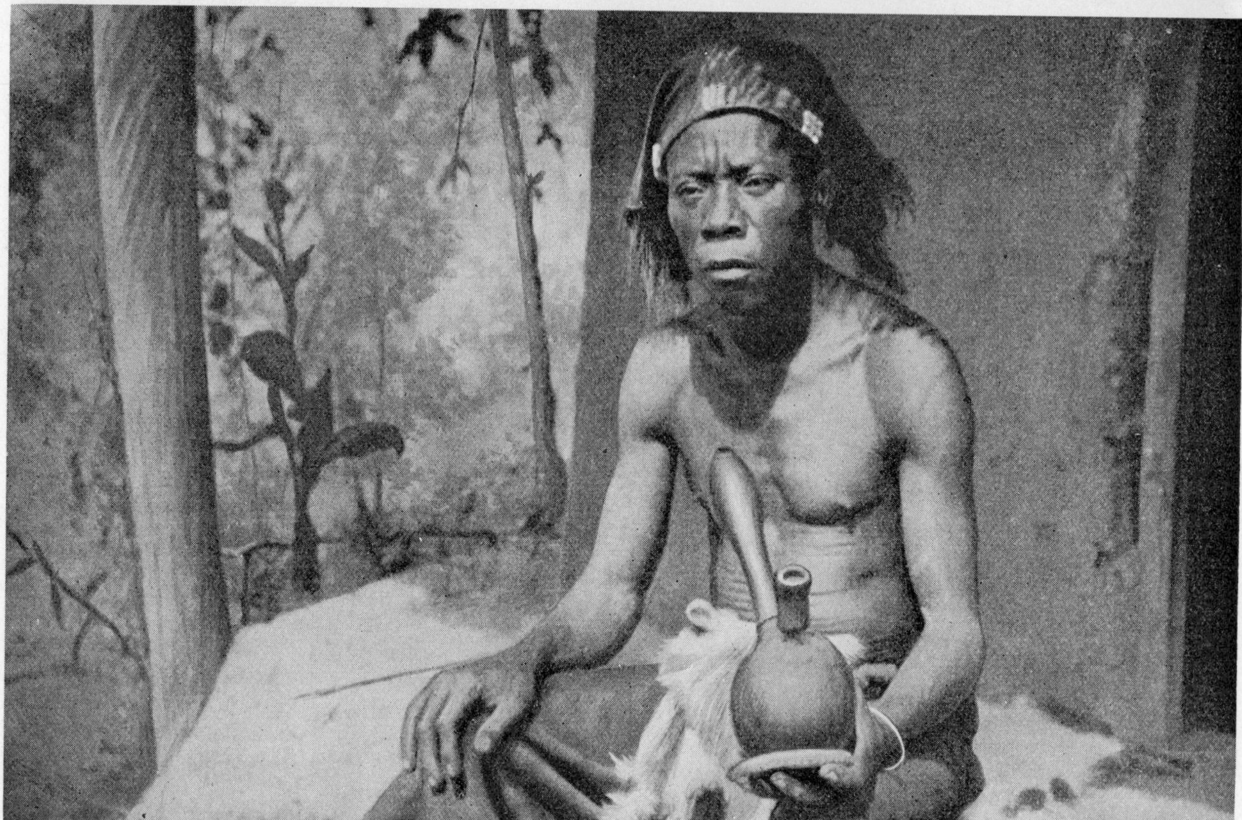

G. P. A.

A SAVAGE PRACTITIONER OF THE HEALING ART

The medicine man is a very powerful personage, the practitioner of the healing art and kindred mysteries. He is initiated into the secrets of his profession with elaborate rites, he wears a special dress, and he usually carries the instruments of his craft in a medicine bag. He performs his marvels by a variety of means—by incantations, by ventriloquism, by sleight of hand, by suggestion, and so forth. The upper photograph shows natives of the Molungo tribe of Central Africa spellbound before the medicine man, engaged in driving out particularly powerful demons. Below is a portrait of the great man in his proper habit for the scaring of devils of sickness and hurt.

the Bathonga of north-east Rhodesia for the Kimberley diamond mines, as they believed that in passing through the Zulu country they became possessed by Zulu ghosts, which they brought back into the Bathonga country. Again, when their warriors went out to war, they were forbidden on their return to cross the borders of their own country until they had undergone an elaborate purification ceremony; otherwise the ghosts of the warriors they had slain which accompanied them would have inflicted disease and other evils on the people.

The action of the indwelling spirit of disease may range from causing the merest local unease to absolute possession in the sense of psychic abnormality, hysteria and its attendant phenomena—a form of mental aberration common in eastern Asia. The ceremonies performed to rid the patient of his disease are no less widely diverse, and vary from gentle persuasion to violent purgatives and emetics physically and the most compelling exorcisms psychically. Sometimes the spirit may be given the opportunity to escape, as by bleeding In certain islands of the Pacific. headache and epilepsy are treated by trephining. Thus in New Britain a hole is scraped in the top of the skull with a stone knife or a piece of shell, and the dura mater exposed so that the spirit may escape. The hole is then covered with a piece of coconut shell, or the scalp may simply be drawn over it. The patient sometimes recovers. On the other hand, violent and nauseating medicine composed of the foulest ingredients may be administered to drive out the spirit of disease in disgust—the theory, if on a different basis, of our allopathic system of medicine, and also a practice of Ancient Egypt. Another form of spiritual purification as a remedy for disease in general use among the Indians of North America was the prolonged steam-bath in the sweat-lodge, an institution probably to be related to our Turkish bath through north-east Asia.

E.N.A.

STATUE THAT KEEPS DISEASE OUT OF A CITY

This fine figure of an elephant carved in stone is a conspicuous landmark in the city of Chieng mai, an important teak centre of Siam. It is regarded with the greatest veneration by the inhabitants for they believe that it is this stone elephant that protects their city from diseases of all kinds. The statue itself is known as the 'Guardian of the City.'

It would seem that some peoples, like the Anglo Saxon already mentioned, think the spirits adhere to the skin. Hence ceremonies of fumigation and brushing or castigation are often employed. In the Malay Peninsula the medicine man brushes down the patient with leaves seven times; the Blandas of Selangor burn benzoin gum to drive the spirits away. In ancient Sparta at an annual festival in the temple of Artemis Orthia boys were severely beaten, a test of endurance which perhaps arose from a purification ceremony intended for the protection of the whole community. Ceremonial bathing is also practised—a common and obvious form of purification. In Murray Island a man who had been bewitched and was unconscious was healed by a ceremony in which the medicine man, after being anointed with coconut oil by his attendant as he approached the patient, lying on the ground with closed eyes, gazed steadily at the body and then spat and blew upon his hands. He then moved his hands with a steady motion towards the patient as if conveying some invisible force to him. After crying out in a loud voice he rushed to the sea with the patient and they bathed. The patient was then massaged, an operation which was repeated daily if necessary.

Fire is a powerful purificatory and protective agent. Even if not specially mentioned, disease-spirits, it may be assumed, are to be included among the evils averted by the periodic performance of protective fire rites. Fire, and objects heated in a fire, are, however, also specifically used to drive away the disease of an individual. An interesting and instructive ceremony is performed in the Malay Peninsula on the occasion of childbirth. If a woman dies in childbed, it is believed that she becomes a ghost or demon whose aim it is to steal the new-born child and harm the mother. The mother and child are, therefore, placed on a platform under which a strong fire is built. This is kept up for some days. In one case, a few years ago, the result was fatal to the mother. The participants in the ceremony were indicted for murder, and an effort was made to suppress the custom. Passing through flames or smoke is effective as a prophylactic. One of the sixteenth-century European travellers in Persia records that certain members of his caravan, after staying the night in a caravanserai, built a fire in the courtyard in the morning and leaped through the flames before they started on their day's journey. Thus they rendered impotent any evil spiritual influence which might have attached to them from their night's lodging. Similarly, the Scottish shepherd used to make his sheep pass through the smoke of the ceremonial fires, which were at one time lit on stated occasions, to ensure their future immunity from disease. In fact it would not be too much to say that all the great ceremonial fire-festivals once celebrated in Europe, Beltane on May 1st, at Midsummer, at the November feast of the dead on All Souls, and the Christmas and New Year bonfires, inasmuch as they were connected with reverence for the dead, included disease and pestilence as not the least of the evils they were intended to drive away from the farmer and his family, his cattle, sheep and crops.

CALLING ON THE DEVILS TO WARD OFF ILLS

Wearing a head-dress decked with hornbill feathers and wild boar's tusks, and a sword decorated with a tiger's tooth, this high priest of Kachin, Burma, is invoking the 'nats' or devils to accept a sacrifice. Nearly all a Kachin's actions are prefaced by consultation with the nats. If he wishes to be protected from disease or other ills, the nats are invariably approached.

It is to be observed that, as in the use of fire, measures taken to cure or protect the individual may be extended to protect the whole community. An interesting ceremony, of wide distribution, but with

Cambridge University Press

According to Dr. C. G. Seligman, in his authoritative work 'The Veddas,' this primitive people of Ceylon believe that the spirits of their dead have power to affect their lives for good or ill, and in the latter event must be propitiated. This man is reciting an invocation to ascertain which spirit is responsible for an illness that has overtaken him. The bow so carefully balanced will swing to and fro when the name of that spirit is spoken.

E.N.A.

BLIND FAITH THAT HOPES TO WARD OFF THE INVISIBLE MALIGNITY

In parts of India particular diseases—cholera, for example, and smallpox—are attributed to particular supernatural agencies or deities, and these must be placated by ritual services originating in fear, no heed being given to scientific methods of prevention or cure. When an outbreak of smallpox occurs, the goddess of smallpox is carried abroad, accompanied by attendants grotesquely masked and attired in weird vestments, the most distinctive of which is an enormous helmet swathed round the brim with material with weeper-like ends hanging down below the waist.

Driving Out the Devils of Disease

SUMMARY TREATMENT OF INFLUENZA GERMS IN JAPAN

E.N.A

Japan has every reason to be proud of the contributions to medical knowledge made by her men of science since she opened her gates to foreign influences and learning. Not yet, however, have Western methods spread throughout the land, and this quite recent photograph shows two local notabilities of a small country town driving the devils of disease down the main entrance steps of an hotel where several guests had fallen victims to an epidemic of influenza.

local variations, is found in eastern Asia in which disease is charmed from the patient along streamers into some object such as a model human figure. In the Malay Peninsula there are twelve of these made of coloured rice and standing on a tray. These figures are then put on a little boat, which is placed on the river and left to float away. On the Mekong river this ceremony is performed annually, and the boats, each with its lighted lamp, float away at night, carrying all the evils and diseases of the village. In the Nicobar Islands a similar purification ceremony takes place in the course of the annual Monsoon Festivals.

Bamboos decorated with bunches of leaves of various palms are erected on the beach as 'scare-devils,' and for three nights in succession the witch doctors catch, beat and spear the evil spirits and bind them with thongs fashioned from a particular creeper. The devils are then placed on a raft rigged like a ship with sails of palm leaf and with palm leaf torches tied on to it, and when the wind is favourable this is towed out by swimmers beyond where the surf breaks. When night falls the torches are lighted and the ship with its load of evil spirits is set adrift, to be slowly borne away by tide and breeze.

And finally may be mentioned the ceremony of the Scapegoat—a ceremony in which the disease is transferred to an animal. Among the Hottentots an ox is slaughtered while the patient holds his hand on the leg of the beast. In Bechuanaland the ceremony is communal. The paramount chief is seated on the body of a bull which lies stretched on the ground. Its head is forced into a pond until it drowns. As a substitute for the chief, it expiates the sins of the community and frees them from the ills which would be their consequence. The idea of the scapegoat survived in a number of European seasonal festivals, especially in Germany. At Easter or Whitsuntide a man or a woman was dressed up to represent 'Winter' or 'Death,' and after a day of carnival he was chased from the village or district and was then burned or buried in effigy. (See pages 12 and 15.) Thus the people even 'chased out Death.'

THE CEREMONIAL USE OF EFFIGIES

EXHAUSTIVE study of the many purposes for which effigies of men and animals have been employed at one time or another would carry us back to prehistoric times, when they were important adjuncts of sympathetic magic. Here they are considered only as they are found in use today, as one feature in the many and varied funeral customs which form the subject of other chapters in this work.

THAT death is the portal of another life closely resembling this one was the view of very primitive times. It is shared in our own age by those spiritualists who, from their communications with the dead, have pieced together a picture of existence on the Other Side differing little in many aspects from the life of the quick. Early man could not conceive the human soul surviving apart from the human body, and the concern of those left behind was to see that the corpse was protected in every way. Wives were killed or burned so that the dead man should still have the comfort of matrimony; food was provided him, in some cases at regular intervals by means of a tube or narrow passage into the grave—many traces of this custom are to be found in prehistoric tombs in the British Isles—his arms and household utensils were interred with him; and to this day the Patagonians kill horses at the grave of their dead chief so that he may ride to Alhuemapu, or country of the dead.

Over six hundred years ago Marco Polo described the funeral rites of the Chinese in Hang-chau, which, in that unchanging land, are still carried out to-day. 'When they come to the burning place they take representations of things cut out of parchment, such as caparisoned horses, male and female slaves, camels, armour, suits of cloth of gold (and money), in great quantities, and these they put on the fire along with the corpse that they may all burn with it; and they tell you that the dead man shall have all these slaves and animals in which the effigies are burned alive in flesh and blood, and the money in gold, at his disposal in the next world.' In every modern Chinese city the manufacture of these paper effigies remains an important industry.

FUNERAL EFFIGY OF A BRITISH KING
This saturnine figure in wig and ruffles is a wax effigy of Charles II. It forms one of a collection of funeral effigies of British monarchs and other notabilities kept in a secluded chamber in Westminster Abbey.

To preserve the reputation of the deceased—perhaps, too, to distract the attention of evil spirits from his remains—the employment of effigies is almost universal. The Romans had waxen masks made which were brought out and paraded on state occasions. All our own Sovereigns up to and including Queen Anne had effigies made of them before they were buried. For several centuries they were fashioned of *cuir bouilli*—leather soaked in hot water to render it pliable. When this particular art of modelling was lost, wax was employed for making the effigies. In Westminster Abbey there is an upper room where these funeral effigies are preserved. The most notable is that of King Charles II. There are ten other figures, beginning with Queen Elizabeth and ending with Lord Nelson, but neither of these, the first and last, is really a funeral effigy. Here is General Monk, who brought the Stuarts back, sunk to four feet, a headless James I, William III and Queen Mary, that Duchess of Richmond and Lennox who figures as Britannia on our coinage, and Queen Anne.

To-day the use of funeral effigies is preserved in several forms throughout the world. The Patagonians, already referred to, wait a whole year after the death of their chief, then collect his bones and arrange them in the form of an effigy, which they then proceed to dress in the deceased's best garments, with beads and feathers. The ceremony is completed by burying the effigy in a square pit round which dead horses are placed, set upright on their feet by sticks. Among the Melanesians of

THE RICHER THE CHIEF THE BIGGER THE EFFIGY
In the district of the Waterfalls, Belgian Congo, when a chief dies his body is placed on a grate made of reed stalks and roasted until it is mummified, the widow or the next of kin tending the fire. It is then dressed in all the dead man's clothes. If the chief was rich and so the possessor of an extensive wardrobe his effigy may assume such fantastically huge dimensions as are shown in the photograph. After the details of the face have been painted in, and the tribal marks tattooed on the stomach, the finished effigy is carried round the village.

the Solomon Islands there is a curious custom which embraces the idea underlying the use of funeral effigies. 'The mourners,' we are told, 'having hung up a dead man's arms on his house, make great lamentations; all remains afterwards untouched, the house goes to ruin, mantled, as time goes on, with the vines of growing yams—a picturesque and perhaps indeed a touching sight.' Some Eskimo shut the dead man's body up in his house, leaving by his side as a funeral effigy the head of a dog which shall guide him on his last journey, along with his tools and kayak. The Sea Dyaks set a chief adrift in a war canoe with his weapons.

So deep-rooted in modern man is the instinct to link himself up with the departed that it is recorded that at Lord Palmerston's funeral one of the mourners was seen to drop his watch and jewelry into the open grave—so that 'Pam' presumably should be able to tell the time in that eternity where time is not, and have the means of providing himself with some of his accustomed luxuries. This happened as lately as 1865, and comparatively recently at Paignton, Devonshire, a lady left food and wine in the vault where her mother lay buried—thereby attracting all the hungry of the neighbourhood. In France, on All Souls' Day, this ancient practice still survives, and cakes and confectionery are carried to the graves in the great Parisian cemetery of Père Lachaise. Thousands of lives are sacrificed in the Dark Continent of Africa each year, in spite of all efforts to stop the practice, so that the departed shall not be without his companions in the other world.

According to the ritual of the Lake-Wake that portion which deals with the 'laying out or streaking of the Body' provides for the presence of certain functionaries called Sin Eaters, who presumably took upon themselves for the occasion the identity of the deceased and his responsibilities—which is the idea underlying the use of effigies at funerals. Mary Webb in her famous novel 'Precious Bane' makes use of this Sin-Eating custom, which was prevalent in Shropshire.

Beck & Macgregor

'TOMBSTONES' FROM AN INDIAN BORDERLAND

These figures are life-sized funeral effigies from Kafiristan, the north-west boundary of India. They are rough-hewn from the deodar with axes and finished off with knives. The couple represents a man (left) and a woman, the single figure a woman on a throne.

The most fantastic use of effigies at funerals to-day is that employed in a certain district of the Belgian Congo. Lest men who call themselves civilized should feel unduly superior when they read of these savage rites, they should remember that our own mortuary ceremonial of hearses and weepers and trappings of woe is really equally incongruous. In Catterate, in the district of the Waterfalls, the body of a dead chief is placed on a kind of grate made of tressed reed sticks. Underneath this the widow or the nearest relative keeps a big fire burning. The body is turned carefully upon a spit until it assumes the mummified appearance of overdone meat. It is then dressed in all the clothes belonging to the dead man. As the wealth of a Boer farmer is said to be ascertainable by the size of the dung heap outside his farm, so here the importance of the deceased chief is to be gauged by the dimensions that his effigy assumes. The richer he was, the more stuffs, linen and cloths he left behind, the huger will become his effigy, until it assumes the gigantic proportions given in the illustration. A very rich chief will in his effigy become three or four times life-size.

This dressing having been done, experts then paint in the various details of the face, and other specialists tattoo characteristic tribal marks with dye-stuffs on the abdomen. When everything is ready the mummy is carried in procession around the whole village, and so at last to the burying ground. Above the grave the family erect a little temple made of wood sticks and covered with reeds, and food and drink are regularly brought to the grave by relatives. The funeral ceremony ends with a wild burst of shouting and the beating of tom-toms and finally a dance and a feast.

RAINED ON BY MANNA FROM AN EARTHLY HEAVEN

Whenever a man of Siam thinks that he has grown too rich for the peace of his soul he first goes out and spends all his superfluous money on food and clothing. He then kneels (top) before an image of Phya Yomaraj, the King of the Devils, tells him that he is going to give his substance to the poor, and offers prayers and praise. Finally he mounts a high platform (bottom), accompanied by others in the same predicament, and from this eminence the penitents fling down their purchases to be scrambled for by the assembled poor below.

GIVEN TO THE FLAMES BUT DESTINED TO RISE AGAIN

This prostrate flaming effigy is Phya Yomaraj, the Siamese King of the Devils. After he has enacted his appointed part his image is pushed over by the crowd and the broken giant burnt with much rejoicing. This great idol is set up from time to time by those who wish to divest themselves of their wealth for the benefit of the poor, so that they may ensure recognition for themselves when they appear before Phya Yomaraj seeking entrance into Heaven. The effigy destroyed, the sometime Dives must again become rich before another image may be erected.

In Siam an effigy is employed in what may be called an anticipatory funeral rite. The ceremony is a curious mixture of barbaric paganism and the purest ethics. In this respect it is reminiscent of the worship of the Aztec, who mingled with the most appalling blood rites teachings almost as altruistic as those of Jesus Christ.

The Siamese believe literally in the divine dictum that it is more difficult for a rich man to enter the Kingdom of Heaven than for a camel to pass through the eye of a needle. What in European countries has been cynically called 'fire insurance' has induced many a rich man on his death bed to leave his wealth to charity or church. But the Siamese faith is either more fervid or simpler. They believe in shedding their superfluous goods during their lifetime, when real self-denial is entailed thereby. Whenever their accumulation of real or personal property becomes too big, so as to threaten their welfare hereafter, they perform this curious ceremony.

The first step is to erect a great image of enormous stature. This idol is called the King of the Devils and stands 75 feet high. Round this gather all those whose fate hereafter has not been placed in jeopardy by the possession of too much of this world's goods. They pray and sing, begging benefits from Phya Yomaraj, as the idol is called in the native tongue. Then the conscience-stricken rich man plays his part. He has already rid himself of his superfluity of wealth by making huge purchases of food, clothing and fruit. He approaches the idol and, kneeling down, informs the King of the Devils that he is about to give his substance to the poor. Prayers and praises to Phya Yomaraj are then offered. Afterwards the penitent, with his fellow conscience-stricken rich men, mounts the high platform built for the express purpose. From here the penitents throw down the gifts they have purchased to members of the poorer class below. Instantly the dignity of the scene is disturbed by a kind of scrimmage. The populace fight merrily to get possession of the offerings. Special hooks are even manufactured and employed so that the distributed goods can be raked in more readily.

Phya Yomaraj has now played his part. As the guardian of the dead he has been propitiated. He will see to it that the penitent's access to the next world will not be hampered by his wealth. There is a rush and the King of the Devils is flung to the ground. The shattered remains are then burned amidst great rejoicings. Before another celebration of the kind can be performed, the residents of Siam have to accumulate more riches.

There are now in the British Museum some very remarkable funeral effigies from Kafiristan, which lies midway between the Imperial northern outpost of Chitral and Afghanistan. The district, made famous in one of Rudyard Kipling's stories, is still practically unknown country. It takes its name from the fact that its untameable inhabitants are Kafirs, or unbelievers. They are a light-coloured race claiming descent from the Greeks of Alexander the Great. Many of their customs are very primitive, and especially peculiar are those relating to funerals.

F. H. Byron

A CLUSTER OF SACRED PALACES BUILT ONLY TO BE BURNT

In Burma the funeral of a Buddhist monk who has gained renown by his ascetic life and been over twenty Lents a monk is marked by great splendour. Among its striking features are the pyathats (top), elaborate bamboo structures adorned with coloured paper, tinsel, and pictures of events in the life of Buddha. Palatial though these are, they are burnt down at the end of the festival. Disciples of the dead man are housed in specially built rest-houses called mandats (bottom), each containing a cradle on which to rest the coffin during its progress.

F. H. Byron

READY TO SPEED THE HOLY DEAD TO THE FUNERAL PYRE

This colossal elephant car is typical of the tumbrils seen during the obsequies of celebrated monks in Burma; the coffin rests in the pagoda-like howdah. On these occasions the streets are alive with enormous gaily decorated effigies of elephants, tigers, and other animals mounted on cars. The Burmese believe that great merit attaches to those who help in conveying the coffin from one resting point to another. To each end of those cars upon which the coffin is to be carried stout ropes are fastened, and a tug-of-war decides who shall obtain the privilege.

Gerard Goschen

PASSING THROUGH WATER TO BECOME PURE

The people of the little island of Bali, east of Java, though physically like the Javanese, differ considerably in customs. The Balinese retain the older forms of Hinduism, and cremate their dead or effigies of them. The rites connected with the cremation ceremony include purification by passing through water, and here Balinese are walking through the river for that purpose.

Round stones are used for the eyes. These effigies are held in superstitious veneration, and in that wild tangle of cliff and ice-field, the inhabitants ascribe all the dangers of sudden storms, avalanches and landslides to any mishandling of them.

The most elaborate use of effigies in funerals is peculiar to Burma. A Buddhist monk is known in the Burmese language as Hpongyi, and if he is celebrated for his ascetic life and has spent more than twenty Lents as a monk, his funeral festival is known as a Hpongyi Byan. The ceremony is one of extraordinary pomp and elaborate detail. Funds for the performance of the rite are collected from the monk's pupils, who are, of course, scattered all over the country. Meanwhile the corpse is embalmed in wood, oil and honey. As no monk may be burnt during the Buddhist Lent—that is from the full moon of July to the full moon of October—the body may be kept for a considerable time. At last, when sufficient funds have been gathered, a large open space close to the town is selected, and on it enormous Pyathats and Mandats are erected. The Pyathats are huge buildings from forty to fifty feet high, lofty bamboo structures of elaborate design richly decorated with coloured paper, tinsel and pictures of scenes from the life of Buddha. The Mandats are more like Burmese rest-houses, and, intended for the use of the dead monk's disciples and pupils and for the purposes

The village Shenitans, or cemeteries, are formed on almost inaccessible shelves on the cliff side. These, though chosen as close as possible to the villages, are not held sacred. They are merely places to be avoided because the dead are not buried but placed in very rough, far from air-tight, wooden boxes which are distinctly insanitary. Only a very rich or influential man gets one of those boxes to himself. At the time of the interment a straw effigy of the deceased is burned above the grave, followed by a feast given to the village by his relatives. One year later an effigy, like those given in the illustrations in page 61, is set up on the shelf where the body lies. They are made from the deodar tree and are fashioned only with axes and knives.

of rest and meditation, are adorned with silken curtains, tinsel, velvet carpets, and embroidery of oriental design. Each of them contains a cot or large cradle on which the sacred remains rest for at least ten minutes during some time of the eight day ceremonies. A portion of the Mandat is curtained off for the use of other Hpongyis.

Every day of the festival is devoted to feasting and amusement. Troupes are engaged to entertain the guests with music dance and song, and bullock cart and horse races contribute to the uproar. Gaily decorated effigies of elephants with their howdahs, tigers, peacocks, all of exaggerated size, are mounted on carts. Some of these are utilised for bearing the sacred coffin in the procession. To settle who shall

'KING OF THE DEVILS': MONSTER SIAMESE EFFIGY

This great image is the Siamese King of the Devils, Phya Yomaraj. In accordance with the Siamese belief that entrance into heaven is jeopardised by riches, the wealthy at various stages of their lives give away their surplus to the poor. As the guardian of the dead, Phya Yomaraj has to be propitiated in this manner. In the case of old men, the performance of this ceremony may be looked upon in the nature of a funeral rite, or at least of one performed in preparation for a more or less imminent passage to the next world.

Gerard Goscher

A STAGE IN THE BODY'S LAST JOURNEY

In Bali before cremation the body is placed under a special shelter, such as is shown in the photograph, which is erected on land belonging to the dead person's family. In this various religious and domestic formalities are performed before the body is transferred to the funeral car. Cremation is an expensive process, and on this account may be postponed for years. Sometimes all vestiges of the body save the bones have disappeared, and then little effigies of the dead person are burnt instead. The same applies to persons who have died in far-off places

Gerard Goschen

HEARSE SERVES FOR FUNERAL PYRE

The funeral car used by the Balinese has a lofty spire made of bamboo and rattans, towering tier upon tier in the manner of a pagoda. The car is drawn by rattan ropes to the scene of the cremation, and there set alight. The body is utterly consumed

achieve the great merit of drawing the sacred coffin, a species of tug-of-war is engaged in. Ropes are attached to each end of the cart with its effigy and crowds pull on the ropes strenuously. The struggle lasts until the victors succeed in wrenching the vehicle away from the vanquished. It is then proudly drawn on its way from one Pyathat or Mandat to another, being moved in the course of this progress to various other carts. The women are allowed to share in this rite of drawing or carrying the coffin. The effigies employed are extraordinary works of art.

On the eighth day of the festival the gilded coffin is taken to the funeral pyre to be burnt. If the dead monk is of very high standing, the fuel used is sandalwood, and the pyre is always decorated with gold and silver tinsel, silk, white calico, and palm and plantain leaves. When it has been consumed by the flames, the charred bones of the monk are reverently gathered up and carefully interned in a pagoda close to the deceased monk's monastery. These bones are disposed of according to the sanctity of the deceased, sometimes being ground into powder and moulded into an image of Buddha, which, daintily gilded, is then presented to the dead Hpongyi's monastery.

THE most extraordinary part of the ceremony is the burning of the Pyathats, some of which rise to a height of nearly a hundred feet—elaborate buildings merely erected for the purpose of being destroyed. Strong ropes, sometimes made of wire and a hundred yards long, are fixed from the Pyathat to different parts of the ground. Rockets are suspended from these ropes. At the right moment in the obsequies a rocket is fired by means of a long taper. Propelled along the rope, it strikes the Pyathat with a resounding crack. As each rocket plunges into this edifice of paper and bamboo, the crowd cheers itself hoarse. If the pyrotechnic expert has done his job badly, and the rocket sputters and stops half-way up the rope, shouts of derision rise from the mob. The rockets are made of large bamboos, measuring as much as four or five feet in length, and having been hollowed out, are filled with gunpowder and bound round with bamboo straps. They are usually painted and mounted with cardboard or metal cut-outs, representing fabulous beasts. Great honour accrues to the maker of the rocket which first fires the Pyathat.

Inevitably, under this bombardment, the Pyathat catches fire. Flames rise, licking the tinsel and gold leaf, the paper and silken trappings. The tall spires totter and dissolve. The miniature city, raised simply to do honour to the dead Hpongyi, vanishes in smoke. The excitement of the crowd rises to its height as the last Pyathat tumbles in. Only then is the ceremony over and the crowds, chanting songs, prepare for their journey homewards.

Such examples, which might be multiplied indefinitely, will serve to illustrate how by means of the crudest symbols mankind has managed to represent more clearly, and hence in the long run to elevate and purify, the deepest emotions touching the ever-present problem of the meaning of death

HOLY WEEK AND ITS CEREMONIALS

EVERY religion has its feasts and fasts, ritual observance of which is enjoined upon its adherents, and such ceremonies lead to the institution of complementary customs outside church or temple. Here some of the religious customs connected with the Christian Holy Week are described. Passion Plays form the subject of another chapter, as do also the purely lay customs attaching to Eastertide

EASTER, the most triumphant of all Christian Church festivals, is marked by almost all sects of Christians with striking and elaborate celebrations. The contrast between the long fast during Lent, the tragic events of Holy Week, the crime of Good Friday, and the sudden, startling gladness of the Resurrection, lends itself readily to the purposes of ecclesiastical pageantry. The Puritans made little of Easter; their spiritual descendants, the Free or Nonconformist bodies in Britain, the Lutherans, Zwinglians and Calvinists of the Continent, follow their example. But the Roman Catholic Church and all those in the Church of England who call themselves Anglican Catholics do everything possible to bring out its significance by picturesque and stimulating ceremonies.

In many churches there are dramatic representations of the death on the Cross and the burial, followed by that of the empty tomb. As the scene in the stable at Bethlehem is reproduced at Christmas for the edification of worshippers, so the grave in the garden is shown at Easter, a symbol of despair on Good Friday and of victory on Easter Day. No effort is spared to make the difference between the emotions of these occasions vivid and enduringly impressive. The services in St. Peter's at Rome on Good Friday may be taken as illustrating to the highest degree of effectiveness what is aimed at among Catholics all over the world. Signs of mourning are to be seen throughout the Basilica. Desolation and gloom are suggested in all kinds of ways. Neither the Pope nor the Cardinals nor the Bishops wear their rings of office; they dress in purple, the colour of grief. The Papal Guard appear with reversed arms. The Pope, after his shoes have been taken off, goes to the partly-veiled crucifix and kisses it. The Miserere is sung in the afternoon to a crowded congregation in the Sistine Chapel

ON Easter Sunday everything is reversed. Cannon are fired early in the morning to announce the good news. St. Peter's is in a blaze of light. All ecclesiastics wear their most splendid vestments. The music is of the most joyful character. Carried in his high chair above the heads of all the others, the Pope celebrates Mass, and then from the balcony over the main entrance he gives his blessing to a vast crowd outside. Such, with variations of magnificence, are the Easter ceremonies in all Catholic churches. But there are certain special celebrations peculiar to certain places, with their origins far in the past, which have particular interest, not historical only, but because they throw light on the mental condition of large numbers of people to-day.

The most remarkable of these takes place in Seville. Hundreds of years ago the members of a number of religious orders in that city were instructed, as a penance, to walk in solemn procession to the cathedral on the night following Holy Thursday and preceding Good Friday. These orders were known as 'Cofradias' (confraternities), and they exist still. They even wear still, when they are engaged on duties of pity and kindness, the dress of the Middle Ages penitent with a big 'extinguisher' head-covering, coming down over their faces, of which nothing can be seen but their eyes, glittering through narrow slits in the coarse cloth. Wearing this costume and carrying lighted tapers, the members of the 'Cofradias' continue every year the practice of their predecessors

George Long

ANCIENT GARB IN SEVILLE'S HOLY WEEK

The dresses of the various confraternities of Seville seen in Holy Week differ greatly in colour and details. The cream-coloured robe with purple buttons and cord and purple cap of the member of the Brotherhood of Our Lady of Hope (right) is in striking contrast to the deep crimson robe and red hood (left).

Topical Press

ONE OF THE MANY IMAGES OF THE VIRGIN BORNE IN THE HOLY WEEK PROCESSIONS OF SEVILLE

Seville is famous for its sacred images, and in the ceremonies of Holy Week figures of Christ and the Virgin are taken out of the churches and carried in procession. These images are among the most treasured possessions of the churches of Spain's southern capital. Some of the Madonnas are robed in rich stuffs covered with gold and jewels, and glitter with costly rings and bracelets. For the processions the images are mounted on platforms, and these are placed not on wheels but on men's shoulders. Impatient crowds wait outside the churches for the moment when the figures are brought out into the street. After the singing of traditional airs the images start their toilsome journey to the cathedral. The photograph shows the image of the Virgin of Refuge.

centuries back. They are all laymen, and they include numbers of the wealthy and aristocratic people of the city It is scarcely an exaggeration to say that all who do not take part in the processions look on at them, so there is no going to bed on Good Friday night in Seville.

For two days no wheeled traffic has been allowed in the streets. This does not matter so much in the capital of southern Spain as it might elsewhere, for the Sevillians are not much given to driving, except in the main carriage throughfare on Sundays and holidays, and the principal streets are really too narrow for vehicles. This helps to give the place its lounging, gossiping Moorish character and makes it so delightful unless you happen to be in a hurry and want to pass through the throng. But to be in a hurry in Seville is unpardonable; it is to miss the whole charm of the city.

If the processions were arranged by people who had any sense of time and attached any value to it, they would be all over in an hour, instead of taking up five or six. The distance traversed is short, but the pace at which the processionists move is very slow, stops are frequent, and the last thing that occurs to anyone is that the business might be got through more quickly Why should it? The spring nights in Andalusia are soft and warm. There are delicious scents in the air, scent of roses and carnations, scent of orange trees. Besides, no one ever has thought of going home on these occasions before dawn at earliest. Why should anyone now?

George Long

SYMBOL OF ANCIENT ROME SURVIVES IN MODERN SEVILLE

Seville is a city of many confraternities. The dress of the Brotherhood of the Sacred Spear Wound (above) is very striking, the robes cream-coloured and the cap and bib scarlet. Roman military emblems, such as the S.P.Q.R. banner, are common. Below, a confraternity is seen leaving San Lorenzo, the church that owns the famous image of 'Jesus of Great Power.'

Not until after midnight do the brethren of the Orders begin to assemble in their churches. You see them leisurely parading, strange sinister figures in their dress, that is so unpleasantly associated in our minds with the Spanish Inquisition. Their monkish robes are of black, white or purple; these are surmounted by the tall conical hoods described already. Let us follow some of them to the church of San Lorenzo, which owns the most famous of all Seville's images, 'Jesus of Great Power.' These images, Saviours and Madonnas, are an important part of the processions. Their platforms are carried on the shoulders of men, who shuffle along under their heavy burdens in the ancient traditional way. As we go towards San Lorenzo we see that the cafés and wine shops are still open and well filled. Tobacconists are doing a brisk trade in cigarettes. In the square before the church there is a crowd already; it grows larger every minute, though it still wants half an hour of two a.m., the hour at which the procession comes forth. The crowd is lively, even noisy. It chatters and jokes. It cries

E.N.A.

ONE OF THE STRANGEST USES OF A FIREWORK DISPLAY

On Holy Saturday in Florence, when the cathedral Mass reaches the 'Gloria,' a fire in the form of a dove is lighted at the altar and conducted outside by a wire to this car, where it sets off the fireworks with which the car is covered. The car was presented to Florence by a family one of whose ancestors had brought from the Holy Sepulchre stoves which were used for the fire for the Easter lights. People vied with each other to be the first to light a candle at the sacred fire, and when a descendant of the donor did this, a firework display was inaugurated

impatiently for the doors to open. At last two o'clock strikes. The lights are put out. There are some cat-calls and demands for the image to appear. In a few moments the great doors of the church swing slowly back. The 'penitents' are seen massed within. They begin to stream out.

Above the heads of the crowd we can only see the points of their hoods and the yellow patches which their tapers make in the darkness. But when the platform with the image is borne forth, it can be seen plainly by all. A silence falls upon the people Every man takes his hat off. Women bow their heads. Almost everybody is muttering something in the nature of a prayer—or is it an incantation? Then suddenly the silence is torn by a voice, metallic, unmelodious, but wonderfully flexible. It sings a hymn in praise of the Saviour to a melody that is unmistakably Moorish—a florid, yet monotonous Arab chant. It is the custom to welcome the images with these traditional airs. Well-known singers are engaged to sing them at certain points; at other points they may be sung by unknown people in the crowd.

THE singing relieves the tension. Talk and laughter begin again. The image is moved on. The crowd breaks up. A rush is made now for the Plaza de la Constitucion, where stands have been put up and seats are sold at high prices, from which all the processions can be seen as they pass through the square To-night there are six brotherhoods moving towards the cathedral, each from a different church and each with two images. These include several famous Virgins in costly robes of brocade stiff with gold and covered with jewels—not tinsel and paste, but the real thing. Diamonds glitter on the necks and stomachers of these figures. Rings of great worth adorn their fingers. Bracelets, given in gratitude for prayers answered, hang on their wrists. Their value runs into hundreds of thousands of pounds.

Now, as we take our seats in the Plaza, it is just on three. Boys are crying programmes and caramels. There is a cheerful buzz of talk and laughter. One cheeky urchin lights his stump of cigar at the flare of a penitent's taper. No one is shocked.

There are two youngsters just in front of us who might have sat as models to Murillo ; they play and squabble without ceasing. There are long intervals between the processions, and they frequently halt, either because the streets leading to the cathedral are blocked or because the carriers of the platforms must be given frequent rests. From twenty to as many as forty in number, they are hidden, as they move, by the valance of the platform. When they come into sight now and then, mopping their faces, to get a little air, we can see they are working hard. They give the platforms a curious jerky movement, like that of huge insects with innumerable unconnected legs.

The scene leaves behind an imperishable memory. In spite of the many jarring notes in it, the effect is certainly impressive, though it belongs to a different age and to a state of mind totally unlike that of the twentieth century. The penitents' costumes are some of them almost beautiful. Each 'Cofradia' has its own cross and banner and blazons its device upon the robes of its members. Women walk in the processions as well as men (only a small number, though), and children also. One feels sorry for the tiny boys and girls, toddling along wearily. Perhaps it is the sight of them and the feeling of sympathy with them which makes us feel weary ourselves. Let us go to our hotel, then, though it is scarcely five o'clock. No one else seems to be leaving. We might misquote Wordsworth : 'Dear God, the very houses seem *awake !*' We fall asleep with the sound of the bands which accompany the processions and of metallic voices chanting Moorish melodies still in our ears.

Evidently there is a fascination in the scene. Next evening, that of Good Friday, we are watching more processions of exactly the same kind. This time the seats in the Plaza are full at six and remain well filled until towards midnight. In a box are the mayor and town councillors, not paying very much attention to the 'Cofradias,' smoking innumerable cigarettes. Daylight is fading as the cloaked and hooded figures move interminably on. The moon lends to Seville's famous tower, the Giralda, a fairy, far-off loveliness. The Scenes of the Passions on the platforms draw to a close. Last of all comes Death, a grisly figure triumphing at the foot of the Cross. But only for the moment. On Sunday we shall celebrate the discomfiture of Death. The veil which has hidden the altar screen all the week will be lifted. The golden bells will clang joyously. The great organ will fill the whole church with triumphant harmonies of faith and thankfulness.

In many other places there are parades of penitents in more or less the same costume as that which the confraternities of Seville wear. They are to be seen in Rome even. At Palermo in Sicily the penitents carry on their hoods crowns of thorns : they

E.N.A.

THE EXPLOSION OF 'THE CAR' IN FLORENCE

The fireworks are seen exploding on the car outside Florence cathedral (see previous page), and the populace watch the leaping flames with joy. Their delight on this occasion is doubled if the Little Dove has performed its journey from the high altar to the car without a hitch, for this is regarded as an omen that the coming harvest will be fruitful.

Central News

Topical Press

TWENTIETH CENTURY PENITENTS WHO MAINTAIN MEDIEVAL HABITS AND SYMBOLISM

Among the most remarkable features of the Holy Week celebrations are the processions of the confraternities in Seville, which originated in a penance imposed upon certain religious orders many centuries ago. Having assembled in their various churches early on Good Friday morning, the confraternities walk in procession to the cathedral, wearing medieval penitent's dress. A long pointed hood is drawn over their faces, with slits for the eyes. The upper photograph shows a procession of the Nazarene Confraternity, and the lower a group of hooded figures halted before an image of the Dying Christ.

George Long

CARRIER OF THE CROSS IN A SEVILLE HOLY WEEK PROCESSION

Magnificent jewelled crosses such as the one seen here are conspicuous features of the Holy Week processions of the Confraternities in Seville. It is considered a great honour to carry the cross on these occasions, and the man to whom the coveted privilege is granted walks barefooted, just as did the penitents from whom the observance is believed to have originated. The other members of the brotherhood wear buckled shoes and carry each a lighted candle, with the exception of those directly escorting the cross-bearer, who are equipped with long wands.

have also ropes round their necks which are looped about their hands, clasped on their breasts in the attitude of prayer. Thus they cannot release their hands from this attitude. Sometimes the emotion aroused by Christ's suffering expresses itself in more dramatic form. On the evening of Good Friday another procession moves through ancient streets lighted by torches as well as by tremendous starlight. In Monaco the Stations of the Cross are acted, also by members of a brotherhood. Costumes and 'properties' have all been used for years which go back beyond living memory. One curious feature of this Passion Play is that at each Station a different actor takes the part of Christ. All, however, wear the same dress of scarlet, open at the breast to show splashes of red paint on the flesh to resemble blood. Hair and beard are white; on the head is the crown of thorns. Pontius Pilate has an open umbrella held over him by an attendant. Four gowned lawyers who act as his advisers have on their heads the biretta of the French advocate. The Roman captain also wears a lawyer's black gown. A slave carrying the basin in which the Governor washes his hands of the whole business is habited in a white satin cloak. King Herod, who gets into the picture somehow, has an 18th century wig and flowered waistcoat, a scarlet gown and a gilt paper crown. Adam and Eve are there, too, fully dressed in the Louis Quinze style.

P. & A.

PENITENTS OF ROME MARCH WHERE THE EARLY MARTYRS DIED

Seville is by no means the only place where processions of penitents in medieval dress take place during Holy Week. Palermo, in Sicily, and Monaco are other towns that have them. In Rome, too, in Holy Week, mystic figures in cassock and cowl parade the streets carrying crucifixes and great lanterns. The photograph shows such a party about to enter the Coliseum.

As the procession moves from point to point, Christ is attacked by Jews and Roman soldiers, all the movements and acting being regulated by tradition many centuries old.

There are not many religious ceremonies peculiar to Holy Saturday. This is, however, a great occasion in Florence. Since the eleventh century fire for the Easter Lights (which have all been put out before Good Friday and so must be re-lit) was obtained from stoves brought in 1099 from the Holy Sepulchre by a Florentine who went to Jerusalem with the most celebrated of the Crusades. These were given to the municipality, and by them presented to the principal church in the city. They had already become objects of adoration among large numbers of the pious inhabitants. The municipality ordered that the fire, when it had been created by means of these stoves, should be taken to the cathedral and other churches. As it was carried round, numbers of people lighted candles at it and supposed they were glorifying God by going about with these. It was considered lucky to be the first to light a candle in such a way.

One year—it was the year 1300—a young man belonging to the family of the donor of the sacred stoves succeeded in being the first; his relations were so pleased that they decided to show their gratitude by a display of fireworks when Holy Saturday came round again. This became an annual custom with

Keystone

HOLY WEEK DEVOTION AT THE PASSAGE OF THE CROSS

When the cowled figures that are so frequent and picturesque a sight in Rome during the celebration of Holy Week walk through the streets in procession, their passage is the occasion of the most fervent manifestations of piety on the part of the assembled populace. One and all salute the crucifix with every circumstance of devotion. The old and infirm bow reverently to the Cross as it is being carried past them held aloft in the hands of its strangely garbed bearer, while those who are able kneel before the sacred symbol.

them and more of a show every year. At last they asked permission of the municipality to build a car covered with harmless explosives which should be set off by the sacred fire at the moment when the Gloria of High Mass begins. At first the car was burned each time, but the family resolved after a while to build a more solid and decorative 'carro' that should be used year after year. It has many times been renewed in the course of centuries, and is now in no way remarkable. But the ceremony of letting off the fireworks with which it is filled in the square before the cathedral is one that always attracts a large concourse of spectators.

Drawn by white oxen, the car arrives in front of the cathedral. There it waits until the moment comes for the Archbishop of Florence to set light to a dove which is at the end of a wire running from the high altar to the doors, and then outside to the car. As soon as it has been kindled the dove starts along the wire, wobbles, stops, goes on again, wobbles again, gets to the end of its journey, and sets the fireworks off. If it is very slow and stops often, the omen is considered a bad one. If it travels without interruption, the people say the next harvest will be a good one. After the display on the Piazza del Duomo the car is taken to a corner near where the old house of the family which provided it used to stand. There some more crackers are fired, and the programme ends.

Quite as impressive as any Easter ceremony is the midnight service in a Russian Orthodox Church. For an hour or so before twelve o'clock there is sonorous chanting by the deep thrilling voices of the choir, all men. Then the lights are all lowered, the music sinks until it can hardly be heard. As twelve begins to strike the lights go up, the organ and the choir unite in psalms of victory, the priests and the members of the congregation kiss one another and say 'Christ is risen,' to which the reply 'He is risen indeed' must be returned. In the streets this used to be done also. After the service feasting begins at once; it goes on all next day and the day after. Special dishes and cakes are eaten, there is much drunkenness. The beauty of the Mass which ushers in Easter is too often forgotten in the pleasures of unrestrained appetite.

HABIT AND CUSTOM IN THE ART OF FISHING

FISHING in some form is a very ancient pursuit, depending upon simple means. The later developments of fishing into a specialised form of hunting by water led to the introduction of more elaborate implements, some of which are described here. The chief varieties of hunting on the land, whether for food or for sport, are dealt with in other chapters in this Section

FROM time immemorial man has hunted and fished. Around these pursuits there grew up a ritual of experience, but as long as they remained the only means of filling the larder, they were merely hunting and fishing. When they were followed, not for the simple reason that man was hungry but because the ritual lingered, they became sports.

So to-day we have the ceremony of fox hunting and stag hunting and fly fishing—though everybody knows that we could exterminate Reynard more quickly with a gun, that venison could be procured far more efficiently and far more economically than by pursuing stags with hounds, and that there are dozens of quicker ways of transferring a fish from his native stream to the dinner table than by the orthodox method of the hook and the artificial fly.

But there are the sacred rules of sport. Your true fisherman, as distinguished from the low fellow who is merely hungry and wants something to eat, has laid down decrees more exacting than the laws of the Medes and Persians, in accordance with which alone the sport may be pursued. And this is the underlying principle. On biting at an artificial fly the fish, with unerring instinct, immediately detects the game which has been put on him and spits it out. Before he can complete these capers the skill of the angler comes into play, and the fish ought to be hooked in the lip. In this position the hook can be removed without fatal results.

The growth of the angler's religion is very much like the growth of any other religion. If you are curious to trace it you have only to read Izaak Walton's 'Compleat Angler,' the seventeenth-century treatise which for the mere literary person is the Bible of Fishing. For your real sportsman Izaak is little better than the common poacher who puts quicklime into an empty whisky bottle, fills it up with water, corks it swiftly, and then throws it into a pool, where the gases generated cause it to explode, with the consequent killing and stunning of all the fish in the neighbourhood. Did not Izaak Walton shamelessly advocate the use of live grasshoppers as bait, and did he not tell us that 'a black snail with his belly slit to show the white' was a lure that was 'choicely good'?

M. Steedman

FISHING BY TORCHLIGHT IN HAWAII

The Hawaiians have always had to rely upon the sea for a great part of their food, and a flair for fishing is innate in them. They are skilful in all branches of the craft, and their knowledge of the habitat and habits of fishes is amazing.

BUT it is with the men throughout the world whose souls have never been lifted to the higher idealism of a hook and an artificial fly that we are concerned The poacher with his ready-made bomb of quicklime, once a popular device in England and Ireland, merely follows a method which is met with all over the earth. How often during the war were Mills bombs used for this purpose? How many a mess has been supplied with fresh-water fish by this means, with the O.C., perhaps himself in peaceful times the most rigorous of sportsmen, partaking of the dishes, and careful not to inquire how they happened to appear on the menu?

To this day fishermen in Co. Wicklow, Ireland, catch salmon by methods which offend against all the sporting canons. Not far from Woodenbridge on the river Avoca, close to that spot made famous by Thomas Moore's 'Meeting of the Waters,' there are certain ochre mines. The deposit from these mines seeps through into the river and is

N. B Baboneau

POISONING THE WATER FOR AN EASY CATCH

The natives of North Borneo sometimes catch fish by drugging them with the juice of a poisonous root called tuba. Having found a quiet reach, the fishing party build a bamboo platform in the water, and on this they pound bundles of the root. The juice drops through the interstices of the platform into the water below and the fish are gradually stupefied. When the poison has worked long enough to render the fish easy to catch, the party jump into the water and secure their haul. Poisoning by tuba has no effect on the food value of the fish

carried down towards its mouth at Arklow. The salmon coming in from the sea strike this polluted water, which acts upon them very much in the same way as an anaesthetic. They cease to swim and float up to the surface, where the fishermen secure them.

While the Wicklow fishermen merely take with thankfulness what the gods send them, and cannot be accused of drugging the fish, the Pagans of North Borneo deliberately employ this method to secure food. Mr. Owen Rutter, in his work on the 'Pagans of North Borneo,' describes how this is done.

LARGE hauls of fish are made by the use of the tuba root (Derris elliptica, a poisonous root used also as an abortive medicine by the Papar women). For this a considerable party assembles, each person bringing his own bundle of tuba, which is pounded on a bamboo platform built over a pool or quiet reach, so that the milky pulp falls into the pool below and stupefies the fish, though it does not render them unfit for eating. As soon as the poison begins to take effect, everyone dives and dives again, shouting with glee as they come up with fish in their hands. Tuba fishing is the nearest thing to a river picnic that the Pagan knows. Fish caught in this way may be preserved by being split open, salted, and allowed to dry in the sun.

In the Nicobar Islands, formed in common with the Andaman Islands in the bay of Bengal by the submarine spurs of the Himalayas, fish-doping is also employed. Owing to the unquiet sea there are no good spawning grounds near the islands. As a consequence fish is a luxury—so much so that the trading firms have to supply their own men with an allowance of dried fish. The Nicobarese have therefore to snatch what opportunities present themselves in order to garner the harvest of the seas, and they are not hampered by any consideration of the strict ritual of the sport.

They watch for a reach of comparatively shallow water at high tide. Shortly before the tide turns a great number of men and women will get some way out on the water in a kind of chain. Here they will splash about and keep dashing small boughs of trees into the water to prevent the fish that have come along with the tide from returning with it again. By this means they gradually drive the fish towards the shore. Some are safely cabined in shallow pools or are stranded on the sands and so are easily caught. Others, however, find a refuge in a pool of some depth left behind by the retreating tide. Just as our own mackerel fishers keep splashing the contents of their seines to prevent the fish from escaping from the net until it has been drawn close, so the Nicobarese

E.N.A.

J. Hornell

THE DIFFICULT ART OF SHOOTING FISH WITH BOW AND CROSSBOW

Among primitive races one of the most widespread and at the same time most difficult methods of catching fish is that of killing or wounding them with arrows shot from a bow. The Pagans of North Borneo use their bows and arrows almost entirely for fishing; they never carry them as weapons The upper photograph shows Papuan boys using little bows and arrows for shooting fish that have been left in pools on a reef. Below, a Malabar native is seen employing an antiquated Portuguese crossbow for the same purpose

Col. F. D. Fayrer

FISHING WITH SPEARS ON AN INDIAN LAKE

Catching fish by impaling them on spears is a practice found in many parts of the world. Familiar instances are the salmon-spearing of Scotland and the eel-spearing on the mud flats of estuaries in Tasmania. The Black Bhils of Rajputana are particularly expert at this kind of fishing. The spear they use is a very long pole, measuring about twice the height of the fisherman, and topped with a formidable barb. A party of Bhils is here seen engaged in fish-spearing in a lake from a primitive log raft. Note the barbed ends.

surround this pool and drive its captives into the centre. Next they sprinkle on the water a powder made of grated kinyav seeds mixed with ashes.

The completion of the catch is interesting. In his book on the Nicobar Islands Mr. Whitehead gives a native's description of what happens. 'Some big fish die, others do not, and these last we shoot with bow and arrow, or strike them with dahs (choppers). We are a long time over it, for we have to wait for the different kinds of eels to come up, and when they do come out we strike them with a dah. Then we go home and gut and scrape the fish, and put them on a split stick and roast them.'

One might be rashly led to assume that the use of the bow and arrow for securing fish—a method so difficult that it might be said to rank with the sacred hook and artificial fly—is peculiar to the Nicobarese But this is not so. It would appear to be common to the primitive races throughout the world. In one of our illustrations we give an extraordinary picture of a native using an ancient Portuguese cross-bow—what a history must lie behind that bow—to stock his larder from the waters.

E.N.A.

AN ARTIFICIAL FISHING POOL IN THE SOUTH SEAS

The natives of the South Sea Islands have an ingenious method of providing themselves with good fishing grounds. They fence in a part of the sea between the reefs and the shore, with the result that the shoreward stretch becomes a well-stocked fishing pool when the tide goes out The photograph shows one of these native fisheries in the Solomon Islands.

In North Borneo, indeed, the Pagans only know and use the bow as part of their piscatorial equipment or for jungle traps. Authorities have argued that the absence among the Pagans of the bow and arrow as a portable weapon is evidence against any comparatively recent migration from Asia, or any intimate contact with the Chinese. With the bows used for fishing or spring traps the arrow is invariably attached to the bow by a strand of rattan. It is argued from these facts that the stock from which the Pagans of Borneo sprang had not learned the use of the bow when the cleavage took place—assuming the theory that the present Pagan tribes inhabiting North Borneo are the descendants of Indonesian immigrants from the mainland of Asia—and also that they never had any opportunity of acquiring the use of a weapon so valuable and efficient since they came to the island

Readers of R. D. Blackmore's classic, 'Lorna Doone,' will remember how John Ridd, when he was a small boy, went fishing for loaches in Bagworthy Water, and so found his way to the Doone valley and had his first interview with Lorna. They will recall, too, how his fishing tackle consisted of 'a three-pronged fork' firmly bound to a rod with cord The method he used to catch those loaches is still common throughout the world for very much bigger fish. In Tasmania to this day one of the favourite night sports is eel-spearing on the mud flats of the estuaries The equipment consists of a boat of shallow draught a lantern and a trident-shaped spear of seven or eight

SKILLED CASTING OF THE FISHING NET IN THE PACIFIC ISLANDS
After taking his stand on the rocks with his net carefully folded over his arm, this Hawaiian fisherman has been patiently scanning the waters until by their movement or by the actual shining of the fish he knows that the moment for action has come. Then with the uncanny skill of his race he casts his net in such a way that it opens wide and falls into the water in the correct position ; and seldom does he draw it out empty The net used in this kind of fishing is of Japanese origin.

prongs pressed close together with a long handle. The lighted lantern is placed over the bow of the boat as it approaches the flats, and there near the light, spear in hand, the fisherman takes up his position. Very soon the eels, attracted by the light—just as they are off the Cobb at Lyme Regis—begin to gather. The fisherman then plunges in his spear in the hope of impaling the eel he has selected. Novices, however, find themselves at first baulked by the refraction of the light, and it is some time before they become proficient. Salmon are sometimes speared by torch-light both in Scotland and in Ireland

Spearing as a means of catching fish is used in the Indian Archipelago, in the South Seas, in Africa and South America. The Eskimo, of course, use the same weapon for their bigger game—a harpoon, after all, being a spear. They, however, to meet the particular difficulty of their sea hunting have invented some ingenious improvements. Some of their harpoons, for example, have detachable points to which an inflated sealskin is fastened. When the quarry is struck the floating skin serves to tire it out, marks its course, and buoys it up when dead.

Except for the bow and arrow there is hardly a mechanical device for catching fish which is not employed in home waters in some form or other. Fishing traps, for instance, embody a principle, like the one used in our lobster pots, which is common to all of them. The fish can get in, but they cannot swim out again. Mr. I. H. N. Evans describes an ingenious trap used among the Tempasuk Dusuns.

This is a bottomless conical basket of natural rattan twigs. The reflex thorns of the plant are left adhering on the inside the strands of rattan being so arranged that the thorns point backwards—that is, towards the apex of the trap. Walls of stones with small holes

J. Hornell

WHERE FISH ARE LURED INTO TRAPS OR FRIGHTENED TO THEIR DOOM

Some strange methods of fishing are found in India. In some tidal waters the fish are shepherded by means of long stretches of palisading (bottom) into a kind of corral, in which they are enticed into traps set in quiet corners. When the tide goes out they are left stranded in the traps. Sometimes a couple of canoes fitted with net screens are moored close together with a space between (top). The fish are frightened into leaping out of the water and land in the canoes, the nets preventing them from jumping right across the boats.

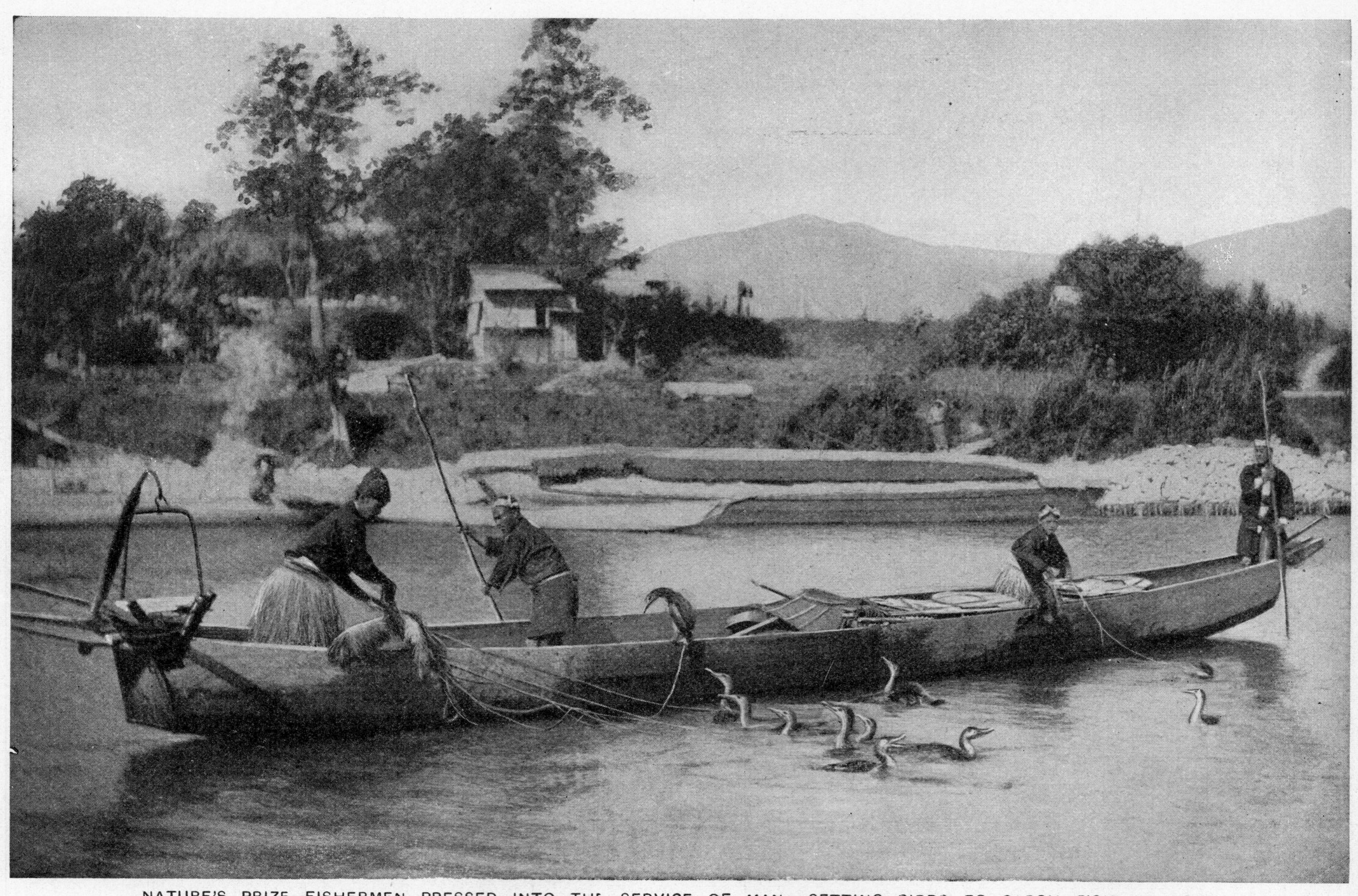

NATURE'S PRIZE FISHERMEN PRESSED INTO THE SERVICE OF MAN: SETTING BIRDS TO CATCH FISH IN JAPAN

Fishing with cormorants is practised in Japan and China. In Japan it takes place only at night, and a great brazier in the form of an iron basket is placed on the bows of each vessel of the cormorant fleet. The birds are controlled by reins attached to a small collar round the neck, which prevents all but the tiniest fish from being swallowed outright. The man in the bows, who gets the full benefit of the light of the brazier, may have charge of as many as a dozen birds. When a cormorant has filled its gullet it is hauled on board, and with a firm pressure of the hand forced to disgorge its booty. A Japanese cormorant boat with its attendant birds is here seen preparing for the night's work

in them at intervals are built at right angles across the river to receive the traps. These are inserted with their openings facing up-stream, so that fish descending the river put their heads into what appear to them to be breaches in the wall, but are unable to withdraw again owing to the thorns of the traps catching them under their scales

TICKLING is another device which most country-bred boys at home have tried upon their native trout. It is almost universal among primitive people, who have brought it to a fine art. A writer describes how he once saw a Dusun of Merak-Perak, in the Marudu district, dive down into a pool and, after two consecutive efforts, come up with three fish of approximately two pounds each, one held in his mouth and one in each hand. Like the English boy, he gently cajoles the fish with his finger-tips, until he can get the final grip on the gills.

But there are two curious methods of fishing for which we have no parallels at home. One comes from Guiana, in South America. Veracity is not supposed to be the strong point of fishermen, and this story might suggest the inventive genius of another Baron Munchausen, but it is none the less a fact. The native Indians possess the singular ability to 'call' fish. They stand motionless and emit a peculiar whistle which brings the fish to the surface, where they are easily caught.

The other method referred to is peculiar to China and Japan. While the use of the hawk in hunting is as ancient as history, it has been left to the East to use birds for the purposes of fishing. The Chinese and Japanese use cormorants in fleets. In China the fisherman proceeds with eight or ten of the birds sitting on perches projecting out of a boat. On reaching a suitable spot he rests on his oars and the cormorants swim away and begin diving.

Each bird has a tight-fitting ring, usually of bast, round his neck, low down near the body. This is to prevent him swallowing. Birds work in flocks, and are trained to return to their masters when they have caught a fish. He either hooks them by the leg or holds out a bamboo for them to perch on. The bird returns to the boat and is quickly made to disgorge his catch, and then is flung back into the water to get on with the job.

These birds are bred in captivity and are very tame. They have more white on them than the cormorants round the British shores. Sometimes several fishermen combine and work in a circle, with birds diving inside. Sometimes the birds are used to drive the fish towards nets set up across the creek or stream being worked.

In Japan the cormorants are captured wild and afterwards tamed. They are not allowed to dive freely into the water, but are controlled by a kind of harness made of fine cords. The Japanese, moreover, only use these birds at night. There is an interesting description extant of cormorant fishing at Gifu near Nagoya—said to be the place where the best fishing of this kind can be witnessed.

In the leading boat stands the 'Captain of the Cormorants.' In his hand are twelve cords, and at the end of each a large, truculent-looking bird. The boats are poled slowly down current, the birds diving and swimming under water all the time. On returning to the surface, if a bird has a sizeable fish he is pulled into the boat and the fish is removed. Sometimes these cormorants catch the same eel, and a great fight takes place.

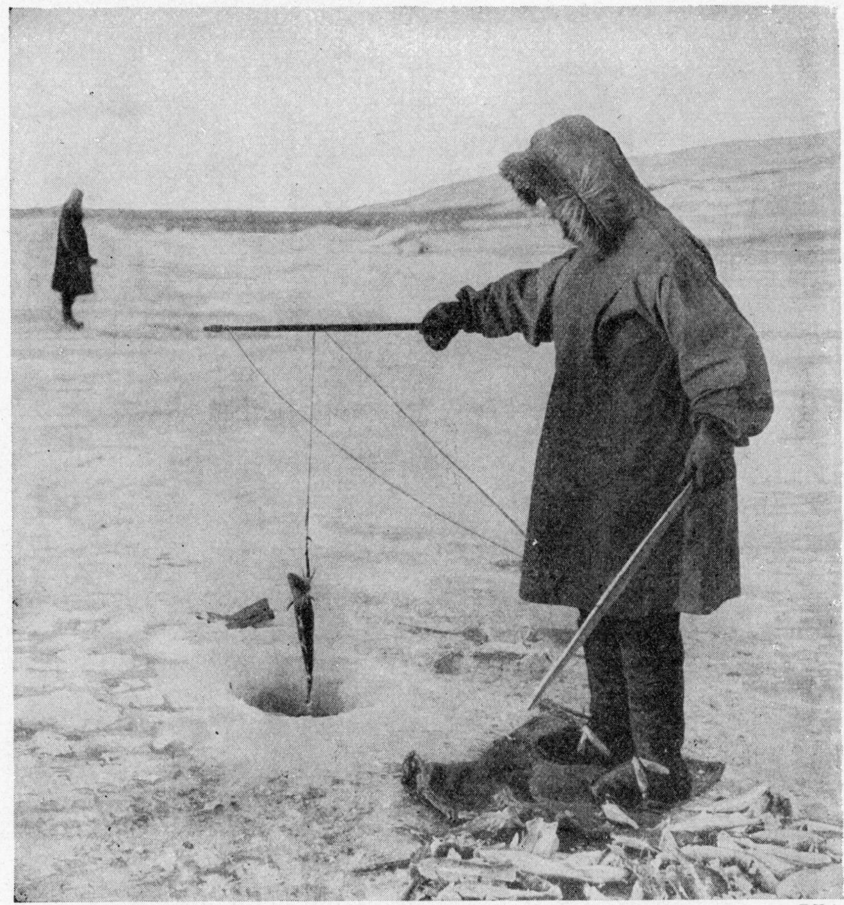

E.N.A.

FISHING UNDER DIFFICULTIES IN THE FROZEN NORTH

The Eskimo live largely on fish, but in the cold regions that they inhabit the waters are frozen over for several months in the year, and the only way then to get at the fish is to cut a hole in the ice. An Eskimo is here seen fishing through a hole he has made in a frozen river. His catch is small cod, and his skill has produced a heap of fish

E.N.A.

CAUGHT IN THE TOILS OF A LIVING PALISADE

In Fiji a vine rope, over a mile long (top), is used as a guide-line for the fisherfolk, who form themselves into a great horseshoe. As the ends of the rope are hauled in from the net, which is made fast to two boats, the horseshoe becomes smaller and smaller until the men, beating the water as they close in on the boats, stand shoulder to shoulder and no fish of any size can pass. The catch is generally so heavy that it takes all the men to lift it from the boat (bottom) The process is an elaborate one and is carried out on traditional lines

E.N.A.

LANDING THE MONSTER FISH OF THE MEDITERRANEAN

The tunny fishery was systematically carried on in classical Roman times, and it is still one of the key industries of southern Italy and the Mediterranean. One of the largest of food fishes, sometimes measuring over ten feet and weighing nearly half a ton, the tunny demands exceptionally strong tackle. Gangs of men on capstans and winches haul in the immense nets. The fish are finally despatched with lances and harpoons, as seen on the right. Note the turmoil of the water in this Sardinian catch caused by the threshing of the great fish.

Among the Japanese a certain ceremonial pertains with regard to these cormorants. Birds take rank and precedence according to the date of taming. The senior bird is sent last into the water and is allowed out first of all the fleet. He is honoured, moreover, by a perch in the prow. All other birds have their proper places, and woe betide any bird who gets on the wrong perch.

But the true angler, who would die sooner than pull a fish out of the water except by means of a hook and artificial fly, must not imagine that it is only among the white races that rules of sport have grown up around fishing. Quite recently a disturbance arising from a breach of sporting etiquette among the Samoans was solemnly inquired into by a much puzzled Royal Commission.

In that land bonito, or large mackerel, fishing is regarded not merely as a means of getting food, but also as a sporting pastime. It is governed by numerous rules of etiquette, hereditary rites and ceremonial. To drop a fish after striking the hook, which is made of turtle shell with a pearl shell haft, being liable to alarm the whole shoal, is considered a most clumsy misdemeanour, and by immemorial custom anyone so doing, be he the highest chief in the land, must submit meekly to abuse from the occupants of the other canoes in the fishing fleet. This is part of the game. Should he repeat the offence, the offender will seize his paddle and make his hardest for the land.

The sporting sense of comradeship engendered among the Samoans is seen from the fact that before the fleet of canoes that has been engaged in the mackerel fishing returns to the shore, it pauses outside the reef. There those anglers who have been unlucky are given a share of the catch, and the master fisherman makes a speech thanking everyone for the good sportsmanship he has displayed.

Col. F. D. Fayrer

A HINDU SADHU WITH ALL HIS WORLDLY POSSESSIONS

Complete detachment from all worldly interests and material associations is a first rule of the ascetic life in all religions, involving obligations of chastity, poverty, and—in the conventual life—obedience. Begging bowl of wood, coconut shell or brass, water pot and staff are the only possessions permitted to the itinerant mendicant devotee in India, with tattered woollen robe for only garment, if indeed he does not go naked. They rely exclusively on charity for their support, begging once a day for food either personally or vicariously through a disciple.

HERMITS, FAKIRS AND ASCETICS OF TO-DAY

In the following pages those extremists are dealt with who carry renunciation of the world and mortification of the body to unreasonable lengths in their desire for spiritual exaltation and hope of heaven. The reasonable compromise between the claims of body and of soul offered by monasticism and the conventual system both in Christian and non-Christian communities forms the subject of later chapters.

FROM its earliest beginnings religious enthusiasm has expressed itself in many curious ways: few are more remarkable than the practices of the ascetic and the religious devotee. In all the great religions—even that of Mahomet, though the Prophet set his face against asceticism—men, and women, too, have withdrawn themselves from this world to contemplate the next, and, in contempt for the claims of their bodies, have inflicted upon themselves neglect and indignity, pain and even mutilation. 'The world forgetting, by the world forgot' expresses an ideal no less powerful in religious experience than in human love. The hermit is as fervent in his desire to be alone at one with God as the lover in his longing for union in solitude with the object of his affection. And, indeed, when the psychological factors underlying each case are taken into account, there is every reason to admit the essential unity of the craving for a mystic bond which inspired the love, for instance, of Dante for Beatrice, the feeling of brotherhood for all living things of S. Francis of Assisi, and the overwhelming impulse towards solitude which drove the members of the early Christian Church into the waste places of the Egyptian desert.

Extremes of religious fervour and eroticism are undoubtedly often closely akin—pathological states which take their spring from hyperexcitation of the emotions, and may by force of circumstance be turned into either channel. The great waves of religious enthusiasm which swept over medieval Europe from time to time, as, for instance, in the earlier Crusades, or the Children's Crusade, were fostered by the unbalanced state of mind of the populace due to their malnutrition and adverse conditions of life. The history of the Flagellantes and some of the happenings recorded in connexion with the revivalism in England and Wales in the eighteenth and nineteenth centuries show how narrow is the dividing line between the ecstatic and the erotic. It is not without significance that the religious exaltation which finds expression in a life of devotion and self-abnegation lived either in solitude or in a community, but as one set apart, occurs in modern times with greatest frequency in India among a population highly-strung, sensuous and passionate.

To fly from the world, to give the mind to contemplation and subject the body to privation, either for a period or permanently, is a practice that has been followed by some of the world's greatest teachers and leaders. Elijah sojourned seven years in the desert, and Christ himself abode in the wilderness and was tempted of the devil. Buddha withdrew from his family and his great possessions that he might

A. Schalek

SEEKING HEAVEN ON HIS HEAD

Some of the austerities practised by Hindu ascetics seem to defy natural laws. By training himself to maintain this unnatural position for long periods together, this man has achieved a triumph of bodily discipline, but how it facilitates pious meditation baffles understanding.

VERSE-SINGING MAHOMEDAN FAKIR

Intoning verses of the Koran and of Persian poetry is the method by which some itinerant dervishes beguile alms from the public. The axe borne by this Persian fanatic is evidence of his conservatism, since he carries it only because his father did before him. Only the Mahomedan ascetics are correctly named fakirs.

give himself up to meditation and more nearly attain perfection. In later time the Emperor Charles V and Tolstoi renounced great worldly position for the sake of the things of the spirit.

On the other hand, John the Baptist, who clothed himself with skins and lived on locusts and wild honey, withdrew from participation in the life of his fellow men in the hope that he might lead them from the vanities of their day back to a simpler form of life—that of the nomad desert tribe, which he exemplified in his dress and mode of living. He belongs to a type, sufficiently common in history, whose objective is reform rather than personal salvation.

ASCETICISM, of which the practices of the early Christian recluse and the modern fakir are examples, and with which monasticism in both its ancient and its modern form is a compromise, is based upon the theological doctrine which puts the body and soul in opposition. By the performance of various devotional and disciplinary exercises, meditation, penances, fasting and the like, of a more or less painful nature, the weaknesses of the flesh are purged away and the soul benefited by being brought into a state more fitted for the life to come. It is sometimes said that asceticism is confined to the higher religions and comes into existence only when belief has become reflective. Although it may be the fact that the theological doctrine emerges relatively late into consciousness, there can be little doubt that both the beliefs which give rise to these practices and the temperaments which are receptive of their suggestion are seen at a much earlier stage in the development of religion.

It is unnecessary to dwell in detail on the resemblances between the ascetic practices of the more advanced religions and the prophylactic magic of primitive belief. It will suffice to point, as examples, to the fasting and castigation to which recluses have subjected themselves. These are methods employed by primitive peoples to drive away spirits, in particular the spirits of disease. By a natural transference of idea it comes about that primitive peoples and ascetics alike employ these methods to guard themselves against the attacks of such spirits. In the latter case, however, the theory of penance obscures the earlier conception.

The idea of seclusion by which the ascetic hopes to rid himself of the influences of this world, as well as secure the opportunity for pious devotion, also figures in primitive belief. It is at once a means and a mark of separation from the influences, especially spiritual influences, of a previous stage of existence. In Africa it is common to find the bride-to-be secluded from the light of the sun for a considerable period before marriage, while both sexes undergo a period of seclusion before their initiation to adult life and full membership of the tribe. The seclusion is a preparation for a new life, which they reach through the portals of death as represented by the initiation ceremony.

The nearest approach to the ascetic of the higher religions, however, is to be found in the medicine man. The shaman or medicine man sometimes inherits his office, sometimes is chosen on account of a peculiar aptitude for the office—a peculiarity in mental temperament which at times goes so far as a marked tendency to hysteria and epilepsy. In either case it commonly happens that the shaman has something peculiar in his mental make-up, a fact also noted in many ascetics, both ancient and modern. In Egypt, for instance, the claim to sanctity of the holy man in the eyes of the populace depends largely on the fact of his mental instability, and even, in some cases, lunacy.

When an individual is about to enter upon the career of a medicine man he places himself under the tutelage of one of the practitioners of the art, just as in India or in Egypt an aspirant to the career of ascetic will attach himself to a holy man. He then enters as a probation upon a period of solitude in the woods. This period may last for some weeks, and involves considerable hardship as well as semi-starvation. During this period the probationer will hear the voice of the spirits, some of which will eventually attach themselves to him permanently as his helpers. This period of seclusion may be repeated for several seasons before the shaman's training is complete.

From this brief and much generalised account of the shaman's character and training, which applies, with variation in detail, more particularly to the medicine man in north-east Asia and north-west America, it is evident that both the temperament and the practices of the ascetic are to some extent to be found in the more primitive forms of religion.

There can be little doubt that the movement towards a solitary life of asceticism in the early Christian Church originated, whether directly or indirectly, from the idea of purification and protection from the evil influences of everyday life. It began in Egypt, where at Alexandria the Christians found themselves in the midst of many strange rites and even stranger philosophies—of one school it is said the members strove to attain the idea of perfection through a state of contemplation each of his own navel. From this welter of beliefs S. Anthony and S. Simon Stylites passed with many followers to the desert in order to save their souls by devotional exercise in a state of solitude. Out of this through the Coenobites grew the monastic system as a compromise for the weaker brethren. How one saint stood for forty years on a pillar, how another passed the remainder of his life in ceaseless prostrations, and others gave themselves up to strange manifestations of devotion and penance, is sufficiently well-known.

Thenceforth the call to the life of a hermit, with its accompanying discipline of self-castigation, fasting, the hair-shirt and the hard bed of the stone cell or cave, advanced pari passu with Christianity. We are told of the hardships the saints voluntarily

SNAKE-PROOF ASCETIC OF PERSIA

Snake charming is a special function of some of the mendicant dervishes of North Africa, and in the East Mahomedan fakirs are credited with exceptional powers of handling poisonous snakes. This dignified individual with a handful of pet snakes for companions is an itinerant beggar in the Anglo-Persian oil fields region.

H. von Perckhammer

WHERE PROTRACTED ORISONS ARE THE ONLY OCCUPATION

Most Buddhist religious orders adopt the communal life of monasticism, but the eremitical life has its followers among the adherents of that religion. Thus near the summit of a mountain west of Peking is the Buddhist monastery Tjae-tai-tse, or monastery of regular terraces, and from this a narrow path winds upwards to a hermit's cave. The present occupant has lived there for forty-seven years without once leaving the mountain top. One of his devotions is to sit for days in one position mumbling incessant prayers.

endured in Ireland. For no less than seven years did S. Kevin stand in one position without sleep and with his arm outstretched in one direction; S. Mochua endured life in a stone prison in which there was only one small hole, through which food was passed barely sufficient to keep him alive; and another saint was suspended by shackles under his armpits for seven years—a feat of endurance rivalled in modern times by a similar exhibition of piety—the hook-swinging ceremonies of Indian devotees.

It would be tempting to look for the germ of the idea of Christian practice among the Semitic peoples with whom the Christians came into contact; for although Mahomet, as has already been said, set his face against asceticism, 'the Holy Man' of the Moslem world is a survival of an earlier practice which persisted in Mahomedanism. It is more probable, however, that the idea came from India; for Strabo, quoting Megasthenes, speaks of sects in India who inhabited the forests, wore clothes of bark, and refrained from sexual experience: while two sophists of Taxila are said to have stood on one leg all day and to have lain on the ground exposed to the weather at night. Philostratus, too, in his life of Appollonius of Tyana, speaks of feats of a spiritualistic or magical nature in India which bear a close resemblance to some of the performances attributed to modern ascetics.

An early record of the religious devotee comes from Japan. It is stated by early Chinese travellers that the Japanese used to appoint a man, known as the 'abstainer,' to whom it was not permitted to wash, to comb his hair, to eat flesh, or to approach woman. When the country was prosperous, he was rewarded, when prosperity failed, he was punished. There is no other record of this official, and it may be that we have here an ill-informed account of a school of hereditary priests known to have been in existence at an early period of Japan's history, though subsequently to the Chinese record. These priests claimed to be descended from the god Futo-dama. Their duties were connected with the king, and especially with the building of a royal palace, when they had to keep ceremonially pure, and eat

H. von Perckhammer

ALONE WITH HIS GREAT MASTER ON THE MOUNTAIN TOP

The cave occupied by the hermit shown here and in the opposite page penetrates deep into the interior of the mountain and is entered through a decidedly imposing arched portal. At the entrance are three representations of the five hundred disciples of Buddha painted in glaring colours. Almost the only glimpses the hermit obtains of the great world outside is when he emerges from his cave and, robed and mitred, stands outside the archway to address invocations to the Buddha and to perform certain customary rites.

the life of the religious devotee was a revolt against caste, and, indeed, it is not uncommon for men of advancing years to retire from active life and take up the life of religion with the object, inter alia, of ridding themselves of the restrictions of caste.

Followers of the ascetic life are found among both Hindus and Mahomedans, the former being known generically as Sadhu, the latter as Fakirs, a term popularly, but erroneously, applied to both. Many famous ascetics of the past have been members of the Moslem community, and their shrines are still regarded with much reverence.

Hindu ascetics are divided into a number of sects. These, for the most part, are to be distinguished by their dress. The robes of one of the largest and most important are of salmon colour, but they may be of skins, one sect wearing the tiger skin instead of the more usual robes. Some go naked. Their foreheads bear a mark of sanctity made with coloured earth and frequently their bodies are smeared with ashes.

It is usual for an ascetic to spend some considerable period in solitary meditation in a forest before he enters upon his career of itinerant mendicancy, and the aspirant to a religious life has usually passed some time as the disciple of a holy man, after a species

no flesh but that which had been cooked at the sacred fire.

In modern times India has always been noted for the number of its ascetics and the extraordinary practices by which they have manifested their piety. Although they are said to be decreasing, it is estimated that they still number over four millions. As they subsist entirely on alms, this is a serious burden on a country in which the general average of wealth is low.

Although asceticism finds no place in the Vedas, the earliest religious poems of India, it makes its appearance early in the sacred literature as a recognized 'way of life.' Bodily penance is required of all four orders into which society is divided under the caste system. In the Code of Manu formal rules for ascetics are laid down in which their mode of life, diet, dress, devotions and meditations are prescribed in detail.

The ascetic life was at first limited to the highest order, the Brahmin, but it was later thrown open to all. This is a matter of no little interest, as

H. von Perckhammer

MUMMIFIED HERMIT AND HIS FINAL RESTING-PLACE

Cremation of their dead is the usual custom of Buddhist priests, but the Tjae-tai-tse monastery priests preserve the bodies of the hermits as mummies, the latest remaining as shown here until his successor dies and takes his place. His body is then placed in a sitting position in a casket (top) and preserved in a vault beside his predecessors.

W. Bosshard

TYPES OF WANDERING RELIGIOUS MENDICANTS WHO TRAVEL OVER INDIA

Yoga—the Sanskrit word for effort—is the name of one of the six orthodox systems of Hindu philosophy. Its professors, yogis, practise asceticism and various penances believed to confer supernatural powers. Some of them, like the white-bearded yogi (top left), claim hypnotic influence; others, like the sturdy fellow beside him, are jovial rascals with a gift of repartee and a fund of risky stories; all are itinerant mendicants, and when old age puts an end to their wanderings they settle down in some ruined shrine and are venerated as local saints.

E.N.A

WISDOM AND HOLINESS SET IN A LONELY CELL IN THE MOUNTAINS OF RUMANIA

One need not go to the Far East to find deeply religious men electing to live in solitude and thereby acquiring wide reputation for sagacity as well as saintliness. At Oltenia, high up in the Carpathians, a Rumanian hermit has lived for many years in this cell hewn from the living rock and bare of everything save actual necessaries. But though aloof he is not inaccessible, and the peasantry from far and near come to him for spiritual counsel and temporal advice.

of initiation or baptism, during which the sacred thread worn round the waist has been taken off and burnt, this symbolising the abrogation of caste.

THE ascetic discipline of India is severe. It entails a life of continuous self-denial and poverty, as well as entire dependence upon alms. The robes worn must be mean and tattered, and may not be of anything but wool. The devotee must not carry anything but a begging bowl of wood, coconut-shell or brass, a water-pot and a staff, which some sects are said to worship. Nor may he beg more than once a day, and then it must be after, not before or during the meal of those whom he approaches. Often, however, when, as frequently happens, the holy man has vowed himself to the immobile life of meditation, the offerings of those acquiring merit will be brought to him, or fetched by his disciple. One sect is said to have acquired an extraordinary taste for the flesh of human corpses, which they obtain from graveyards and rivers.

The bodily discipline to which the Hindu ascetics submit is almost incredible, but it is well attested. Hook-swinging, in which steel hooks are inserted in the muscles of the back of the devotees and they are then swung in the air is however a specific act of worship and strictly an ascetic discipline Another practice is to hold the arms above the head for a protracted period until the muscles become stiff and the limbs cannot be lowered. The votary may stand for a prolonged period on one leg, or the hands may remain clenched until the nails of the fingers grow right through the flesh. A regular form of endurance is the exposure to 'five fires,' in which the devotee stands between four fires and in the blazing sun. Some may vow themselves to silence, or to go upon a pilgrimage to a holy place, in which every foot of the way is covered by a series of continuous prostrations. A favourite manifestation of piety is to lie night and day without cessation on a plank through which spikes, nails and other sharp implements have been driven, so that the body rests upon their points. One holy man is said to have lain on such a bed for a period of thirty-five years without intermission.

The ascetic life is not confined to men but is also open to women, but owing to the social conditions of India they have not as a rule taken up the life of itinerant mendicancy. One woman of Benares lived in seclusion in a pit for no less than thirty-eight years.

When Buddhism passed from India to Tibet, it carried with it the practice of the ascetic life. Of a number of religious orders which were formed, one in particular followed the life of the hermit. It failed to be popular, a matter which need not cause surprise in view of climatic conditions, and reverted to the

Special Press

FIRE-PROOF HOLY MEN OF FIJI DEMONSTRATING THEIR POWERS

Fire-walking is one of the feats of endurance credited on well-supported testimony to the ascetics of India, both Hindu and Mahomedan. In this ceremony stones are heated to a great temperature and the performer walks over them barefoot without sustaining injury. Difficult of explanation as the performance is, persons capable of it certainly still exist in Fiji, as shown by this photograph of the ceremony in progress at the celebrations in 1924 of the fiftieth anniversary of the establishment of British control over the islands

Ullstein

MONGOLIAN EXORCIST AND HIS MAGIC DRUM

The shaman, a holy man of northern Asia, acquires magical powers after a period of seclusion and self-discipline, in the course of which he enters into touch with the world of spirits. Shamanism is also found in Tibet. This Mongolian shaman is displaying the magic drum with which he drives away evil spirits.

common life of monasticism followed by other orders. The religious life in one part of Tibet, at least, is closely bound up with the original spirit worship, which was not entirely superseded by Buddhism, and it is among these monks or lamas that travellers have reported such extraordinary practices in self-mutila tion as running sharp spikes through the tongue, ripping up the abdomen with a sword, and so forth. It is said that no mark of mutilation is to be seen after the instrument has been withdrawn. Performances hardly less marvellous have at times been credited to the ascetics of India. There is well supported testimony that both Hindu and Mahomedan are able to perform the fire-walk ceremony, in which the holy man, sometimes his followers as well, passes over stone at white heat with bare feet and receive no injury.

The Mahomedan fakir is credited with a great variety of powers which those in search of primitive traits in the more advanced religions might well consider bring him within affinity to the medicine man. For he is credited with power to heal the sick, cause rain in dry places, pass over the sea and fly over the land. Some of the holy men of India are held, too, to have special powers in handling poisonous snakes. Here they come closely into relation with the fakirs of other parts of the Moslem world, where snake charming is a special function of some of the mendicant members of the Dervish orders.

The Dervish Orders do not, as a rule, practise seclusion from the world. The members withdraw to a solitary cell, in which they may remain, fasting day by day, for as much as forty days. Frequently the Orders carry on the vocations of everyday life, except when required for religious observances. In virtue of these exercises, however, frequently of a severe and exacting nature, they may well be regarded as ascetic. The performances of the Dancing Dervishes of Constantinople are well known. In a famous observance in Cairo the head of the Order, mounted on horseback, rode on the bodies of the devotees as they lay prostrated on the ground. The mendicant fakirs, who are noted for their importunity throughout Egypt and Turkey, were regarded, more especially in Egypt and North Africa, as possessing marvellous powers. Living entirely on alms, clad in ragged woollen garments, and carrying a staff with rags of many colours fluttering from its top, they performed on feast days and at private entertainments, when they produced spiritistic phenomena, divined by various means, and performed feats of magic rivalling those of the itinerant conjurors of India.

WHY WE TOUCH WOOD AND COLD IRON

OF the many common superstitions which are instinctively observed in the daily life of even the most intelligent persons, that of touching wood to avert the consequences of a boast is perhaps the least understood and one of the oldest. Related methods of warding off ill fate and ill luck are analysed in the chapters on Mascots and Luck Bringers, Outwitting the Force of Evil, and other persistent superstitions

THE actual reasons why we still entertain certain superstitions, or at least instinctively practise their outward observances, are capable of being referred to ideas so primitive that when they are explained they are apt to seem far-fetched to those unaccustomed to probing into the origins of folk-belief. Why, for example, in certain circumstances do we exclaim 'touch wood,' and extend our hands to the nearest chair or table, or 'cold iron,' and grasp a poker, or fumble for the keys or knives in our pockets?

The persistent 'ceremonial' touching of wood so universally indulged in is usually associated with a boastful exclamation, or a statement regarding future possible luck or good fortune. 'This has been a good year,' we may say, 'but I believe next year will be a better one—touch wood,' or 'such and such an affair has proceeded just as I wished it to so far, and I am sure will turn out to my benefit,' and we tap circumspectly on the desk or hastily lay a palm on the nearest wooden fitting.

The act is obviously of the nature of a charm to avert untoward occurrence or evil hap. The notion underlying it is the very ancient one that when we boast we lay ourselves open to the caprice of certain Fates or Powers, who, jealous of man's happiness or prosperity, are ever ready to inflict reverses upon him or destroy the work of his hands through sheer caprice. To prevent such a contingency we touch wood—but why wood?

To discover the original reason for the custom we must hark back to those early circumstances in which man paid reverence to trees of various species. Certain trees were identified with certain deities. In Greece, for example, the oak was sacred to Zeus, while in Britain it was dedicated to a Celtic deity whose precise identity is still a matter of conjecture. The ash tree was sacred to Thor, the Norse god of thunder, and the sycamore to the Egyptian goddess Hathor.

BUT the cult of the oak tree became almost universal throughout Europe, and was associated with the early European sky god. It was observed that the oak was the tree most commonly struck by lightning, and from this it was inferred that it was the particular shrine or dwelling-place of the sky-and-thunder god, and therefore the especial repository of his virtues and life-giving qualities. The parasites of the oak, the ivy and the mistletoe, partook of the attributes of the tree round which they coiled, the bird which sang in its branches was inspired by the oracular spirit of the god in the oak, as were its leaves when they whispered in the breeze and communicated the secrets of the deity whose spirit dwelt in the trunk.

To avert evil through boasting it was essential to employ the aid of sympathetic magic and to touch the oak or other sacred tree in order that one might be inoculated by its divine virtue and thus be rendered immune from the vengeful essence or emanation of the irritable sky god who punished boasters either with the lightning stroke or by sending down some dire and disastrous influence. Communion with the virtue of the sacred tree made man immune from the dreaded stroke of fate on the principle that 'like cures like,' which lies at the roots of the idea of sympathetic magic. Just as it was believed a wound might be healed by bathing it in water in which the wounding weapon had been dipped—'a hair of the dog that bit you' expresses a similar principle—so the power communicated by the mere touching of the sacred tree was sufficient to ward off or neutralise the full force of the divine influence from which its virtue descended.

AS time proceeded and the original idea grew vague and confused, it came to be thought that the touching of wood of any kind sufficed to neutralise the danger inherent in a boast. Man was thought to be surrounded by impish supernatural agencies only too ready to take advantage of any rash statement for his undoing, and if a vaunting wish were expressed these might discern the weak spot in the human armour and pierce it, were not the ceremonial rite of wood-touching observed.

To wear the leaves of the sacred tree was as efficacious as to touch it, and this is still practised by certain barbarous peoples. Mariner says that in the Tonga Islands green leaves are worn round the neck by the priests as marks of submission and humility, as well as fear, toward the gods. On the fords of the Calabar River in West Africa the natives are in the habit of plucking a leaf and rubbing the forehead with it to avert danger from crocodiles when crossing. In the Nicobar Islands people thought to be possessed of a devil are beaten with branches. The Fijians cast a twig on the spot where a man has been clubbed to death so that they may avoid a similar fate.

Old Evelyn tells us that in Wales the ash tree was regarded as so sacred that one was planted in every churchyard as a warning to evil spirits and that

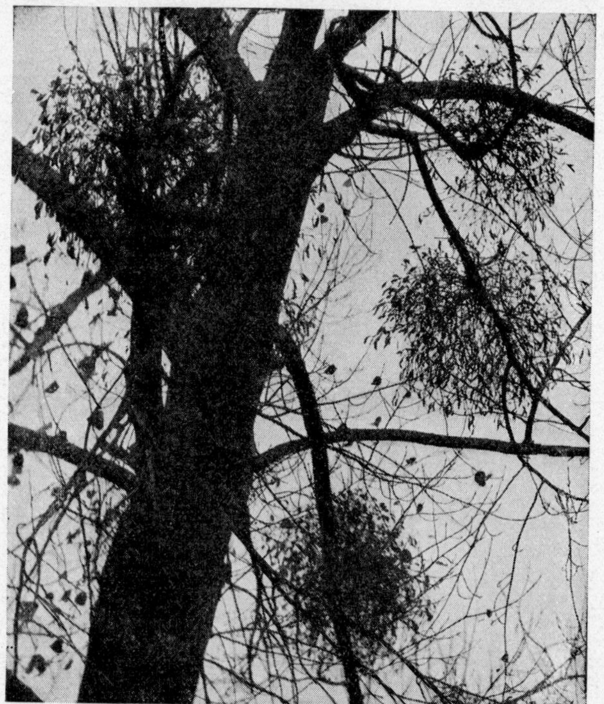

Topical

crosses made of its wood were worn by the people. This would seem to be a fairly late example of the survival of the group of ideas associated with the touching of the sacred wood.

GRASPING cold iron is a custom much in the same category, although its observance is now almost confined to children. If one is being chased and he can reach and touch any iron implement he cannot be harmed or made captive in a game. When a bargain is being made, if one of the parties cries 'touch cold iron' the other cannot withdraw from the compact. Among the last generation of fishermen on the east coast of Scotland, if the names of the minister, the cat, the fox or the hare were mentioned while at sea the crew instantly clapped hands on the thwarts, crying 'cauld iron!' An entirely different set of words had to be used for certain persons or creatures whilst at sea, the minister being known as 'the Black Man,' the hare as 'Sandy,' and the cat as 'Theebit.' The implication is that a different set of powers was recognized as ruling on the water and that their taboos must be respected.

But why should iron be regarded as a magical substance capable of protection or of averting evil

Dixon Scott

SACRED TREE OF THE SKY GOD, TO WHOM THE MODERN WORLD PAYS UNWITTING DUE

In Celtic mythology the sky god was associated with the oak, and so with the parasites mistletoe (above) and ivy. The god punished boasting by lightning stroke, as evidenced by the frequent blasting of the oak tree, but by touching the tree and so doing reverence at the shrine of the god, evil might be averted. In time this form of sympathetic magic was amplified into touching any kind of wood, and so lived on as a simple but surprisingly persistent superstition.

W. F. Taylor

LATE FORM OF AN ANCIENT CELTIC SUPERSTITION AMONG MODERN CELTS

The idea of the sacredness of a particular tree spread to other trees, among them the ash, which, in Scandinavian mythology, was personified as Yggdrasil, in whom all existence was rooted. In Welsh churchyards, as seen in this photograph of the ancient abbey church of Strata Florida, Cardiganshire, ash trees were planted to ward off evil spirits, and their wood provided crosses which acted as amulets.

consequences? For an explanation we must revert to the age when the bronze-using peoples of Europe first encountered the iron-using folk, who first employed the iron civilization of Hallstadt or La Tène, at some time about the ninth century B.C. It was quickly discovered in combat that the leaf-shaped bronze sword was easily shivered by a strong blow from the blade of an iron sword, and as barbarous man imputes any extraordinary result to magic, he concluded that an especial magical virtue resided in the metal from which the victorious weapon was made.

It is, however, obvious that an entire group of ideas and superstitions was connected with the use of iron, just as was the case with the use of obsidian as a weapon and social implement in ancient Mexico. In the latter instance obsidian glass was first regarded as magical because from it were made the spears and arrows that slew those animals the flesh and blood of which kept the savage in life. As time proceeded all objects made from obsidian came to have a sacred significance, knives of sacrifice were made from it, and mirrors in which sorcerers could descry future events. Some of the gods, even, were thought to be composed of obsidian, that is, the stone was deified, and a special cult grew up around it. It was regarded as the great provider of sacrificial blood by which the gods were kept in life, and which, magically turned into the ever-needed rain, thereby ensured the growth of the crops and the continuance of the human race.

A similar set of ideas was associated with flint by primitive man in Europe, and these seem in a measure to have been passed on to the iron-using folk, though in a manner somewhat weakened in its sanction, for though we hear of gods made of flint and gods whose blood was dropped from the sky in the form of flint flakes or thunderbolts, there are no traces of deities made of iron There were, however, gods, like Vulcan and Thor who cultivated the art of the blacksmith, and who made and cast thunderbolts, so that the analogy is complete enough.

To touch iron, therefore, or to invoke it was to place oneself under the protection of the gods presiding over that metal, and to ask their aid against the powers of an older and banished religion, whose deities were regarded as lurking nigh in spiteful readiness to work woe upon those who had deserted their worship. This theory seems to be amply illustrated by the case of the fishermen alluded to, who feared even the names of those beings that were evidently the gods of the deserted faith, and who invoked the magical substance of a later cultus when their unlucky names were spoken. For the fox, the hare and the cat, it is known, were all symbolic or totemic animals of ancient British tribes who had once been users of bronze. The fox was specially invoked in the ancient British rite of Bealtainn ; the hare, Cæsar tells us, was sacred to the Britons and might not be eaten by them ; and the cat was the totem of the ancient Catti, from whom are descended the Keiths and MacIntoshes.

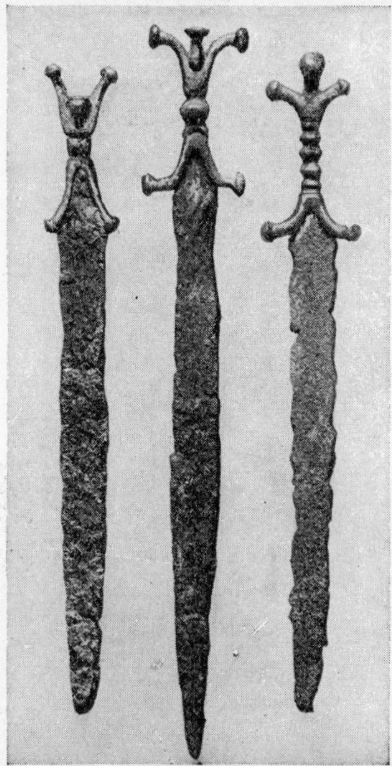

Thus, when anything savouring of the uncanny, unlucky or supernatural is uttered, people cry 'cold iron' and grasp the nearest iron implement to avert the evil. To swear to a bargain or compact by cold iron is evidently a relic of the period when barter was concluded by the invocation of a metal symbolic of the faith of the bargainers, just as in the Middle Ages buyers and sellers swore by the Cross that they would keep faith with each other.

British Museum and 'The Times

WHY IRON CAME TO POSSESS MAGIC QUALITIES

The superstitions which became attached to iron are almost as numerous and persistent as those connected with wood. Their explanation is clear. When the bronze-using peoples of the ninth century B.C. clashed with those of the new-born Iron Age they were confounded by the apparently magical powers of the new iron swords (actual examples above). A modern survival of this respect for iron is the sailor's resort to the 'cauld iron' of his ship when words of ill-omen are spoken, a superstition which applied particularly to the crews of sailing ships.

HEAD-DRESSES: THEIR VARIETY AND PURPOSE

HEAD-COVERINGS for protective purposes may have preceded those used for decoration, but prehistoric sites reveal both varieties and the question remains open. Certainly from remote times head-dresses have been symbols of social or professional distinction. These aspects are further discussed in the chapter on Distinctions of Rank

IN the ritual of manners, the head has always played a supreme part. To the hands are assigned the symbols of betrothal and marriage; to the wrists, the arms and the ankles the merely decorative ornaments; to the neck, round which was once worn the collar of servitude, the orders of chivalry and the chains of municipal office; to the left knee the blazon of the Garter. But it is the head that wears the crown.

There is a whole world of history and tradition in the dressing and ornamentation of that seat of human majesty—the head. The civilized man, who has his hair cut short and rings the changes on the very limited products of the hatter—the woman, who bobs and shingles or whatever is the mode of the day, and, more sophisticated than the male, devotes much time to the purchase of her hats—may wrinkle the lip of scorn and superiority at the sight of the queer head-dresses worn by savage peoples. But our judges and barristers still wear wigs, and still on the head of our king when he opens Parliaments, glistens that symbol of authority—the crown.

We uncover that seat of dignity to show reverence to our God, our women-folk and our ruler. Because the brazen of her sex went uncovered in the early Christian days, S. Paul ordained that woman should not go bareheaded, and to this day, if she would avoid the scandal of being turned out of church, she must make her devotions in a hat.

Dignity—the sort of dignity which requires to be dressed and distinguished for fear of escaping notice—still turns to the head. A gentleman was no gentleman until the middle of the eighteenth century unless he wore a wig, and one of the most pathetic memorials ever presented to a sovereign was that sent to King George III in the year 1765 by the Master Peruke-Makers of the metropolis, in which they besought him to see to it that the despicable fashion of a gentleman wearing his own hair was put down, so that his humble petitioners might stave off bankruptcy. We might still be sporting wigs to-day (our legal luminaries being distinguished by wearing their own hair) had it not been for some unworthy humorist, obviously without the virtue of dignity, who promptly sent a petition to His Majesty from the Master Body-Carpenters of the metropolis imploring King George to wear a wooden leg.

Still the servants of the Crown distinguish themselves from ordinary people by making their servants wear the cockade, which is the final evolution of the medieval chaperon—the cape and hood worn separately and then joined together for convenience, the peak of the hood lengthened grotesquely until it had to be twisted round the head, leaving the cape protruding like a cock's comb, so to the turban-like hat with the hood peak already twisted and fixed, and finally to the cockade. The chaperon in the Middle Ages was made in the colours of the servant's lord, and in this guise it appears on the cloaks of the Knights of the Garter, and, according to one authority, in the button worn by the members of the Legion of Honour and other foreign orders.

The truth is that, however superior civilized man may think himself, he must still be dressing his head. So in the Services we have

PLUMED HEAD-DRESS OF THE YOUNGEST SERVICE
Feathers have been used in ceremonial head-dress from very ancient times the world over. They are a prominent feature in primitive ceremonial headgear. British field-marshals also wear them, and officers of the Royal Air Force, as seen here, sport a plume in their full-dress hats.

E.N.A.

TRADITIONAL HEAD-DRESS OF TUNIS

The Jews, ever tenacious of their customs, have never become absorbed by the people of the countries in which they have settled. This curious embroidered cone-shaped hat is of a fashion long affected by Jewesses of Tunis and parts of Algeria.

cocked hats, and our field-marshals are as resplendent as birds of paradise, and when recently they had to invent a ceremonial dress for the Royal Air Force, the gentleman responsible, who would have turned up his nose at Zulus and Red Indians and the Dyaks of Borneo, almost inevitably added a plume to the officer's head-gear.

What sources of habit and custom were tapped for the Royal Air Force ceremonial plume it might be difficult to say, but some of these sources are very ancient. According to one authority the Damara women wear a head-dress which is derived from the three-pointed Norseman's helmet. The surmise on which this conclusion is based is interesting.

According to Professor Schwarz, the Damara tribe originally lived on the shores of Lake Tritonis in Libya. The lake was associated with the goddess Athena, and the Damara women wore on their woolly hair a helmet similar to the one in which the goddess is usually depicted. When early in the fifth century of our era the Vandals conquered Carthage, the women changed the fashion of their hats to the three-pointed Norseman type, adding at the same time, out of envy for the long tresses of their Vandal sisters, hairs from the tails of cows. When, a hundred years later, Belisarius wiped out the Vandals in the name of the Eastern Roman Empire, the Damaras, it is presumed, fled southwards across the Dark Continent.

In the course of time, still clinging to their Vandal head-dress, they came up against the Hottentots in Damaraland. Here they remained until 1916, when, in the midst of the war, they migrated to Lake Mgami, where they were employed by the Batawana as cattle herds. They have 'made good,' and now own vast herds of their own. Into the middle of the Bechuanaland Protectorate they have introduced the three-pointed helmet of the Norsemen and the long, false tresses of cows' hair which mimic the locks of the Vandal women.

Among the Bantu or native races of South Africa, the Zulus—that great fighting race which under Chaka and Dingaan arose to such military pre-eminence—pay great attention to the head. The woolly hair of the women is worked up into a long knob not unlike a maize-cob, which stands out stiffly from the middle of the skull. Their hair-dressing is an art. The men who hold tribal rank are distinguished by their head-rings, which belong, of course, to the same family as our crowns and coronets.

With the native tribes of Angola, again, the dressing of the head is an elaborate affair. The woman's own hair is plaited with shell and fibre ornaments, and the general effect after this stiffening and decoration is that of some freakishly shaped hat. The native belles of Kenya wear extraordinary ornamentations that have the general appearance of small baskets filled with vegetables. One particularly beautiful

E.N.A.

BUTTERFLY CAP OF NORMANDY

Some of the most elaborate and picturesque head-dresses to be found in Europe are those which are worn by the peasant women of Normandy when they are dressed up for important occasions. This winged example in lace is well named the butterfly of Avranches.

head-dress of African natives is that worn by the lion-hunters of the Nandi. It is a tall, cone-shaped busby, and is used to distinguish the chieftain and the head-man from the common herd.

The hat is much in use in Southern Nigeria, though neither in shape nor in the material of its construction does it bear much resemblance to any headgear favoured by Europeans. The Olowa or Owo in full ceremonial wears a cone-shaped hat, elaborately ornamented, with a superimposed structure which gives to the whole an effect remotely resembling a bishop's mitre. Its bizarre appearance is enhanced by the fibre streamers which hang down from under it over the face of the wearer. King Walter Obi Amobi, ruler of Onitsha, on the other hand, wears what is clearly an imitation of the coronets of our own period—probably regarded as the *dernier cri* of fashion in Onitsha. The king of Enogu, another native Nigerian state, wears on state occasions a very elaborate hat which with its trimmings looks for all the world like a lampshade closed at the top.

Properly speaking, the mask is to be regarded as a form of head-dress, and those worn by the African witch doctors and certain races in Asia and Melanesia form a curious link with European custom. The masked ball, or masquerade, first appeared in Europe in medieval times, flourished in Italy in the fifteenth century, became an innovation in the French court under the patronage of Catherine de Medici, and finally blossomed out in England under the patronage of Henry VIII. So popular did it become here that no royal progress, no public occasion of any kind was thought properly seasoned unless a masquerade was held. The Chelsea Arts Ball may be regarded as the lineal descendant of these masques.

Wide World Photo

LION'S MANE BUSBY OF AFRICAN LION-HUNTER

Tanganyika territory is infested with lions, and a body of 'lion police' is enrolled from the Masai and Nandi tribes to protect the inhabitants. This young Masai warrior has succeeded in spearing his first lion, and may therefore wear its mane as a head-dress

'VIKING' HELMETS IN THE HEART OF AFRICA

These are Damara women of South Africa wearing their characteristic three-pointed helmets and false hair made from cow's tails. It has been suggested that the fashion indicates contact in ancient times with the Vandals and their long-haired women in Carthage.

But long before their first appearance in Europe these 'masques' were being performed with elaborate ritual by the Dyaks of the Borneo jungle and are still so to-day. Laden down with banana plumes, the dancers wear on their heads horrible looking masks made out of light-weight white wood and covered with goats' hair. Some of these masks are real works of art, showing a very high standard of execution. The Dyak masquerades are not merely performances of mingled instrumental music, dialogue and declamation, such as Ben Jonson occasionally contributed to, but are in the nature of religious observances.

There is a striking resemblance between these Dyak masquerades and the weird dances of the Papuans. The latter inhabitants of New Guinea use dry lalang grass instead of banana leaves for their ceremonial dresses. The head-dresses are fantastic

E.N.A

Planet News and Central News

AFRICAN KINGS AND HEAD-MEN AND THE HATS THEY WEAR

A large portfolio could easily be filled with pictures of the peculiar head-dresses worn in Southern Nigeria. To give three instances, Paramount Chief Auyama, King of Enogu (bottom left), wears on state occasions a hat which by its shape and elaborate fringe trimmings reminds one of a lampshade. King Walter Obi Amobi, ruler of Onitsha (bottom right), when in full ceremonial dress wears on his head what looks like a modern peer's coronet, while the close-fitting shell head-dresses worn by Kavirondo head-men in Kenya (top) are also surprising and original.

R. St. Barbe Baker

HEAD ADORNMENT OF THE OLOWO OF OWO OF SOUTHERN NIGERIA

The Southern Provinces of Nigeria are a region of strange headgear, and among the many remarkable examples of hats that can be seen here not the least striking is the head-dress worn by the Olowo of Owo, who is a very important personage in these parts. When this potentate is in full ceremonial dress he wears an elaborately ornamented conical hat. To add to the effect, the hat itself is surmounted by a tall additional structure, the whole remotely resembling a bishop's mitre. From under the hat fibre streamers fall down in front of the wearer's face.

E.N.A.

GORGEOUS FEATHER HEAD-DRESSES OF TANGANYIKA WARRIORS

Feathers, fibres, shells, and a vast variety of other materials go to the making of the strange head-dresses that are affected by many of the tribes scattered over the Dark Continent. The photograph shows Wagaya warriors of Tanganyika wearing elaborate feather head-dresses A not uncommon feature is the streamers hanging down in front of the face.

and some of them are of enormous size. The men who wear these masks are called 'Kaiva Kuku,' and are supposed to represent the spirits of the dead ancestors of the village. A woman, a girl or an uninitiated boy meeting with one of them immediately turns his or her back or bolts into the nearest house, for to see them is supposed to be unlucky.

The head-dresses represent such subjects as the setting sun and the crescent moon, a heron or a stork. In some cases the head-dress, made of fibres covered with soft, downy white feathers, is surmounted by the totem mask. When fully dressed to represent their ancestral daemons, the performers' bodies are almost completely concealed. In addition to their monstrous headgear and mask they wear a red fibre apron, and their breasts, backs and limbs are adorned with shapes cut out of sago leaves and stuck all over with red, white and blue-black seeds which represent animals or plants. The feet and hands are invariably covered with clay.

In the Nosuland district of China—the 'bogey land' of the Chinese, peopled by a wild and primitive race—there are some extraordinary head-dresses used. Mr. S. Pollard, in his book In Unknown China gives an interesting description of one. He was staying at a farm for the night, and his host's daughter-in-law joined the family group round the fire.

She had on a blue jacket and a quilted skirt, and wore an enormous head-dress. This latter was made by winding layer after layer of dark, blue native cloth around a small frame. Sometimes nearly a hundred feet of this cloth is so wound round the head. The width of the cloth is a little more than a foot. The weight of the head-dress is nearly six pounds and must be a great burden till one is used to it. The women, however, do not seem to mind it, and as a crown to their tall figures, the head-dresses are most striking and picturesque.

Among our own rude ancestors the wearing of the horn used to be a symbol of nuptial blindness, but among this strange Chinese race it is an emblem of distinction. The same author describes a scene one night when a man showed him how

to put up the Nosu poke to the left of my hair. Just what the origin of the head horns is one does not know. In Nosuland it is the men who wear the horn. South of the Yangtse, among another tribe, the Flowery Miao, it is the women who wear the exalted horn as the sign of motherhood. Very occasionally a Miao man may be seen with one, but this is rare

In the lands bordering upon Tibet, where the races are so strangely mixed—the descendants of Alexander the Great's soldiers being said to be responsible for the Caucasian strain so often met with—many curious head-dresses may be found. The women porters, for example, of the Yangtze-Nekong divide have pigtails which are swollen to positively grotesque dimensions by the addition of wool plaited in with the hair. When this has been made up, the whole is bound up on the top of the head, where it forms a huge and cumbersome bulk.

Courtesy of London Missionary Society

TOWERING FEATHER HEAD-DRESS OF THE PAPUANS

As among so many primitive races, feathers are a very widely used and important item in the composition of the head-dresses of the Papuans of New Guinea. Some of the Papuan head-dresses are most elaborate affairs, not only as regards decoration but also in size, often running to an enormous height and girth. The head-dress shown here is a characteristic example of those worn by the Papuans for their ceremonial occasions The whole structure sometimes reaches a height of as much as eight or even ten feet.

Robert Moore

Traditional head-dresses are often very cumbersome. In Mongolia every woman who is married wears a head-dress of some kind, the value of which is commensurate with the wealth of the family. It is presented to her by her husband when she marries. It has to be worn continuously ; it must not be discarded even while the woman is employed about her domestic duties. Some of these Mongolian female head-dresses are immensely valuable. That shown (right) is of gold, silver and beaded coral. The Karo Batak woman's (left) is not so valuable, but is very heavy, being made of stout cloth. Her enormous earrings weigh about two pounds each.

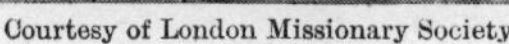

Courtesy of London Missionary Society

BLANKETS, BEADS, FEATHERS AND HAIR IN THE HEADGEAR OF THREE CONTINENTS

The picturesque though unwieldy head-dress of the Pueblo Indian chief (right) is only worn on ceremonial occasions. It is ornamented with buffalo horns and eagle's feathers. The Papuan exquisite (left) devotes the utmost care to the decoration of his hair. This he combs up with a three-toothed comb, parting it back from his forehead so as to allow for the adjustment of his feather head ornaments. Round his forehead he binds a frontlet of beads or shells. In his case the head adornment consists almost entirely of the elaborate dressing of the hair, the extraneous embellishments being no more than a few feathers.

E.N.A.

CARRYING HIS WORLDLY WEALTH UPON HIS HEAD

This venerable-looking personage with his very decorative head-dress is the king of one of the various orders of begging monks that are found in many parts of India. Apart from his head-dress he wears scarcely any clothes at all. India is a paradise for beggars, who constitute a regular professional class, and demand alms with a pertinacity that has to be seen to be believed. The begging monk of India, no less than his lay counterpart, is never allowed to be without food or the other necessaries of life.

E.N.A

A BASKET FOR HEADWEAR IN JAPAN

Though much peculiar headgear is found in the countries of the Far East, it would be exceedingly difficult to imagine head-covering stranger than that shown here. The wearer of this basket is performing as a street musician as a self-imposed penance for some misdeed. His takings go to a charity.

The Tibetan males also dress their heads elaborately. From the mistresses of their hearts they expect not only kisses, but what may be called hairdressing attentions. The girls take their lovers' heads upon their laps and carefully perform this rite. It must take a long time, for the sham queue—made of blue wool and carefully plaited—has first to be unwound and detached. Then the real hair is combed out, buttered (butter plays a part in almost every detail of life in Tibet) and re-plaited. Next the false queue, with its section of elephant's tusk threaded on to it, is hooked into position, and finally the whole is rebound on the top of the head.

The feathered head-dresses of the Indians of the American continent are as ancient as the Aztec of Mexico, whose elaborate feather-work excited the admiration of the Spanish conquerors. Examples which still possess their ancient vivid colouring may be seen in the British Museum. Among the Eskimo women, coloured ribbons in the hair are used to indicate their position in the body politic. Red is used for girls, blue for married women, and green for those who are neither widows nor maids. The hair in which these extraordinary insignia are braided is dragged out on both sides over the ears so tightly that nearly all Eskimo women get bald places at an early age, and are said, by one unkind explorer, to come in time to resemble nothing so much as the bladder-nose seal. In North Greenland, oddly enough, though different coloured ribbons are used to bind the krilledik or hair-knot, the colours have no significance, and their use elsewhere among the Eskimos is regarded as a foolish custom 'imitated from foreigners.'

All this 'ritual of the head' among savage peoples may strike the sophisticated reader as bizarre and fantastic. But let him remember with humility that it was a young assistant in a London hat-shop who imposed upon the world that monstrosity, the top-hat, without which no ceremony not requiring the trimmings of pure pageantry is to-day considered complete. The inventor, who was discharged for producing this outrage, caused such a riot when he walked abroad that the police had to intervene, and charged him before the magistrates with creating a breach of the peace. But there is little comfort to our national pride in this story, for despite that gesture of aesthetic protest, the top-hat became the fashion and survives to-day, surely the most ridiculous of head-dresses, as the symbol of dignity and respectability.

Topical

ENGLISHMAN'S HAT OF CEREMONY

About 1792 men began to wear beaver hats resembling the modern top-hat, but ornamented with strings and tassels. It was not, however, until about 1840 that the modern top-hat was first worn in England. Invented by a young London hatter's assistant, it has held the field as a ceremonial head-dress

POPULAR CUSTOMS OF EASTERTIDE

APART from its religious significance, Eastertide is full of secular interest, for many of the customs then observed are survivals of pagan rites associated with spring (see page 13). Equally picturesque are the charities of ancient origin which fall due at this season. Religious aspects of Easter are dealt with in the chapters on Holy Week Ceremonials and Passion Plays.

ALL customs, all traditions, had their origin in popular imagination. For this reason those events which most powerfully stir imagination are accompanied by the largest number of celebrations and festivities. Especially festivities. For the mass of mankind, finding life as a rule so monotonous, yet at the same time uncertain, turns always to holiday-making, to eating and drinking, on occasions when it can escape from its usual daily routine. No festival in the year touched the imagination of the Age of Faith more closely than did Easter. The marvellous nature of the occurrence commemorated, the dramatic manner of its happening, the contrast between Good Friday's sadness and the triumph of the Resurrection, combined to take possession of the medieval mind. This caused Easter to be marked by numberless customs and ceremonies quite part from those of the Church.

Many of these had, as one would expect, a charitable origin. Thankfulness for the rising of the crucified made people think of the poor. For example, at St. Bartholomew's, Smithfield, one of London's largest and noblest churches, the terms of a will made centuries ago are still fulfilled. A number of sixpences and Hot Cross buns are laid upon tombs in the churchyard and a number of poor men and women are invited to pick them up. Unfortunately, sixpence does not purchase now, as it did when the kindly arrangement was thought of, a joint of meat or half a sack of flour.

Here is another example of Easter bounty of ancient origin being kept up. At Biddenden, in Kent, there still takes place a distribution on Easter Sunday in the afternoon of small cakes with the figures of two women, side by side and very close together, printed on them. These are paid for out of the rent of fields known as the Bread and Cheese Land (for loaves and cheese were once given away as well). Who originally left these lands for the purpose is not known, nor can the date of the bequest be fixed. But it has been made quite plain that the figures on the cakes do not represent twin sisters who created the charity several centuries ago. This was the general belief for a long time (it is still held by a great many), but it was effectually disposed of by the discovery that the cakes were not ornamented with the impress of the two women until after the middle of the 18th century, that is to say, after the annual distribution had been taking place for two or three hundred years. It is now supposed that the figures were meant to be those of poor widows, typical recipients of the cakes.

Yet another bequest of this kind continues to be carried out at a little place called Ufton, between Reading and Newbury, in Berkshire. This has been traced as far back as the year 1583. Loaves of bread to the number of 164 are given away to selected persons, and nine necessitous persons receive five yards of flannel and eleven yards of calico apiece.

TWICKENHAM, in Middlesex, used to have two immense cakes baked and cut up in church on Easter Day and divided among young people. The Puritans put an end to this in 1645; they called it a 'superstitious relic.' Parliament ordered that loaves of bread should be bought and given to the poor. It did not order them to be scrambled for. No doubt it was during the merry times after the Restoration that the custom arose of throwing them from the parish church steeple and letting those who were most active in the crowd below carry them off. A like custom prevailed once in Paddington, when it was a village near London; this could be remembered by persons living in the early years of the 19th century.

Topical

EASTERTIDE ALMS ON A CITY TOMBSTONE

An ancient Good Friday custom is still kept up at St. Bartholomew's, Smithfield, in accordance with a centuries-old bequest. Sixpences placed on the tombstone of the benefactor are picked up by the poor of the parish. A widow is here seen picking up her sixpence.

George Long

THE TICHBORNE DOLE: BLESSING THE FLOUR FOR A MEDIEVAL CHARITY

Although Easter itself is a very favourite date for medieval doles, some of these old charities are dispensed during the preceding season of Lent. The Tichborne Dole is distributed every Lady Day, March 25th, when a ton and a half of flour is given away to the poor of the village, each man receiving a gallon and each woman and child half a gallon. The flour is placed in a great bin in the church porch, and is blessed with due rites by the family chaplain. The dole is served by the revenues of a piece of land, which, according to legend, was set aside for this purpose by a wicked twelfth-century Tichborne at the dying request of his pious wife. In the photograph the boy dressed as an acolyte is the heir of the Tichborne family.

Popular Customs of Eastertide

The greatest of the Church's festivals, Easter became naturally enough a holiday-time. The long fast of Lent was over, mourning had been turned into joy: also it was the end of winter, flowers were appearing, trees were putting on their leaves, the sun shone with spring splendour. Indeed, it was supposed that on Easter Sunday the sun rose earlier than the calendar indicated and blazed with a specially rich fire—and even 'danced.'

> No sun upon an Easter Day
> Is half so fine a sight.

(as the bride) sang Suckling in his Ballad upon a Wedding.

In the 'Mirror of the Months' an author wrote:

> Now at last the Easter week is arrived and the poor have for once in the year the best of it—setting all things but their own sovereign will at a wise defiance. The journeyman who works on Easter Monday should lose his *caste* and be sent to the Coventry of mechanics, wherever that may be . . . on Easter Monday ranks change places; Jobson is as good as Sir John; the 'rude mechanical' is 'monarch of all he surveys' . . All the narrow lanes and blind alleys of our metropolis pour forth their dingy denizens into the suburban fields and villages in search of amusement.

One form of pastime which has happily been abandoned for a long time was the baiting of an unfortunate stag by crowds of Cockney 'sportsmen' in Epping Forest. This was the survival of the yearly insistence upon the right of Londoners to chase game in the woods and warrens around the city, a right granted to them by the King in 1226. In order to preserve this the Lord Mayor and Aldermen made a point throughout the Middle Ages of hunting in Epping Forest, which was the easiest for them to get at, every Easter Monday. A writer describing the scene in a London newspaper of 1826 could not hide its foolish and rowdy character. By nine o'clock in the morning 'the huntsmen of the east' were to be seen, some on horseback, some in gigs, cabs, job-coaches, some on foot. For hours they hung about, awaiting the arrival of their quarry. They had to wait until the afternoon, for various public houses around the Forest had laid in vast amounts of food and drink—'boiled beef and fat hams, beer and brandy in abundance'; and innkeepers wanted these to be consumed before the hunt began. So the stag was taken round in a cart from one public house to another and exhibited at threepence a head all the morning. At half past two it was turned out and the hunters formed up in two long lines, between which the animal was expected to run. It did not hurry itself; it walked and ambled until it caught sight of the hounds, and then it

George Long

Topical

MYSTERY OF THE 'TWINS' ON AN EASTER CAKE

Biddenden, in Kent, has long been known for its Easter dole of bread and cheese and cakes. The charity was instituted some hundred of years ago by twin sisters of the village, the necessary funds being provided from the rents of what are still known as the Bread and Cheese Land. The quaint female figures stamped on the Biddenden Cake (left) were long thought to represent the creators of the dole, but are probably an illustration of those who benefit by it. On the right are seen boys receiving their portion.

E.N.A.

EASTER EGGS OF EASTERN EUROPE

These highly decorative objects are Easter eggs from the Bukowina district of Rumania. Eggs play a large part in many of the Eastertide customs, and vary widely in colour and ornamentation. One of the commonest forms is the hen's egg dyed a bright colour.

dashed through one line, knocking several sportsmen down, and disappeared. What happened to it the writer did not know, for he and most of the other hunters went back to London early to attend the Lady Mayoress's ball at the Mansion House!

Everyone tried to find some exciting form of amusement at Easter. In the midlands and north of England there was 'lifting' (carrying on crossed hands). On Easter Monday men lifted every woman they met; on the Tuesday women did their best to lift men. There were ball games in which priests took part with their flocks, who were still chuckling over the jokes and often salacious stories which it was customary, before the Reformation, to put into Easter sermons. In the county of Durham young men took the buckles off girls' shoes on the Monday; on the next day the girls claimed the same privilege. Then they all met together and made merry and redeemed their buckles by 'forfeits.' What was the original meaning of these alternating playful attacks by men on women and by women on men cannot now be even guessed at. In some places it was even customary for wives to beat their husbands on Easter Tuesday and for husbands to inflict the same chastisement on the day after. But this was all done in the way of kindness and as part of the jollification for which Easter gave excuse.

All who could took part in it. Even

> The old wives get merry
> With spiced ale or sherry,

as verses in a collection of 1708 put it, and to this day the tradition of holiday-making and feasting and drinking more than usual is kept up. No longer

> On Easter Sunday is the pudding seen
> To which the Tansy lends her sober green,

and if it were seen, we should probably dislike the flavour of the herb tansy, supposed to be among the 'bitter herbs' on the sponge which was held up to Christ on the Cross as a restorative; we should decline to eat it. But within the last half-century it was still eaten. Eggs and bacon, the well-to-do Englishman's habitual breakfast and the favourite dinner of the agricultural labourer's family when they can afford it, seem to have had a semi-religious origin as an Easter dish. A gammon was on every table as evidence that the householder was no Jew, and with it went the eggs, which had been regarded

E.N.A.

TRICKED OUT IN ALL THEIR EASTER FINERY

In the Spreewald, a woodland district outside Berlin, Easter observances can be seen in rich variety. The peasants bring out their traditional costumes and celebrate the occasion in the time-honoured ways. The photograph shows little girls in gala head-dresses with symbolic Easter gifts, including Easter eggs.

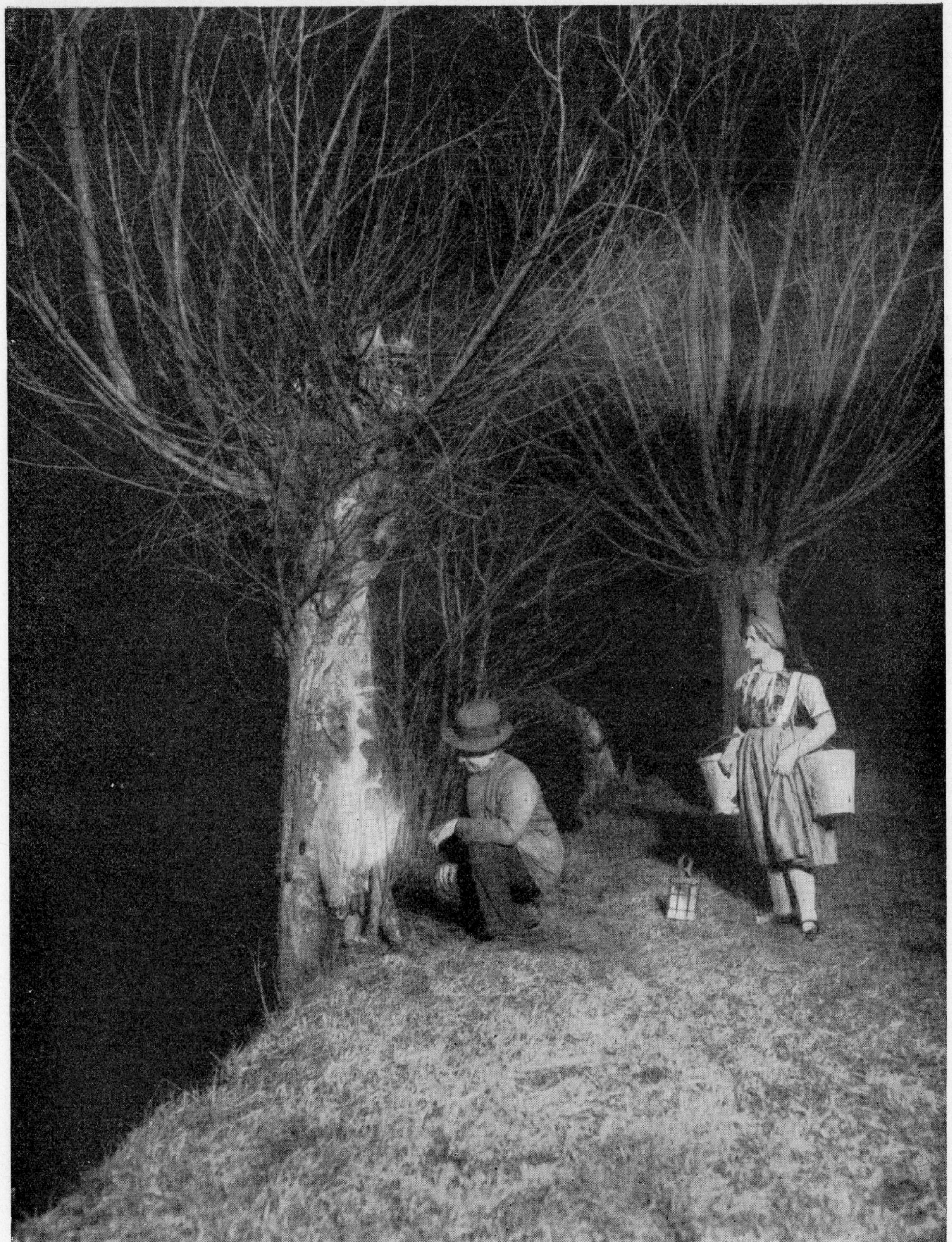

E.N.A.

WONDER-WORKING LIGHT OF THE EASTER FIRE

One of the many picturesque Easter customs observed by the peasants in that home of Easter celebrations, the Spreewald, near Berlin, is that connected with the Easter fire and Easter water. Having chosen a particular spot by the side of a river, they proceed to kindle a fire close to the water's edge. When the fire is thoroughly well alight they scoop up water from the stream in the belief that, through having been subjected to the light of the Easter fire, it has gained the power of healing disease.

E.N.A.

YOUTHFUL PARTICIPANTS IN A CHRISTIANISED FORM OF A PAGAN CELEBRATION

Throughout Germany Easter eggs have always played a very prominent part in the Eastertide celebrations. In some parts eggs were the reward for prowess shown in connexion with the Easter fires. At Althenneberg, in Upper Bavaria, for instance, a wooden cross swathed in straw was formerly burnt on a bonfire, and the man who first reached the fire and kindled it was given coloured eggs at the church door. Young people of Hirschberg, in the Prussian province of Silesia, are here seen parading the streets offering their Easter eggs for sale.

from very ancient times, long before Christianity, as emblems of the universe and of the continuity of life.

The Easter egg's history can thus be traced back to the Egyptians and Persians of pre-Christian ages. Most of us think of it as being made of sugar or chocolate, filling the windows of large and small shops at widely differing prices. These are merely imitation Easter eggs. The real thing must be a hen's egg; it must be hard-boiled and coloured. The proper way to colour it is to dip it into cochineal or some other vegetable dye, and then it ought to be rolled down a hill along with many others. If yours be unbroken, it is one of the winners and you will have good luck till next Easter. If its shell is cracked, then you must tell yourself you have no belief in luck at all. 'Pace eggs,' they are called in Lancashire; in Northumberland, where they are 'jaaped' instead of 'rolled,' pace becomes 'paste.' Rightly, they should be 'Pasque eggs.' One name for Easter is derived from the Greek 'pascha' (meaning 'pass-over,' which points to a confusion between the Jewish and the Christian festivals); hence the 'paschal lamb' and the French Pâques.

In German-speaking countries eggs are as much a part of the Easter celebrations as in England. In France, Italy, Spain, they are scarcely seen. Most French confectioners' shops are filled at Easter-time with fish made of sweetmeats. These are called 'poissons d'Avril' and have sometimes been considered to have a connexion with Easter. But none is clear. In the German Spreewald, a district not far from Berlin, young people's Easter games and customs characteristic of those in many other parts can be seen to-day. Eggs have a prominent part in them. One peculiar trick is performed by these children. They light an 'Easter fire' by the side of a stream or pond. The water in which it shines is supposed to possess healing power. Many scoop it up and use it for themselves or for sick friends. In some of the Spreewald villages the women wear at Easter the old traditional costumes with head-dresses designed by far-off Wendish ancestors. Very pretty they look in them, too. Polish girls also put on antique frocks and veil their heads in muslin when they take part in the Easter procession. Saxon boys and girls roll their eggs, just as English north-country children do. In Prussia they may be seen taking around their eggs for sale, instead of begging for them as the English custom used to be.

Singing enters largely into German Easter festivities. In Tirol the peasants (who are German still, though now under Italian rule) make music with their guitars and go about from village to village, welcomed by the inhabitants and escorted by bands of children with pinewood torches to light them on their way. In England there are survivals of Easter singing practices. At South Shields thousands of

Topical Press

E.N.A.

CLEAR YOUNG VOICES LIFTED UP TO WELCOME EASTER

Singing is a common feature of the Easter festivities of Germany, and in certain special forms survives in some parts of **England.** At Beverley, in Yorkshire, every Easter morning the choir boys mount the Minster tower and from their lofty perch sing hymns (top), as do those of Magdalen College, Oxford, on May morning. The Spreewald, near Berlin, a region noted for its wealth of Easter observances, affords another instance of Easter singing. **Girls perambulate the district on Easter Sunday, singing outside the houses** of the old and sick (bottom).

E.N.A.

ETIQUETTE OF COYNESS IN WATER-SPRINKLING CEREMONY

In Hungary the old-fashioned custom still prevails of sprinkling the village girls with water from the well on Easter Monday. Although it is considered a disgrace for a maiden not to be sprinkled by her lover on this occasion, custom demands that she should show every sign of reluctance. She struggles with her would-be captor, and in the end may have to be forcibly dragged to the appointed spot. In the upper photograph a girl is being taken to the well, and in the lower she is being sprinkled.

W. S. Campbe .

CARRYING ON HIGH THE ROYAL GIFT OF THE MAUNDY

On Maundy Thursday, the day before Good Friday, the distribution of the Maundy money takes place with great ceremony at Westminster Abbey. The doles are brought to Westminster by Yeomen of the Guard and are distributed by the Lord High Almoner. A detachment of the Yeomen of the Guard are here seen arriving in the Abbot's Courtyard at Westminster from St. James's Palace. One of their number carries the alms dish high above his head, laden with the Maundy money contained in purses, the strings of which hang over the edge of the dish.

Topical Press

PENNIES FROM THEIR SOVEREIGN'S BOUNTY

These two old people are among the fortunate recipients of the Maundy money. The gift is made to as many aged men and women as there are years in the sovereign's age, at the rate of one penny for each year. Formerly food was also given, but this has been replaced by a money payment in addition to the Maundy pennies.

sovereigns had another duty to perform on Good Friday; they had to 'creep to the Cross.' It is true a special carpet was laid for them to creep on, but they did actually go down on all-fours, which signified 'a humbling of themselves to Christ before the Cross,' and they then kissed it 'in memorie of our redemption made upon it.' That was how Henry the Eighth understood it.

The ceremony of giving money to poor folk on Maundy Thursday has, on the contrary, always been kept up by English sovereigns. This takes place on the day before Good Friday; it commemorates the washing of the disciples' feet by Jesus on the eve of the Crucifixion, though there is nothing in the present-day proceedings to indicate this, since the 'act of humility' was left out a very long time ago. Up to the reign of Dutch William the sovereign actually did wash the feet (though in a perfunctory way) of a number of poor men. But the Protestant Prince of Orange told the Archbishop of York that, as he was Lord High Almoner, he must do it. That went on for a good many years, then the washing was given up altogether. Also the distribution of food was altered to a money payment in addition to the 'Maundy money' which all the old people receive. This is specially struck by the Mint, as it differs from the ordinary coinage.

'Maundy' is derived from an old word meaning 'basket'; the poor brought with them baskets in which to take away the provisions given to them. What these were in 1731 we learn from the Court Circular of the time. For forty-eight men and forty-eight women—the number was always that of the sovereign's years, and George the Second was in his 49th year—there were provided 'boiled beef and shoulders of mutton and small bowls of ale which is called dinner; after that large wooden platters of fish and loaves, viz. undressed, one large old ling and one large dried cod; twelve red herrings and twelve white herrings, and four half-quartern loaves.'

Once it was the Christian duty of all men of high rank and great wealth to go through this symbolical feet-washing ceremonial. The Pope keeps up the practice, but has substituted for the poor men thirteen bishops. Twelve represent the Apostles and the thirteenth an angel who once appeared (in the 6th century) while the performance went on. But they were really poor folk who were having their feet washed then.

school-children gather in the market place to sing, many of them wearing curious garments and garlands of flowers. At Beverley, in Yorkshire, boys go to the top of the Minster tower and sing hymns.

Good Friday customs were once almost as numerous and as well honoured as those of Eastertide. Now scarcely any survive excepting the hot cross bun, which is eaten only in England, by the way. Once there was careful baking of bread as well as buns on Good Friday, and loaves were put aside to be kept all the year and used in miraculous ways. If you were seized with sudden illness, you could have a piece cut off and soaked in water. Drinking the water would make you quite well. It was wise, too, to keep a few eggs laid on Good Friday as fire extinguishers. They could be trusted to put out the flames of any ordinary conflagration.

AGAIN, if you suffered from rheumatism, you could take a ring to Court on Good Friday and get the King or the Queen—either would do—to bless it. That would cure you very soon. Less than a hundred years ago it was still believed in Suffolk that if nine young bachelors in a parish gave each a crooked sixpence and had the coins made into a silver ring, it would relieve any young woman who happened to be afflicted with cramp. And, of course, there are many people to-day who believe that certain kinds of rings will keep off certain ailments—even though they have not been blessed by king or queen. The

CUSTOMS OF COURTESY

STUDY of the daily routine of representative men and women is an important branch of cultural anthropology. Here we are concerned chiefly with the etiquette that governs the exchange of salutations among various peoples. Other aspects of racial manners are dealt with in later chapters on Distinctions of Rank and differences in the Standards of Decency and Decorum.

'MANNERS maketh Man' is an old saying which time has familiarised; but man's conception of etiquette varies so very widely in different parts of the world that the proverb needs some modification. For instance, the use of the handkerchief is usually associated with polite society, and especially with the fairer sex; but in Montenegro the fingers are used by the ladies, handkerchiefs being reserved for officers of the army. Numerous customs have become so well known or so familiar that their original meaning has been obscured. The casual invitation to 'Come and have a shake-down' alludes to the period when a bed meant a litter of straw. Similarly the handshake, which implies friendship, arose from the fact that the knight of the medieval period had to remove his gauntlet to offer his hand; an act of faith, since a blow on his right hand might disable him for life.

Many and varied are the forms of ceremonial greeting. 'Good-bye' is a corruption of 'God be with you,' and the Irish peasant's 'May your shadow never grow less' refers to an old-time belief whereby practitioners of the Black Arts were compelled to run through a subterranean hall with the Devil after them, and if he could catch their shadow or part of it they became first-rate magicians. The saying really means may you escape wholly and entirely the clutches of the foul fiend. The loss of Peter Pan's shadow is an important episode in Barrie's play of that name. Another kind of greeting is to be found in the Albanian mountains, where the stranger is welcomed with the words, 'Bread, salt and my heart,' indicating the most lavish hospitality the Albanian can offer; while certain sects among the Montenegrins will introduce their wives with the words 'My wife, if you will excuse me.' This practice is a surviving relic of an era when the unmarried were regarded as perfect and the married as sinful—a species of Manichaeism. Numerous savages have ceremonial forms of greeting and farewell, and perhaps one of the strangest is the leave-taking of the Lengua Indians of the Paraguayan Chaco. When the guest is ready to start a dialogue ensues:

Guest. I am going to leave.
Host. You are going to leave.
Guest. I am going by the straight road.
Host. You are going by the straight road.

This repetition proceeds for some time until the host feels that the forms of politeness have been duly complied with, when he says 'Go.'

ANOTHER curious custom amongst primitives is greeting by excessive weeping. The pigmy Andamanese weep at a wedding, on seeing friends and at a funeral; Ainu women take great delight in falling on the necks of friends they have not seen for a long time and addressing them in voices choked with sobs, while the Tupi Indians of the Chaco region of South America adopt the same practice.

Topical Press

HERE'S A HAND, MY TRUSTY FRIEND'
Western etiquette prescribes that in hand-shaking the right hand, ungloved, shall be used. This custom is a relic of medieval times, when a knight arriving in friendship laid aside his weapon, removed his gauntlet and showed his sword hand empty and unprotected.

Drinking healths was a Roman custom, and in England the Saxons followed the habit. The Loving Cup, which is still used at the banquets of the City Guilds, is a large cup filled with wine passed round at great dinners from guest to guest. In olden times, and the custom is kept up to-day, a man's immediate neighbours on the right and left rose with him when he drank to protect him from the dagger of the assassin. The stirrup cup has been immortalised by Scott in the lines

> Lord Marmion's bugles blow to horse;
> Then came the stirrup cup in course;
> Between the Baron and his host
> No point of courtesy was lost.

It is really nothing more than the last glass

Topical Press and P. & A.

A STIRRUP CUP TO SPEED THE PARTING GUEST

Strictly speaking, the term stirrup cup means the cup of wine offered in olden days to a guest when he mounted his horse preparatory to departure. The custom is a very widespread one. Thus the Swanetians (right), inhabitants of an extremely remote valley high up in the Caucasus Mountains, are toasting some departing travellers, pledging them in vodka from a ram's horn. In Great Britain when hounds meet in private grounds the owner usually offers a stirrup cup to the huntsman and others gathered for the hunt.

prior to the general good-night. In Scotland the stirrup cup is more usually known under the sobriquet of the 'Deoch and Doris,' and in France, in the Ardennes, as the Gloria, the last of a series of cups of coffee, laced with brandy.

Ceremonial drinking is not, however, confined to Europe, and in the South Seas the presentation of kava to strangers and to kings was hedged about with ritual. In Samoa the youngest and fairest of the female sex chewed the kava root, which was then placed in a bowl and kneaded, the solid particles removed, and the resultant liquid left to clear. In Fiji these functions were performed by the men, and a cup-bearer presented it to the stranger or the chief.

ANOTHER European custom closely associated with drinking which persists to-day, and which was introduced by the Vikings and Norsemen, is that of the ladies retiring after dinner and leaving the men to drink. It is said that the Vikings always dismissed the women from their drinking parties, since in those rough times the women were frequently the cause of brawling and fighting.

The custom of 'sending a person to Coventry' arose from the fact that the citizens of Coventry had at one time a great dislike to soldiers, and if a woman of that town was seen speaking to one she was immediately cut off from all social intercourse. Amongst the Australian aborigines a ban of silence is sometimes imposed upon the women, who dare not break it under penalty of death. Release is effected by the husband passing his hand across the lips of the woman, who has afterwards to bathe to cleanse herself from the sin of loquacity.

The practice of 'chucking a person under the chin' recalls to English readers the days when the young squire indulged in that pleasant pastime with the buxom lassies of the countryside; but it is part of the social etiquette of the Koiari tribe of British New Guinea to salute by chucking under the chin.

Kissing, the most popular of the salutations, is practically restricted to Europe; but in Turkey wives salute their husbands by kissing their beards. In Japan maidens should beware of the fact that the word kiss does not appear in the vocabulary, the practice of kissing in that country being regarded as revolting and immodest.

In Polynesia the kiss is replaced by rubbing noses, the salute by smelling or sniffing, in contradistinction to that of kissing, the salute by tasting. The Maori

Thos. McMahon (S. & G.

CUP-BEARER ON BENDED KNEE SERVES A FIJIAN CHIEF

Ceremonial kava-drinking is a custom widespread throughout Melanesia and Indonesia. Kava is a plant of the pepper family, and the root is pounded or chewed, mixed with water, and allowed to ferment, an intoxicating beverage resulting which has useful medicinal qualities and is supposed to contribute to longevity. On formal occasions it is offered to guests with a good deal of ceremony, to the highest in rank first, in a cup of coconut shell which from saturation and frequent use comes to resemble tortoise shell.

Mondiale

NATIVE LADIES OF NEW ZEALAND EXCHANGING FRIENDLY GREETINGS BY THE NOSE

If traced back to their actual origin all forms of salutation among the peoples of the world will be found to have their root in the instinctive animal use of the sense of feeling, smelling or tasting to test the nature and quality of another animal encountered for the first time. The kiss is a refined method of testing by taste, and as a salute is unknown among savage races and unpractised by many others. The greeting used by Polynesians and some other peoples is generally, but inaccurately, described as rubbing noses. Actually the nostrils are pressed together and the practice is drawn from the animal use of the sense of smell. Among the Maori of New Zealand the salute is accompanied by a queer dog-like howl that further emphasises its animal derivation.

of New Zealand, when they meet, rub their noses together and utter a strange, dog-like howl. This curious practice is remarkable for its similarity to that of certain animals, and is only found among primitive peoples. The Eskimo add to this pastime the disgusting habit of licking the face and hands of the visitor, while in Lapland the practice of rubbing noses is accompanied by a pantomine of leaping and jumping.

The formal and ceremonious act of kissing the hand has some curious variants. In Fiji it was the custom to smell the hand of the honoured guest, and amongst the Andamanese persons greeting each other after a long absence, or at a leave-taking, invariably blow upon the hand. The Nandi, a wild tribe of Uganda, spit upon the hand before offering it to a friend; this practice is supposed to bring good luck and avert evil. Amongst the Masai, a kindred people, there is a form of ceremonious salutation in which young girls file past the visitor with a mincing, half-dancing step, holding a bunch of grass in one hand as a token of good will. At this ceremony the hand is offered; but, nevertheless, it is better to spit upon a Masai damsel than to embrace her.

NICE POINTS OF CONDUCT IN NYASALAND

Among the Henga tribe of Nyasaland the small courtesies of daily life are rather elaborately punctilious. Thus, the method of offering and accepting anything is for the man to place his left hand on his right arm while delivering the article with his right hand, and for the woman to receive it with both hands. Persons of both sexes kneel when meeting on the road (top).

The embrace has a wide distribution, and is found amongst the lowest of mankind, but in Greece it is customary for the priests to touch the ground with the fingers before embracing anyone they wish to do special honour to.

The more ceremonious forms of salutation, such as the bow, which may be of the hasty nod variety, or accompanied by those genuflexions of the body which one usually associates with obsequious servility, are usually found in the East. In Southern India the Tamils prostrate themselves at the feet of a benefactor or persons whom they wish to solicit. The Todas, a wild people of the Nilgiri Hills of Southern India, have a curious form of salutation called 'kalmel-pudithti,' or 'leg up he puts.' It consists of a woman saluting her older male relatives by bowing down and placing the foot to her forehead.

Amongst the hairy Ainu, the aboriginal inhabitants of Japan, salutations are of a most ceremonious kind. Before entering a house the Ainu man gives a low cough, waits a few moments, walks in and sits down cross-legged before the owner. He then stretches forward his hands as though praying, while his host performs similar exercises, not a word being spoken. He next gently rubs his hands together and calls

E.N.A. and Sport & General

G.P.A.

SALUTATIONS PRESCRIBED BY POLITENESS IN THE COURTEOUS EAST

Politeness is a marked characteristic of oriental society, the initial exchange of verbal compliments and the attitudes to be adopted being matters most carefully prescribed. Chinese gentlemen when meeting at the new year beamingly shake hands with themselves. Japanese ladies bow low, with their hands resting on their knees, while smiling amiably into one another's faces. In Buddhist temple precincts genuflection almost amounting to prostration is the correct thing, and priests when meeting will crouch to the ground and touch the earth with their hands.

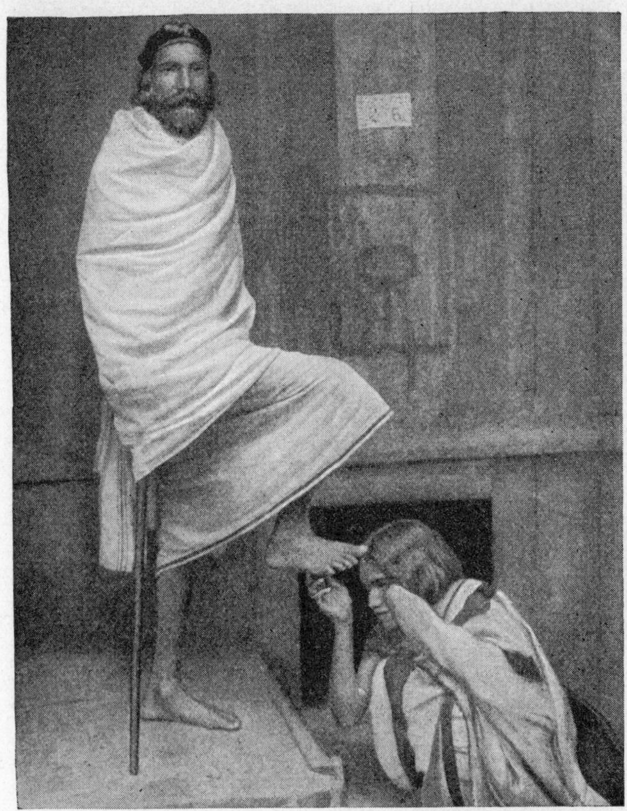

Sports & General and C. Carthrew

Col. F. D. Fayrer

COURTESY MEET AND PROPER FOR WIFE, WARRIOR AND SUBJECT

Removal of the shoes before entering sacred precincts is a very ancient, widespread custom. It is sometimes exacted as a social habit, as by an Indian prince at Udaipur, outside whose reception hall visitors and guests are required to leave their shoes. Much more abject humility is exacted from Toda women (top left), for they have to kneel and place their husband's foot upon their forehead. In Kenya tribal custom secures safe passage through strange villages for natives who cover their spear head with a pompon (top right) in token that they come in peace.

Keystone

SIOUX CHIEFS SMOKE THE PIPE OF PEACE

Among the American Indians ceremonial pipe-smoking at tribal councils is almost a religious rite, and at inter-tribal conferences circulating the pipe of peace has actual sacramental significance. In some tribes the charge of the sacred pipe is committed to a particular selected individual for a specified time, and during this he is under obligation of fasting and continence.

down heavenly blessings on his host and the occupants of the house ; the formal salutations closing by both host and guest stroking their beards and looking attentively and respectfully at each other. After these preliminaries business can be discussed. It is curious to note that the Ainu idols are saluted in an exactly similar manner, and that, therefore, this form of salutation is in a sense religious. Ainu women, however, have a different form of salutation. On entering a house they must remove their headgear, while they draw the index finger of the right hand up the middle and left of the shoulder, and then from left to right across the upper lip, ending by stroking and smoothing the forelocks of the hair. They then await the invitation of their lords and masters to speak. When leaving the house, Ainu women have to walk backwards, as it would be considered disrespectful to turn their backs on their menfolk.

Smoking and offering snuff often form the prelude to polite conversation amongst peoples all over the world. With the Hopi Indians of America, pipe smoking is almost a religious ceremony, and any person invited to join in the tribal council and partake of the circulating pipe is indeed honoured. In Tibet the ritual act of hospitality is the offer of tea, everyone carrying his own wooden cup at his belt. Nevertheless, tobacco pouches and snuff boxes are often exchanged and form the usual welcome to the stranger, accompanied by those stereotyped phrases anent the weather and the crops common among pastoral peoples all over the world.

Sometimes, ignorance of modes of address and procedure among primitive peoples leads to awkward results. A recent explorer amongst the Eskimo, on arriving at a village, asked one of the girls to help him off with his heavy outer clothing, a request customary enough amongst most Northern peoples ; it was, however, construed by the bystanders as an offer of marriage, and the unfortunate explorer was pursued by the girl's mother with the offer of her daughter's hand during the whole length of his visit. In India it is customary to keep the honoured guest waiting before admittance to the master of the house. An Englishman who was not acquainted with this custom of the country, after waiting half-an-hour, left the house in a rage, only to find his host very apologetic in the drive, where he explained that what was intended was not an insult, but an honour.

Customs of courtesy are so numerous and so varied, so strange and yet so natural, that we are apt to forget they have, in the majority of cases, a deeper inner meaning, the outcome of traditional lore framed by etiquette.

INITIATION AND OTHER CEREMONIES OF PUBERTY

THE root idea of the customs connected with puberty is that of dying to childhood and being born again to adult life, although among primitive peoples the initiatory rites for boys are largely concerned with testing their powers of enduring pain. Religious and other aspects of the subject are touched upon in the chapters on Ceremonial Circumcision, Mystical Societies and Secret Societies.

THE ideas behind the ceremonies or initiations which savage and barbarous peoples undergo at the dawn of manhood and womanhood are symbolic of entrance to the adult condition and the putting-off of the childish state. Primitive peoples occasionally dramatise the circumstances of adoption into the new adult life with its responsibilities, social and sexual, though the preliminary actions gone through or the trials endured are sometimes intended either as a rehearsal of the ceremony of initiation or a hardening process for the battle of life.

Puberty initiation among some savage peoples is accompanied by rites so ghastly and barbarous that most observers who have recorded them hesitate to describe them in all their hideous details. Such rites usually take place in the 'men's house' of the village, are thus taboo to women, and frequently result in maiming the unhappy victims for life. As examples of some of the less horrible of these practices, certain South American tribes in the Amazon region hang up the initiate by the lips with fish-hooks and leave him suspended for hours as a test of his manhood and endurance, while among the people of Borneo beatings of a nature so severe are administered as often to end in death or entire disablement. Scarification of a most dreadful kind is common in the puberty rites of central African communities, while tooth-filing and shaving the head are encountered among many barbarous peoples throughout the world. Frightful obscenities, too, often accompany the more strictly social ritual, and wild orgies, the details of which it is impossible to describe, are often indulged in.

ON the other hand, these initiations of young people at the age of puberty are often combined with excellent advice as to the duties of manhood and womanhood, the feminine lore of the women of the tribe being passed on to the maidens, and the tribal history and secrets of the men to the boys. Continuity of tradition and tribal cohesion are thus ensured. The tests of endurance gone through, fasting and purification and severe beatings, are applied with the object of freeing the candidate from the old taboos of childhood, and fumigation and seclusion are also often employed for this purpose. As one sex is regarded as taboo against the other, the ceremony is also directed against the dangers of sexual contact in adult life. Thus the girls must on no account see or be seen by males, nor may the boys have any association with females, in the great majority of instances.

Moreover, personal identity undergoes a very real transformation at puberty. In the ceremonies connected with the East African tribe of the Wanika the boys are smeared all over with white earth so that they cannot be recognized, and names are often changed at puberty, especially among the Australian tribes. Sometimes, too, part of the body is scarified as a renunciation of the 'old man' or old personality; for example a tooth is knocked out, or circumcision is performed. There are also, in some cases, specific rites to ensure a new supply of manly strength, as that known among the Central Australians as Engwara, in which the boy to be initiated is drenched with the blood of adult men. Fasting is often prescribed to prevent dangerous influences entering the system with the food at a peculiarly perilous stage in the adolescent's life-history.

THE novelty of the adult life is often emphasised by the supposed reception of an external soul or guardian spirit, the boy not being regarded as a human entity or person before puberty initiation. The lad retires to a solitary place and remains for days without food. Visions descend upon him, induced doubtless by exhaustion, and his tutelary spirit reveals itself to him in dreams, usually in animal form, remaining with him in after-life as a guide, philosopher and friend. The Australians believe that an ancestral spirit enters each child at conception and is also outwardly materialised in a 'churinga' or sacred object, often a piece of stone or slate. These are treasured and held sacred by the tribe, are alluded to by them as 'grandfathers,' and shown to the boys at initiation as their 'ancestors.'

Throughout Melanesia and the Indonesian Archipelago puberty rites begin when the lad shows signs of a beard. He is hidden in a tabooed spot in the bush and carefully instructed in the moral code, social customs and sacred legends peculiar to the clan. In short, the young man is taken out of the family and made one with the community.

Perhaps the most complete example of a puberty initiation rite extant is that still maintained by the Queensland tribes of Australia, and known as 'Bora.' In a clearing in the woods a short pole is erected, and from this centre a track is led into the bush. The rudely sculptured figure of Baiamai, the divine culture-hero, is erected in this sacred enclosure. He it was who slew Dhurmoolan, who was formerly

Columbia

LION-KILLERS OF TANGANYIKA WHO DRESS UP AS WOMEN IN ORDER TO BECOME MEN

Youths of the Nandi tribe, one of the most warlike races of the lion country of the Tanganyika plains, cannot qualify as full-grown hunters until they have masqueraded for some time as women. Shortly before undergoing the first initiatory rite they are presented with young girls' garments and ornaments. These they wear until the rite is performed. They then change into women's clothes, which are provided by their mothers, and put on skull-like straw masks, adorned with straw streamers, as shown in this photograph taken by Paul Hoeffler for 'Africa Speaks.' For several months they wear this costume, and only when they have performed certain stated tasks can they discard their unmanly garments and unwieldy head-dresses and receive adult status. These changes of garments may be intended to disguise the wearer against demons at a critical time.

regarded as actually re-creating men at the time of initiation, but who occasionally devoured the neophyte. Other mystic figures are scattered about the enclosure, representing the sun and the moon and the great snake, fashioned from a mound of earth

The ceremony takes place in the spring, the men being attired in full tribal regalia. The boys are seated in a circle, each painted with red ochre, his hair decorated with swans' feathers and dressed in the warrior's kilted garb. They are accompanied by their sisters and brothers-in-law, who act as their guardians during the ceremony.

Bull-roarers—instruments which make a loud roaring noise when swung—are now sounded to herald the approach of the god, and burning brands cast in make-believe of his fiery descent. The guardians each seize a lad and carry him along the mystic path, to the accompaniment of a terrific din. The boys are carried for some miles into the bush, where they are instructed in the secrets of tribal sodality. Eventually they are carried back to the enclosure, where they behold the mystery plays representing the myth or story of Dhurmoolan, which are danced out before them. These are explained to them, a tooth is extracted by way of sacrifice, and they are then regarded as initiates, or full men.

In Victoria the blackfellows employ somewhat different rites. Boys of thirteen are removed from the camp by old men for a month and are instructed in the legends and secrets of the tribe. A tooth is then knocked out and the lad is restored to his family, but at the age of eighteen he is again removed and the initiation is completed. Among the Xarra river tribes the boy is daubed with clay—a rite also found in connexion with the ancient Greek ceremonies of initiation—and his hair is shaved off. No one speaks to him until his hair begins to grow, when the women wash and paint him and dance before him. It is obvious that many of these ceremonies are merely fragmentary and degenerate parts of some more ancient and complete initiatory drama or system.

The boys of the Bechuana tribes are stripped and placed in a row before an equal number of men. First they dance the Koha dance, with sandals on their hands, and are asked whether they will worthily perform certain tasks of manhood, such as 'Will you watch the cattle well?' 'Will you guard the chief well?' As they reply the lesson of undertaking their duties is 'thrashed into' them with elastic rods, their backs being scarred for life, yet they must continue to dance and look happy without the slightest murmuring. The boys of the Kosa tribe, in South Africa, live by themselves for two months, and are smeared with white clay and wear a peculiar head-dress. During this period they can steal what they choose, provided they are not caught in the act, and eventually are brought before the old men of the tribe, who lecture them on the responsibilities and duties of manhood. They are then permitted all kinds of immorality without let or hindrance.

E.N.A.

A STAGE IN THE MAKING OF A WARRIOR

This Masai boy of East Africa has recently been initiated into manhood. Therefore, in accordance with custom, he is dressed like a woman, wears earrings, and has whitened his face with chalk. Not until his wounds have healed may he don the dress and ornaments proper to a warrior.

Among the Indians of North America the most typical puberty rites were those associated with female life, but others appertaining to the male sex were not wanting. The Omaha brave was initiated at fourteen into the mysteries of the rite known as Non-Zhin-Zhon, which brought with it communications from the supernatural powers. For four days and nights, his head daubed with clay, he must sing the tribal prayer-song with tears and sighs, until the vision of his guardian is vouchsafed him and its sacred song is revealed to him, which is for ever after to be the medium of communication between him and the unseen. He is then informed by his manitou or patron spirit whether he is to be a warrior, a hunter, or a medicine man. The Tuscarora boys are given a bark to chew which induces raving intoxication and subsequent visions. But, on the whole, male initiation in America is strangely uniform. Indeed, as Hutton Webster has well said, the vision among the American Indians has become 'the regular puberty ordeal,' although in California the vision-experience and the puberty initiation are quite distinct, the former in that region being an exclusive prerogative of the medicine man. Other Indians, notably the Crows and Plains Indians, seek

E.N.A.

PARSEE CHILDREN PUTTING ON THE SACRED SHIRT OF NEW BIRTH

Parsees are initiated into the religion of Zoroaster usually between the ages of seven and eleven. The chief feature of the Nav-Jote ceremony, as it is called, is the investiture of the neophyte with the sudra, or sacred shirt, and the kusti, or sacred thread. The latter is a cord of seventy-two threads, representing the seventy-two chapters of the Yasna, a part of the Zend-Avesta. Nav-Jote means new birth, and signifies that the initiate is reborn when he assumes life's responsibilities. A Parsee girl and boy are here seen undergoing the rite.

the vision-experience at a much later date in life than puberty, and among the Kwakiutl of the north-west coast the guardian spirit is acquired by marriage, by killing its owner, or by purchase, and has nothing whatsoever to do with puberty initiation.

But, as has been said, the puberty initiation of the girl is of much more importance among the American Indians. The following is a typical story of an Indian girl's puberty vigil.

Catherine Wabose, when about thirteen years of age, left her mother's lodge and built a small one for herself. After a fast of four days she was visited by her mother, who gave her a little snow-water to drink. On the eve of the sixth day, while still fasting, she was conscious of a superhuman voice, which invited her to walk along a shining path, which led forward and upward. There she first met the 'Everlasting Standing Woman,' who gave her her 'supernatural' name. She next met the 'Little Man Spirit,' who told her that his name would be the name of her first son. She was next addressed by the 'Bright Blue Sky,' who endowed her with the gift of life. She was then encircled by bright points of light and by sharp, painless instruments, but, mounting upon a fish-like animal, she swam through the air back to her lodge. On the sixth day she experienced a repetition of the vision. On the seventh day she was fed with a little pounded corn in snow-water. After the seventh day she beheld a large round object like a stone descend from the sky and enter the lodge. It conferred upon her the gift of prophecy, and by virtue of this she assumed the rank of a prophetess upon her return to the tribe.

The Thlinket Indian maiden was usually confined in a small outhouse for six months, wearing a peculiar cloak or hood as a badge of her condition. During this isolation she was kept very busy sewing squirrel skins into blankets to teach her industry and patience. She fasted, and the water she drank must be poured out three times to teach her self-denial. She must exercise great care in the choice of food when at last she did eat, as fatty meats might make her fat for the remainder of her life. Indeed, whatever she did during the period of her seclusion she would, it was believed, continue to do so throughout life, the superstition being much the same as that by which children are told that what they 'do' on their birthdays they will 'do' for the rest of the year. By some tribes the girl was even made to pick the spines off a pine tree for days on end to inculcate habits of industry. At the conclusion of her ordeal she was dressed in her best, heralds sang her praises as healthy and active, and, other things being equal, she soon achieved the state of married squawhood.

POMP OF A HINDU GIRL'S FAREWELL TO CHILDHOOD

This young Hindu girl on her gorgeous dais is celebrating her attainment of womanhood. Round her neck she wears garlands of freshly **plucked flowers.** The dais is encrusted with pearls and beads. Over her head on the top of the dais is a representation of Vishnu in his character of protector from evil, flanked on either hand by a figure of a musician. The elaborate figure of a bird in front of the girl is in silver filigree, and is fitted with compartments for holding perfumes and other things needed for the ceremony.

Francis Birtles

SEQUENCE OF TORMENTS ENDURED UNFLINCHINGLY ON MANHOOD'S THRESHOLD

Among the aborigines of Arnhem Land, in North Australia, boys who have reached the age of adolescence are subjected to very severe tests of endurance when they come to be initiated into manhood. First, the candidates lie flat on their backs in the mosquito-infested jungle with the sun beating full on their naked bodies (top). At a later stage of the proceedings bull ants and other noxious insects are strewn over them (centre), the faces of the candidates being covered with tree bark to protect their eyes. When the ceremonies are complete (bottom) nourishment is offered by waiting women, on whom the new-made men may now look. Some die before the initiatory period is complete, so strenuous is the discipline.

Among other Indian tribes the girl must carry out rigorous ceremonies of purification, bathing ceaselessly, living upon ceremonial food and wearing cloth made of the inner bark of the maple, which was supposed to confer peculiar sanctity. She must not touch her hair or face, or these would decay. Among the Hupa Indians of California she must be 'danced over' by the men and women of the tribe for nine nights, at the conclusion of which she whips herself with strands of maple bark, gazing into polished abalone shells held by the women, to catch a glimpse of the supernatural world. After a final bath she is a free woman.

With some primitive peoples the puberty ceremonies of initiation prepare the young people for marital responsibilities, and some of the rites associated with them are believed to assist future sexual relations. Circumcision and the artificial rupture of the hymen are not infrequent. This is sometimes combined, as in Central Australia, with a ceremonial act of intercourse which is regarded as preparatory to married life, the dangers of which it is supposed to lessen by the ritual breaking of taboos. Among other peoples a mere rehearsal or dramatisation of the act suffices. With the Ceramese, one of the old women ceremonially perforates a leaf with her fingers, after which the young woman may associate with any man she pleases. Boys, among the Galelas of Halamera, have their faces painted red, the colour of women's blood, to inoculate them against feminine contacts and the dangers of effeminacy thought to be resident therein. They are also made to sit in the broiling sun as a method of counter-irritation against the 'fires' of love and to neutralise its perils. The future sexual power of the young people, too, is frequently assisted either by symbolic dance or drama among the older people, or by an actual and quite 'sacred' ceremony of tribal promiscuity, undertaken for this specific purpose.

PUBERTY initiation is, indeed, sometimes regarded as a preliminary marriage ceremony in which a boy or girl is regarded as having been wedded to the opposite sex in general, the later actual marriage rite confining him or her to one individual in particular. Among the Central Australian tribes the puberty ceremony for girls is actually their marriage rite. As regards the boys, their future mothers-in-law run off with them, but are chased by the men, who recover the lad, the rite indicating an approach to marriage. Among the Kamilaroi of Australia the men of the clan to which his wife must belong by totemic law bear off the newly initiated boy from the women of his own clan.

But on the whole the idea residing beneath puberty rites is that of putting away the old life of childhood and surveillance by women and the acceptance of the manly life. That the main theme of this idea survives, although its original and perfected ceremonial has been lost and become degraded, is sufficiently clear from the examples quoted. That, however, there was one original rite for boys and another for girls is equally clear, and that these were, at a remote period, fully formulated and later disseminated from a common centre seems highly probable. The circumstance that girls in North America were isolated in huts and girls in New Ireland were confined during puberty in small cages kept in the dark, from which both were released only to bathe, renders it clear that the thousands of miles which separate the actors in these observances do not preclude their close resemblance nor the reference of them to a very remote common origin. The practice, too, in North America and Australia, of smearing boys at the stage of puberty with clay and the occurrence of this feature in ancient Greece is eloquent of a common origin in a distant past.

THE ancient mysteries of initiation in Egypt, it is known, originally applied to the dead alone, and only at a later period were they associated with the justified living. They were connected with the theory or belief in the necessity for a spiritual rebirth after death, and it seems possible from their correspondence with the savage initiatory rites of puberty that it was once believed among barbarous peoples that the young must, on reaching man's estate, undergo the initiation essential to the welfare of a resurrected spirit. Ceremonially the boy 'died' at puberty, and was born again as a man. It was, in short, a psychic, if not a physical death. The Australian blackfellows, for instance, in some cases make their initiates believe they are really dead, and their mothers loudly lament them. They become new persons and change their names. Congoese boys and girls at puberty form a secret society called N'Kimba and are supposed to die and rise again, and take new names. Jonathan Carver witnessed an initiation among the Great Lakes Indians in which the candidate was told by the chief that he would be struck dead and instantly restored to life. The lad fell as if lifeless and rose in a few moments, none the worse. It is obvious, too, from the belief that the spirits of ancestors are sometimes believed to enter the initiate that the original ceremony, the full details of which can only be gleaned through comparisons among existing rites, was in some manner connected with the belief in reincarnation.

Apart from this, the accepted reason in the savage mind for a belief in a psychical death for boys at puberty is not so clear. In the opinion of the present writer the boy 'died' to the women's clan or sex, of which hitherto he had been a member, and must be 'reborn' into the men's clan or sex before he could be regarded as partaking of the male virtues. It cannot be too strongly asserted, for the proper comprehension of these primitive ideas, that early man regarded woman as a being of a separate type or clan from himself, and therefore as surrounded by taboos of the most fatal description, with which the younger boys who were under her tutelage were infected. Thus it was essential, to rid him of effeminate contagions, bodily and mental, that the candidate should become an entirely new individual.

P. and A. (Carl von Hoffman

ZULU FORM OF MARRIAGE BY CAPTURE: BRIDESMAIDS 'RESCUING' THE BRIDE FROM THE GROOM

Among the various ceremonies that are performed on the occasion of a Zulu wedding one of the most striking is the enacting of the attempted rescue of the bride, who, according to old tradition, is supposed to have been stolen from her people by the bridegroom. The bridesmaids, acting together in accordance with a preconcerted plan, make a determined rush as if to free the bride from her captor. In this united effort the bride, too, takes part, in order to make it clear that she herself has joined in this dash for freedom. This strange episode in the nuptial ceremonies of the Zulus, like so many similar features in the marriage customs of other peoples, is a survival of the generally obsolete marriage by capture.

THE VARIOUS FORMS OF MARRIAGE

MARRIAGE, as distinct from mere mating, is a lasting union, and the main varieties it presents are discussed in this chapter, which is to be regarded as a preliminary discussion of the whole subject. In its monogamous form it may be regarded as the primeval foundation upon which the human family is based. The specific aspects of Polygamy and Polyandry are enlarged upon in the chapter under that heading, and many separate chapters deal with marriage ceremonies.

TO barbarous or savage man marriage has an altogether different meaning from that which it has for ourselves. We regard it as a happy contract and union between two persons for mutual comfort and support, while he considers it primarily as the breaking of a taboo between the sexes which may be fraught with consequences most dangerous to himself. Woman, in the eyes of primitive man, is an uncanny being surrounded by magical influences, and these may contaminate him and make him effeminate unless he employ proper safeguards.

He is indeed environed by prohibitions arising out of obscure and deep-lying human instincts, and in view of this general attitude his outlook on marriage is naturally a somewhat timorous one.

In his eyes the female sex is surrounded by a completely different set of laws from those he practises and recognizes and, if he is not to infringe these, he must tread warily. He realizes the necessity for female companionship and assistance, just as does civilized man, yet his training leads him to believe that he is forming a union with a creature fundamentally different from himself, whom he regards as a member almost of another order; for the idea of sex solidarity and sex diversity among primitive peoples is far stronger than can well be realized by the members of a modern civilized community.

It is this ancient and indurated opinion that lies at the basis of most of the different forms of marital arrangement to be found among primitive human communities, which scientific writers on the subject formerly, and rather erroneously, labelled as 'marriage by capture,' 'marriage by purchase,' and so forth.

Marriage by capture, so-called, was for at least a century a favourite theory among social historians, but it has now been demonstrated to belong to a group of ideas profoundly different in their origin from the mere crude desire to steal a helpmeet. All primitive marital customs, in short, are rather designed to neutralise the supposed dangerous influence which the sexes possess for each other, and the peril involved in the breaking of personal and sex taboos. To minimise this, an extraordinary degree of bashfulness is assumed on the part of the bride, and on the approach of her suitor, or his envoy, the women of the tribe resist him in the instinctive belief that the solidarity of their sex is threatened. In some cases, as among the Roro of British New Guinea, a party of the groom's male friends raid the bride's house by mimic assault and carry her off, struggling and screaming.

EVEN if a price be paid for the girl, in some instances force must be employed to carry her off, as among the Wakamba of East Africa. With the Samoyeds, Kalmucks and other northern Asiatic tribes, the same custom prevails, and even a century ago in Wales it was not unknown. The groom appeared on horseback and demanded the bride. Her parents gave him a positive refusal, a scuffle ensued, and the girl was mounted on a horse behind her father, to be pursued by the suitor and his adherents who finally seized her and bore her off.

In Greenland a couple of old women are despatched to the house of the girl to negotiate a marriage and, on hearing the proposal, etiquette enjoins that she

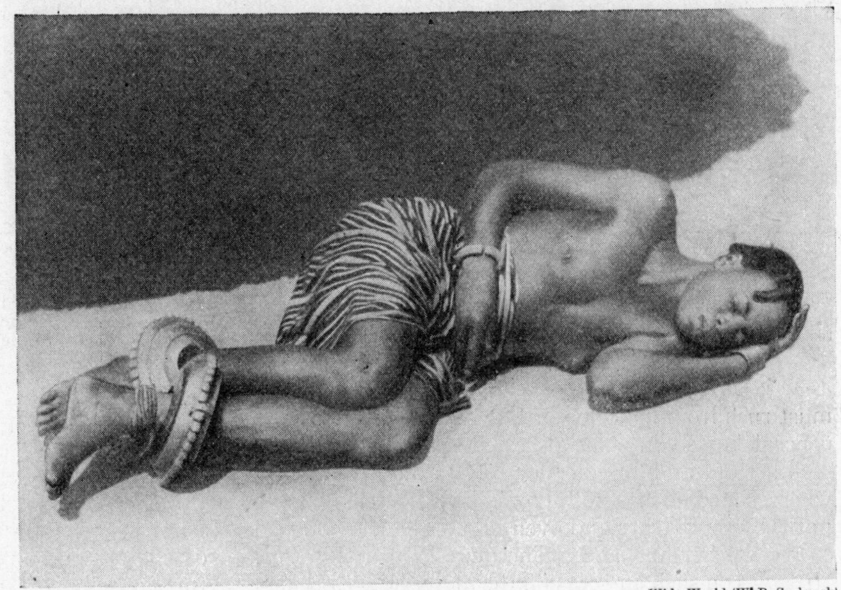

Wide World (W. B. Seabrook)

UNWIELDY WEDDING RINGS OF AN AFRICAN CHIEF'S WIFE

The heavy ornamental brass anklets worn by this Yafouba woman of West Africa indicate that she is a favoured wife of a chief of the tribe. The anklets weigh fifteen pounds each, are welded on, and must never be removed. The wearing of these unwieldy ornaments, burdensome though it may be, exempts the woman for life from all heavy work.

P. and A. (Carl von Hoffman)

STRANGE ADORNMENTS OF A 'CAPTURED' BRIDE

The couple here seen are the bride-to-be and the bride's father at the Zulu wedding illustrated in page 140. Apart from her magnificent ostrich feathers, the most notable features of the bride's dress are the tasselled veil and the balloon-like objects round her head. These are the bladders of goats that have been sacrificed to the spirits of her ancestors.

must rush from her igloo or hut, tearing her hair, and conceal herself in some deserted spot. The women seek her out and drag her forcibly to the suitor's hut, where she crouches sulkily for days, refusing food, until, by reproaches and even blows, she is compelled to receive her husband. The more vigorously a girl struggles on such an occasion the more she is esteemed ever after among the women of the Bedouins of Sinai, and among those of the Mezeyne tribe of that region she is actually encouraged to run away after betrothal and hide herself in the mountains, repeatedly attempting to escape even after marriage, as custom has dictated that a bashful young woman should.

Perhaps the most primitive example of the practice is to be found among certain Australian tribes, where the man drags the woman to his hut with extraordinary violence. But careful observers have been at pains to make it clear that this cannot be described as 'marriage by capture,' but merely as the formal and accepted manner of breaking down sex resistance. Capture proper is, indeed, of the rarest occurrence among the Australian blacks, and it is not in any case a mode of marriage, but only a method of obtaining a wife, or, rather, a female slave without marital rights. As Crawley remarks, it is 'evident that it is not the tribe from which the bride is abducted, nor primarily her father and kindred, but her sex,' as is abundantly proved by the circumstance that in many cases the women of the tribe assemble to obstruct and revile the bridegroom. The mere fact of hostile capture in certain instances cannot prove a rule, is actually rare, and is merely an attendant circumstance of invasion. 'When carefully examined, most of the old examples adduced as instances of "marriage by capture" turn out to be either mere inferences of such, or cases of connubial and formal capture or . . . elopements.' 'The possession of a stolen woman,' says Westermarck, 'would lead to constant attacks, hence the tribes set themselves very generally against the practice.'

'Connubial capture' may be described as that form of marriage as found among the Karens of Siam, where the man fights with a picked champion for his bride, overcomes him, and carries her off from her parents' hut, the affair being conditioned by the ability of the suitor to prove his strength. 'Formal capture,' on the other hand, is merely ceremonial, and previously arranged, as in several of the instances already alluded to. The theory that marriage by capture is associated with exogamy, or the law which compels a man to marry outwith his tribe, has been almost exploded by the discovery that certain endogamous or in-marrying peoples, like the Maoris and Ahts, practise it.

Among the Mosquito Indians of Colombia, even after the wedding is arranged and the presents have been proffered, custom compels the man to seize the girl and make off with her. A rescue is attempted by her female relatives, and serious results sometimes ensue. The Indians of the Uapès river, in Brazil, who possess a very elaborate system of taboos, recognize no other ceremony of marriage than that of carrying off the bride by force, or at least making a show of doing so, and where such an arrangement is found it may reasonably be concluded that the idea of the sex taboo has been weakened. In some parts of Polynesia, as, for example, Fiji and Samoa, the same custom prevails, and traces of it are said to occur in certain districts in Russia and Finland to this day, elopement taking place when the bridegroom cannot afford to pay the fixed purchase sum. Indeed, vestiges of the rite of marriage by capture still remain in the marital ceremonies of the Russians.

Nowadays, however, marriage by capture alone is in the main uncommon. Among most uncivilized peoples to-day it is usually incumbent on the man to pay some compensation for his bride. This was described by the late Lord Abercromby as 'marriage

Mondiale

E.N.A.

HOW SOME BRIDEGROOMS OF EUROPE 'STEAL' THEIR BRIDES

Wedding customs obtaining in various countries of Europe furnish examples of what has been called 'marriage by capture.' In Hungary the Magyar bridegroom (top), bearing the bride's banner, embroidered by herself and her first gift to the groom, rides with his party to the group where the bride is dancing, seizes the bride, mounts her on one of the horses, and rides off. The Rumanian bridegroom (bottom), also carrying a banner, rides with his party to the bride's house, captures her, and carries her on his horse to the village.

E.N.A.

PRICE PAID IN CATTLE BY A ZULU BRIDEGROOM

The actual wedding ceremony of the Zulus is a very picturesque function (top), and is generally the occasion of a large concourse of members of the tribe. Below is seen a young Zulu brave bringing his bridal gift of cattle. Cattle are formally made over to the bride's father by the bridegroom before the wedding. Gifts are also exchanged between the bride and the bridegroom, but these are of little intrinsic value, though made significant through personal association. Beads, as having been in actual physical contact with both the parties, are commonly given.

Keystone

with capture,' by which he meant the ceremonial capture of a bride for whom compensation was paid, a circumstance which clearly reveals the ceremonial character of the 'capture' side of the contract.

But as regards marriage by purchase, we must also use caution in our description of this form or mode of approaching union, for the bride-gift has its origin not so much in the idea of purchase or barter as in the notion of tendering a pledge or part of oneself. In other words, the sex taboo between the pair has to be broken by tendering some article which has had a close physical association with the givers; that is, the act has more of a religious and personal significance than one of barter. Buying and selling among primitive peoples have not the same sordid and material significance as among

E.N.A.

WHERE MATCHMAKING IS PRACTISED AS A PROFESSION

When a marriage is contemplated in Japan the matter is placed by the parents in the hands of a marriage broker. This functionary arranges for the two young people to meet at the tea-house (bottom), so that they may see whether they like one another. If the affair proceeds satisfactorily the bride-to-be serves the ceremonial tea to the prospective bridegroom (top).

E.N.A

CHILDHOOD SACRIFICED UPON THE HYMENEAL ALTAR

On April 1, 1930, the Child Marriage Restraint Act came into force in India, prohibiting the marriage of males under the age of 18 and of females under 14. Hindu devotion to old tradition led to a remarkable increase in the number of child marriages celebrated just before the act became effective, and here we see a child bride in the Madras presidency sharing her wedding meal with her tall bridegroom on her left hand, and on her right her little brother, who has just been married to the small girl standing behind him.

civilized communities, and this view is strengthened by the fact that the gifts made have often no real intrinsic value, though where there has been contact with civilization they usually tend to grow more costly in the material sense.

For example, among the Kaffirs of South Africa it has been observed that the cattle paid for the bride are held in trust for her by her male relatives should she be left a widow, but the actual betrothal gift consists merely of beads, proving that the former gift-custom is only a later development of the latter. The girl also tenders beads to the man; that is, each gives the other something which has had an actual physical association with the giver, as lovers in ancient Europe exchanged their rings.

Prices as now paid among uncivilized people for their spouses are astonishingly high when compared with their actual personal wealth, but vary, of course, with the desirability of the bride and her rank. In British Columbia and Vancouver Island the price tendered by an Indian for a wife ranges from £20 to £40 of our currency, and among the Californian Indians ten or twelve ponies is regarded as a fair price for an attractive girl. The Navahos of New Mexico consider this exorbitant unless in the case of a girl possessing unusual beauty, industry and skill.

Cattle are the general currency among the negroes of South Africa, as among the primitive Romans, who coined the term 'pecunia' (money) from their word for cattle; and the Kaffirs usually pay from five to ten cows for a wife. Among poorer tribes, like the Damara, one cow is generally regarded as sufficient to purchase a daughter from her father, although in Uganda needles, ammunition, or even clothing are frequently tendered and accepted for a promising damsel.

Col. F. D. Fayrer

YOUTHFUL HINDU BRIDEGROOM OF CENTRAL INDIA AND HIS WEDDING GARMENT

In the Laws of Manu, which form the basis of Hindu law, eight kinds of marriage are enumerated. They include marriage by purchase, fraud, ravishment, consent of the girl, and gift of her to the bridegroom by her father without bargain or recompense. The last is the form of marriage in common use among orthodox Hindus. Marriage ceremonies are very numerous and varied. For Hindus generally the most important consists in the bridegroom taking the bride's hand and walking seven steps. In some parts the only ceremony is a feast for the two families.

E.N.A.

SIMPLE FOLK WHOSE MARRIAGE RITES ARE REDUCED TO THE LOWEST TERMS

The aboriginal race inhabiting the Andaman Islands comprises what is considered to be the last pure remnant of palaeolithic man, and al their customs are primitive in the extreme. For example, when the elders of a sept learn that a young couple desire to be married the bride is taken to a newly made empty hut and made to sit down. The bridegroom runs away into the jungle, but after some pretended hesitation is brought in and made to sit down on the bride's lap. That is the whole ceremony. This photograph shows a group after such an event

In northern Asia large prices are often given for wives, as much as 3,000 roubles being paid among the Baskirs, though in Tartary parents, in time of stress, will sell a daughter for a few pounds of butter. The Samoyedes and Ostiaks reckon the bride-price by reindeer, and some low-caste Indian tribes will barter their female relatives for a basket or two of rice and a few rupees. As showing the extraordinary distance sometimes covered by 'bartered brides,' and that a commerce existed in selling or exchanging women, apart from marital purchase, Charlevoix, the Jesuit missionary (died 1761), mentions that he met a Huron Indian woman whom he had known personally in America, in the interior of Siberia. She had been passed from tribe to tribe by barter and had crossed from America to Asia.

Among the Polynesians canoes, pigs and guns were formerly the media of barter for a wife. Sometimes the price is paid in instalments, as among the people of Unyoro in Central Africa. In Japan the system of present-giving which prevails is doubtless a survival of a time when the transaction was one of ordinary bargaining.

Marriage by service, where the man serves the bride's father in lieu of purchase price, is familiar to us from certain instances in the Scriptures. It was by no means confined to the Semitic races, but was, and is, common to the uncivilized races of America, Africa and Asia. Usually it is an expedient resorted to by those who cannot afford the bride-price, but in some instances it is formal and must be adhered to, be the suitor rich or poor, as among certain of the Kamchadale tribes. The custom prevails among the Bushmen and the Fuegians of Tierra del Fuego.

Simple exchange of women, as sister for sister or daughter for daughter, is, of course, probably the most primitive form of purchasing a wife, and is the rule rather than the exception among the Australian blacks and in Sumatra. Nor is the purchase of a wife on credit unknown, custom in this case demanding that the wife and her children cannot leave the parental roof-tree until the price is paid in full. In some Central African communities when a poor man is unable to procure sufficient cattle to pay for a spouse, he may purchase one by the payment of instalments, but the children born in the meantime are the property of the wife's father, although they may be redeemed by the payment of a cow apiece.

It must not be inferred, however, that the purchase of marriageable girls is a universal human custom. Among many uncivilized communities the suitor gives preliminary presents to the parents in order to dispose them favourably to the match, and not as a bride-price. The Ainu of Japan, for example, do not buy their wives, but make presents of tobacco and liquor to the parents, and no stipulated price is fixed beforehand. Certain South American tribes, too, cultivate the practice of present-giving by the suitor rather as a proof of his ability to keep a wife than as a means of barter. Wife purchase does not exist among the Yukonikhotana of Alaska, and the rather debased Wintun Indians of California procure their wives for nothing, the lack of provender probably acting as an incentive to the parents to part with their daughters. The Andaman Islanders, the Chittagong hill people and the cave-dwellers of the Aru Archipelago also make no payment for the bride, probably for similar reasons, or because their culture is so primitive that they have not as yet reached the stage of marriage by barter.

But, generally speaking, marriage by purchase may be said to succeed formal marriage by capture as a social custom, and the latter has largely survived along with the former, in a symbolical sense. The purchase or present may have originated in a desire to escape the parental vengeance. Thus among the Ahts elopement is followed by a present to the father, and the same holds good among the Araucanians of Chile and in New Guinea. The decay of marriage by purchase, which was in itself the resultant of the exchange of the taboo-breaking gift, is witnessed in the adoption of a bridal portion among races emerging from barbarism to civilization, which is either a payment made by the bridegroom and returned to him as the bride's jointure, or the settlement of a sum upon her by the bride's father, which latter custom is regarded as having arisen out of the earlier usage of returning the suitor's gift

E.N.A.

HIGHLY SOPHISTICATED MARRIAGE IN CONSERVATIVE CHINA

Marriage has always been celebrated with much ceremonial among the Chinese, but it is remarkable how completely that most conservative people is discarding centuries-old traditions in favour of the customs of the sophisticated West. Thus at the civil wedding of a Chinese diplomat the bride wore the bridal white of the Occident, disregarding the fact that white is the conventional wear for mourning in China, while the bridegroom wore the uniform of the diplomatic corps and his men friends donned European evening dress

E.N.A

WHERE BEAUTY IS NOT WOMAN'S ONLY DOWER
Among the Ouled Nails of Algeria it is the custom of the young women to adorn their head-dress with as many coins as they can accumulate. A girl thus advertises the dowry she will bring to her bridegroom. The custom is paralleled among many other peoples. It may be regarded as a variety of marriage by purchase.

But the practice of employing go-betweens to arrange a marriage is widespread, both among savages and more civilized nations. It is common in the Mahomedan world, where Jewish marriage-brokers are frequently called in to facilitate preliminaries. When a Turkish or Persian girl is of marriageable age, Jewish agents are called in to look for a suitable parti for her, and when he is found they discourse in a fulsome strain upon the girl's surpassing beauty and talents, employing every art of the Oriental imagination to interest the possible suitor.

Although elsewhere in this work the principal types of marriage relations are dealt with in separate chapters, it may be well to enumerate them here. Monogamy, the union of a single pair, is by far the most common form of marital arrangement. Oddly enough, it is found at the lowest stage of man's development as well as at the highest. Man in the hunting stage has little need of a plurality of wives, or for the increased labour value they bring him.

Polygamy or polygyny, a plurality of wives, is a practice now chiefly confined to savage or barbarous peoples. Its chief home, at the present period, is Africa, although in India and other parts of Asia it is still widely recognized. But the majority of thinking Mahomedans have rejected it, and among semi-civilized peoples it is on the decline. Many races, too, in a condition of almost abject savagery are monogamous, as the Hill Dyaks and the Marquesan Islanders, and some Australian tribes are also 'convinced' monogamists. Even where polygamy is permitted by custom or law it is by no means so generally practised as is often supposed, and economic conditions alone compel the greater number of the human race to eschew it.

The marriage-broker or middleman is usually the product of a fairly high state of civilization, although, as has been seen, female agents are employed by the Eskimo. In Japan marriages are almost invariably arranged by the parents with the aid of a professional middleman known as the 'nakodo,' as it is considered highly improper that any marital compact should be made by the parties or their relatives alone. Among the lower classes such unaided unions are regarded with contempt, and are described by the disdainful term 'yago,' which means 'meeting on a moor,' or 'casual.' The business of the middleman is to make known to each contracting party the good and bad qualities of the other, his or her habits, virtues or vices, and bodily ailments, and to do his utmost in reason to bring the affair to a happy conclusion. He also arranges for a meeting between the pair, and if dissatisfaction occurs the business proceeds no farther.

Polyandry, the marriage of one woman with more than one husband, is a much rarer form of marital relationship, and is confined to Tibet, where it is most common, the Aleutian Islands, some Orinoco tribes and the mountain communities of the Bantu race. The Todas of the Nilgiri Hills, in India, have a form of polyandry, as have certain tribes of southern India, and traces of the custom are encountered elsewhere. Polyandry is most usually the marriage of one woman with a family of brothers, and is generally dictated by the poverty of the countries in which it prevails, and by a scarcity of women brought about by a striking disproportion of female births, or, as is suspected in the case of Tibet, by the absorption of a large proportion of women by the Lama nunneries, though this may be questioned.

NATIONAL DANCES OF EUROPE

UNTIL its modern development as a pastime and an art the connexion between dancing, pagan and Christian religions, and the drama was very close, and clear evidence of all these influences may be seen in the national dances here described. Separate chapters deal with Folk dances of the British Isles, with Modern Social Dancing and the Ballet, and also with savage and ritual dances.

DANCING has been called a necessity of human nature. Ruskin compared a child dancing to 'a lamb leaping or a fawn at play.' Max Beerbohm has imagined the first dancers to have been perhaps Greek vintners who jumped about because the earth was so bounteous—perhaps because they had enjoyed its bounty a little too freely Children certainly dance naturally ; so do primitive peoples everywhere, though usually their movements are regulated by strict rule. Dancing was employed, like the earliest music, to express emotions and to put the mind into certain states. There were, and still are, war dances as well as love, funeral dances in contrast with wedding dances, dances appropriate to the detection of witchcraft as well as those which fit in with the gaiety of a feast.

But if dancing for joy is a necessity of human nature, it is also one of human nature's severest tests. It can so easily be abused, it degenerates so easily into impropriety or rowdiness. Plato suggested that persons guilty of unseemly dancing should be banished from his Ideal Commonwealth. The Puritans would have none of it. 'Dancing hall' acquired at one time much the same significance as 'gambling hell.' But the degenerate dancers are found in cities. The country dance is a different thing altogether. It seems to grow out of the soil ; it is as healthy as flowers and trees. Cicero said angrily in decadent Rome that 'no sane man danced unless he were smitten with temporary madness.' Peasant dances are eminently sane and delightful. Most of them have developed from the earliest of concerted movements, the round.

Photopress

EXPERT EXPONENTS OF THE HIGHLAND FLING

Scotland is comparatively rich in national dances, having reels, strathspeys, sword dances, funeral dances called Latewakes, and the sixteenth-century Salmon dance. Besides these there is the Highland fling, a Celtic dance which, despite its usual Scottish appellation, Scotland shares with Denmark as a national dance.

This was very simple. The dancers took hands, formed a circle, and moved round, giving little jumps, performing elementary 'steps' with their feet. Here we have the basis on which a great many national dances in Europe have been built up. Often they have been elaborated and almost transformed. One which keeps its original character fairly well is the Rumanian and Bulgarian hora (it is danced, indeed, in all the Balkan countries). For this the music, rather solemn, is started by a piper. Young men join hands in a ring, they take some steps to the left, they stamp their feet. Then a pause and on they go again.

Now the mandolin player strikes in with a livelier air, but the bagpipes do not respond. Then the strings of the mandolin are struck three times with energy, the young men at the same time stamping and looking at the girls who wait to join them The girls hesitate, they consult one another, then they run forward, form a ring round the young men. Again the vigorous thrum-thrum of the strings and the two circles break up, partners are taken and the dance proper begins. It has many figures. In one the couples face one another and gaze into

J. Clair-Guyot.

BRETON REJOICING IN THE BRETON DANCE

Bretons are exceedingly tenacious of their old customs and traditions, and all details in their popular celebrations remain precisely what they were centuries ago. A visit of the President of the Republic to Quimper in 1930 was made the occasion of a wonderful exhibition of Breton dances, performed in the main square by men and women attired in the national costume.

each other's eyes. If they showed any affection, or even interest, this would have a charming effect. But when they go through it mechanically, expressing no emotion at all, it looks absurd.

In Serbia the kolo (meaning a circle) has much the same character, except that the men and women do not often hold hands in the ordinary way; sometimes the men hold their partners by the belt or they pass their hands through the arms and behind the backs of the women to clasp the hands of those who come next. The women dancers on special occasions wear exquisitely embroidered bodices and much artificial jewellery, with big gilt crowns and flowers of paper. So deeply attached are the Dalmatians to this dance that they tell the following story about it:

A Serbian chieftain in revolt against the Turks, then the rulers of the country, was captured and pretended to be dead. The Turkish governor ordered him to be buried. But the governor's wife suspected that he might be shamming and recommended various tests. First, a fire was lighted on his breast: he lay perfectly still. Then a snake was laid over him, pins were driven in under his finger and toe nails: he did not flinch. Then the old woman said: 'Let the most beautiful girl we have dance the kolo round him with companions. If he is not dead she will force him to smile.' The dance began. The captive heard the tinkle of the bells round her neck, the rustle of her silk trousers. He smiled and the girl saw it. But she pitied him and quickly threw her handkerchief over his face. So he still passed for a corpse and was thrown into the sea. He swam ashore, broke into the governor's house, killed him and his 'Turkish vixen,' carried off the girl and made her his wife!

In the south-western part of France (Gascony) another kind of round is popular. This has a leader who may set either a furious or a gentle pace and who sometimes leads the other dancers a rare dance (here is the origin of the phrase which signifies causing a lot of trouble or a wearisome pursuit). To begin with, the movements are graceful and rhythmic, but they grow wilder and faster. The dancers must run, jump, climb over obstacles, twist and turn. Never must they loose their clasp of each other's hands or fail to do exactly what their leader does. This variation is to be seen in the Balkans also. Italian peasants in Sardinia have a much simpler form of rondo. The young men and the girls form up in two lines, holding hands, then the lines are joined at each end and the circle goes round, the dancers advance towards each other and retire, all rather slowly, while a group of singers chant curious Moorish airs. M. Gaston Vuillier, the leading French authority on the subject, saw this dance in Sardinia and described the music as 'the most extraordinary kind imaginable, hardly like the sound of a human voice, but a sort of musical buzzing.'

In France there is usually dancing after a rustic wedding, and sometimes the old marriage round may be seen, with its ancient verses addressed to bridegroom and bride (this is also played as a children's game). But the bourrée in the Centre (especially the Auvergne), and the farandole in the South are more popular with peasants in out-of-the way districts, where alone national dances are any longer to be seen. In the farandole the dancers are joined by handkerchiefs held in their hands and form a long chain. They spin round under each other's arms and then 'follow my leader,' as in the Gascon ronde. Suddenly a couple will stop and, with arms lifted, hands clasped, will form an arch. All the others must pass under this. At the end the last couple stops and all the rest have to wind round them. The confusion seems inextricable, but somehow they unwind themselves and break up rather breathless and in the best of humour. The bourrée is a clumsier affair. If it is danced indoors the stamping of heavy feet (in wooden shoes, perhaps) gives it a noisy and even monotonous character. Yet the peasants make it light and graceful when they dance it on grass. M. Vuillier saw a group of shepherds skipping through it to the soft music of reed pipes one evening in the Auvergne. The effect was delightful.

The gavotte and minuet in France were not national but Court dances of our own age. The gavotte and minuet were never danced anywhere but in ball-rooms. Nothing of the kind has survived among the mass of the people save a certain grace in bowing and dropping curtseys. The characteristics of French folk-dancing are seen in the branle (which was once known in England as the brawl, the nearest that could be got to the French pronunciation). Each part of the country had a branle of its own. Often it began with a slow movement for the older people, then a livelier one for the more recently married, then one in which the boys and girls could let off their energy; finally, all would take hands and go round in a ring. Sometimes a less varied and wholly unimaginative branle may be seen. In one part of Brittany the couples stand behind one another and simply move jerkily from left to right and from right to left; in another part the couple take hands as in skating, the woman's right in the man's right, his left holding her left. Each pair in turn does a little performance, the rest clapping their hands in time with the music. All sorts of variations could be introduced

E.N.A

EXHIBITION PERFORMANCE OF THE BOURREE, A PEASANTS' DANCE OF CENTRAL FRANCE

In Central France, and especially the Auvergne—a former province now represented by the departments of Cantal, Puy-de-Dôme and part of Haute Loire—the bourrée is still popular with the peasantry. Generically this is a clog dance, and ifperformed in doors in wooden shoes may be a somewhat heavy-footed, noisy and monotonous exercise. In the right environment—danced on smooth turf in the mellow light of evening to the thin music of reed pipes—it is a very different thing, a light and graceful exercise quite charming to watch.

QUAINT TRADITIONAL MAKE-UP FOR A BASQUE ANIMAL DANCE

Almost every kind of dance found in primitive cultures, from the corrobboree of the Australian blackfellow to the terpsichorean evolutions of the Red Indian, is known and practised by the Basques. They have action dances representing agriculture and the vintage, variants of the Pyrrhic dance of the ancient Greeks, religious dances, war dances like the Scottish sword dance, and numerous animal dances. In one of these, as shown here and in the opposite page, a star part is played by the hobby horse; the performer is exchanging compliments with English morris dancers at a folk-dancing competition at Bayonne.

Keystone

DANCE IN WHICH BASQUE GRACE AND ENERGY FIND THEIR FULLEST EXPRESSION

Among other characteristics for which the Basques are remarkable special mention is universally made of their physical strength and agility, which find expression in all kinds of games and exercises. Dancing figures largely in their social life, and in this they display a natural aptitude for pirouetting, revolving on the tip of the toes and other gymnastic movements which many professional ballet dancers acquire only by long and painful practice. Nothing could be more gay and easy than the freedom with which this young Basque twirls his lacy draperies

into this go-as-you-please kind of dance. One was a violent throwing out of the leg, known as 'the cow's kick'; another was the imitation of the actions of washerwomen; others required the dancers to carry torches (as in one of Sir Edward German's Henry VIII dances), or to wear monk's robes.

It was a monk who long ago wrote a book of etiquette for dancers of the branle. 'Do not look at your feet to see if you are doing the steps properly,' he counselled, 'but keep your head up and look about you confidently. Do not use your handkerchief more than you are obliged, and take care that you have a clean one. See that your stockings do not slip down, and that your shoes are not soiled.' If it seems surprising that a monk should give advice about dancing, we must remember that King David danced before the Ark of the Covenant and that the Church once seems to have used dancing as an aid to religion. We get a reminder of this in the choir boys' dance before the high altar in Seville cathedral on several occasions during the year, in the dances at Saragossa on the feast-day of Our Lady of the Pillar, in the Christmas Eve 'jotas' performed in Aragon. At Echternach, in the Ardennes, there is also a yearly dancing procession of pilgrims to the shrine of a saint; this has gone on for many centuries. Thousands of people take part in it. The Seville cathedral performances are given by two sets of half a dozen choir boys.

Spain is the land which, above all others, we associate with folk-dancing. Cervantes, author of 'Don Quixote,' the greatest Spanish classic, wrote that 'never was Spanish woman born that was not born to dance.' A lesser writer speaks of the power of the fandango over the ears and soul of every Spaniard—'like an electric shock it touches all hearts.' Certainly there is a compelling melody in the airs of Spanish dances which sets feet tapping and heads nodding. This has been illustrated by an amusing anecdote, invented, but not impossible. Once the Vatican, pained by the passion for dancing to which Spaniards were slaves, determined to forbid the fandango. A Papal Consistory was about to pronounce the decree when one of the cardinals asked if any member of the Court had seen this dance. No one had, so he suggested it would only be fair, before condemning it, to let it appear before its judges. Two dancers from Spain were sent for. At first the cardinals frowned, then they smiled, then they began to keep time with the music, at last they could not sit still any longer, they jumped up and danced! It was impossible to proscribe the fandango after that.

To give an account of it is not easy. The movements of the dancers, a man and a woman, begin gently and gracefully; their bodies swaying, pliant and lithe; their eyes are tender. Gradually they quicken up, their eyes flash, their steps are vigorous, though always graceful. The castanets they carry click rapidly, the dance ends in a whirl of motion that would be violent and unpleasing if it were not so perfectly controlled. The bolero is quieter. Danced as a rule by several pairs, its steps are gliding and sinuous. The dancers attitudinise and pose, with inimitable charm and grace. The cachuca is danced by a single performer, either man or woman. It begins like the fandango, easily and slowly, becoming faster and faster, the castanets clattering with more and more noise. The head is poised now proudly, now pleadingly; chest and shoulders are moved in unison with the feet and fingers.

E.N.A.

AN HISTORIC DANCE IN MODERN FORM

Said to have been invented by a twelfth-century poet and musician named Aben Jot, the jota is a characteristic dance with song of Aragon, with many local variations. It is danced by men and women in couples, facing one another but separately without joining hands, and in its oldest form its movements are restrained. The modern tendency is to dance it with much greater abandon, as suggested by this lively young lady, La Argentina.

Less exciting is the jota (pronounced chota, ch as in loch), especially that of Aragon, which has music of a church-like character and is even danced at funerals as an expression of sorrow. Men and women dance separately, without holding hands; their movements are slow, lacking in animation. That is the traditional way to dance the jota, but there are other ways, and if young people try it they make it much more lively. While it is danced, couplets are sung, topical sometimes, often satirical, and perhaps painfully personal. For example:

> Your arms are lovely, like sausages they look,
> Hung from the kitchen ceiling by the cook.

It was very common at one period for song and dance to be mixed. This explains the 'tra-la-la,' the 'derry-down-derry,' and the 'hey-nonny-no' in so many English ballads. These sounds were made to accompany the dance steps which the singer took.

The most truly national dances of Spain, the seguidillas, which vary, like the French branles, according to locality, are also accompanied by verses sung by dancers and lookers-on. Most of them are little love-songs of this nature: 'My heart flew into your bosom. You clipped its wings, so it stayed there. Now it has made itself at home and will stay there for ever.' A feature of the

Martin Munkacsy

SWAYING BODIES AND BILLOWING SKIRTS IN THE ANDALUSIAN DANCE

In tew parts of Spain is dancing more truly expressive of passion and imagination than in Seville. The peculiar style of the Seville dancers would not perhaps appeal to everybody, consisting as it does chiefly in swaying the body and tapping with the feet, but the arrogant postures and swirling dresses of the dancers earn the Spaniard's highest praise ; in a phrase of the country the dancers ' have honey in their hips.' Girls are here seen at a Seville thé dansant dancing to the thrum of the guitar and the insistent click of the castanets.

E.N.A

A NATION'S SOUL IN SUPPLE MOVEMENT AND LANGUOROUS GRACE: THE FANDANGO

The fandango is one of the best known and most popular of modern Spanish dances. Above all others, it is a part of the nation's life, and expresses to the full the character of the people. No occasion of rejoicing is considered complete without the fandango. It is danced by two people, the rhythm being marked by the snapping of fingers, the tapping of heels, and the click of castanets. Beginning slowly, the dance grows gradually quicker until the pace becomes terrific. The partners alternately tease, beseech, and pursue each other. The fandango has one striking feature, which it shares with the seguidilla. Towards the close of each measure the music stops suddenly, and the dancers stand rigid, to bound into movement when the music strikes up again.

seguidilla is the sudden stopping of one step and the motionless attitude of the dancers until they begin the next. They must try to stand exactly as they are when the music changes; they must appear to have been turned into statues. Arms raised, one foot off the ground, bending or standing upright, not a muscle must be moved. That is the ideal, and it is surprising how often the dancers come very near to it. The actual steps are simple. Men and women alternately follow and retreat from one another. It is the sudden stop and the equally sudden return to life of the motionless figures that make the seguidilla interesting.

Of Italian national dances the tarantella is the best known. This belongs to the south, especially to Naples. Its name is connected with the poisonous spider the tarantula; its bite was said to be curable only by dancing so vigorously that the poison was sweated out of the body. Another story was that the poison caused convulsive movements, something like those of dancing. However, though its origin is doubtful, there is no doubt as to the popularity of the tarantella. It is danced to the tapping and tinkling of tambourines, usually by a man and a woman

Mondiale

DANCE RHYTHMS, GRAVE AND GAY, IN A TZIGANE HOMELAND

The people of Hungary, which is an important centre of the gipsies, are passionately fond of music and dancing. Their national dance, the **czardas,** has two movements—the one stately and the other sprightly—and it is this alternation of reckless delight with slow melancholy cadences that gives the dance its fascination. A quaint variation is the umbrella dance (top). The lower photograph shows peasants of Mezökövesd dancing in traditional costumes, which, in the case of the women especially, are beautifully embroidered

Sport & General and E.N.A

WILD WHIRLING OF THE SOUTH AND STAIDNESS OF THE NORTH

'Hora' is a Turkish word meaning 'dance,' but the Balkan Christians apply it to one special dance. In their hora the dancers torm a ring and hold hands or girdles They step to and fro and then revolve, at first slowly, but gradually increasing the pace. The tunes used for the hora vary, the music of the Bulgarian dance being wild and often in minor keys. Pipes and mandolins are the instruments. The lower photograph shows a company of Bulgarian peasants dancing the hora. Above are seen Danish dancers performing a sedate folk dance.

E.N.A.

DANCES OF TWO NEIGHBOUR STATES OF CENTRAL EUROPE

The sword dance of Czechoslovakia (bottom) is a totally different kind of dance from that of Scotland. In the latter the swords are laid crosswise on the ground and the performers dance between the blades, whereas the Czechoslovakian sword dancers hold the weapons in their hands. In one respect the Czechoslovakian dance resembles the Scottish, for both are danced to the music of the bagpipes. Among the peasants of Rumania dancing is a favourite amusement. The upper photograph shows Rumanian country folk dancing the batuta.

E.N.A.

GAY AND UNDAUNTED AFTER CENTURIES OF WOE

For several centuries the Estonians lived a troubled life under foreign masters, but throughout their long struggle for freedom they have clung very tenaciously to their national customs. The festivities connected with the various seasons, for instance, are observed with great detail. Estonian peasants are here seen in their traditional dress and on Midsummer day.

though sometimes by women alone, in which case it loses much of its fascination. For it really is an acted love scene. All the emotions of hope, despair, jealousy, devotion are portrayed. First, the man is victor over the woman, she kneels to him. But at the end he is kneeling to her, and she bidding him rise with a gesture of generous affection.

FARTHER south, in Sicily, there are folk-dances of great antiquity which are still kept up with little alteration. In the Siciliana a man begins by asking a lady to dance, with exaggerated politeness. They each hold one end of a handkerchief. When they have danced awhile, the man bows again and leaves his partner. She trips and pirouettes around until she sees a man to her liking. Him she invites to dance. Meanwhile, her late partner has taken the floor with another lady. So it continues until at the close of the evening all dance together, including the married folks who, up to now, have danced only with each other. At Messina there is a dance called the ruggera, in which two women and two men move round and round in a circle, each singing in turn a song, and contorting both bodies and features in a grotesque way.

Hungarian music is so largely made up of dances that one would expect to find Hungary a country where a great deal of dancing can be seen. But one must travel a good deal over the Puszta, the steppes, to find the old dances. The most famous of Hungarian measures is the czardas (stardas). First, the partners walk with stately step, then the man puts the lady into position, holding her hand at a level with her eyes. They go through some complicated steps to music in a minor key, then the air becomes more animated, their steps quicken, faster and faster they whirl, wilder and wilder sound the violins. The end is a climax of excitement, and often exhaustion for musicians and dancers alike.

A village dance in Czechoslovakia is a pleasant spectacle. The women are in dresses which they have made themselves, taking ten or a dozen years perhaps to finish them, or else inherited, elaborate and beautiful triumphs of the needlewoman's art. The men are in embroidered shirts, velvet waistcoats with silver buttons, long coats and knee breeches, with gay handkerchiefs which they fasten in their belts. The dances in which they take part have a charm, too, all of their own. From Bohemia came the polka. The name means half-a-step, and it was supposed to have been invented by a peasant girl whom a composer heard humming while she tripped about, taking half-steps. But there is much that resembles it in some of the more ancient Bohemian dances, which can still be seen at times. One of these is the sword dance, which is still done in the manner prescribed by tradition, though it might be described rather as a cudgel dance.

Another kind of sword dance, with two crossed sticks on the ground and steps taken in between them, is popular in the Basque country, both of France and of Spain. This is but one of many that can still be seen there, all dating back a very long way. So fond are the Basques of dancing that it has been said 'a child of these parts can dance before it learns to say " father."' The same might almost be said of the children in Bavaria. That part of the German Reich (State) is famous for its peasant dances. They are more vigorous than graceful, but the costumes and the jollity of the dancers lend them an inescapable charm. There is much slapping of their thighs by the men and a continual rhythmic clatter of their wooden-soled shoes. The steps are elaborate, and great pains are taken to reach perfection in their performance. Competitions in this 'Schuh-plattling' are held in all districts; at these it can be seen in its highest developments. But a village inn or the kitchen of any big farm will give opportunity to see it in even pleasanter circumstances. It really is a living part of the Bavarian peasant's existence.

RAIN-MAKERS AND RAIN-MAKING CEREMONIES

To the inhabitants of a northern clime rarely subject to drought, ceremonies and processes for inducing rainfall may seem futile, but in earlier times and in large areas of the present-day world the very existence of the tribe or group is seen to depend upon rain. So, as here described, magic is called to the rescue. Other life essentials in which magic plays its part are discussed in chapters on Magic and the Means of Life, Magic in Love and War, and others.

Only those who have experienced conditions in regions in which rainfall is small, and that of a seasonal character, can appreciate to the full all that water means to a primitive people. In the modern civilized community interference with the water supply, owing, for instance, to a severe frost or a prolonged drought, may cause inconvenience or even a shortage of certain food-stuffs, but beyond the loss to agriculture, the community as a whole suffers little. In the case of a primitive tribe, however, its very existence depends upon water supply. Living in isolation on its own ranging ground, it cannot encroach on that of its neighbours, nor look to them for assistance, even if they should be in better case than itself. In a hunting community, such as that of the Bushmen of the Kalahari Desert, which depends to a very small degree upon vegetable foods, the camp is invariably near a water hole to which game resorts. Should that water hole fail, it may not be easy to find another not already occupied by another tribal group. The disaster following upon a failure of rain in an agricultural community may be even more overwhelming. The appalling dimensions it may assume is shown by the mortality in the Indian famines, even up to the latter part of the last century.

In any primitive community, then, even in a temperate climate, water is a matter of anxiety. That it was so to our ancestors, even in the moist climate of Britain, may be inferred from the number of Holy Wells scattered up and down the country. Each of these was once the shrine of a water deity, to whom reverence was paid to ensure the well-being and fertility of flocks, herds and crops. In the drier regions of the earth, such as the arid areas of North and Central America, water was, it is no exaggeration to say, the pivotal factor in the culture and thought of the people.

On the other hand the rapidity with which vegetation recovers and the earth is clothed in green when once the rainy season sets in—even more, say, in Australia after a drought which has lasted three or four years—has impressed upon the mind of man the fertilising power of the rain and confirmed his belief in the reality of a magic power which, in his conception, lies at the back of all processes of growth and increase in nature.

E.N.A

HIGH PRIEST OF THE SNAKES

Indians of the Smoki tribe of Arizona have an elaborate dance ritual with live snakes, the main purpose of which is an invocation to the gods who control rain and fertility. The face and body of this priest are ceremonially whitened.

If, however, primitive man believes in a spiritual power which lies behind the rain and all that it brings forth with its fertilising qualities, just as he thinks there are spiritual powers animating the other phenomena of the material world which he sees around him, it is equally his belief that this power is susceptible of magical control by himself, or rather by those who are specially qualified to exercise that control.

In view of all these conditions, it is not surprising to find that among peoples of the simpler cultures—food-gatherers, hunting peoples and agriculturists of the simpler type—anyone who lays claim to the power to control the supply of rain will hold a position of commanding influence and importance in the group. At certain seasons—when rain-making ceremonies take place—he will represent the community. He dominates the situation and holds the fate of the group in his hand ; as he may perform, or refrain from performing, the necessary act, so he may demand such reward as he thinks fit. Among the Swazis the cattle sacrificed to procure rain had to be of a particular colour. These herds belonged to the king, who received vast amounts for each victim. If he were not satisfied with what he received, he threatened that unless he were given what he demanded, he would bind up the skin, thus by the exercise of his magical powers rendering the proper performance of the rite impossible.

There is thus good ground for the view which has been put forward that the power of the kingship has been built up largely on the influence acquired by the magician who represents the group in magical ceremonies, and particularly in the one of most vital import—rain-making.

Among the Wambugwe of Central East Africa the principal function of the chief was rain-making, and among the Zulus the rain-maker was always a member of the Royal House, lest anyone outside exercising the function should acquire too great power.

Some of the fundamental conceptions implicit in the belief that it is possible to control the fall of rain are well exemplified in practices found among the Australian tribes. There, although rain-making, like other forms of magic, may be practised by anyone, for instance by such a simple charm as singing an incantation over a bandicoot, the more serious ceremonies are left to the specialist. The sacred character of these ceremonies is indicated by their traditional connexion with the Alcheringa, the fabulous ' once-upon-a-time ' of the Australian tribesman. These ceremonies are performed by members of the rain-water totem kin, and by them only, because, say the Arunta, the secret was imparted to their ancestors in the Alcheringa. On the other hand, among the Kaitish, it is said, the ceremonies are performed at the place where in the Alcheringa the old men drew water from their whiskers, these whiskers now being represented by the sacred stones over which water is poured in the ceremonies.

When it is proposed to perform rain-making ceremonies among the Arunta, notice is sent to all members of the rain-water kin, who assemble at the

Topical

HISTORIC DANCE OF THE SNAKES WHO BRING FERTILITY TO THE ARIZONA DESERT

The ceremonial dances of the Hopi and other Indians of New Mexico and Arizona are of great antiquity and are based upon folk legends whose origins are lost. The principal ceremony still performed among all the tribes, with serious and religious purpose, is some form of snake dance, often with live snakes. These priests of the Smoki tribe wearing antelope horns are leaving the kiva, or temple (see page 166), to take their place in the great snake dance performed in June each year. The masks are intended to be suggestive of their tribal ancestors.

MYSTERIOUS WEATHER-CHARMING RITUAL OF A LITTLE-KNOWN RACE

The Baining tribe, who live in the interior of the Gazelle Peninsula of New Britain, are entirely different from the rest of the New Britain peoples, and their customs have been but little studied. Among them an elaborate two-part fire dance is apparently a fertility festival. The ritual of the second part of the dance, in which these enormous hats, made of beaten tree bark and supported with long strings of fibre, are worn, is supposed to have a magical effect on the weather and other conditions. This dance continues for hours at a time, and is performed round a log fire while women beat sticks on the ground and chant. The head-dresses are symbolical both in shape and decoration.

H. J. Shepstone

RAIN-MAKER OF THE PUEBLO INDIANS OF ARIZONA DESCENDING TO THE RITUAL CHAMBER

In the arid regions of Arizona and New Mexico rain is of vital importance, and many of the Indian tribes practise elaborate rain-making ceremonies. Among the Hopi people underground altars to the rain god (see page 166) are maintained at which one of the tribal priests performs semi-secret rites at intervals, as in this pueblo, or adobe village, at Walpi built high on a rock above the sandy plain. A complete ritual, performed annually, includes the Katchina and other dances with masks and a flute ceremony, in addition to the snake dance.

camp. The most significant feature of the ceremony which follows is that on the final morning at daybreak, when the ceremony is declared over, the men rush from a shelter, specially built for the purpose, screaming like plover.

In this ceremony, which is simple as rain-making ceremonies go, the performers, as members of the rain-water totem, identify themselves completely with the events they wish to bring about. They are the rain. When they burst from the shelter in the morning they dramatise the rainstorm, which is usually accompanied by the cries of the plover they imitate. The cry of the plover is heard again in the ceremony of the Kaitish tribes where, however, the dramatisation takes a different form. For here the fall of rain is imitated by water which the leader pours on himself, the stones and the ground.

At the risk of being tedious, it is worth while to glance briefly at two other Australian ceremonies for their bearing on the development of conceptions in rain-making which appear in other parts of the world and at very different levels of culture.

Among the Queensland tribes a great part is played in the ceremonies by the rain stick. This is a stick about twenty inches long to which are fastened three stones, usually of quartz crystal, and hair from the beard. Three or four sticks may be used. All taking part repair to a pool, in which one member of the group dives with a hollow log, which he fixes to the bottom. Then all go into the water and, forming a circle round the leader, who holds the rain stick aloft, they splash water on it. They sing, and after singing is over, the man in the centre dives and attaches the rain stick to the hollow log. When he comes up he climbs out and spits out the water he has swallowed on to the dry land. The performance is repeated for each rain stick.

There can be little question that this custom may well have a phallic significance. A parallel may be cited from India, where in the Bombay Presidency, for instance, among the potters and Chudbudki Joshis, a phallus of Shiva in mud is made on a board and water poured on it as it is carried from house to house, while for several days Brahmins and high caste Hindus pour water over it at the temple.

The second of the Australian ceremonies in question is the practice of the Dieri, among whom the whole tribe and not a section takes part. The Dieri appear to recognize spirits, the 'mura-mura,' who dwell in the sky and make the clouds bring forth rain. It is reported that they pray to these to give them success in rain-making. Here, apparently, is the rudimentary idea of a rain god.

It has already been mentioned that in Australia rain making may be practised by anyone who has knowledge of the necessary magical formula or charm. It may be thought that the specialist group in rain-

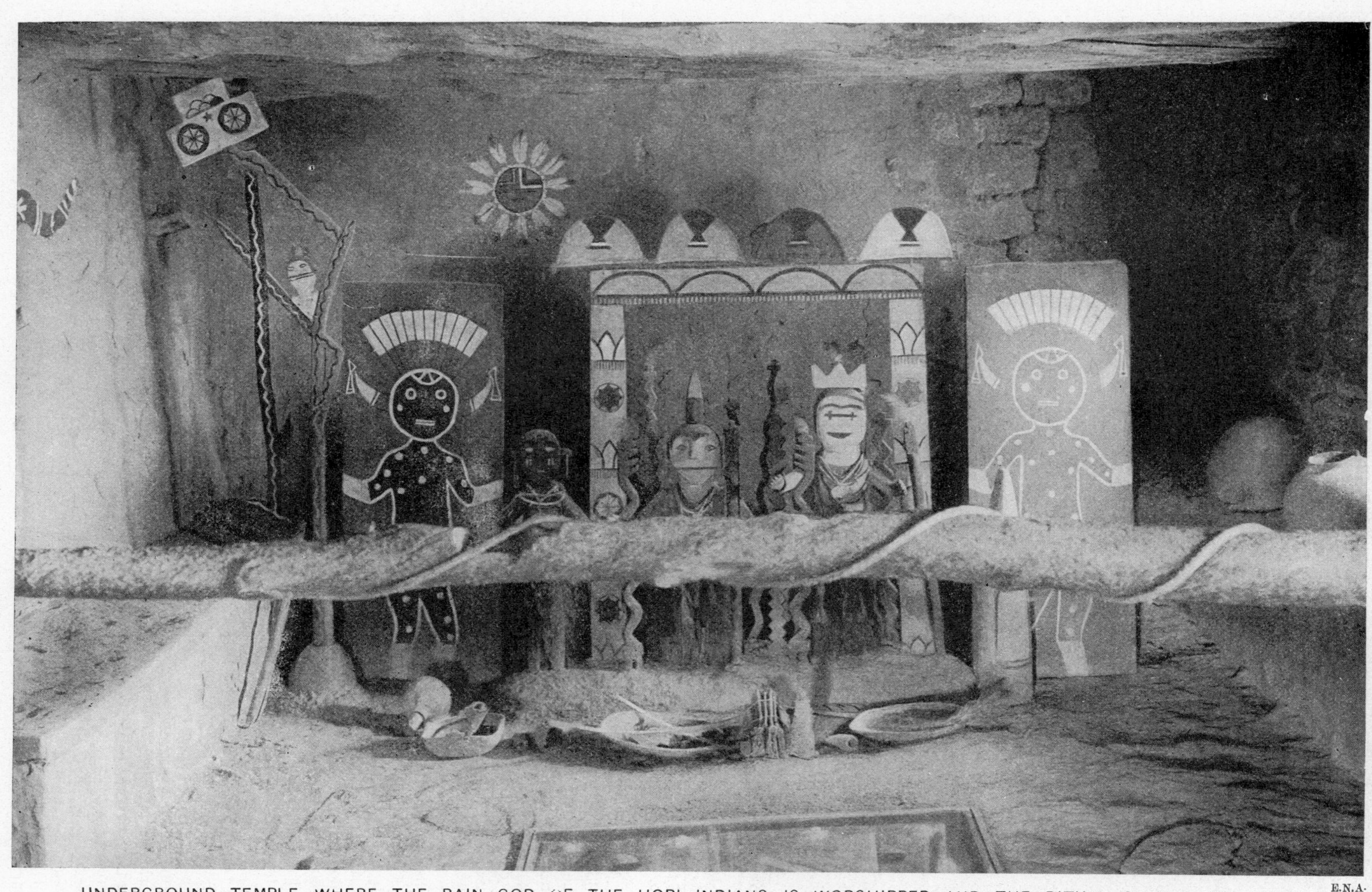

E.N.A.

UNDERGROUND TEMPLE WHERE THE RAIN GOD OF THE HOPI INDIANS IS WORSHIPPED AND THE RITUAL SNAKES ARE KEPT

In all primitive races the primal need is water, since without it food fails and the tribe dies out. In dry and semi-sterile countries such as the south-western districts of the United States and the central and northern regions of Australia, water-holes are strictly guarded and kept secret, and magic, generally religious in character, is devised to placate the gods of rain and induce their beneficent activities. The Hopi, or Moqui, Indians of the pueblo district of Arizona have underground temples or kivas, where enshrined figures and emblems of wind, rain and storm of the rain god and his snake, with offering dishes in front, are the subject of secret ritual. In another chamber, known as the kisi, numbers of live snakes of many different varieties are kept. The snakes in these ceremonies are probably of totemic significance, the tribe using them being a 'people of the snake.'

making is a gradual development, through accumulated experience and through training, in the correct and most efficient procedure—a view to which customs connected with the preparation for entering the ranks of medicine men in some parts of the world might lend support. It is probable, however, that the reverse is the case. The knowledge of the rain-makers is esoteric and not on a par with the simple charm which might be within the grasp of anyone. As was seen in the case of the Arunta rain-water totem kin, it is a secret transmitted to the group from the time of the Alcheringa. Anyone may whistle for a wind, but to control the weather it was necessary to go to the specialist, the witch, or at least so it was believed even up to the last century on the north coast of Scotland.

E.N.A.

ZULU WITCH DOCTOR INVOKES THE STORM

In all important crises of tribal and individual life among agricultural and hunting peoples the man of magic is the man of the hour. Claiming to control the needed rain, he is usually shrewd enough to delay his ceremonies until a weather change appears likely. This does not detract from the dramatic force of the attitude adopted by this Zulu 'making rain.'

The idea that rain-making is the exclusive property of a group is found in what is perhaps the best known of all rain-making ceremonies—the snake dance of the Hopi Indians, who live in what is known as the arid region of the south-western United States. This dance has now become a well-known attraction for tourists, but is still carried out in all its traditional elaboration. Among the more prominent features are the sand pictures of the altar, which in the symbolism of the ceremony represent the six quarters of the heavens, the wind, the rain, clouds, lightning, and the crops for which the benefit is sought. The second remarkable feature is the part played by the snakes, which in the course of the sixteen days' ceremony are caught, washed and carried about, at one time in their mouths, by the participants. The dance is the property of the snake society. There are a number of societies of a similar kind among the Hopis themselves, and among other tribes. The societies are undoubtedly totemic in origin ; but their connexion with rain has given them an overwhelming importance in the social and religious organization owing to climatic conditions which have made interest in the rainfall all-absorbing.

In the Arunta ceremony, although the whole kin took part, one old man was singled out as leader or chief rain-maker. Speaking generally, when a tribe as a whole takes part and the ceremony is performed on behalf of the community as a whole, this duty devolves upon the magician in chief, either the king or his representative. In India, when the Meitheis strip themselves naked, and, standing in the roadway, curse and revile one another (nudity, bad language and mutual casting of filth are strong rain charms, especially in India), the Raja takes his place at their head. The custom that the king should be the chief rain-maker is only in accordance with the belief that the prosperity of his land is bound up closely with him, and that his is the responsibility. Hence the many customs that have been interpreted as meaning that the king, as representing the god, was once sacrificed

F. E. Williams

LABORATORY OF THE AUSTRALIAN RAIN-MAKER

Among the Australian aborigines one or more of the old men are chosen as principal rain 'magickers.' This is the laboratory of a rain-maker of the River Morehead district, Queensland. His stones, torches, trough, pointing-sticks and other objects are important items in his mystic processes.

down from generation to generation which enabled the rain-maker to perform his function, it was customary to put him to death before old age crept on him and his powers failed. Among the Shilluk tribes of the upper Nile the rain-maker was held responsible for drought, and if he failed to break it they ripped up his abdomen, where it was believed he kept the winds.

Rain-making charms and customs surviving in Europe, which perhaps represent an even older stratum of belief than those found among many savages, certainly seem to point to a time when the leader of the rain-making ceremony was the victim, and perhaps also the representative of the god.

in order to secure the fertility of his realm. Thus it is frequently found that either the king or the medicine man is held responsible for either a drought or the failure to produce an adequate supply of rain when it is wanted. Among certain West African tribes, the chief was beaten in the event of rain failing, and among the Dinkas, who believed that a spirit was handed

Epiphany customs of Eastern Europe are clearly ceremonies to secure rain supply. Such an interpretation might be placed upon that in which the head of the Greek Church at Constantinople blesses the waters of the Bosporus. At Bukarest the elaborate Epiphany ceremony at the river in which the king and the dignitaries of the church take part, it has

Sport and General

RAIN THAT IS WELCOMED WITH CARNIVAL AND FEASTING

Evidences of the fundamental importance of the supply of water from the heavens are not lacking in peoples of higher culture than the so-called savage. In Burma the coming of the rains is made the occasion of much rejoicing, in which religion plays its part. At Mandalay a huge Buddhist carnival is held with appropriate ceremonies and dances, which are performed in the courtyard of the largest temple of the city. Here popular dances of the rain carnival are seen in progress.

E.N.A.

CHRISTIAN CEREMONY WHICH PERHAPS ORIGINATED IN CHARMING FOR RAIN

The picturesque Epiphany ceremonials of the Orthodox church at Bukarest include the incident here illustrated. The waters of the river Dimboitza having been blessed, the king throws in a cross, which is retrieved by the white-garbed priests standing in the shallows. It has been suggested that this rite replaces a far more primitive one in which a victim, representing the rain god, or perhaps his principal priest, was thrown into the river as a sacrifice.

been suggested, may have taken the place of a rite in which the man was cast into the water. At one festival in Greece children go in procession from well to well, and at each the leader, who is decorated with flowers and garlands, is drenched with water. Many similar customs in the Near East might be quoted. One of the most significant, perhaps, is the custom on SS. Peter and Paul's day of casting the images of these saints into the river, a custom also found in India with the image of Indra. Some traces are even to be found in Britain, for at harvest time it was a common practice for women to try to drench the last sheaf or 'corn dolly' with water, while the man carrying it tried to prevent them. In Wales, the man carrying the sheaf, if caught, was bound with straw ropes and thrown into a stream. Lastly, perhaps, it is worth mentioning the 'Beating the Bounds' custom of a certain parish in Devonshire, where at a certain spot one of the boys taking part in the procedure was rolled in a brook.

Enough has been said in what precedes to indicate some of the essential features of the rain-making ceremony. It begins in, and up to a certain level of thought is, pure magic. It aims at producing a fall of rain by simulating its action or its appearance, as in the Arunta dramatisation, or the ceremony of the Natchez Indians, in the course of which water is blown in a mist-like cloud out of finely perforated pipes held in the mouth. Water may be splashed over the person, or it may be poured on stones which are perhaps conceived as having an indwelling spirit to be influenced thereby or thought to be the image of a god.

The Dieri belief in the 'mura-mura' who dwell in the sky (see p. 165) is a conception toward which an Indian belief approximates, for it is thought that rain is due to the good offices of Indra, who fights with, and overcomes, the demons in the sky who prevent rain. In Africa in particular do we find the rain god who is propitiated by sacrifice. He is usually conceived in association with the hill tops. This conception of a rain god may have been reached by way of the tree and ancestor cult, for among the Akikuyu offerings for rain are placed at the foot of a tree in which a spirit dwells, while among the Zulu, maidens, to procure rain, make offerings and pour beer for their ancestors at the roots of a tree.

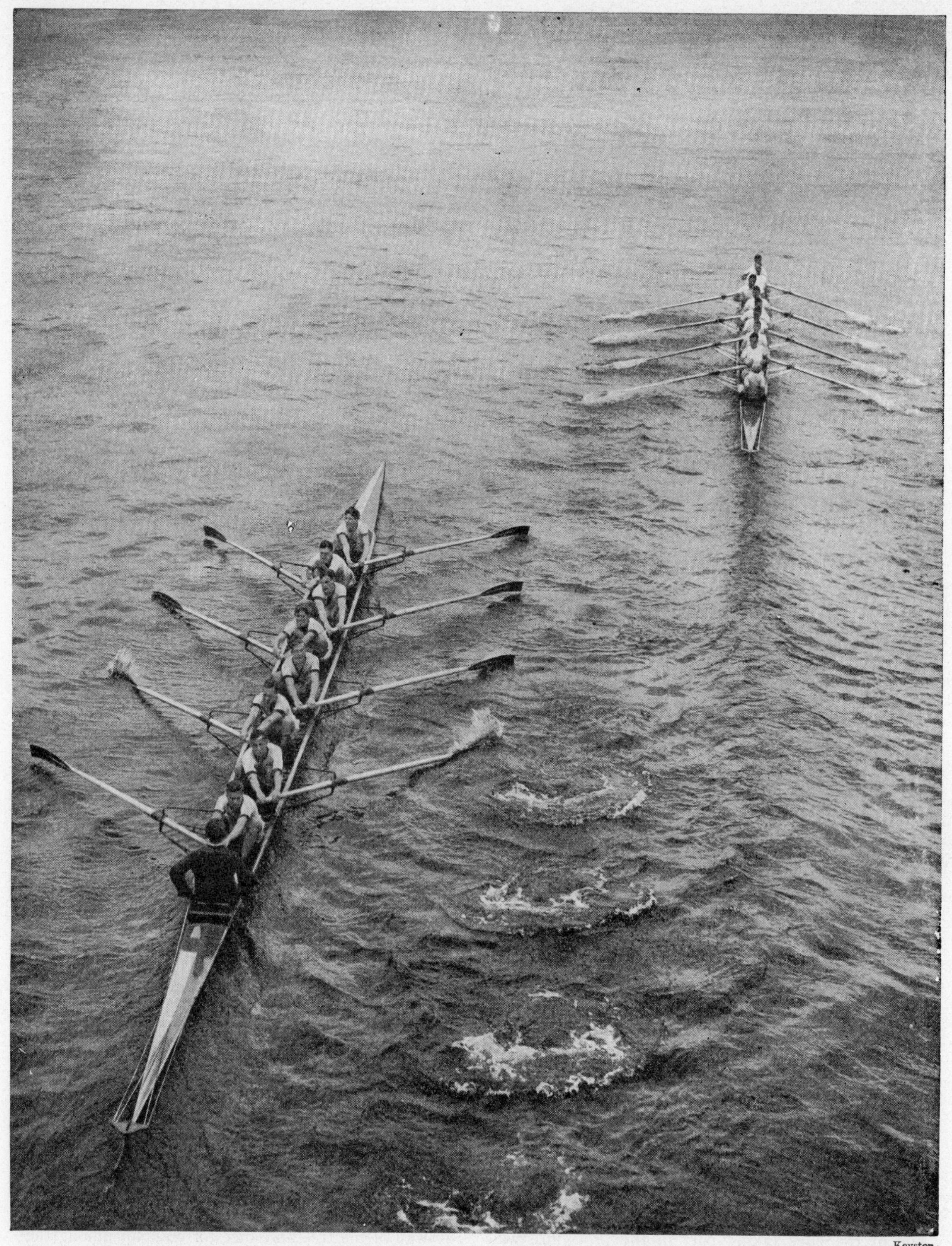

Keystone

LAST LAP OF THE BRITISH BOAT RACE: CAMBRIDGE LEADING AT BARNES BRIDGE

Next to the Derby the sporting event which holds the greatest popular interest in the British Isles is the boat race between the universities of Oxford and Cambridge. Each crew consists of eight oars and a coxswain and the race is rowed over a course of 4¼ miles on the Thames from Putney to Mortlake. The race was instituted in 1829, became an annual event in 1856, and up to 1930, when, as shown here, victory fell to the Cambridge crew, each university had won on forty occasions, while there was one dead heat.

BOATING AND BOAT-RACING THE WORLD OVER

IN view of the keen interest now taken in all forms of sport and exercise it is a little odd perhaps that man's fundamental sporting instinct did not find expression in boat-racing at a much earlier date than it actually did. All aspects of the sport are envisaged here, and reference should also be made to the chapters on National Sports of Europe and Savage Sport and Play.

ROWING, like hunting and fishing, derives its origin as a sport from the practical side of life. In this it is unlike cricket, football and all ball games, and those other sports which might be catalogued under the heading of self-defence, such as fencing, wrestling, boxing and shooting. Man—and this is particularly true of the English, who even invented a sport of eating and fasting—naturally tends to make a pleasure of his labours, and inevitably the toil on sea and river and lake has been sweetened universally by turning the daily task and the common round into a sporting competition. Hence have arisen yacht-racing, motor-racing, and, first of all, rowing.

The great part that rowing played in the social scheme of things at one time may be demonstrated by some curious statistics. An average of the calculations made as to the population of London in the reign of Queen Elizabeth places the figure somewhere in the neighbourhood of 150,000. John Taylor, the water poet, writing in 1613, declares that during Queen Elizabeth's reign ' the number of watermen, and those that live and are maintained by them, and by the only labour of the oar and scull, betwixt the bridges of Windsor and Gravesend, cannot be fewer than 40,000.' This means in effect that at least a fourth of the population lived by their aquatic labours.

In these circumstances it was only a matter of time before rowing became sublimated into a sport. From the earliest days, of course, there must have been friendly competitions among the watermen of the Thames, but it was left to Thomas Doggett to lay the foundations of that modern rowing which includes the classic struggle each year between Oxford and Cambridge. Doggett was what we should call nowadays a ' character ' actor, who made the first serious study of make-up. Born in Dublin, he migrated to London and became manager of Drury Lane. He was an ardent politician and an enthusiastic supporter of the Hanoverian succession. To commemorate the accession of King George the First to the British throne on August 1, 1714, he left at his death a sum of money, the interest of which was to be appropriated annually, for ever, to the purchase of a waterman's coat and badge to be rowed for on the anniversary of that blessed day. With that minute attention to matters of dress which distinguished

E.N.A.

ALL-RUSH BOAT OF BOLIVIAN WATERS

A solid bundle of rushes was, like the unhollowed tree trunk, among the earliest means of conveyance on water. The ancient Egyptians are known to have had rush boats, and canoes cunningly woven from rushes and bound with cord over a framework are very commonly used in Bolivia. The boat here seen is on Lake Titicaca.

Photopress

THAMES RACE THAT IS TWO CENTURIES OLD

Thomas Doggett was an actor who in 1715 founded a prize for rowing to commemorate George I's accession to the British throne. It consisted of an orange coat and silver badge, and was to be competed for by six young Thames watermen who were less than twelve months out of their apprenticeship. The race is still rowed annually from London Bridge to Chelsea.

him as an actor, and in accordance with his political principles he directed that the coat should be of an orange colour, and the badge should represent the White Horse of Hanover. The race, for which six young watermen, whose apprenticeships end in the same year, are eligible, still takes place on the old course, against the tide, from The Old Swan at London Bridge to The White Swan at Chelsea.

For well over a hundred years this race remained the great aquatic struggle on the Thames. In 1829, however, there occurred an event which was destined to eclipse the importance of the race for Doggett's coat and badge. This was a match rowed between crews representing Oxford and Cambridge at Henley. It was not until 1856 that the event became an annual affair, fought out on the present $4\frac{1}{4}$-mile course from Putney to Mortlake. It has now become, perhaps, the greatest sporting event of the year. Since the war, during the continuation of which the race was abandoned, Oxford have been singularly unfortunate. One of the most curious features of the race nowadays is the passionate partisanship shown by the London population, only a very small proportion of whom have any connexion with either University.

'The' Boat-race is, of course, merely an extension of the Lent and May inter-collegiate races at the two Universities—the 'Bumping' races—from the competitors in which the 'Blues' are selected. It is a mistake, however, to imagine that the home country has an historical monopoly of boat-racing. Twenty-three years before the struggle between Oxford and Cambridge on the Thames became an annual event, the famous regatta on the Parramatta river at Sydney had been started, and it has been held there ever since. A year later, in 1834, the equally famous Hobart Regatta was inaugurated in Tasmania.

Boat-racing, indeed, has been a favourite sport in Tasmania from a very early date, long before there was one purely racing craft in the colony. When Hobart had become an important whaling station, and the wharves of the port were packed with vessels, nearly thirty crews would take part in a five-oar whalers' race at the Hobart Regatta. It was Sir John Franklin, the famous Polar explorer, at that time Governor of Tasmania, who promoted this aquatic tournament to commemorate, on January 26th, the discovery of the island by Tasman in 1642.

English people remain so intensely insular that many of them still imagine that rowing is a monopoly of our Universities and such big public schools as Eton. For them, Henley Regatta, with its famous Diamond Sculls, the Wingfield Sculls for the amateur championship of the Thames, and perhaps the world's sculling championship, complete all the world's programmes of rowing races which matter. They would probably be surprised to learn that in Australia the sport has been developed on lines very similar to those of our International Rugby Match. Since 1878 there have been inter-state championship races between rival eights which are perhaps the most notable events of their kind in the world.

To show the extraordinary keenness displayed by the Australians for the sport of rowing, it is only necessary to record a few illuminating facts. In 1906, before the Trans-Continental railway was built, when the race was held in Perth, Western Australia, the Queensland eight travelled 3,000 miles to the race, and the South Australian crew from the neighbouring state had a four-days' ocean voyage to get to the course. Under existing arrangements the races, held at the close of the rowing season—about May—are rowed in each capital in turn, and to secure to itself this right each state must be represented each year. Mr. Gordon Inglis, in his excellent book on Australian sport, commenting on this famous aquatic contest, remarks: 'I can recall no more stimulating memory than an inter-state race of a few years back when the picked eights of six Australian States were rowing side by side on the broad waters of the Parramatta. This is, I think, the best rowing course in Australia, all things considered—i.e. straightness, accessibility, accommodation for the steamers, smoothness of water, etc.' The race is for three miles, and the rivalry between the crews is so strong that the race for fifth place is sometimes keener than that for the first.

Rowing, indeed, in the Antipodes has been brought to such a fine art that for many years it seemed as if Australia had a mortgage on the world's Professional Sculling title. From 1908 to 1911 R. Arnst, a New Zealander, who until two years before he won the title had never been in a boat, held the world's championship.

It is not only in the British Empire that boat-racing has taken deep root. It is being popularised in several European countries, and in the United States of America, where the annual contest between Harvard and Yale mimics the struggle between Oxford and Cambridge. In all marine sports, indeed, the United States takes a leading part. Since 1851, when the race was inaugurated, they have held the America Cup presented by our Royal Yacht Squadron, in spite of the efforts of Sir Thomas Lipton, Lord Dunraven, and others to wrest it from their grasp. To them also belongs the honour of inaugurating two new branches of aquatic sport—an International Lifeboat race in New York Harbour, and canoe-racing, which, at their instigation, is henceforth to be included in the programme of the Olympic Games.

Canoe-racing in the United States has developed under the guidance of the American Canoe Association, founded in 1880. Clubs have been formed all over the country, but only here and there are 'war canoes' used—that is to say, canoes manned by nine men and propelled by paddles. Canoe-racing is essentially a sailing sport. From 1909 to 1917 the rules of the association forbade the use of a sail area larger than ninety square feet, but since that year, as the canoes themselves have tended to grow bigger, a sliding-scale sail area has been permitted. The decked sailing canoe has been recognized as the finest type of canoe-sailing machine, but none the less it has been frequently out-manoeuvred at regattas by the open, or cruising, canoe rigged with lateen sails and steered by means of a paddle.

The use of a canoe propelled by a paddle in contradistinction to the boat propelled by oars might also be made a method of dividing the human race. The canoe is, of course, indigenous to America, where the skill of the Red man is still remembered in the pages of history and romance, and also to South America, Africa, parts of Asia, and Polynesia. The best built canoes are those constructed in the Fiji Islands. The Fijians, indeed, are wonderful boat-builders, and they handle their craft with amazing skill. The speed they are able to develop suggests that here we might easily find competitors worthy to pick up the gage thrown down by the United States for the Olympic Sports of 1932.

In Bolivia the canoes are ingeniously hand-woven from rushes. The natives use them with great skill on Lake Titicaca, and during the summer months—November to May—traffic above the great Zarawes swamps is largely carried out by these vessels because of the floods resulting from the summer inundations. In Liberia until comparatively recent years the only method of locomotion, besides porterage and

Photopress

BOATING DRESS OF AN OLDEN DAY

So fervent a supporter of the Hanoverian succession was Thomas Doggett, that he made the badge included in the rowing prize named after him a huge affair bearing the White Horse of Hanover. Officials of the race are here seen wearing their badges.

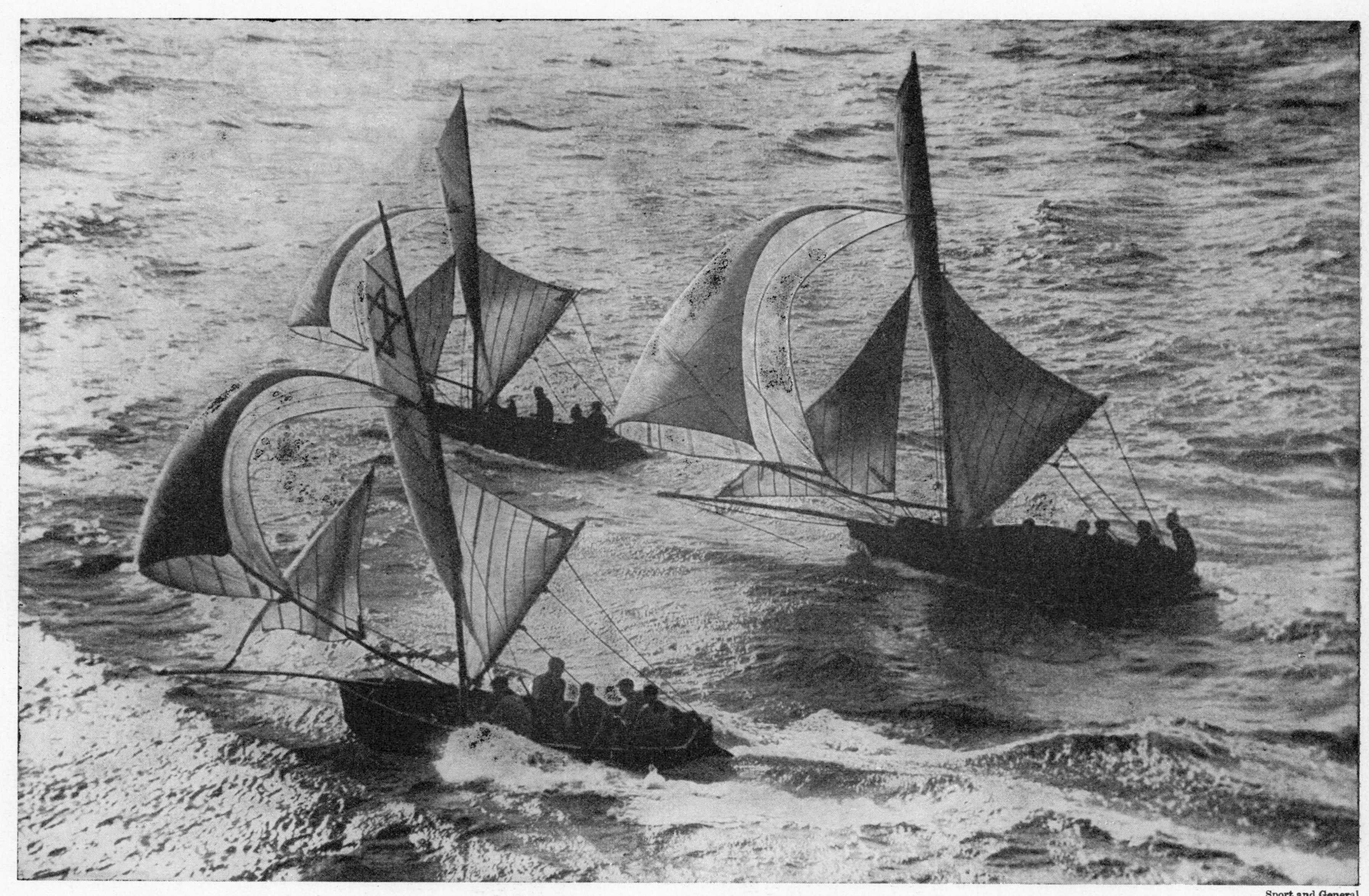

Sport and General

YACHTING IN SYDNEY HARBOUR: SPECTACULAR RACE OF THE EIGHTEEN-FOOTERS FOR THE HONOUR OF QUEENSHIP

By common consent Sydney harbour is one of the most magnificent harbours in the world, but besides its facilities for commerce, it is also the scene of exciting yacht races. Of these the race of eighteen-foot sailing boats for the title of queen of the harbour is both a highly picturesque and a keenly contested sporting event. To see the boats taking part in this trial of speed and skill in full career, their sails bellying in the wind, is a spectacle to make the blood tingle. It has been said that the visitor who once tries surf-bathing on a Sydney beach wishes to live all his days on a Pacific beach; the same might also be said of one who had witnessed the race of the eighteen-footers in Sydney harbour.

walking, was the canoe—a dug-out, or a tree trunk hollowed to the requisite thinness by fire and adzing.

In his 'Through Asia,' Sven Hedin describes the canoes used at Lop-Nor, the lake system in the Gobi Desert in east Turkistan. The canoes vary very much in size, but three men working hard can hew one out of a poplar in five days. They never use sails, but always row with an oar with a thin broad blade. There are usually two rowers to each canoe, and they generally kneel facing the way they are going. The canoes used by the Inthas, the pile-dwellers on Inle Lake in the southern Shan States of Burma, are unique, not only because of their shape, but also on account of their method of propulsion. Their crews are the only rowers in the world who make direct use of the leg-drive, about which every coach on the bank of the Thames, the Cam and the Isis shouts himself hoarse each year. Balanced on one leg, sometimes with, and sometimes without, a supporting rail, they twist the other round their six-foot paddle, lean forward, and with a backward kick propel the canoe at an astonishing pace. Their trained crews exhibit a precision of body swing and a regularity of stroke that characterise the rowing of a University Eight, and now that canoeing has been raised to the dignity of a sport by inclusion in the Olympic Games, regatta committees might well pay attention to this method of propulsion. Punting is, of course, another method of propelling a boat which has been popularised into a sport among the white races; but experts who have watched them declare that the boatmen of the Yangtse-Kiang could give points to most of our crack punters.

Keystone

YALE UNIVERSITY CREW OUT FOR A PRACTICE RUN

The boat-race between the universities of Yale and Harvard dates back to 1855, a year before the Oxford and Cambridge boat-race became an annual event, and with few exceptions it has been rowed every year from 1864. Over this long period the contests have run very evenly, Yale having only a few more wins to her credit than Harvard.

The simplicity of the canoe, its lightness, and therefore the ease with which it can be transported across obstacles, have given it an almost universal use. By its means Englishmen have explored such inaccessible stretches of water as the Jordan, the Kishon, the Abana and the Pharpar at Damascus, as well as the lake of Galilee. The record canoe trip in New Zealand was carried out some years ago from the terminal face of the Tasman Glacier to the lower reaches of the Waitaki. The last sixty miles of this trip were covered in eight hours. Canoeing in New Zealand, though of late years it has declined in popularity, is a very exciting sport, especially in the western rivers of the Southern Island with their rapids and broken water and 'leaping bars.'

Among the Lomani of the south-west Congo, and also among the natives of Fernando Po, square-

Topical Press

EIGHT-OARED BOAT RACES, HEAVY AND LIGHT, ON FRESH WATER AND SALT

Inter-collegiate boat races are held at both Oxford and Cambridge in the Lent and summer terms. Owing to the narrowness of the waterways these are 'bumping races,' the boats starting at equal distances in line ahead and striving to overtake one another. In the event of a 'bump' being effected the successful boat starts above its defeated rival in the next race. An international race for ships' life-boats was inaugurated in the United States of America in 1927; the lower photograph, taken from the statue of Liberty, shows the first race in progress.

Central Press

YACHT-RACING IN THE SOLENT: SPORT FOR THE WEALTHY

In this photograph Sir Thomas Lipton's Shamrock V (right foreground) is taking the lead from Westward at Cowes during a race for big yachts in August, 1929. Sir Thomas Lipton has built five Shamrocks for his gallant attempts to gain the America cup. This famous trophy was originally named the Queen's Cup, and was offered by the Royal Yacht Squadron in 1851 for an international race over a course round the Isle of Wight. It was won by the U.S.A schooner yacht America, was presented to the New York Yacht Club, and has been held against all challengers ever since.

Courtesy of C.P.R.

E.N.A.

FRAIL CANOES THAT CAN SHOW A TURN OF SPEED AND RIDE IN ROUGH WATERS

Though frail in appearance, the canoe is marvellously waterworthy. It is the one type of primitive boat that has been adopted by civilized peoples. From the Red Indian's birch-bark canoe developed the popular Canadian variety. As regards the dug-out, the savage found that it took a very large log to make a canoe wide enough to be stable, so he devised the outrigger, a pole fastened parallel with the boat. The upper photograph shows a Canadian canoe on the rapids of a Canadian river. Below is a racing outrigger of Santa Cruz.

Swedish Travel Bureau

LIGHTNING SPEED BOATS OF THE WATER AND THE ICE

For speed there is not very much to choose between the ice yacht and the motor boat. Both are terrifically fast. With a high wind an ice yacht can move at about ninety miles an hour. Sir Henry Segrave's motor boat speed record was 98·76 miles per hour, but this has been exceeded by Mr. Kaye Don. The upper photograph shows ice yachting in Sweden. In the lower Mr. Don is seen driving 'Miss England II' on Lough Neagh in Ulster at a speed of 107 miles an hour

ended canoes are employed. Elsewhere in the Congo the canoes, however long and shapely they may be, are nothing but hollowed-out tree stems. Wonderful effects and wonderful craft are produced with this medium. The prow is sometimes carved into a long beak or crocodile head. The biggest canoes manufactured among the Congo natives are probably those made by the Ngonbe, but some very fine canoes were formerly possessed by the Kongo people, some of them capable of seating sixty men.

Man, eternally adapting himself to his environment, has invented other craft besides boats and canoes when his environment did not readily supply him with the material he required. Among the Shilluk tribe in Central Africa boats are constructed of fascines of reeds tied together, because of the lack of wood. In appearance they resemble the 'felucca,' being long and narrow. These vessels are easily constructed, ride the water perfectly, and can transport as many as fifteen people with their kit. On the Euphrates, while the builders still make boats and coracles from the poplar wood so common in the Euphrates valley, pitching them outside and in, as Noah did, with bitumen from Hit, the most typical boats are gourd-like vessels, round in shape, called gufas. They are manipulated with poles with astonishing skill, and sometimes surprising speeds are obtained.

Even when winter comes man has devised an ingenious system of navigating the frozen rivers and lakes. Everybody will remember how Mr. Fogg, in Jules Verne's romance, kept within his programme for getting round the world in eighty days by crossing a part of Canada in a sledge with a sail. This sport and its kindred one of ice-yacht racing has become very popular in Canada of late years. In England ice-yacht sailing on Windermere has developed into a feature of the winter season in the Lake District.

In his march of progress Man has raised many memorials to his triumphs. The motor car and steam engine are there as records of his attempts to annihilate space. The aeroplane symbolises his conquest of the air. But these are but the inventions of yesterday. In the boat we have the oldest memorial of his triumph over the shackles with which Nature has sought to trammel him.

E.N.A.

WHERE CANOES ARE PADDLED BY LEG INSTEAD OF BY HAND

In the southern Shan States of Burma the Intha tribe have a remarkable way of propelling their canoes. They use paddles six feet long, but instead of manipulating them with their hands they work them with their legs. The canoeist stands firmly on one leg, and, curling the other round the paddle, proceeds to kick backwards with it. The Inthas can paddle in this way for several hours, and develop tremendous pace. The lower photograph shows an Intha canoe race, while above is a close view of these leg-paddlers.

TREE AND PLATFORM BURIAL

CUSTOMS observed at death and burial provide a wide field for investigation, one of the most interesting of which is entered upon here. It is also touched upon in the chapter on Red Indian Burials. Separate chapters deal with such topics as Graves and their Decoration, How the Nations Mourn their Heroes, European Death and Burial Customs, as well as similar customs in other lands.

IN that area of Central Australia where the Arunta people still perpetuate immemorial native customs, travellers occasionally have their attention drawn to strange, nest-like bundles of boughs and twigs among the branches of trees. When one of these is examined it may be found to contain the little bones of a child, which are left undisturbed. Natives will explain that ghosts haunt certain trees, and express the belief that in the course of time the winsome spirit of the baby will effect a reunion with the mother and be reborn.

In the case of an adult the corpse is sometimes placed in a nest-like structure, and sometimes in a hollowed log which is deposited in the fork of a tree, or tied to branches overhanging a pool or stream. The near male relatives keep watch for a considerable period, no woman being allowed to approach the tree until the log coffin rots and its fragments fall with the bones into the water. It is believed by the natives that after the bones drop down to lie in the pool, or be carried away in a flood when rain comes, the deceased will be born again. Sometimes, however, after the body has lain for a period among the branches of a tree, the medicine man and near relatives take down the bones and rake them out on the ground. Then they are smashed into fragments, and these are placed in a vessel and carried to an ant hill, in which they are buried. The right arm bone is, however, reserved for special treatment. First of all it is carefully wrapped up and deposited in the hollow of a gum tree. Then, in time, it is taken out to be used in the final mourning ceremonies, which include solemn dances of painted men. In the end the bone is broken with a club and buried hastily and secretly in a hole in the ground in association with the dead person's totem.

Another custom is to give partial ground burial to the log coffin, which is left in an erect position until the flesh decays. During the elaborate and prolonged mourning ceremonies men and women wail and gash themselves, making offerings of blood to the deceased.

IN the Americas, before the Red Indians began to adopt the funerary customs of the white man, tree burials were fairly common, especially among the western tribes, but rarely, if ever, in the eastern portion of the continent, although timber was there in greatest abundance. The mourners, like the Australians, scarified and mutilated their bodies. There are many records of American tree burials. One tells of a Sioux sacred place in which in a hackberry tree, elevated about twenty feet from the ground, lay a corpse wrapped in a blanket on a kind of rack made of broken tent poles, while there were attached to it the cup, moccasins, etc., which had been used during life. Another record tells of the tree burials of the Blackfeet Indians of Montana, and makes reference to the custom of placing small toys beside the corpses of children. 'The Dakotas,' wrote Dr. L. S. Turner, of the United States Army, in one of his records, 'bury their dead in the tops of trees when limbs can be found sufficiently horizontal to support scaffolding on which to lay the body.' The Loucheux Indians of Canada, according to W. L. Hardisty, enclosed a corpse in a neatly hollowed log which was

E.N.A.

PLATFORM SHRINE OF THE SOLOMON ISLANDERS

The natives of the Solomon Islands fear ghosts. If a chief has been powerful in life it is believed that his ghost will be equally potent after his death. The shrine containing his skull or cremated body is therefore set up on high in a secluded place, and gifts of food are placed near it to appease the spirit of the departed. The relic case seen here is on Tendao Island.

Francis Birtles

FUNERAL SCENES AT AN ABORIGINAL TREE-TOP BURIAL IN AUSTRALIA

In Arnhem Land, North Australia, the aborigines use tree-top burial, partly with a view to securing the corpse from the attacks of the dingo and partly to satisfy the requirements of half-forgotten tradition. The lower photograph shows bearers with a body ready to set out for the burial place. The woman, to express her grief for her son's death, has cut herself with a stone knife, whitened her body and strewn earth over her head. Above, a native funeral party is departing for their camp after having placed their burden in the trees.

Dr. W. D. Walker

CORPSE'S LOFTY RESTING-PLACE THAT NO MAN MAY APPROACH

When a death occurs in the Wurramurra tribe of North Australia the corpse is placed on a platform in a tree and covered with branches. Poles are bound all round to keep off birds of prey. The body is then left until it has become mummified by the sun. During this process no member of the tribe may mention the name of the departed or set eyes on the tree; the guide of the taker of this photograph refused to go near it. When mummification is judged to be complete the remains are taken down and buried with elaborate and prolonged ceremony.

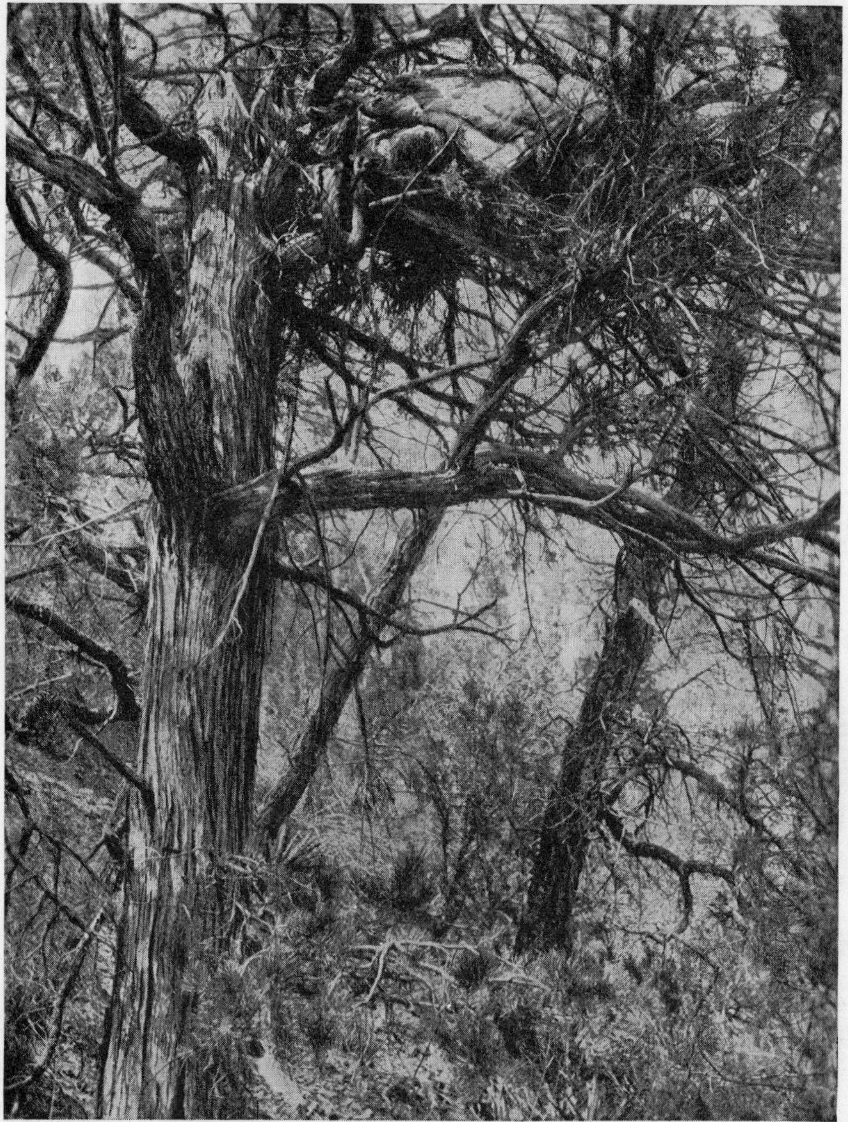

American Field Museum

APACHE INDIAN LYING LIKE A WARRIOR TAKING HIS REST

Tree burial was formerly common with the North American Indians, and although the eastern part of the continent is the more heavily timbered, it was among the tribes of the western plains that the practice was more prevalent. The Apaches, for instance, of New Mexico, Arizona and Texas buried their dead in trees. An Apache brave is here seen laid to rest high among the branches.

suspended from two or more trees about six feet from the ground.

Tree burials were formerly common in the Minahassa area in the Philippine Islands among the indigenous people, but, according to tribal tradition, strangers arrived before the Spaniards had been heard of, and taught the natives to deposit the bones of their dead in stone urns.

Tree burials were likewise common until recently among the Malayo-Siamese folk of the ancient Malayan kingdom of Patani. If a person died a good death, or was of high rank, a coffin was constructed and either erected on a platform among trees or suspended from branches. When the flesh decayed the bones were taken down to be burned and deposited in a temple. The bodies of those who died a bad death were wrapped up in a bundle, shaped like a cigar and strengthened with bamboo poles, and either placed in the fork of a tree or suspended between two trees and left undisturbed. A 'bad death' was usually one caused by violence or in punishment for some crime. There are records of the prevalence in ancient times of the tree burial custom among the Scythians and among the Colchians, who, according to Herodotus, were the descendants of colonists from ancient Egypt.

MEMORIES of very ancient tree burials appear to survive in ancient Egyptian myths regarding the god Osiris and in ancient Anatolian myths regarding the god Attis. According to Plutarch, the body of the slain Osiris drifted across the Mediterranean to the coast of Palestine, and after it had been washed ashore a tree grew up and enclosed it. The King of Byblos had the tree cut down and fashioned into a pillar to support his house or temple. That this myth was known to the Egyptians themselves is made evident by a Dendera temple representation of the Osirian coffin in a tree. A bird in the branches is the soul of Osiris—'the solitary one in the acacia.' Firmicus Maternus tells that an Egyptian ceremony was to hollow out a tree in which was placed a wooden image of Osiris. When a year had gone past, the image was ceremonially burned. A Pyramid inscription (c. 2600 B.C.) which appears to refer to this antique custom is translated as follows by Professor Breasted: 'Hail to thee, Sycamore, which encloses the god, under which the gods of the Nether Sky stand, whose tips are scorched, whose middle is burned, who art just in suffering!' The tree is referred to as 'the gracious damsel (goddess)' which 'was made for his soul of Gehesti—thy soul, O Osiris.' In Pluarch's myth the sacred tree is the 'erica.' The Phrygian god Attis was, after death, transformed into a pine tree, and it was customary to fasten to a sacred tree an image of Attis, which was preserved for a year and then burned.

There are many Western stories of ghosts and deities inhabiting trees and of trees growing from the graves of lovers and entwining their branches. Coffins were made of the wood of a sacred tree—a relic of the tree-burying custom. According to an ancient Chinese sage, 'pines and cypresses possess great vitality and coffins made from them facilitate the return of the dead to life.'

The disposal of the dead on platforms is a custom sometimes found to be closely related to that of tree burial. Indeed American recorders of Red Indian customs have stated that platforms were substitutes for trees. 'Should no tree be growing in the selected spot,' writes one, 'an artificial platform is made for the body.' Another record, dealing with the customs of the Choctaw Indians of Carolina, states that

the body of the deceased was exposed upon a bark scaffolding erected upon poles, or secured upon the limbs of trees, where it was left to waste to a skeleton. The bones were subsequently removed either to the former house of the deceased, or to a small bark-house by its side. . . . In this manner the skeletons of the whole family were preserved from generation to generation. . . . After the lapse of a number of years, or in a season of public insecurity, or on abandoning a settlement, it was customary to collect these skeletons from the whole community around and consign them to a common resting place.

On the north-west coast of America canoes were used instead of platforms. The Chinooks, for instance, laid a corpse wrapped in blankets in a canoe, which was 'then raised up and placed on two parallel bars, elevated four or five feet from the ground, and supported by being inserted through holes mortised at the top of four stout posts previously firmly planted in the earth. Around these holes were hung blankets and all the cooking utensils of the deceased.' At the end of a year the bones were 'buried in a box in the earth directly under the canoe.' According to George Gibbs, who investigated the burial customs of the Indians of Oregon and Washington Territory, 'the common mode of disposing of the dead among the fishing tribes was in canoes.' He tells of a cemetery in which there were formerly to be seen about 3,000 canoes perched on poles and containing the bones of the dead. An interesting fact was that canoes and platforms were usually laid east and west, as were also the bone houses.

In British New Guinea the Kiwai natives erect a platform, usually of a canoe board, oriented east and west and supported by four forked poles. On it is placed the body of the dead, with the head towards the setting sun, so that the spirit (urio) may be drawn towards the Elysium of Adiri. The near relatives attend to the body until the flesh has decayed. Then the bones are taken down, washed, laid on a mat in their natural order and buried. Sometimes a coconut tree is planted at the head of the grave and another at the foot. Another custom is to retain the skull, which is placed in a dwelling house or on a platform.

E.N.A.

HOW THEY BURY THEIR DEAD IN A PACIFIC ISLAND

The custom of platform burial is found over a wide range—in North America, Australia and many of the islands of the Pacific Ocean. Where head-hunting is practised the head or skull is removed subsequently. Sometimes the platform is reserved for one corpse, sometimes it is used for a number. The photograph shows a platform for dead bodies in New Guinea.

Paramount

DEAD, BUT WITH ALL THE GEAR OF LIFE ABOUT HIM

The Ojibway Indians bury their dead on platforms. Here is seen a dead Ojibway chief laid upon his high couch. At his head is his ceremonial head-dress. Disposed about the scaffolding of the platform are the dead man's snow-shoes, cooking utensils, and other gear that he used in life, while at the base of the platform gather the mourners.

In Dutch New Guinea it is customary to dispose of the dead at dawn. Sometimes a body placed in a canoe is buried; sometimes it is elevated on supports. Coffins made of pieces of old canoes may still be seen in a grove, supported on trestles of crossed sticks, about four feet from the ground. When the body decays the skull is taken out to be preserved. On Rossel Island chiefs alone are honoured with tree or platform burials. Women wail and mutilate themselves during the mourning ceremonies. In the Solomons one of the customs is to deposit a wrapped body in a canoe, which is elevated on 'forked sticks.' The body is left for about a year, and then the skull is removed and placed in the figure of a sword-fish or bonito. Lofty platforms are also known in localities, but usually only the bodies of chiefs and other important men are deposited upon them, the bodies of commoners being thrown into the sea. Distant Easter Island had a cultural connexion with the Solomons, and there a disposal custom was to elevate a wrapped corpse on four forked stakes for about three years, after which the bones were removed.

A pathetic account of a ceremony connected with the skull of a child is given by Professor G. Landtman. The maternal uncle approaches the bereaved parents, carrying the skull on a mat and rocking it gently to and fro while he murmurs in pidgin English, 'You been stop here two three week for me fellow (us); me been make dance for you; me sorry (feel grief for you); you spirit now; you go place belong you . . . straight along that line (the coast-line in a westerly direction); place belong you other end; that's Adiri there.'

Pope's lines about the 'poor Indian's' idea of the future state:

> He thinks, admitted to that equal sky,
> His faithful dog will bear him company—

are recalled by the custom in this area of providing platforms for those old dogs which had proved themselves 'exceptionally fierce in fighting pigs.' The natives fear, however, that, if they were thrown into the sea, these canine veterans of the hunt might be transformed into dangerous shark-like monsters.

Francis Birtles

MOUNTING GUARD OVER HIS SON'S GRAVE

Although the natives of Arnhem Land, North Australia, practise tree burial, this is not the only means they use of disposing of their dead. Sometimes they build graves on low platforms, like that here seen. These they make of earth, stones, brushwood, logs, and branches, closely compacted, and strong enough to resist the attacks of animal marauders.

J. Hornell

PLATFORM GRAVE IN A SACRED GROVE BESTREWN WITH DEAD MEN'S BONES

In some of the islands of Polynesia very high burial platforms are met with, the rule in these cases being—the higher the platform the more exalted the rank of the departed. In the Marquesas the platforms are of no great height. They are built of large stones, arranged in such a way as to present a flat top, and are grouped about the sacred place. Each platform accommodates several bodies. The photograph shows one of these Marquesan stone platforms with its freight of skulls and bones in the Houmi valley, Nukahiva.

In Polynesia elevated platforms were used in those areas in which the bodies of chiefs and aristocrats were dried and embalmed, the mummy being afterwards placed in a canoe or cave, or suspended from the rafters of a dwelling house. In Samoa one of the customs was to expose a body on an elevated platform in a forest until it decayed. Then the bones were removed and buried secretly.

An interesting aspect of platform burials in the Melanesian island groups of New Ireland and New Hanover was the custom of elevating the platform on poles in accordance with the rank of deceased. The highest platforms were erected for those of highest rank. In Seran, Dutch East Indies, the bodies of chiefs and priests were given platform burial, the heads being subsequently removed to be deposited in a stone coffin. An old custom in the interior of Burma and in some parts of Assam was to place the bodies of commoners on elevated platforms of wood and those of chiefs and priests on platforms of stone. In eastern Madagascar one of the fashions was to place coffins on a platform 'in the midst of a palisade roofed over with leaves.' The disposal of the dead on platforms inside houses has been reported as one of the East African customs. A record from the Kasempa district of Northern Rhodesia deals with the disposal of the body of a chief. It is placed in a 'chitala'—a kind of coffin raised on piles, well off the ground, within the hut of the deceased.

Various theories have been advanced to explain the platform burial. One is that it was simply a form of tree burial; another is that it had origin in the custom of mummification, the bier, or bed, on which the corpse was embalmed being the prototype of the platform. A third view is that the act of placing the wrapped body on a stage supported by Y-shaped stakes was a ceremonial raising of the deceased to the 'sky world,' the platform being representative of the sky and the forked stakes of its supporting pillars. The elevating of canoes would thus suggest the provision for the ghost of the 'ghost of a vessel' in which to cross the Sea of Death, or sail along 'the waters above the firmament,' whence, as was believed, comes the rain and even the rivers. The preservation of skulls may have been connected with the widespread belief that the soul was in the head. In various localities the platform custom was mixed with other fashions of disposing of the dead in the interests of the soul's welfare.

E.N.A.

VESTIGE OF THE ANCIENT FEASTS OF THE DEAD: A BRETON PARDON

The Pardons of Brittany take place annually on saints' days at various churches and shrines. They are regarded as relics of the ancient feasts of the dead. Some attract the faithful from far and near; in others the appeal is local. The peasants make an elaborate toilet for these occasions, and some wonderful costumes and headgear are to be seen. One of the most notable Pardons is that of S. Anne d'Auray. The photograph shows the procession leaving the church of S. Anne, outside Auray, with the image of the patron borne on men's shoulders.

BRITTANY'S PICTURESQUE 'PARDONS'

PILGRIMAGES, processions and other ceremonies are performed in honour of the saints or with a view to invoking their aid in almost every quarter of the globe, but the particular variety of local pilgrimage known as the ' Pardon ' is peculiar to Brittany. Other such observances are discussed in chapters on Pilgrims and Pilgrimages, Ceremonies of Saints' Days, Holy Week and others.

IN no part of Europe are people so solemnly and superstitiously attached to ancient religious rites and customs as they are in Brittany. The Bretons do not merely practise religion ; they believe in it. They suppose that saints can cure illness ; they think that miracles still happen ; they will tell you that men and women long since dead may be met with still walking the earth. It is sometimes suggested that nowadays they keep up their Pardons (pilgrimages) rather as holidays, as occasions for making an excursion and drinking more than usual, than as religious exercises. This may be true of a minority, but one has only to attend some of these Pardons to be convinced that the mass of those who take part in them are genuinely hopeful of spiritual advantage. A Breton author has written that ' they are not pretexts for feasting, like the Flemish *kermesses* in Belgium, neither are they revels like the Paris *foires* (fairs). Their attraction comes from a higher source. They are the last lingering relics of the ancient Feasts of the Dead. There is little laughter at them, there is much prayer.'

For over two hundred years these processions and ceremonies have been unchanged. Everything is regulated by tradition. The local costumes that are worn are those of the seventeenth century. No innovation is ever proposed. If any were, it would be rejected with indignation. For the Pardon has formed so prominent and so picturesque a feature in the life of the peasants and fisherfolk that they are jealous of any alteration in even the smallest detail. From their childhood they have been present at them year after year. They look forward to the summer day when they will meet their friends and sit through the familiar services and enjoy the amusements hallowed by custom, and perhaps win some favour from the saint in whose honour the pilgrims assemble. Most of them have hard lives ; the Pardons shine out from the grey monotony of the rest of the year.

AMONG the most celebrated of the Pardons in the north of Brittany are those of Guingamp and Morlaix, known as the Pardons of Fire. Though they are connected by medieval tradition with a confused and foolish legend of a half-wit who stole a finger of Saint John, preserved as a wonder-working relic, and presented it to his parish church, the lighting of fires is clearly a survival of some ancient Festival of the Sun. The legend explains it by telling how, when the holy finger was placed on the altar, the candles blazed suddenly, lit by an unseen hand. But that is evidently an effort to give a Christian significance to an observance of pagan origin. The fires are lit on the Eve of S. John (June 23) in the market-place of Guingamp at night and on a hill nearer Morlaix about five o'clock in the afternoon.

THE former is by far the finer spectacle. During the day three heaps of dry gorse and bracken are built up in the market-place, forming the points of a triangle. Towards these at nightfall vast numbers of people make their way through the dark, narrow streets. Each parish sends a procession with priests and banners and statues and relic cases. Each procession sings as it passes on its way among the crowds of onlookers, all good Catholics among them carrying lighted candles. These must be lit by a priest standing at the high altar in the church, which is decorated with flowers and illuminated inside and out with little coloured lamps. The church is dedicated to Our Lady of Good Help. Locally she is known as ' Madame Marie de Bon Secours,' and an image of her in a dress of embroidered satin and a crown that sparkles with precious stones is the most prominent object in the procession to the market-place. Arrived there, the image is taken to one of the heaps of fuel, to which a priest puts a light. This is an anxious moment, for if the gorse does not flare at once, that is regarded as a sign of misfortune. Very seldom, however, does that happen. Great care is taken to ensure good luck by seeing that the fuel is dry ! Then the other piles, known as the Tantads (fire-heaps), are set fire to, and all blaze up briskly, throwing a red glare on the crowd and the old roofs and house-fronts, while the jubilant song of triumph rises from the faithful.

The other celebration takes place near the church and little town of Saint-Jean-de-Doigt (Saint-John-of-the-Finger), some ten miles from Morlaix and close to Plougaznou, on the sea. To this out-of-the-way place come hundreds of pilgrims, who are catered for by innkeepers from the towns with the aid of cooking-stoves built up with stones from the beach ; on these they cook sausages, turn pancakes, make pasties, roast potatoes, and boil water for coffee. Before the sun has got low the processions arrive with their immense banners, one especially heavy which only the strongest of men can carry. Bearers of it have been killed by the bursting of blood vessels. There is keen competition among the younger men for the distinction of bearing it. They practise for months beforehand every Sunday with a long pole that equals the banner's weight. The one who secures the coveted honour is watched very carefully on the great day, and severely censured if he does not acquit himself well.

E.N.A

PILGRIMS TAKING THEIR EASE BEFORE THE RIGOURS OF THE PARDON

A day or even two days before the actual date of the Pardon of S. Anne d'Auray pilgrims begin to arrive in great numbers in order to have time to gain the indulgences that are then granted. These early comers bring their food and cooking utensils with them and camp out in the fields and under the trees near the famous shrine. On such occasions the peasants wear their traditional costumes, and the scene presented is picturesque in the extreme.

Up the hill go the processions, up go the pilgrims from other parts, up go the blind folk, who come in large numbers, hoping to receive their sight when the fire is lit, up go the beggars, who gather for all the Pardons, exhibiting their sores and deformities and sometimes demanding charity as 'the right of the poor.' On the summit is a huge pile of gorse to which each parish has made its contribution and which has been decorated with flowers, ribbons and wreaths the evening before. From the top of this stack to the top of the church steeple runs a rope, a survival (now without purpose) from the time when an angel was sent along it to light the fire, just as the dove is sent from the High Altar in Florence carrying the flame for the 'scoppio del carro' (as described in pages 75 and 77). Now the ignition is done by a rocket which is called the Dragon, the last of a display of fireworks always given as a preliminary excitement.

As the stack catches, the cry goes up 'An Tan! An Tan!' (The Fire! The Fire!). It is the immemorial cry of pagan worshippers, heard in the dim twilight of European humanity, still cherished and repeated at this supposedly Christian celebration.

There is a fire lighted also at the Pardon of Saint Nicodemus on the first Saturday of August not far from Pontivy, which is forty-five miles south of Guingamp, and once was evidently another centre of fire worship. But the most attractive feature here is that animals are brought in from all the districts round to be blessed with elaborate ceremony. It is known, indeed, as the Pardon des Bêtes, which are far more interesting and familiar to the pilgrims than Saint Nicodemus. Saint Cornély, the patron of all horned animals, who shares with the other the honours of the occasion, is much more the man for their money. He presides over similar Pardons at Carnac, St. Herbot and Chapelle-des-Marais. At Toulpoen there is a pretty Birds' Pardon. It must be more difficult to collect starlings and thrushes and blackbirds, wrens and finches, tits and jays, than it is to drive in the farm animals which are to receive Saint Cornély's benediction. These fill the fields for some distance around the chapel where the festival Mass is said. The lowing of cows, the bleating of sheep and goats, mix with the neighing of farm horses and the grunting and squeaking of big and little pigs. After Mass a procession comes out of the chapel, headed by the beadle and two drummers. The two saints are impersonated. Priests carry the consecrated wafer and other holy objects. Gold and silver-

Donald McLeish

I CLIMAX OF THE PARDON: BENEDICTION FROM THE STEPS OF THE CHURCH

The supreme moment of the Pardon of S. Anne d'Auray has arrived. **Benediction is to be given on the steps of the pilgrimage church.** Supported by all his attendant clergy and servers, the priest stands in the porch carrying the Host under the canopy. With a noble gesture he raises high the monstrance, and with it makes the sign of the cross before the throng of pilgrims assembled outside the building. The Pardon, which is to mean so much to all the faithful who have attended it, is finished.

Donald McLeish

PILGRIMS MOUNTING THE SACRED STAIRS TO GAIN INDULGENCE

It is possible to gain indulgences at the Pardon of S. Anne d'Auray by mounting the Scala Sancta, or Sacred Stairs, that lead to the open-air platform from which Mass is sung. The pilgrims have to go up the stairs on their knees, and for every step thus laboriously ascended an indulgence is granted. Naturally the mounting of the Scala Sancta is a lengthy proceeding, and the stairs are always crowded not only on the actual day of the Pardon but also a day or two before.

threaded banners glitter in the golden air. The flames of great candles flicker wanly in the sunlight.

When the animals have all been blessed, the fire is lit by means of three circles of crackers ; these are set off by an angel provided with a taper which comes along a rope from the chapel, as once used to happen at Saint-Jean-du-Doigt. These circles are of very ancient origin ; they are known to have been used by sun-worshippers in other parts of Europe (Swabia, for instance). They must have been in use long before the angel was thought of. And no doubt the pagans who used them made the occasion one for drinking cider, as the Bretons of to-day do in simple tents like tunnels of tree-boughs covered with sheets. At rough tables running the whole length of these sit the cider-drinkers. Many of them are in exquisite costumes made long ago and carefully preserved for holiday wear. The women wear hoods, white for the younger ones, black lined with scarlet for the wrinkled and old. The men in local dress mostly have on white cloth jackets, edged with black velvet and embroidered in orange or blue.

South of Morlaix, east of Pontivy, lies Locronan on the road between Quimper and Brest. Here lived Saint Ronan, the Hermit of the Mountains, and here every seven years is held a Pardon—the Pardon of the Mountain. The pilgrims follow a path said to have been used by the saint; it runs through the four parishes that were sanctuaries affording safe refuge when there stood in the centre of them a monastery enjoying privileges and dispensing protection. This belt of security was called 'Minihy.' Another name for this Pardon of Locronan is the 'Tromenia,' originally Tro-minihy, the Town of the Refuge. Beginning on the second Sunday in July, it lasts for some days and is attended still by large numbers of people, although the out-of-the-way spot where it takes place is not easy to get at. As the pilgrims go up the mountain they pass numbers of huts containing small shrines of saints. The pious ones stop at each, say a prayer before the little figure on a rough altar, and put some coins into the contribution plate under the eye of a careful watcher. Another attendant on the shrine sings in praise of the saint and exhibits relics to anyone simple enough to believe in their efficacy. This is the commercial side of the pilgrimage. There is not much drinking or junketing. The pilgrims must keep silence—that, at any rate, is what tradition enjoins upon them.

E.N.A.

A DRAUGHT OF THE WONDER-WORKING WATERS

Throughout Brittany there is a strong belief in the beneficial powers of the various springs named after saints. Specially notable in this respect is the fountain of S. Anne d'Auray, which is regarded as sovereign against present and future ills, and the drinking of its waters is an important feature of the Pardon. The little girl here seen is drinking at the sacred spring.

Most of them obey it as they go up to the strange stone, shaped like some monster of the early world, which is supposed by them now to be the body of Saint Ronan and the cart on which it lay, both turned into granite. It is considered certain that this stone must have been the object of heathen worship long before Christianity. It may have been a symbol of fruitfulness, for childless women used to sleep on it three nights running in the hope of curing their sterility, and young wives came from far distant places to rub themselves against it. These beliefs are not yet dead in the Breton mind. To many—men as well as women—they are as firmly held as those which take them, after they have visited the sacred stone, to the

E.N.A.

BEGGARS' BENCH' AT THE FOOT OF A CALVARY

A Pardon is usually a rich harvest time for the beggars, who in many parts demand charity as their right. The photograph shows beggars at Landernau, in Finistère, on the day of the Pardon, entrenched at the foot of the Calvary outside the church of S. Eloy. Everyone entering the church, unless he or she would have bad luck, must give alms.

W. F. Taylo.

WITH THEIR BANNERS PROUDLY FLYING THE BRETON PEASANTS MARCH

The peasants of Brittany are as devoted to their religion and their religious customs as they are to their traditional costumes. To carry one of the richly wrought banners or to help in carrying the image of the patron saint is to them a coveted distinction. Here is seen a Pardon procession at La Forêt, near Concarneau. Down the middle of the street walk the men, bearing crucifixes, banners, and the figure of the saint, while on either side are the women and girls, also with banners.

church in the little town that bears Saint Ronan's name. Here there are long services.

Then with the usual banners and the usual priestly robes, with images and relics as elsewhere, The Tour of the Refuge begins. Along the roads, through the lanes, over the meadows, on paths across marshland, the pardoners tramp in the hot sunshine till they come to another shrine of Saint Ronan on high ground overlooking Douarnenez Bay. From an open-air pulpit a sermon is preached to the weary folk who sit on the grass all round. Then they make their way back to Locronan in the cool freshness of the early summer night.

Now we travel west till we have passed Quimper and Lorient and come nearly to Vannes. We will stop at Auray, where are the chapel and the sacred fountain of Saint Anne, commemorating an appearance made by her to a poor peasant. This pilgrimage still draws a very large number of people from the district known as Morbihan, and from farther afield as well. They are drawn partly by the grant of 'indulgences' for visiting the chapel and for going up the Scala Sancta (Sacred Stairs) barefooted and with many stops for prayer. The steps are crowded on July 24, the day of the Pardon; there are many on them the day previous and even two days before. Those who come early camp out under trees, in the fields, lighting fires and sitting round them after dark.

Seeing these costumes of the past, the long-haired men, the rosaries passing through horny fingers, these cudgels called 'penn-baz,' these rugged faces in the firelight, one could imagine oneself back in the middle ages, watching a bivouac of peasants, driven from their hamlets by the tide of war or gathering in some lonely spot to plot revolt against their feudal lords. Passing among them, one comes more completely under this illusion. They are not talking on the subjects which are usually talked about. You hear nothing of politics, or industry, or local affairs. You may hear thanks given to God for a good harvest of grain or abundance of apples on the trees, but most frequently you will be listening to voices which relate miracles or re-tell old legends of the faith.

The 'penn-baz' it should be said, was a formidable club of oak or holly which the peasants wore fastened to the wrists by leathern thongs. Not very long ago these were used every year at the Pardon of Saint Servais or Gelvest (whose business it is to protect the growing crops). There used to be a free fight in the church between bands of desperadoes from Vannes and from the district farther west which is known as Cornouailles. It was a regular part of

E.N.A.

'PARDON OF THE BEASTS': BLESSING THE ANIMALS AT CARNAC

According to the legend, S. Cornély was saved from enemy soldiers by cattle, and so out of gratitude for his delivery he became the patron saint of horned animals. The most prominent feature of the pardons with which he is associated is the blessing of his protégés, farm animals being brought from miles round for this purpose. The photograph shows cattle and horses being blessed at the church door at Carnac. High above the porch the saint in effigy stretches forth his hands in blessing over pictured cattle.

the celebration. It had to be stopped by the authorities, civil and ecclesiastical combined, so many heads were broken, so many arms and legs fractured. But the older folk say that their crops have never been the same since! The saint is displeased because the 'penn-baz' no longer cracks skulls in his honour, and he does not take as much care of the young corn as he once did!

On the day of the Pardon of S. Anne d'Auray, after buying candles and souvenirs and the little favours of red and blue worsted which are worn in hats as token of having made pilgrimages, the pilgrims go to the fountain, where they hope, by drinking or washing with the water, to be cured of present ills or saved from future misfortunes. The belief in the healing powers of the springs named after saints is strangely persistent. Stories are told, wherever peasants gather, of miraculous cures. Bites by mad dogs are healed by one saint, boils by another; if you buy a little muslin bag of earth from the tomb of Saint Govéry and tie it round the neck of anyone suffering from fever, recovery will be rapid. As for Saint Yves of Kermartin, he will cure anything or put right any piece of injustice. He was a lawyer, according to tradition—the only lawyer ever canonised; he still sits in the seat of a judge, according to popular belief, giving to the poor their rights and spurning bribes from the guilty rich.

From S. Anne's fountain the pilgrims go to her chapel for Mass, which is sung at an open-air altar on a platform at the top of the sacred stairs. As

E.N.A.

WHEN THE WOMEN BRING OUT THEIR MOST TREASURED ATTIRE

The Pardons of Finistère are noted for the magnificent costumes worn, particularly by the women who carry the saint's image or the banner. Only once in the year do these gorgeous silk gowns trimmed with rich lace, these elaborate scarves and heavily brocaded aprons come out —for the day of the Pardon. During the rest of the year they remain in jealously guarded presses. The upper photograph shows the statue of the saint being carried by the women of Juch, and in the lower is seen a Pardon procession at Plouneour-Trez.

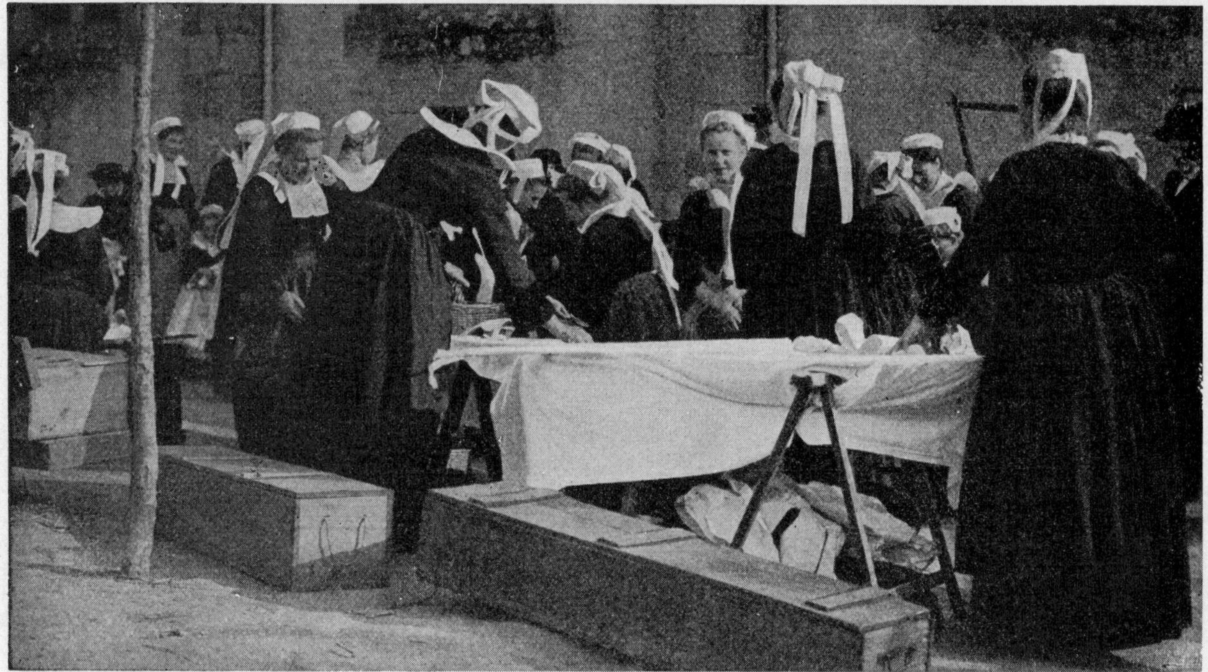

Humphrey Joel

FAIR AND FEASTING FOR THE PARDONERS

Although the Pardons are by no means pretexts for feasting, yet food and drink have to be supplied. Pilgrims from afar who have brought no provisions with them will need refreshment, as well as those living in the district who do not wish to waste time by going home to their meals. Ample provision is therefore made for open-air eating and drinking. Women of Benodet, in their spotless white caps, are here seen busy laying the refreshment tables that will be besieged as soon as Mass is over. With some of the Pardons fairs and side shows are associated.

many as 20,000 people can be collected within hearing distance, and often there have been almost as many as that. Then all walk in procession round the chapel. Those who have been saved from danger by the saint bring emblems of their peril. Here a man who escaped from a shipwreck carries the model of a ship, there a woman who almost died of fever holds up a model coffin. People who were crippled and have recovered the use of their legs have their crutches over their shoulders, those whose houses have been burned bring the rope or the ladder which enabled them to escape from the flames. All their good fortune they attribute to Saint Anne. She has another well-attended Pardon at La Palude, near Douarnenez, on the last Sunday of August. This for a curious reason attracts an unusually large concourse of beggars, 'an abusive and repulsive horde.' The reason is that ages ago beggars were called the Kings of La Palude—on Saturdays only. Now they pester everybody on the day before the Pardon, which is a Saturday, but they must not be seen on the Sunday. All must have cleared off before the Pardon begins.

Many pilgrims come in advance and sleep in tents or under the sky ; many come from Douarnenez by road and return at night ; many take the 'pilgrim path' through the woods at first, then over the smooth, hard sand of the sea shore, then across dreary moorland baked by the fierce autumn sun. The splendid costumes of Finisterre are seen here to the greatest advantage. For example, the women who carry Saint Anne's statue and her banner wear cherry-coloured silk gowns, with trimming of gold lace, silver lace scarves, and aprons of gold tissue or rich silk brocade. Every family preserves its gown in a press that is opened only once a year for the Sunday of Saint Anne. It is worn by the eldest daughter or daughter-in-law. The sight of these women in their magnificent dresses moving majestically through the glittering scene to the chanting of litanies and the muffled beat of drums is something that can never be forgotten.

LESS gorgeous as a spectacle but amusing and in its way unique is the Pardon of Pont-Aven, in Lower Brittany. This takes place in the middle of September and is famous for its wrestling and dancing competitions. These begin as soon as Mass is over. What each wrestler tries to do is to get a firm hold of his adversary's thick shirt and lift him by it so as to throw him to the ground. Both shoulders must touch before the thrown man can be counted out. In the dancing there is less excitement and no picturesqueness, though it is certainly curious to watch. Men and women form up in lines and very solemnly, without a smile or any expression of enjoyment, they jig and jog about to the music of discordant bagpipes.

To lovers of children one of the most charming of the Pardons is that of Les Bébés at St. Léger, a little place not far from Pont-Aven. In a wood there is a well, and to this in the month of June hundreds of babies and tiny children are brought by their parents to be bathed in the holy waters and so preserved from sickness and accident all through the year to come.

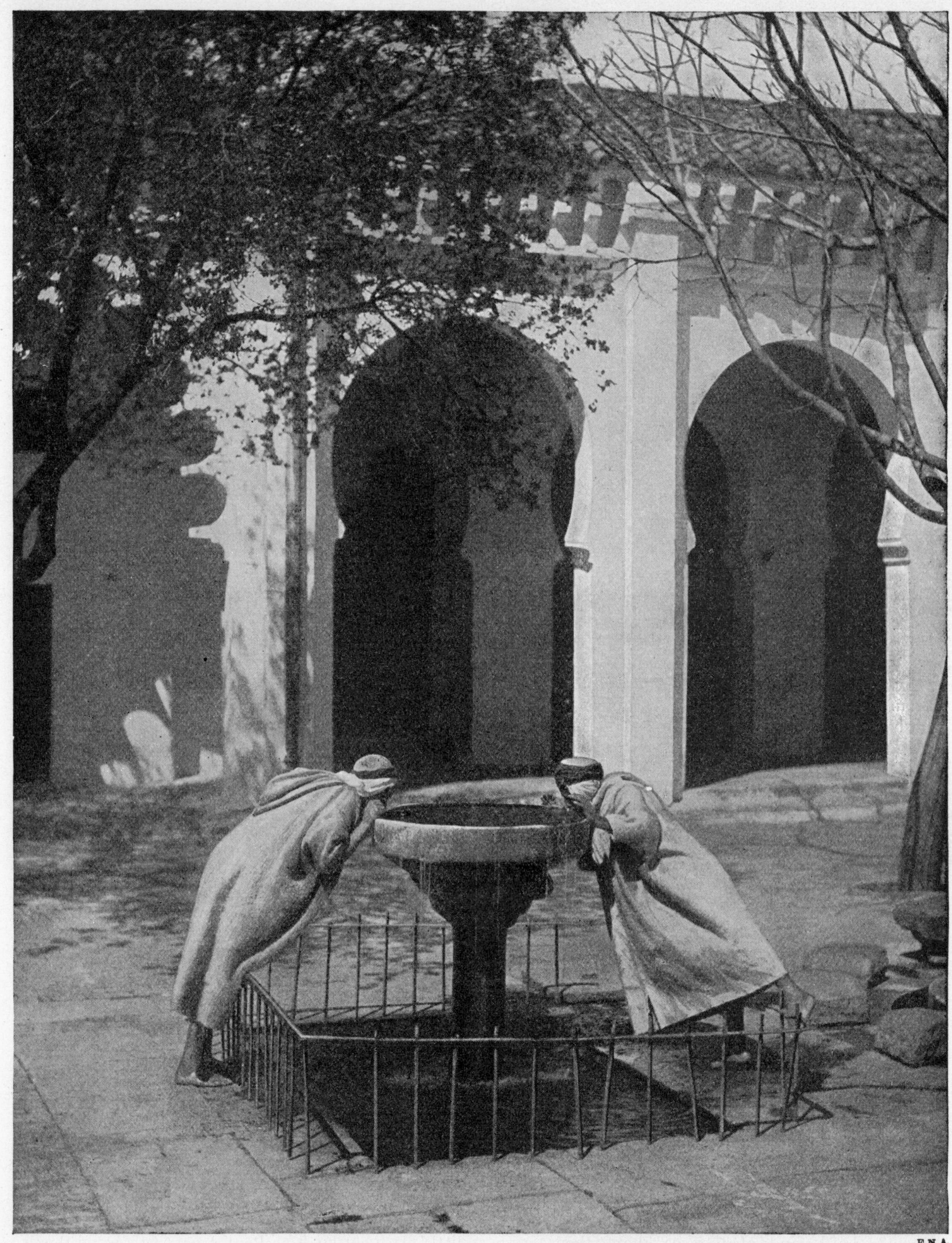

E.N.A.

MAKING THEMSELVES PURE IN READINESS FOR PRAYER

Islam is a highly organized religion, and its worship and ritual are governed by precise rules. When a Mahomedan must recite the creed, how often he must pray—these and other such matters are minutely prescribed. Before he prays he has first to make himself legally pure by performing what is called the lesser ablution. This consists in washing the face, the forearms, and the feet. Only after 'legal pollution' is complete washing of the body enjoined The photograph shows Arabs of Algeria performing their ablutions in the courtyard of a mosque.

PRAYER AND ITS MANY FORMS

A GENERAL description is given here of the devotional acts observed by many non-Christian religions, from the community prayers of Buddhists and Mahomedans to merely mechanical devotions. No criticism of the act of prayer in any of its forms is to be implied, for the Lama with his whirling prayer-wheel may be no less sincere in his devotions than the members of a European fashionable congregation.

THE act of prayer in all religions forms the most crucial moment of faith. The spectator who has seen the devotees of Islam at mass prayer in mosque or in the open may be intensely antagonistic to the tenets of that religion, yet he will be impressed by the act of devotion and sympathetic to the solemnity of the worshippers. That is perhaps the most inspiring form which prayer takes in any non-Christian religion, and is excelled only by the noble conception of reverence presented annually on Armistice Day by the whole of the British Empire, irrespective of their religions, in the 'two minutes' silence.'

It would seem that in passing through the jungle of conjectures to the light of truth, man has carried with him the burrs, not easily to be shaken off, of many curious conceptions. It has been truly said that he who never prays or goes to church, or uses the name of his Maker except in conjunction with an oath, and yet keeps in his waistcoat pocket a lucky sixpence is, in essence, religious. 'He has but exchanged belief in the Living God for belief in the omniscience and almightiness of a coin.' That the worship of the dead influenced the mind of man, and is still to be found among primitive races, cannot be denied. Even in England, today, this survives in many curious forms. Luck has come to be associated with the dead, who are supposed to have a beneficent or evil effect upon the fortunes of the living.

Not long ago it was recorded in the Press that after a motor bus had collided with a tree, as a result of which many of the passengers were killed, the crowd, immediately attracted to the spot, stripped off pieces of the bark to preserve as charms. Our official hangmen are still pestered for sections of the rope which has sent a murderer to his account. Among the sailors of the Orkney and Shetland Islands it was deemed unlucky, till recently, to rescue a man from drowning, since the sea was entitled to certain victims and, if disappointed, would avenge itself on those who interfered. This idea of the ever-watchful presence of the dead, ready to take offence at human actions, has a remarkable illustration in the customs prevailing in the Solomon Islands. Here, if a man falls into a river and is attacked by a shark, he is not allowed to escape but, should he gain the shore, is flung back again to propitiate the unseen powers. In both these last-mentioned customs we can trace the evolution of the worship of the dead to a conception of some power associated with the particular spot where the accident took place.

THE development of prayer as an aid to worship has inevitably followed the same road as man has pursued in his search for God. The question whether the muttering of a magic spell preceded prayer or the reverse can probably be answered in the same way; namely, that man in the process of discovering the proper use of prayer to the Divine Father brought with him from his remote past many 'survivals' of cults long forgotten.

When man simply worshipped the dead, his god or gods were even such as he—equal, not superior. The consequence was that the god was sometimes treated with extraordinary familiarity in the prayers of his worshippers. Among the Egyptians, where the worship of the dead survived in an exaggerated form, the bullying manner of the faithful towards their god excited the wonder of classical antiquity. The Zulu says to his ancestral ghost, 'Help me, or you will feed on nettles'; the primitive Australian exclaims to the 'dead hand' that he carries about with him as a sort of divining rod, 'Guide me aright, or I will throw you to the dogs!' To this day in remote

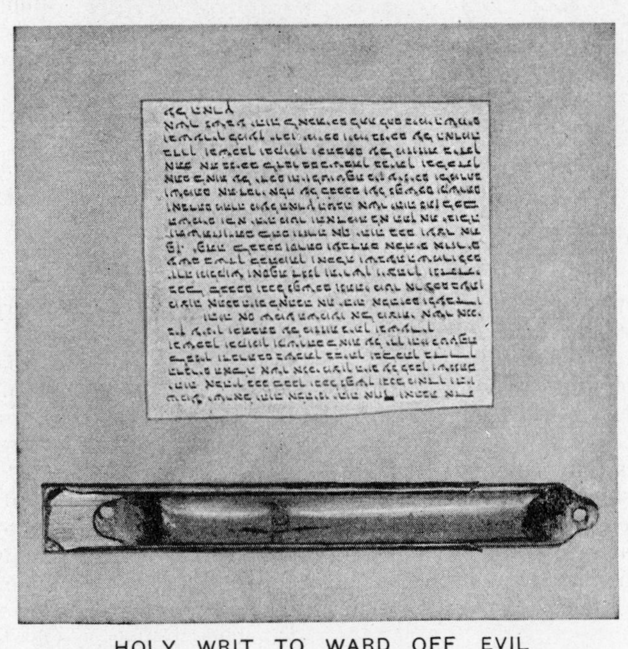

HOLY WRIT TO WARD OFF EVIL

The wearing of prayers and other holy writings as amulets is not uncommon. Mahomedans carry extracts from the Koran. Apart from their phylacteries, orthodox Jews fix on the doorpost of their dwelling rooms tubes containing the text of passages of Scripture. Such a case with its contents, from a London house, is seen here.

Keystone

ISLAM AMONG THE INFIDELS : THE MUEZZIN AT WOKING

The muezzin, so picturesque a figure in Mahomedan countries, loses something of his glamour when divorced from his characteristic setting. At Woking this official, while performing his religious functions, merely exchanges his hat for a turban and puts on a voluminous robe over his everyday clothes. He is here seen calling the faithful to prayer on the occasion of a festival.

districts in Italy men and woman adopt an attitude which can only be called hectoring towards a saint whom they regard as being backward in providing them with the blessings they desire ; and the Indian hedge-priest uses much the same tone.

THIS 'bargaining note' is common to all forms of prayer where the worshipper places the object of his adoration on the same level as himself—or almost on the same level. The curious rite of 'killing the Sacred Bear' described in our chapter on Magic and the Means of Life affords an excellent illustration of this.

Such prayers to the bear, who is deified, appear not only all along the northern region of the Old World from Behring Straits to Lapland, but are common to the American Indians. Prayers are always part of the ceremony. Whales are treated much in the same way in north-eastern Siberia and among the inhabitants of the isle of St. Mary to the north of Madagascar. In the latter instance the natives, having singled out the young whales for attack, offer a humble prayer to the mothers beseeching their pardon, stating the necessity which drives them to kill their progeny, and requesting that the mothers will be pleased to go below while the deed is doing, so that their maternal feelings may not be outraged by witnessing what must cause them so much uneasiness. In West Africa the natives, after killing a female hippopotamus, first disembowel it, then stepping naked into the hollow of the ribs, pray to the soul of the dead animal not to bear them a grudge for having killed her and so blighted her hopes of future maternity ; and they further entreat the ghost not to stir up other hippopotamuses to avenge her death by biting at and capsizing their canoes.

This propitiation of wild animals by hunters would appear to be universal among primitive peoples. The bargaining prayer appears again among those inhabitants of the earth who still believe that the beneficent functions of nature can be made to operate by invocations of a higher power. In Africa one of the chief attributes of the witch doctor is that of rainmaker. In almost every instance he is necessarily the king or the chief. Chaka, the famous Zulu despot, used to declare that he was the only diviner in the country, for if he allowed rivals his life would be insecure. In times of drought, prayers would be made to the king. Another form of bargaining prayer is for success in battle. In the island of Timor, in the Malay Archipelago, the high priest remains praying in the temple while war is being waged. In the Kei Islands, when the warriors have departed, the women anoint certain baskets containing fruits and stones. To these they offer up the following prayer: 'Oh lord sun, moon, let the bullets rebound from our husbands, brothers, betrothed, and other relations, just as raindrops rebound from these objects which are smeared with oil.'

Sport & General

Photopress

PRAYER ORDAINED IN THE HEART OF ARABIA PERFORMED IN AN ENGLISH TOWN

Like other parts of Mahomedan worship, the prostrations performed at certain intervals are carried out in accordance with strict rules. Some of the niceties of Mahomedan ritual may be seen at Woking, where the festivals are often attended by a sprinkling of unbelievers. The photographs show stages in the celebration of the festival of Eid-ul-Fitr. The worshippers, having removed their shoes, stand with hands raised during the progress of the prayers (top), and at another stage all prostrate themselves, their heads touching the ground (bottom).

B.N.A

SERRIED RANKS BOWED DOWN IN PRAYER DURING ISLAM'S GREAT FAST

The Mahomedan fast of Ramadan is very severe. It lasts for a month, and during each day neither food nor drink may be taken from sunrise to sunset. Ramadan was the month in which the Koran was revealed to the Prophet. Among the Berbers of North Africa the marabouts, reverenced as living saints, are strict observers of the fast. A company of these devotees are here seen in the second posture of their great prayer during the fast (top), and also in the third posture, of complete prostration (bottom).

It is where the worshipper regards the object of his adoration as his superior that we reach the Christian idea of prayer—a service of praise, supplication and thanksgiving. When considering the abnormal forms that praying takes among non-Christian races we must remember those herculean spiritual exercises in which our Puritans indulged. Did not Johnstone of Warriston remain on his knees in prayer from six o'clock in the morning till eight o'clock in the evening? The 'minutes' of the meeting of the Westminster Assembly of Divines in 1643 record that 'Mr. Marshall prayed large two hours most divinely. After, Mr. Arrowsmith preached one hour, then a psalm, thereafter Mr. Vine prayed near two hours and Mr. Palmer preached one hour, and Mr. Seaman prayed near two hours, then a psalm.'

To these heroes of extemporary prayer the mechanical device employed by the Lamaist Buddhists would seem a blasphemous mockery, and Europeans in general are inclined to smile when they hear about praying-wheels. This attitude is all very well for sects unhampered by a liturgy, but it must be remembered that there is a very considerable Buddhist liturgy, and that the disseminators of the faith were faced with a population who could neither read nor write. It was to meet this difficulty that the ingenious contrivance of the praying-wheel was first invented, however much it may have been turned to other uses since. The method by which the praying wheel is employed is as follows: Strips of paper bearing a manifold repetition of the words 'The Jewel in the Lotus, Amen,' are wrapped round cylinders of all sizes—from hand mills to wind or water mills. As the wheel revolves, these uncoil and the prayer is considered to be offered.

E.N.A.

MACHINE FOR ADORING THE BUDDHA

The praying-wheel used by the Buddhists of Tibet consists of a cylinder round which are wound strips of very thin paper inscribed with repetitions of the sacred mantra, 'Oh, the jewel in the lotus.' Each revolution of the cylinder counts as a prayer uttered.

E.N.A.

CALLING THE FAITHFUL TO PRAYER

The muezzin is the mosque official whose duty it is to proclaim the times of prayer. He is appointed by the imam of the mosque, and by virtue of his office is entitled to a place in Paradise. The call to prayer is sounded from the minaret.

THERE is a sense in which modern Jewry presents a curious parallel to the prayer-wheel, if we can compare a fixed device with one that revolves In the home of orthodox Jews throughout the world will be found little metal prayer-cases fixed to the lintels or the doorposts of the rooms. They are semi-tubular in form and contain a small piece of parchment or paper printed in Hebrew characters and rolled to fit inside the container. The printed matter is a copy of one of the most familiar of the daily prayers used by the Jews, and on the back of the roll is printed one of the names of God. Usually a slit is pierced in the metal cover to allow that name to show, or, as in the sample which illustrates this chapter, the name itself is embossed on the metal. The writer has seen exactly similar

G. P. Skrine

SINGING THEIR WAY FROM CENTRAL ASIA TO THE HOLY CITY OF MECCA

Some of the dervishes, such as the Senussi, are strict Mahomedans. Others adhere nominally to the Koran, but are tinged with Hindu pantheism and mysticism. Some live more or less like the Christian monastic orders; others are hermits. Perhaps the best-known of these religious devotees are the dancing dervishes, who worship by lacerating their bodies and swallowing glass and live coals. The holy men here seen, at Aksu, in Sinkiang, are singing dervishes. They travel all over Asia, making their devotions and supporting themselves by singing.

prayer-cases in the homes of rich English Jews and in the homes of the poorest inhabitants of Eastern and North African ghettos. The orthodox Jew salutes this case, or rather the name of God upon it, every time he goes in at the door.

In the four precepts of the Prophet which constitute the religious duties of a Mussulman—prayer, fasting, alms and the pilgrimage to Mecca—prayer comes first. According to the legend of Mahomet's mystical journey from Mecca to Jerusalem, the Deity commanded him to impose on his disciples a daily obligation of fifty prayers. On the advice of Moses, however, he applied for an alleviation of this intolerable burden, and the number was finally reduced to five. Every devout Mahomedan to-day, regardless of business, plea sure, time or place—at daybreak, at noon, in the afternoon, in the evening, and at the first watch of the night—turns his face to Mecca and makes his prayer to that supreme Being of whom Mahomet is the Prophet. According to the Koran, these prayers should be prefaced by the cleansing of the hands, the face and of the body, sand being allowed to be used for the purpose where no water is available. In his book, Savage Abyssinia, Mr. James E. Baum gives a description of this hour of prayer as it occurs in that semi-Christianised outpost of Africa:

> Gleaming on the hilltop, to the north-westward, the village of Sheikh Hussein stood, the six tombs of the Sheikhs glistening like alabaster in the light of the dying sun. It was the hour of Moslem prayer and the mullahs, as I sat on a rock overlooking the plains below, began the evening chant. The wind was from the right direction, and the Mohammedan prayer floated up from below, dim, faint, barely audible for the distance was four or five miles.
>
> 'Allah il Allah. Allah il Allah'—interminably.

When the devout Moslem makes his devotions in a mosque—though any spot, whether it be his sitting-room or the street, is as efficacious for prayer as the official church—he first removes his sandals, or whatever he is wearing on his feet. On entering the main body of the building he prostrates himself on a praying-rug. These rugs, as the pews used to be until recently in English churches, are the private property of the individual. The vast floor space of the mosque of Santa Sofia is completely covered

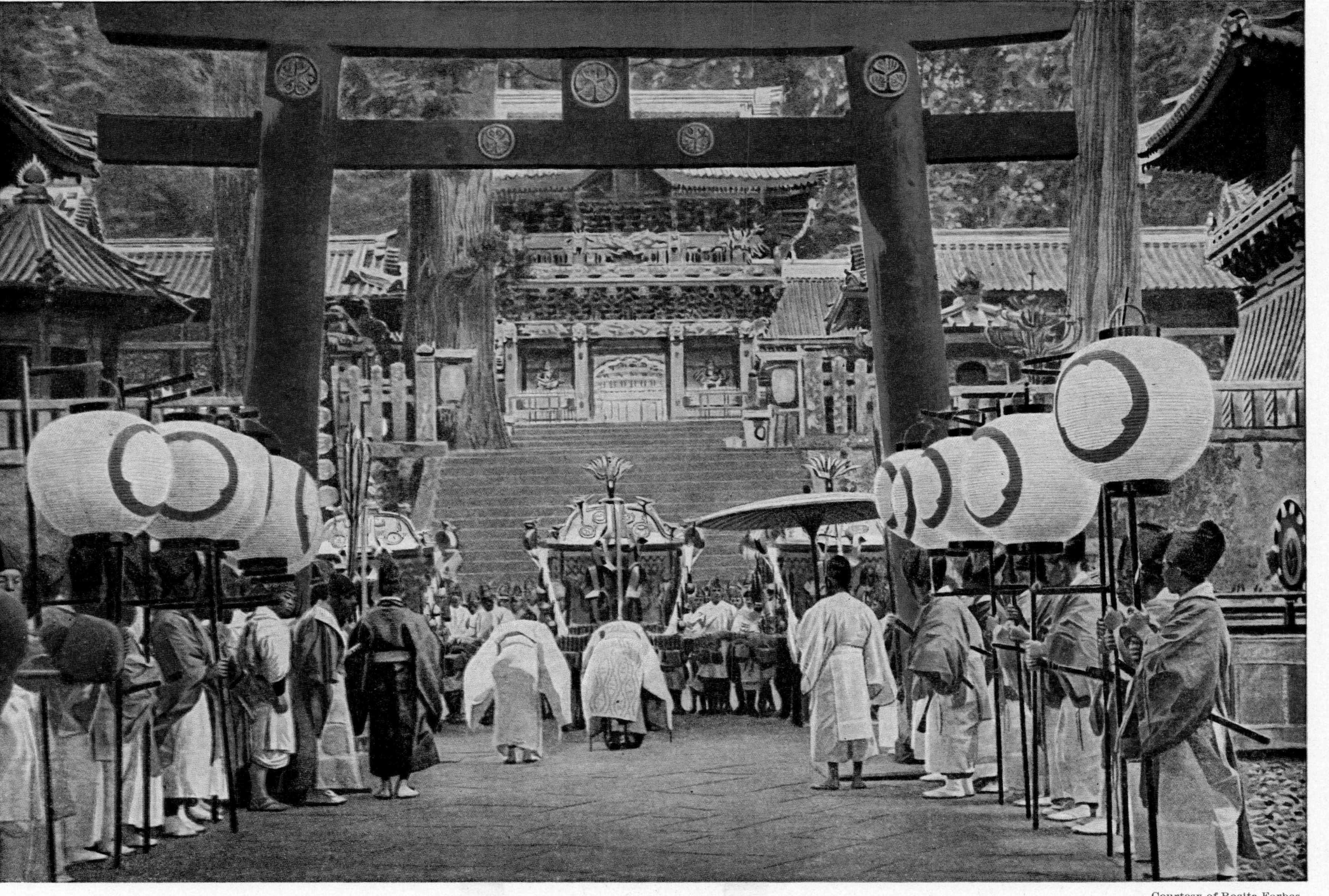

Courtesy of Rosita Forbes

PRAYING THROUGH THE MEDIUM OF DEIFIED MEN: SHINTO PROCESSION AT NIKKO

Shintoism is the national religion of Japan. Its Mecca is the great Ieyasu temple at Nikko, the 'Wonder of Unsleeping Eyes,' to which once a year pilgrims come from all parts of Japan. A mighty flight of steps leads to the gorgeously ornamented central building. The chief deity of Shintoism is the sun goddess, Amaterasu. There are no idols. The deity is invoked through the medium of countless inferior beings, of whom the majority are deified men. Gaily decorated litters, purporting to contain these intangible beings, are carried about from shrine to shrine. A litter, with its imaginary burden, is here seen on its arrival at the temple, accompanied by priests in conical hats carrying lanterns.

Mondiale

FLAGS THAT FLUTTER THE MESSAGES OF THE FAITHFUL TO HEAVEN

Not only is Tibet the home of the praying-wheel, the machine that sends up a prayer with every revolution. In and about the monasteries in that land of mystery and monasteries may be seen strings of flags fluttering in the breeze, and sometimes lofty poles flying flags along a part of the whole of their length. On each of these flags is inscribed a prayer, and it is thought that, as the wind stirs the flags, the prayers that are written on them are wafted up to Heaven.

E.N.A

TEMPLE-SIDE TREE WHOSE EVERY LEAF CARRIES A PRAYER

The vast majority of the Sinhalese, the dominant native stock of Ceylon, are Buddhists, but with their traditional Buddhism is mingled a good deal of spirit worship. In Ceylon, as in Tibet, the practice obtains of inscribing flags with prayers and then hanging them up so that the prayers may be floated to their destination. The photograph shows a structure in the form of a very symmetrical tree hung thickly with these prayer-flags; it stands by the side of a Buddhist temple on Slave Island, near Colombo.

with these rugs, which are largely manufactured in Persia, though they are also made in Constantinople. The praying-rug is carried by the devout Moslem. It is probable that the 'bed' described in our Lord's miracle which the man 'took up' was exactly similar to one of these praying-rugs.

There is a certain amount of controversy about the origin of these prayer-rugs. It is most likely that they were first made in Persia, which is to-day the great source of supply. The wools of Asia Minor, Persia, the Caucasus and Central Asia are naturally extremely well adapted to carpet knotting, which under the influence of Mongolian art evolved in the Middle East. The oldest known carpets, however—those at Konia in Asia Minor in the Mosque of Ala ed Din—appear to date from the erection of the mosque in the thirteenth century, and no Persian carpets of this date are known. On the other hand, Persian manuscripts of the fourteenth and fifteenth centuries in the British Museum illustrate carpets, and all the designs of the Asia Minor carpets are largely based on Persian originals. It is fairly safe to say, therefore, that the original prayer-rugs came from Persia. At the Exhibition of Persian Art held in London in

Photopress

Keystone

TWO WAYS OF PRAYER IN JAPAN—SILENT, AND WITH MUSIC

Very striking contrasts in the manner of praying are sometimes found existing almost side by side. The upper photograph shows boys and girls of the Musachino Youth Society, wearing white sweaters, bowed in silent prayer for the emperor Yoshihito's recovery from what proved to be his last illness. Below are seen devout members of the Nichiren sect of Buddhism praying for the same purpose. Standing almost naked in the surf at Nayama, near the Imperial villa, where the emperor lay dying, they make music lustily, beating these fan-shaped instruments.

E.N.A.

BUDDHIST PRIEST OF CAMBODIA SEATED IN THE CHAIR OF PRAYER

Though Brahminism is the religion of the Cambodian court, Buddhism is the dominant creed of the people. The bonzes, or Buddhist priests, have no money or possessions of their own. They live by alms alone, and in return teach the children to read and write. The dress of the bonzes of Cambodia consists of a long yellow robe, which is worn so as to leave the right shoulder bare. The photograph shows a bonze sitting cross-legged on the cushioned back of his grotesquely fashioned and elaborately carved prayer-chair.

1931 there were a number of beautiful specimens of these rugs clearly made for use of the Shi-ites—the famous Mahomedan sect.

Community prayers are of course a feature of non-Christian races as they are of our own, and in some instances, especially among certain sects in India, they are employed very much as Oliver Cromwell used them to excite the fervour of his troops. What we call nowadays 'mass suggestion' is brought into operation by prayers and rites among all the primitive races of the world. Here prayer treads upon the fringe of the magic spell, in the lower forms of religion being almost always associated with superstitious practices. It is employed among other aids to fanaticism derived from early paganism in the degrading rites of Siva and the Tantrism of Nepal.

One of the most picturesque illustrations of man's attempts to make contact through prayer with the Supreme Being is to be seen at the Buddhist Temple of Bodh-Nath—the largest and perhaps the oldest temple in Nepal, and the most venerated shrine of the Buddhist world outside Lhasa. Mr. A. E. Powell gives a vivid picture of the scene in his book, The Last Home of Mystery:

> Immense throngs of Tibetan pilgrims visit this ancient tope each year, the terrible journey over the main range of the Himalayas from Lhasa to Khatmandu taking fifty days. Squat men with yellow skins, slanting eyes, and flat noses, in fur caps, red quilted coats and high boots, long-haired, greasy and verminous, sometimes accompanied by their women-folk and children, usually followed by shaggy and ferocious dogs, they pour down from the northern passes by the tens of thousands, drums, gongs, and coach-horns sounding, to pitch their black tents on the plain beside the stupa, to say their simple prayers and make their simple offerings, to circumambulate the sacred spot, often on their bellies, twirling their prayer-wheels and chanting the interminable 'Om mani padme hum' (Oh, the jewel in the heart of the lotus, Amen) which is the shibboleth of their faith.

The universality of prayer is one of the most remarkable features of the human race. Christians and non-Christians alike, throughout the world, recognizing their own insufficiency, send up their petitions to a Higher Power for help and guidance. Behind the practice there must be the belief or the hope that the petitions will be answered. In view of this, one may question Tennyson's rather sententious remark that the world is backward in realizing all that 'may be wrought by prayer.'

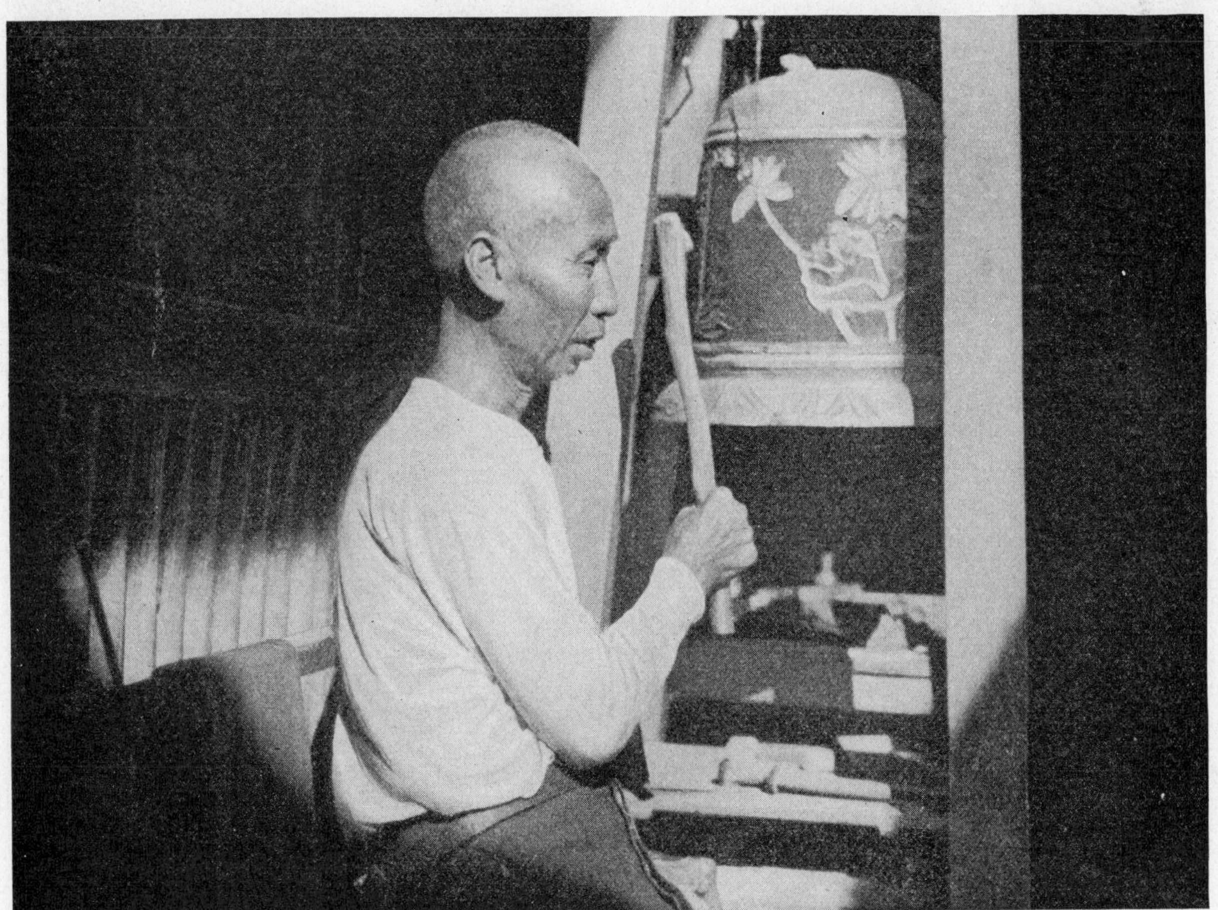

Francis Birtles

PRAYER WAFTED ON EVER-WIDENING WAVES OF SOUND

Music is an important feature of the temple services of the Chinese. Processions round the temple to the accompaniment of chants form a large part of the complicated ritual, the instrumental side of the music consisting in the beating of deep-voiced bells, gongs and drums. Most of the bells used in the temple worship of the Chinese are wonderfully resonant and mellow in tone and of exquisite workmanship. The bell here seen is in a Chinese joss-house.

Topical Press

DECORATING THE MASCOT OF THE IRISH GUARDS ON S. PATRICK'S DAY

The shamrock is a plant of many picturesque associations, among which the stories of S. Patrick plucking a leaf to illustrate the doctrine of the Trinity and of his adoption of it as the badge of Ireland are familiar. When on S. Patrick's Day sprigs of shamrock are presented to the Irish Guards, the distribution is general and all ranks participate. Nor is that important animal, the mascot of the regiment, omitted. The noble Irish wolfhound is always allotted its proper share and is decorated with due ceremony.

THE MASCOT OR LUCK-BRINGER

FROM earliest times man has endeavoured to control chance, and in this quest he has adopted some fantastic expedients. Further information on the methods that have been used for averting evil and inducing good can be gathered from the chapters on Outwitting the Forces of Evil, Superstitions of the Sea, Superstitions about Animals, Superstitions about Numbers, and Magic in Love and War.

OVER and over again scientific argument has demonstrated that there is no place for chance in the chain of causation ; and still mankind clings to a belief in luck. We may no longer sacrifice in the Temple of Fortune as our forefathers did in the time of the Romans, and the mascot on the car may be disclaimed as merely an ornament which follows the dictates of fashion ; but not many walk beneath a ladder without a qualm, and most of us prefer not to be the thirteenth at table. From the day when palaeolithic man first smeared red pigment on the bodies of his dead to ensure their vigour in a future life or painted the figure of a bison transfixed by a dart on the wall of his cave in the certain hope of a like result in his hunting, down to these days of lucky pigs and four-leaved clover, the belief has been held, sometimes more, sometimes less seriously, that inanimate objects may possess or become endowed with certain qualities which will ensure a happy event for the fortunate individuals with whom they are associated.

The belief that certain material objects have power to affect the future course of events appears to go back to the earliest times of which we have evidence. It is a legitimate inference that the shells found in association with human remains of palaeolithic age were placed there as luck-bringers. All the world over, and in all times of which we have any interpretable record, shells, and particularly the cowrie, are given a magical significance or put to uses with a magical connotation. Most frequently they are strung in necklaces, when they serve as a protective charm. They may be incorporated in woven material worn on the body or used to cover other objects, often of a ceremonial character. Cowries will be found inserted in the carved wooden figures of West Africa which often have a magical or religious import. There they must, obviously, represent a part of the female body. Instances of their use could be multiplied almost indefinitely ; but from what has been said it is evident that probability is in favour of the view that the people who lived in Western Europe, perhaps twenty thousand years ago, believed in the efficacy of the luck-bringer.

NOR is it any exaggeration to say that some form of the belief is found in every part of the world. It is peculiarly prevalent in West Africa and India, and it is almost universal among the Slav peoples. In the more highly developed communities of western civilization it is found among the peasantry as a living belief ; but it is not confined to them. Among the more educated and upper classes it exists, although it may be regarded half humorously. How near the surface it lies was seen in the recrudescence of the mascot during the war and in the years immediately following, when white heather, the swastika, lucky pigs, elephant's hair rings, pocket pieces and the like were to be seen on every side in the shops and on the person.

It has been noted that the use of the mascot is particularly prevalent among certain classes and in certain callings—shepherds, sailors, miners, actors, beggars, gypsies and members of the criminal classes. The piece of coal carried in the burglar's pocket is a well-known instance. Dustmen are said to be peculiarly addicted to the brass finger-ring, but this is probably only a specialised instance of its use as a charm against rheumatism.

Perhaps it may not seem remarkable that the belief in the mascot should have flourished

WELFARE SYMBOL IN WORLD-WIDE USE

Endless speculation has been indulged in concerning the original significance of the swastika, which has been used as a symbol of welfare from a very early period. Probably it has some association with the sun and with fecundity. It appeared first in the Bronze Age, and now appears as a decorative touch in women's clothes and jewelry.

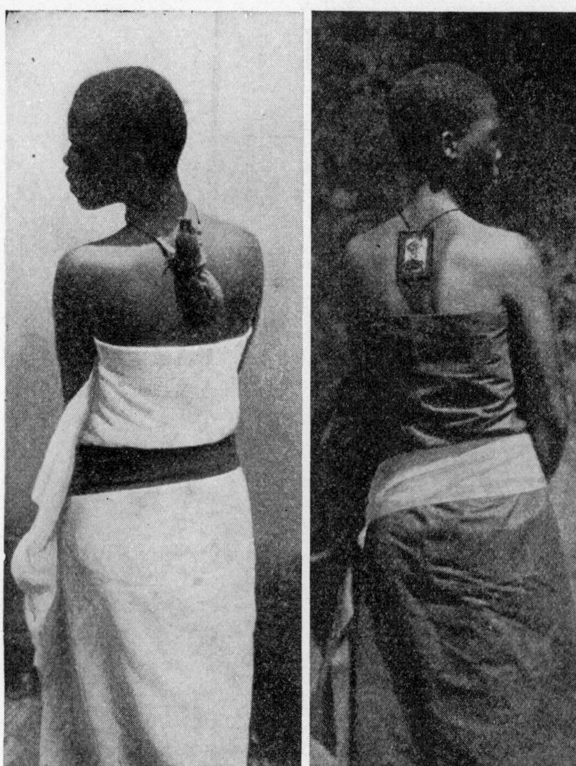

MAKING AN AFRICAN FETISH CHRISTIAN
After becoming Christians the Baganda women of Uganda held fast to their local fetishes. Their traditional charm, worn on the back, was composed of cowrie shells and bewitched hairs and bones (left). Now they have been persuaded to substitute a little picture of Christ, printed on calico (right).

during the war if the psychological factors involved are taken into account. Faith in the lucky charm is based upon the incalculable. Where, in the chances of war, so many factors are unknown, on the one side is the hope that something favourable may turn up ; on the other the still stronger desire that something may intervene to disintegrate the conditions which in combination will bring about disaster. In either case the mascot is the efficient agent. It need hardly be said that among the more highly educated this crude conception does not rise above the threshold of consciousness. Otherwise it would be rejected immediately. It is, probably, all the more firmly rooted for that very reason, and certainly it corresponds entirely to the mental attitude of the savage who lives in a world of spiritual forces which he, too, finds incalculable.

How it is possible to believe that material objects affect the course of events to the advantage of an individual or individuals—a belief so obviously irrational when analysed—becomes more readily comprehensible when it is brought into relation with the general body of belief of the primitive, the savage and the semi-civilized. Accompanying the belief in the world of spirits is an equally strong belief in the possibility that spirits may be controlled by various methods. Of such methods, one is to secure the assistance of a spirit sufficiently powerful to protect and advance the interests of the person with whom it is associated. An example which could hardly be bettered, though it does not belong to a society primitive in the strict sense, is the witch's familiar, the spirits in the form of a cat, dog, or other animal who in sixteenth and seventeenth-century Europe were believed to assist and support the witches in their nefarious deeds. In the more primitive form of the belief, however, the spirit is not visualised. It is vaguely conceived as some ' power ' resident in a material object—a stick, a stone, a shell and the like. If that object presents some striking peculiarity, it may be in form or colour, it is adopted as what we would call a mascot or charm, and the person who has associated this object with himself then counts upon securing its assistance for his protection.

It requires but a slight knowledge of the character of primitive belief to realize that the basic attitude towards the spirit world is one of fear rather than of worship or adoration. These phases of belief belong to a higher plane. To the primitive mind, even if it recognize a high god or gods, it is the spirit world around that is the matter of immediate concern, and it is conceived on the whole as inimical.

Kurt Lubinski

HOW SUPERSTITION IS TURNED TO ACCOUNT
In its passage down the centuries the Christianity of Abyssinia has become deeply tinged with superstition through contact with negro tribes. Doubtless, therefore, this Abyssinian begging monk has small difficulty in disposing of his stock of amulets, which purport to bring good health to the wearer.

Topical Press

ANIMAL MASCOTS CHERISHED BY BRITISH SOLDIERS AND SAILORS

Although not perhaps frankly acknowledged, it is lingering belief in some intimate spiritual relation between mankind and various animals and birds that lies behind the adoption of animals as mascots among civilized people to-day. Above are the black cat—proverbially a luck-bringing animal—carried on Discovery II, the ship in which Sir Douglas Mawson sailed for the Antarctic in 1929, and the monkey mascot of H.M.S. Calcutta. Below is the goat of the Royal Welch Regiment, one of several British regiments to select that creature as a mascot.

Keystone

AFRICAN FOOTBALL PLAYERS WITH MASCOTS NATIVE AND PERSONAL

The mascot has a prominent place in the world of sport. In this photograph showing the South African football team at Waterloo station, in the centre is the captain, with Felix the Cat and the Association's flag. The player on his right has a doll representing Cupid, while the one on his left holds a figure which is, or exactly resembles, a native African fetish.

An eastern ruler when sent to England some years ago as a small boy in order to be educated was unable to sleep until a copy of the Koran had been procured to be placed under his pillow to scare away the demons.

Although it may be convenient to discriminate between an amulet and a talisman, it must be remembered that the distinction between an influence which is protective only and one which is positively helpful is not one which it would always be easy to maintain in practice. It certainly would not be present to the primitive mind. The distinction between good and bad spirits is one which is made by the civilized observer rather than by the savage. To the latter all spirits are potentially harmful, and some are actually and actively inimical. They become good to him when they have been won over to his side by some propitiatory means, positively bad when they act on behalf of his enemies to his detriment. His mascot is a talisman in so far as the spirit or influence it embodies may be used to secure his advantage or harm his enemies, an amulet in so far as it is able to protect him from the attacks of other spirits, and especially those which would bring him misfortune at the bidding of an enemy. It is therefore commonly found that the enumeration of the virtues and magical functions of an amulet will close with the term 'luck-bringer.' Thus among the Japanese it is customary for adults to carry in a bundle about the person some thirty of the inscribed paper charms sold at the temples. These protect him against various misfortunes and illnesses, but in general terms they 'secure good luck.'

Still more is this the case at a more advanced stage, when possibly in the official, and certainly in the popular theology the spirits for the most part have become devils and demons. This, on the whole, is the attitude of the populace of Islam and among some of the peasant populations of India. It follows, therefore, that the luck-bringer is more commonly an averter of evil than a helpful influence.

A distinction is sometimes drawn between the amulet, the charm and the talisman on the ground of their function. It is held that the amulet is protective only, while the talisman is helpful and brings good luck in a positive sense. 'Charm' in this connexion is perhaps less strongly associated with the implication of a beneficial influence. The term is also used to denote an incantation. In eastern countries it is the practice to transcribe the incantation on a piece of parchment or paper, or on a jewel or precious stone, which is used then as an amulet. Verses from the Koran may take the place of the incantation. The Koran itself is sometimes regarded as an amulet, as other sacred writings have been.

The nature and special virtue of an amulet, like Mr. Sam Weller's spelling, may depend very much on the choice of the individual. Usually it is a portable object. This, however, is not invariably essential—witness the animal mascot. Psychologically speaking, the sole requirement is that it should appeal to the imagination of the owner, so that he may attach it to himself and assimilate it as part of his ideational complex. Hence it would not be surprising to find any object derived from the animal, vegetable or mineral kingdom in use as a mascot, an infinite variety of statements as to its powers, and an equal number of reasons for its adoption. There are, however, a large number of amulets which, owing to their material or their form, are widely recognized as having certain specific virtues. It is not always clear on what this rests, but the usual and reasonably probable explanation is that their virtue is due to a mysterious spiritual influence—'mana,' as it is generally called, after the name given it by natives of the Pacific Islands. In some cases, on the other hand, the influence of sympathetic magic may be inferred. The richly decorated silver hunting rings, set with a piece of boar's tusk, worn in Austria in the seventeenth century were clearly intended to bestow upon the wearer the strength and valour of the boar, as well as protect him from its attacks and give him luck in hunting. In India a charm made from the tiger's skin, claws or whiskers confers bravery and cleverness, which are supposed to be the qualities of this animal. The fetish of West Africa, however, in which a spirit is enclosed in some material object, and is under the control of its owner and maker, is typically an artificial mascot, and suggests that the 'mana' idea is in all probability the more widely prevalent conception. This view at least would gain the greater support from the ideas apparently embodied in a large number of individual mascots.

The animal mascot has been made familiar to many by the goat which is the regimental mascot of the Royal Welch Fusiliers. At one time the Northamptonshire Regiment kept a Himalayan bear. Goats are often found in stables with valuable horses, but this has a practical rather than a magical object, as the horses will follow it in case of fire. A clearer case is sometimes found in the southern counties of England, where many cowmen will not stay on a farm unless a goat is kept with the cattle. This ensures their fertility. An analogous custom is found in Northern France and Northern Germany. Monkeys, marmosets, and other small animals of an exotic origin are frequently carried by women, half as pets, half as mascots.

The animal mascot opens an interesting chapter in the history of religion, for it is possible to follow it up in various forms through the companion bird or animal of the Greek gods—the owl of Athena, the eagle of Zeus, the bear of Artemis—and the animal-headed gods of Egypt to the animal spirit-helper of the Indian tribes of North America and of the Pagan tribes of Borneo. Here the revelation of a spirit-helper in animal form in a dream is believed to create a special relation between the dreamer and animals of the same species which endures throughout his life. In the Banks Islands the relation between the man and his spirit-helper is so close that if the latter is supposed to die, the man also dies.

EGYPTIAN beliefs, in which amulets played a great part, would certainly appear to have transmitted their influence to the modern mascot, whatever may be the channel by which that influence has come. For in the horns (a charm against the evil eye), the crescent and the horseshoe we may discern a vestige of the representation of the cow-goddess Hathor.

Not only while they are alive, but even after their death, animals may serve as mascots. Fur and feather, beaks, claws and teeth are all made into charms. In India, when hunting the tiger, it is almost

W. Bosshard

ARMED WITH CHARMS TO DRIVE AWAY DEMONS

In Central Asia the belief in the protective powers of amulets is very strong. These parents have seen to it that their little son shall have a good start in life. Round his neck they have hung amulets containing passages from the sacred writings, while on his arms are wooden beads which are to guard him against sickness and evil spirits.

Keystone

SUPERSTITION THAT DEFIES THE MARCH OF INTELLECT

Popularly known as 'thunderbolts,' but actually weapons—axes and arrow heads—fashioned by the hand of man, Stone Age implements were long credited with magical properties and worn as protective amulets. Protective powers, again, are vaguely attributed by many people to the 'mascots' affixed to motor cars—decorative radiator caps, of which this glass racehorse, with mounted jockey, is an example.

impossible to secure the whiskers and claws of the kill, as these are almost always removed by the native assistants for use as charms. The Nambudiri Brahmin wears a piece of yak skin with the sacred thread which girdles his waist. Rings made from elephant's hair, such as can now be bought in London shops as 'lucky,' are worn by the Shan woman of Burma who has lost a child to ensure that the next will not die. If an amulet is made from an animal substance, its potency is increased if it can be fashioned in the form of the animal. Among the Shans the toe of the elephant is a favourite charm. It is frequently carved in the semblance of an elephant.

The vegetable world, with its many examples of eccentric growth, is a fruitful source of charms. The mountain ash, especially in Scotland, is effective against witches. Perhaps the best known vegetable charm is the mandrake, familiar from a certain passage in the Scriptures, and still, on account of the peculiar shape of the root, regarded in the East as possessing magical powers. In medieval times it was believed that it shrieked as it was drawn from the earth, causing instant death to all who heard it. It was therefore recommended that those who sought it should stop their ears while it was pulled up by a dog, which would immediately fall dead.

Stones of unusual or eccentric shape are naturally in frequent use as amulets. Flint implements, arrow heads and celts, are mounted and worn as charms. Among the peasantry, who know them as 'elf-shots,' they are reputed to have protective powers, especially from lightning, whence the name 'thunderbolt.' They are also medicinal. For this purpose water poured on them is given to cattle. Each of the precious stones has its special virtue and confers certain qualities on the wearer or assures good fortune. In the Moslem world 'The Nine Stones' and 'The Five Stones' are groups of certain precious stones which bring good luck to the wearer.

The magical quality of natural objects is enhanced if they are imitated in material which itself has magical power, such as the precious metals or precious and semi-precious stones. In Naples the sprig of rue, which is both protective and a luck bringer, is a favourite ornament in silver; and the pointing hand, a protection against the evil eye, is made in coral, which in itself is also a protection against that evil influence.

The list of objects and materials used for amuletic purposes might be prolonged to an almost incredible length. Enough has been said to indicate the main features of this remarkable and extraordinarily persistent belief. This persistence may perhaps best be illustrated by a final reference to two of the most popular of the mascots of the present day. The lucky pig charm in this country goes back at least to the Iron Age, for images of the pig have been found in graves dating from long before the Roman invasion. The second charm in question is the swastika, the bent-legged cross which is found as a magic and lucky symbol all over the world. After the war it was adopted as the badge of organized anti-semitism in Central Europe: it was in use in Troy long before the existence of the city which was besieged.

'BEATING THE BOUNDS' IN TOWN AND COUNTRY

SUCH civic or municipal customs as beating the bounds and riding the marches die hard, and even if they fall into disuse they are apt to be revived as soon as a favourable opportunity offers. Further information on picturesque survivals of a like nature will be found in the chapters on Customs of Famous Cities, Customs of Parliament, and Lawyers, their Customs and Traditions.

MAN, as he has passed on his long pilgrimage from a nomad state to a settled community, has brought with him habits and customs which apparently he cannot shed. These burrs of the Past cling to him, and neither the passage of time nor the growth of education can rid him of them.

Still in the Commination Service we curse him who removeth his neighbour's landmark, though the Land Registry and a legal deed of conveyance are much more efficient means of preventing us from encroaching upon the real estate of our neighbours than the simple stone to which reference is made in the Ash Wednesday denunciation of 'God's anger and judgement against sinners.' And the idea of that simple stone—as a sacred symbol of the respect we ought to pay to property—remains with us to-day in the ancient ceremonies of 'beating the bounds.'

Rites as ancient as the recorded history of mankind, religious observances, legal formulae, are all bound up in these ceremonies. Hebrew rites, imparted to us through the Bible, and pre-Christian-Roman practice, have grafted these customs upon the western world. About the time of what we now call the Rogation Days—the Monday, Tuesday and Wednesday before Ascension Day—it was the ancient Roman rule to celebrate the Terminalia and Ambarvalia, festivals in honour of the god Terminus and the goddess Ceres.

In the fifth century Bishop Mamercus of Vienna took these customs, which still survived, and gave them a Christian flavour. There had been frequent earthquakes, which had injured property and destroyed the crops. During the Rogation Days, therefore, Mamercus ordained that there should be solemn processions and supplications. This religious variation of a practice already in existence spread to other dioceses, and in the eighth or ninth century was formally adopted by the Church. It emphasised, perhaps, more the ancient festival of Ceres—the asking of God's blessing on the rising produce of the earth—than that of the Terminalia, which, in effect, was intended to preserve in all classes of the community a correct knowledge and due respect for the bounds of parochial and individual property.

IT is interesting to note, before leaving the religious aspect of these Rogation Week ceremonies, how the cult of Ceres became expanded, and how among the insecurities of the medieval world the prayers to God contained in the Rogation Litanies ask not only His blessings upon the fruits of the earth, but His protection from the evils of pestilence and slaughter. The old Gallican Rogation Litany talks about the 'crash of the falling world,' and that of York beseeches the Almighty to 'deliver us from the persecutions of the Pagans and all our enemies.' The pagans in this case were the Danes, probably in the first instance the dreaded heathen king, Penda. The use of the word 'pagan' in this connexion embodies whole centuries of tradition and habit. The Roman soldier in his military pride used to refer to the civilian as 'paganus'—a mere yokel. When in the Christian era everyone became a 'soldier of Christ,' the name stuck and was applied to those who were not Christians.

What may be called the cult of Terminus was celebrated in its Christian

Keystone

LINKS WITH LONDON'S HISTORY

Much London history has centred in the Chapel of the Savoy since its original building by John of Gaunt. It was constituted a parish church in 1564, and the perambulation of the boundaries by wardens and choir boys is carried out annually.

Topical Press

form with great pomp and circumstance before the Reformation. The lord of the manor, with a large banner, priests in surplices, and other persons with hand-bells, banners and staves, walked in procession round the parish, stopping at crosses and forming crosses on the ground. Strictly speaking, ecclesiastic Rogation Days were fast days, but old heathen habits were too strong, and besides saying or singing 'gospels to the corn,' the members of the procession indulged in 'drinkings and good cheer.'

THESE practices were known under several names—'processioning,' 'Rogationing,' 'perambulating' and 'ganging the boundaries'—'gangen' being the Saxon word 'to go.' In pre-Norman times the Rogation Days were known as 'Gange days.' When the Reformation rapidly swept away 'vain ceremonies,' what was considered the useful part of these perambulations was still retained. By the injunctions of Queen Elizabeth it was required that, in order to retain the perambulation of the circuits of parishes, the people should once in the year, at the time accustomed, with the curate and substantial men of the parish, walk about the parishes as they were accustomed, and at their return to the church make their common prayers. The curate on these perambulations was at certain convenient places to admonish the people to give thanks to God, as they beheld His benefits, and for the increase and abundance of the fruits of the earth.

There was no public provision of refreshments, but in the old days this cheerful part of the ceremony

Topical Press

DELIMITING THE FRONTIERS OF A LONDON RIVERSIDE PARISH

Of all London parishes, that of S. Clement Danes is most punctilious in preserving the minutiae of its traditional customs, including the annual beating of the bounds. Formerly there were seventy boundary stones, each marked with the anchor sign of the parish. Twenty-five of these still remain, and each of them is struck by the choir boys (top) with rods that in olden days were used for their own chastisement. Finally they embark in a boat and beat their riverine boundary line along the middle of the Thames.

Keystone

BEATING THE THAMES-SIDE BOUNDARY MARK OUTSIDE THE TOWER OF LONDON

As might be expected, several very old customs are religiously kept up at the Tower of London. For example, it is one of the only four districts in London where the curfew is still rung every night at sunset—a custom once enjoined by law upon all parishes. Annually, too, upon Ascension Day a perambulation of the boundaries of the precincts is made by the residents and their children, when the latter, boys and girls alike, beat the boundary stones with long wands.

seems rarely to have been neglected. At Edgecot, in Bucks, there was an acre of land called 'Gang-Monday land.' It was let for three pounds a year, and this money was used by the parish officers to provide cakes and beer for those who took part in the annual perambulation of the parish. At Clifton Reynes, in the same county, a bequest of land for a similar purpose directs that 'one small loaf, a piece of cheese and a pint of ale' should be given to every married person, and half a pint of ale, with the loaf and cheese, to every unmarried person, resident in Clifton, when they walked the parish boundaries in Rogation Week.

One of the objects of the perambulation was to establish the bounds of the parish. Many difficulties arose in the course of time. A landowner might put up a fence, but it was held that if in the perambulation the fence was broken down, the parishioners responsible could not be sued for damages. If a canal had been cut across the boundary some of the parishioners had to pass through the water. The obstacle of a river was surmounted by boats, or some of the party stripped and swam along it. More often, however, the older members of the perambulation took a mean advantage of the younger generation present, and the parochial boundaries were established by throwing small boys into the water at certain places.

Small boys, indeed, figure largely in these old 'ganging' ceremonies, and some of their experiences were not intended to be pleasant. Upon reaching a boundary, they were often beaten, so that the whereabouts of the boundary would continue to be impressed vividly upon their minds. In these days when we question the dictum about sparing the rod and spoiling the child, the beating is a purely formal one. In one of the illustrations we show a party of Boy Scouts performing the ceremony at the Otterspool boundary post at Liverpool, treating one of their members very gently with their Scout staves.

BUMPING was another memoria technica. The boy was held upside-down and his head banged on the ground. This method is adopted at several places in the country, one of the most curious being near Clacton, where the boundary crosses the railway to London. The victim, if not 'bumped off,' has his head at any rate brought in violent contact with the permanent way. There was a house in Buckinghamshire which had an oven so placed that it passed across the parish boundary line. Into this annually a boy was thrust to preserve the integrity of the parish. If the oven happened to be in use, he was made to scramble over the roof.

Once it is recorded that in the perambulation of St. George's, Hanover Square, the procession found their way blocked by a nobleman's carriage. The coachman refused to move without instructions from his master, who was paying a visit at a neighbouring

Keystone

OLD POMP AND CIRCUMSTANCE AT THE PERAMBULATION OF THE TOWER PRECINCTS

At the Tower of London the actual beating of the stones that mark the boundaries of the precincts is performed by the children of the residents, as shown in the previous page. This resident population is a large one, comprising the Governor, Constable and Lieutenant, the Beef-eaters or Yeomen of the Guard, the Wardens or Extraordinary of the Guard, the garrison and a large number of officials. The ceremony of beating the bounds ends with the singing of the national anthem by the entire company present, led by the choir, in cassock and surplice. There are two ecclesiastical buildings within the walls, the Chapel of S. John in the White Tower—the oldest church in London—and the Chapel of S. Peter ad Vincula, which is one of the Chapels Royal.

house. The door of the coach was therefore opened and the procession passed through the vehicle one by one. Many of these customs have, of course, fallen into abeyance, but at a recent carnival at Wokingham an illustration of the old practice was given, when instead of a small boy the mayor of the town was 'bumped' on the boundary stone.

At Great Bentley, near Colchester, the boundary line meanders through a creek. In the 'ganging' ceremony, lately revived after fifty years, a boy is 'bumped' by being held over the side of the boat upside-down.

But boys are not the only sufferers at these ceremonies. In two cases at least members of the softer sex are chosen, probably with the idea that they are more likely to remember the indignity and hand down the tradition to their children. Annually, when the perambulation of the boundary of the Chapel of the Savoy is held, a lady is solemnly 'bumped' on the Embankment At East Barnet, too, where the ancient ritual has been revived after a lapse of nearly a hundred years, a girl is bumped on the boundary stone

Topical Press

BEATING A BOY AND BUMPING A GIRL ON THE BOUNDS

It is not always the boundaries that are beaten. Sometimes boys are the victims, though such whippings are nowadays purely formal. The upper photograph shows a Wolf Cub on the Otterspool (Liverpool) boundary post under the staves of older Scouts. Women and girls figure in some of these ceremonies. Below a girl is seen being bumped on a boundary stone at East Barnet.

One feature is common to all these ceremonies, some of which follow local tradition and hold their perambulations at times other than the Rogation Days preceding Holy Thursday. The 'gangers' are always armed with sticks with which they strike the boundary line or the boundary stones. The most thoroughgoing performance of this ritual is in the parish of S. Clement Danes in London. Here choir boys in their surplices and mortarboards march round the limits of the parish, their course taking them through the Temple Gardens, where one of them has to be held upside-down to enable him to reach the boundary stone, which is underground. At another spot, the

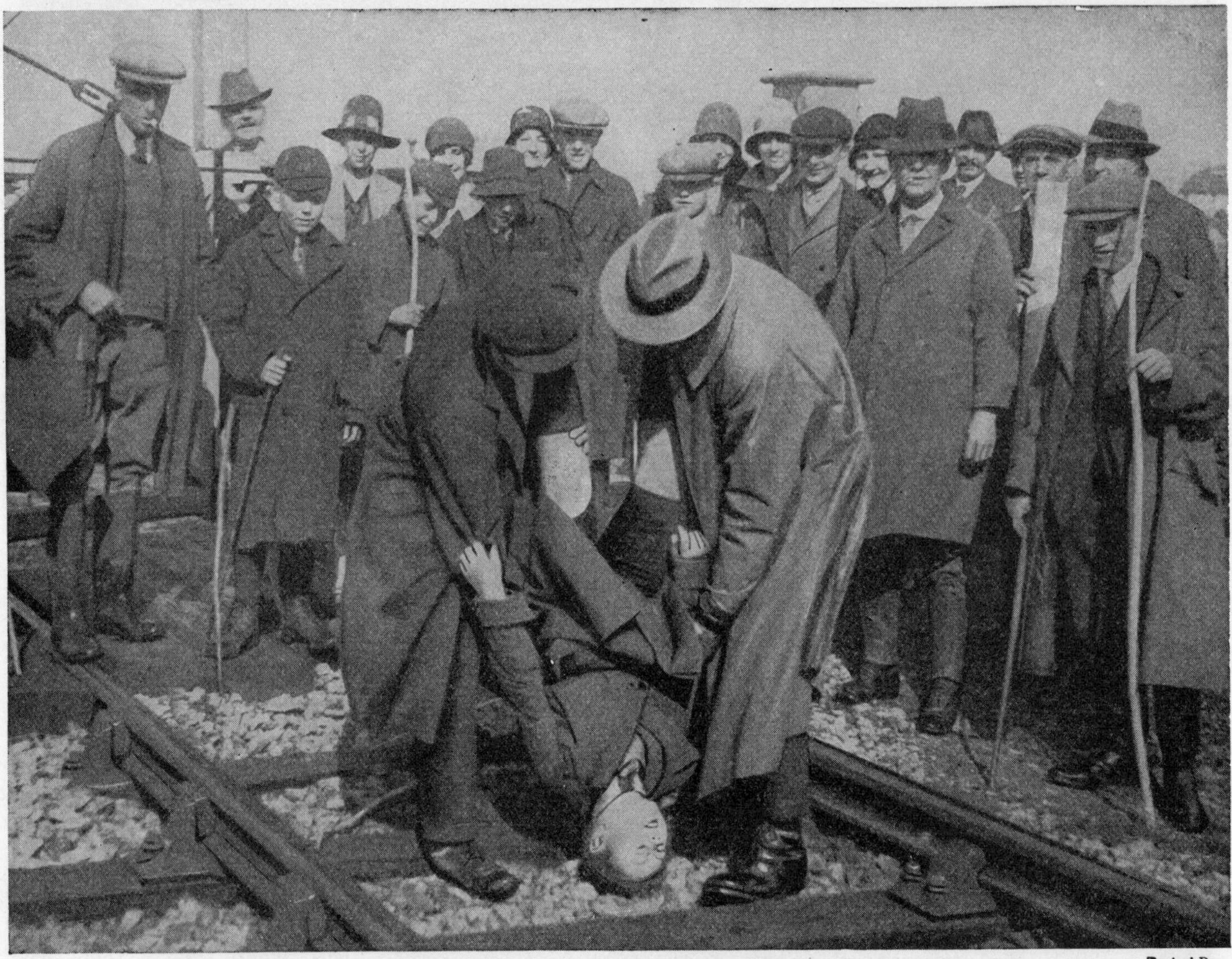

Topical Press

WHERE BOUNDARIES RUN THROUGH HOUSE AND CREEK AND OVER RAILWAY

Sometimes the perambulation of the boundaries leads to strange complications. At Great Bentley, near Colchester, for instance, the boundary not only runs through a house, through which the procession solemnly files, but also along a creek and over the railway line. When the processionists reach the water they get into boats. At the creek boundary a boy is bumped by being held upside-down over the side of a boat (top), and where the boundary crosses the railway there also a boy is bumped (bottom). A similar custom in Devonshire is referred to in page 169.

Topical Press

STRANGE RITES OF BOUNDS IN THE WEST COUNTRY AND THE EAST

Among the many curious ceremonies observed in establishing boundaries, one at Truro is notable. A man deliberately 'trespasses' on land belonging to the city. At once he is ceremonially arrested by the police and the harbour master. If he pretends to show fight he is frog-marched or carried off the scene (top left). At Wokingham, instead of a boy or a girl, the mayor himself has been bumped (top right). At Leighton Buzzard a boy stands on his head at a certain stage of the proceedings (bottom).

Topical Press

THE STANDARD BEARER RIDES THE MARCHES AT SELKIRK

The patrolling of the burgh boundaries is the Scottish equivalent of beating the bounds, and the ceremony is still kept up in several parts of Scotland. It is usually known as riding the marches or common riding. At Selkirk, as at Hawick, the common riding is strongly tinged with memories of Flodden. A mounted standard bearer takes the chief part in the Selkirk ceremony. Carrying a war-worn colour, he rides round the boundaries, completing the journey and so winding up the proceedings at the toll-house. He is here seen arriving at his goal.

boundary stone having disappeared in the process of making one of the Temple tennis courts, the hole which once held it is well and truly beaten. To complete the circuit of the parish the 'gangers' have to take boat into the middle of the Thames, where they thresh the water with their sticks. At the Tower of London the perambulation and beating are carried out by the residents and their children. The ceremony always ends with the singing of God Save the King by the Beefeaters and the choir and the others present.

So difficult a matter is it to eradicate ancient traditions and customs from the mind of man that even after the lapse of many years the annual practice of beating the bounds has been revived in the West Country. After thirty-five years the ceremony now takes place at Falmouth, each of the boundaries, both on land and water, being visited in succession. At Truro the rite is performed every six years. The beating of the water bounds here, which only dates back to 1703, has a curious feature. A member of the public formally 'trespasses' on Truro land, and is promptly arrested by the police and the harbour master. To give a touch of verisimilitude to the proceedings he 'resists' arrest, and is duly frog-marched away. Part of the ceremony consists in the town clerk reading a declaration of the city's rights at the boundary stone.

A modern note has crept into some of the more elaborate performances of this rite in Scotland and the north of England. In the old days the riding of the Berwick boundary was really a ride, the distance having to be covered being all of twelve miles. Nowadays, however, the mayor and his procession make their way to Canty's Brig in motor cars, though

Topical Press

MOTOR CARS AND A HORSE, PIPES AND A BOAT, MARK SCOTTISH BOUNDS

A quaint ceremony is observed at Greenock to establish the town's claim to the waterworks on the Renfrewshire Hills. Civic dignitaries proceed in small boats along the swiftly flowing aqueduct that brings the water to the burgh, to the stirring music of a pipe band (bottom). Unfortunately the motor car is robbing some of the northern boundary ridings of their picturesqueness. At Berwick-upon-Tweed what was formerly a dashing cavalcade has latterly become a mere procession of cars, sometimes accompanied by no more than a single horseman (top).

Topical Press

CORNET' AND BANNER AT HAWICK'S COMMON RIDING

The inspection of the boundaries and the memory of a victory snatched in the hour of defeat are combined in one celebration at Hawick. Shortly after Flodden the youth of Hawick surprised an English band and captured a banner, and it is a copy of this flag that figures in the Hawick ceremonies. Here the 'Cornet,' or leader, is planting the banner in the Teviot.

occasionally these boundary riders are accompanied by gentlemen on horseback. The whipping of boys at every boundary stone used to be a part of the ceremony, and was not a mere formality.

At Morpeth the 'riding' continues to be done in the old style. As many as a hundred horsemen, usually accompanied by a detachment of yeomanry, ride up the station bank out of the town on their tour of the common boundaries.

Over the border, Selkirk mingle with their Common Riding a commemoration of the tragic Flodden Field—that disastrous battle in 1513 when James IV of Scotland, ten leading nobles and ten thousand of his army were slain. A tattered standard, which symbolises the return of the standard-bearer from Flodden, is carried on horseback, and the celebrations culminate with his arrival at the toll-house.

Greenock's 'ganging' ceremonies have one peculiar feature. The property of the town includes the waterworks on the Renfrewshire Hills. To mark their claim, the Provost and some of the city fathers sail along the aqueduct, or cut, which conveys the water for the distance of six and a half miles from Loch Thom to the town. The boats move along with the current, and pipe music is supplied for the 'skirting' party by a band, which marches on the pathway alongside the cut.

Linlithgow have their perambulation or 'Riding of the Marches,' as it is called, on 'the first Tuesday in June which follows the second Thursday.' According to local tradition several of the old burgh charters depend upon the performance of this rite. The custom can be traced back to 1541, but its origin is probably very much older.

The Common Riding ceremonies at Hawick are among the most popular festivals on the Border. Each year a 'Cornet' is elected whose duty it is to bear round the boundaries the Common Flag, of royal blue and old gold, a replica of the original which was captured from the English by the youths of Hawick in 1514. The proceedings begin as early as six o'clock with what is called the 'snuffing ceremony.' The Cornet is accompanied on his ride by a right- and left-hand man, and is supported by a troop of other horsemen.

All this 'beating,' 'ganging,' 'bumping,' 'riding,' mingles curiously with the pattern of modern life, and the philosopher might find in it an illustration for a sermon preached from the text of Napoleon's dictum that 'men are led by toys.' There have been waves of rationalism which have now and again threatened the traditional habits and customs of the people. In 1834, for example, a cry was raised against the symbols of municipal existence. It was the popular thing then for corporations to sell their insignia and get rid of their maces and gold chains. But hard on the heels of this reformation—this cutting away of dead wood, as it was regarded—came the counter-revolution. Towns which had sold their maces bought new ones, and mayors went once more in purple and fine linen. It would seem to be the same with these ancient boundary ceremonies, which, instead of falling into desuetude, have of late years been revived all over the country.

THE VEIL AND ITS SIGNIFICANCE

It is in its association with the mysteries of marriage, its prophylactic use against supernatural evil agencies, and its bearing upon the seclusion of women, that the veil is considered in the following pages. Other aspects in which it may be regarded are treated in chapters on the Separation of the Sexes and Woman's Status in Primitive Society.

All the world loves a lover, and there is perhaps no more popular spectacle than the ravishing bride in her bridal veil. The use of the veil in wedding ceremonies is not by any means confined to Europe, but is found in China, Burma, Korea, Manchuria, Persia and other countries. Sometimes customs connected with the wearing of the veil vary from the accepted standard in Europe; for instance, in Cappadocia the bride is obliged to wear her veil for forty days after her wedding. Amongst the Chinese the groom does not see his bride till he lifts the red silk veil which she wears on arrival at his house. The veil worn by the bride in England is supposed to be derived from the canopy held over Jews at their wedding ceremonies, though a more reasonable supposition would place it as a descendant of the wimple.

The bridal veil has, however, a deeper significance than its appearance warrants. With primitive peoples marriage is a time when evil spirits and influences are rampant, and extraordinary care must be taken to ensure happiness in married life, and its corollary, an abundance of children. Amongst the Arab tribes of Morocco great precautions are taken with the bride, who is carried to her home, closely veiled, in a box amidst great noise and bustle, to the accompaniment of rifle shots. The noise is intended to frighten away the evil spirits, and the concealment of the bride to protect her friends from her glance, which might be dangerous at such a critical period in her nuptials. Catholic brides of Scutari used to be closely veiled until they reached the altar, when, since they were safe in church, the veil might be raised. In Melanesia the bride is carried to her home wrapped in many mats, with palm fans held about her face so that her glance may not fall by chance on any unwary bystander and so bewitch him.

Formerly Montenegrin brides were so closely veiled when fetched from their homes that there is a tradition of two brides being accidentally exchanged; the prospective grooms had, of course, never seen the girls before. It is said that two parties bringing brides from afar had to spend the night on the mountain-side. They met and encamped, the two brides sleeping together. In the morning each party rode off with the wrong girl, and as the girls were married immediately on arrival, and as nobody had ever seen them before, the mistake was not discovered until some days later.

Sight in primitive science is a method of contagion, and while there are dreaded influences at work during wedding ceremonies which necessitate the veiling of the bride, there is also a very prevalent superstition that the life or soul may escape or be charmed away through the mouth or nostrils. For this reason the Sultan of Darfur, in the Sudan, usually swathes his face in muslin, particular attention being paid to the vulnerable organs—the nose and mouth. The Sultans of Bornu and Wadai speak from behind a curtain, while the King of Jebu, on the west coast of Africa, might be seen by nobody, conversation being carried on from behind a screen. Good-looking Arab men and women frequently muffle up their faces to escape the influences of the evil eye, and in the Balkans the Montenegrin says 'My soul was in my nose all the time' when speaking of an escape from danger; while his Moslem sisters, if surprised unveiled, will invariably stuff something into their mouths so that the dread glance of the stranger may not charm their souls from them.

The name Tuareg is applied, as a term of opprobrium, to certain nomadic peoples who inhabit the Central Sahara. Though nominally Moslems, Tuareg

H. Manuel

HAPPIEST USE OF THE VEIL

A transparent veil held in place upon the head by a wreath of orange blossom is a traditional item of a bride's wedding dress in England. Formerly the bride arrived at the church with the veil covering the face, throwing it back after the ceremony, but changing fashion is abrogating this touch of symbolism.

E. Hudson

OUTDOOR GARB FOR ORTHODOX TURKISH WOMEN

Islamic law requires the complete seclusion of women, and when walking abroad Turkish women used invariably to conceal figure and face under feridjé, or mantle, and yashmak, or veil. With the abolition of the Khalifate the rule has been relaxed, but even in Constantinople the custom dies hard, as this photograph shows.

women do not wear the veil, and enjoy great freedom of action. The veil is, however, worn by the men; it consists of a strip of thin cloth worn round the head in such a manner as to form a hood over the eyes and a covering over the mouth and nostrils. Only a narrow slit is left open for the eyes, and the veil, once adopted, is never removed. Tuareg men usually don the veil in the early twenties, and sleep, eat, drink and die wearing it. If a Tuareg man wishes to remove his veil he is careful to see that no onlooker can by any chance be present, and the care with which the nostrils and mouth are protected leaves little doubt as to its significance; it is, in fact, a protection against evil supernatural forces which might be expected to attack the warriors who are known all over the Sahara and the Sudan as the 'veiled ones,' and are dreaded for their raiding propensities and their great bravery. The mysterious veil of the menfolk, and the large measure of freedom enjoyed by the women, so unusual in Moslem countries, have gained for them a notoriety amongst their Mahomedan neighbours and others to which perhaps their prowess in battle does not entitle them.

CLOSELY associated with the significance of the veil as a protecting garment from the hidden evil which surrounds the unwary is its religious significance, relics of which are still to be found in use to-day. For instance, the nuptial canopy of the Jews must in some way be associated with the veil with which the ark is covered. Scriptural authority enjoins veiling on women from a very early period, and early Christian women went veiled to church; a relic of this custom is the habit of women wearing hats in church while men remove them. Professed nuns wore veils, and set the fashion in head-rail through the succeeding centuries. In Spain to-day the black lace mantilla, which is in all essentials a veil, is considered, with the accompaniment of black clothes, the only reverent wear in the house of God; for this reason, also, the wedding dress of a Spanish bride is of black satin. The origin of the widow's veil has also a religious significance, since it was the practice in medieval times for widow ladies to withdraw into convents on the death of their husbands, where, though they might not become professed nuns, they adopted the veil as part of their costume.

The Moslem religion enjoins on women the wearing of the veil and a secluded life. It is distinctly stated in the Koran that it is neither lawful nor decent for a woman who is a true believer to uncover herself before any man other than her husband, brother or father. Amongst the Sarts of Turkistan the women will not go into the street without the veil. This species of veil is woven of black horsehair, and

H. A. Bernatzik

CHRISTIAN BRIDAL FASHION IN ALBANIA

Christianity and Islam live side by side in Albania so amicably that mixed marriages are common, and Christian and Moslem have the same national customs. Thus nearly all Albanian women go closely veiled out of doors, and a Christian bride, like the girl shown here, lowers her veil before meeting her bridegroom.

Emil Fischer (E.N.A.)

HEAD VEIL AS WORN BY THE WOMEN OF TRANSYLVANIA

In Rumania both prince and peasant have an innate love of the beautiful, which is exemplified by the exquisite and elaborate costumes that are met with in all parts of the country. This Saxon lady of Transylvania is no exception to the rule. The pretty head veil she is wearing, known as the marama, sets off to perfection the charming gown with its richly decorative embroideries. The handsome brooch and belt are hand-wrought and set with jewels. Both are heirlooms, being handed down from mother to daughter for generations.

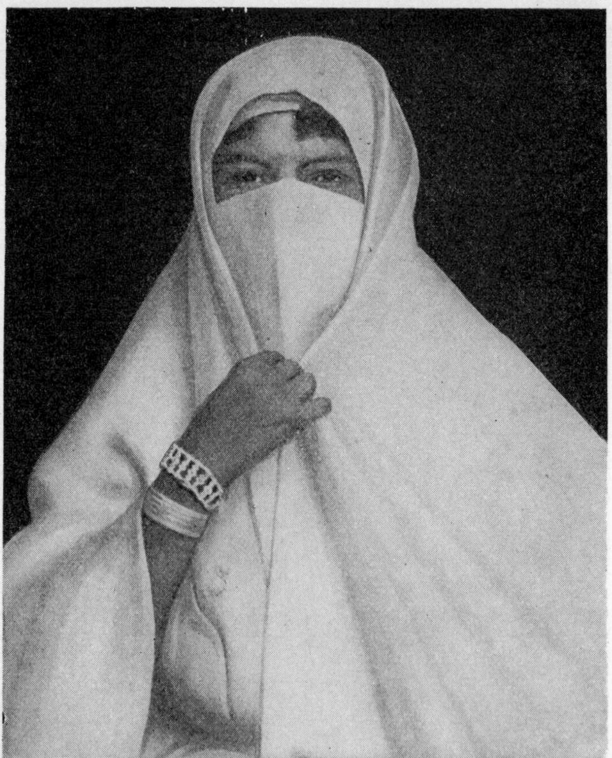

Wide World

CONTRASTING WAYS OF WEARING THE VEIL IN AFRICA AND EUROPE

Innumerable are the ways adopted by women for wearing the veil. The yashmak of the Moslems, as seen on the Egyptian water carrier (top left) and the Moorish woman of Egypt (top right), leaves the eyes uncovered. The lower photograph shows a bridal procession in the Spreewald, outside Berlin, a district known as the Venice of Germany, where the ancient costumes and customs are sedulously preserved. The women are attired in their traditional dress, and the bride's veil completely covers her face and is arranged over an elaborate framework.

Dr. A. L. Strong

HIDEOUS VEILS BEHIND WHICH FEMALE MODESTY RETIRES IN TURKISTAN

Islam was introduced into Turkistan early in the eighth century and spread widely, notwithstanding Buddhist influence emanating from Tibet. The veil—' parandja '—worn by the women is a hideous thing woven of black horsehair which completely covers the face, as shown by the figure on the right. Over this the khalat is drawn, a robe with long sleeves which are tied together at the ends and dangle down behind. Women are beginning to discard the 'parandja,' but they draw their shawls close round their head when they encounter men.

made in great quantities in Bokhara. Over the veil is thrown a dark blue or dark green robe called the khalat, the sleeves of which, tied together at the ends, dangle behind. The Jewish women of Bokhara also adopt this costume and find in it the safety they might otherwise desperately need; for under Mahomedan law it is death to lift the veil of a woman.

EGYPTIAN ladies wear a veil which consists of a long strip of white muslin concealing the whole face except the eyes and reaching nearly to the feet. It is suspended at the top by means of a narrow band which passes round the forehead. Sometimes at funeral ceremonies Egyptian women will tear their veils off and rend their garments, a custom recalling a similar practice recorded in the Bible and undoubtedly of great antiquity. Amongst the poorer classes the veil is sometimes dispensed with for reasons of economy; nevertheless the Egyptian peasant woman is only perfectly happy when her face is covered.

When Persian women go out they are concealed from head to foot in a shapeless black ' chadar ' or cloak, their faces being covered with a white silk veil. The women of this country are very superstitious, and have a firm belief in the dread powers of the evil eye, various amulets and charms being worn to protect them from supernatural influences; but these beliefs have little to do with veiling, since in Persia the tenets of the Prophet are very strictly adhered to.

Turkey is, or, rather, was, the spiritual home of the Moslem faith, since the Khalif was a direct lineal descendant of Mahomet. It is therefore necessary to examine rather more closely the veiling and seclusion of women in that country. Under Islamic laws a man may marry four wives and possess an unlimited number of concubines; but it is the exception to find a Turk, wealthy or poor, with more than one wife. The reason for this is obvious—the expense of keeping up the separate establishment to which each hanŭm or wife is entitled is prohibitive. Every Turkish home, however poor, is divided into two parts, the haremlik and the selamlik; the former for the women, the latter for the men. The rules of admittance to the haremlik are very strict even for the husband, who must not enter should he see a pair of shoes outside the door—it is perhaps needless to say shoes worn by the fairer sex. When the hanŭm goes out, her dress consists of the feridjé or mantle, a loose-sleeved garment reaching to the ankles, and the yashmak or veil. The materials used in making these vary according to the taste and wealth of the owner, but the yashmak is usually made of two pieces of silk, which are attached to a small cap worn for the purpose of supporting the veil, which covers the face up to the lower part of the nose. It will be noticed that here, again, the

C. P. Skrine

W. Bossnard

MODERATION AND TASTE IN TURKISTAN VEILS

While Mahomedan women in Chinese Turkistan all wear the veil they do not carry the rule to extremes. Witness the women on their way to market at Yarkand (top), and the tasteful veil with an embroidered cap affected by the lady of Khotan (bottom).

mouth and nostrils seem to be the vulnerable points in a Turkish woman's attire.

It is a complete misconception of the facts of Moslem life to imagine that Mahomedan women are restricted to a life of utter degradation amid the gloomy walls of the haremlik. Turkish women enjoy a full measure of protection under Moslem law, and may own property in their own right, and are not subject to the laws of coverture. In matters of divorce they have considerable freedom. Many Moslem women enjoy the privilege of safety conveyed by wearing the yashmak and feridjé. It should be remembered that in the East, amongst a mixed population of Moslem, Christian and Jew such as that which throngs the streets of Constantinople, an unveiled woman, even if attended by a duenna, is not safe from insult or perhaps molestation. But by hiding their natural charms from the curiosity of the impertinent in the veil and cloak of Islamic custom they are perfectly safe whatever provocation they may give. In fact numerous Christian women in the Balkans and in Asia Minor adopt the habit of Islam as a measure of precaution; for instance, in Albania Roman Catholic girls are kept in great seclusion, and usually go out veiled.

The younger and more progressive people of Afghanistan have advocated a greater freedom for women in the matter of the veil. This movement is, however, supposed to have been the main cause of the downfall of King Amanullah, until recently the

Georges Scott

VEILED SPEARMEN OF THE NORTH AFRICAN DESERT

Among the Islamised Tuaregs of the Sahara the veil is worn not by the women but by the men. Used to protect the wearer from the sand, and even more from evil, it shades the eyes and covers the mouth and nostrils. A Tuareg is rarely, if ever, seen without his veil; he wears it day and night, and when he dies it is buried with him. These desert nomads are fearless fighters. They almost live in the saddle, raiding trade routes and levying blackmail on caravans. To the Arabs they are known as the 'veiled ones.'

E.N.A.

FEMALE SANCTITY CONCEALED BEHIND A GHOSTLY CLOAK AND VEIL

It is generally supposed by people who are not Moslems that only men make the pilgrimage to Mecca. This, however, is not the fact. Married women are allowed to perform this crowning obligation of Islam provided they are accompanied by their husbands. This rather gruesome white garb is the conventional costume of a Mahomedan Indian pilgrim who has reached Mecca and returned to her home, the pilgrim in this instance being a woman of the lower middle class living in the neighbourhood of New Delhi.

E.N.A

VEILED LADIES OF CAWNPORE TAKING A WALK ABROAD

Although the movement for the emancipation of women from rigid seclusion is spreading throughout India, the greater number, both Moslem and Hindu, still adhere to the purdah custom, especially in the north. Only a few years ago no purdashin would have left the house on foot, even though veiled as heavily as these two native ladies of Cawnpore ; nor would one have tolerated such a violation of her privacy as the taking of her photograph, since her portrait might thus be seen by strange men.

sovereign of this mountain kingdom, who strongly supported the emancipation of women, while his wilder subjects preferred the custom of their forefathers.

The situation is somewhat different in Turkey. With the downfall of the Khalifate the religious reason for the seclusion of women has been somewhat obscured. Kemal Pasha, the present dictator, has urged the greater freedom of women, and his own wife has appeared at public gatherings unveiled ; but the emancipation of women in Asiatic Turkey has made little progress, and in the absence of a rapid increase in the benefits of civilization in those regions, it is not to be supposed that the custom of centuries will disappear in a day.

THE new fight for freedom and the fulfilment of national aspirations in British India has resulted in a measure of emancipation for Moslem and Hindu women, who have, in some cases, abandoned the veil and the secluded life of harem and zenana ; but by far the greater number are still secluded. Amongst Mahomedans of the North every woman accepts the rules of gosha, the state of being hidden. The breaking of gosha is not only a disgrace, it is also sufficient excuse for a divorce. For instance, should a Mahomedan woman of good position be photographed she would have committed a breach of gosha and be liable to divorce by her husband because her portrait might be seen by strange men.

The rules governing the lives of secluded women in India are far stricter than those of the Turks. A purdahshin or secluded woman of India may not leave the house on foot, however heavily veiled, but has to ride in a closed carriage or bullock cart. With the Hindus of the north, women are confined in the zenana ; but in the south rigid seclusion is not practised ; nevertheless Hindu ladies observe a certain amount of retirement and shrink from publicity. Some of the wives of the Hindu Rajas and Princes of the south have been present at social functions behind semi-transparent curtains, the light being so arranged that their forms were not distinguishable. In the north, however, the Hindu woman is as rigidly secluded as her Mahomedan sister.

The history of the veil is obscure ; but it is unquestionably bound up with the mysteries of marriage rites, the evil eye, and the seclusion of women. Formerly, no doubt Eastern women welcomed the idea and habit of the veil ; but with the passage of time and the ever-increasing benefits of civilization the need for the secluded life and shrouded habit has passed, and with the means of Western education at hand and the example of Western emancipation before their eyes our Oriental sisters are ever claiming for themselves a greater share in the public life, which means for them an end to seclusion and equality with their menfolk.

In primitive life the veil has as its significance protection at times of great susceptibility to danger from outward supernatural agencies ; in religious life the significance is its close association with the predominant faiths of the World, Christianity and Islam.

SURVIVAL OF TREE WORSHIP: MAYPOLE DANCING AT AN ENGLISH VILLAGE FESTIVAL

Probably tree worship is at the bottom of most of the rites and ceremonies associated with May Day. Within the tree, according to the primitive notion, resided the kindly spirit that scattered fruitfulness, and so to plant a may-tree or to set up a maypole was to display a visible sign of the blessings which the tree spirit had in its power to bestow. In Europe this idea of the tree spirit survives as little more than a traditional rite, but in other countries we still find a very real belief in it. In the England of today the maypole is reared expressly for the occasion, although not so very long ago permanent maypoles were not uncommon.

MAY DAY AND THE MAYPOLE

LIKE so many other picturesque customs, the festivities associated with May Day have in recent times obtained a new lease of life, and observances that had fallen into abeyance have been widely revived. Other Surviving Customs of Springtide are dealt with in a chapter bearing that title, and further information on related subjects is contained in the chapters on British Folk Dances and Tree and Stone Worship.

THE Great War, which swept like a scourge over mankind, obliterated in the process many habits and customs deep-rooted in tradition. The fact that any survived must be ascribed to the stubbornly retentive memory of the human race, which subconsciously still tends to reproduce in some form or another all the hopes and dreams of its primitive beginnings. Of these survivals, none is more extraordinary than that of the rites associated with May Day.

Towards the end of April, ordinary statistical observation shows that the number of marriages increases, reaching its peak on April 30th. This is due to the prejudice against May marriages. They are supposed to be unlucky, but why they are unlucky, probably not one of the couples who hurry to get married before the expiration of April, or postpone their wedding until the beginning of June, really knows.

About the origin of the name ' May ' itself there is still some doubt. The poet Ovid suggested three interpretations—' majestas,' or the sovereign power of the Roman people; ' majores,' or the senatorial power in the original constitution of Rome, in contradistinction to 'juniores,' or the inferior branch of the Roman legislature, from which the succeeding month possibly took its name; and thirdly, from Maia, the mother, by Jupiter, of the god Hermes or Mercury. What concerns the aspirants for matrimonial bliss, however, is the fact that the month was under the protection of Apollo, and that during its course the Lemuria, the festival held to propitiate the ghosts of the dead, was celebrated. It was on this account that Ovid, writing one thousand nine hundred years ago, declared that the month was ill-omened for marriages, and so crystallised in the mind of man this curious inhibition.

Even during the Great War part of the May Day rites were still carried on by children, those natural repositories of tradition, and since the war many of the customs which had fallen into abeyance have been revived. Still within thirty-five miles of London the children dress themselves up with flowers and garlands, and go from door to door collecting money. The songs they sing vary with the neighbourhood, but here is the first verse of a typical one :

Good-morning, Ladies and Gentlemen,
I wish you a happy day.
I've come to show you my garland,
Because it is May Day.

The song usually ends with a business appeal, ' Please give us a halfpenny, and we'll all run away.'

THE cynic, who regards carol singing merely as a shameless exploitation of the adult population by the younger generation, and the celebration of Guy Fawkes' Day as organized solely in the interests of the manufacturers of pyrotechnics, may look upon this pretty rite purely as a money-making affair. It is possible that the children, apart from the fun of dressing up and weaving garlands of spring flowers, also so regard it. But its origin takes us back not only to the classic observances practised at this season of the year in honour of Flora, the goddess who presided over fruits and flowers, but to those primitive times when man in his search for God made offerings to the spirit of fertility. Those garlands with which the children still adorn themselves are the same garlands which once adorned the maypoles, not only on every village green, but in every town. In London the memory of these vanished maypoles yet survives in the name of the parish of St. Andrew

Topical Press

MAY DAY DEW TO KEEP THEM BEAUTIFUL

In many country places the old belief still obtains that bathing the face with dew from the grass on May Day morning will ensure a good complexion. In the Isle of Man May Day dew was also supposed to bring women good luck and to protect them from the malignity of witches.

Keystone

CROWNING LONDON'S MAY QUEEN ON HAYES COMMON

The May Queen of London festival takes place on Hayes Common, near Bromley, Kent, on May Day, if that day falls on a Saturday, or otherwise on the first Saturday after May Day. It begins with a procession of May Queens from various places in and around London, attended by their maids of honour. Arrived at the common, the prettiest of the May Queens is crowned May Queen by a girl dressed like a boy, called the Prince of Merrie England, who is usually the May Queen of the previous year. As noted in pages 9 and 236, the festival is essentially primitive and pagan.

Undershaft—the shaft which was yearly on May morning erected 'in the midst of the street before the south door of the said church'; which shaft, 'when it was set on end and fixed in the ground, was higher than the church steeple.'

According to Sir James Frazer, the maypole and all the rites associated with it are a survival of primitive tree worship. The tree was supposed to embody the beneficent spirit which gave rain and sunshine, made the crops grow, the herbs multiply, and women bear offspring. The planting of a may tree before every house, or the rearing of it on the village green, was to bring home to every inhabitant the blessing which the tree spirit had the power to bestow. Outside Europe this belief in the tree spirit survives as a real faith and not merely as a traditional rite, the origin of which has been completely obscured.

On the Gold Coast the negroes sacrifice at the foot of certain tall trees, which, if felled, they hold, would lead to the destruction of all the fruits of the earth. Throughout northern India this worship exists today, and in the month of February libations are poured at the foot of the sacred tree, a red or yellow string is bound about the trunk, and prayers are offered to it for the fruitfulness of women, animals and crops. The coconut, too, is esteemed one of the most sacred fruits and, as the symbol of fertility, is kept enshrined throughout Upper India and presented by the priests to women who desire to become mothers.

The Maoris in former times used to ascribe to trees the power of making women fruitful. These trees were associated 'with the navel-strings of definite mythical ancestors, as indeed the navel-strings of all children used to be hung up on them down to quite recent times. A barren woman had to embrace such a tree with her arms, and she received a male or female child according as she embraced the east or the west side.' Is it possible that in the story of Jacob and his flocks, given in the thirtieth chapter of Genesis—the story which tells how Jacob took rods of green poplar and of the hazel and chestnut

Keystone

PRETTY PAGEANTRY OF THE MAY QUEEN'S DRIVE OF TRIUMPH

One of the many picturesque sights of May Day is the procession from the parish church at Hayes, near Bromley, Kent, led by the May Queen of London. The queen who has been adjudged to be the fairest sits in her gaily decorated car, with crown on head and sceptre in hand. The girls—some of them quite tiny ones—composing her retinue carry garlands and little banners dedicated to beauty, flowers, music and other subjects meet for the occasion. The car is drawn not by horses, but by members of the queen's suite.

Keystone

MAY PROCESSION IN DUBLIN IN HONOUR OF THE BLESSED VIRGIN MARY

To the Blessed Virgin Mary Roman Catholic theologians ascribe what is called hyperdulia, that is, the highest veneration, while dulia, which is a lesser reverence, is paid to the saints generally. Supreme worship (latreia) is restricted to God alone. In the Roman Catholic Church the whole month of May is sacred to the Blessed Virgin, and consequently May is a month in which processions in honour of the Virgin are specially numerous. Children, and particularly girls, figure largely in these processions, and to this fact is due a large measure of their picturesqueness. The girls wear veils, and in the front of the procession seen here a tiny maid lifts hers to take a peep.

Topical Press

LISTENING TO MAGDALEN HYMNS IN THE EARLY MORNING OF MAY DAY

A quaint old May Day custom is still kept up at Magdalen College, Oxford, whose chapel is famous for the beauty of its choral services. At six o'clock in the morning a short religious service is held on the top of Magdalen Tower, at which several hymns are sung. Large crowds, as seen in this photograph, assemble on Magdalen Bridge at this early hour to hear the choir singing from their lofty perch. A similar service is held on the top of the old Bargate at Southampton; a like custom followed at Easter is noted in page 121.

tree—we have a record of the invocation of the fertile powers of the tree spirit?

The relics of tree worship in modern Europe take three forms. The tree spirit or the spirit of vegetation is sometimes represented simply by a tree, bough or flower—the maypole hung with garlands. In England the maypole in many parts of the country was a fixture from year to year. Less than thirty years ago there were some still in existence. In London in 1661, after the Restoration, an enormous one was erected at the opening of Little Drury Lane, opposite Somerset House. There it remained until 1717, when it was purchased by Sir Isaac Newton and transported to Wanstead, in Essex, where it was used as a support for the great telescope which had been presented to the Royal Society by the French astronomer, M. Hugon.

In Upper Bavaria it is the custom to renew the maypole every three or four years, but as the whole rite depended upon the maypole being a living tree and not merely a dead staff, a bunch of dark green foliage was left at the top. In England the 'fixtures' were annually scraped. It is interesting to note that while in Provence and in most of the countries of central Europe these maypoles are set up on May morning, in Sweden and in some parts of Bohemia the celebrations take place on the eve of S. John, June 23rd, an account of which appears in a later chapter of this work.

How the magic properties of the maypole are still associated with May Day celebrations is to be seen in several parts of Europe. In certain districts of Germany on the first of May the peasants set up may trees or may bushes at the doors of stables and byres, one for each horse and cow; this is thought to make the cows yield much milk. A similar custom used to prevail in Ireland. To the fertilising powers of the tree spirit must be also ascribed the Bavarian custom of setting up a may bush at the house of newly married pairs. Among the South Slavonians a barren woman, following the same principle, places a new chemise upon a fruitful tree upon the eve of S. George's day. Next morning, before sunrise, she examines the garment, and if she finds some

Topical Press.

ANCIENT MAY DAY CUSTOMS IN THE WEST COUNTRY

The hobby-horse is a conspicuous feature of the May Day celebrations both at Padstow and at Minehead. The operator of the Padstow hobby-horse (top) is enclosed in a canvas frame stretched over a hoop. Wearing a mask fitted with snapping jaws, and crowned with a sugar-loaf cap, he prances through the streets, accompanied by a man in woman's clothes, who dances and waves a 'club' consisting of a soft pad on a wooden handle. The Minehead hobby-horse (bottom) goes round collecting money from the town and neighbouring villages.

living creature has crept on it, she hopes that her wish to have a child will be fulfilled within the year. Swedish peasants stick a leafy branch at each corner of their cornfields, believing that this will ensure an abundant crop.

International Graphic Press

DANCING ROUND THE MAYPOLE IN TIROL

In that stronghold of old customs, Tirol, May Day is celebrated with many quaint ceremonies. The Tirolese still burn out the witches on May Day by setting fire to bundles of resinous twigs on poles to the clanging of bells and clashing of pots and pans. Entire villages, too, turn out to take part in costume dances round the maypole.

The second method of representing the tree spirit is by a tree, bough or flower combined with a human form, or the representation of a human form. In our own country the garlanded children who go about on May Day sometimes carry a doll, whom they call the Lady of the May. At Thann, in Alsace, a girl called the Little May Rose, dressed in white, carries a small may tree, gay with garlands and ribbons. In another part of France, in addition to the may tree, a lad wrapped in leaves and called 'Father May' is led about. A similar custom prevails in northern Bavaria, where a man enveloped in straw from head to foot, in such a way that the ears of corn unite above his head to form a crown, dances round the maypole. Among the Slavs of Carinthia —the celebrations here take place on S. George's Day—the chief figure in the maypole procession is known as the 'Green George'—a lad clad from head to foot in green birch branches. At the end of the proceedings he, or a very cunningly contrived effigy of him, is ducked in an adjacent river or pond, with the express intention of ensuring rain to make the fields and meadows green in summer. This Green George festival is also carried out among the gypsies in Transylvania and Roumania, either on Easter Monday or S. George's Day.

E.N.A.

CAVALCADE OF MAY KINGS IN CZECHOSLOVAKIA

There are May Kings as well as May Queens. At Ellgoth, in Silesia, the youth who succeeds in snatching a cloth from a pole at the gallop and plunging it in the Oder is king. At a similar contest in Czechoslovakia two groups of horsemen strive to capture each other's king. The king and his retinue are here seen riding past.

Mannhardt, commenting on this practice of including a living person or puppet with the tree or bough in the May rite, says:

> We may conclude that these begging processions with May trees or May boughs from door to door (bringing the May or summer) had everywhere originally a serious and, so to speak, sacramental significance; people really believed that the god of growth was present unseen in the bough; by the procession it was brought to each house to bestow his blessing. The names May, Father May, May Lady, Queen of the May, by which the anthropomorphic spirit of vegetation is often denoted, show that the idea of the spirit of vegetation of the season is blent with a personification of the season at which his powers are most strikingly manifested.

The third form of symbolising the spirit of vegetation is particularly interesting. In

E.N.A.

MAY DAY DANCE AT A GIRLS' SCHOOL IN JAPAN

Just as May Day dancing is often seen at English girls' schools, so at similar establishments in Japan dancing is common on May Day. The maids of Japan may be the equals of their Western sisters in grace and exactitude, but they surpass them in picturesqueness of dress, their many-coloured attire rivalling the hues of the flowers and butterflies.

this the bough or flower is entirely omitted, and the tree spirit is represented by a living person only. This is the origin of our English Jack-in-the-Green, who in some parts of the country still strutted his hour upon the May stage in the earlier years of the present century. These mummers used to be selected almost entirely from among the chimney sweepers. Sometimes he was encased in a wicker framework covered with holly and ivy and surmounted by a crown of flowers and ribbons. It is interesting to recall that the presence of these Jack-in-the-Greens in London in 1827 was made the excuse for a very effective piece of propaganda against the employment of small boys to climb chimneys. Charles Lamb lent his aid, and the whole contributions were combined in the 'Chimney Sweepers' Friends and Climbing Boys Album,' which was largely instrumental in the abolition of a system which condemned 'the poorest and weakest of British-born subjects to unnatural, unnecessary and unjustifiable personal slavery and moral degradation.'

Jack-in-the-Greens figure in the May celebrations on S. George's Day in several parts of Russia. In Ruhla he is dressed up by the children from among their number, and he is known as the Little Leaf Man. Covered with branches, he is led with singing and dancing from house to house, where gifts of food are asked for. At the final ceremony the whole party sprinkle the Leaf Man with water and feast on the food they have collected.

In some parts of Europe these rites are postponed till Whitsuntide, and the personification of the spirit of vegetation is sometimes called the Whitsuntide King. For the selection of the king various methods are employed. At Ellgoth, in Silesia, it is called the Kings' Race. A pole, with a cloth tied to it, is set up in a meadow and the young men ride past it on horseback, each trying to pluck away the cloth as he gallops by. The one who succeeds in carrying it off and dipping it in the neighbouring Oder is proclaimed king. Here, according to Frazer, the pole is a substitute for a may tree. The election of a May Queen is common in France, has been revived in England, and has been rendered generally familiar in this country by a very bad poem by a famous poet.

In the south-east of Ireland it used to be the custom on May Day to choose the prettiest girl to be queen of the district for twelve months. She was crowned with wild flowers; feasting, dancing, and rustic sports followed, and were closed by a grand procession in the evening. During her year of office she presided over rural gatherings of young people at dances and merry-makings. If she married before next May Day, her authority was at an end, but her successor was not elected till that day came round.

In some parts of England on May Day the spirit of vegetation is represented by a king and queen who march at the head of the garlanded procession. At Halford, in south Warwickshire, these proceedings used to close with tea for the mummers in the local school house. In the Highlands, and in the Isle of Man, these spring ceremonies take place on S. Bride's Day—February 1—and the great authority on the subject points out that S. Bride, or S. Bridget, is obviously an old heathen goddess of fertility disguised in a threadbare Christian cloak. 'Probably,' says Sir James Frazer, 'she is no other than Brigit, the Celtic Goddess of Fire, and apparently of the crops.'

Apart from what may be called the sacramental aspect of these May Day customs is the modern development which consecrates the first of May to Labour. How this was evolved is not quite clear. Before the Reformation, May Day was certainly a holiday, and we have the authority of both Chaucer and Shakespeare for a universal observance of the rite. Revived by Charles the Second, it later fell into disuse among the fashionable. Associated with it, however, had been the Robin Hood Games—in Scotland these were linked up with the sports of the 'Abbot of Unreason.' As Robin Hood has always been romantically associated with the protection of the poor and struggling against the rich and highly placed, this memory perhaps has consecrated May Day in the minds of the toilers.

At a very early date the day appears to have been

Keystone

Keystone

PAPER CARP FOR THE JAPANESE BOYS' FESTIVAL IN MAY

In almost every garden in Japan during the month of May an immense paper carp is displayed (bottom). The fifth of May is the Boys' Festival, and on that day these fantastic figures are flown from flagstaffs (top). The Japanese regard the carp as the symbol of courage, because it is supposed to be the only fish that swims upstream, and in this manner Japanese fathers seek to impress upon their sons that they must be as brave in facing life as the carp is in making its way against the current.

Keystone

CELEBRATING THE FIRST OF MAY AS LABOUR DAY IN GERMANY

As in most of the other countries of Europe, the first day of May is observed as Labour day in Germany. Indeed, the custom of celebrating May Day in this way may be said to date from the Berlin Labour Congress, which was held in 1890. On May Day processions and demonstrations are organized in the various European centres, with a view to setting forth the ideals and ambitions cherished by Labour. The photograph shows a demonstration of the Communists at the Lustgarten, in Berlin, on Labour day.

Keystone

LABOUR PROCESSION ENTERING HYDE PARK ON MAY DAY

Apart from its association with the rites and ceremonies of primitive tree worship, May Day is now a day specially set apart for Labour demonstrations. How exactly the first of May came to be celebrated as Labour day is not clear. Before the Reformation the day was observed as a holiday. It was, too, the occasion of the old Robin Hood Games, and perhaps it was its association with that redoubtable champion of the struggling poor that may have led to its being adopted as the day for putting forward the aims of Labour.

used for united celebrations by various trades. Until the nineteenth century the milkmaids used to march in procession through the streets of London. It would be carrying the science of association too far perhaps to ascribe this demonstration to the old Saxon name of the month, but it is a fact that May was known to them as Tri-milchi—or 'three-milk month,' when cows were milked three times a day. More probably the milkmaids were merely celebrating unconsciously the old worship of the tree spirit.

We know, too, according to an old authority, that 'the Printers' Journeymen, with the Founders and Ink-makers, have every year a general feast which is kept in the Stationers' Hall on May Day.' Labour Day, as we know it now, developed during the last years of Queen Victoria's reign. The amazing growth of what may be called Labour interests through the Trade Unions, which has twice put a Labour Government in power during the last decade, is demonstrated by the manner in which this day has been fastened on the calendar.

Finally, there is to be noted the practice which is still carried out in the country of girls bathing their faces with the dew from the grass on May morning. Did not Pepys note in his diary: 'My wife away down with Jane and W. Hewer to Woolwich, in order to a little ayre, and to lie there tonight and so to gather May dew tomorrow morning, which Mrs. Turner hath taught her is the only thing in the world to wash her face with; and I am contented with it.' So strong is the hold of tradition on the human race, that even now there are girls to be found in the country who believe that this washing with May dew will make them beautiful.

E.N.A.

QUAINT KARELIAN COURTSHIP AND BETROTHAL CUSTOMS

The Finns of Karelia have a summary way of dealing with suitors. The girl's father lights a candle before the icon. If his daughter lets it burn, her suitor is accepted. If she blows it out (top), he is refused. When an engagement is decided upon, the bride-to-be sits in the women's corner (bottom), while her mother, with the weepers, approaches her from the other corner. The betrothal song is then wept three times—a general weeping, then one for the bridegroom's people, and finally one for the people of the house.

NORTH EUROPEAN MARRIAGE CUSTOMS

THE marriage customs of Europe vary so widely and spring from so many sources that it is more satisfactory to deal with them in groups, one of the most characteristic of which is presented here. Other chapters in later pages are devoted to the Wedding Ceremonies of Central Europe, South European Marriage Customs and those of France and Spain.

THROUGHOUT the greater part of northern Europe marriage customs present a general similarity. This is due in no small degree to the fact that the population of a great part of the area—Sweden, Norway and Denmark, with their outposts in Iceland, the Faroes and the Swedish parts of Finland—are predominantly and characteristically of the Nordic stock. Their isolation socially and economically, at any rate until comparatively recent times, has enabled them to preserve traditions and customs which they had inherited in common from their Teutonic ancestors. In their marriage customs, as distinct from the marriage ceremony—in which they follow the office of the Lutheran or the Roman church, as the case may be—they still retain many observances which can only be explained as survivals from an earlier form of belief and a society organized on a different basis from that of to-day. In northern Europe paganism long survived the introduction of the Christian religion, and here perhaps more than anywhere else the Church was long compelled to ignore, if not actually to approve, many of the observances of the older cults.

In northern Russia marriage customs, though showing Teutonic influence, are markedly affected by the mixture of the races of which the population is composed. Among the Lapps of Norway, Sweden and Lapland, and the Finns of Finland, East Karelia and Latvia, racial inheritance and primitive economic and social conditions have all played their part in determining and preserving the distinctive character of their observances in marriage.

WHEN Scandinavian custom as a whole is brought under consideration it is significant that in the preliminaries leading up to courtship and marriage the most interested parties, the future bride and bridegroom, as a rule play a very minor part. The negotiations are carried on by others, on the side of the girl by her family, on the side of the man by a representative who may be a friend or even his own father. In Russia before the war the go-between was even more important. Indeed they formed a class who made it their business to introduce suitable ' partis ' one to another and negotiate the terms of marriage, drawing a percentage on the marriage settlement. For this development we may perhaps look to the Eastern strain in Russian custom, but among the Scandinavians it may reasonably be attributed to their Nordic ancestry.

The Nordic peoples, wherever we encounter them in the early stages of their history, were a conquering race, and like other conquering races they made every effort to keep the racial strain pure from contamination by marriage with inferior stock. Among the Teutonic peoples marriage came to depend on status, which in its ultimate derivation was a distinction of race. When a class of noblemen was gradually differentiated from the freemen, suitability in marriage depended on social position, and inequality was an absolute bar. This has been the rule among the European aristocracy; it was rigidly observed in Sweden until comparatively recently; and in England and Germany it is only since the war that it has begun generally to break down. By custom it has come to be recognized that a man might marry a woman of inferior social position without the couple incurring the certainty of social ostracism, though this form of marriage was not welcomed by other members of the family and the social group to which the man belonged. Among crowned heads and members of Royal families morganatic marriages, in which the left hand was used in place of the right in the marriage ceremony, sanctioned with the rites of the Church an unequal union which was not recognized by the laws of the state.

THE morganatic marriage, essentially an institution of a Nordic group, may serve to emphasise the fact that with the Nordic peoples, marriage, in addition to being a matter of status, was a concern of the group rather than of the individual. It is the survival of the interest of the group which still in northern Europe requires the negotiations for marriage to be discussed by representatives rather than by the individuals most concerned.

Among the Teutonic peoples two forms of marriage were followed. In one of these the rights of the group were recognized by the payment of a bride-price, which served to fix the status of the parties by compensating the group for the loss of one of its members and providing for the woman in case of a dissolution of the marriage. In Scandinavia, somewhere between the sixth and ninth centuries, the bride-price passed from the group and was handed to the bride. In modern marriage it survives in appropriate conditions in the marriage settlement. The second form of marriage was marriage by capture. This method of obtaining a bride survived in Scandinavia until quite late times. It was a common custom for the would-be bridegroom to capture his bride at the very door of the church as she was about to be married to another, and in a church in Gothland a bundle of spears is still kept which were formerly used as candle holders—the marriages taking place at night —but were available for defence in case of attack.

E.N.A

KARELIAN WEDDING: WAKING THE BRIDE AND PRAYING AT DAWN

Before a wedding in Karelia the bridesmaids and bridegroom rise very early on a Sunday morning, and, after baking bread sufficient for all those who are going to be present at the wedding, go to the bride-to-be's house to wake her, preceded by the weepers (top). At daybreak the bride prays with her kinsfolk (bottom), all turning towards the east. The men stand at their devotions with hands folded, while the women kneel, bowing their heads low in the light of the rising sun.

WASHING THE BRIDE AND THE INCANTATION IN KARELIA

When a Karelian girl is betrothed her girl friends take her to the wash-basin, where a weeping song is sung (top). The bride-to-be is then supposed to be so tired that she cannot walk and asks for a horse. On the wedding day the master of ceremonies (bottom), holding a knife between his teeth, a torch in his left hand, and an axe in his right, walks round the bridegroom's people, making cuts in the ground and praying. The sign of the cross is made three times before performing this pagan rite.

E.N.A.

THE KARELIAN BRIDE CRAVES A BLESSING ON HER JOURNEY

In Karelia on the day of the wedding the bride, kneeling on a rug outside her parents' home, bows low to all present and requests them to bless the wedding journey. The master of ceremonies then lights three pieces of amadou, a fungus used as tinder, of which the bride and bridegroom each swallow a piece. This functionary does not attend the Christian ceremony. He merely sees that the old heathenish customs are carried out. The lower photograph shows the bride, completely veiled, leaving her home for the church.

Other traces may still be seen in the fact that in some districts the bride approaches the church walking between two men, or a man and a woman, who hold her arm as she advances with every sign of reluctance and sometimes simulating resistance. It is perhaps significant that in many weddings in Norway the bride's party follows that of the bridegroom in the procession to the church instead of preceding — a curious and unusual position of inferiority.

A secondary consequence of the insistence on status was the need for publicity. Betrothal, which was once looked upon as nearly equal in importance to the marriage ceremony and might in case of necessity take its place, was in the presence of as many witnesses as possible. At the actual marriage ceremony members of both groups were present as witnesses — the true function of the wedding guest—and, what is more, they were required to be in a position to testify as to consummation, or at any rate to have seen the married couple under the one blanket. This was of importance in a society which might in future require evidence as to the status of the married pair and the inheritance and status of their children—a purpose fulfilled in modern times among ourselves by registration, but for which provision was still made in the traditional manner in northern Europe up till recent times. At Skäne up till the beginning of the nineteenth century the bridal pair were married in the presence of the guests, and at Bohuslan not long ago the guests entered the bridal chamber after the couple had gone to bed.

E.N.A.

THE MOTHER REFUSES TO BE COMFORTED

After a Karelian wedding there is a general exodus to the husband's home, but the bride's mother refuses to go. She sits disconsolate apart and gives herself up to weeping; not until the bridegroom's people have offered her a suitable bribe can she be induced to move. Below, the bride, arrived at her future home, is seen bowing to her mother-in-law.

We may turn to a more detailed examination of the customs of each of the countries in northern Europe in turn, with the prefatory caution that changes are taking place rapidly, and in recent years, especially in Norway and Russia, many of these customs have fallen into disuse.

In Sweden, if a youth and a maiden eat of the same loaf of bread it is said that they are sure to fall in love with one another.

E.N.A.

WEDDING CROWN OF NORWEGIAN BRIDE

The silver crown of complicated pattern seen on the head of this Norwegian bride is a characteristic feature of wedding costume in northern Europe. In Norway such a crown is often kept in the church for brides who cannot afford to buy one.

Here at the outset we are met by a memory of a traditional form of marriage, eating together, 'confarreatio,' being one of several forms of marriage among the Romans. Be this as it may, when once a man has determined upon the lady of his choice, the question of marriage is opened with her family by a friend. If the proposal is agreeable to the family and the girl, he is presented to the family on the following Sunday. At this stage the young people are not permitted either to converse or to approach one another. If the offer is accepted a feast, called 'yes-ale,' is held, and the suitor gives the lady a silver goblet containing coins wrapped in paper. Then follows the betrothal, when they exchange presents in the presence of the pastor, the witness for the community, as already indicated.

In Western Gothland the woman gives the man a shirt which she has made with her own hands. This he must wear on the wedding day, but not afterwards until the day he is buried in it. Whatever the youth may present to his lady love, he must not give her scissors or a knife, for they will cut the friendship; nor shoes, for then she would walk away from him; nor a handkerchief, for with this she would wipe away her love for him. Frequently a considerable time must elapse before the wedding takes place, but as it approaches great preparations are made, for not infrequently the celebrations are prolonged. At one time in Norway a fortnight was not considered excessive. It is common throughout Scandinavia that the guests, in thus expressing the feeling of solidarity which once animated the tribal group, help towards the expense by bringing a large supply of provisions with them, but in south Sweden, when they depart each takes a ring of wheaten bread and a flask of brandy, so that they may share with any friend they may meet.

DRESSING the bride is a matter of considerable importance. Her dress is of black with artificial flowers and a liberal display of ribbons and embroidery. She wears a girdle and a more or less elaborate head-dress. This may be merely a fillet of myrtle or of tinsel, but the ambition of every bride is to have the elaborate silver crown of traditional pattern, a characteristic ornament of the wedding costume throughout northern Europe. Indeed, so important is this considered that in Norway it is a common practice to keep a silver crown at the church which is lent to girls who are too poor to provide a coronet of their own. This elaborate silver head-dress is of course a symbol of the chastity upon which Nordic peoples have set such store. In the Russian marriage ceremony, at one stage of the proceedings the officiating priest crowns both bride and bridegroom each with a crown. This observance, however, obviously has a different intention from the bride's crown. It has been suggested that it is a form of disguise, a protection against the spirits of evil.

The shoes of the bride are also a matter to which great attention must be paid. They must have neither buckle, strap, button nor other fastening if she hopes for easy delivery in childbirth. It is usual for the shoes to be placed on her feet by two members of the bridegroom's party. When they are on her feet her father places a silver coin in the right shoe and her mother a gold coin in the left. This ensures her future prosperity. Every girl hopes that a gentle rain will wet her crown, for then she will one day be a rich woman. This is no doubt a fertility charm both for herself and her holding. When her shoes have been put on in due order, she visits the cowhouse, where, if she milks one cow, the milk will never be lacking in her new home.

During the marriage ceremony the bridesmaids hold a canopy of shawls over the bride. This keeps away evils from above, and is a matter of no little importance in many districts. Possibly the crown in the Russian marriage ceremony may have similar intention. In the Swedish communities of Finland, when the bride and bridegroom take a meal together after the wedding ceremony, at a table set out of doors, a canopy is fixed over their heads, and a similar canopy is arranged to protect them in the bridal chamber.

When the bride goes to her husband's house, his mother meets her at the door with a lighted candle. She must touch the flame with her hand. This no doubt with the intention that the fire should drive away finally any evil spiritual influence which may still cling to her from her former life.

Keystone

MARRIED LOVERS IN A SWEDISH FOREST

This youthful Swedish bride and bridegroom are wearing the traditional costume of the country. In Sweden when a youth has found the lady of his choice he employs a third party to open up negotiations. If all goes well, he is introduced to his future bride's family and presents her with a goblet containing coins.

TURNING now to Norway. It was customary for wedding parties to proceed to the church by boat, a practice for which geographical conditions must obviously be held responsible. The bridesmaids may wear green, in other countries considered an unlucky colour, and green may even appear in the bride's dress. In the celebrations which follow the ceremony, dancing and drinking brandy are the principal features in the entertainment. There is, however, one piece of ceremonial which needs more particular mention. In this the bride 'dances off her crown.' She stands blindfolded in the centre of a ring of dancing maidens, and taking off her crown, she places it on the head of whomsoever she may catch. This girl, who will be the next to follow her example and get married, now takes her place in the centre of the ring, and the dance goes on until the other members of the party have been crowned. In the meantime a similar ceremony goes on in an adjoining room, where the bridegroom dances with each of his friends in turn. He is then hoisted on their shoulders and a scuffle follows between the single and married men for his person. At the conclusion of the ceremony the pair are sometimes addressed as 'young father' and 'young mother.' Probably, then, this is to be regarded as an instance of a struggle between two sides acting as a fertility charm. The bride and groom then change into their everyday clothes for the rest of the merrymaking.

In the Torna district the pastor conducts the wife and the husband to the bridal chamber, where he delivers a suitable oration, and the guests throng in to give the couple their good wishes, whereupon the bridegroom hands every man a glass of brandy and the bride gives every woman a glass of wine. It is hardly necessary to point out that this is another instance of witness as to consummation. In Bohuslan and the Swedish parts of Finland the day after the wedding the bride sometimes hides away and a search ensues. When she is found she is escorted home in state and a ceremonial drinking follows, after which each guest places a coin on the wedding cake.

Photopress

CROWNING THE BRIDE AND BRIDEGROOM AT A RUSSIAN WEDDING

The marriage ceremony of the Greek Orthodox Church is as ornate as are the vestments worn by the bearded clergy and the architecture and appointments characteristic of the churches of that communion. The photograph shows a particularly striking stage of the wedding rite. The bride and bridegroom stand behind the priest, each holding a lighted candle, while crowns are poised over their heads in readiness to be placed in position at the appointed moment. The crowns may perhaps be a form of disguise, to protect the couple from evil spirits.

The question of wedding presents is not without interest. In Sweden in many parts it was the custom for the bride and bridegroom to take their seats on a dais under a canopy, while the wedding presents were arrayed on a silk-covered bench before them. In Finland, however, it was a convenient and ingenious way of raising funds. The bridegroom and bride sat arrayed in full splendour, while the bride held a rich shawl over her knees. As each guest present filed past the pair he or she laid a piece of money on the shawl.

In Denmark the feature which is perhaps most worthy of remark is the exceptional position of the bridegroom. Invitations to the wedding are given out through a friend of the bridegroom, who rides round to the invited guests in person, asking them to the wedding in a set speech and pressing them not to fail to attend. In accordance with this is the custom for the wedding feast to take place at the house of the groom. After the wedding feast the company begin to dance, and, significantly enough, when about two hours have elapsed the groom must take the bride's crown from her head. The bride heads the procession to the church, walking between two 'bride-women,' of whom one is her tire woman.

Among the Lapps the conditions of marriage are much affected by the nomadic habits necessitated by their culture, which is based on fishing and the reindeer. Marriage negotiations are opened by the father of the would-be groom, but the young Lapp looks out for a girl who is well stocked with reindeer. Even so, marriage does not, as a rule, take place for some years after betrothal. This is to some extent due to the expense of courtship, as the young man has to travel long distances to pay the frequent visits to his future bride which are expected of him, and also has to make frequent gifts to her and her relatives. Even after marriage he is not allowed to take his bride to his own home. For at least a year he must reside with her parents. The woman is usually considerably older than the man, a feature of marriage which also appears in the Iceland marriage, where, indeed, it is common for a woman to have quite a large family before the marriage ceremony with the father of her children takes place.

In Russia the traditional marriage customs had very largely disappeared, even before the War. The ceremony—now being dispensed with even more frequently as a result of the hostility of the Soviet Government to all religious influence—was in accordance with the rite of the Orthodox church, which probably provided the colour needed to give the emotional outlet which the other peoples of northern Europe found in tradition.

CERTAIN of the Russian traditional marriage customs point to a very early type in social organization. A position of exceptional importance is assigned to the bride's brother. This is generally explained as a survival of the importance of the mother's kin. It would certainly appear that in early times the Russian woman was polyandrous. As the guardian and protector of the woman the brother played an important part at the wedding. When the bridegroom arrived at the bride's house he found the brother sitting at her side with a naked sword. When requested by the groom to surrender his seat he refused unless he received payment. In old days the betrothed maiden, as a token of her complete submission to the bridegroom, presented him on her wedding day with a whip which she had made with her own hands, and he gave her a gentle stroke on the shoulders. She was then required to lay her head on her husband's shoe as a sign of obedience. The bridegroom gave her bread and salt as a sign that he would give her subsistence and an almond cake in earnest of his intention to provide her with luxuries.

Among the Finns of East Karelia marriage customs still retain much that is relatively primitive. This is hardly a matter for surprise, as it is only within recent times that they have been converted to the Orthodox Church, and less than a hundred years ago they celebrated pagan festivals side by side with the feasts of the Church. It is also possible that many features in their marriage customs bearing a close resemblance to those of Russia are derived from a common source. Such, for instance, is the bride's bath, which in both countries is of great importance in the ceremonies preceding marriage. She is formally escorted to the bath by her friends, and it is then that the Russian girl looses her plaited hair which is the sign of her maidenhood, distributing the ribbons with which it is decked among her friends.

Both in Russia and among the Finns the bride displays the greatest reluctance to leave her home. She spends her time for some days before the marriage in tears and lamentation. Her friends endeavour to console her, and at the same time she receives something in the nature of an elaborate course of instruction in the future duties of life. When she leaves the house her mother and the neighbours indulge in loud weeping. Both on the journey to the church and on the return home the face of the bride is closely veiled. In conjunction with the weeping of the bride, her mother and the neighbours, this has very strongly the appearance of a memory of marriage by capture.

Shepstone

WARM CLOTHING AND GOOD CHEER AT A WEDDING FEAST IN LAPLAND

Among the Lapps marriages seldom take place until several years after the betrothal. This is largely due to the heavy expenses to which the prospective bridegroom is put during courtship. As likely as not he lives a considerable distance from his lady-love, and, apart from the cost of travelling, he is expected to make frequent presents to her as well as to her relatives. After the wedding he may not take his bride to his own home; he has to live with the bride's parents for at least a year.

Major K. K. Horn

WEIRD CEREMONY AT A LAMASERY IN TIBET: THE DEVIL DANCE IN FULL SWING

At the Lamaist monastery of Choni, in Tibet, a devil dance takes place every September. During the dance a very peculiar ceremony is performed. A little figure of human shape, made of flour and dyed red, having been placed on the ground, is dismembered by one of the priests and the fragments thrown among the spectators. This figure is an effigy of a false emperor of Tibet. At certain stages of the dance copper trumpets, some nine or ten feet long, are sounded, which, together with the other strange instruments of the orchestra, combine to make a terrific din. The old women regard the dance with the greatest awe; the younger generation treat it as an amusing performance.

DEVIL AND OTHER SPIRIT DANCES

ALTHOUGH the devil dances of Tibet and Mongolia are familiar it may not be so well known that these performances are not merely mask dances, but ritual dances originally designed to exorcise evil spirits. Animals figure largely in many of the dances that form an integral part of Oriental religious and secular drama, and these are dealt with in the chapter on Animal Dances of the East.

To the plain man who lives in the matter-of-fact surroundings of our modern civilization there is perhaps nothing that could seem more absurd than the belief that it is possible to cure disease by dressing up in hideous masks and fancy costumes and dancing in front of the patient; for in appearance 'devil dancing' amounts to no more than that. It is a term applied to certain ceremonies of exorcism found in the East—Tibet, India, Ceylon—in which dancers wear hideous and grotesque masks. Yet, when we understand the nature of these curious beliefs and allow the premises from which they set out, we see that the peoples who hold them are only acting in accordance with the strictly logical conclusions which follow. Many of the peoples among whom devil dances and dances of a kindred nature are to be observed are neither primitive nor savages, and, curiously enough, in these conceptions, which seem to us bizarre or merely childish, they approach most nearly to the advanced ideas of modern psychology and therapeutics. For such success as in many cases they undeniably achieve is based upon suggestion, the method of modern psychotherapy.

To understand the nature of devil dancing and allied forms of dancing, it is necessary in the first place to appreciate that its employment is dependent upon a certain theory of the nature of disease. It is believed that disease, or some forms of disease, is caused by a spirit which has taken possession of the patient, and in order that he may recover, the spirit must be exorcised. Dancing is not the only form of exorcism; nor does it always constitute the whole of the rite; but it is found very frequently as one stage or as an important element in the ritual of healing.

Mejrabpom-Russ

MASK OF MONGOLIAN DEVIL DANCER

This terrifying personage is a Buddhist priest attached to the great monastery of Usersky-Dazan, near Urga, in Mongolia. The mask he is wearing is the devil mask in which he takes part in the dances of the Tsam, performed at the Buddhist autumn festival.

The peoples with whom we are here dealing, even those whose culture is of the simplest, are neither children nor fools, though some writers speak of them as if their mentality were childish, and although they must admit occasional failure on the part of the medicine men and their therapeutic measures (a failure attributed to more powerful magic), a continuous run of failures would have serious results—for the medicine man. Ritual dancing of this type, it is known, has been practised from time immemorial; the first recorded case of possession in China goes back to 500 B.C., the Wu priesthood, whose speciality is spirit dancing, were in existence in 180 B.C., and Marco Polo, the Venetian traveller, describes a dance of this character which he saw in that country in the thirteenth century. The explanation of its persistence must be sought in the fact that in certain forms of disease the ceremony as a whole, not merely the dancing, does work—by suggestion. Many forms of disease are susceptible to treatment by suggestion, but more particularly those forms of mental aberration to which the term 'possession' is applied.

It would take too long and it would lead us too far from the main line of our subject to enter fully into the nature of 'possession.' For our present purpose it may be defined as an alteration of the personality such as takes place when a spiritualistic medium in a trance is said to be under the influence of a spirit control. Closely akin in certain respects are certain hysterical and epileptic affections which produce a superficially similar condition. These phenomena are of world-wide occurrence, and appear in all grades of civilization. They are particularly prevalent among primitive and semi-civilized peoples owing to their inferior mental stability and their peculiar

W. F. Taylor

susceptibility to mental suggestion. The Malay will run amok, killing any chance person he meets, as the result of a trivial or fancied slight; and among many peoples it is found impossible to save a man who has made up his mind that someone has willed his death (called by one authority thanatomania). He will even name the exact day of his decease, and the event will justify him. It is among peoples of such mentality, and particularly in dealing with this class of affection, that the magical treatment of the dance is effectual.

But why, it may be asked, should the dance be used to effect a cure? Here, again, it is tempting to wander down a fascinating by-path to discuss the physiological and psychological effects of dancing, and the part they have played in the history of religion. It must suffice, however, to indicate briefly that certain physical and mental phenomena, so closely resembling one another as to be regarded as identical, are the cause and the effect of certain forms of the dance.

In those who are of normal constitution dancing produces a state of mental exhilaration; it will even act as an aphrodisiac. Hence the orgiastic dance and the results which were believed to follow on the dances of the Witches' Sabbath. That dancing will produce a state of exaltation was well known in classical times, and the ecstatic dance was a central

G.P.A.

AIDS TO ECSTASY: AFRICAN SPIRIT DANCERS' OUTFITS

The fetish men of the Chokwe tribe of West Africa work themselves up into a state of great excitement when they are performing their professional dances. In their frenzy they go through the most extraordinary evolutions, and jump in and out of the crowd of spectators. They have a large assortment of masks to choose from for these dances, the form seen here (top) being one of the most popular. The lower photograph shows a group of Molungo devil dancers of East Africa, wearing the masks and fibre costumes used in their dances.

W. Pudovkin

DEATH SYMBOLS FOR THE DEVIL DANCE IN A HIDDEN TEMPLE OF MONGOLIA

Over the ceremonies performed during the festival of Tsam broods the melancholy influence of death, for the celebration marks the end of summer, the autumn season of death in the fields. Everything possible is done to emphasise the presence of the god of death. Mongolia is a land where the priesthood flourishes, and the Lamas are the performers in the drama that is enacted on this occasion. Of the strange masks and head-dresses worn by the priests for the Tsam dances many have a direct bearing on the actual ritual as well as some association with spirits of the underworld. In this group of Lamas at the monastery of Usersky-Dazan it will be noticed that the decoration of some of the head-dresses takes the **form of human skulls.**

G.P.A.

PRIESTESS OF SUMATRA IN A STATE OF POSSESSION EXORCISING EVIL SPIRITS

Among the Karo Battaks of Sumatra dancing figures in the ceremonies performed for exorcising evil spirits. The magician is not the only intermediary between the living and the dead. Sometimes a woman is employed. The photograph shows a priestess engaged in capturing evil spirits in the house of a chieftain who had been greatly tormented by them. On this particular occasion the medium started by dancing. She seemed hysterical, and as the music began to grow lively fell into a trance. In the end she crouched wearily on the floor.

feature in the mystic rites of Dionysus and other cults. In the mentally unstable the effect may become acute. Religious revivals in the Middle Ages and in modern times, as among certain religious sects in Russia and among the so-called 'Shakers' of America, have produced epidemics of semi-maniacal dancing.

AMONG primitive peoples, hysterical and epileptic affections and allied mental disturbances sometimes manifest themselves in convulsions, violent muscular reactions and dancing. Not uncommonly these manifestations become epidemic. Several cases of such epidemics are recorded from Africa. Such phenomena are to be regarded as cases of 'involuntary' possession. On the other hand the shamans of Siberia (see pages 100 and 29) and medicine men elsewhere, especially in the Malay Peninsula, Indonesia and the Pacific Islands, habitually induce a form of voluntary possession by dancing.

They dance violently until they fall into a somnambulistic, hypnotic or cataleptic state in which they divine, prophesy, or heal disease, whichever may have been the object of their performance. Even persons who may be perfectly normal will fall into this unconscious state. Among the Veddas, the wild tribes of Ceylon, there is a medicine man whose function it is to dance these invocatory dances to the spirits of the dead for divinatory purposes; but the ordinary members of the tribe may also perform these dances. Then they, too, fall into a cataleptic state. Yet on examination they have been found to show no hysterical or neurotic tendency whatsoever.

It has been noted that among the people who hold this type of belief certain forms of the dance, comparable to the ecstatic dance, invariably terminate in collapse. In fact the dance is one of the regular methods by which prophets, diviners and magicians attain that cataleptic state in which the spirits through whose aid they perform their magical functions enter into the tenancy of their bodies. They are then endowed with the power of that spirit, and it enables them to control the spirit causing the illness they are to cure. They drive it from the body of the patient. On the other hand, following another line of thought, in cases of involuntary possession, if the patient at one stage of the ritual of exorcism can be induced to fall into the state of collapse, the spirit will leave him. Sometimes the suggestibility of the patient is such that mere

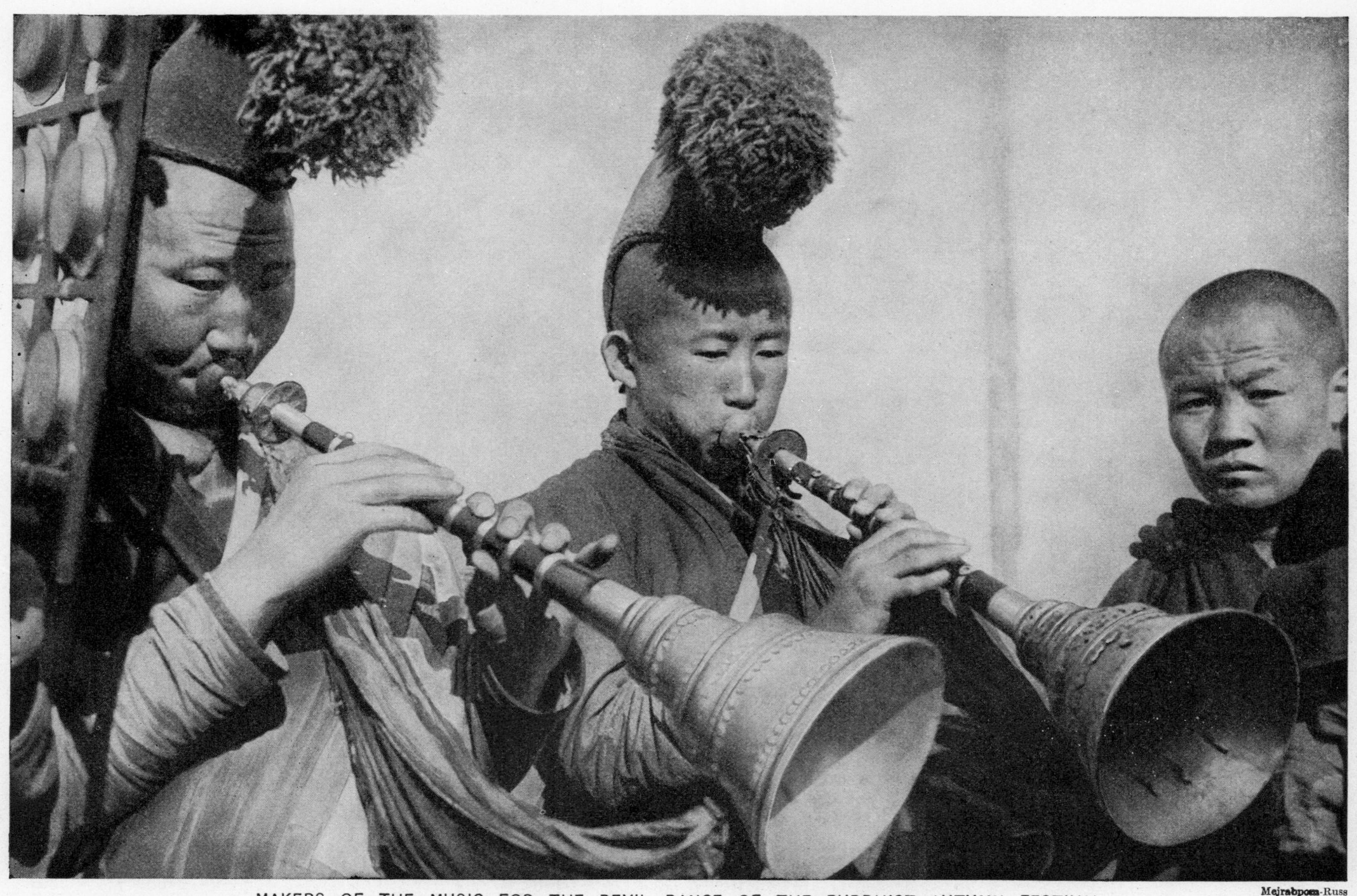

Mejrabpom-Russ

MAKERS OF THE MUSIC FOR THE DEVIL DANCE OF THE BUDDHIST AUTUMN FESTIVAL

The most important event in the Buddhist calendar is the Tsam festival, which is celebrated every autumn. Its outstanding feature is a mystery dance-play performed by Lamas wearing extraordinary masks. This goes on all day, and in every step there is a symbolical significance. A favourite scene for this ceremony is a monastery some twenty miles from Urga. The ceremonial represents life and death, and shows the final exorcising of evil by good after a lengthy conflict. To and fro the devil dancers move, to the strident tones of ancient horns and gong-like metal drums. The photograph shows two of the musicians at the dance held at the lamasery of Usersky-Dazan, in Mongolia.

imitation suffices. Thus in Madagascar when any individual is possessed and begins to dance, the other members of the village gather round him and by imitating his motions bring him relief.

The occurrence of dancing as a form of exorcism for involuntary possession has been recorded from many widely separated parts of Africa. The principal features of the ceremony as it is found among the Bathonga of north-eastern Rhodesia may be mentioned as typical. Among these people spirit possession at one time attained the dimensions of an epidemic. It takes the form of a settled melancholia, or, less frequently, perhaps, of a dancing frenzy. It is caused by spirits, mostly Zulu spirits who attack and enter the Bathonga as they cross Zulu country on their way to and from the mines in which they serve as labourers. The ceremony of exorcism lasts sometimes for as much as seven or nine days. The patient sits in his hut surrounded by the exorcists, who beat their drums and tambourines, shake rattles and sing songs with the intention of forcing the indwelling spirit to reveal his name through the mouth of the patient. Knowledge of the name is essential for successful treatment. When the spirit has spoken, it is asked what it wants, the reply being sometimes 'blood,' when a goat would be brought. The intention of the rite is fulfilled when the patient has been aroused to dance violently, this dance ending in his falling into a cataleptic state, in which he sometimes suffers injuries, such as falling into the flames of the fire, without heed. While he is in this state the spirit leaves him. If it has asked for blood, the patient will suck blood from the goat violently, and in the vomiting which follows the spirit departs. Anyone who has been cured of his distemper by this rite is regarded as peculiarly fitted to take part in healing others who may suffer in the same way. Here we see the beginning of a 'school' analogous to the troupes of dancers elsewhere.

TREADING A SOLEMN AND STATELY MEASURE

Wearing gorgeous robes surmounted by an ugly mask, this Lama is enacting his appointed part in the Tsam dances, which are a prominent feature of one of the great Buddhist festivals of Mongolia. The mask is intended not merely to strike fear, but also to attain a more important end, the expression of the dancer's identity with the underworld spirit he represents.

Before leaving the subject of the exorcism of involuntary possession and its incidence in Africa, there are two points to which attention may be called, as they are an almost invariable feature of exorcists' ritual dances elsewhere. The first is that the aim of the exorcist is to induce or compel the possessing spirit to reveal its name through the mouth of the patient. This is in accordance with the well-known magical principle that knowledge of a name gives power over the owner of that name. Secondly, the use of drums, rattles and other forms of musical instrument is also in accord with a magical principle, namely, that the noise of musical instruments is powerful in its effect on spirits. Hence the use of the church bell. The Siberian shaman in the course of his ceremonial beats his magical drum and jingles the metal rattles and bells fastened to his robe, as further described in the chapter on Drums, Secular and Sacred. The two principles are combined in exorcist's ceremonies found among the peoples of the western Sudan. While the spirit is being exorcised a Sudanese fiddle or guitar is played. For each

W. Pudowkin

FIRE PLAYS ITS PART IN THE MONGOLIAN DEVIL DANCING FESTIVAL

Disguised by masks, some of which represent devils and others animal spirits, Mongolian Lamas are here seen (bottom) marching in procession into the courtyard of the monastery of Usersky-Dazan to take part in the dances of the Buddhist autumn festival. A feature which appears in other devil dances, including those of Australia, is the lighting of a ceremonial bonfire. The upper photograph shows priests, some in their everyday garb, some wearing masks, others holding aloft mystic banners, gathering round in readiness for the lighting of the fire.

F. Kingdon Ward

LAY COPYISTS OF THE LAMASERY DANCERS OF TIBET

Among the many picturesque figures encountered by the traveller in Tibet are the itinerant devil dancers, who go from village to village and from rest-house to rest-house giving imitations of the devil dances performed at the monasteries. These wanderers wear wooden masks of a traditional design. The masks, which are frequently heirlooms, bear a far more pleasing expression than do the majority of those used at the lamasery dances. Round their waists the dancers wear girdles of yaks' tails, which add greatly to the effect of their peculiar evolutions.

E. O. Hoppé

MEDICINE MEN OF MALABAR WHO DANCE DISEASE AWAY

When a native of Malabar is seriously ill and ordinary means of cure seem to be unavailing, friends send for the devil dancers, who by their wild evolutions endeavour to drive out the devils of disease from the sufferer. These dancing medicine men, who are always members of the same family, go through extraordinary contortions to the accompaniment of strange music. They paint their faces lizard green. The dancer in this photograph is performing the Ottam Thullal dance at Trivandrum, Southern India.

disease there is a special musical phrase which expresses its name. When this phrase is played the patient falls into convulsions and the spirit leaves him. Thus when Saul was possessed of an evil spirit, David played on the harp before him.

We now turn to the form of dance of which the aim is primarily to throw the exorcist, and not the patient, into an abnormal state in which he attains the power to perform his function. Here the induced trance is employed to get into touch with the spirits. Among the Punans of Borneo the medicine man dances until he has worked himself up into a state of abnormal excitement. He then fights with a sword against the spirits who are drawing away his patient's soul from his body. Sometimes the excitement of the combat is such that the patient rises up and dances side by side with the medicine man to help him until he falls down in a state of exhaustion.

Among the Veddas of Ceylon, as already mentioned, there is always an expert in each village whose business it is to know the correct method of invocation for the spirits of the dead in solemn ritual dances. He calls upon the spirits to accept the people's offerings, and this the spirit does, speaking in a guttural voice through the shaman. He also tells them whether he will assist them in hunting and sometimes where the game is to be found. In another dance, held on the fifth day after a death, in which the shaman holds a large ceremonial arrow, the spirits tell the dancers whether there will be a plenty of yams, of game and of honey. The use of the bow to detect the source of illness is illustrated in page 59. When the shaman dances to cure sickness, a bead necklace, bangles and the leaves of a certain tree are placed in a basket. As the shaman is possessed, he raises this basket over the patient's head.

It is said that among the Veddas a woman may also act as shaman and enter into communion with the spirits; but the statement needs confirmation. There are certainly women shamans in Siberia, and also in Borneo. Among the Melanaus, a woman who has been possessed acquires powers to help others. She acts as the leader of the dance in a ceremony which is held in the hut of the sick person, singing an archaic chant of which the language is hardly understood. When she is dancing madly, with flying hair, another woman whirls the patient round in a cone of shavings. Then the medicine women one by one are whirled in the cone until each falls in a faint or staggers round the room in a state of giddiness and hysteria.

We pass now to the dances to which the term 'devil dance' is more specifically applied. But first attention may be called to an interesting form occurring among the Australian aborigines. The 'Molonga' is performed with infallible accuracy, because it is believed that 'Molonga' will punish any mistake by inflicting death on the men of the tribe and by carrying off the women and children. The dance lasts about five nights, of which the first four may be regarded as preparatory to the fifth. On this night 'Molonga,' the devil himself, appears. He rushes in without warning and, made hideous by grease and red paint, charges the dancers, who retreat before him in panic, while the women and children shriek in alarm. The dance terminates in a grand conflagration in which the sticks used in controlling the rhythmical performances are thrown on the fire, while all the performers dance round it. It will hardly be necessary to recall that the witches' dance at the Sabbath took place in the presence of the devil, their leader.

The performance of 'devil dances' has been made familiar from its occurrence in the Far East. There it extends from China, through Tibet, to Ceylon. In Tibet the Lamas give entertainments in which the performers wear hideous masks, representing the demons of the underworld. The masks are in the form of men, beasts and ogres of hideous monstrosity. These demons are the nature spirits which Tibetans worshipped before the introduction of Buddhism. One of the principal characters is a black-hatted 'Chief of the Wizards,' who dances frantically to

Sport & General

DEVIL DANCERS AT THE PERAHERA FESTIVAL IN CEYLON

The devil dancers of Ceylon are in great request at religious festivals. Of these the most important is the Perahera, which is celebrated every year from the new to the full moon in July and August, and is regarded as the great Buddhist holiday. On this occasion the precious relic of the Buddhists, the Sacred Tooth, is taken from the Temple at Kandy, the old capital, and carried in procession. Thousands of people assemble, and during the holiday performances of devil dancers are the order of the day.

Photopress

BROWN BODIES GLISTENING UNDER A TRACERY OF SILVER LEAVES

The dress and ornaments affected by the devil dancers of Ceylon are fantastic in the extreme. Although the dancers are all men, in appearance they are far more like women, for they wear skirts elaborately frilled and pleated. Over the upper part of their bodies, which is left bare, they bind a curious decoration of leaflike silver open-work. The chief dancers have magnificent silver head-dresses, while the subordinate performers wear the plainest of turbans. The girdles of the chief dancers are very massive and complicated affairs.

quick music in clouds of incense burning in censers.

The wearing of masks, which is a distinctive feature of these dances, is to be noted. No doubt there is the intention to strike fear into the heart of the beholder ; but that is a secondary consideration. Nor is it likely that they are used merely as a protective disguise. Probably, like the shaman's trance, they are intended to secure the merger of the identity of the dancer and the spirit each represents—the underlying conception of the use of masks in most primitive dances and ceremonies. The Kobéua Indians of north-west Brazil say that the masks they use in their dance represent demons, which are incorporated in the masks ; but when they wear them themselves, the demon of the mask passes into him who wears it.

In Malabar, where the exorcism of devils by dancing occurs among the Nayars, a woman is usually the patient possessed of a devil. An elaborate dance called Kolam, or Ottam Thullal has to be performed. The whole village shares in the expense, which is considerable. The performers are a medicine man accompanied by twelve assistants, each wearing a mask with a distinct expression and painted for the occasion. At night the patient is brought by her mother to the dancing place in front of the house, which is brilliantly illuminated. The whole village assembles, and as the girl sits there alone, or with the support of her mother, each dancer in turn executes a terrifying dance before her, until at last she becomes hysterical. Then the demon reveals his name and whence he came, thus rendering himself incapable of any further harm.

In South Canara devil dancing is the function of three special castes, who allow their hair to grow long so that it may float out in the dance, a custom of magical significance which occurs elsewhere in India in a similar context. A special feature of their dance is a beautiful curved steel sword, which is waved about while the dance goes on. The dance begins at nine o'clock in the evening with a performance by the chief assistant of the exorcist. He imitates the motions of demons, but does not become fully possessed. This is left for the chief, who is a man of the lowest class. He dances naked save for a waist cloth, while his face is painted with ochre and he wears a metal mask. He works himself up to a frenzy to the beating of tom-toms and the howling of the spectators.

For the origin of the ' devil dance ' as it exists in the East we should perhaps look to China, where the belief in malevolent spirits is rife, and dancing under the influence of spirit possession has long been a prominent feature in the cult of the Wu priesthood, who have been powerful in China for over two thousand years. For the weirder features and the exploitation of the mask we may perhaps look to the cruder animistic beliefs of Tibet.

THE MYSTERIES OF TABOO

At almost every turn, and especially at times of difficulty, the primitive mind applies the principle of taboo. The whole life of the savage is indeed regulated by it. Aspects of the subject are elaborated in chapters dealing with crucial periods in the life of the individual, such as Initiation and Other Ceremonies of Puberty, The Separation of the Sexes and others covering marriage and death customs.

The traveller who wanders about the trim suburbs of Honolulu is constantly faced by a notice board set up at the entrance of some tempting garden and bearing on it the single word KAPU. Like the 'tapu' of New Zealand or the 'tambu' of Melanesia, this is but a variant of 'tabu,' the form of Oceanic speech used in the island of Tonga, whence Captain Cook brought it back to adorn the English language under the more homely spelling of 'taboo.' Now the American landowner who addresses this curt notice to native trespassers has really no business to use so strong an expression ; for he is virtually saying, 'This is holy ground!' He ought to mean, in fact, that persons who are rash enough to intrude will not only be duly prosecuted and punished in this world but will likewise be eternally damned in the next. Indeed, in the olden days if a Hawaiian chief who ruled by divine right had hoisted such a danger signal his subjects to a man would have credited him with the power of blasting the offender alike in body and in soul. In modern eyes, however, neither the institution of private property nor the law itself can claim a sacredness so absolute as to involve the direct authority of Heaven.

In its ultimate derivation taboo seems to mean 'marked off,' just as our word sacred may have originally meant 'cut off'; that which is so demarcated and set apart being the supernatural in all its manifestations, whether good or bad. In the Pacific region the word which comes nearest to our 'natural,' and is regularly opposed to taboo, is "noa,' that is common or ordinary. The savage observes that both men and things have their more or less regular habits of behaviour, and so long as they keep to these, he for his part can hope to accommodate his habits to theirs. Within this limit of the habitual, then, life is pretty safe, though no doubt correspondingly humdrum. Beyond it, on the contrary, all is uncertain ; and when the unknown has to be met, the first rule is 'Beware!'

Taboo, then, is just this preliminary counsel of prudence. Discretion is the better part of primitive religion ; though it can ripen into a genuine reverence as the conviction grows that behind the mystery lies an influence or being that is not only incalculably powerful but also incalculably good. The original reaction, however, towards the uncanny leaves it doubtful whether harm or help is likely to be forthcoming ; and, if man were all coward—and in any case he is decidedly not all hero—one might have expected him to give a wide berth to whatever baffles common sense. But, apart from the fact that troubles are apt to come uninvited, we are one and all compounded of cross-impulses, such as fear and hope, disquiet and curiosity. Shout at a flock of sheep and they will start running, but presently they will stop to gaze round in search of the cause of the disturbance. A more intelligent animal exhibits even more clearly a like interplay of tendencies making severally for repulsion and attraction. Thus there is the well-known story of the ape at the Zoo which, when required to retire into the sleeping-place where he could be shut up for the night, refused to leave the outer cage, and sat on a lofty perch gibbering defiance. It was only necessary, however, for the keeper to enter, and, gazing down a drain-pipe, to pretend a moment later to start back in horror.

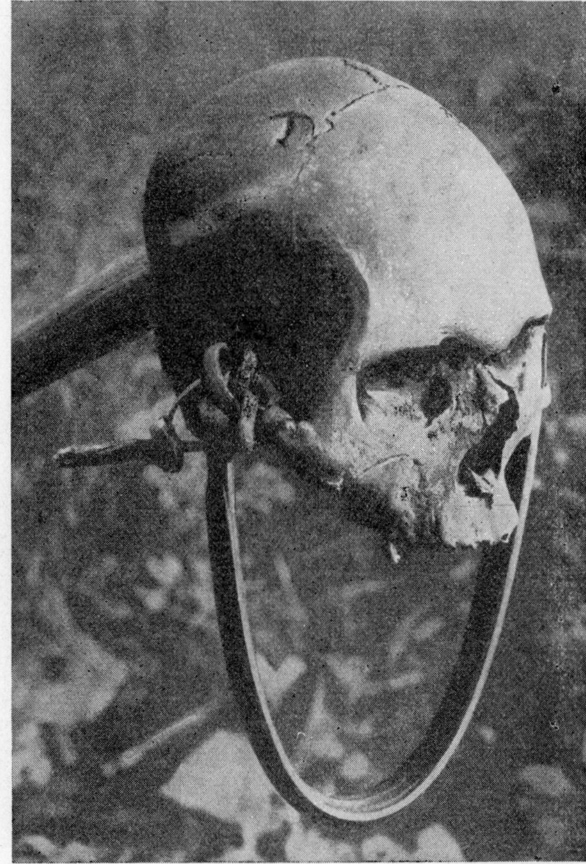

SAVAGE 'NO THOROUGHFARE' SIGN

A skull impaled upon a pole is the sinister signal adopted by head-hunters in Central New Guinea as a warning against trespassers. Such grim sentinels as this are frequently used to indicate those prohibitions, common among primitive peoples, which we call taboos.

Thereupon the ape descended slowly and took a cautious peep for himself, only to bolt instantly with a cry of terror into the safe retreat provided by the inner compartment. So too, then, there is for the primitive mind an intriguing as well as a purely alarming side to any experience of the unfamiliar; so that the taboo sign by no means implies an absolute ban on contact, but simply enjoins a wise circumspection in the manner of approach. Thus more especially does the notice apply to idle meddlers. There is no admission to the world of the sacred except on business. An unlimited liability attaches to this kind of venture, and, if any profit is to come of it, the perpetual watchword must be 'Attention!' What the Roman called 'profane' persons—as we should say, worldlings—had better keep at a respectful distance.

One series of experiences to which every savage is normally subject will serve excellently as illustrations of the general nature of taboo. There are at least four occasions in the course of his earthly career, namely, when he is born, when at puberty he is initiated or made into a man, when he marries, and, finally, when he departs this life, which are deemed so critical as to demand special precautions on the part of all concerned. They are, in a word, sacramental seasons, and a corresponding mood and behaviour are needed if the slippery ground is to be safely crossed on this pilgrim's progress. Society in its religious capacity sympathises with the human weakness associated with birth and death, or again with the shyness incidental to the assumption of the responsibilities of manhood and marriage. So a scheme of rites is devised to permit a certain retirement from worldly affairs. It is in its way a reciprocal relation that is thus set up, because just as the subject of the experience, together with those in immediate touch with him, is held to be in a spiritually delicate condition requiring freedom from disturbance, so ordinary folk engaged in the common round do not want to be troubled by the presence of such mystic invalids in the midst of their daily bustle. It is thus to their mutual satisfaction that they should keep away from each other. What the profane man finds good company is bad company for the sacred man, and vice versa.

First of all, then, a man has to be born, and in so doing is a trouble not only to himself but to his parents, and more especially to his mother. The latter as soon as she knows that a baby is coming must practise various avoidances to keep herself and her precious burden from harm—not mere physical harm, but the thousand immeasurable risks that lurk in the unknown. Indeed, her views as to the nature of conception may be so pre-scientific that she may ascribe it to the influence of some animal or plant. Thus a woman on Mota in the New Hebrides found an animal in her loincloth and tried

Wide World

TABOO-TROUBLED PASSAGE FROM BOYHOOD TO MANHOOD

Among primitive peoples adolescence is a period of taboos. The candidate for initiation is regarded as a being apart, neither boy nor man, and all manner of avoidances and tests of endurance are inflicted upon him, as described in pages 135 to 139. Here is seen a group of Ibibio natives of Southern Nigeria, enveloped in closely woven garments of curious stripe, about to take part in the ceremonies of initiating novices.

E.N.A.

FACE UPON WHICH A BRIDEGROOM-TO-BE MAY NOT GAZE

In accordance with the custom of his tribe this young Zulu warrior has to walk three times round the kraal of his future mother-in-law while she crouches on all fours at the entrance to her home. It is taboo for him to look upon her face, and so he holds his shield before his eyes until he has passed her. In his right hand he grasps a staff with which to ward off any of her relatives who may try to knock the shield away.

to carry it back in her hands to show it to the village, but lo! when she opened her hands it had disappeared. Clearly this was no common beast, and it was incumbent on her coming child never to eat such meat for the rest of its life; for in a similar case an eel-child all unwittingly tasted eel in a mixed grill and promptly went mad.

Again, what the mother eats may affect the looks of the child, so that a Kaffir mother who does not want her baby to have too large an under-lip must never touch the underlip of a pig. In general, pregnancy is a period of seclusion; and, though many of the accompanying restrictions are to our mind unnecessary and even absurd, there is sound experience at the back of the system as a whole. Indeed, there is practically much to be said for trying to meet and satisfy the nervous imaginings that are so regular a symptom of that condition; while as a matter of scientific fact it is not impossible that the mental impressions of the mother may in certain circumstances be reflected in her offspring, as folk-belief has always held.

Passing on to the actual birth, the cleansing of the child is treated not merely as a physical but likewise as a spiritual necessity, and it is duly baptized or, it may be, half choked by a prolonged fumigation. When the infant cries in the smoke, the Kaffir mother calls out, 'There goes the wizard'; just as at a christening the nurse may be heard to rejoice in baby's lusty protests as a sign that the devil is being expelled. Again, it may be thought expedient to perform a ceremony to purify the mother's milk before it can be safely drunk. Too many indeed to mention are the taboos which the savage mother must observe until some rite of purification restores her to her workaday status.

Nor is the father immune from similar restraints, but on the contrary is often subjected to a confinement almost as strict as his wife's, at any rate on the non-physical side. Much cheap fun has been made of the custom known as the 'couvade,' from the French word 'couver,' to go broody in the manner of a sitting hen. Thus Strabo, the ancient geographer, wrote that in Spain when a child is born it is the man who is brought to bed. As a matter of fact the Brazilian native does take to his hammock on such occasions, because if up and about he would be bound to do something unsuitable—to use a cutting tool, for

Mondiale

PRAYING AT THE PLACE THAT NONE BUT HE MAY APPROACH

In or near every Maori village of the olden type there was a sacred place, a tuahu or altar, where religious ceremonies were performed and the assistance or protection of the gods was invoked. The tuahu took many forms. Sometimes it was a stone or rock, sometimes a tree or a flax bush, sometimes a carved figure, and always the place was taboo to all save the priest. A Maori tribal priest is here seen with hand raised over such a sacred stone, addressing a prayer to some deity whom he wishes to propitiate.

instance—that might jeopardise the welfare of the child. Papa, mamma and baby must all lie low until the domestic crisis is over. It is holiday for them all, in the primitive sense of the word, that implies a fast rather than a feast.

Next, puberty is eminently a time of taboo. Our educational experts have but recently come to realize that this organic crisis is likewise a moral one ; so that it is highly inadvisable to force the young during the period in which they are storing energy to be expended later with renewed vigour on a plane of fuller life and greater responsibility. The novice who undergoes initiation must retire to the wilderness, where austerities of all kinds are imposed on him by his elders as a preparation for the stern duties of manhood. In the meantime, however, he is regarded as neither man nor boy, but an intermediate being, a sort of embryo on its way to be born into a new condition ; and the metaphor of a new life is variously enacted by ritual means. Nay, so whole-heartedly does the savage enter into the spirit of his drama that when the probation is over and the boy become man —the convert, as one might say—comes home in triumph to don the accoutrements of a warrior, his own mother is not supposed to recognize him. He is as strangely different as a butterfly that has emerged from the chrysalis, for his soul has found wings. His new personality is sundered from his old by a sort of hiatus in the sense-bound experience of ordinary existence, during which he has been withdrawn into the subliminal depths where the deferred instincts of sex and parenthood are sprouting as inevitably as the down on the young man's chin. It is quite a fitting symbol that on his return the regenerated one should simulate complete loss of memory as regards common things and even words. On the other hand, the spiritual experiences of his stage of transition abide with him, so that, for example, if fasting has brought him a vision of the animal destined to be his mystic guardian and helper—his ' genius,' as the Romans said—he must make it his private taboo for the rest of his days, refraining from injuring or eating it, or even from mentioning it casually.

MARRIAGE, the third of these typical sacraments, needs a long chapter to itself. Suffice it to say that honeymooning is not a modern invention, since as far back as we can penetrate into the mists of human history it has been plain to all that, without some gradual progress of mutual adjustment involving

Mondiale

HOW A MAORI UNDER TABOO IS KEPT ALIVE

A Maori who had come into contact with the dead was taboo. He was cut off from almost all communication with his fellows. He was not even allowed to touch food with his hands. It was laid before him on the ground, and he had to sit or kneel, with his hands held behind his back, and eat it as well as he could. Sometimes, as seen here, he might be fed by another person, but the feeder had to be careful not to touch the tabooed man. In earlier times the person offering the food had to be naked lest contamination should pass from clothes.

some liberation from the stale round of the day's work the couple must miss that slow-dawning sense of a larger life in store for them and theirs which is the true consecration of their union. Sometimes among savages the period between betrothal and marriage is stressed as taboo, and sometimes that between actual mating and the birth of the first child. In any case, bride and bridegroom are by means of all sorts of ritual prescriptions marked off as involved in the holy state of matrimony—holy for themselves, but for their neighbours unclean in the ceremonial sense that they had better keep clear of whatever is thus set apart.

This double aspect of the matter will explain, by the by, those contradictory features so often noticeable in marriage ceremonies, for it may chance that either of the happy (or unhappy) pair is now touched for luck, and now pelted to avert misfortune. It is a mistake to try to put too precise a meaning on such customs, which arise in the first instance out of a thoroughly confused state of mind on the part of all concerned, in which not only allied feelings such as fear and respect are mingled, but there is a downright pivoting between opposite tendencies, fear and hope, tears and laughter. A sort of hysteria, an upsetting of the normal equilibrium, is bound to occur when the clash of interests, traditions, temperaments involved in a marriage has to be overcome by a sort of humouring process.

Not only are the two sexes designed by nature to be different though complementary, so that a certain reserve in their dealings with each other, a certain concession to each other's privacy is desirable, but the two families have to learn to tolerate more or less discordant ways and become friendly. Curiously enough, savage society often seems to contemplate the other possibility of their becoming too friendly, though this is but one side of the relation of mutual aloofness typified by the polite distance maintained between the son-in-law and his wife's mother. It is felt in such a case that too near is too far. Social beings though we essentially are, we individually need to guard the approaches to our own soul-world, and never is this more urgently required than in times of emotional stress, when the only remedy is quiet as a means of self-concentration.

Finally, death might seem an end rather than a period of transition were it not that, from the earliest cavemen onwards, the forefathers of our race have

Copyright, Capt. Frank Hurley

WARDING OFF TABOOS AFTER LIFE IS ENDED

In the 'long houses' of the head-hunters of New Guinea a cubicle is allotted to each dead warrior. Here the skulls of his victims are displayed in racks, and beneath each rack is hung a carved shield representing the spirit of the warrior. This arrangement is believed to ensure that the victims' spirits will be enslaved to the warrior's.

had imagination enough to reckon on a future life, and have organized their funeral rites on that comforting supposition. On the other hand, death always comes as a sudden break with present existence, and just as those who are left behind need time in which to turn round and face the new situation, so the deceased himself might be expected to linger on the threshold of that other world. So closely indeed is the attitude of the mourners reflected in the mood attributed to the dead man that the conventional term of mourning usually sets the limit to his spell of hesitation. Thus for a year, it may be, the shade still haunts its former place of abode, so that a second and concluding funeral may be required to send it away, whether to dwell with the ancestors for ever or else to return in due course as a reincarnating spirit. During the same interval the bereaved relatives must faithfully wear the trappings of affliction and otherwise mark themselves off as disinclined to mix with their fellows. Nay, the ghost would resent any carelessness in this respect ; and an Australian widow who, being dark-skinned, wore white gypsum as her mourning garb, explained that this was to catch her late husband's eye and to assure him of her sorrow at his loss.

A day arrives, however, when, however regretfully, the living must cease to look back, in order once more to attend to the mundane affairs so long interrupted; while in turn the widow herself may wish to remarry or perhaps as the wife of her deceased husband's brother may go on to bear children that continue the former's name. As for the ghost, it, too, must abandon its half-way standing and, after a tender parting, go for good.

If indeed it 'walks' after that, there is something wrong with it. Either the funeral rites were scamped and those responsible are in for trouble, or it has its own reasons for being unquiet, as, for instance, after a suicide when a stake at the cross-roads might be needed to 'lay' it. Nay, all unburied dead, like unbaptized infants, pine in the homeless middle state, whereas those who have been duly seen off on their passage—sometimes with the fare actually provided in cash—are sure of a welcome among the shades, with or without the possibility of an eventual re-birth, when the cycle is resumed and the re-invigorated spirit by way of the taboos of infancy prepares once more for life and its troubles.

Here, then, are four crises, of which two in modern eyes are natural events, namely birth and death, and two social mechanisms, namely education and marriage, that the savage prefers to class as mysteries, perhaps not without reason. Though they primarily concern the individual, they likewise affect his intimates, so that one and all are simultaneously provided with an off-time for spiritual rest and refreshment. It is hard to say whether they take it, or it is conceded by the rest, who, after all, have no use for those whose heart is for the time being not in their daily work. Instead of merely smiling, then, at the eccentricities of the taboo system with its tendency to perpetuate the accidental phantasies and phobias to which we all give way when temporarily off our balance, one should note rather the essential needs of the human spirit to which these rough-and-ready Sabbath-ordinances minister with marked success, and can test for himself the value of the primitive view that there are difficult times when it is best to have it out with oneself in quiet and alone.

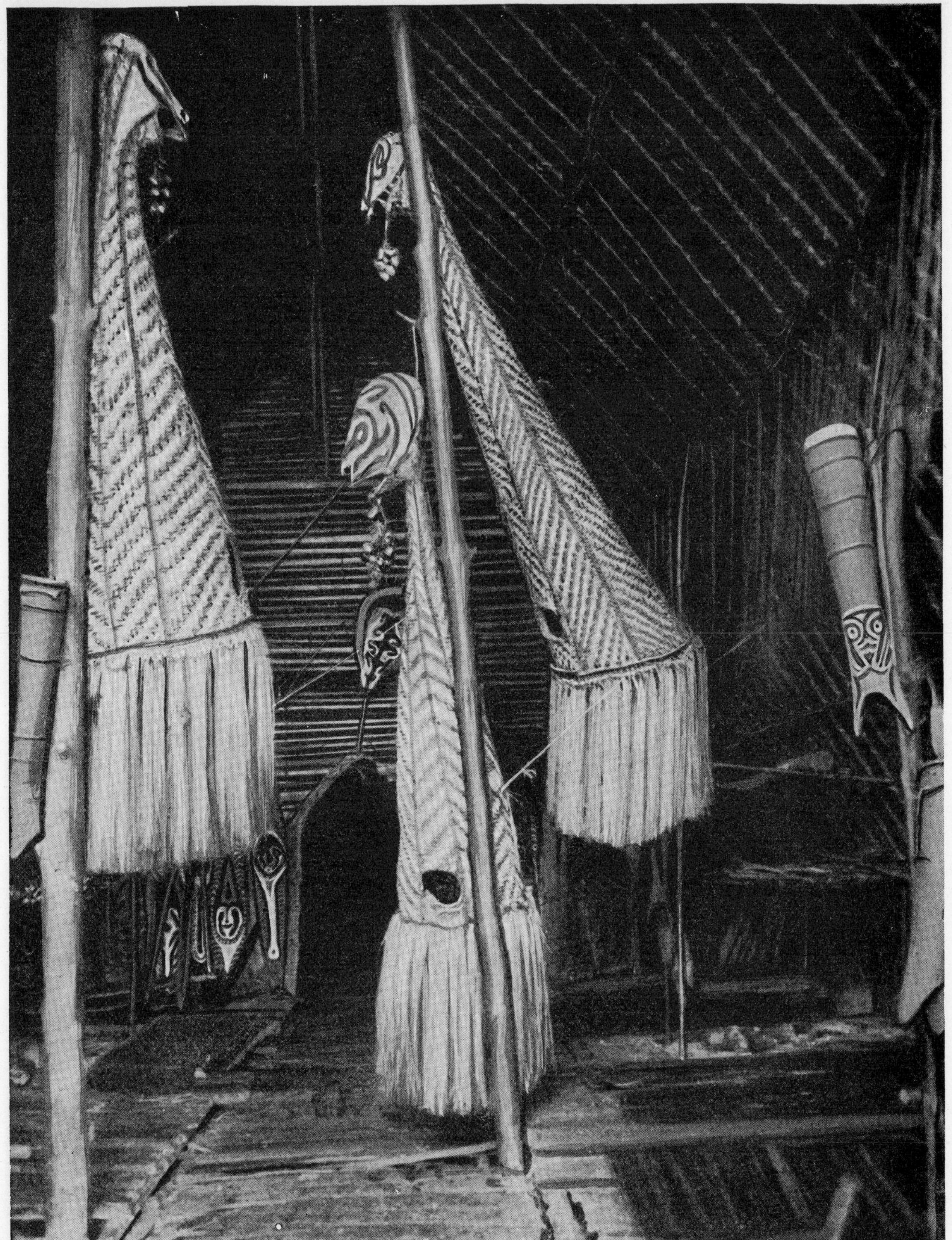

Captain Frank Hurley

DRESS USED IN PUTTING A TABOO ON A CEREMONIAL FRUIT TREE

In order to secure ample supplies of fruit for their great ceremonies the head-hunters of New Guinea resort to the following expedient. They place a taboo on the tree that produces the fruit. To achieve this the priests dress themselves in tall extinguisher-like straw costumes, surmounted by a mask from whose under jaw hangs a bunch of fruit and with a fringe round the bottom, and, thus arrayed, they dance round the tree. No sooner has this rite been accomplished than the fruit becomes forbidden fruit and none dare eat it.

Dr R. R. Marett

PLAY THAT MAKES FOR PROFICIENCY IN THE SERIOUS WORK OF LIFE

Many savage children at a very early age acquire remarkable skill in making and using miniature weapons—bows and arrows, it may be, or blow-pipes or, as here in Australia, spear and 'wommera,' the method of use of which is explained and illustrated in page 4. The lower photograph shows a young aboriginal of Central Australia whose proficiency with this singular weapon secured him a couple of plump young kangaroos. Above are two little boys of the Northern Territory who, though hardly more than babies, are already serious in their play at sport.

CHILDHOOD GAMES OF SAVAGES

COMPARATIVELY little attention has been paid to the childhood of the savage, which nevertheless is an important subject for ethnographical study. In their games, as shown in this chapter, they display a significant kinship with civilized children. The illustrations in pages 277 to 279 and 281 to 282 are taken from 'Savage Childhood,' by Dudley Kidd (A. & C. Black). Adult aspects of the subject are dealt with in the chapter on Savage Sport and Play.

WHEN Homer, in the midst of a description of battle, compares an onslaught to that of the sea which destroys the sand walls and towers shaped by children, the homely simile reminds us that, although manners and customs may have changed greatly throughout the ages, there has been little alteration in child behaviour. We find, too, remarkable resemblances in the habits of youngsters in various parts of the world and in various states of society and different climates. In their games we detect a similar love of 'make believe,' a similar spirit of fun, even when it involves discomfort in others, a similar tendency to imitate their elders and a similar enjoyment of entertaining recreation.

Eskimo children have games in which they impersonate animals and hunters, take delight in mimicry of wild bears, turning at bay to fight fiercely, or raiding little snow-houses or camps to slay and devour; the boys have their little kayaks (covered canoes), their little spears and bows and arrows and their little sledges; while the instinct of the 'eternal feminine' is manifested by the girls with their little dolls of bone or driftwood, clad in reindeer clothes. Even in the land of eternal snow the sport of snowballing never loses its attractions, and tobogganing is almost always in season.

In hot New Guinea, where snow never falls, the naked youngsters may be seen pelting each other with balls of mud and becoming gloriously dirty; they engage, too, in a kind of tobogganing by racing along a beach and throwing themselves flat at the edge of a muddy slope, to slide down quickly on their bare stomachs. They can, however, complete their fun in a recreation denied by Jack Frost to the Eskimo children, by romping and bathing in the warm waters of the sea.

No children have a greater variety of games than those of the savage Papuans in this part of the world, and nowhere are they more earnest and active in the quest of recreation and amusement. They have to make their own toys, and at an early age acquire wonderful skill in shaping imitation weapons. With their little bows and arrows they march out to attack an enemy, which is sometimes represented by an old ants' nest either on the ground or on a tree. This game is usually played when dusk comes on or in moonlight. The little arrows are tipped with resin and set aglow, and there is active competition in causing the dry heap to break into flame. The thick, damp foliage prevents trees and bushes catching fire. Papuan children like 'playing with fire,' and a favoured sport is to make bonfires of dry coconut leaves and husks and use them in obstacle races, successful competitors having to leap through the flames and smoke.

A BEACH game resembles our own Prisoners' Base. Two parties oppose one another in lines at right angles to the sea, and as a competitor runs towards a given point efforts are made to intercept and catch him. Then all join hands and go through somewhat complicated spiral evolutions, shouting calls which

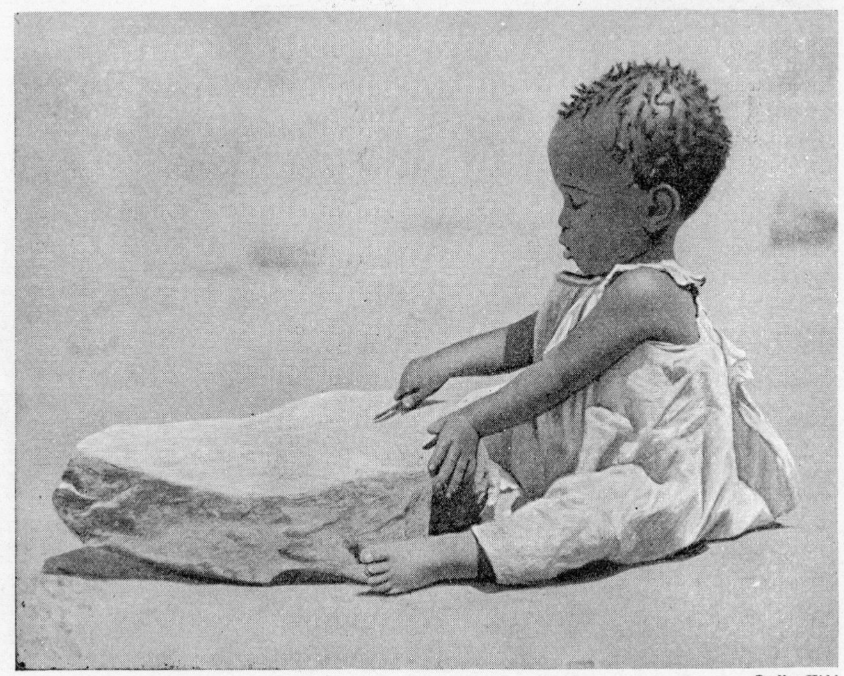

Dudley Kidd

LITTLE THINGS TO OCCUPY LITTLE MINDS

African babies are engaging little creatures. The shape and figure of their bodies are usually perfect in their baby proportions, and a strangely thoughtful expression is commonly seen on their faces as they sit bolt upright on the floor, amusing themselves with a bit of stick and a stone or some equally simple toy. Despite the wise look on their faces their minds are nearly a blank

A New Guinea land game, which has been compared to our own children's greatly favoured Nuts in May, or, as it is called in some localities, Knots of May, is taken part in by boys carrying long grass stalks with plumes. They scamper round in circles, waving their 'wands' and shouting lines of folk-verse, and then suddenly squat down in groups. After a brief pause, during which they repeat more lines, they leap to their feet, run round in a circle, and, scooping handfuls of sand as they go, throw them behind against a follower. These Papuan children also take delight in imitating their elders as agriculturists, fighters and fishers. They are wonderfully expert in the management of the small canoes which they shape with their own hands.

But we must go to the islands of Polynesia to see youngsters imitating their elders as daring surf riders, swimming out with a board and mounting on it on the crest of a billow to be swept towards the beach. In Tahiti one can still see native children on the old Polynesian swing—a single rope attached to the branch of a tree with a short stick fastened at the lower end to serve as a seat on which the swinger sits astride. The Polynesian youngsters also like walking on stilts, as did those whom the first Christian missionaries found on many of the South Sea Islands. They also continue to fly their own peculiar kind of kite, which was made originally of a light native cloth. Some of the youngsters of Polynesia and Melanesia display strong and decided artistic leanings. In New Guinea when the tide goes out the talented few give great delight to their companions by drawing figures of fish, animals and human beings on the sand either

have a significance in folk-tales. In the end each player obtains release by giving, in demand for his name, that of some animal, insect, or inanimate object. Ball games are popular, one being to keep a ball in the air as long as possible either by striking it upwards as it descends, or by 'heading' it in our Association football fashion. The youngsters manufacture their own balls by pleating strips of strong and pliable leaves and stalks of creepers. They also make swings of creepers, and utilise fallen trunks of trees for 'see-saw.' At an early age they learn to swim, and a popular sea game is to pretend to be porpoises, imitating realistically that tumbling fish. The shark may be impersonated by a swift swimmer, who gives chase to the other 'fish.'

Dudley Kidd

HOME-MADE AMUSEMENTS WHERE NO TOY-SHOPS ARE

Making toys by modelling them in clay which is then dried in the sun or baked in a fire is a childhood amusement widespread in Africa. Boys make clay oxen with sprawling legs and thick horns, and other animals—often comical caricatures yet with their peculiar features well preserved. Another game (top) common where ant-heaps abound is King of the Castle.

Dudley Kidd

AFRICAN VERSIONS OF GAMES WELL KNOWN IN EUROPE

African children are fond of building toy huts with the materials used for real huts, the girls making little houses for their dolls (bottom), and the boys small cattle kraals for their clay cattle. A droll animal game is Frogs (centre), in which little boys imitate frogs to perfection. In a round game popular in Basutoland the children sit in a circle (top) and pass a stone or a grain of corn from hand to hand, one child guessing in which hand it is when all shuffling is stopped; if he guesses correctly he changes places with the child in whose hand the object was found.

Dykes

FINALE OF A BALLET OF O'GIDI GIRLS IN A NIGERIAN VILLAGE

Dancing is a never failing source of delight to African children. In nearly all native dances the action of the arms and trunk is more important than that of the legs and feet, posturing and fantastic contortions forming the major part of the exercise, which grows wilder as it nears its end, as in the corybantic revel shown here. There are dances for boys only and others for girls alone; when both sexes dance together the boys and girls keep the lines separate, never joining hands or touching one another.

with pointed sticks or with their fingers. The competitive spirit is never absent in this educative recreation.

African native children model animals in clay and use them in their games, after drying them in the warm sunshine or baking them in a fire. A merry game is played with a herd of clay cows and a few clay lions. One group of boys takes charge of the cows and another of the beasts of prey. When the herd is taken to pasture by the 'cow boys' the 'lion boys' prowl around to make an attack. If a 'lion boy' darts out from a hiding-place, the 'cow boy' may run with his toys in another direction, but he may be intercepted by another 'lion boy.' The game goes on merrily until either many 'cows' are captured or the 'lions' are driven away.

Travellers who are expert in modelling animals in clay soon make friends with negro village children, and through them get into the good graces of the elders, which is often fortunate, especially if assistance is required in taking a motor car across a river or through a belt of forest.

Negro girls show a preference for clay dolls, using beads for eyes and fibres of wool for hair, and then dressing them with little pieces of cloth. These they nurse, pretend to feed and wash, behaving in a spirit of delightful 'make believe' as affectionate little mothers. Mr. Dudley Kidd tells how the boys tease the girls by saying, 'Oh! Your stupid dolls are made of clay; they are not alive.' But the girls protest indignantly that they are truly alive, and mock at the boys' clay animals, with the result that the boys in turn feel hurt, going the length, perhaps, of asserting that if their clay cows were broken, blood would flow. The girls also make dolls' houses, and engage in the work of mothers, grinding corn, baking cakes and engaging in other household work, singing work-songs the while.

ROUTLEDGE tells us that among the Wakikuyu of East Africa he saw as many as twenty-two children sitting quietly, content to watch a few little girls playing as workers, and he wondered at their quiet apathy. Mr. A. C. Hollis has found the children of Kenya Colony inclined to be individually more active. The girls make dolls by utilising elongated fruits of a tree, and the boys engage in pastoral pursuits in imitation of their elders. Canon Roscoe has found the children of Central Africa very imitative. Those of the Banyankole have warfare games and engage in wrestling, spear throwing and shooting at a mark with arrows. Among the Bakitara the youngsters amuse themselves similarly, and have a game resembling nine-pins or skittles. They also love guessing games, one being for a child to hold something behind his back, while another guesses in which hand it is grasped. A quiet game is for a couple of competitors to spin the stones of a wild fruit. Each time a stone is knocked down a point is won. Some children are clever at sleight of hand tricks. Racing, sham fights and wrestling are in particular favoured among the boys of the Bagesu and other Uganda peoples.

Among the games of the Bantu children observed by Mr. Dugald Campbell was 'see-saw.' The boys drive a peg into a tree stump and cut a hole in a plank or log to accommodate the peg, so that they may swing up and down. Blind Man's Buff, which the youngsters know as 'Kaffi,' creates much fun. A ball game which demands a good deal of energy and skill is called 'Mupila.' According to Campbell, 'one strikes a ball hard on the ground, and as it rebounds they all jump and clap their hands, after which each springs into the air to catch the returning ball.' The rule is that a boy cannot catch the ball until he has first jumped and clapped his hands together.

Another African ball game, which is described by Mr. James B. Baird, is played by opposing sides, which may sometimes be each quite large. The aim is to obtain possession of a ball, which is kept as much as possible in the air. The game begins by a player throwing the ball to another on his own side. When this is done all, except the one who holds the ball, clap their hands once and perhaps also stamp their feet. Up the ball goes again, passed to another, and the rivals, having all clapped, leap and rush to intercept it. Those who are quick of hand and eye soon become prominent, and the game goes on merrily. When the players on one side have kept the ball for a certain number of rounds, there is a pause while they sing a victory song, clapping their hands to keep time. Then the game proceeds again.

Where ant-hills abound and are sometimes about ten feet high, boys play a kind of King of the Castle game, one taking his stand upon the summit, while the others endeavour to dislodge him. Like the South Seas boys, those of Africa make and use stilts. Sometimes

Dudley Kidd

American Museum of Natural History

STRING GAME LOVED BY BABES IN EVERY COUNTRY

Cat's cradle is a game of world-wide distribution. As played by these three Kaffir girls (top) in Natal, the first four moves were exactly the same as those made in Europe. In Melanesia the game is popular with the Manus children when they tire of more strenuous play (below). They know many varieties of the string formations and begin to play it while still virtually babies.

Dudley Kidd

DARK HORSES IN AN AFRICAN VILLAGE

As a rule only very young European children play at horses, and then confine themselves to 'driving.' African boys carry the game further; two of them compose the steed, the hinder boy resting his hands on the shoulders of the one in front, thus providing a 'back' which the third boy may bestride.

there are hill-climbing competitions on hands and knees. A more trying contest is witnessed when boys run, holding in front of their bodies sticks grasped firmly in both hands. As they proceed they leap into the air and over the stick which, while still running, they raise up their backs, pass over their heads and bring down to the first position. This is a rather difficult feat, but some dark boys become very clever performers.

THERE are various war games, one of which is called 'Fita'; it is quite realistic, for the rival parties go into separate camps and engage in scouting, manoeuvring and in fighting, which sometimes becomes rough enough to cripple some of the combatants. In an imitation war-dance a boy may receive a cut or bruise, but he invariably makes light of it, considering it warrior-like to endure pain with simulated unconcern. A favourite game with toy bows and arrows is Shooting the Pumpkin. One boy rolls a pumpkin along the ground, usually down a gentle slope, and the others give chase, discharging arrows. Campbell records that he has seen a pumpkin 'stuck with arrows like a pin-cushion.'

Top spinning is popular with youngsters, who construct tops by carving big hard seeds. One game is to spin a number of tops in a hollow, and the best top is the one which knocks out most of the others. This game is called 'Mpeta.' Another top game, called 'Nsikwa,' may be played by two boys or by two groups of boys. The rivals take up position in lines about ten feet apart. Each player sets up in front of him a bit of maize-cob, and the tops of either side are then spun and sent travelling across towards the bits of maize-cob of the opponents, which it is hoped to overthrow. The winners are those whose tops are most skilfully directed. Much amusement is aroused among the onlookers, and the players shout defiantly or in disappointment, as the case may be.

A GAME which is very widespread in Africa, and is called 'Morabaraba' in Basutoland and 'Tsoro' in Gazaland, is referred to by Mr. Dudley Kidd as 'a modified game of solitaire.' It may be played with four, six or eight rows of small holes, which are sometimes made in a shady place on the ground. In the four-row game each competitor is in charge of two rows. The 'men' used are seeds, small stones, etc., of distinguishable colours. Each hole on either side receives its 'man' except one. Then moves are made according to the rules, and 'men' are 'taken' until a player secures his opponent's last one. This game is played also on a slab of stone or a plank of wood in which rows of holes have been made.

Animal games as played by negro youngsters are often most exciting to them. A boy may pretend to be a crocodile, and hide either almost wholly submerged in a pool, or among bushes and long grass on a river bank. The others go to bathe or to draw water, and suddenly the 'crocodile boy' darts from his hiding-place to seize a victim. Another game is a variety of hide-and-seek. One boy is a lion and other boys are deer, who hide in long grass. The 'lion boy' has to prowl about in search of the 'deer boys.' Sometimes a single boy hides as a goat or deer, and all the others, impersonating hunters, set out in search of him. When a boy, playing as a lion, whirls a bull-roarer (a piece of wood attached to a cord) the sound made resembles somewhat the roaring of a lion, and little children are terrified. Another animal game is the stealthy raid of a hyena which seeks to seize village poultry. The boy who acts the part of the hyena hides in long grass and occasionally yelps and whines like one. Other boys are the poultry, and one, impersonating the cock, utters a 'ko-ko-li-li-ko'—the equivalent of our 'cock-a-doodle-do'—when the hyena comes in sight. The alarm is raised, and the boys and girls who are the 'householders' come out to ascertain why the cock has been crowing in the middle of the night. If the hyena pounces upon the boy who impersonates the cock before he can crow he wins and the cock is 'out.' Another boy acts as cock if the game is continued.

The game formerly familiar in this country as Dish-a-loof, Hard Knuckles, Hot Cockles, Dump, etc., is well known to Basuto and Fingo children. One lays down a hand, another places his upon it, a third his on that, and so on. Then the hand at the bottom is pulled out and placed on the top, and others follow in rotation. The African method is for each boy to grip and pinch the skin on the back of another boy's hand. When a pile of hands is made, a song is sung. A signal is then given and all quickly withdraw their hands. Sometimes pieces of skin are torn off. In our own Dish-a-loof game the worst punishment was when a particularly hard and heavy hand was slapped down on another, making blood spurt from the finger tips of the victim. Evidently Dish-a-loof, now rarely played, is a savage survival.

One of the simplest and perhaps one of the oldest African games is dancing hand-in-hand round a tree. A dancer who touches the trunk is disqualified and must 'fall out.' A sort of leap-frog, and another game in which the boys advance in imitation of frogs, are both favoured by Bantu youngsters. Some boys trace out labyrinths on sand, and competitors try in turn to trace their way into the centre. Cat's cradle contests are common in Natal and in some other areas.

Among the Naga tribes of Manipur, India, the children spin tops, walk on stilts, and imitate their elders as wrestlers, runners and jumpers. According to Seligman, the boys of the Veddas of Ceylon make toy bows and arrows with remarkable skill, while the girls play at housekeeping with little utensils of clay of their own shaping. Australian black children of both sexes live in the women's camp until they are about twelve years of age, when the boys are removed to a special camp to be trained by men. The youngsters have not many amusements, but as they are invariably found to be cheerful and bright, it is evident that they live quite happily. A common game is to imitate animals, including the jumping kangaroo and the scampering emu, which are chased by the young hunters. Boys and girls imitate the women in their customary tasks, and go out into the scrub with digging sticks to search for edible roots and bulbs.

RED Indian children in Canada and the United States are fond of games like cat's cradle and another resembling battledore and shuttlecock. Girls imitate their mothers by nursing dolls and engaging in cooking, while boys play as warriors with toy weapons, and set out on their own hunting expeditions. An interesting fact about the savage peoples in various parts of the world is that they are very kind and often indulgent to their children, and rarely chastise them. They also take great interest in their games.

Photopress

WATER-BABIES FROLICKING IN WEST INDIAN SHALLOWS

Water has an irresistible attraction for boys the world over, and wherever river or sea—and climatic conditions—render it practicable, they will spend hours over their bathing, playing games on the sand between the periods spent in the water. In the West Indies the native boys are notoriously expert swimmers and divers, and gather quantities of coins tossed to them by passengers on the big ships visiting the harbours. These merry urchins splashing in shallow water were 'shot' by a camera-man at Macaripe Bay, North Trinidad.

Courtesy of Imperial War Graves Commission

THEIR BODIES ARE BURIED IN PEACE, BUT THEIR NAME LIVETH FOR EVERMORE'

The Imperial War Graves Commission was established in 1917 to care for the graves of British soldiers who fell in the Great War. It has charge of over 1,600 cemeteries, chiefly in France and Flanders. Wherever possible, two central monuments have been erected in each cemetery—the Stone of Remembrance, designed by Sir Edwin Lutyens, and the Cross of Sacrifice, designed by Sir Reginald Blomfield, to which latter is fixed a crusader's sword in bronze. All the graves conform to a uniform plan, irrespective of rank. On the headstone appear the badge of the **regiment or unit,** the name and date of death of the soldier, the symbol of his faith, and an inscription chosen by his relatives. **The photograph shows the British war cemetery at Abbeville.**

HOW NATIONS MOURN THEIR HEROES

EVERY people has its own variety of funerary customs, and these are studied in other chapters of this section, such as European Death and Burial Customs. Here we are concerned with those solemn manifestations of national grief which the wars and catastrophes of the modern world have occasioned Another aspect of the same subject provides the material for a chapter on Customs of Armistice Day

THE evolution of funeral rites through the ages forms a curious commentary on the influences by which man is swayed. The hope of primitive man that he would survive after death logically enough made him pay particular attention to the corpse of the deceased. The tombs of heroes contained all the paraphernalia the dead man had used in life, and when the sepulchre of Childeric, king of the Franks, was opened, there were found, not only his spear, his sword, his other weapons, but even his horse's head.

This attribution of a special sanctity to the body survived, oddly enough, when man accepted the doctrine that an immortal part of him, called the soul, for which the body was merely a prison-house during life, lived on after death. Among the Romans a hero who was to be given the honour of a public funeral was kept seven or eight days, was washed at regular intervals during that period with hot water, and, in case he might be merely sleeping, was hailed with shouts by his assembled friends. This 'conclamatio' ended, the body, together with the couch on which it had been lying, was carried to the rostra, where the nearest of kin pronounced the funeral oration, and afterwards to the funeral pyre, where the ashes were subsequently gathered and placed in a tomb. In the case of a national hero, such as an emperor, an apotheosis was usually part of the ceremony. In like manner the Christian Church made the resurrection of the body a dogma of their faith. Only the Magi among the Medes and Persians seem to have bowed to logic and, admitting the body was but an empty shell, left it to be consumed by birds of prey or dogs.

J. B. F. Thompson

THOUGH FEW, NEVER FORGOTTEN

Nearly every town and village in the kingdom has its war memorial, bearing lists of names of its gallant dead, and at these monuments services are held every Armistice Day. In the tiny village of Little Hampden, though there are only three names to be commemorated, these are inscribed on the local memorial stone, here seen.

Nowadays, in civilized countries, the funeral is largely a memorial service in which we recall the virtues of the deceased. When we lay the mortal remains of one who has done great service to his country in their last resting-place, the pride and pomp of the ceremony are really the apotheosis of the dead man's civic virtues. Inevitably such ceremonies have been used as propaganda. In Ireland, during the Sinn Fein troubles, Dublin, which a writer once claimed to be the city of splendid funerals, was the scene of many such obsequies, intended not so much to express the public grief as to propagate a hatred of English dominance. During the Suffragette riots before the Great War the leaders of the movement took a leaf from the Irish book and made very effective use of funerals. Londoners still recall the impressiveness of the funeral accorded to Miss Davis, who, in order to propagate her belief in Woman's Rights, flung herself in front of the King's horse at the Derby and was killed. Even the Salvation Army have made effective use of the funeral for the same purpose, and there must be many middle-aged people who will recollect the immense cortège which followed to his grave the remains of an ex-burglar who, 'saved' and reformed, had spent the last days of his life in that kindly home of Christian charity in Argyll Square.

The Great War, with its glorious records of selfless sacrifice, inevitably lent emphasis to all those rites which can be reasonably associated with the burying of the dead. For the first time in history a united attempt was made to see that no man, however humble, no matter what his rank, should be

Walter Scott

TOMB OF THE UNKNOWN WARRIOR IN WESTMINSTER ABBEY

On November 11, 1920, the second anniversary of the armistice, the body of one of the British Empire's sons, unknown by name or rank, taken from a war cemetery in France, was laid to rest in the nave of Westminster Abbey. The Unknown Warrior is the type of those who fell unidentified in the Great War. The interment took place in the presence of King George V, the ministers of state, the chiefs of the forces, and a great concourse of the nation. The body lies beneath a black marble slab bearing an inscription in letters of brass.

'The Times'

HOW FIFTY-SIX THOUSAND GALLANT DEAD ARE COMMEMORATED

The magnificent arch spanning the Menin road at Ypres, at the point known to all serving soldiers as the Menin Gate, was unveiled in 1927 in memory of the British soldiers who fought there. The memorial has a double significance. It commemorates not only the armies of the British Empire that held the Ypres salient, but also those fifty-six thousand men who died there but who have no known graves. The names of these are recorded on the stones of the 'hall,' the staircases, and the pillars. The photograph shows the ceremony of the unveiling.

forgotten. An organization was set up, financed by the Government, whose business it has been to see that the last resting-place of every rank and rating should be consecrated and made inviolate for all time. The War Graves Commission have reverently collected most of the dead from every one of the tortured battlefields and placed them in those wonderful cemeteries which will permanently keep green the memory of our heroes. Those acres of crosses constitute one of the most moving sights in the world. Our American Allies collected their own dead where possible, and transported them to America.

One aspect of the manner in which, after the Great War, the English people sought to do honour to their dead heroes may be dealt with here conveniently. It was an innovation in funeral rites. On November 11, 1920, on the second anniversary of the Armistice, a coffin containing the body of the Unknown Warrior—one of the unidentified dead who had fallen in France—was laid to rest in Westminster Abbey. Covered with the Union Jack, with Admirals of the Fleet and Field-Marshals as pall-bearers, the Unknown—that representative of all those who had fallen in doing their duty—was lowered into the vault in the Empire's historic Pantheon. His Majesty, wearing the uniform of a Field-Marshal, occupied the position as chief mourner in these common rites, placing a wreath of laurel leaves and crimson flowers on the coffin.

This impressive piece of symbolism has been imitated by all the countries that were allied with us during the great struggle. Until recently it used to be part of the official duty of any distinguished foreigner visiting this country on state matters to lay a wreath on the tomb of the Unknown Warrior as well as on the Cenotaph. But this custom has now been abandoned, on the ground that it tended to keep alive in a tormented post-war world the restless passions of that universal conflict.

Connected with the honours that a nation pays to its dead heroes is the wonderful annual ceremony at the Cenotaph, which is the subject of a separate chapter.

While the Cenotaph in London is the chief war memorial in the kingdom, there is hardly a hamlet which has not erected a memorial to its own gallant dead. In the very small village of Little Hampden, which consists of a few cottages surrounding one of the most beautiful commons in the country, there is a stone which bears simply three names. Small as is the number, they are not to be forgotten. These local memorials are annually the scenes on

Topical Press

STONE WARRIORS THREE ON A BATTLEFIELD OF FRANCE

This sculptured group is known as the Soissons Trinity. It forms the central feature of the British war memorial at Soissons erected in remembrance of those who fought in the Soissons sector and whose graves are unknown, and was unveiled in 1928. The Trinity is the work of Mr. Eric Kennington (assisted by Mr. Herbert Hart), who, after being invalided home in 1915, was an official artist on the Western front during 1917 and 1918. Starkly noble in design, it depicts three soldiers standing at the foot of a newly made grave, marked by a rifle and steel helmet.

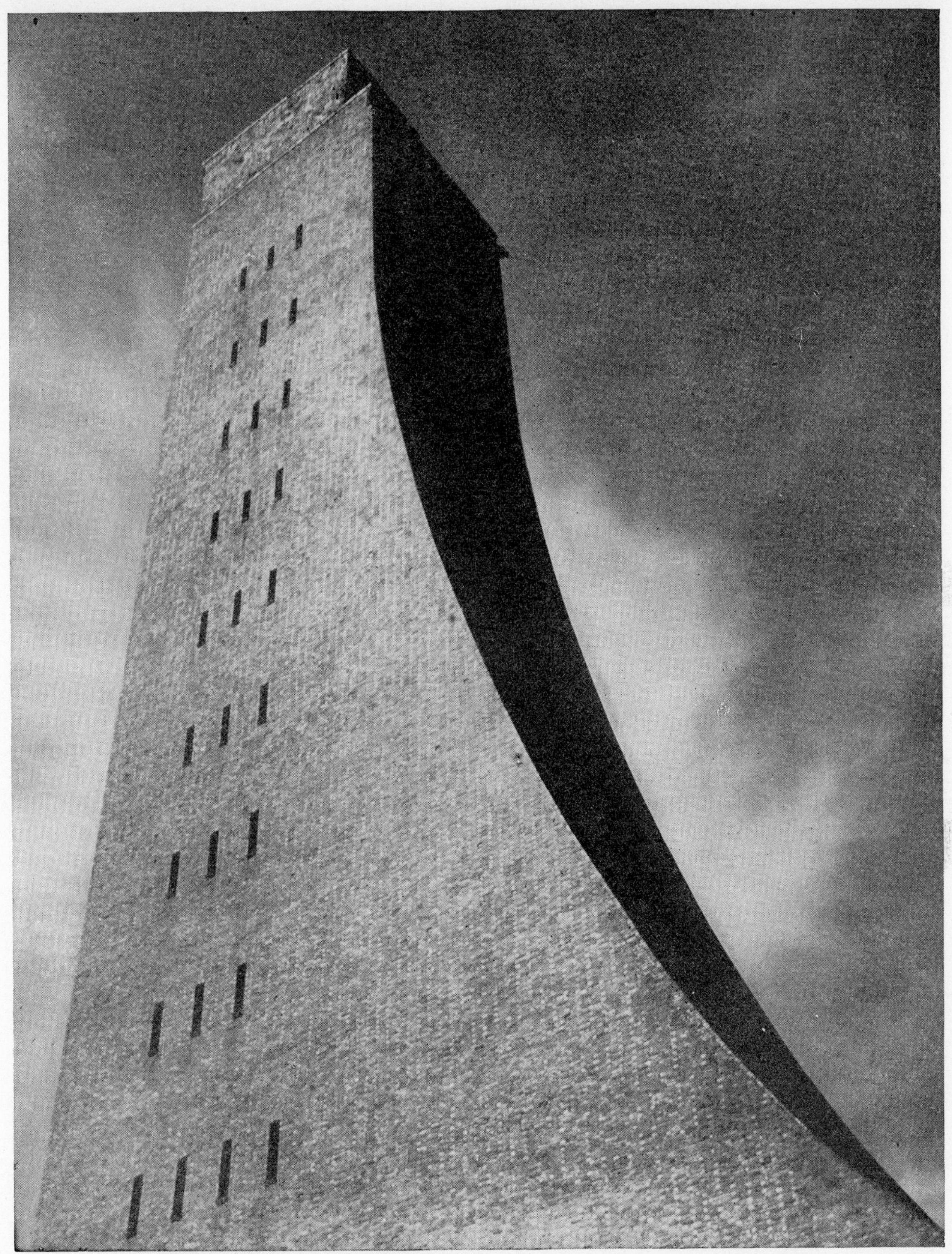

MONUMENT TO THE GERMAN SEAMEN WHO DIED IN THE GREAT WAR

At Labo, near Kiel, close to the shore, stands one **of the most extraordinary examples** of ultra-modern architecture **ever creat**ed by the hand **of** man out of brick and stone and concrete—the German naval war memorial. Built in the form of a wedge, narrow at the top and widening **gradually in a curve** to **the** base, it towers to **a** height of over three hundred feet. The face of this mammoth building is severely plain, being broken only by slit-like openings. Inside there is a vast hall that can hold ten thousand people.

Sport & General

stereotyped designs the architect, Herr G. A. Munzer, has achieved an epic in stone. It stands on the seashore, 300 feet high, and contained within it is a hall which will hold ten thousand people. Less striking perhaps, but remarkably beautiful, is the War Memorial Arch at New Delhi. This is the work of Sir Edwin Lutyens, and stands at the entrance of the King's Way leading to the Viceroy's House. It was unveiled on February 12, 1931, with ceremonies which included 'silence,' the laying of wreaths, and the lighting of a 'Fire of Remembrance.'

As the Great War has receded into the past the figures that played the foremost parts in its operations have one by one left the stage. In January, 1928, Field-Marshal Earl Haig

Armistice Day of processions and services, in which all those who died in the great struggle are recalled.

Other monuments there are to our heroes. One of the most beautiful is the Menin Gate, erected by Great Britain at Ypres, to the memory of 'the Armies of the British Empire who stood here from 1914 to 1918, and to those of their Dead who have no known graves.' It was fitting that such a monument should be raised on such a spot, for it was in defending the Ypres Salient that Great Britain suffered approximately one quarter of her total losses in all theatres of the Great War, in every part of the world by land or sea. Here about a million of the Empire's soldiers were wounded, and a quarter of a million died. Of these latter, 56,000, whose names are engraved on the Memorial, have no ascertainable graves.

Striking, impressive—representing the ultra-modern development of architecture—is the German Naval War Memorial at Labo, near Kiel. In breaking away from all the old

POMP AND SIMPLICITY AT A FIELD-MARSHAL'S FUNERAL

Although the obsequies of Earl Haig of Bemersyde were marked by a great military procession (bottom) to Westminster Abbey, where a memorial service was held, the last rites were verv simple. The great soldier was quietly laid to rest at Dryburgh Abbey, the coffin being drawn from St. Boswells on a farm wagon (top), led and escorted by Bemersyde men.

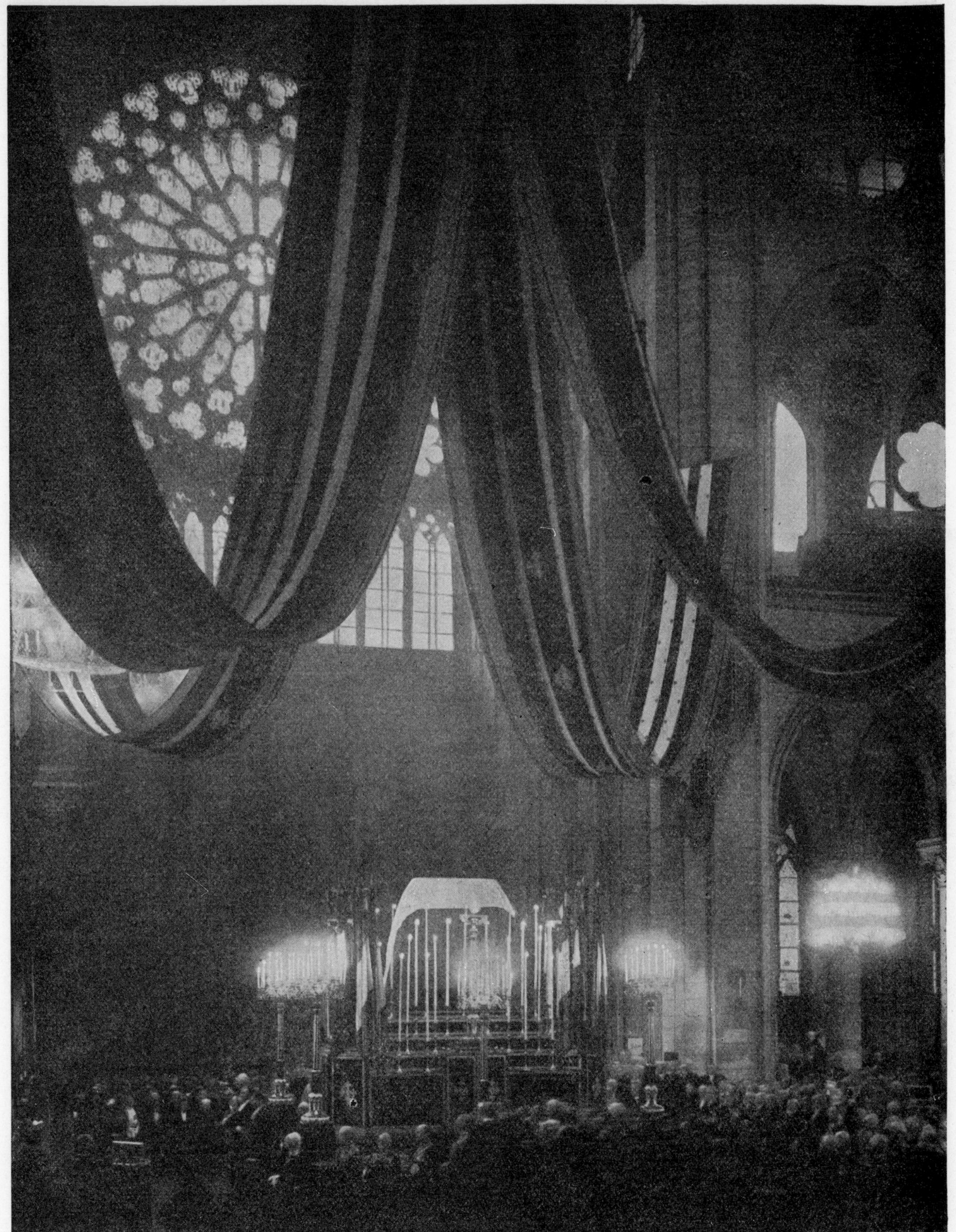

Henri Manuel

IMPRESSIVE SPECTACLE OF THE LYING-IN-STATE OF MARSHAL FOCH IN NOTRE DAME DE PARIS

The French have a genius for ceremonial, and this was exemplified to the full in the scenes witnessed at the funeral of Marshal Foch. Before being conveyed to its last resting place in Les Invalides the body lay in state in Notre Dame. Here the spectacle was impressive in the extreme. The vast building was thronged with those who had come to pay the last honours to the dead soldier. The coffin rested on a catafalque nearly twenty feet high, while overhead hung great black draperies, their gloom relieved by the light of the candles and clustered tapers round the coffin.

Agence Rol

MARSHAL JOFFRE'S FUNERAL: THE HALT BY NIGHT AT THE ARC DE TRIOMPHE

On the evening of January 6, 1931, the body of Marshal Joffre was removed from the Ecole Militaire, where it had been lying in state, to Notre Dame. On the way the cortège passed beneath the Arc de Triomphe, and here a dramatic incident took place. Close to the Arch is the grave of France's Unknown Warrior, where the Fire of Remembrance burns day and night. The coffin was halted by the side of the grave, a minute's silence was observed, and a military salute fired. Then the procession went on to the cathedral, where it remained through the night.

passed away. Experts may argue as to his claim to be placed among the list of great soldiers; but no general, not even Napoleon, so won the esteem and affection of the men whom he led to victory. He accomplished this not so much during the War as afterwards. When Waterloo was fought, no state provision was made for the soldiers who had brought Napoleon at last to his knees. The public subscribed half a million of money, and with that inadequate gesture allowed the claims of these men to pass out of their minds. Earl Haig was the only British commander-in-chief who after the war which had won him fame and rank devoted his life to the interests of his comrades.

It was due to him that the British Legion was founded, that those poppy factories where disabled ex-service men make the flowers of remembrance to be sold on Armistice Day were established, that an organization was set up which has seen to it that the claims of ex-service men are not conveniently forgotten now that the need for their courage has passed. Lord Haig devoted all his days to the interests of the Legion; it was fitting, therefore, that his obsequies should be made the occasion for a great demonstration by the organization he had inspired. Five thousand members of the Legion, drawn mainly from the metropolitan area, with the standards of their respective branches, lined the route along the Mall as the coffin, draped in the Union Jack, was drawn through Whitehall to Westminster for the memorial service. It was symbolical of the innate simplicity of Lord Haig's character that the last rites should have been almost primitive. The body was taken to St. Boswell's, and there placed on an ordinary farm wagon drawn by two horses. A guard of only a dozen soldiers marched by the side of the wagon, but following behind were thousands of those ex-service men to whose interests he had devoted so much of his life. In Dryburgh Abbey, Haig of Bemersyde was laid to rest.

P. & A.

HOW FRANCE HONOURED A GREAT SOLDIER

At the lying-in-state of Marshal Joffre the body rested on a plain black bier. On the ground at the foot of the bier was a cushion on which lay the Marshal's baton. Surrounding the bier were other cushions, each bearing insignia. On either side, in front of the bier, were two old mortars, with steel breastplates and morions, tokens of the warfare of earlier days.

A little more than a year later Marshal Foch, who had commanded the Allied Forces in France in the last great days of the War, passed away. Of all the scenes at that remarkable funeral, perhaps the most moving and the most dramatic was that which took place at the Arc de Triomphe. Here the coffin was halted in front of the tomb of the Unknown Warrior, where the Fires of Remembrance burn day and night. It was 'la suprême rencontre.' Preceded by the clergy, the cortège, after a discourse by the French Prime Minister, made its way to Les Invalides, where the greatest soldier of France lies buried. The route was guarded by troops, and the gun-carriage was followed by French and foreign marshals and generals. Then came the President of the Republic, foreign princes, members of the Government, and relatives. The French have a genius for ceremonial, and nothing was wanting to make the last honours done to the man who had helped to save France at once impressive and moving.

Foch died on March 20, 1929. Less than two years later the man whose command he had taken over passed away. With the death of Marshal

Photopress

NATIONAL RESPONSE TO A NATIONAL CALAMITY: VICTIMS OF THE GREAT AIR TRAGEDY LYING IN STATE

The great British airship R101, which left Cardington on the evening of October 4, 1930, for an experimental flight to India via Egypt, crashed near Allonne, a few miles south of Beauvais, in the north of France, early the following morning, and was destroyed by fire. Of her complement of fifty-four passengers and crew, forty-eight perished. The victims included Lord Thomson, the air minister, Sir Sefton Brancker, the director of civil aviation, and other high officials of the Air Ministry. In this disaster Britain lost the flower of her resources, personal and material, in the airship branch of aviation. After lying in state at Beauvais the bodies of the victims were conveyed to England, where, on October 10, they again lay in state in Westminster Hall.

Joffre all the controversies which had collected about his name were suddenly forgotten. He was remembered only as 'Papa Joffre,' the stout, benevolent, phlegmatic figure who in the hour of his country's greatest danger had remained cool, serene, immovable, and from disaster had plucked the laurels of the Marne. His obsequies were a pageant which expressed the debt owed to him by the Allied Nations. As a unique gesture the band of our Brigade of Guards was sent to take part in the procession, and the Lord Mayor of London, in full state panoply, accompanied by the Sheriffs and attended by the City Marshal, the Bearer of the Mace and the Bearer of the Sword of State, also attended. Lord Allenby was one of the pall-bearers and sat beside the catafalque in Notre Dame. Representatives of the Navy, the Army and the Air Force and of the British Legion took part. After lying in state in Notre Dame the coffin was transferred to the Invalides, where a funeral oration was delivered by the Minister of War, and then finally to the place of interment in the grounds of the dead Marshal's home at Louveciennes.

Undoubtedly the most impressive public funeral witnessed in England in the present century was that accorded to Queen Victoria when, in 1901, she laid down the crown whose dignity and prestige she had done so much to enhance during her reign of 63 years. Nothing was omitted of the pomp and pageantry befitting the obsequies of the ruler of the greatest Empire in the world. But far more impressive than thunder of guns, roll of drums, funeral marches, splendour of uniforms of soldiers and sailors, and of kings and princes from every sovereign state, were the silence and the grief of the black-garbed hundreds of thousands of her subjects who thronged every yard along the line of route.

A FUNERAL which stirred much emotion in England was that of the victims of the R101 disaster. The bodies of the forty-seven dead were brought from Boulogne to Dover in H.M.S. Tempest on October 7, 1930, reaching London at one o'clock the following morning. Late as the hour was, enormous crowds, which included the Prime Minister, were waiting to pay their respects. At Westminster Hall the dead lay in state, and then made their last journey to Cardington, where, in one great grave, they were laid to rest side by side—Air Minister, Air Marshal, Aircraftsman.

Monuments and cenotaphs are erected by nations in honour of their great dead; but it is doubtful if these alone would preserve the names of the heroes in the public mind. Millions who have never seen the pillar in Trafalgar Square or the tomb in St. Paul's cherish the heroic virtues of Nelson; and it is not the memorial erected among the ice-bound fastnesses of the Antarctic, which few are ever likely to see, that will keep green for all time the memory of the heroic action of that 'very gallant gentleman,' Oates, who gave his life in a vain attempt to save those of Captain Scott and his other comrades.

Topical Press

PER ARDUA AD ASTRA

The memorial to the men of the Royal Air Force on the Victoria Embankment is an effective piece of symbolism. Poised on the globe surmounting the obelisk beside the Thames a great golden eagle spreads its wings as if on the point of upward flight

BRETON SAILORMEN'S SUPPLICATION FOR FAIR WEATHER AND GOOD HARVEST FROM THE SEA

Donald McLeish

Bretons are a deeply religious people, and besides their picturesque 'Pardons,' described in a separate chapter, they have many customs to which Roman Catholic ritual imparts much beauty and colour. Notable among these is the annual blessing of the sea at Douarnenez in Finistère. The town is the centre of the sardine fishery, with an active coasting trade and a minor shipbuilding industry. The prosperity of the people is thus inseparably associated with the sea, and they are piously punctilious in invoking the blessing of heaven upon it. This photograph shows a section of the procession at the annual ceremony, with French blue-jackets carrying a model of a fishing boat; the banner borne before them has the appropriate picture of Christ stilling the tempest.

BELIEFS AND SUPERSTITIONS OF THE SEA

NEVER is it more difficult to draw a line between ignorant credulity and enlightened faith than when considering the beliefs and superstitions prevalent among those whose occupation is on the sea. Some of these superstitions are noted in the chapter on Why We Touch Wood and Cold Iron; here insistence is laid rather upon the more serious beliefs that underlie traditional customs.

WHEN man first launched himself trembling upon the sea he brought with him all those fears and aspirations which then constituted his religion. He who had sought to placate the spirit of fertility by ceremonies and sacrifices so that the hunter might prosper or the harvest might not fail—who had ascribed to all the forces of nature by which he benefited or suffered, presiding, unseen genii who must be humbly worshipped, inevitably surrounded the new element which he was trying to conquer with a network of superstition.

When the science of meteorology was unguessed at the uncertain moods of the ocean suggested a presiding deity, irritable and quick to wrath. Solomon, who with all his wisdom had not foreseen the modern oil-powered, turbine-driven vessel with its automatic steering gear, which has reduced the labours of a sailor during a voyage to a minimum, leaving the real tasks to be done by the engineers and mechanics in harbour, accounted the way of a ship upon the sea as one of the great mysteries of the world. The God of the mariner who made the storms to rise, who drowned or wrecked, or brought the hopes of the fishermen to naught, was a very real and terrible being. The English, with their trick of making a jest of what they secretly fear, have preserved to this day in their nautical terminology their conception of this old sea god ; for Davy Jones and his ' locker, to which the dead sailor is committed, is only Poseidon and Neptune and the other sea gods under another name.

THE theology of the sea had its scapegoat like that of the land. In classical times a young man was thrown into the sea with the prayer ' Be thou our offscouring,' a ceremony by which the people were supposed to rid themselves of the evils by which they were beset. Among the Leucadians—in the Ionian island sacred to the memory of Sappho—this rite was performed under more humane conditions. Though hurled from the Lovers' Leap, the victim's fall was broken by a number of live birds and feathers being attached to him, and a flotilla of small boats waited below to catch him in case he drowned. In the British Isles and as lately as within the last century Orkney and Shetland fishermen hesitated before they rescued a comrade who had fallen overboard. The sea god had claimed his victim, and they feared it might go ill with themselves if they interfered. Among the native races of the South Seas this practice still survives and a drowning man is left to drown, and even flung back into the water if he should manage to swim ashore.

The beautiful Catholic rites which form part of the Breton customs—the blessing of the sea at Douarnenez and the feast of Saintes Maries de la Mer at Camargue—is a Christianised version of a rite as old as man's connexion with the ocean. The Indians in British Columbia, who depend largely on the produce of the waters for their food, go through a ceremony which is partly magical and partly religious in order to induce the fish to appear. A Nootka wizard will make an image of a swimming fish and, while all the assembled tribe raise their voices in prayer, places it in the water facing the direction from which the fish are most likely to come. In the same way the islanders of Torres Straits use models of dugong and turtles to charm these creatures to their destruction.

THOSE who get a picture of the average sailor from the rousing chorus of a sea chanty, in which the material side of their lives is perhaps over-emphasised, do not realize the spiritual instincts of awe and reverence which is part of their make-up. This is apparent more in Catholic countries perhaps, and especially in France, where the Virgin is the patron saint of sailors. At Fécamp, in Normandy, the fishermen climb up to the little stone church of Notre Dame de Salut on the top of the cliff enclosing the harbour to make their devotions before sailing on their perilous voyages. Votive tablets of gratitude—' Merci à Marie '—for protections and blessings received, line the walls of all the ancient churches along the northern coast of France. Large gilt statues of the Virgin standing outside are features of these seaport churches. La Chapelle Notre Dame stands high on the cliffs above the lovely little fishing village of Etretat. The fishermen making and mending their nets in picturesque attitudes on the stony beach may be noticed lifting their eyes reverently to the church of their guardian saint if a storm seems to be brewing. We may trace perhaps the relics of sympathetic magic in the practice of Danish sailors, who always have a ship hanging from the roof of their particular churches. An example of this is to be seen in the Scandinavian Sailors' Church at Poplar in East London.

Plato's story of Atlantis, a submerged country beneath the Atlantic, gave rise to superstitious beliefs, which have continued, that there are houses, enchanted castles and churches to be seen in the ocean depths. It is easy to understand that the sailor, before steamships rushed him over the water at express speed, made imaginary pictures looking down into ocean depths, just as children see forms in the fire.

Sailors and fishermen believe that the sound of bells rises from the sea ; they may be from a submerged church or bells lost in a wreck. Baltic fishermen believe they can hear the bells of Vineta. A Norman fisherman will not set out to sea if he hears the muffled peal of the Jersey bells which were lost in a storm. Bells are believed to quiet a storm. At Malta the bells are rung during a gale, and this custom prevails in Sicily, Sardinia and Tuscany.

The mariner's belief in a country beneath the ocean led to a belief, not altogether a superstition, that it was peopled by men and women and sea animals resembling those on land. Hence we have mermaids, mermen and sea animals like the sea serpent, sea wolf and sea hog. These animals do exist, and there are circumstantial accounts of mermaids and mermen found washed ashore. A so-called mermaid is exhibited at Bombay, a creature with the upper part like a human being and the lower part like a fish.

The mermaid is beloved of poets and painters. She is always bewitchingly beautiful, and sits on a rock combing her tresses and carefully hiding her fish's tail. Susceptible sailors on lonely craft are lured to their doom as she sings with the voice of a siren. She may choose one for a lover and take him down to her apartment below the sea. Folk-tales abound regarding mermaids and sirens and naiads, whose allurements sailors profess to dread. Irish fishermen are said to have a particular dread of these ladies of the sea. Harlem boasts the story of a sea-woman who came ashore and became like other women. She lived for fifteen years, died in the odour of sanctity and was buried at Harlem.

The Gunnar's Stone in West Gothland marks the spot where a famous knight, Sir Gunnar, was captured by a mermaid. Swedish fisherman salute the stone for good luck. The Icelanders have many stories of mermaids.

We can understand how the sailor or fisherman in his midnight watches has his imagination stirred until he fancies he sees forms standing on cliff or headland or phantom ships rising out of the sea. These may be explained by atmospheric effects or lights and shadows on the rocks. Most sailors are poets by nature as well as romancers, and prefer to think that they have seen apparitions, and, indeed, to-day the landsman confirms the sailor's belief in the supernatural. The legend of the Flying Dutchman is well known. He is the 'wandering Jew' of the ocean. For sacrilegious behaviour to a Divine Being who visited his deck in a storm, this wicked Dutchman was condemned to sail the seas for ever in his phantom ship. This happened at the Cape of Good Hope. English and American sailors spin

Keystone

QUAINT TRAVESTY OF HOMAGE TO THE SEA-GODS OF OLD

Faint memories of classical mythology are quaintly preserved in a farcical custom kept up by British sailors when crossing the line of the equator. Envoys from Father Neptune board the vessel and announce to the captain the sea-god's intention to hold a court and investiture on the quarter-deck. In due course these heralds are followed by Neptune himself, a grave, bearded figure, crowned and carrying his trident, and accompanied by his consort with flowing tresses and robed in trailing seaweeds, his chaplain, surgeon, barber, police and sea-dogs.

Keyston

RITUAL SHAVE AND BATH ON FIRST CROSSING THE LINE

Following the ceremony on the quarter-deck, at which ladies who never before have crossed the line are baptized with equatorial water and invested with the Order of the Mermaid, Neptune and his retinue proceed to the forecastle, where trial is made as to which persons on board are also novices. These are then seized by the barber and his assistant, generously lathered with soft soap, shaved with a gigantic razor and then flung into a bath of sea water previously prepared, in which they are ducked by the expectant sea-dogs.

yarns about this mysterious mariner. No old sailor or fisherman 'worth his salt' would admit that he had no faith in the phantom ship of the Flying Dutchman. The French believe firmly in his existence, as do German and Dutch sailors, and mariners in the Indian ocean dread the appearance of his phantom ship, as it indicates shipwreck or disaster. There are many stories told by mariners of spectre ships. Cornish sailors are said to see them shrouded in mist before a wreck occurs, and the sailors who perish in the wreck are seen on the spectre ship.

Many superstitions are connected with mysterious lights at sea, the most widely known being S. Elmo's light. Columbus and his mariners saw it above the mast on their second voyage when the ship was in peril and they rejoiced, believing that S. Elmo, their patron saint, was protecting them. Sailors in some countries think these spectral lights are from souls in pain, or caused by drowned sailors trying to get on board. In the island of Batz the lights are said to indicate an evil spirit, a kind of will-o'-the-wisp luring mariners into danger. In Portugal, Germany,

Topical Press

GIVING LUCK TO A STEAMSHIP FOR THE TRANSATLANTIC TRADE

There is a widespread belief among sailors that it is unlucky to sail in a vessel that has not been christened. The usual practice is to name the ship while breaking a bottle of wine against her prow immediately before she is launched. In Brittany the sponsors lick up some of the wine so spilt, and also gather up crumbs of biscuit that have been ceremoniously crushed upon the deck.

Great Britain and America they are held to be harbingers of fair weather.

Cornish fishermen believe in Jack Harry's Lights, so called from the man who first saw them. They are generally seen before a gale, and are said to appear on a phantom ship resembling the one which is doomed to destruction in the gale. The relatives of sailors have professed to see the forms of those who are drowned standing on the deck of the phantom ship.

The influence of tides on human destiny, particularly as regards birth and death, is a superstition as firmly held today by seafaring people as ever it was. As Sir James Fraser points out, 'In the flowing tide they see not merely a symbol, but a cause of exuberance, of prosperity, and of life, while in the ebbing tide they discern a real agent as well as an emblem of failure, of weakness and of death.' Shakespeare makes Mistress Quickly, when describing the death of Falstaff, declare 'A 'parted even just between twelve and one, even at the turning of the tide,' and Dickens makes Peggotty remark 'People can't die along the coast except when the tide's pretty nigh out. They can't be born unless it's pretty nigh in —not properly born till flood.' This belief is met with all over the world, and is as ancient as the days of Aristotle, to whom by some it is attributed. The tides are also held to influence the forces of nature in their operation on land. The Breton peasant only sows his clover when the tide is coming in. If by any chance he should sow it at low water or with the ebb it will either wither or the cows that feed on it will burst. Butter must be made just when the tide is beginning to flow. It is solemnly held that water drawn from the well or milk extracted from the cow while the tide is rising will boil up in a pot or saucepan and flow into the fire.

ONE of the most widespread superstitions with regard to the sea is that a child born in a caul cannot be drowned. By a process of association the caul itself has come to have magical properties of life-saving, and they still command a price among some seafaring folk. Another obstinately persistent belief which neither time nor education has been able to eradicate is in the effect produced by certain waves. Occult virtues are attributed to the third wave, which makes the loudest noise. The ninth wave is believed to have special virtues by the Welsh and Scandinavian sailors. English sailors are said to dread the ninth wave and make the sign of the cross when they see it coming. Before the mariner's compass was invented fishermen took the mother wave as a guide and would find their way by it in a dense fog. This custom is well known in the Shetland Islands.

In Morocco, the Berber tribes believed that the great spirit created the ocean of sweet water, but to punish its arrogance in flooding the land it was made salty. A similar legend exists among the Moslems.

Courtesy of 'Syren and Shipping'

PRAYERS FOR THE SOULS OF DEPARTED JAPANESE SHIPS

Most sailors believe that a ship has personality, but in Japan the idea goes much further, and the belief is held that the soul of a ship survives after 'death.' In December, 1930, the members of the Osaka Shipbreakers' Guild actually attended a ceremony, performed by the Buddhist high priest, of prayers for the souls of 109 steamers broken up in their yards during the previous seven years and for the souls of ten workmen accidentally killed during the operations. Named photographs of the 109 steamers were hung round the walls (top).

E.N.A.

Alfieri

BENEDICTION SERVICES IN FRENCH AND ENGLISH WATERS

At the ceremony of blessing the sea at Saintes Maries de la Mer in Camargue, southern France, the effigies of the two saints who give the town its name are carried from the church in a model of a boat and set on a temporary altar in the water. Seaside benediction ceremonies are not unknown in England, being performed, for example, at Hastings at Rogation-tide, when clergy and choir go down to the shore and hold a special service there asking a blessing on the harvest of the sea.

We all acknowledge the medicinal and antiseptic virtues of salt and the value of sea bathing, but sailors and fishermen invest the cures with superstition. In Trėquier, sea water is used as a purgative, but the patient must blow on it before drinking to dispel impurities. Breton sailors use sea water for eye disease, but it must be taken from the ebbing tide. Scottish sailors use it for spinal trouble, but the water must be taken from the rising tide. In Sweden a belief survives that a sea bather should have beside him a knife or other metal instrument to ward off attacks from marine animals. Solway fishermen believe that it affords protection to throw three white stones into the water and repeat an incantation.

Sailors have a supreme faith in this constituent of their native element. It is lucky to carry salt in the pocket when embarking. Few Isle of Man fishermen would go aboard without their 'salt.' Ship carpenters believe that a sprinkling of salt between the timbers and planks helps to preserve the ship from disaster.

J. Clair-Guyot

BIDDING GOD-SPEED TO THE FISHING FLEET

Saint Malo is rich in seafaring traditions of great antiquity. Many of the inhabitants are employed in the Newfoundland cod fishery, and a very moving ceremony is invariably performed before the departure of the fishing fleet for the northern waters. A high ecclesiastical dignitary—in this instance the Archbishop of Rennes—goes aboard a coastal motor boat and is carried slowly along the line of schooners in the harbour, blessing each vessel as he passes.

SCIENCE may explain the tides and foretell the hurricane, but the old superstitions die a hard death. A midshipman will listen to the tales of an old salt about omens and unlucky days with secret credence. Friday is considered the sailor's most unlucky day by Protestant and Roman Catholic sailors alike, because it was the day of the Crucifixion. We recall the untimely death of Lord Byron. Though he believed the superstition he defied it by sailing to Greece on a Friday. The tragic sequel came in the poet's death at Missolonghi. The last day of the year and Candlemas Day are also a sailor's unlucky days.

Sailors consider it very unlucky to lose a mop or a bucket at sea, or to throw a cat overboard—even newborn kittens—while to lose or damage the ship's flag portends disaster. The ill luck supposed to be attaching to the shooting of an albatross is largely a literary invention due to Coleridge's 'Ancient Mariner.' Captain George Shelvocke wrote an entertaining account of his buccaneering voyage round the world in the beginning of the eighteenth century. In the course of that narrative he described how in passing through the straits of La Maire the ship was followed by a solitary black albatross 'hovering about as if he had lost himself.' Hatley, the second captain, thinking this was a sinister omen, managed after several attempts to shoot it, in the hope that a fair wind would result. Coleridge read the account of this incident, and at Wordsworth's suggestion gave it the twist by which his hero was pursued by the tutelary spirits of the South Seas to avenge the crime.

It is considered a bad omen also to sail in an unchristened boat or ship; hence the elaborate ceremonies of christening ships in various countries. In Catholic Ireland it was believed that the Titanic went down because the Protestant workmen in the Belfast yards chalked upon her hull before she was launched that famous politico-theological phrase which condemns the Pope to the infernal regions. A boat is christened in Brittany with picturesque rites. A bottle of wine is broken on the prow, some biscuit crushed on the deck, and the godparents of the vessel gather the crumbs and lick up the wine. A very curious custom is connected with marriage. Some fishermen hang an effigy of an oil-clad fisherman at the mast head of a trawler, signifying that a member of the crew is about to be married. This is a sign of good luck to the bridal pair.

Topical Press

FRIENDLY GESTURE TO A NAUTICAL BENEDICK

As a signal of good wishes to a comrade about to be married, fishermen in some parts of England and Scotland hoist an effigy of him in oilskins to the masthead of the trawler. The inscription chosen here, 'Every dog has his day,' though well meant, seems liable to misconstruction.

As mentioned in the chapter on the Mascot, seafaring men constitute one of the classes among whom the mascot is particularly prevalent, and all the world over sailors and fishermen have their good omens and luck-bringers. Their belief in the prophylactic efficacy of touching wood and cold iron is referred to in the chapter on that subject. The Pomeranians think it brings good luck to use some stolen timber in building a boat. Greenock fishermen take it as a good omen if a fly falls into a glass from which they are about to drink. Old sailors say it brings luck to hide a coin under the mast. Ships' mascots are very popular to-day. It is said that American sailors will not join a vessel which has not a mascot on board

Birds play an important part as omens of the sea. Squalls are expected when the stormy petrels, Mother Carey's chickens, come flying round the ship in the Southern Seas. It is unlucky to kill one. The osprey is regarded by the fishermen of the New England coast as a sure harbinger of good weather, and to kill one is certain to be attended with unpleasant consequences. In the Baltic the tern has a similar significance, as has the swan. The flying of sea birds inland is believed to herald a hurricane by sailors in Scotland, Brittany and Spain. Flocks of seagulls seeking the shore warn fishermen of 'nasty' weather. Even prosaic Londoners have their imagination stirred when the Serpentine is covered with seagulls—conditions, it is thought, must be bad on the river and out at sea.

THE visits of porpoises, or sea hogs, are held in some parts to predict bad weather, and in others they are good omens. A recent visitor to Fécamp, the Normandy port for the great fishing vessels sailing to and from the Newfoundland and Greenland cod fisheries, witnessed an exciting scene on the arrival of porpoises. There was a general stampede to the beach to watch these ugly creatures disporting themselves with amusing antics in the sea, and they were hailed by the fisherfolk with rapture as the harbingers of a good season.

Among the most curious legends of the sea which still exist—it has, indeed, been made the subject of a film during recent years—is that of the Sargasso Sea. This is a tract in the North Atlantic ocean discovered by Columbus and so named on account of the seaweed, with berry-like air vessels, that floats in island masses hundreds of square miles in area. Many sailors believe that thousands of derelict ships—the accumulated wreckage of many centuries, caught and trapped—are huddled together here.

Life at sea, like everything else in the world, is becoming mechanised ; but the sea itself still evokes a sense of mystery, and while man preserves his feelings of awe in the presence of that sublime pageant of the ocean, it is unlikely that he will shed many of his strange superstitions and the habits and customs to which they have given rise.

MAN'S USE OF ANIMALS

BESIDES their functions as helpers of man in his labours and leisure, as here described, animals play an important part in many sports. Information on this aspect of the subject will be found in the chapters on Hunting the Tame and the Wild, and on National Sports of Europe. There are also many superstitions about animals, which are dealt with in a special chapter.

THE extent to which human beings use domesticated animals has been suggested as a test of civilization. Certainly the races lowest in the scale are those which have none, while the most highly civilized have a great many. This is true of the nations in past ages as well as at the present time. It is curious that all domesticated animals have been known as far back as we have any record of man's life. Since history began not a single new one of any real value has been added to the list.

Some philosophers have been inclined to think man's use of animals unfortunate, not alone because animals have suffered through it, but because it has had also a doubtful effect on humanity. Sir Arthur Helps in his Talks on Animals and their Masters, a characteristic example of Victorian thinking, made one of his characters say: 'I sometimes think it was a misfortune for the world that the horse was ever subjugated. The horse is the animal that has been the worst treated by man and his subjugation has not been altogether a gain to mankind.' The speaker went on to suggest that the homes of the Mexicans and Peruvians before the Spanish conquest of South and Central America, and before any horses were known in those parts, were superior to the dwellings of the poor in London and other great cities. But the argument will not bear being pressed far.

WE shall consider here man's use of animals for help in his labour and for amusement and for the enhancement of his dignity. Their use for food and for clothing is excluded from our view; it will be touched upon in other places. First, then, among the creatures that have been tamed and trained by man for his own purposes comes the horse. Almost everywhere he has been, and still over a large part of the earth he is, the chief carrier of burdens, the principal aid to travel. He is being superseded by the motor. Already he has become a rare object in city streets. But there are still many employments in which he is found irreplaceable so far. Visit a training stable filled with racehorses or with hunters, and you will see them treated with the most careful attention, reared in luxury yet under severe discipline, no expense spared to fit them for their careers. They appear to enjoy their lives. Even when they are straining every muscle under the jockey's whip or the fox-hunter's spur, they seem to share in the excitement of the race or chase. Lying with broken backs or legs on the Grand National Steeplechase course, they must excite sympathy, but racing has no other ordeals for them so severe as this.

Far more to be pitied are the horses that still carry cavalrymen and drag batteries of guns on battlefields. In many minds the Great War left no more sad or sickening recollection than that of wounded and dead horses. They are used for police also in almost all countries. In Germany they go through a strenuous preparation for duties during civil disturbance. They must learn to stand quiet during salvoes of fire and every kind of disturbing noise.

Polo ponies have, on the whole, a good time, though the pace they must show is very hot while it lasts. Pit ponies, on the other hand, lead monotonous and risky lives in darkness far below the surface. There are some 56,000 of them in the collieries of Britain and they die at the rate of about 10,000 a year. Their usual life is seven years, far less than the normal span of a pony. But they never come into the daylight, they breathe always the air of the mine. Whether their lot is less irksome than that of horses trained to perform in circuses is a matter of opinion. Unfortunately we cannot ask them about it.

Many accomplishments of the circus horse are unnatural and must have been painfully acquired. Far happier, we would think, the farm horses, ploughing the fields or harrowing, enjoying the sunshine and the healthy air, and then, when crops have been cut, carrying the sweet-scented hay and the golden grain to the stack-yard. Even the horses on the tow-paths of rivers or canals, though their work is heavy and their hours all that God sends of daylight, are more to be envied than those which prance and curvet in sawdust rings under the glare of artificial light and with myriad eyes upon them.

NEXT to the horse, man depends upon the ox to help to drag heavy carts and furrow the land for sowing. Not, however, in northern Europe as a rule. Few people from Britain, where this use of oxen is scarcely known, can have seen for the first time beautiful yokes of large creamy beasts in Italy, or of darker, stockier animals in the south of France, without a glow of admiration and pleasure.

Nor can the evolutions of a long span of oxen, twelve or fourteen pairs, perhaps, on the South African veldt be watched without a thrill, especially at a spruit, where they must go carefully down steep banks and then up the other side, or at a river, where they may have to swim. Thrills there are, too, in the bull-ring · popular still in Spain and in South America is the spectacle of bull-fighting. But it is hard to imagine a worse use to which these animals could be put than irritating, tormenting, wounding them, and then having them killed by the espada (swordsman), intent only on making a large income by exhibiting his skill.

In Italy buffaloes are also used for draught, in Spain and Greece, too, as well as in India, Persia, Egypt, and the near Eastern countries. They are gentle creatures with those whom they know and trust. They are full of pluck and can defend themselves against tigers; they will even form squares around their herdsmen to protect them. It is curious that the bison, which is so closely related to the buffalo, has never been brought into subjection by mankind. Even the yak of Tibet has been domesticated, and in Turkistan the creature of this species known as the 'grunting ox' is most useful as a burden carrier. But this black yak with long shaggy hair on its belly and flanks can only live in a high latitude. Below a certain level it pines and dies.

Donkeys and mules are widely used both for riding and driving. Here again, however, the north of Europe is exceptional. In Scandinavia there were at a recent date no donkeys at all. Spain is more than any other in Europe the country of the ass; to Central and South America the Spaniards took it, and it still remains the principal beast of burden there. When you see a camel train in the East, you will frequently notice that it is led by a donkey. The swaying, spiteful, spitting camels follow it readily. No doubt the donkey would give the camel a better character than human beings do. No one has a good word for it. It is called morose, discontented, a perpetual grumbler and shirker. It will not come at call; it has to be fetched when it is wanted. It cannot be talked to; every order must be enforced by a tug at its nose-rope. Its bite is severe and sometimes dangerous. Even camel drivers seldom feel any affection for their animals. Yet gratitude is due to them, for without their assistance it would be impossible to travel across dry sandy deserts unless railways were laid, and in few places is there traffic enough to warrant that. Their capacity for going without water for a long time, their swiftness when ridden light, and their willingness to let themselves be heavily laden, are of infinite usefulness

THE elephant in eastern lands is of equal value where heavy tasks are concerned He is used also to lend dignity to unimpressive human beings, who, perched on his back in a howdah, appear more 'heaven-born' than they do on the ground. But the elephant's real value is in industry. He piles timber with his trunk, he drags immensely heavy loads. When a bulky vehicle has been overturned or has got stuck the elephant's tusks and trunk serve, it has been said, 'as lever, screw-jack, dog-hooks, and crane all at once.' These huge beasts show a high degree of intelligence and arouse a great deal of affection.

Topical Press

WHERE THE HORSE STILL HAS HIS PRICE

Although the engine is rapidly displacing the horse, considerable business is done at Barnet horse fair, which is held every year in September. The horses come from places as far apart as the New Forest, Wales, Scotland, and Ireland. The very best of the animals are snapped up by keen buyers before they reach the fair, many of the horses being brought long distances by road.

Central News

AS STEADY IN THE DIN OF CITIES AS IN THE FURROW

The police horse has to be very carefully trained for its multifarious duties. Its gentleness when used in keeping back the crowd during public functions is well known. It must be able to stand firm amidst the noise and bustle of traffic, and has to be inured to even greater disturbances. The lower photograph shows a test being carried out by the Munich mounted police, in which rockets are being exploded among the horses. Very different from this scene of commotion is the quiet silhouette of a ploughing team seen in the upper photograph.

They remember kindness and they do not forget injuries. Their gratitude and their revenge are alike liable to take singular forms. A professor who gave an elephant a cayenne-pepper sandwich to see how the creature liked it had a stream of dirty water poured over him from its trunk. Mahouts (attendants) who have not fed them properly, or have vented spite on them, have been 'savaged' and even trampled to death. For all their apparent calm, these monsters seem to have in their blood a touch of the tropical sun, fierce and maddening.

The elephant can live only in hot climates. The reindeer, on the contrary, must live in lands where for a large part of the year snow and ice are the rule. They are harnessed to sleighs and make long journeys, sustained only by the moss which they find under the snow. In the extreme north of Europe, in vast areas of Russia and Siberia, amid the mountains of the Yukon, they are most valuable for winter journeying.

Across snow dog-trains are also used to carry the lighter forms of transport. But for the 'huskies,' arctic exploration would hardly have been possible. An Eskimo dog can drag a load of 160 pounds and can do just on seven miles an hour. Going at about the same pace, reindeer will drag 240 pounds. These

'The Times'

WHEN WINTER MAKES HEAVY GOING FOR THE HORSES OF THE WOODMAN'S TEAM

Britain is justly proud of the magnificent horses that are employed for cartage and heavy work on her farms and estates. The three chief strains used are the Shire, the Clydesdale, and the Suffolk punch. Of these the Shire horse is the biggest and the heaviest, standing as much as seventeen hands high and weighing up to 2,200 pounds. It is bred chiefly in Lincolnshire, Cambridgeshire and Leicestershire. The largest horse in the world, it is the direct descendant of the old English war-horse and is as docile as it is strong. The Clydesdale takes the place of the Shire in Scotland. Very different in appearance from either of these is the noticeably chubby Suffolk punch. It is an extremely hardy horse, very active, and excellent for hauling purposes.

sleigh dogs are attractive and intelligent, affectionate to their owners, and ready to make friends. This is more than can be said for most of the dogs which help to get small carts along in Holland and Belgium; work does not seem to improve their tempers, or perhaps it is that they are trained to be distrustful and surly. In Britain a law prohibits the use of dogs for any kind of draught labour. This does not prevent their being employed in a number of other ways. Sheep-dogs are trained to watch flocks, to gather them together when they are spread over the hills or dales, to drive them along the roads and prevent them from straying. Marvellous the quickness with which they understand a wave of the hand or a whistle! Sheep-dog trials have of late years given a great many people an insight into the clever work done by these animals, formerly known to a few only. In most countries watch-dogs are familiar members of households, especially in secluded spots, though they are found protecting city dwellings also.

E. Watts

P. & A.

USING BULLS FOR ENTERTAINMENT, QUIET OR FURIOUS

In Pamplona, just before the bull-fighting season opens, the young men of the city chase the bulls through the streets (bottom). Crowds watch the proceedings from behind barricades erected in the streets and from balconies and windows. The performing bull (top) is a not uncommon sight in India. The animals are taken from village to village, and earn a fair living for their masters.

Dogs are used in many forms of sport. Greyhounds and a smaller breed of the same build are taught to race. Some run to handkerchiefs waved by their owners, some chase hares or rabbits. The Waterloo Cup, which is run for every year in February, near Liverpool, is the Greyhound Derby. During the past few years dog racing with an artificial hare has become a popular pastime. Worked by electricity, the stuffed quarry goes at a pace rather faster than a real hare and is never supposed to be caught. Occasionally a dog does get it—and must be sorely disappointed! Fox-hounds, stag-hounds, harriers and beagles (the latter two for hare-hunting) still exist in large

W. F. Taylor

E.N.A

DONKEYS OF TWO CONTINENTS IN STRANGE GUISE

In Persia one frequently sees what appear to be bushes moving along the road. At a closer view these prove to be stacks of camelthorn, a desert product used as fuel, loaded on donkeys (top). The peasants of the Ile de Ré, off La Rochelle, have the curious custom of encasing the forelegs of their donkeys in trousers (bottom).

numbers in England, nowhere else to any extent. Even in England a sentiment has grown up that the cruelty of pursuing animals until they are exhausted and then giving them over to a horrible death is out of key with the spirit of the time. Otter-hounds are going out of use for this reason, and the upkeep by the sovereign of a pack of stag-worriers (the Royal Buckhounds) was dropped many years ago in deference to popular feeling. This does not resent the occasional use of bloodhounds for tracking down escaped prisoners or fugitive criminals or lost persons, but this is not often resorted to. Newfoundland dogs were once kept in some places to rescue people from drowning, and the dogs of St. Bernard are famous for their skill and persistence in finding travellers lost in the snows. But they are seldom heard of now.

Dogs are still used as rat catchers, but the public contests in which black-and-tan terriers were set to fight with large numbers in a ratpit have long ceased. A hundred years ago high prices were paid for seats at these elevating performances—five shillings for a stall, three shillings for the pit (equal to at least a pound and twelve shillings of our money). A really good dog could kill a hundred rats in less than a quarter of an hour. The sport of bull-baiting by dogs has also died out, so has the use of long-bodied dogs to turn spits on which joints roasted before the fire. But the pointer and setter are still seen in the autumn fields with shooting parties—or to better advantage with a single 'gun,' walking leisurely through the woods and across the stubble; the spaniel and the retriever (so-called because it retrieves, that is, finds and brings to its owner game which he has brought down) are by no means extinct; and plucky little fox terriers continue to be put into

Topical

ELEPHANTS AND CAMELS IN THE RING AND AT THE RACE MEETING

Fights between animals have long been a favourite entertainment in India. The beasts do not fight to the death, for the Hindu religion forbids the taking of animal life, but they are usually dragged from the ring utterly exhausted. Elephant and buffalo fights are fairly general; fights between elephants are an ancient form of sport; the duel staged before the Viceroy at Baroda (top) has parallels in ancient Mogul manuscripts. The Arabian camel or dromedary, as used by the camel corps, can develop very fair speed, and is often raced in Egypt (bottom).

the 'earths,' or holes, in which hunted foxes have taken refuge, in order to drive them out.

The principal use of dogs, however, is as companions or pets. The Friend of Man, the dog has been called. Unfortunate are those who have not enjoyed that form of friendship. There are fashions in this, as in everything else. Tastes alter from age to age. In the later 19th century pugs were the usual favourites of old ladies. Today these animals are scarcely ever seen. As men's companions, fox terriers or Irish terriers were at one time almost compulsory. Now there is a much wider range of choice. Scotch terriers of various kinds have become very popular. The old lady's pet is now a Pekinese or a toy Pomeranian or some other very diminutive breed. Pekinese dogs were once held in very high honour by the Chinese. Long ago an Emperor made one a doctor of letters and ordained that others should have the rank and precedence of mandarins! Evidently the Chinese were once very fond of dogs, not only cooked but alive. They eat them still. The very idea of such a thing causes Britons to shudder. They could as soon almost think of eating human children. Nowhere is a whole people so warmly attached to dogs as in England.

No bond of sympathy between people of different ranks in life is stronger than their common fondness for and interest in their dogs. It is rare to find dogs treated as anything but members of the family. The days when they were usually kennelled outside have been a long while gone.

Cats are now as highly respected and as affectionately treated as dogs, a great change from the way they were generally harried and hunted up to the last quarter of the 19th century. What has brought about the change it is difficult to say. It may be the general strengthening of humane sentiment. It certainly is not due to any effort made by cats to ingratiate themselves or to 'pay for their keep'!

No one has ever yet induced a cat to do anything useful except catch mice, which it does to satisfy its own instincts, not from any desire to be obliging to its owners. Dogs are loved because they are dependent on mankind, cats for the opposite reason: they are so entirely independent that they compel admiration, and we are moved to grateful tenderness by any slight advance on their part, even by a haughty recognition of kindness received, or a readiness to purr gently in reply to our advances. They must find it hard to reconcile the human commendation they receive for killing mice with the taste some humans have for keeping white mice, and even white rats, as pets. Rabbits, also, are used in this way, and many species of birds, especially parrots, parrakeets, cockatoos, canaries. The keeping of native British song-birds in cages was common at one time,

Willis Eadon

ELEPHANT TRANSPORT IN THE STREET OF AN ENGLISH CITY

Of the two species of elephants, the African is valued chiefly for its ivory, and the Indian for its prowess as a draught animal. The enormous strength of the elephant enables it to drag very heavy loads. In such countries as Burma elephants do almost all the handling of the forest timber. These intelligent beasts haul the logs to the stream, and with their trunks pile the squared logs and stack the sawn planks. An elephant is here seen in unusual surroundings, amid electric trams and motor lorries, harnessed to a heavily laden lorry in Sheffield.

Dr. Habberton Lulham

HAPPY WITH HIS MASTER BY HIS SIDE AND HIS CHARGES WITHIN EYESHOT

Sheep-dogs are among the most intelligent of dogs. A flock of sheep, say, is scattered far and wide over hill and dale. With a few quick and clever manœuvres the sheep-dog will gather them together and marshal them, thus compacted, through gates and fields and along the road. And woe betide the sheep that attempts to stray. This remarkable aptitude for herding sheep and cattle is doubtless an adaptation of primitive hunting instincts. The sheep-dog displays the utmost devotion to its master, whose slightest signal it at once obeys.

but has been successfully frowned on. It is now regarded as 'low'—nothing can long survive in England under that ban. Canaries are used in another way; they are taken down into coal mines as a means of detecting the presence of dangerous air, to which they are more susceptible than men. This is analogous to the use of mice in submarines.

Birds are not only kept for the pleasure of their songs, the oddness of their appearance and remarks, or the beauty that is in their plumage or their movements (peacocks and swans). They are trained to perform in a good many ways—especially in India, where, too, in certain districts, as in parts of China and Japan, cormorants and pelicans are taught to catch fish for their owners' benefit, as described in pages 86 to 89. Birds are used also for man's amusement by being set on to fight. Cock-fighting has almost ceased in England, but it is kept up in the East, where combats between quails and black partridges are staged as well. Hawks are in a good many lands still sent up in pursuit of other birds, but now only as a sport, not because the prey brought down are wanted for food. Sport is killing without the spur of hunger or from any need to kill. The shooter treats pheasants, grouse, partridges, pigeons, woodcock, snipe, simply as moving targets. The hunter looks upon stag, fox or hare as the object which will set in motion the hounds and give him a good gallop. In India the cheetah is trained to kill antelope and black buck, and an arduous business it is to catch and control these hunting leopards.

Courage and care in as high a degree are required by the snake-charmer, who uses serpents as his means of a livelihood. As a protection against snakes the mongoose is domesticated. Because it has thick fur and adopts a rapid method of attack it can, as a rule, kill snakes; but the popular belief is that it eats a plant which confers on it immunity from the poison of snake-bite and also makes its breath so

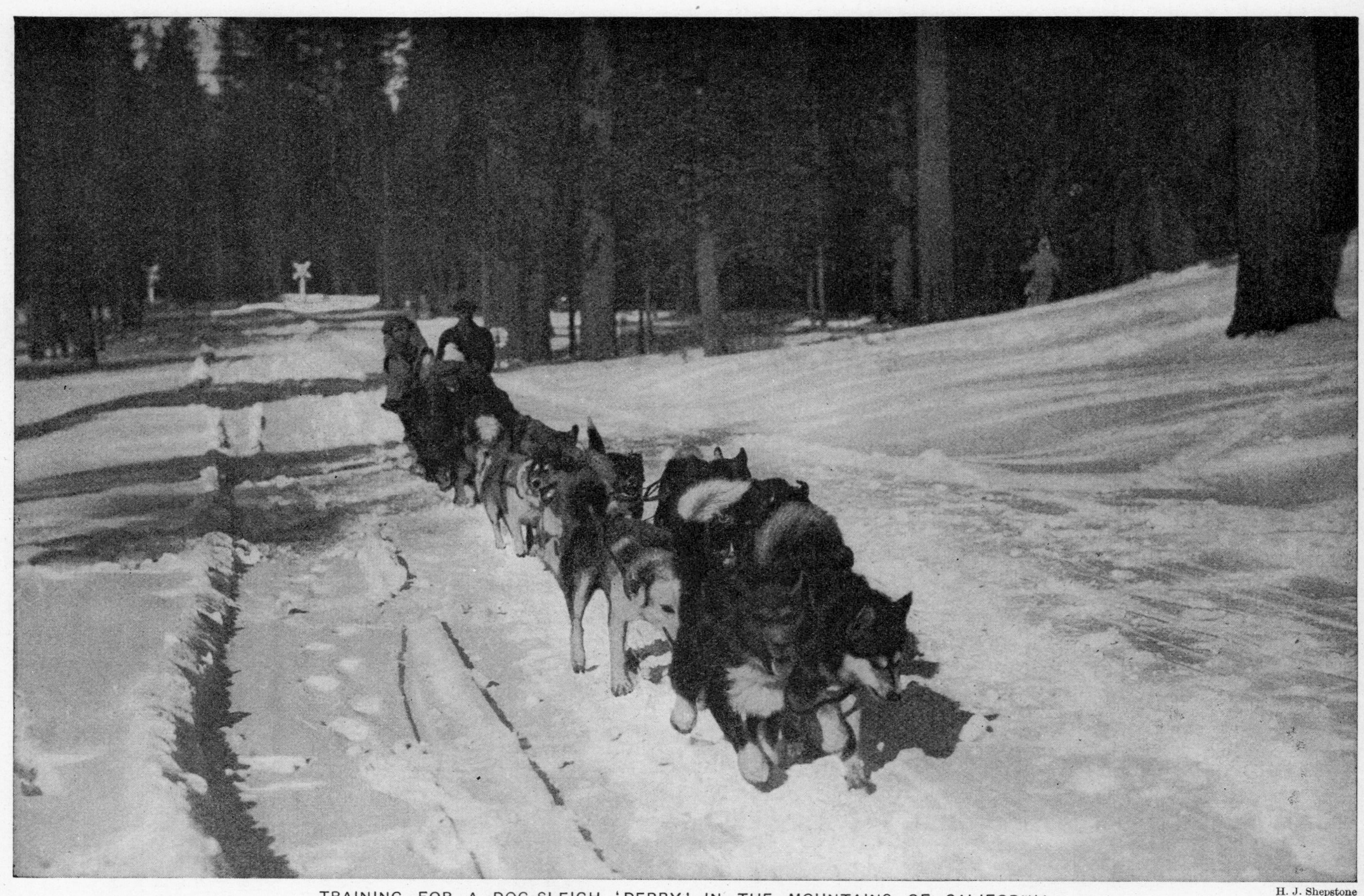

H. J. Shepstone

TRAINING FOR A DOG-SLEIGH 'DERBY' IN THE MOUNTAINS OF CALIFORNIA

With its thick coat, usually tawny in colour though sometimes black and white, its fine bushy tail, and its sturdy build, the Eskimo dog is a handsome animal. There is a good deal of the wolf in its composition; instead of barking it howls like a wolf. It is used for drawing sleighs, about eight being usually yoked together. For this work two types of dogs are used, the malamute and the husky. Over soft snow the husky is preferred, while the malamute, which has comparatively short legs, is better when the snow is hard. Of late years dog-sleigh racing with these animals has become a very popular sport in Canada and other countries where snow is abundant. These races are over long distances, and take several days.

Topical

DOG-DRAWN MILK CARTS OF THE NETHERLANDS

In Holland and Belgium it has long been the custom to employ dogs as draught animals. Securely strapped between the shafts of long, low carts, dogs could formerly be seen struggling along with all manner of quite heavy loads—great tanks full of fish, towering piles of vegetables from the market gardens—indeed, almost all the tradesmen's goods in the Netherlands were conveyed to the customers' houses by means of these dog-drawn carts. Nowadays, however, dogs are no longer used for such heavy work, but only for drawing light milk carts.

offensive that it can paralyse snakes before it strikes them dead.

Many animals are trained by man to perform in public in such a fashion as to appear either very clever (that is, very human) or very ridiculous. Bears are led about still and forced to dance in a clumsy manner, monkeys perched on the backs of goats are common sights in the East. Even sea lions have appeared on the stages of European variety theatres. The learned pig used to be a familiar ' turn ' in circuses and at country fairs until the trick by which he appeared to spell words was revealed by Lord George Sanger. Pigs (as well as dogs) are used in countries where truffles are found to smell out this variety of tuber so highly esteemed by gourmets and show where it lies hidden.

THE domestication of bees in order that they may make money for the owners of their hives is another instance of animals being used to produce food, as the silkworm is an instance of their being kept so that they may produce material for clothing. These differ from the use of animals for food or for clothing, and therefore come properly into our list of examples of man's use of animals. The list is almost concluded with the mention of the tame gold-fish and carp kept in houses and ponds and the extraction from the bodies of certain animals of remedies for certain ailments. This medicinal use is not as common as it used to be, but the writer has been told by a man not very old that, as a boy, doctors in the Windsor district used to pay him half-a-crown for a viper, from which, it was said, they would make a decoction that was a cure for viper-bite.

Our survey cannot be brought to an end, however, without mention of a use of animals on which there is very great difference of opinion. Vivisection, the infliction on dogs, cats, rats, mice, rabbits, of diseases, the subjecting of pigeons and other creatures to temporary starvation, all the experiments which are made with a view to widening knowledge about the effect of various ills and various treatments on the human body—these must be added to our list, but without further description or comment. To go into details would be revolting; to offer to decide the question whether such use of animals is necessary and has given useful results would be an impertinence. It is a matter on which all must make up their minds for themselves.

Altieri

ASCENSION-TIDE WELL-DRESSING: THE BISHOP OF DERBY BLESSING A WELL IN MEMORY OF DELIVERANCE FROM THE BLACK DEATH

The annual custom of dressing the wells on Ascension Day can be seen to great advantage in the Derbyshire village of Tissington, near Ashbourne. In the 14th century epidemic of the Black Death Tissington was the only locality untouched in Derbyshire, and the festival was founded, it is said, in gratitude for this escape. Some think it was but revived then, since similar customs persist in Derbyshire without the plague legend. The decoration usually consists of a picture within an ornamental frame, surmounted by a Bible text. The designs are made with flowers and flower petals, buds, leaves, moss, lichen, and grains of rice, arranged in trays spread with moistened clay. Detail of one of the designs is shown in page 319.

WELL-DRESSING AND HOLY WELLS

THE subject of this chapter has two aspects. It is partly a seasonal festival and partly a survival of a form of primitive nature worship. It is therefore convenient to discuss with it holy wells and wishing wells and springs venerated in earlier days as the abode of the supernatural. The association of water with religious rites is considered under Baptismal Rites and The Pilgrimage in Europe.

THE picturesque old custom of well-dressing, which is still observed every summer in Derbyshire, is one of the most charming survivals that still remain among us, and attracts large crowds of interested visitors. It is even more important to the serious thinker, because it is a fragment of the world-wide cult of holy wells and magic springs, traces of which are found in every clime and among men of all races. Its origin goes back to the childhood of mankind, before the dawn of history, and affords valuable clues to the origins of belief.

Water is a primary human need; without it both animal and plant life are equally impossible, as we have already noted in the chapter on Rain-makers and Rain-making Ceremonies. Although this is a fact all over the world, it is much more obviously true in the arid countries of the East, where from time immemorial to own a well and to possess the surrounding country have been synonymous terms. So vital is the need for water that fights for wells have been frequent from the days of Abraham until to-day. Even now it is dangerous to approach a well in the Arabian desert, because if Arabs are already in possession, they are likely to fire on strangers. In antiquity wells, streams and pools were regarded as infested by local nature spirits, kind or cruel, to whom sacrifices were made. Thus in the days of Homer the rivers Xanthos and Scamander were each provided with a priest and appeased by sacrifices, but they were certainly not more venerated than is the Ganges to-day. That river attracts vast hordes of pilgrims to Benares who believe that they will make sure of paradise by bathing in its waters. Wells and streams are widely venerated in India, although it is a dragon rather than a nymph that is believed to watch over them.

The subject is so vast that British observances will be described first, and then a return made to the wider aspect.

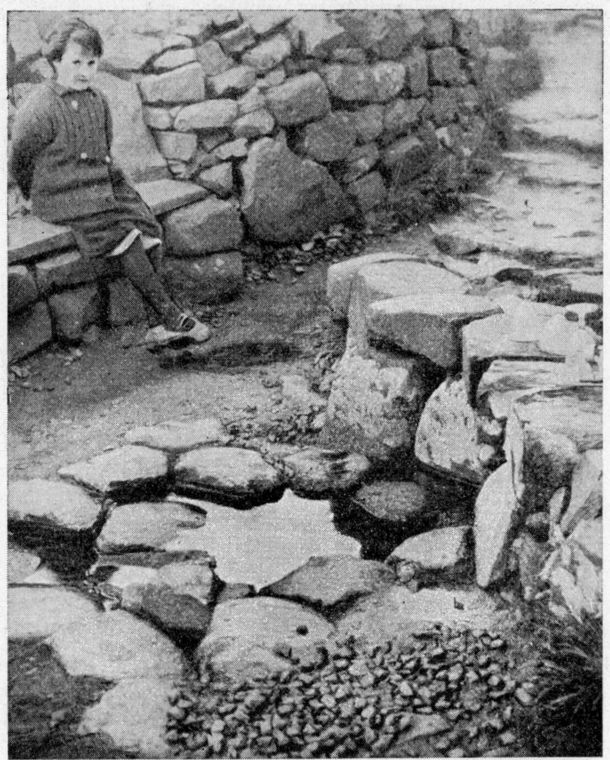

W. F. Taylor

WISHING WELL ON THE GIANT'S CAUSEWAY

Ireland is a country very rich in magic springs and holy wells, and Irish folklore abounds in stories of the beings that are supposed to dwell in them. This little Irish maid, sitting beside the wishing well on the Giant's Causeway, is puzzling her head what to wish.

ONE of the best known ceremonies of this kind is the Tissington well-dressing, which takes place every summer on Ascension Day. The wells are adorned with flowers, and a religious service is held at each in turn. The decorations are wonderful, and form a most beautiful example of an ancient local art performed by very skilled craftsmen. Large wooden frames are spread with moist clay, which is smoothed flat and forms the background for the designs. The usual plan consists of a Bible text at the top, with an appropriate picture below, the whole enclosed in an ornamental border. It is really a mosaic of flower petals, buds, leaves, berries, mosses, and grains of rice or corn, which are packed closely together to form designs in vivid natural colours. Some of the colour effects are astonishingly fine, the tender blue of wild hyacinth or dog-violet, the vivid green of the young larch, the hazel and umber of lichens and berries, or the pink flush of apple blossom. At a short distance the designs could be mistaken for paintings, though the glowing colours put to shame the best efforts of the artist's colourman. Each of the five wells has a different subject.

Very large crowds resort to Buxton every summer to see the ceremony at the historic S. Ann's Well, which is decorated in the same way. This well was renowned for its healing virtues in Roman times, and has been resorted to

Topical

WHERE ONCE THE ROMANS BROUGHT THEIR SICK AND HALT TO BE HEALED

S. Ann's Well at Buxton was known as far back as Roman times, when it was famed for its healing properties. Later a chapel was built over it, and the shrine became renowned far and wide for the wonderful cures effected by its holy waters. Large numbers of crutches, bandages, and other offerings were deposited in the building as witnesses to the gratitude of sufferers who had been healed. The chapel was subsequently demolished, and the custom of well-dressing was established. The ceremony of blessing the well takes place every summer.

ever since. At the time of the Reformation a chapel had been erected over it, and was full of crutches and other tokens left behind by those who had gained benefit from it, just as we can see at Lourdes to-day. Sometimes they offered gifts to the goddess of the well. There is an ancient Roman well dedicated to Coventina on the line of the Roman Wall near Chollerford (Northumberland) in which an enormous number of Roman coins, vases, beads, rings and other objects of value were found; and at Bourbonne-les-Bains, in the department of the Haute Marne (France), a Roman well was discovered in 1875 containing 4,000 bronze, 300 silver, and even a few gold coins, ranging from the reign of Augustus to that of Honorius.

In each case the dates of the coins are in sequence over a long period, which suggests that they were thrown in as gifts one or more at a time, and are not a hoard which was hidden for safety. In 1870 S. Querdon's Well at Troqueer (Kirkcudbrightshire) was cleaned out, and hundreds of coins were found, dating from about the period of Queen Elizabeth to that of George III. This idea of making a gift to the spirit of the well is found far and wide. When travelling in Africa during the last decade the writer saw a bush beside a well which was covered with rags tied on. Exactly the same thing can be seen to-day at the Holy Well of Doon, in Donegal. Clustered round the well are a number of votive crutches, and the bushes near by are covered with rags, which—as in Africa—are really gifts to the spirit of the well. There is another wishing well at Innis Maree, Ross-shire (Scotland), and here also a gift is affixed to the adjacent tree; Queen Victoria is recorded to have attached a coin to comply with this ancient custom (September, 1877).

While holy and magic wells are found all over the world, it may be of some interest to state what a large number we have in Great Britain. They are most plentiful in the Celtic districts, Cornwall being by far the richest district in England, and they are exceedingly common in Wales, Scotland

and Ireland. There are about five hundred in England, and perhaps as many in Scotland. Over seventy of these are dedicated to the Virgin, and about fifty are consecrated to various saints by name. A very interesting example is S. Mungo's Well, in the south-east chapel of Glasgow cathedral, which tradition insists was once a Celtic holy well in the centre of a stone circle and used for 'Druidical' lustrations. When the saint had converted the heathen he built his church on the very site of their holy place and incorporated the well within the edifice.

Exactly the same legend is told of the very ancient holy well in the crypt of Winchester cathedral, which is still pointed out to visitors as the 'Druid Well.' Proof is lacking, but the legend is likely enough, since it is known that the early Christians often erected their churches on the sites of heathen temples, and even S. Paul's cathedral is believed to stand on the site of a Roman temple.

REBEKAH AT THE WELL
AND SHE GAVE HIM DRINK

Topical

Alfieri

TRIUMPHS OF A BEAUTIFUL RURAL CRAFT

At the Derbyshire market town of Wirksworth the ceremony of well-dressing is observed at Ascension-tide in thanksgiving for the bringing of water into the town. The decoration of the Wirksworth wells (top) is done with flowers and laurel leaves. The lower photograph shows a veteran craftsman belonging to the village of Tissington dressing one of the five wells there.

The holy wells of Wales are too numerous to mention in detail, but two in the north are of special interest. S. Elian's Well (Denbighshire) is remarkable in that it is a cursing well, and will make an enemy pine away if his name is inscribed on a pebble which is thrown into the water together with a pin ; or the latter can be cast in by itself, provided the name is announced of the person to be blasted. This was done in England two thousand years ago, and in the Roman bath at Bath a piece of lead was discovered, inscribed in Latin *backwards* thus : 'May he who carried off Vilbia waste away like that dumb water, save only he who . . . her.' The missing word has rusted out. There must be a thrilling drama of love and hate behind these words written nearly twenty centuries ago.

George Long, from 'The Folklore Calendar'

PRINCE'S DEVICE ON A HOLY WELL

Harbledown, near Canterbury, has a famous holy well. It is called the Black Prince's well from the fact that water from it was sent to that prince during his last illness. Over the top of the well is a stone on which are carved the badge and motto of the Prince of Wales.

The celebrated S. Winifred's Well, at Holywell, Flintshire, has been aptly styled 'The Lourdes of Wales,' and attracts large numbers of devout and ailing pilgrims. The annual opening on May 1 is celebrated with processions and festivities of quite a Continental type, and this is continued at the Feast of S. Winifred in June and November, when very large crowds attend and the bones of the saint are exhibited to the devout. There is the usual collection of discarded crutches left behind by those claiming to have been cured. The origin of the well is explained by legend thus. S. Winifred was a holy virgin who lived in the seventh century. She was sought in marriage by a chieftain named Caradoc, but refused him, as she was vowed to chastity. He sought to abduct her, and she fled from him, whereupon he pursued her and struck off her head with his sword. The severed member rolled down the hill, and at the spot where it came to rest the holy well gushed out. The maiden was miraculously restored to life, and the murderer fell dead. This type of legend is very common, and twenty-six holy wells in England are said to have sprung from the spot where some saint was martyred, buried or rested.

It is interesting to record that modern Greek peasants still dread the Nymphs or 'Nereids of the River or Spring,' and no cautious man will ford a river without first crossing himself three times. Children who are sent to draw water from a well are taught to spit three times into the spring before filling their pitchers, and vague tales are still current of children who neglected this safeguard and were dragged into the water by the nymphs. Similar beliefs were held by country folk in remote parts of Wales a century ago.

The same idea is found in the Celtic legends of the water kelpie, water horse or water bull, which we find in Wales, the Isle of Man and Scotland. This corresponds to the Icelandic Nikr, the Swedish water demon of the same name, and the German river spirit known as Neck; all of which strive to seize and drag down those who bathe.

The legends are still believed in Scotland, and as recently as 1930 an old fisherman in Skye gave the writer a description of a water kelpie he had seen in Loch Corrusk many years before when out on a deer-poaching excursion. Though a horse, the kelpie was credited with powers of speech, but the fisherman did not wait for conversation.

Other lakes specially mentioned as the abode of the dreaded Each Uisge or water horse are Lochs Ness, Rannoch and Awe, and the Pontage Pool on the Esk, in Forfarshire.

We have shown that wells, streams and pools have been venerated as the abode of supernatural beings, who are to be propitiated by rites or offerings, but how and where did the idea arise? There can be little doubt that it was beneath the burning eastern sun, in those arid lands which have been the cradle of the world's great religious systems. It is in the desert that the almost miraculous power of water is most clearly demonstrated, both in saving the lives of men and beasts who are dying of thirst, and in creating a green oasis in the midst of desolation. This idea of the magic power of water is found in the ritual of nearly every religious cult. We see it in the rite of baptism, in the use of holy water, in the ceremonial washings of Islam, and in the lustrations of pagan systems both ancient and modern. Its origin is found in that primitive nature worship which may have been the mother of all cults, and traces of which are found everywhere. It regarded the sun as being the all-father and the earth as the all-mother. The symbol of the former was the lingam or phallus, which was usually represented by a tall, straight tree, especially the date palm, also by a pillar, a cone or an upright serpent. The sign of the earth-mother was a well or cleft in the rock from which water flowed. This dual idea of the sacred tree and the fountain of life is found almost all over the world. Yggdrasil was the world-tree of Scandinavian mythology, and under each of its three roots was a fountain of marvellous virtues ; the sacred well of Connla in the old Irish legend was overshadowed by nine mystic hazel trees whose nuts were filled with knowledge. When the Persians burned the Temples on the Acropolis, at Athens, in 480 B.C., it is recorded that they destroyed the sacred olive tree of the goddess Athena, in the Erechtheion. In the same sacred enclosure was the holy well of Poseidon, which the sea god had produced by striking the rock with his trident. The olive tree has, of course, disappeared, but the sacred spring is still shown ; it has now shrunk to a mere trickle.

This idea was very common in the childhood of the world. We find it in that superb creation poem with which our Bible begins. In Genesis ii, 9-10, we read : 'The tree of life also in the midst of the garden, and the tree of knowledge of good and evil. And a river went out of Eden to water the garden.' Here we have an earthly paradise with a wonderful river and two magic trees. One of them (like that of Connla) gave knowledge to him who ate of its fruit.

The Eden of Celtic mythology was Avalon, that 'Deep meadowed island, fair with orchard lawns,' to which the souls of the heroes were wafted, and here, also, we find a very ancient holy well and a sacred or magic tree. Though both are associated by Christian tradition with Joseph of Arimathea, it seems highly probable that they were objects of veneration centuries before the birth of Christ. It is definitely stated by the present owners of the Chalice Well that the masonry of the well is pre-Roman ; and though, of course, the Holy Thorns at present visible are comparatively recent cuttings, they doubtless descend from an original miraculous tree of high antiquity. We know that the medieval Holy Thorn was hewn down by a Puritan, but slips taken from it have grown and 'still blossom at Christmas in honour of the Nativity,' as the legend

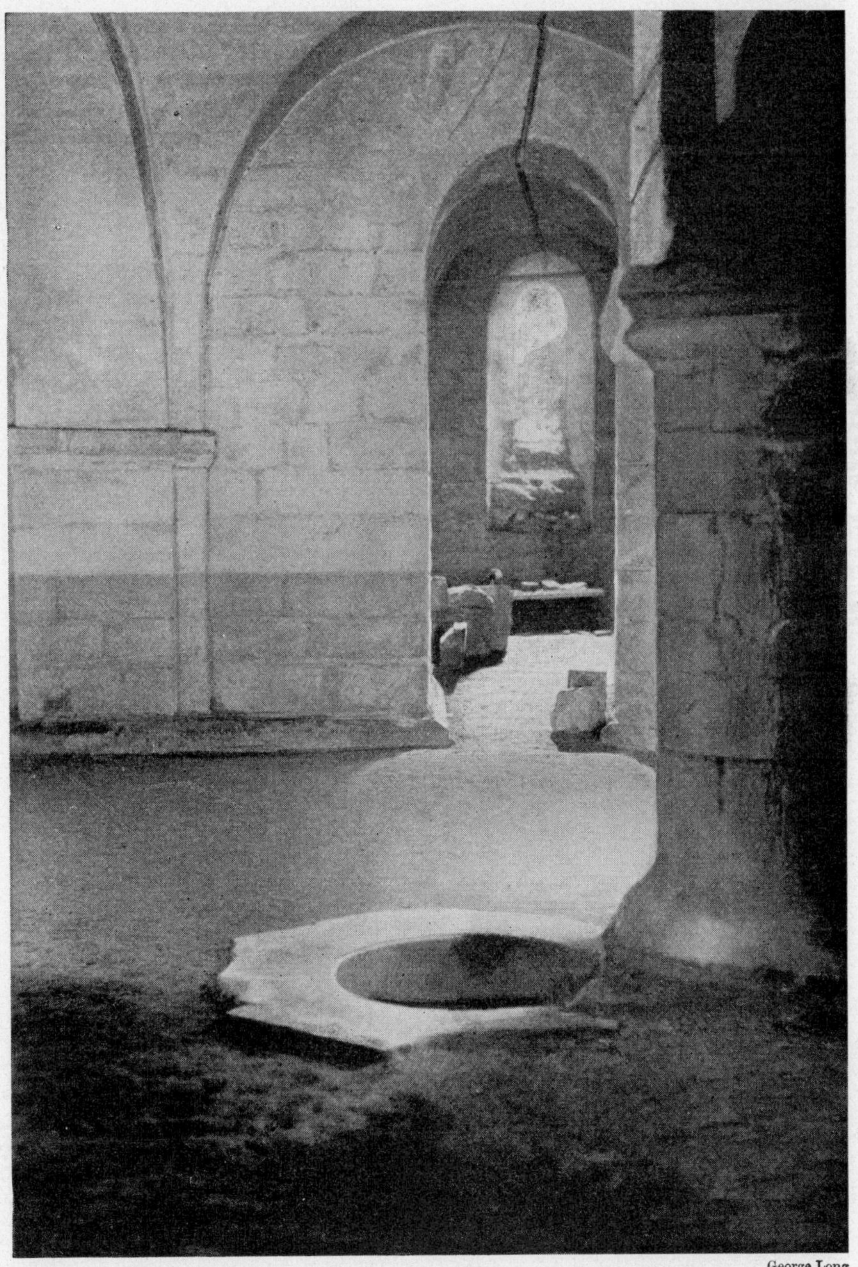

George Long

'DRUID WELL' IN WINCHESTER CATHEDRAL CRYPT

It is a well-known fact that in the early days of Christianity churches were frequently built on the sites of heathen temples. Where a holy well existed, it is probable that this would be incorporated in the building. Thus, according to tradition, the holy well in the crypt of Winchester cathedral was formerly a Celtic holy well, and to this day it is known as the 'Druid Well'

W. F. Taylor

STRANGE RITES THAT MUST BE PERFORMED TO APPEASE THE WATER SPIRIT

Apart from holy wells which have properties of curing disease and other infirmities, many waters exist that are regarded as possessing the power of granting the wishes of those who duly carry out certain necessary formalities. The ceremonies that have to be performed to produce the desired results vary in different localities, and are dictated by the tradition that the water is the abode of a supernatural being who has to be propitiated. Often gifts are brought to the well, such articles as coins or pins being thrown into the water. At the wishing well at Upwey, in Dorsetshire, here seen, the procedure is very simple. All that the visitor has to do is to take a glass of the water, drink some of it and throw the rest over his shoulder, and then wish.

of the thorn insists. Today the ancient well has been fitted with a beautiful lid, which was dedicated in 1919 by Archdeacon Farrar as a thank-offering for peace.

We find a very similar legend about the holy well of S. Mullen at Listerling (Co. Kilkenny). It is overshadowed by a fine hawthorn, which it is said sprang from the saint's staff—like the Holy Thorn. But the most ancient and interesting of the sacred waters of Ireland is to be found at Saint's Island, in Lough Derg, near Donegal. It is thronged by the devout from June 15 till the end of August, and has been resorted to by Christian pilgrims for fourteen centuries. As long ago as 1840 the annual total of visitors was nineteen thousand, most of whom walked thither barefoot. The ritual comprises prayer, fasting, and bathing in Lough Derg. Pilgrims still resort to Croagh Patrick, a picturesque mountain in Co. Mayo, upon which the saint is said to have collected all the snakes in Ireland before driving them into the sea. The sacred sites include two

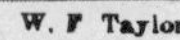

W. F Taylor

J Dixon-Scott

WATERS OF ANCIENT SANCTITY AND MAGIC IN SCOTLAND

Of the many British wells that are credited with holy or magical properties most are to be found in the Celtic districts. In England, for instance, the greatest number are met with in Cornwall, and they are plentiful in Wales, Ireland and Scotland. Some of these are healing wells, and others wishing wells. The upper photograph shows the well of S. Ignatius, at Strathglass, Inverness-shire, which is held in great favour by Roman Catholics. Below is seen S. Anthony's Well, an ancient wishing well on the slopes of Arthur's Seat, Edinburgh.

WONDER-WORKING WATERS DISCOVERED IN A DREAM

There is a famous healing well in Rumania. It is only a few years ago since its thaumaturgic qualities were discovered, and now it is a great resort of pilgrims and hundreds of cures are reported every year. It owes its discovery to a dream. A little blind girl who lived at Smeeni dreamed that if she bathed in the waters of a certain local well her sight would be restored. She told her dream to her relatives, who were so impressed that they decided to take the child to the well, where her dream came true.

George Long, from 'The Folklore Calendar'

CHALICE WELL AT GLASTONBURY

At the foot of Glastonbury Tor is a spring, which is said to mark the spot where Joseph of Arimathea buried the Holy Grail. Its waters are reddish, and from this fact the well is sometimes called the Blood Spring. The well-cover only dates from 1919.

holy wells, and a station called S. Patrick's Bed beside which are two old trees. These are covered with votive offerings left by pilgrims, rags, locks of hair, pins, needles, etc., which they say are placed on the tree to remind the saint that they have visited the place. The splendid conical profile of the mountain renders it highly probable that it was an ancient pagan high place for the worship of the Sun God and Earth-Mother centuries before S. Patrick came to Ireland.

We even find holy wells in the bowels of the earth. Harold Bayley mentions several which are to be found in the ancient dene holes, or prehistoric subterranean galleries found in Kent, Surrey, etc. There is one in the Chislehurst labyrinth, 70 feet deep and lined with Roman cement. He considers they were put there for ritualistic reasons, and that the well which he mentions in the Great Pyramid had the same purpose. It is an interesting speculation, but as the main purpose of these excavations is not established, we cannot be certain. But this we do know. To-day the worship of water is a creed outworn, but it is at once the oldest and the most widely diffused of the symbols of Creative Power which have been venerated by mankind. It has received the homage of philosophers and poets, as well as that of the uncultured and Philistines, and its observance has endured for millenniums and has not vanished yet

ROMANY RITES AND CUSTOMS

THE gypsies are known the world over not only as inveterate wanderers, but also as accomplished dancers and musicians. Their distinctive customs observed at betrothal, marriage and death may be compared with those treated in other chapters on these subjects. Nomadism is also discussed in the chapters on The Ways of Nomadic Life and The Pedlar.

IN every country in Europe are found the wandering and trading Romany people, perpetuating their own peculiar customs and habits of life and speaking their own language among themselves. Originally they came from north-western India, but when they first appeared in the Aegean area some five centuries ago and told they had come from 'Little Egypt' the Greeks called them 'Gyphtos'—Egyptians—a name that has clung, for to us they are still the 'Gypsies.' In the Romany language 'rom' means 'husband' and 'romni' 'wife.' Non-gypsies are referred to as 'bu'no'—'busno'—the equivalent of 'impure,' 'gajo'—'gacho'—the generic term for 'gentile gentlemen,' or 'tororo,' which means 'poor and pitiful.' In their migrations, often forced by persecution and repressive laws, the Romany have remained a people apart, ignoring national boundaries and retaining, with their traditional manners and mental habits, their Eastern physical characters, for the pure Romany, black-haired, brown-eyed, and with olive complexion, remain distinctive and recognizable among the indigenous dark types of European countries.

They have ever been an industrious people, and before the development and extension of centralised and specialised industries and rapid transport filled a really useful and necessary part in the commercial life of many countries. When cheap china utensils had not yet largely replaced those of tin, the Romany were in great demand as tinkers or 'tinklers'—small smiths with their open-air forges, who repaired pots and kettles, manufactured tin pails, drinking cups, skewers, sieves, etc., sharpened knives and scissors, and as pedlars of baskets, woven chairs, matting, horn and wooden spoons, clothes pegs, and so on. Withal, they have ever been shrewd and cunning horse dealers, and at fairs and markets not only prominent in a trading capacity, but as musicians and picturesquely-attired dancers, adorned with jingling bangles, while their women have achieved fame as wonderful soothsayers and fortune-tellers. One industry which has failed to attract them is agriculture, mainly because it is unsuited to their nomadic habits.

THE Romany find 'the call of the wild' irresistible, confessing to being unable to keep still—to an inner urge to move on and keep moving. Many have settled down from time to time to live in houses, but individual members of families that have thus become sedentary often revert to the ancestral habits. Not a few frankly dislike house-life. Rodney Smith, the Gypsy Evangelist, has told in this connexion that he prevailed upon his brother to occupy a comfortable cottage, but on visiting him some months later found him in a camp in the garden, his explanation being that he found the house too cold! The true tent-gypsy prefers the free and wandering open-air life and in winter may regard a wagon as sufficiently luxurious and comfortable. Others who occupy houses during the cold months are wont to take to the road in early summer.

There can be no doubt that the Romany are happy and contented in their congenial camps. As a rhymer has said of them:

If you call a gypsy a vagabond,
I think you do him wrong,
For he never goes a-travelling
But he takes his home along.

F. R. Hinkins

A ROMANY CHI OF THE NEW FOREST

The New Forest is a favourite camping ground for the Romany. These care-free wanderers are very fond of tobacco, which they usually smoke in a pipe. Indeed, a well-seasoned pipe is the inseparable companion of most gypsies of both sexes, young and old.

F. R. Hinkins

SUMMER-TIDE HOME OF THE ROMANY TENT-DWELLERS

Although many gypsies live in caravans, the natural dwelling of the Romany is a tent. The summer tent is a very simple affair Two rows of rods are fixed into the ground. The tops are bent over till they meet, and are then tied together. Over this framework are hung coarse cloths, which are fastened together at the top and pegged to the ground at the bottom. Sometimes a bank of earth is raised or a trench dug round the outside, to carry the rain away. Gypsies seldom use tables or chairs. At their meals they usually sit on the ground.

The Romany nomads have their distinctive and picturesque immemorial customs, including those connected with marriage. First comes the betrothal ceremony, following upon the mutual attraction of couples, or an arrangement between the parents. In England a Romany girl may make the initial deliberate approach, signifying her consent to marry the young man by handing him a red string or cord, or by throwing over a hedge to him a cake containing coins. In eastern Europe a girl is said to delay her final decision until she has performed a mysterious ceremony which enables her to peer into the future, going to cross-roads for this purpose and hoping to see in a dream or vision the form of her future husband. During the ceremony she pricks with a needle the little finger of her left hand, letting the blood fall on the ground. She must afterwards collect the blood-stained dust and throw it into a river, lest evil spirits should lick up the blood and work a spell against her.

When the preliminary formal advance is made by a young man, he purchases two red kerchiefs which he fastens to his jacket. If the girl he loves accepts one, the couple are formally betrothed. In the event of a young man visiting a camp to court a girl who happens to be already promised to another, he is quickly made aware of the true state of affairs, for the girl leaves the family tent and, seating herself a short distance from the camp, loosens her hair to let it fall round her and covers her face with her hands.

A FORMAL betrothal ceremony before witnesses is of very simple character. The girl may just drink from a cup and then hand it to her lover. When he drinks from it, too, the act is regarded as one of 'covenanting.' Another binding ceremony is to eat a cake together. In Spain the betrothal ceremony often takes place, as a result of parental agreement, when a girl is only 14 years of age and the youth about the same age or a little older. The marriage is not celebrated, however, until the contracting parties are 16. Among the 'Coppersmiths,' the Romany people who caused such a stir in England by their sudden arrival in the year before the outbreak of the Great War, old-world betrothal and marriage customs have had tardy survival. According to their own confessions, one of their methods of arranging a match is by means of a dowry payment. The father of a youth visits a camp to procure a bride for him, declaring, 'I have lost a little cow.' Someone with an unbetrothed daughter responds by saying, 'You can have the lost one for a sum of money.' If an agreement is reached, the bride-price is paid and a date fixed for the marriage. Except in the case of very youthful betrothals, engagements do not last long. Pre-nuptial chastity is invariably strictly observed. Parents usually object to any displays of affection before marriage and lovers are rarely left together. An English Romany woman not long ago informed a student of her people's manners and customs that she and her husband had never once been out by themselves, and had not kissed each other before they were married, and she told this not as something out of the ordinary, but to illustrate what was customary among the northern Herons, Boswells and Grays.

THE marriage ceremony is found to vary somewhat not only in different areas, but in different families. An essential feature everywhere, however, is the clasping of hands in the presence of witnesses, while a Romany chief makes a solemn, if brief, declaration that the contracting parties take each other as man and wife. Marriages by clasping hands over a tongs held by a gypsy grandfather or leader, or by jumping over a tongs have been reported as a Romany custom surviving in Scotland. This ceremony may be related to one reported from Ireland, where the tinker couple leap hand-in-hand over the 'budget'—the box containing the tinsmith's implements. In England and Wales a young couple may be united in a 'broomstick' or a 'besom' marriage. A flowering broom is supposed to be particularly lucky, but one with pods may be regarded as the next best thing. In her description of this custom a Romany woman has told: 'De old gran'father he held de stick dis way (one end resting on the ground), den de bride's girl jumped over it, and den de bridegroom, den de bride, and last de bridegroom's man.' The besom ceremony is of like character. In his description of one which took place in Yorkshire an eye-witness has related that he found the Romany campers making merry in a big sand-pit, a musician playing a fiddle, and the younger people dancing hilariously. Suddenly, by order of the chief, the fun ceased and his people arranged themselves in two opposite rows about six feet apart. 'Half-way down between these rows two gypsies held up a broomstick about eighteen inches above the ground.' In response to a call from the chief, the bridegroom, wearing a green velveteen coat and a red kerchief round his neck, came from his tent, stepped over the broomstick, paused and turned round. The bride was next summoned from her tent and, advancing, she stepped over the broomstick as soon as she had clasped the right hand of the bridegroom. Then the young man embraced and kissed her, the chief declaring them to be married. The usual announcement by a chief or grandfather is,

F. R. Hinkins

HOW THE ROMANY GO INTO WINTER QUARTERS

The winter form of gypsy tent is slightly more elaborate than that used for the warm weather. It is built on the same principle, the chief difference being that a chimney is provided, so that in very cold weather the fire may be lighted inside the tent. Like the main tent, the chimney is made of cloths stretched over a framework, but the poles used for it are higher.

Dr. P. Habberton Lulham

ROMANY GIRLS OF THE ENGLISH COUNTRYSIDE: A DANCE TO THE MOVING MUSIC OF THE FIDDLE

The gypsies are famous for their music, which is very wild and stirring, as well as for their dancing. The instrument they chiefly affect is the violin, though they are at home with many. They play entirely by ear, and their technique is marked by extraordinary accuracy. It is in central and south-eastern Europe that the finest gypsy music can be heard, notably among the Hungarian tzigane, but the music played by some of the English, Scottish and Welsh gypsies is often of a very high standard of excellence. Romany dancing is as stimulating as Romany music, and a gypsy dance performed in the proper surroundings to gypsy music is an experience, once enjoyed, never forgotten.

Sport and General

RELIC OF ANCESTRAL CREMATION CUSTOM AMONG THE GYPSIES

When a Romany dies it is a common custom to destroy all his or her belongings. This may be due to a fear that ghosts may haunt them, or it may be done to ensure that the deceased is as well equipped in the next world as in this. Often the wagon in which the departed lived is burnt with the whole of its contents. Any fragments that remain over are either buried or else thrown into a river. Even if the whole of a dead Romany's possessions are not destroyed, it is usual to burn at least the clothes and bedding.

'Nē! Kaná romadí šan' (There now: you are married). An old custom is for the young husband to put a rush-ring on the bride's marriage finger, replacing it later with one of gold. Romany women treasure the 'rush-ring' as a luck-bringing amulet. Feasting, drinking and dancing follow the marriage ceremony. A custom still prevalent is to carry a young wife to the tent erected by the husband. Church weddings are nowadays more common than formerly, but on returning to the camp the old ceremonies prevail and lavish hospitality is extended to everyone.

Cases of polygamy have been known in comparatively recent times, a well-attested instance in England being that of old Dick Heron, who had two wives. There have also been cases of temporary marriages in some families. Divorce, according to old Romany law, was carried out with ceremony. In Scotland a formal separation required the sacrifice of a horse, round which the couple marched 'by the left' or 'against the sun.' Separation rites, however, have been unknown among the Romany of England during the past century.

In Romany customs attending birth there are interesting survivals. The first covering of a baby is usually something belonging to the father. Then a garment specially made for the little one is used, but it is ceremonially burned after a period—usually now after baptism. On leaving the tent or wagon for the first time after the birth the mother lays the baby on the ground and steps over it three times backwards and forwards. The little one is then lifted by the father, who puts round the neck a red cord as a means of warding off the influence of the evil eye. For thirty days after birth the mother does no work and must not touch any food or food utensils used by others. The cups, plates, etc., reserved for herself are destroyed after the period of the 'taboo' has expired. Certain ceremonies are observed in the washing of a young infant, and in the cutting of its hair, which is burned, lest evil spirits should, by obtaining a little, work spells that would injure the little one. If a child is stillborn, or dies soon after birth, milk offerings are poured upon the grave on perhaps as many as nine successive nights.

Romany methods of disposing of the dead may vary in different areas. There are, however, definite ceremonies which are still observed by the conservative Romany groups in England and the Near East. If a death takes place in a tent, it is an invariable

F. R. Hinkins

GYPSY WAYS OF PREPARING AND PROVIDING A MEAL

One of the most important articles in a Romany camp is the stewpot, which is seldom, if ever, empty. Hares, rabbits, geese, mallards, pheasants —nothing furred or feathered comes amiss to the pot. Nor is the gypsy particular how these are obtained, the men being usually inveterate poachers. Among special gypsy delicacies is the hedgehog, which, prepared in the gypsy way and cooked in an open pan over the fire, makes a very tender dish. The upper photograph shows a gypsy woman preparing a hedgehog for a meal, while below are seen two men poaching.

Dr. P. Habberton Lulham

LIFE RUNS GLADLY UNDER THE SUN AND IN THE WIND ON THE HEATH

Although gypsies have been known to live in houses, as a rule they soon tire of this confinement, finding the call of the open road irresistible, whether they are caravan-dwellers, or of those who live in tents. It is this content with simple things that makes the Romany such a happy-go-lucky race. It is this easy-going temperament, too, that has prevented them from moving with the general march of progress. So long as they have the sky and the sun and the stars overhead, and the moor and the heath for their resting-place, they are satisfied.

Topical

ROMANY BROTH CEREMONY

At Baildon, in Yorkshire, an old gypsy custom is observed. On a giant tripod a huge cauldron is rigged up, and this is filled with broth, which is ladled out in cups to the spectators, the king and queen of the gypsies, in full regalia, serving out the first lots.

custom to cut an opening in the side and take the body through it into the open air. It is feared that if the dead were carried through the door the ghost might afterwards enter the tent and disturb the living.

The temporary opening is quickly sewn up to prevent such a calamity. Women wash the corpse with salt water, which is afterwards given to the domesticated animals so that they may wax stronger. It is believed that in former times the Romany cremated their dead, but this custom has long been extinct.

The death-watch is, however, still observed before and after the coffin has been made or purchased by the mourners. A special tent is erected over the remains of the departed, and near it sit two watchers, who are relieved by others every few hours during the day-time and night-time. When darkness falls a lantern is suspended over the coffin, and it is kept alight till dawn. The watchers sit beside a fire, and their subdued conversation is mainly regarding the deceased, whose merits are extolled. When they have kept watch for a specified time, another two men are awakened to take their places. It is customary to terminate one spell of watching at midnight and another when the first streak of dawn appears in the eastern sky. In some Romany camps the immemorial custom of wailing is observed by the women immediately after death occurs and when the body is being carried away. Some gypsies have been accustomed to bury their dead in secret places, and cases have been reported from Wales and America

Topical

CHRISTIAN RITES AT A ROMANY WEDDING IN SCOTLAND

The gypsies have no special religion of their own. If they conform to any it is usually that of the country in which they are living. They like having their babies christened, for they regard baptism as a kind of charm, and they will often have the ceremony repeated. Church weddings are increasingly popular. Their own marriage ceremony varies in different districts and even in different families. Clasping hands in the presence of witnesses is an almost universal feature. Sometimes hands are joined, or the couple jump, over a pair of tongs.

Dr. P. Habberton Lulham

KENTISH GYPSY LADS IN A FRIENDLY SPARRING MATCH

Among the earliest writers to draw attention to the English gypsies was George Borrow, in his 'Lavengro' and 'The Romany Rye.' He wandered about England in gypsy fashion, making friends with the Romany and learning their language and their ways. The gypsies are very proficient at boxing, and 'Lavengro' contains one of the finest descriptions ever written of a fight with fists, between the author himself and the truculent gypsy known as the Flaming Tinman. Borrow's glorification of boxing in 'Lavengro' was at first very distasteful to the critics, but the book has since become a classic.

F. R. Hinkins

HOW THE GYPSIES FOLLOW THEIR LEADER

The Romany have special ways of showing which route their leaders have taken. The sign they make is called a pateran. Sometimes they scratch a cross, or lay a long and a short stick crosswise on the road, and the long arm points the way. Sometimes bundles of grasses or twigs are arranged on the ground. A gypsy is here seen (top) laying a pateran, and (bottom) 'reading' one.

for the deceased, and in comparatively recent Romany funeral processions the men have been seen with red ribbons in their button-holes or pinned to their coats. 'Each mourner,' says an observer, 'wore a scrap of crimson and the hearse was decked with red plumes.' When a 'King of the Gypsies' was buried at Norwood during Queen Victoria's reign, the chief mourners wore green velveteen coats with half-crowns for buttons, and red vests with buttons of sixpences. The use of red suggests a lingering belief that this colour imparts vitality to the dead as well as the living. A curious old Romany belief was that there should be no iron nails in a coffin, or in the shoes of the well-clad dead man in the coffin. A subdued mourning nowadays takes place at a grave, but in the Balkans the older custom of wailing is still observed, the women uttering 'terrible and lamentable cries.' Some sections of English gypsies continue to visit the graves once a year, generally about Christmas time, to mourn over them. The Romany respect for the dead is so profound that an oath by a grandfather is binding; to break it would bring calamity.

An ancient custom which has persisted till our own time is that of collecting and destroying all the belongings of the deceased after the funeral has taken place, lest the ghost should return to search for them, or, as some think, for the purpose of releasing the 'ghosts of each particular article so that in

of burials by the roadside. But nowadays it is customary to have graves in the cemeteries of the people among whom the Romany may chance to be. Night burials were formerly favoured by some gypsies, but it is uncertain whether this is an ancestral or a comparatively modern custom—in short, a rite forced upon the Romany by those who insisted that their dead should be interred in unconsecrated ground on the north side of the churchyard.

The custom of wearing red as a mourning colour appears, however, to be essentially a Romany one. There are records of the use of red death 'clothes'

the Other-world the departed may be provided with all the things he or she requires there. What appears to be a relic of the ancestral cremation custom is to set fire to all the property of the deceased. Recent cases are known of wagons, costing as much as £80, being burned with their contents, after the crockery had been smashed, the pots and pans cracked or broken, and even the harness cut and torn. Some bury the ashes and unburned remnants, while others cast them into a river. Romany mourners have been known to travel many miles to throw the destroyed belongings of the deceased into the Tyne or Mersey.

E. O. Hoppé

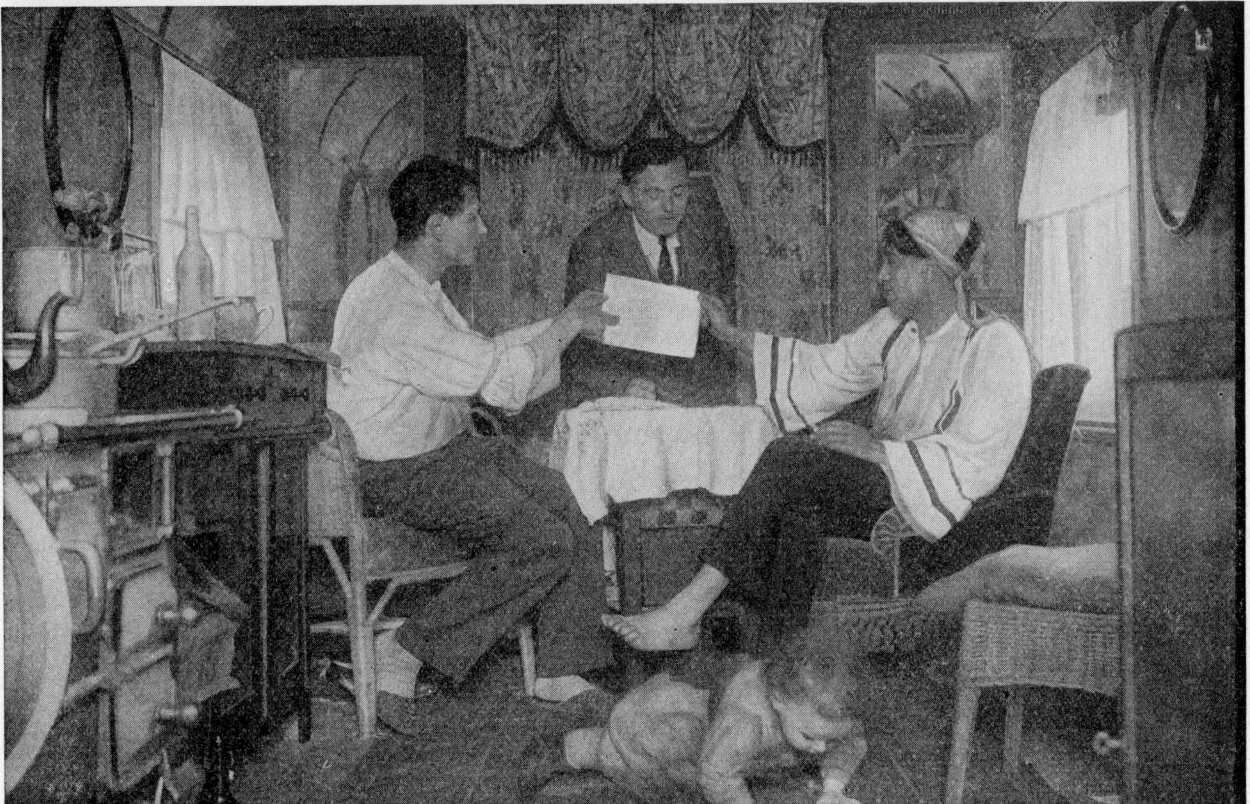

Keystone

ROMANY OF GERMANY INDOORS AND ON THE ROAD

There are now very few gypsies left in Berlin, whereas formerly there were encampments in the very heart of the city. The tents or caravans were stationed in the courtyards of dilapidated old tenement houses, and there the gypsies lived rent and rate free until the police drove them away. The interior of one of these caravans is seen here (bottom). Germany is also the home of some of those most picturesque members of an honourable gypsy calling, the ursari, or bear leaders (top). The bears are caught young, and when trained to dance and perform tricks bring in a good deal of money to their masters.

E. Watts

STICK DANCE OF THE GYPSIES OF INDIA

In every continent gypsies are to be found. Asia has untold thousands—in Persia, Syria, Anatolia, Turkistan, Siberia, etc. India has its full quota of gypsy tribes. Indeed, it is generally believed that north-western India was the original home of the Romany. Of the host of itinerant dancers, musicians, and other entertainers that may be met in India, not a few are gypsies. The band of Indian gypsies here seen, each member holding two sticks crossed, are about to begin the kolata dance, in which the performers strike one another's sticks.

E.N.A.

SPELLBOUND BY THEIR FATHER'S MUSIC

While Bohemia has produced such composers of world-wide fame as Dvorak and Smetana, the caravans of the Bohemian gypsies house many a skilled executant, the violin being their favourite instrument. Without being such accomplished musicians as the Hungarian tzigane, the Bohemian gypsies hold a high place among the itinerant music-makers of the world.

Among Romany groups which do not perpetuate the old custom of destroying relics wholesale it is still considered necessary to burn the bedding and garments of the deceased. In former times breakages and burnings often reduced a family to poverty.

In the Near East the funeral feast is still sometimes observed with dinners at intervals after interment 'for the repose of the dead.' Here also the old Romany belief obtains that the soul must linger about the grave until the body decays. Fires are lighted every seventh day for a year and into these fragments of food offerings are cast. When at length the soul sets out on its last journey to the 'Land of the Dead' it must cross seven mountains and seven deserts, facing a wind which cuts like a knife, or creeping between ravines that may clash together. A great serpent haunts this perilous way and must be avoided or propitiated. Even after death the Romany are thus adventurous wanderers.

THE SEPARATION OF THE SEXES

MOTIVES of jealousy and fear, in addition to the obvious principles of sex, are here disclosed as among the root causes of the custom of segregation of the sexes. The practice is further considered in the chapter on Women's Status in Primitive Society, while some of the religious aspects are treated in the chapters on Monasticism in Christendom and on Monks and Nuns of Non-Christian Religions.

FROM time immemorial it has been the custom over a great part of the East for woman, where social and economic conditions allow, to live a life of seclusion, taking no part in the public and social activities in which men engage. This separation of the sexes extended to relations within the house; for, as a general rule, the woman was not allowed to enter her husband's apartments; nor did she take any part in a common hospitality. She entertained her own sex exclusively in her quarters, while her husband welcomed his friends on his side of the house. In no circumstances was a male guest invited to visit the women's apartments.

Sexual jealousy unquestionably has been responsible in a large measure for the extreme care with which Eastern races have guarded their women-folk, keeping them in seclusion and requiring them to go veiled when in public; while the conviction of the inferiority of women as a sex—some Islamic sects say that women have no souls—has debarred them from overt participation in affairs. While each of these factors must be taken into account in estimating the position of women in the East, it would be a mistake to accord solely to either or to both in combination the custom of keeping the sexes apart. The causes, social and psychological, lie deeper.

The seclusion of the harem has exercised a fascination over the minds of Eastern story-tellers and Western writers which has tended to obscure the fact that it is no more than a highly developed form of provision for certain relations in which the sexes may stand to one another. In some form or other these are found in many parts of the world, and may vary from avoidance of the most trivial acts—and that perhaps only temporarily and at certain times and seasons—to the complete severance of all intercourse such as prevails in the monastic systems of the Orthodox and Catholic Churches. They are to be seen in the subordinate position assigned to women in the Early and Medieval Church, in the latter, incongruously enough, a position almost of degradation. They linger on in the custom of the Churches which assigns a separate portion of the building to each sex at divine service, and in the exclusion of women from Freemasonry and similar associations—a direct derivative from the East.

In certain cases separation of the sexes is an obvious measure of convenience. In polygamous marriage, for instance, it is not unusual that accommodation should be provided for each wife. In the Zulu kraal each wife has her own hut in which she brings up her family, while the husband has his hut apart; or separate provision may be made for a certain class. The young Masai warriors live apart in a common house until they attain that stage in social grading at which they may marry. This is in conformity with the common taboo against women which is a frequent accompaniment of preparations for war; but in this instance in practice it is neutralised by the fact that the warriors are habitually visited by the ladies of their choice.

AN institution which conforms more strictly to the requirements of the separation of the sexes is that of the club, bachelors', or men's house, such as is found particularly in New Guinea and Melanesia. Here it is customary for the men to assemble for

Sir Henry Barwel.

HOUSE FOR UNMARRIED MALES ONLY

What may be called a bachelors' house is sometimes found among certain tribes in Burma, New Guinea, and elsewhere. When a boy reaches puberty he is sent to live with the unmarried males in this building, which no woman may approach. The building seen here is a Papuan bachelors' house.

Ewing Galloway, N.Y.

WHERE DEATH IS THE PENALTY IMPOSED ON A WOMAN TRESPASSER

In the New Hebrides the differentiation between the sexes is very sharply defined, the separation taking place at an extremely early age A son is taken away from his mother as soon as possible after birth, and is sent to the men's compound, where he is brought up by his father. No woman is allowed in the men's compound. If a woman trespasses there, the penalty for this breach of the rules is death. The women live in their own compound with the girl babies The photograph shows a men's compound in Atshin Island, in the New Hebrides group.

social intercourse; it is the centre of their lives; some, if not all, sleep there, and to it women are not admitted. In fact in Fiji it is not considered respectable that a married man should sleep at home with too great frequency: he is expected to make use of the two men's houses which each village provides. In the Carolines there is a common sleeping house for men and one for women. The Sandwich Islanders' homestead made provision for separate sleeping houses and separate eating houses for each sex.

The age at which the separation of the sexes takes place and the male enters the club house varies. In the New Hebrides it is early—as soon as possible after birth—but here the differentiation of the sexes is very strongly marked. It serves to show the degree to which sex avoidance may be carried between the members of the same family. Neither mother nor sister dares make use of a common noun which forms part of the boy's name; if he should come to his father's house for food, he may not eat it if his sister is in the house. If his mother brings him food she must not hand it to him, but lays it on the ground at his feet; and she addresses him in the distant terms of set formality. If his sister meet him on a path, she must run away and hide; while if he himself finds her footsteps in the sand, he turns aside in order not to follow them.

In Polynesia the taboos are so strong as to create a gulf between man and wife. As it has been said, they can never eat together, nor play at the same fireside with their children, nor may the woman even cook at the same fire as her husband. The heaviest curse that can be laid upon a man is 'May you become a bottle to hold water for your mother,' or 'May you be roasted as food for your mother.' The Zulu woman must not mention her husband's name, but speaks of him as 'the father of So-and-so.' The separation of the sexes may be even more than lifelong. The Egyptian husband, if exceptionally the two sexes are buried together, is separated from his wife by a wall within the tomb; and after death,

STRICT SEGREGATION OF THE SEXES AMONG INDIAN MOSLEMS

The purdah system can be seen in its strictest application among the Mahomedans of India. On Fridays, when the Moslem women of Delhi assemble for prayer at the Jama Masjid, or Great Mosque, they are separated by a screen from the men. If there is not room for all the men, those for whom there is not accommodation below must stand, as shown here, on the surrounding walls. A Moslem woman who visits the mosque wears a robe called the burkha, which covers her completely, save for small openings over her face to enable her to breathe and see.

E N.A

Dr. Wirz

TASKS THAT ARE PERFORMED ONLY BY WOMEN IN AFRICA AND NEW GUINEA

In most communities the occupations followed by men and women are more or less clearly defined. Among primitive peoples agriculture is generally the women's domain and hunting or cattle keeping the men's. So rigidly is the distinction made among the cattle-breeding Bantu tribes of Africa that no man would think of using the hoeing stick. The upper photograph shows Kaffir women hoeing mealies, while below are seen Mentawei women of Dutch New Guinea setting out on a fishing expedition. Among the Mentawei, a very primitive tribe, fishing is the women's occupation, the men being hunters. Moreover, the women wear a special banana strip garment for the purpose.

E. N. A.

SEXES SEPARATED IN CHURCH: A CUSTOM OF TRANSYLVANIA

The custom of separating the sexes is found in almost every relation of life. In the domain of religion especially it is by no means uncommon. In some religious communions, and in certain churches, it is usual for a separate portion of the sacred building to be set aside for each sex while divine service is in progress. Among the Saxons of Transylvania, for instance, the women always sit apart from the men in church. The women here seen wearing hats are unmarried; the wearing of the head veil, or marama, is the mark of a married woman.

according to some Moslem theologians, there is no place for the woman in Paradise.

It is hardly necessary to add that the regulation which excludes the female sex from the club house also extends to the men's secret societies, dances and entertainments—a feature which appears among the tribes of California, one of the few instances in which the American Indian affords an example of discrimination between the sexes in social organization. In West Africa a function of several of the secret societies is to keep the women in subjection through fear of the retribution with which the society would visit them in case of any misdemeanour. On the other hand, among some of the West African tribes the women themselves have secret societies to which men are not admitted.

It has been noted that in those societies in which separation of the sexes is at all a prominent feature—Islam, India, China, Melanesia and Australia, to name some instances only—it is accompanied by an inferiority in position of the female sex; and some attempt has been made to relate both these social characters with economic conditions. It is evident that in certain types of society, e.g. a community living predominantly by hunting or sea-fishing, the main occupation, by its very nature, excludes the female from participation, and thereby leads to a certain consolidation of sex interests. Still more is this the case where ritual is involved. Among the Todas of India, the main occupation of the tribe being the care of cattle and the sacred ritual of the dairy, the women, to whom this is taboo, are practically excluded from tribal activities.

Again among all peoples, but particularly among peoples of less advanced culture, the occupations

Paul L. Hoefler

Paul L. Hoefler

DOING MAN'S WORK IN THE LION COUNTRY OF TANGANYIKA

Among the Masai of Tanganyika Territory the occupational separation of the sexes is very clear. The women stay at home and busy themselves with agricultural work, while the men are cattle breeders and lion hunters. No woman is allowed near the cattle, which are kept within thorn enclosures (bottom). Masai boys are entrusted with the care of cattle at a very early age. The young cattle herdsman seen in the upper photograph is only about twelve years old, yet is sole guardian of an enormous herd.

A. L. Strong

HOLY GROUND OF ISLAM WHICH THE FOOT OF WOMAN MAY NOT TREAD

Now the chief city of the Soviet republic of Uzbegistan, Samarkand was the capital of the Tatar conqueror, Timur, who was buried here. It is a city of magnificent buildings, and was once the centre of the intellectual life of Mahomedan Asia. Although its mosques and colleges are falling into ruins, even now no Moslem enters the city without feeling that he is on holy ground. The great mosque of Shah Zindeh, the companion of Timur, retains to this day much of its ancient splendour, being one of the finest buildings in Central Asia. Women may not enter it.

Topical Press

FEAR THAT KEEPS THE MEN AND WOMEN APART

The attitude observed by savage man towards the opposite sex is dictated largely by motives of fear and awe. To him woman is dangerous and unfathomable, and for this reason she must be hedged off from contact with man and from his activit es. Particularly must this be done at times of sexual crisis. Then the separation of the sexes becomes doubly strict. The young girls here seen belong to a tribe of East Africa. For a period of six months they are required by their religion to cover their heads and bodies with this strange garb.

Mondiale

HUNGARIAN FOLK WHO SECLUDE THEIR YOUNG GIRLS

Mezökövesd, in western Hungary, is inhabited by a people called Matyok, who are a branch of the Palocz race. The Matyok are exclusive and very conservative, clinging to their ancestral customs with the utmost tenacity. They are artists in embroidery and are noted for their highly decorative dress. Among them the separation of the sexes is very marked. The young girls do not mix with men at all, and when they attend church have a separate service to themselves. A party of Matyok women are here seen in gala costume at the church.

of men and women are more or less strictly defined. Each sex shows a reluctance to take part in the occupations of the other, even if they are not actually debarred by an actual taboo. Agriculture, especially in its early stages, is essentially a woman's occupation; the care of cattle belongs to men. But among the cow-keeping Bantu tribes of Africa no woman is allowed to touch the men's cattle, while no man would use the characteristically feminine implement, the hoe or digging stick. In fact, evidence is not wanting that agriculture itself is something of a woman's 'mystery.' Hence originated the fertility cult of the miniature 'Garden of Adonis' of the East which women cultivated, perhaps as far back as twelve hundred years before Christ, if we may so conclude from utensils of clay recently found in Palestine, and the secret rites of the mystic cults of Greece and the 'Bona Dea' of Rome, from which men were excluded. It was the intrusion of Clodius at the latter when conducted by Caesar's wife that nearly caused a revolution.

A more detailed examination of such instances as these reveal that it is not economic conditions that lead to the discrimination between the sexes, but that sexual taboo governs, rather than is governed by, or arises out of, these conditions.

The relation of women to sacred objects with which men are particularly associated is significant. No woman may look upon a sacred bull-roarer of the Australian tribes, and in the Marquesas not only was it forbidden for a woman to approach the place of the sacred dance; if she set her foot on the shadow of the trees which surrounded it the penalty was death.

At one of the most critical periods of life, the time of initiation, both male and female novices were rigorously precluded from the company of the other sex. Precautions were taken not only against their meeting, but against even the sight of the other sex. They were therefore taken into the bush for the whole period of their instruction and preparation. In the New Hebrides, if a woman, even accidentally, saw one of the newly initiated boys before he had been washed, she was buried alive.

It has been mentioned that the Polynesian husband and wife may not eat together. That the sexes may not take food together is a prohibition that is almost universal outside Western civilization. It still survives in the Balkans, where it may be, but is not necessarily, due to Islam. In Albania the men eat apart, except that it is customary that a woman who has taken a vow of perpetual virginity, and is thereby entitled to take her part in the activities of the men, which consist largely of tribal feuds, may also share their meals. In Serbia the woman eats a meal with her husband and is waited upon for the only time in her life on her wedding day. A memory of such a prohibition may linger in the Brandenburg popular belief that if lovers or husband and wife eat from the same dish they will quarrel.

Some peoples will not eat food prepared by, or from the hands of, a woman; but this feeling is stronger and more widely spread at the sexual crises. Among the Chippeway Indians the menstruous woman must cook her food at a separate fire, and no man will accept food from a pregnant woman. Food which is regarded as specially that of women, or female animals, to many are taboo.

The separation of the sexes is, for obvious reasons, more marked at times of sexual crisis. It is a common custom that special huts should be provided for menstruous women, and a woman is surrounded by her own sex only at childbirth, when she becomes and continues unclean for a varying period. Among the Basutos, a man is not admitted to see his wife and child until a period of four days has elapsed.

The attitude of savage and semi-civilized man towards the opposite sex is dominated by his extraordinary fear of menstruation and his awe of the mystery of sex. Woman is dangerous, and therefore she is debarred from participation in man's activities, from the objects which he holds sacred, and as far as possible from personal contact, especially at the times of sexual crisis. Only very slowly and in certain societies has this feeling partially broken down. The separation of the sexes on the side of the man is an expression of the solidarity of sex which is based on fear. It may have been reinforced by economic and social conditions; for in studying a custom such as this in isolation and divorced from its context, general statements without qualification are not without danger. Substantially, however, man's attitude of fear towards the unfathomed, mysterious and spiritually dangerous sex is fundamental.

On the other hand, as most of our knowledge of these practices is derived from the observations of male travellers and investigators, we know little of the women's side. That women, too, have a sense of solidarity cannot be denied. It finds expression at the time of sexual crisis, when they withdraw from the society of men, in their women's societies and dances, and in other matters. When it is said that a man refrains from visiting his wife except secretly and at night it gives his side of what perhaps the woman regards as a prohibition analogous to her exclusion from the man's quarters. In the East this feeling on the part of the woman has been reinforced by male jealousy. The rapidity with which the restrictions of the veil are breaking down in Islam, especially in Turkey, suggests, not that jealousy is no longer a male attribute, but that women themselves are removing the barriers which separate the sexes.

Keystone

BREAKING DOWN THE BARRIERS OF THE SEXES IN THE TURKEY OF TODAY

The care with which the Eastern races have guarded their womenfolk is doubtless due in great measure to sexual jealousy. They have kept them in seclusion, and they have insisted on their wearing veils when exposed to the public view. But this attitude is altering, particularly in Turkey, which under the republic is becoming Westernised with astonishing rapidity. Here the women themselves are taking a hand in the change. The photograph shows a group of Turkish women wearing the dress of various periods, ranging from the yashmak and feriji, or cloak, down to the quite modern Western costume, with face uncovered and short skirts.

Clarendon Press

HOW ASHANTI WIDOWS KEEP THE SPIRITS OF THEIR DEAD HUSBANDS AT BAY

These photographs, taken from Captain R. S. Rattray's work 'Religion and Art in Ashanti,' show how the widows of that country protect themselves from the spirits of their dead partners. Small brass basins on the head indicate that the husband belonged to a particular clan. Strands of palm fibre fastened above the elbow float behind in funerary dance rites, and indicate the desire for wings to fly after the departed one. Seeds and leaves carried in the left hand act as an antidote against the spirit, while the cane in the right signifies the loss of a husband.

WIDOWHOOD AMONG THE CIVILIZED AND SAVAGE

THROUGHOUT the world, in parts both civilized and primitive, the breaking up of the marriage state by the loss of a husband is fundamental. In consequence, as detailed here, the etiquette of widowhood is rigid and complicated. This subject is so closely related to DEATH AND BURIAL CUSTOMS that most of the chapters appearing under that section have some bearing upon it.

WHEN Mr. Woolley's excavators laid bare the cemetery area at Ur they discovered, neatly arranged in a rectangular compartment twenty-seven feet by twenty-five, the remains of seventy-four human beings—sixty-eight women and six men. The heads of some of the women may be seen by the curious in a glass case at the British Museum; heads flattened and distorted by the weight of the accumulated débris of five and a half millennia, yet still bearing around their brows jewelled circlets and tinsel flowers.

We do not know, we probably never shall know for certain, the why and wherefore of this massacre of women; but from the knowledge derived from similar discoveries made elsewhere it is reasonable to suppose that some, at any rate, of the slaughtered sixty-eight were the wives of some monarch or great chieftain, and that on his death they died in order that their lord and master might not voyage alone and unattended into the land of the shades.

Similar deeds of blood were enacted in India until a century or so ago; and it is said that even today, in out-of-the-way corners of the peninsula, the Indian widow still on occasion mounts the funeral pyre of her husband and is joined with him in death. In Peru, when an Inca was 'called home to the mansions of his father, the Sun,' his favourite wives and concubines, sometimes to the number of several hundred, were immolated on his tomb; and we are told that there was the keenest competition among the harem inmates to give the last proof of conjugal affection. In Fiji the wives of the deceased were either strangled or buried alive; and as far apart as China and West Africa we find instances of widow-sacrifice.

THE explanation of the custom is simple. Unsophisticated man, confronted by the awe-inspiring fact of death, bereft suddenly of loved ones whom henceforth he meets only in sleep, not unnaturally supposes that death is the gateway to another existence in which the dead have the same needs and desires as they experienced and expressed when alive. Hence it is that we find in the graves of primitive peoples cooking pots and drinking vessels, weapons of the chase, fire-making implements, and—the bones of women.

With the growth of more humane sentiments and of a greater respect for human life the actual sacrifice was no longer insisted upon. But still the widow was a pathetic figure, for upon her head were centred the superstitious fancies of her neighbours. These were, and are, mainly the result of the primitive belief that death entails a degree of uncleanness. The corpse is unclean, and to touch it means defilement. The clothes in which it is wrapped, the hut which gives it shelter, the weapons and vessels that it has used, and in particular the woman who has had so frequent and close a contact with it for so long—all are unclean.

Only by the performance of certain rites, some arduous, even dangerous, some trivial, only by the passing of a certain time, can the defilement be wiped out and the evil influence nullified. Then, too, death frightens the savage. Seeing one of his companions suddenly stricken down by the invisible finger of disease, he not only surmises that death is contagious

E.N.A

WHERE THE WIDOW'S VEIL IS WHITE

This lady of Csokol in Hungary, in accordance with the custom of her part of the ancient kingdom—and other parts of the world—is dressed in white raiment as a sign of mourning, and her 'weeds' lack the normal funerary melancholy.

Dorien Leigh

WHEN THE DAYS OF MOURNING END WITH AUSTRALIAN WIDOWS

In Melville Island, off the coast of Northern Territory, the most elaborate system of earth burial known among the Australian aboriginals occurs. Tall, highly decorated posts are erected beside the graves, round which the mourners dance, being careful to yell loudly as they approach in order to scare evil spirits away. During widowhood the women smear their faces with pipeclay, and when the period of mourning ends they again visit the burial place and intimate the fact to their departed spouses by rubbing off the pipeclay over their graves.

and that, therefore, the corpse is to be avoided, but that the spirits are angry and must be propitiated. He sees to it, therefore, that the widow performs to the full the rites prescribed by tradition, for only in this way may the angry ones be appeased.

Among the Arunta of Central Australia, when a man dies custom requires that his wives should smear their hair, faces and breasts with clay and preserve silence for a certain period—sometimes as long as twelve months. During this time their only means of expressing themselves is by gesture—of hands and fingers and arms. The Yoruba widow mourns her husband for three months, during which she must not plait her hair, take a bath or remove the clothes that she had on when her husband died. Her bed is a mat of rags, and she is confined to her hut during the daytime and allowed to leave it only very rarely after dark. In Papua the widow lies beside her husband's grave during her mourning period, also of three months, covered by a mat and by a roof of branches. On the west coast of Africa widows among the Minas are shut up for six months in the hut beneath which is the grave containing the remains of their husbands. Elsewhere the body remains unburied in the hut, guarded by the widow; and only when the bones alone are left is she relieved of her ghastly vigil.

Among the Takulli, says Westermarck, a widow is compelled by her husband's kinsfolk to lie on his funeral pyre until the heat becomes unbearable. Then after the body has been consumed she gathers up the ashes, places them in a small basket, and carries them about with her for two or three years, until the expiration of which time she must not think of remarriage.

THE first duty of a widow in Portuguese East Africa is to take a sweat-bath, followed by a thorough fumigation by a fire made from dry grass. Then, having donned a waistband of reeds, she crawls, wailing the while, through the hut she had occupied with the dead man. This done, the hut is destroyed, for it is considered highly dangerous to sleep on ground where a corpse has lain. The Melanesian widow smears her body with mud and then puts on a costume of grass; the widows of the Upper Congo cover themselves with white clay; and those of the Torres Straits, where the ordinary feminine dress is an ample petticoat, make a special garment of banana leaves, passed between the legs and fastened to the waistband. Finally, in India the widow shaves her head, gives her jewels and valuables to the needy, retires from social life, and devotes herself to menial duties in her late husband's family.

Such are some of the customs enjoined upon the widow—customs that have grown up in the course of ages and which are enjoined upon her by the voice of the community and of her own conscience.

The belief that widows are haunted by the spirits of their late husbands is very widespread. In the preface to one of his lesser-known novels Sir Walter Scott tells of a pirate who was at length caught and hanged for his crimes. He was affianced to an Orkney girl, and she went up to London to see him before his death. Arriving too late, she had the courage to request a sight of her lover's dead body; and then, touching the hand of the corpse, she formally resumed the troth-plight which she had bestowed. 'Without going through this ceremony,' says Sir Walter, 'she could not, according to the superstition of the country, have escaped a visit from the ghost of her departed lover, in the event of her bestowing upon any living suitor the faith which she had plighted to the dead.'

THE belief is now rarely met with in Western lands, although Hartland tells us that as late as 1912, at Macon, in Georgia, U.S.A., the second husband of a lady was granted a decree of divorce on the ground that the ghost of her first husband haunted both his wife and himself, with the result that they found it utterly impossible to live together.

E.N.A.

TALISMANIC RELICS OF HER DEAR DEPARTED

Among the Andamanese, custom prescribes that six months after the burial of a man his bones are dug up and washed in the sea; his skull is given to his widow, who carries it about suspended round her neck. His jaw-bones are given to the next principal mourner.

E.N.A.

QUEERLY DISTORTED SENTIMENT IN SAVAGE LIFE

Preservation of a dead man's bones is customary among many primitive peoples. In the Trobriands the skull is made into a lime pot to be used by the widow, and the jaw-bones are turned into a neck ornament for her to hang upon her breast.

Among primitive peoples, however, the case is very different. The Ewhe of Togoland believe implicitly in the possibility of conjugal relations between the widow and her deceased spouse, and as such intercourse would mean death to the living participant, the most elaborate precautions are taken to thwart the dead man in his desires. For six weeks after her husband's death the widow lays aside clothing and ornaments and goes entirely naked, spending the period in the hut beneath the floor of which the man is buried, leaving it only for a few minutes at a time. When she does go out it is with bowed head and turned-down eyes, with arms crossed over her breast, and with a club in her hand—the latter to drive away the dead man if she should encounter him in her path. She sleeps on the club in order that he shall not steal it from her in the dark, and she mixes ashes with her food and drink to make them so unpalatable that he will not attempt to share them. At night she keeps an evil-smelling brew smoking on the hearth, so that the deceased may be deterred from returning to his old quarters; and she believes that to answer a call would mean certain death.

We find the same dread and similar precautions in Loango, too. Immediately the corpse of her husband has been laid in the ground, the widow sees that all the openings in her hut are tightly closed, to prevent the dead man's spirit from visiting her by night and thus either compassing her death or engendering some hideous monster. Then the medicine men give her—of course for a consideration—a spell-bound piece of wood wherewith to fasten her hut door, and a fringed cord, likewise enchanted, to hang about her bed to trip up the amorous 'revenant.' If these precautions are deemed insufficient, if the widow is very nervous or the spirit particularly pertinacious, the woman changes her hut and wears different foot-gear in order that her husband shall be unable to trace her by her footprints. If these precautions are considered inadequate the medicine men will organize the village in a spirit-hunt, tracking down the ghost from place to place until, they hope, the neighbourhood is too hot to hold him and he will retire quietly to his grave. If when the thatch has been beaten and the ground swept, spells have been cast and guns discharged—if then the ghost is still feared and his visits expected, nothing remains but to remove the village to another site.

Widows are forbidden to marry a second time in many parts of the world. Hinduism teaches that widowhood is the result of sins committed in a previous incarnation, and the widow, in the higher castes at least, is little but a hopeless drudge, despite the fact that she may have been married when a mere child to a man old enough to be her grandfather. The Chinese have a saying that 'as a faithful minister does not serve two lords, neither may a faithful woman marry a second husband.' Masai widows are not allowed to remarry, although they may cohabit with men of the same age and class as their late husbands; and the same bar is to be found in the Marquesas Islands, among some of the savage tribes of Formosa, and in many other places. Far more often, however, a widow is allowed to remarry after the lapse of a certain period or the performance of a particular ritual.

The end of the mourning period for the Arunta widow is marked by what is called 'trampling the twigs on the grave.' On the appointed day the widow, painted all over with pipeclay and wearing a chaplet of small bones, hair and feathers, proceeds to the camping-ground where her husband had died, and which since his death has been 'burnt out' in order that his spirit may be driven from its old haunts. She is accompanied on her pilgrimage by the adult members of the tribe, and on arrival one and all shout their loudest and beat the air with their hands

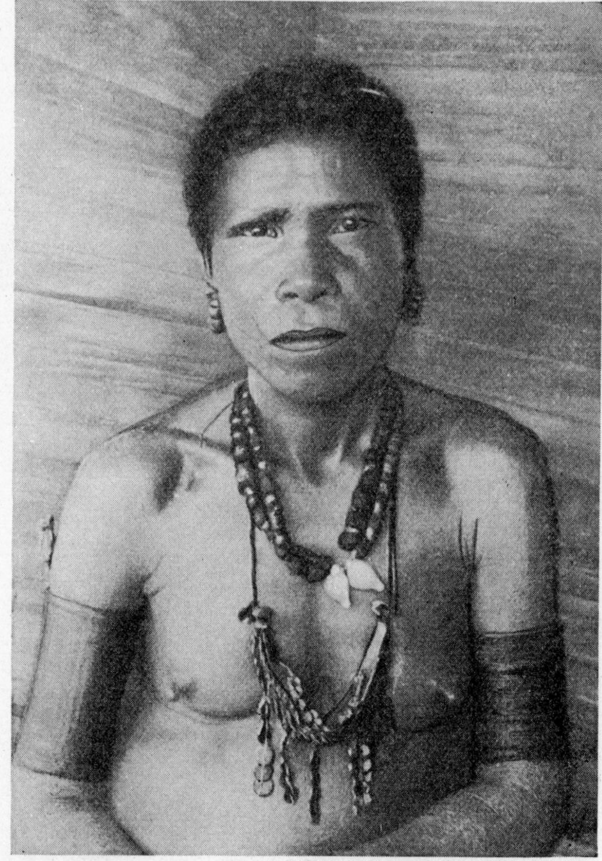

From Malinowski's 'Sexual Life of Savages'

GRADATIONS OF MOURNING DRESS FOR WIDOWS IN THE TROBRIANDS

Trobriand widows wear mourning garb for a period that varies according to the dead husband's status. In full mourning (left) the widow covers her breast with black beads and wears a necklace of balls of her husband's hair, another of rope, another of his calico, and, on top of all, his jaw-bone; her head is clean-shaven and her face blackened. For half-mourning she wears only one necklace and the jaw-bone; her hair is partly grown; she no longer blackens her face, and she carries a sprig of aromatic herbs in her right armlet.

Deaville Walker

PATHETIC VICTIMS OF A VAIN AND IGNORANT SUPERSTITION

One deplorable consequence of child marriage as formerly customary in India was the large number of women who, married in infancy to men many years their senior, were left widows at an early age. For widowhood, according to Hindu doctrine, is the penalty incurred for sins committed in a previous incarnation, entailing hopeless drudgery for the rest of life. Daily along the Ganges scenes like the above could be witnessed—widows bathing in its sacred waters in hope to wash away the sins that had brought such doom upon them.

and spear-throwers—all with the same object of frightening the dead man's spirit. Then from the camp the party run to the actual grave, the leader executing a wide détour as if to head off the spirit and prevent him from doubling back to the camp. Arrived at the grave the men jump vigorously on the brush-wood-covered mound to prevent the spirit getting out, while the women beat the air downwards. Then some of the women displace the men on the grave, and engage in a fierce conflict until their blood drops upon the ground. Finally the widow scratches a hole in the grave, tears her chaplet into fragments, and puts them in the hole. This done, she gets up and carefully scrapes all traces of the clay from her body, although sometimes she leaves a white stripe down her forehead to signify that, though she has completed the period of mourning for her first husband, she is not yet ready to be taken by his successor.

At the end of the customary period of mourning in the Portuguese territory in West Africa the widow goes to a running stream and deposits in mid-river her late husband's bed and one or two of the articles he commonly used. Then she washes herself and sits on the bed. Now the medicine man of the village wades out, dips her three times in the water, and then dresses her in her scanty clothing. Next the bed and the other articles are broken and the bits thrown down-stream. The woman is now conducted out of the river and on the bank is given a raw egg to eat, while the blood of a newly-killed toad or fowl is rubbed on her

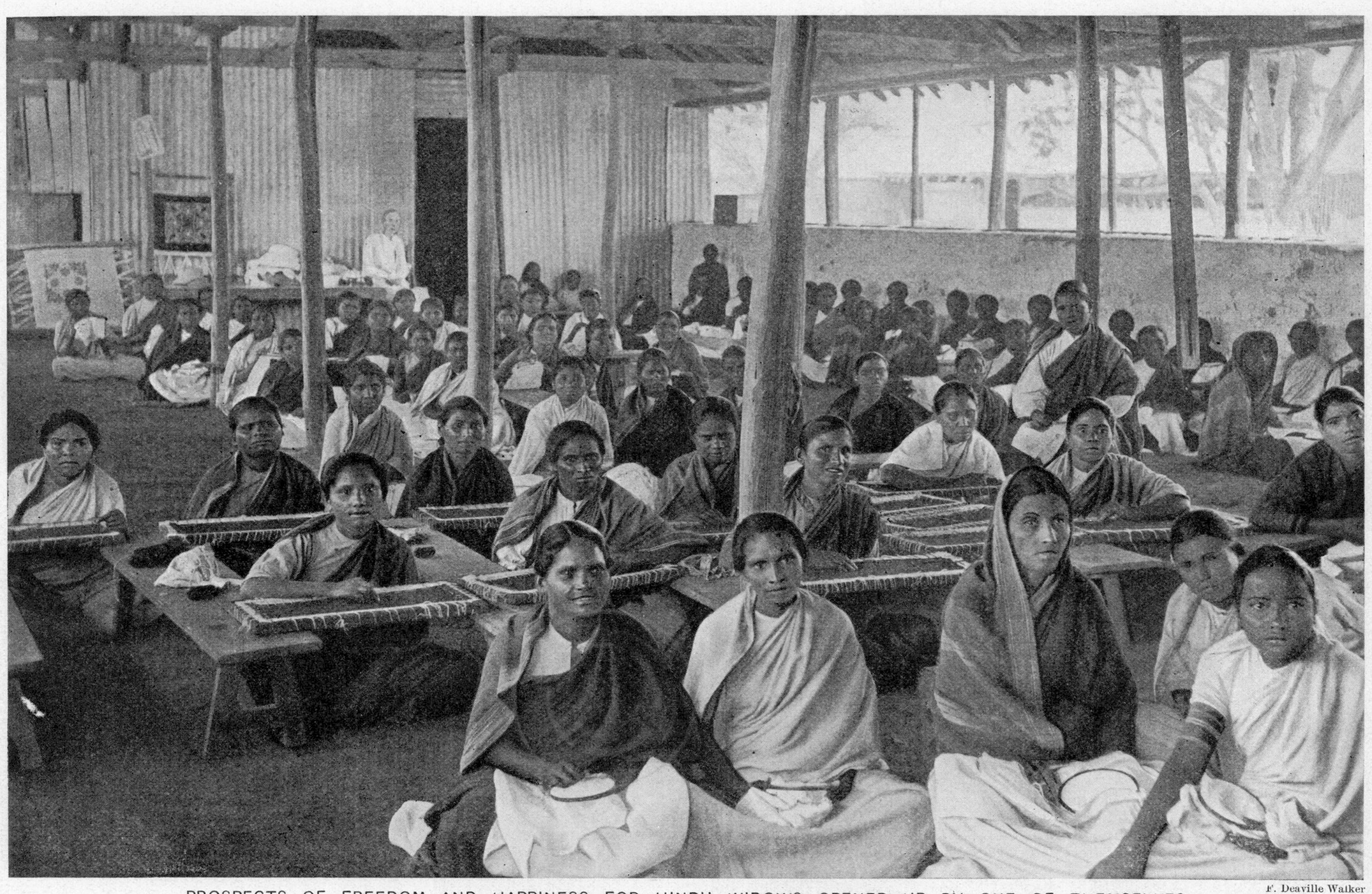

F. Deaville Walker

PROSPECTS OF FREEDOM AND HAPPINESS FOR HINDU WIDOWS OPENED UP BY ONE OF THEMSELVES

Great efforts are being made to ameliorate the lot of Hindu widows. This philanthropic work owes its origin to the various Christian missionary organizations, and while it is now being much helped by the movement for the general emancipation of the women of India, it is still the Christians who do most for the widows. Eminent among them was Pandita Ramabi, herself a Hindu widow, who, converted to Christianity, founded institutions in which widows are taught industries by which they can earn their own living, and having thus secured economic independence can escape from a life of servitude with their husbands' families. In one institution no fewer than 1,500 widows are received, adults, like those shown here, learning weaving, and infants like those shown in the opposite page, for whom school training is provided.

Deaville Walker

HAPPY IN THEIR IGNORANCE OF THE MIGHT-HAVE-BEEN

Preposterous as it may seem to people unfamiliar with facts in Indian life, these eight babies are Hindu widows. But for the beneficent action of Christianity their days would be spent, not in the bright atmosphere of a kindergarten, in the care of a kind-hearted teacher, herself perhaps a widow, but immured in the women's quarters of their dead husbands' families, ill-treated, despised, doomed never to know the happiness of having babies of their own.

lips. After these sacrifices to the memory of her husband the widow returns to the village and there sits on the ground with her legs stretched out in front of her until her deceased husband's brother comes and steps over them. This act, seemingly so strange and meaningless, is symbolical of sexual intercourse, and it may be regarded as an indication to the spirit of the dead man that his one-time rights have been permanently alienated. Sometimes the person performing the act is the one to whom the widow has been assigned as wife, but more often it is a substitute who thus, so it is believed, without harm to himself, renders the marriage innocuous to the new spouse.

WOMEN are not allowed to remain long unmarried in 'tribal' Africa, and Yoruba widows, when the mourning period has come to an end, are then escorted by their relatives to the river to the accompaniment of wails and volleys of gunfire. Arrived at the water they wash their clothes and themselves, after which they return to their suitors' homes and are taken to wife forthwith. The Formosan widow, among certain tribes at least, celebrates the end of her mourning by a second funeral of her husband. The first, or 'green,' funeral is when the body of the newly dead man is dried for nine days before a slow fire, after which it is placed on a platform in the open. Two or three years later, when nothing is left save the bones, there takes place the 'dry' funeral, when the remains are placed in a grave. The widow is then free to marry again if she can find a husband.

A. L. Strong

MOURNING CAPS FOR MONGOLIAN WIDOWS

Head-dresses of astonishing designs, richly adorned with silver and jewelled trimmings, are worn by all Mongolian married women. With widowhood, however, this extravagance is discarded, and far plainer caps are worn—as by the old lady in the foreground here.

P. & A.

EUROPEAN ROYAL LADIES IN FULL PANOPLY OF MOURNING

During this present century, and especially during and since the Great War, there has been a growing tendency in the most highly civilized societies to discount the outward manifestation of grief, and, consequently, for widows to discard the long black veil and the black crape 'weeds' that custom formerly required them to wear for a full twelve months after their husband's death. This full paraphernalia of mourning is still, however, worn at the actual funeral ceremony, as here, for example, at the obsequies of the Duc de Vendôme by his widow and daughter.

Before leaving the subject of remarriage it may be noted that the second marriage of a widow does not as a rule necessitate the elaborate ceremonial that generally attends the first. This is due to the fact that union with a widow is not considered to be so 'dangerous' as with a virgin, who has not been initiated into the mysteries of the married state.

Up to the present we have been concerned almost entirely with the widow in savage society, chiefly because of the wealth of picturesque ritual and fascinating theory that have her for their centre. Her counterpart in the higher cultures is not so colourful a character, but she is just as pathetic, as anyone will admit who watches the gloomy procession through the cemetery gates on a Sunday afternoon—the long train of black-garbed women, many wearing thick and heavy veils, bringing their flowers and plants to lay on the graves of their loved ones. Gifts and garb are alike eloquent, for the former are said by some authorities to be a relic of the age-old custom of placing food and drink on the tomb in order that the spirit of the dead may refresh himself in the intervals of sleep; while the veil very probably has a double origin, in the desire to express sorrow in so obvious a fashion that all (including the mourned) may appreciate its genuineness, and also in the quite contrary desire to disguise oneself in order that the spirit (whose touch, as we have seen, means death) may not seek a renewal of the conjugal relationship.

In Victorian England the widow wore deepest black for a year, and this was followed by a period of half-mourning, when black was varied with lavender, mauve or purple. In the twentieth century we tend to discount the outward show of grief, and perhaps the time is not far distant when the widow will entirely discard the gloomy paraphernalia of widowhood. Nor need we then regret the disappearance of the funerary emblems. The widow's grief is, alas, an ever-recurring phenomenon; it is only the means whereby it finds expression that differ and change.

THE GOLDEN BALLET OF THE EAST

DANCING, drama and religion remain inextricably intertwined in the East, as may be seen in the ballets founded on the Hindu religious epics, one class of which is here described, another being the Javanese form discussed in the chapter on Animal Dances of the East. Further varieties are dealt with in the chapters on Oriental Dances and Devil and Other Spirit Dances.

IN the gorgeous Orient the principal feature of the drama is the Corps de Ballet. Arrayed in cloth of gold, adorned with sparkling and precious jewels, often with no other stage than the natural beauties of a background of tropical verdure, lissom maidens and youths perform the amazing undulations and serpentine movements of age-old dances, which they have been taught from childhood to regard as the perfection of terpsichorean art.

Fundamentally the difference between Western and Oriental drama and dance is one of religion, since the subject-matter of the Eastern drama is invariably chosen from the legends and tales of the culture-heroes associated in story and song with ancient faiths of Hindustan. When, centuries ago, Hindu and Buddhist priests migrated from India to Java and China by way of Siam and Cambodia, they naturally took with them and spread abroad the deathless fables of the Ramayana and the Mahabharata (see page 43). These stories of the exploits of the gods of the Hindu Pantheon particularly lend themselves to dramatic representation, and seem, too, from the numerous sculptured remains on the crumbling temples of Java and Cambodia, to have formed the basic factor in the scenes portrayed in stone by the artists of that era. It need hardly be added, perhaps, that art and religion are as closely connected in the East as they are in the West.

Ewing Galloway

SPIRED HEAD-DRESS OF SIAMESE DANCER

The dresses worn by the royal temple dancers of Siam are magnificent. No jewels are used, but a profusion of tinsel, and less often of gold, contributes to the splendour of the effect. The head-dress is specially remarkable. It is a tall filigree structure of elaborate workmanship, very similar in form to the votive spire seen on Buddhist temples.

When Hindu Java, at the end of the fifteenth century, exchanged its religion for that of its Moslem conquerors, all that was best in Javanese culture migrated to Bali, an island lying directly to the east of Java. The emigrants comprised the priests, Hindu and Buddhist, the aristocracy, and, since Islam forbids the representation of the living form in its art, the artists. The present-day Balinese, descendants of so rich and cultured a stock, possess great physical beauty; they are tall, slender, very graceful, with skins the colour of bronze, wavy black hair, dark, lustrous eyes, and regular features. The heirs of a people who constructed the magnificent Javanese temples could scarcely be bereft of artistic sense, and Balinese art as it appears in temple architecture, sculpture, painting, handicrafts, and, most of all, in the drama and the dance, is of a very high order.

IT may well be that art closely connected with religion is responsible for the gorgeous pageantry of the ancient faith which Bali, alone among the countless islands of Island-India, professes. For here the ancient gods of Hindustan are worshipped with all their wonted magnificence and splendour. As is natural to a people who have preserved their faith through five centuries despite the all-conquering power of Islam, religion plays a very important part in the life of the Balinese, and enters into almost everything they do;

G. H. Malins

THE HERO ARJUNA IS TEMPTED BY EVIL SPIRITS

Bali, east of Java, is famous for its girl ritual dancers. The photograph shows a phase in 'The Temptation of Arjuna,' a ballet from the Mahabharata. The character of Arjuna is one of the noblest in the great epic. One of the five Pandava princes, he is the wielder of the redoubtable bow, Gandiva. Here the evil spirits are represented by girl dancers with gilded. fan-shaped head-dresses.

almost superhuman beings, and who daily watch them performing the striking ritual of the Mudras in the temples, of which there are at least three in every village, should expect a high standard of proficiency in these same gestures from the temple maidens on account of the essential religious basis of the dance ceremonies ; but it is more than curious that in Siam long artificial gold finger-nails should be worn by the dancers in imitation of those of the Buddhist and Hindu priests. Nothing can better illustrate the fundamental importance of the ritual hand gestures in the dance-dramas of the East.

The Pedanda or priest, having made his ablutions, attires himself in white and, seating himself on his mat, recites his prayers to the accompaniment of the Mudras. The actual hand gestures comprise features from religious ritual such as delicately touching with the tips of the fingers the nostrils to simulate breath control, which is supposed to confer occult and psychic powers. Considerable use of cult implements and flowers is found in the Mudras ; for instance, the white champaka flower symbolises the soul. In the Ngili-Atma ritual the Pedanda takes a champaka flower in both hands, describes a half-circle in the air, and places it in his hair. That means that the priest identifies himself, for the time being, with Shiva (a god), whose soul would be in his head, in contradistinction to that of man, whose soul, according to Hindu belief, is in his stomach.

but, as in other parts of the Malay Archipelago, the animism of the aboriginal inhabitants has left a dubious legacy of good and evil spirits, who must be appeased by temples and shrines, offerings and worship. With these the Pedandas, priests of Shiva and Buddha, have little connexion ; their duties lie in keeping the orthodox temple festivals, in directing the dance ceremonies, in their own religious observances, which include the ritual of the Mudras, or ancient hand-gestures, and in teaching and training the temple maidens in the art of the dance, in which the ritual gestures play so important a part.

It is perhaps natural that the simple and lovable people of Bali, who fear and reverence the Pedandas as

Cult implements, which include the censer, chalice, rosary, hand-bell and sacred lamp, have striking similarities with those used in other ritualistic religions ; but the use of flowers in the Mudras is peculiar to Bali, where the ancient ritual gestures of the two great religions of India have perhaps been preserved in greater purity than anywhere else in the East.

The girls chosen for positions as temple dancers are very young, between the ages of four and five, and are carefully trained in deportment, posture and the gyrations which comprise the chief part of the

E. O. Hoppé

A TENSE MOMENT IN THE BALINESE TEMPLE BALLET

The subjects chosen for representation by the temple dancers of Bali are very sensational and highly charged with emotion. The favourite sources of the ballets are the Hindu epics, the Mahabharata and the Ramayana, both of which abound in dramatic situations. One of the girl dancers is here seen in the clutches of a long-haired, long-clawed evil spirit, who in the end appropriately meets with defeat. The performances, usually given in the daytime, are enacted by the side of a temple building or else against a natural background of jungle green.

Ewing Galloway

Dr. S. M. Manton

ARJUNA RESISTS THE TEMPTERS AND TRIUMPHS OVER THE EVIL ONE

The temple dances of the Balinese combine the elements of a mystery play, a religious service, and a gymnastic display. The lower photograph shows the final scene in a ballet from the Mahabharata, the 'Temptation of Arjuna,' in which the hero of the play slays the evil one in the form of a dragon. Another phase of this ballet, in which the noble Arjuna sets his face against the blandishments of his tempters, is illustrated above. The properties used by the performers are provided by the temple authorities.

dance-dramas. To achieve suppleness of limbs and graceful carriage, so necessary for the successful accomplishment of the dance, this training no doubt includes massage of the limbs, an art with which the Oriental is more familiar than we are, and which, owing to the youth of the subject, may be carried to extremes unknown outside the East.

In the Balinese drama, owing to the fact that the dancers' faces are thickly coated with paint and powder, facial expression plays no part; anger, sorrow, hate, envy, pleasure and surprise have to be shown by means of gesture or by conventional signs. Indeed the successful portrayal of the story in these mimetic dances depends upon extreme ability in the ritual gestures. During the dance, which usually occupies some thirty or forty minutes, every muscle is brought into play, and it is amazing to see the gyrations which the little creatures, bound up in gilded clothes like mummies, and painted and powdered beyond belief, perform; but perhaps the most extraordinary feature of the dance is that it is all flat footed. Performed on uneven ground, usually in the temple precincts, the movements of the writhing, quivering, supple-limbed bodies of the little dancers give the impression of unusual grace and subtle charm, while their extraordinary command of the art of gesture, and the prodigies, in this direction, which they are able to perform with their hands convey the meaning of their story to the mind in a fashion both remarkable and strange.

The clothes worn by the girls are temple properties, and comprise tinsel cloths, head-dresses and breast shields cut out of gilded leather, and gaily coloured sarongs or skirts. Fresh-cut lotus flowers are often used in the head-dresses, the lotus flower being especially sacred on account of its association with Vishnu, the lotus-born, one of the Hindu trinity. Flowers, freshly cut, are also used in the temple services, and in the Mudras or devotional exercises of the Pedandas. For the adornment of the person the favourite flower is the scarlet hibiscus, which lends exotic charm to the raven locks of a people whose passion it is to look beautiful.

THE subject-matter of the dance-dramas is often selected from the stories of the Ramayana and the Mahabharata, a favourite being the story of the temptation of Arjuna, the son of the pluvial god Indra and the real hero of the Mahabharata; of undaunted bravery, generous, tender-hearted, forgiving and affectionate, yet of superhuman strength and matchless in arms and athletic exercises, he rarely fails to appeal to the romantic maidens of that island Eden called Bali.

Those dancers who show great promise are attached to the more important temples where the clothes or

Dr. S. M. Manton

AGE-OLD HINDU MYTH IN A DANCE OF TODAY

In the phase here seen of 'The Temptation of Arjuna' the girl dancers are posturing before seated men. Arjuna is a prominent figure in the Mahabharata. This particular example of the ballet is based upon a two-thousand-year-old myth, which received its present form and was adapted for the ritual dance towards the end of the nineteenth century.

E. O. Hoppe

MEMBERS OF THE CORPS DE BALLET OF A BALINESE TEMPLE

From each Balinese girl the Hindu temples in the island exact at least three years' dancing service. Girls between the ages of ten and twenty take part in the temple dancing in the intervals of their domestic activities. They are trained from babyhood, and twist and turn in marvellous contortions. Each dance lasts for thirty or forty minutes. The golden parts of the dresses worn by the performers are cut out in gilded leather. The dancers are swathed in their finery like mummies, and express ritual meanings with their fingers and with arm gestures.

E. O. Hoppé

LOTUS-DECKED HEAD-DRESS OF A TEMPLE BALLERINA OF BALI

The sacred dances of the island of Bali, in the Dutch East Indies, are as notable for the splendour of the spectacle presented as for the exquisite grace of the youthful girl performers. Apart from some of the village dances, in which simpler costumes are worn, the dress of the dancers is gorgeous in the extreme, consisting of brocades and batik heavily overlaid with gold and colour. The galungan, or head-covering, is specially beautiful. It is made of stencilled leather, gilded and coloured, and is adorned with fresh blooms of the sacred lotus flower.

Dr. S. M. Manton

DANCING GIRLS' EVERYDAY DRESS

Only on entering the temple must the women of Bali cover the upper part of their bodies. In this island religion inspires all work and play, and it is in great measure to the training for the ritual dances that the suppleness and grace of the Balinese maidens are due.

vestments are of great richness, the crowns or head-dresses often being constructed of gold, and the breast shields studded with precious stones of great value; but as soon as the girls attain to puberty their service in the temple is at an end, and they return to their native villages trained and tutored in the faith which they profess, the years of training forming the basis of their religious experience, and the beauty and art of the dance, their form of religious expression, a fragrant memory for the years of life before them.

ORIGINALLY Cambodian dancers were, as in Bali, temple dancers, but for many centuries they have been attached to the court of the king of Cambodia, where they form a royal corps de ballet. Here in a land whose crumbling ruins testify to the grandeur, importance and 'glory that was Greece' the beautiful dance-dramas of the East have survived not as a form of religious expression, though the underlying motive is religious, but rather as the supreme achievement of an art long lost, but still pictured and portrayed in stone on the ruined temples which are scattered far and wide over the land.

The ballet consists of some thirty or forty girls chosen for their exceptional beauty and trained from early youth as professional dancers. As in Bali and other parts of the East, the face is so coated with paint and whitened with powder that all facial expression becomes impossible. The action of the drama becomes dependent on the skill of the dancer and her proficiency in the art of gesture. With undulating and serpentine movements, writhing, shuddering and quivering, the girls tell by means of posture and mime the legendary stories of Hindustan, dressed to resemble exactly the mythological figures carved upon their ruined temples.

All the wealth and splendour of Cambodia have been lavished upon the ballet. The dancer's coats are of cloth of gold, sparkling with jewels, the legs are sheathed in gold brocade, and a tiara of gold set with precious stones forms the head-dress, while the gesture language of the hands, in which the girls are remarkably proficient, is in no way impaired by the flashing stones of the gorgeous rings with which their fingers are loaded. The performance usually takes place in a large hall open at the sides to the accompaniment of an orchestra composed of gongs, drums and wooden harmonicas; the latter, a special feature of Cambodian and Siamese orchestras, are made of resonant wood and struck with velvet-padded sticks.

Amongst the Siamese by far the greater proportion of the people are Buddhists; nevertheless the subject-matter of the drama, one of their most cherished and ancient institutions, is confined to the stories of Brahmin mythology, the Ramayana and the Mahabharata, brought to Siam many centuries ago by Hindu priests, and a living testimony to the way in which Buddhist and Hindu philosophy and thought have developed side by side, two religions differing completely in essentials, yet existing together without antagonism. Dancing is here again the principal feature in the dramatic entertainment, and an

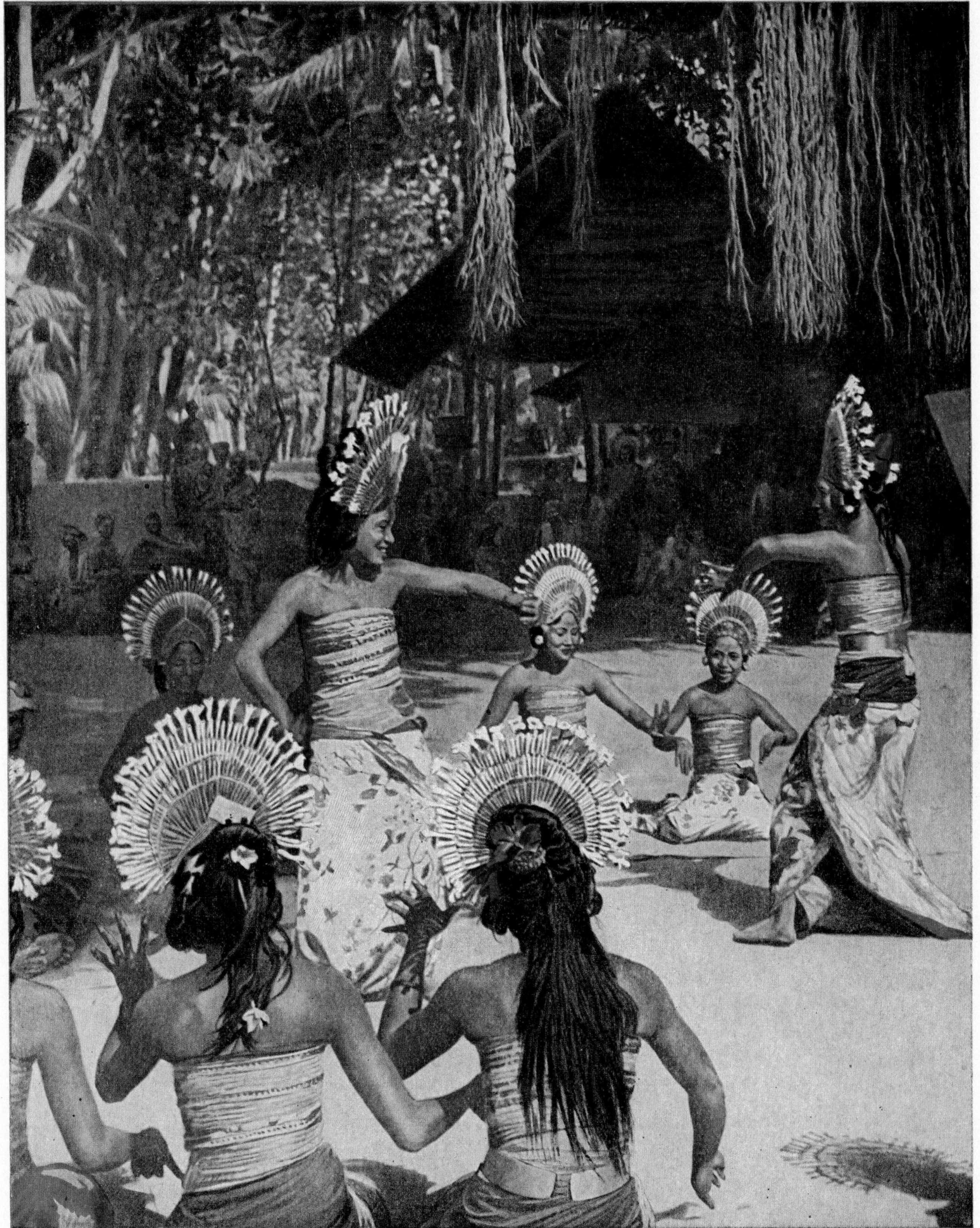

Dr. S. M. Manton

GIRL DANCERS OF BALI IN THE GOLDEN BALLET OF THE TEMPLE

In few parts of the world is the ritual dance carried to such a pitch of complexity and exactitude as in the island of Bali, off the eastern tip of Java. The performances are executed by young girls, arrayed in gowns glittering with gold leaf and tinsel and wearing ornate flower-decked head-dresses. The dancers are dedicated to the temple at the age or four or five, from which time they are trained in their art. Each posture, each swaying of the body, each movement of the fingers, hands and arms, has its special symbolic meaning. The ballet is performed to the plaintive though exciting music of the gamellan (see page 43).

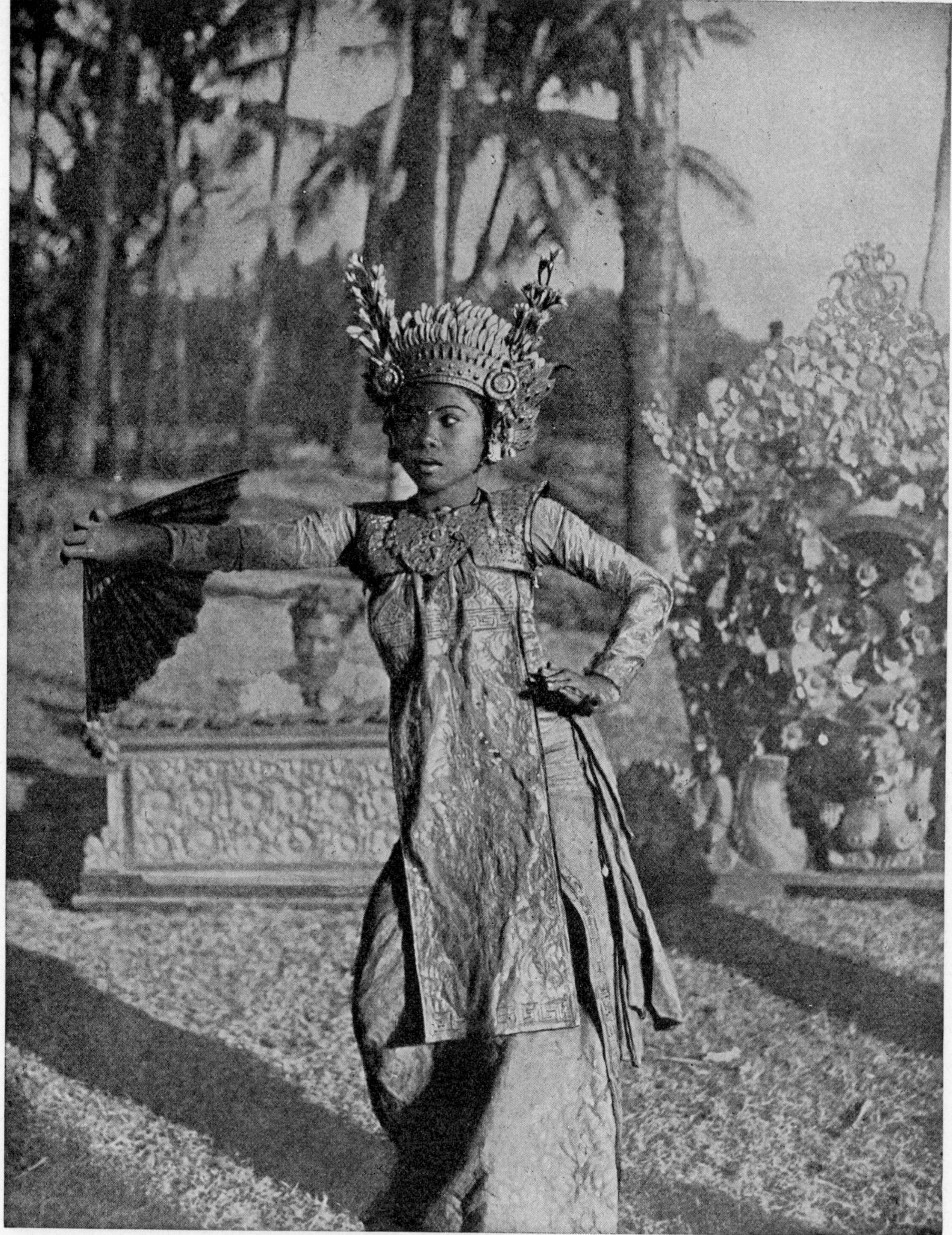

W. O. Burden

BRILLIANT FAN-PLAY AND POSTURING AT A TEMPLE FESTIVAL DANCE

The skilled manipulation of the fan is an important feature in the elaborate temple dances of Bali, and in the clever little hand of the Balinese ballerina the fan can be made to express a world of meaning. The lissomeness of these youthful dancers is the result of a long and exacting training, and every muscle of their bodies is brought into exquisite play. There is no tip-toe dancing. The whole is performed flat-footed and often on uneven ground, but in spite of these apparent handicaps the grace, control and suppleness of the dancers are incomparable.

Ewing Galloway

ROYAL TEMPLE DANCERS OF SIAM INTERPRETING A RELIGIOUS LEGEND

The religion of Siam is Buddhism of the southern variety, similar to that obtaining in Ceylon and Burma. The king is the religious as well as the political head of the country, and Siamese art and literature are mainly religious or inspired by religion. The ritual dances of Siam bear a marked resemblance in steps and postures to those of Cambodia and Bali. The mask is used in these dances for the same purposes as it served in the ancient Greek drama, namely, to emphasise the character presented and also to increase the carrying power of the voice.

Ewing Galloway

Topical Press

POSE AND POISE IN RITUAL DANCES AT BANGKOK

Like so many of the dances of the East, those performed by the royal temple dancers in Siam are very largely exhibitions of posturing. The steps are executed with a gliding motion. The dancers are remarkable for their endurance and for the consummate perfection of their technique. Interspersed between the sections of the main dance are incidental dances depicting such states of mind as love, hate, and so forth. Thus there is a dance of loyalty, a dance of obedience, a dance of respect. The lower photograph shows a dance of loyalty in progress.

Ewing Galloway

SUPPLENESS OF FINGERS AND ARMS IN THE SIAMESE BALLET

Although the Siamese are Buddhists, they go solely to the Mahabharata and the Ramayana for the subjects of their dance-dramas. Unwarlike themselves, they are very fond of themes depicting the triumph of warriors. The performances in the Royal Temple at Bangkok last several hours, and are accompanied by harsh instrumental music and much loud singing. The executants are in the main women, though sometimes a few men are introduced for the less important parts. The female dancers are marvels of suppleness. As the result of years of training they can bend their fingers backwards from the joints and their arms backwards from the elbow with the greatest ease.

endless amount of time and trouble is taken in training the body to the difficult postures and undulations which the art demands. The most important parts are taken by the women, but comic relief is sometimes supplied by two or three men who take the part of modern peasants, a rôle analogous to that of our country bumpkins. The faces of the women are, as in Bali and Cambodia, completely covered with powder and paint, thereby precluding all possibility of facial expression.

The drama is usually played upon a stage open on three sides, while the fourth is reserved for an orchestra consisting of fiddles, drums, gongs and flutes. The music is harsh and discordant and distasteful to the European ear ; no doubt European music has a similar effect, at any rate at first, on the peoples of Siam. The general impression is that Siamese music is played in a minor key ; but this is by no means the fact. Orchestral music is often of a very sprightly nature, and many tunes are played as with the loud pedal down. Harmony is not understood ; but there is simple variation, and time is very carefully kept. Almost every person in Siam is proficient in playing at least one instrument, women usually confining themselves to the stringed instruments such as the Siamese viol or zither. As is perhaps natural among simple peoples, instruments of percussion are the most popular, and there are numerous varieties of drums, gongs, harmonicas or xylophones. The drums most commonly in use are slightly barrelled wooden cylinders, about twice as long as they are broad, closed at both ends by cow-skin drumheads. The fingers or palms of the hands are used in playing, and there is a great deal of gesticulation and flourishing by the performer, who usually works himself into a state of excitement analogous to that of our jazz drummers at home.

Ewing Galloway

DANCERS GRAVEN IN STONE COME TO LIFE IN THE CAMBODIAN TEMPLE TROUPE

Not far from the ruined city of Angkor, the ancient capital of Cambodia, stands the wonderful congeries of temples, Angkor Vat, which, after lying hidden for centuries, has now been cleared of the jungle growth. The principal temple is built in terraces one above the other, and all the available space on the stonework is covered with finely and minutely carved figures. Attached to the main temple is a corps of highly trained female dancers, who in their dress and attitudes imitate as closely as possible the sculptured dancers on the temple walls.

Ewing Galloway

ROYAL CORPS DE BALLET OF CAMBODIA ON THE VERANDA OF THE PALACE

In Cambodia the ballet is part of the king's personal possessions. The dancers, in the words of Pierre Loti, 'undulate like snakes. . . . At times they stretch out their arms, and then the serpentine undulation begins in the fingers of the right hand, flows through the wrist, the forearm, the elbow, the shoulder, crosses the breast and continues on the opposite side, until it dies at last on the finger-tips of the left hand, overloaded with rings.' The performers wear gorgeous dresses of cloth of gold, set with jewels, and golden tiaras.

The orchestra is the natural accompaniment to the drama, and in almost every orchestra the gong, cymbals and clappers find their place. The cymbals, clashed together, mark every embrace of the stage lovers, while the clappers, made of split bamboo and played by some ancient females, probably superannuated dancers to whom nothing remains of their erstwhile beauty save a sense of rhythm, are used for marking time. The principal wind instrument is the 'pi' or pipe, made of ebony, whose notes resemble the Scotch bagpipes.

Singing, which forms a great part of the entertainment, is always slow, loud and of strong nasal intonation. The dancing consists of wreathing the arms with fingers turned back, swaying and writhing the body, and advancing or retiring with gliding motion, the toes turned out widely, and the weight supported on the heel of the foot rather than the toe. The dramatic performances often last for hours, and embody incidental 'pas seul' dances indicative of love, triumph, hate, anger or sorrow, and concerted 'morceaux de ballet' implying the array of armies, flight of angels or struggles with monsters. The dresses of the dancers are similar to those used in Cambodia, though not so gorgeous; tinsel is more common than gold, and precious stones are remarkable for their absence. The head-dress of the dancers calls for some notice on account of its close resemblance to the Pra Pang, or votive spire of the Buddhist temple, emphasising once again the close connexion between the dance-dramas and religion.

The striking similarity between the dance-dramas of Bali, Cambodia and Siam can only be explained by the fact that wherever Buddhist and Hindu thought has migrated there will be found the dancing temple-maiden, and the matter of her dance the ancient myths of Hindustan. And indeed it could not be otherwise where art and religion are so closely intertwined as to be almost one; where drama, story and song, ritual and ceremony point out with such clarity the essential religious importance of the dance, which, popularised for the sake of the people, is in itself the highest achievement of religious expression.

THE DRUM, SACRED AND SECULAR

CONCERNING the use of the drum in various activities of peoples whose culture is still elementary much will be found in the chapters on Rain-makers and Rain-making, Driving out the Devils of Disease, Devil and Other Spirit Dances, and elsewhere. Here it is considered chiefly as a means of long-distance communication and in its magical aspects, including its use in the cult of Shamanism.

WHAT instrument can equal the drum in antiquity? Not even the most primitive races are ignorant of it. In the course of thousands of years it has come to possess a sacred significance as well as a merely secular one. In ancient Egypt it had a religious use, and in old Mexico was in almost continual and monotonous employment as a priestly instrument. But although it is to be encountered pretty widely in America, India, Siberia, Australia and the Pacific archipelagoes, it is chiefly in Africa that its weird tones find employment as the summons of the witch doctor or as the telegraph of the local chiefs.

That the drum is regarded as sacred by some peoples, as having a life of its own, is shown by the recently abandoned custom of the Baganda of Central Africa, who, on re-covering their sacred tympanum with a fresh cow-skin, not only ran the animal's blood into the hollow, but actually beheaded a man and allowed his life-stream to flow into the instrument. They did this so that whenever the drum was beaten the king might get new life from the spirit of the slain man.

But, besides having a soul of its own, the drum of primitive man has a voice, a voice which can reverberate its message across miles of forest and lake, prairie or tundra. Europeans are frequently astonished at the extraordinary rapidity with which messages can be received and replied to by drum-sound. The true home of drum language is Central Africa, east of the chain of the great lakes. By its means the villagers converse in the most intimate manner, inquiring after each other's health, quarrelling, even declaring war by syncopation. But it is notorious that insults expressed in a drum-palaver are punished more rigorously than those conveyed by word of mouth. It is like using bad language over the telephone—a public offence.

WAR DRUM OF THE CITY OF BLOOD

Notable among stationary drums of Africa is this war drum of Benin City. It is carved in panels of grotesque heads and serrated bands, with drumhead of leopard's skin pegged down to the sides. It stands three feet eight inches high on a carved stand with claw feet.

THE drum language of Central Africa consists of beats on different parts of the drum's surface. There are four distinct notes in a drum's register, and these may be imitated by tapping on the cheek with the mouth held open, or indeed may be whistled, so that they actually convey a different medium of communication. The words expressed depend upon the number of taps, the depth or lightness of the note, and the rhythm, long or short, much as in the Morse code of telegraphy. This kind of telegraphy is not only practised in Central Africa, but in Oceania, the Amazon country in South America, in Mexico, and in north-west America.

The forms taken by signal drums are of great variety, and the manner in which they are held and played differs greatly among the peoples who employ them. In the country south of the Congo the drum is usually hung from the body, much as a European drummer might carry it, while to the north of these latitudes it is made to rest on feet or supports. Some African drums are round, like our own, others resemble a wooden box. A simple form is a mere section of tree trunk hollowed out and covered with hide or parchment, while a few are actual tree stumps, excavated and covered with skin, and are thus 'stationary' drums. An extraordinary little signal drum is the bow-drum of the Amadi, Aganda

Wide World

DRUMS THAT ARE BEATEN BY AFRICAN WITCH-DOCTORS TO HELP THEM IN THEIR MAGIC

In many parts of Africa the drum is a conspicuous feature in the life of the natives. Among some tribes it is regarded as sacred and as having powerful qualities of magic. Until quite recent times the Baganda of Central Africa used to behead a man and let his blood flow into their sacred drum. Other tribes use the drum for sending messages, which by this means can be despatched with marvellous rapidity over long distances. Among the peoples who employ the drum for purposes of magic are the Guere, a cannibal tribe of the Ivory Coast. In the photograph of some members of this tribe the drums used by the sorcerers are seen at either side of the group. They are carved out of wood.

and Bangba tribes of the Ubangi river, in which the tympanum is fixed to the inward side of a bow, an arrow being tapped from a cane string so as to beat upon it with reverberant tattooings, capable of being heard a long way off. Such drums are used by hunters in the forest, either to send news of their whereabouts to their friends, or to tell their wives to prepare a meal against their return. Stationary tree-trunk drums are frequently placed near elephant-pits to act as signal stations to the tribe should a passing hunter find that one of these great beasts has fallen into the snare laid for it.

The drums used by the peoples of Oceania are more various in shape than those in use in Africa. Those employed in Java and Sumatra are made of pieces of bamboo so separated from the stem that a joint intervenes, enclosing a hollow space, which is split longitudinally. These are hung on trees and beaten with sticks. Probably in the first instance the stem of the bamboo was employed just as it grew, until it was discovered that the hollow joint with a split in it produced a more resonant sound.

Ewing Galloway

KEEPING THE RHYTHM FOR THE DANCE

Some of the simpler African drums are merely sections of tree trunks hollowed out and covered at one end with hide or parchment. Surprising effects can be got out of them by skilful use of fingers and palm of the hands, without the aid of sticks. The African has a remarkably keen ear for rhythm, which this musician marks not only by means of his drum, but also by singing.

A PERCUSSION instrument that is perhaps unique is preserved in Pedjeng village, in the island of Bali, where, enclosed in a stone tower, about thirty feet high, is an all-metal drum, of kettledrum shape, around the rim of which are a number of fantastically carved human heads. No one knows the origin of this drum or its history. It was there when the famous Dutch botanist, Rumphius, visited Bali in 1750, and it is regarded by the Balinese with great awe, so much so, that when the writer, anxious to see the drum, clambered up the stone-work of the tower to a small opening and not only saw it, but touched it, the natives were awestruck, and said that some great ill luck would occur to him who had done such an impious deed. It is the fact that within an hour a violent thunderstorm came up with remarkable rapidity out of a brilliantly clear sky and a thunderbolt fell which missed the writer's car only by a foot or so!

But wooden drums of various designs have almost superseded the bamboo type in Oceania and the Pacific archipelagos. In the Philippines narrow tree trunks, hollowed out and split lengthwise, are hung from trees, while in Borneo and Java hollow wooden drums, often elaborately carved, are placed in a recumbent position on the ground and beaten with sticks resembling our wooden drumsticks. In the New Hebrides an entire grove of trees is frequently cut down partially and the hollowed stems are turned into drums with longitudinal slits, capable, when beaten together, of a surprising tumult.

The Somalis have drums resembling mortars in shape, while the people of Morocco make drums out of clay. Some Congoese drums are merely earthen pots, the opening of which is covered with skin.

It is perhaps in Siberia that the drum is still employed most particularly for magical purposes. It is connected with the cult of Shamanism, a system of sorcery or spiritism, the practitioners of which pretend to have intercourse with the spirit world. This they carry on by means of a magic drum, which, indeed, is in use among several Arctic peoples, and formerly was in Lapland, where it was prohibited in 1671 by Swedish law.

This instrument is made of a single piece of wood, hollowed in its thickest part in an oval form, the under part of which is convex, in which they make

St. H.

W. F. Taylor

STATIONARY SIGNAL DRUMS AND ORCHESTRAL TYMPANI

Nowhere has the use of the drum as a means of communication over long distances been so wonderfully developed as in Africa. Above are two of the large wooden-framed kettledrums available for such signalling purposes. The lower photograph shows the side drums used in a native band. These are elongated cylinders of wood, suspended from the drummer's neck and struck on both ends with the bare hand. The instruments in the background here are a form of xylophone with bottle-shaped gourds for sound boxes.

two apertures long enough to permit the fingers to pass through, for the purpose of holding it more firmly. The upper part is covered with the skin of the reindeer, on which they paint in red a number of figures, and from whence several brass rings are seen hanging, and some pieces of the bone of the reindeer.

A divining rod is placed on a definite spot, showing from its position after sounding the drum what magic inference might be drawn. By means of the drum the priest could be placed en rapport with the spirit world, and was thus enabled to divine the future; to ascertain synchronous events occurring at remote distances; to forecast the measure of success attending the day's hunting; to heal the sick; or to infect people with disease and cause death. Such a drum is also used by the Eskimo shamans in Greenland. Its shape varies slightly according to locality

The Samoyeds of Siberia use a drum of reindeer skin ornamented with brass rings. The shaman, or medicine man, attended by an assistant, walks round in a circle invoking the presence of the spirits, shaking a large rattle the while. The noise grows louder, and as the spirits are supposed to draw near the sorcerer he addresses them, beating his drum more gently, and pausing in his chant to listen to their answers. Gradually he works himself into a condition of frenzy, beats the drum with great violence, and appears to be possessed by the supernatural influence,

Baron Nordenskiöld

A LADY DRUMMER OF EL GRAN CHACO

Many primitive peoples besides the African employ the great carrying power of drum taps for mutual communication over long distances. In the Gran Chaco region of Argentina, for example, to which this girl belongs, it has been practised for centuries.

writhing and foaming at the mouth. All at once he stops, and oracularly pronounces the will of the spirits. The shaman's office is an hereditary one, but if a member of the tribe should exhibit special qualifications he is adopted into the priesthood, and by fasts, vigils, the use of narcotics and stimulants in the manner employed by the North American Indians he comes to believe that he has been visited by the spirits. He is then adopted as a shaman with midnight ceremonial, and is invested with a magic drum.

The method of playing the magic drum of the Siberian Yakuts requires considerable skill, and a prolonged course of practice is essential to success in it. One shaman told Sternberg that before he entered upon his vocation he was exceedingly ill for two months, during which time he remained unconscious. In the night he heard himself singing shaman's songs. Then spirits appeared to him in the shape of birds, and one in human form, who commanded him to make a drum and the other apparatus.

The drum they preserve with the utmost care. When they desire to know what luck they will have in hunting, or if a person will recover, the shaman kneels down before the drum and beats it, at first with light strokes, then louder, stronger ones. The instrument is cut in one piece out of a thick tree stem, the fibres of which run upward in the same direction as the course of the sun. It is covered with the skin of an animal, and in the bottom holes are cut by which it may be held. Upon the skin are painted the figures of spirits and animals, lands and waters, and on the surface is placed a bundle of metal rings which act as an indicator. When by means of

E.N.A.

WIRELESS TELEPHONY BY A BUNYORO HEADMAN

Uganda is in the heart of the home of the African drum language, by means of which the natives convey messages with astonishing rapidity to other villages surprisingly far away. Words are expressed by drum taps of varying intensity, number and rhythm.

E.N.A.

DRUMS TO CALL FOLK TO CHURCH AND KEEP THE DEVIL AWAY

That noise has efficacy to ward off evil is an idea held by simple folk the world over. In the New Hebrides it is given practical application in these grotesque objects, hollowed logs which the natives beat like drums to frighten evil away. The crude dug-outs of the Fiji Islands shown in the upper photograph are used for summoning purposes. They are beaten with short, heavy mallets. In the old cannibal days they were thumped to summon the natives to their feasts of 'long pig.' Nowadays they are used as church bells, to call them to prayer.

Kurt Lubinski

MEMBERS OF THE SHAMAN PRIESTHOOD WITH THE SPIRIT-INVOKING DRUM

In the cult of Shamanism the drum is the means by which the priests communicate with the spirits. The instrument used by the shamans of Siberia is cut out of a single piece of wood, over which reindeer skin is stretched. The bells on the priest's back (top) are supposed to announce his presence to the spirits. Inside the drum is a wooden sacred image decorated with coloured ribbons. The lower photograph shows a shaman priestess, her face hidden by a mask of black ribbons, whirling in an ecstatic dance under the spirits' influence.

Central News

E.N.A.

EXQUISITE ARTISTRY IN JAPANESE DRUMS

This hour-glass-shaped instrument is one of the hand drums used by the dancers in the No plays of Japan. Above craftsmen are shown putting the finishing touches to the drums intended to furnish the sacred music at the coronation of the Emperor.

beating these move in the direction of a certain figure, the answer is understood to have been given in terms of that figure's symbolical significance. Sometimes the shaman falls into an ecstasy, when he usually places the drum on his head. Then he sings a magical chant, in which the reply is more or less oracularly indicated. Great care is taken that nothing shall touch him during this process, and he may lie in that state for hours, seemingly more dead than alive.

The people of China, Burma and the adjoining countries all employ drums for the purpose of rain-making. These are decorated with little figures of frogs, the animal traditionally associated with flooded rice-fields. Several of the tribes of Central Africa, during a season of drought, beat drums to imitate thunder and induce rainfall by sympathetic magic.

The drum is, in short, regarded by the savage as the larger voice of the king, the priest or the god, as well as a means of communication, and has thus come to be thought of as in itself a thing of almost supernatural character. Its note is perhaps the most solemn and portentous known to man. The hollow beatings of the sacred drums of Africa and India, their monotonous tones and persistent boomings, have been known to stir profoundly even the most unimaginative of Europeans, and travellers and explorers who have traversed the vast forests of the Congo region or the Amazon have written with feeling regarding the note of menace and horror of these instruments, the memory of which they have been conscious of for the remainder of their lives.

MODERN SLAVERY AND SERFDOM

OF all the customs surveyed in this work, trade and ownership in human beings is the most deplorable. Its wide distribution in the world today is indicated here: no little difficulty has been experienced in securing photographs to illustrate the text—encouraging, perhaps, the hope that even those peoples who tolerate serfdom in their midst are ashamed to let the fact become known.

IT will come as a shock to many people to learn that slavery still exists in the world—that human beings are still bought and sold like cattle. It has been customary to assume that Wilberforce abolished the slave trade in 1807, and that since then the iniquitous system, which was adopted from the Greeks and Romans by the European races, has entirely disappeared.

Not only in what the League of Nations has aptly described as its 'classic form'—raiding, capture and exchange for money according to the will of the master—is slavery in existence to-day. Those medieval forms that the system assumed in feudal times—vassalage, villeinage and serfdom—all find their reflection in some part of the world at the present time.

As a nation we can rightly take pride in the fact that not since 1833 has slavery, in its most open and callous form, been allowed to continue within the confines of the British Empire. Long before that our Courts held that a slave setting foot on British ground became instantly a free man. It is unhappily true, however, that under the guise of indentured labour a system bearing a suspicious likeness to slavery has existed. But even where this has been found the Government has done its best to bring about its abolition.

According to the slavery convention of 1926, slavery is defined as the status or condition of a person over whom any or all of the powers attaching to the right of ownership are exercised. Comprehensive as this definition is, it would not seem, on a strict interpretation, to embrace some of the forms of modern economic slavery. When inquiring into the charges of slave-trading brought against Liberia, the International Commission were compelled to ask themselves 'whether practices restrictive of the liberty of persons analogous to slavery, which are apparently temporary but tend to become permanent in practice from lack of power of legal redress on the part of the person involved,' could reasonably be included within the scope of this definition. The ordinary man will have no doubts.

'ADOPTION,' 'peonage,' 'forced labour,' 'indentured labour,' these are all terms that mask slavery, from Hong Kong in the Far East to Liberia on the western coast of Africa. It flourishes not merely among what we call the coloured races, but, bitter as the reflection is, among white men. The invention of the limited liability company clouded the conscience of mankind, and in the economic struggle for dividends the money of quite respectable and kind-hearted members of society was used to propagate those horrors of the Congo and Putumayo which shocked the world in the first decade of the present century.

Most books on modern slavery have of necessity been written at second hand. It has been left to the League of Nations to compile what may be regarded as the first judicial report on modern slavery.

Ewing Galloway

CHAINED SLAVES IN THE 'HOME OF THE FREE'

Irony of fate could hardly have more terrible illustration in real life than the system of slavery established by the free-born descendants of emancipated slaves in a state expressly founded by abolitionists to be the home of the free. This photograph, smuggled out of Liberia as recently as 1930, shows how natives are secured by collars and chains for 'forced labour.'

the human pledge remains in pawn—or in slavery. He gets such formal documents as the following, which, with its pretence of legal phraseology, might be regarded as funny if we do not remember what the transaction implies.

> This to certify that I, Sidi Weah, at Gbowah Section have pawned one girl and one boy to Sergeant Johnny Williams until the amount £13 10s. thirteen pounds ten shillings sterling which I due him be pay to him *at any time.*

The story of Liberian forced labour is a terrible one. By involving a local chief in a fine which he cannot pay, wholesale raids can be carried out. Settlement of the fine can be made only by providing the men needed for a job. And not only men. The black conscripts who

A commission of three investigated the charges on the spot, and their report is there for all the world to read.

The fact that slave-trading is practised in Liberia is of especially tragic interest because of the origin of that state. Between 1820 and 1860 the American Colonisation Society rescued more than eighteen thousand slaves from the Union and repatriated them in Liberia, on the west coast of Africa. This was to be 'the Home of the Free,' as the name of the country signifies. In 1846 Liberia became an independent republic. Its constitution embodied, naturally enough, a provision against all slavery. How these descendants of enfranchised slaves have interpreted that clause is now known to the whole world.

Human flesh is bartered and sold in Liberia under various forms. Sometimes these forms have a legal flavour. Pawning is one of them. A native who has committed a breach of the law has to pay a fine. He must raise the money, of which he has none. He pawns his children. Pawning implies, of course, the right of redemption, but as the native has no money,

Martin Munkacsy

MILITARY SUPERVISION FOR COMMANDEERED LABOUR

Porterage, road making and building are three of the principal public services for which native labour officially 'recruited' is provided in Liberia under compulsory conditions indistinguishable from actual slavery. Natives are here shown pressing concrete bricks and (top) employed in building in Monrovia. Note here the armed guard in charge of the working party.

Capt. K. Amall

Topical Press

RAIDERS HOIST WITH THEIR OWN PETARD IN A SLAVE-RIDDEN LAND

Notwithstanding edicts from the Abyssinian authorities prohibiting slavery many Abyssinian princes own enormous numbers of slaves. The file of men (below) are the bond-servants of one such magnate carrying gifts of food and drink to a camp conference. In the Sudan the British government takes drastic action to suppress the slave trade, and the upper photograph shows how some captured Arab slave-raiders were given a taste of their own medicine by being fastened in the wooden yokes from which the slaves had just been released.

enforce these orders must have a free supply of women. Opposition is met by cruelties as old as the history of human slavery. One ready means of torture for which the appliances are always handy is to light a fire under the victim.

The most profitable employment of these human goods by the people and government of a country whose motto is 'the love of liberty brought us here' is for the labour market in the island of Fernando Po. All the machinery of these transactions—the beatings and burnings and chainings—imitate the features of the classic slave-raiding and slave-trading. Not only are these wretched men sent to Fernando Po for the profit of the Liberian Government officials, but they are retained within the territory of the country for porterage, road construction and barrack building. The Commission found, moreover, that while the American Firestone Plantation Company which operates so effectively in Nigeria, had not consciously employed any but voluntary labour on its leased rubber plantations, it had accepted 'recruits' obtained for it by official methods.

E.N.A.

RAMSHACKLE OUTPOSTS WHERE UNHAPPY HELOTS KEPT CONSTANT VIGIL OVER THE GROWING CROPS

Although some of the slaves in Upper Burma were engaged in domestic work the great majority were employed as agricultural labourers. Here, for example, are three slaves—one male and two female—with their owner on a 'Yi-wa,' the building erected in the fields to house women slaves whose work it was to scare birds off the crops. Slaves were well fed and clothed, but were paid no wages, were beaten savagely if they failed to work satisfactorily, and were hunted and sometimes shot if they tried to escape. Slaves married slaves and their children were born slaves. Some of them were fairly well treated, but on the whole their lives were spent in abject misery, and all, without exception, eagerly sought release.

Modern Slavery and Serfdom

The unfortunate natives of Africa are still exploited as slaves throughout the Dark Continent. The traffic flourishes throughout the West African coast and has not yet been completely suppressed in British protectorates. In Portuguese territory—especially in Angola—natives are recruited, brought down to the coast, and sent to work in Portuguese islands. In a famous libel action which occupied the Courts some years ago it was brought out in evidence that the Portuguese Government had offered two hundred black labourers for £3,550.

This is called 'contract labour,' but as the contracted labourers are taken by force, and in many cases believe themselves submitting to slavery, the title does not seem to matter. Slavery by any other name smells just as foul. In our own unfortunate experiment in South Africa after the Boer War Chinese labourers were signed on for a number of years under the compulsion of the local Chinese authorities. A contract was read to them which they could not understand, and having duly signed, or made their mark 'on the dotted line,' they were shipped to Africa.

WHITE races, it would seem, unlike the Mahomedan races, are shy of engaging openly in the slave trade. Hence these euphemistic names of 'contract labour' and the like. The French, since they assumed authority in Morocco, have suppressed the open slave market, but slave-trading in a covert fashion still continues. Very well-to-do natives will own several slaves, whilst those powerful chiefs the 'Lords of the Atlas' number their serfs by the thousands. It is noteworthy that it was due to French colonial ambition that the slave trade in the Persian Gulf flourished so profitably for the last forty years of the nineteenth century and the first few years of this. To spread French influence the representatives abroad of liberty, equality and fraternity distributed the protection of their flag broadcast. The slave-trader seized upon the gift, and under the protection of that flag thousands of African natives were forcibly seized, trapped or netted and sold in the markets of Arabia and Persia. The British Navy, which had hitherto kept this traffic within bounds, naturally refrained from firing upon the flag of a friendly nation.

IN 'Christian' Abyssinia slavery flourishes on an enormous scale. Some of the Rases or princes are said to own as many as fifteen thousand. As in Liberia, high-sounding edicts have been passed against slavery—the Emperor Menelik even made it a capital offence—but the raiding parties still go out and still the inhuman traffic in black ivory continues. For the world at large, which has difficulty in knowing what is going on, the Abyssinian authorities once published statistics showing how many slaves had been liberated. The total for three years from 1924–26 was 1,109. But it is calculated that there are over two million slaves in the country!

On becoming a member of the League of Nations it was agreed that Abyssinia should 'secure the complete suppression of slavery in all its forms and of the slave trade by land and sea.' Abyssinian slaves now trickle across the frontier, lured by the prospects of free employment in the Sudan cotton plantations. They come in ever-increasing numbers, and Sir Austen Chamberlain, when he was Foreign Secretary, announced that 'in no case has any escaped slave been sent back to Abyssinia.'

While in the British Protectorate of Sierra Leone, where the Government has not yet been able completely to establish its authority, and in the districts already mentioned, the slave traffic goes on, its worst features are to be found on the east coast of Africa, where from time immemorial the Arabs have raided their black brothers. For a century our

F. Kingdon Ward

A SIGHT TO MAKE ANGELS WEEP

Shocking conditions of child slavery exist throughout China, in some regions without any attempt at disguise. This poor mite is one of thousands of girl slaves bought for a song from the Lisu tribesmen and devoted to a life of hopeless misery and degradation in Yunnan.

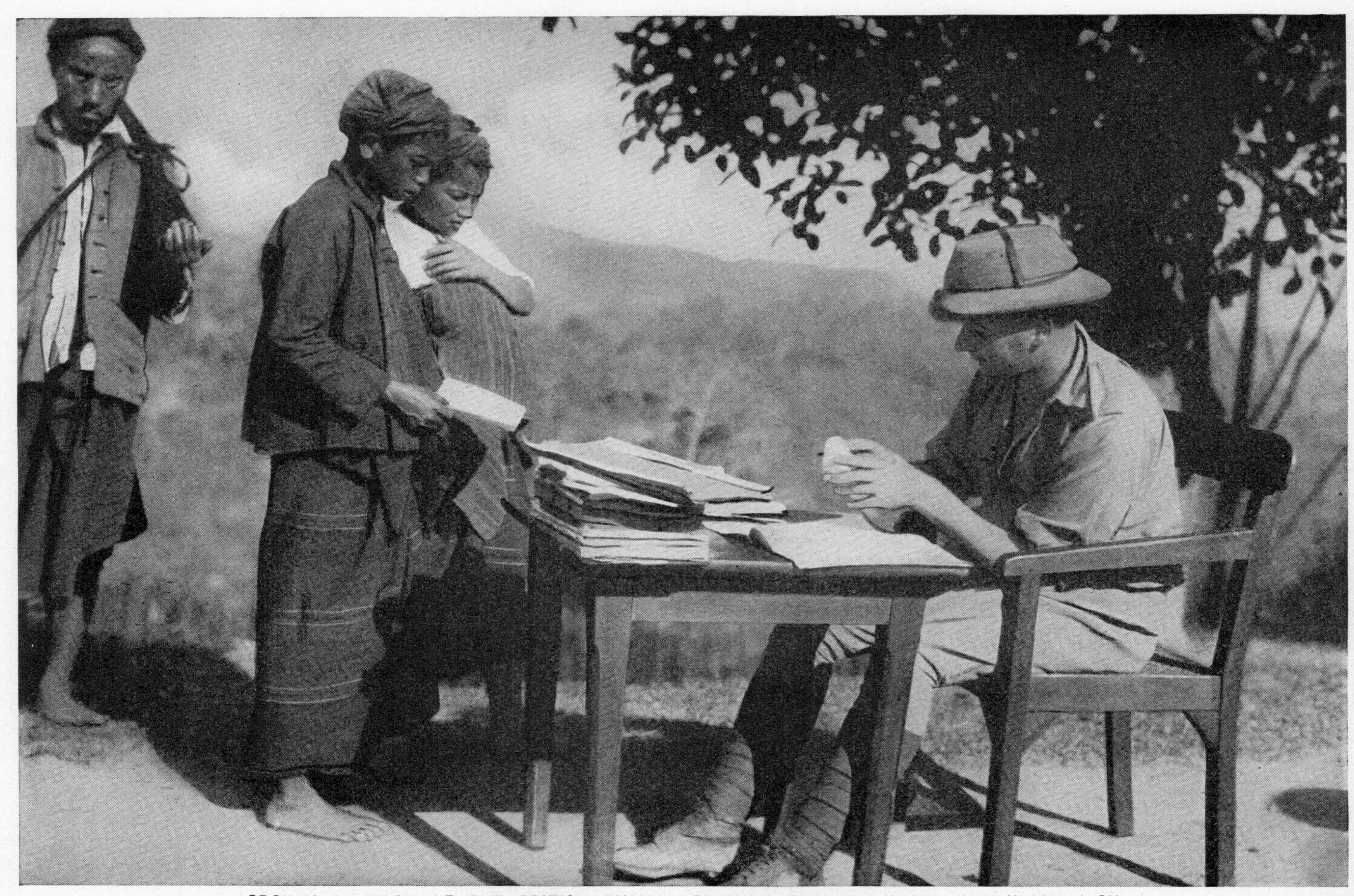

CROWNING MERCY OF THE BRITISH EMPIRE: FREEDOM FOR ALL UNDER THE UNION JACK

In 1925 the then Governor of Burma led an expedition to the Hukwang Valley in Upper Burma to put an end to the slavery and human sacrifice which existed among the Kachins and Nagas who occupied that still unadministered area. Despite the difficulties of the problem a peaceful settlement was effected, and by 1928 both evils had been practically abolished. The slaves were released on payment to their owners of compensation which worked out at about £10 per head, after which each emancipated slave was given a certificate guaranteeing freedom for himself and his descendants for ever and a social status equal to that of all other free men in the valley. Arrangements were made for those who wanted land to get it in the valley or in the British administered area.

Government has made treaties with sultans and chieftains and all the autocratic puppets in the neighbourhood of the Persian Gulf, and by these treaties, if words could accomplish anything, slave-trading has been suppressed.

The last treaty was made in 1927 with the King of the Hejaz, and contained the usual clause for the suppression of the slave-trade. But the slave markets are still held openly with the official recognition of the Government. Indeed, as Lady Simon points out in her book on slavery, it is an absurdity to forbid slave-trading, when slave-owning is permitted. There are said to be seven hundred thousand slaves in Arabia, and as this 'property' must depreciate, efforts will be made to obtain a new supply. The slavers still run down to the African coast with the north-east monsoon, which blows from October to April, and return with the south-west monsoon between May and September, their holds full of black ivory.

F. Kingdon Ward

GIRLHOOD FOR WHICH A HAPPIER DAY HAS DAWNED

By means chiefly of equitable compensation to slave owners the British Government since 1924 has practically put an end to the slavery that had existed for a long period in the Burma Triangle, the wild district between the main branches of the Irawadi river in Upper Burma. These girls belong to the Maru tribe, many of whom were formerly held as slaves by the Kachins.

It may be presumed, perhaps rightly, that the lot of the slave in Arabia or Persia or even Turkey is much better than it would have been in his native country. They are probably fed and treated better, once the brutalities of the raid are over, for the strict Mahomedan is merciful to his dependents, and acquires virtue by the emancipation of his serfs; but this does not affect the great principle of individual freedom which is at stake.

Modern slavery persists in its most horrible form in China, for there it is not adult men or women who are the victims, but little children. There are said to be two millions of these slave children in China. A girl is picked up for a mere song. She is passed from owner to owner as 'property.' She can be, and is, beaten and tortured or even killed without redress or penalty inflicted. Mr. Charles H. Coates, in his 'Red Theology in the Far East,' declares that 'floggings, suspension, the pouring of boiling water over the hands, the amputation of a finger joint, gagging and tying up for torture with hot irons, and similar cruelties are not uncommonly practised upon these children.'

Here is another picture from the same pages. It is the story of a little girl who

> as a child, had been suspended by her owners from the ceiling, hanging by one rope which bound together both wrists and both ankles, and left in that situation all night. By the morning the poor little limbs were so mortified by this ordeal that all four had to be amputated. The foreign doctor who performed the operation secured for the child her freedom and a monetary compensation sufficient for her future from the owners, under threat of publication of the facts.

The usual history of these girl slaves is one for sombre reflection. They are bought cheap when only four or five. Their owners work them for ten years. Then they are sold for marriage or supplied at a price to the brothels of the great cities and ports.

A variation of this open purchasing of little human creatures as property is practised in Shanghai and elsewhere. Contractors hire young children from the country districts, paying their parents for the services of each of them two dollars a month. These children are then hired out to the mills and factories at six dollars a month. The children do not receive this money, and are housed and fed miserably, thereby making a profit for the contractor of four dollars a month. Young boys as recently as 1925 were being sold for ten shillings apiece. Some of them had been slaves for nearly six years. Marks on their bodies indicated that they had been burned with iron rods. As in other countries where slavery flourishes, high-sounding proclamations have been issued in China from time to time, forbidding the practice and enunciating the principles of human freedom, but still the slave trade goes on.

In our own Crown colony, Hong Kong, where according to the law slavery is impossible, the Mui Tsai system is practised. Here slavery is disguised as adoption. A child is pledged to a Chinese man in return for twenty dollars. To redeem her, the mother must pay all the arrears of maintenance. The child is then sold as an adopted daughter to another Chinese man. So, by gradual degrees, rights of absolute property are established. This is, of course, slavery carefully disguised. For years our Government has been struggling in face of the dead-weight of custom to abolish the practice. There are said to be ten thousand of these Mui Tsai in Hong Kong.

ALMOST TOO OLD TO ENJOY THE FRUITS OF FREEDOM

Young, able-bodied male and attractive female slaves were valued at something like £12 apiece, the old and children at £3 or £4. One very pathetic figure seen in the closing stages of the work of slave liberation was this emaciated old slave carried pickaback on the shoulders of his master, who brought him in in the hope of getting some compensation for his release.

Like the Chinese, the Tibetans practise slavery. In the Salween valley on the Tibetan frontier there dwells a curious tribe of dwarfs, known as the dwarf Nung, who are very popular as slaves with the Tibetans. Raiding parties go out frequently to secure a supply of these much-coveted little people. In the triangle of Northern Burma the activities of the British authorities have gradually eradicated the system from the country, though slavery still exists there. In Nepal slave-owning and slave-trading were abolished by 1926 in the course of two years by the courageous conduct of the Prime Minister, His Highness the Maharaja Sir Chandra Shumshere Jung. It is more than probable, however, that in the other states on the northern and north-eastern slopes of the Himalayas bordering on Nepal slavery still lingers.

The truth about the condition of affairs in Russia has been so obscured by propaganda for and against the Soviet Government that it is difficult to decide

Captn. Green

HUMAN CATTLE EMPLOYED IN CARRYING SWINE

Conducted by their owner—the shady-hatted individual holding the spear that proclaims him a headman—these Kachin slaves are carrying pigs to a neighbouring village as part payment of the price of a bride. Pigs are ubiquitous in Kachin villages, living under the floors of the dwelling houses, which, for sanitary purposes, are raised some four feet above the ground. No Kachin, bond or free, is ever seen without his 'dah'—the sword which serves every conceivable purpose to which a blade can be put in peace or war.

what can and what cannot be accepted as a fact. The report of the National Lumber Manufacturers' Association of the United States on the methods of employing labour in Russian timber camps suggests, however, that even in Europe slavery exists today.

It is estimated that some four million prisoners, mostly guilty of political offences, are employed in these camps under conditions so brutal and inhuman that many of them try to injure themselves even by cutting off a hand in the hope of escaping from their misery. Throughout the entire northern region, in the big forest tracts, not only these convicts but exiles and forced labourers toil at the task of cutting the timber with which it is hoped to flood Europe. Reports state that in the freezing cold these unhappy men, half starved for want of food, are made to toil at work far beyond their strength. To some of them as they labour comes the relief of death. The others less fortunate are kept moving by whip or club. For failure to cut the allotted number of logs, these unhappy slaves are punished with the most barbaric cruelty.

There is one aspect of this continuance in the twentieth century of a servile class in the world which cannot be avoided. It is the inevitable consequence of economic conditions. White nations, in the process of imperial expansion, or because of commercial enterprises, have taken over vast tropical and semi-tropical territories. Here either the white man cannot work, or, if he did work, the whole white race might, it is held, lose caste with the huge surrounding black population. The native population may not want to work at the white man's job. What, therefore, is the white man to do?

This problem has arisen in both Kenya and Uganda. In the former, demands have been made by the white men for the legalising of compulsory labour among the natives—a system akin to the corvée which was prevalent in France before the Revolution. The obvious danger of such compulsory labour developing into thinly-disguised slavery has always been present in the minds of the Imperial Government at home. In 1922 the Duke of Devonshire laid down the principles which the British people desire should be followed

E.N.A.

CONSCIENTIOUS SUPPORTERS OF HUMAN SACRIFICE AND SERFDOM

One obstacle to the abolition of slavery among the Nagas of Upper Burma was the belief of those people that the 'nats' or spirits they worshipped must be propitiated by human sacrifice and that otherwise crops would fail and disaster and death would fall upon the villages. Victims for the sacrifice were slaves, of any age and either sex, and their emancipation was thus resisted on religious as well as economic grounds by the more obstinately conservative Nagas—of whom this overseer (left) and village headman (right) are representative figures.

towards the native races under their protection.

It created at the time very violent feelings in Kenya, where the white men considered they had been 'let down' by the Imperial Government. In an area of 224,960 square miles there is a, roughly estimated, population of 3,000,000, of which only 16,000 are Europeans. Only one two-hundredth part of this vast region is at present cultivated entirely by Europeans. Kenya's problem is how to get the most out of this fertile part of the world when it is impossible to make the black population work without some form of coercion. The Duke of Devonshire's pronouncement was directed against the not unnatural tendency of the Europeans to get workmen to help them with their maize, hemp, coffee and wheat crops.

That Declaration is the denial of the right to make use of forced labour, unless such labour is conscripted, as a soldier's services may be conscripted, in a national emergency for the national interests. If followed, it must of necessity make even the taint of slavery impossible under the British flag. In this Declaration it is laid down that

> His Majesty's Government think it necessary definitely to record their considered opinion that the interests of the African natives must be paramount, and that if, and when, those interests and the interests of the immigrant races should conflict, the former should prevail.

That there was need for some declaration of the kind this brief survey of slavery as it exists today, with all its sufferings and cruelty, amply proves.

'FENG-SHUI,' THE CHINESE SYSTEM OF BURIAL DIVINATION

No parallel exists to-day to the Chinese quasi scientific system of interpreting the configuration of the earth in terms of good or of bad luck. The subject is of real importance, because both Feng-Shui in its numerous branches and this belief in the mysterious activity of spirits have influenced the life of the masses in China to an incredible degree.

FENG-SHUI is that most ancient science by the aid of which the Chinese fix the sites and locations of the graves of their relatives, of their temples and shrines, and even of their dwelling-houses. The two words really mean 'wind' and 'water' and signify the influence of climate and environment on any site or building raised by human hands. Out of the superstition associated with natural forces and the elements has arisen a set of rules of the most fantastic and involved description which must be observed in the choice of sites and buildings, and especially in the location of tombs, if evil influences are to be avoided.

Taoism, the ancient philosophy of China, implanted a belief in the Celestial mind that man must live in harmony with nature, and this aroused an extraordinarily keen observation of its functions, the distribution of mountains, the flow of rivers, the effects of winds and rainfall. These were believed to concern the welfare and fate of man in a most intimate degree, and to have magical repercussions on his existence and on the growth and prosperity of the crops.

Therefore it was thought essential that they must be closely studied in order that only the best natural influences might come into contact with humanity. Especially did this seem necessary in connexion with the graves of ancestors, whose welfare in the tomb was thought to react upon their descendants and on the growth of the fruits of the earth. For the Chinese believe that man has two souls, one of which remains in the grave for some time after death, so that an inauspicious burial-place would have evil effects upon the lingering spirit, which would consequently wreak its wrath on its negligent relatives and on the crops they had sown.

Therefore the most pious care is still taken by virtually all classes in China in the choice of the site of a grave, and it is here that the science of Feng-Shui is brought into particular use. A special class of geomancers, who have made a deep study of the science, are called into consultation, an auspicious date for the burial ceremony is fixed, and the search for a favourable site is begun. This is often found to be a task of extraordinary difficulty, because of the disposition of natural objects in the near neighbourhood. No watercourse must run straight toward the spot, as it might carry with it evil influences. A straight road is similarly taboo, as that too much resembles a spear, and therefore a threat! The direction of the winds must be propitious, and no sloping ground must frown above the tomb, lest it carry rain water into the grave and enrage the spirit of the deceased. In short, there is no end to the semi-grotesque, semi-practical 'reasons' which dictate the choice of a site.

THOSE who can face the necessary expense usually select the top of a sloping hillside, as likely to afford dryness, and surround the tomb with a wall in the shape of a horseshoe, with the ends slightly curling outward to keep off the wind, the closed end facing the hill top. Should the site selected have a natural rise at either side of the tomb this is regarded as particularly auspicious, as it is supposed to guard the dead from the influence of evil winds. But should anything in the nature of a gap occur in the surrounding land, this is filled up by a large heap of stones or a wall of earth. The corpse is invariably

OSSUARY URNS FOR THE TOMBLESS DEAD

Probably with an eye to the main chance, Chinese geomancers profess that it is extremely difficult to discover a site for a grave entirely free from deleterious influences attaching to adjacent natural objects. A consequence is that burials are often delayed for long periods, and until a satisfactory site has been found the bones of the dead are kept in jars like these.

CHINESE FAMILY TOMB MOST AUSPICIOUSLY LOCATED

All the important conditions required by the rules of Feng-Shui for a family grave are satisfied in this example in South China. It is set high up on a sloping hillside and enclosed within a wall shaped like a Greek omega, with the open end facing the south, and nothing to impede the entrance of light, heat, warm winds and soft showers. The terraces seen in the immediate vicinity are the banks of paddy or rice fields, and are advantageous as helping to deflect surface water from the tomb.

buried with its feet toward the opening of the horseshoe enclosure.

It is thought desirable that this opening should face the south, so that light, heat, warm winds and soft showers may find entrance to the tomb, and no object of any great size should be permitted to stand in front of it to deflect these. The general idea is that if these good climatic influences find their way to rejoice the spirit of the dead, he will see to it that his descendants enjoy similar good weather for their crops. The crenellations or openings so frequently to be observed in Chinese walls are usually made at the request of relatives whose ancestral tombs have been placed near these walls, so that good influences may pass through the masonry and not be diverted from the dead.

Water is often deflected from the tomb by digging a pond to receive surface moisture from the ground behind or above the building, only the water must not be carried off too swiftly, lest it tend to hurry away good influences. Anything in the shape of a curious natural object in the vicinity of a tomb is closely scrutinised before the site is accepted. A queerly shaped knoll or rock or other landmark may possess some extraordinary occult significance which might have the most disastrous effects, therefore the greatest care is first taken to arrive at its real significance.

The four points of the compass, too, are regarded as supremely ominous for a burial site. In the east lurks the great Blue Dragon, lord of the waters, to the west the White Tiger, ruler of the winds, on the south dwells the Red Bird, and from the north comes the Black Tortoise. If the grave faces the south, some landmark symbolic of the Tiger should stand to the west, or right, and of the Dragon to the east, or left. The Dragon is the more important, while the northern and southern genii are held to be of minor influence. A piece of high ground, a house, or pagoda, may typify these animal guardians, and if this is lacking, cairns roughly resembling them are often raised. Indeed this practice is not confined to tombs, but the good luck of a town or village is frequently enhanced by the erection of such images in the proper situations. If the earth in any neighbourhood appears peculiarly ' vigorous,' that is, if it is undulating or cast in ridges, this is considered a most propitious vicinity for good influences, for a snake-like ridge is thought to typify the celestial dragon from which proceed the vivifying rains. Certain forms of mountains, too, typify the five elements, fire, water, wood, metal and earth, and as one or other of these is thought to predominate in the scenery, good or evil influences prevail.

Along with the four grand points of the compass there are eight subsidiary points, which have affinities with different animals and elements, and which are assiduously examined by the geomancers to discover the influences that emanate from them or that are blown from their direction by the winds. All this notwithstanding, the practitioners of Feng-Shui are compelled to admit on occasion, when the crops fail, or a family is unfortunate, that Providence has overruled the natural conditions. That they have misread the omens they will never confess. But sin or folly on the part of a son or descendant may do much to neutralise the happy conditions of a father's burial-place, and an ancient proverb states that virtue is the foundation of the search for auspicious sites. In imperial times if the burial of a parent was unduly postponed by anyone who was a government servant, he was denied official promotion on that account. Frequently there is much delay in repairing buildings, roads and bridges, and even in digging the earth for agricultural purposes, because of the possible disturbance of good influences and the attraction of evil ones.

If damage is done to a grave by wind or weather, it sometimes becomes necessary to exhume the body and bury it elsewhere, or evil may befall the family to which the deceased belonged. In fact a family or clan overtaken by misfortune will almost certainly attribute this to bad Feng-Shui, and they will invariably find a geomancer to agree with them, for the fees are very considerable.

AMONG the poor peasants of agricultural districts a common graveyard on a deserted site is purchased where the influences are reasonably auspicious, and here the people bring their dead for generations. If the children of a deceased peasant prosper and elect to give him a better tomb they are often put to considerable trouble, as no headstones are erected and the remains must be sought for. But a test is in use which permits of the definite identification of a parent's bones, for a few drops of the son's blood applied to them will be absorbed, otherwise, if the remains are not those of an ancestor, the blood is not absorbed.

If a valley be unfruitful, if a house be unlucky, if a city or village should believe itself to be open to bad influences, the geomancers are called in, and usually prescribe some change, such as the blocking of certain approaches or the removal of obstacles in order that the site may reap the benefit of good Feng-shui.

That the idea arises out of the ancient superstition of animism—that is, the doctrine that everything has an indwelling soul of its own, and is therefore capable of good and evil—there can be little doubt. Every force in nature, according to this belief, was personified, winds, waters, trees, and, indeed, every inanimate object, and although this notion was by no means common to China, it was adopted in the Flowery Kingdom with extraordinary completeness. If the equally powerful incentive of ancestor-worship be added, it becomes clear why the Chinese pay such close attention to the science of Feng-shui, and why even the poorest will part with their last 'cash' to give parents a suitable and auspicious burial-place, for upon the good will of the ancestor the future prosperity of the family is thought to depend.

Especially did those who formerly sought official promotion by the exercise of literature pay the closest attention to the burial sites of their parents, for if they did not do so it was universally held that they would not succeed in their examinations. This was, of course, a logical extension of the idea that agricultural prosperity would not follow were the proper disposal of the ancestor's body not carried out. Many tales are told in China of students who failed miserably in their official examinations because of some trifling oversight in connexion with the position of a father's grave, and the sequel usually narrates that when an auspicious alteration had been effected, they passed with flying colours.

At the same time, sceptics have not been wanting in all ages who seriously questioned the efficacy of Feng-shui. But the power of Taoist superstition—for the geomancers, like all wizards, belong to this sect—is much too great to be questioned with any likelihood of success, and ancestor-worship, upheld by the upper and literary classes, has still so wide a sanction that in all probability it will be able to withstand modernist influences for some generations.

OFFERINGS BEFORE A CHINESE TOMB ALTAR

Large tombs constructed according to the principles of Feng-Shui frequently have an altar, or altars, dedicated to the god of the soil, to whom offerings are made at the time of Ching Ming, the great annual festival of the dead.

Sport & General Press

SOURCE OF THE WONDROUS WATERS OF HEALING: PILGRIMS AT THE GROTTO AT LOURDES

The Grotto at Lourdes is the spot where the Virgin is said to have appeared to the young Bernadette. Here is the very core and centre of the pilgrimage. From this rugged amphitheatre hewn out of the living rock flows the water which has become renowned far and wide for its powers of healing. The Grotto is the actual scene of the cures. The space around it is closely packed with sick people, the more helpless of whom are in invalid chairs. Tired the pilgrims may be after their long and unaccustomed journey, but not so weary as to lose interest. Each eagerly waits for the longed-for miracle to take place. The walls of the grotto are thickly hung with crutches, left behind by those who have been cured of their lameness by the waters of the spring.

THE PILGRIMAGE IN CHRISTENDOM

THE urge to visit holy places, whether for spiritual or physical benefit, is deep-rooted in mankind. Apart from the Christian pilgrimages, described here, as well as in the chapters on The Pardon in Brittany and on Well-dressing and Holy Wells, there are many observed in other religions, the best known being the pilgrimage to Mecca. These last are treated in a separate chapter.

PILGRIMAGES arise from an instinct that is found among the fervent worshippers of every religion, who are impelled by their enthusiasm or their desire for spiritual benefit to visit spots which for them are hallowed by association with specially holy men and women or remarkable events which they call miracles. Long before the coming of Christ there were pilgrimages of this kind in India and in the Mediterranean lands. When Mahomet founded the religion of Islam, he made it a duty for good Mahomedans to make pilgrimage to Mecca, where he was born, just as Christian pilgrims visit Palestine and as in medieval times immense numbers went to Rome.

In the Dark Ages, when Christianity flourished and left its mark ineffaceably upon Europe, the pilgrimage idea spread widely and was put on a business footing. The object of pilgrims generally was to secure relics as well as to obtain 'indulgences' and forgiveness of sins. Relics were accordingly manufactured to meet the demand. Enough bones of saints were sold to make up the skeletons of large armies. As much 'wood of the True Cross' was produced as would have built a fleet of ships. Efforts were occasionally made by sensible and devout leaders in the Church to discourage these superstitious and foolish practices. To an abbess who was disappointed because she could not go to Rome, the learned Alcuin wrote to tell her she was better at home, especially if she expended the sum she had gathered for the journey on the support of the poor. A bishop of Orleans in the ninth century declared that living uprightly would make salvation far more certain than a visit to the Holy City. But protests were vain. Pilgrimages were exciting, a break in the monotony of existence. They had dramatic value, compared with which leading an upright life was dull. So the pilgrims were found by hundreds of thousands in all the countries of Europe, and the habit has persisted among Roman Catholics to this day. The nineteenth century saw it increase. New shrines and fresh 'miracles' were proclaimed, often against the wish of Church authorities.

THE popularity of Lourdes in France now rivals that of the most frequented medieval pilgrimage places. Augustus Hare saw in this a striking evidence of the power of the Roman Catholic religion in France. 'The voice of a child spoke in 1858, and since that time 100,000 persons have annually answered.' (That was in 1890.)

E.N.A.

WHERE THE 'VOICE OF A CHILD SPOKE'

In 1858 Bernadette Soubirous, a fourteen-year-old peasant girl of Lourdes, in the department of Hautes Pyrénées, had a vision. The Blessed Virgin appeared to her and bade her tell the priests to build a chapel by the spring. Before that time Lourdes was known to few; now the famous pilgrimage town is visited yearly by thousands.

The 'child' was a peasant girl who believed that she saw the Blessed Virgin and heard the apparition say: 'Go to the spring, eat grass that grows beside it, pray for mankind, tell the priests to build a chapel here to me. I am the Immaculate Conception.' Lourdes was then an insignificant village. Now it is a large and prosperous town. At its railway station a million travellers alight every year. It has many hotels and restaurants, fine streets and churches. The 'chapel' which the Virgin is supposed to have asked for is a magnificent basilica. Nearly 2,000 bishops have stayed at Lourdes, including some eighty cardinals. News of the cures effected at the spring and shrine are authenticated by doctors and circulated among the faithful everywhere. Invalids and sick persons in every stage of disability and exhaustion are taken there by pious relatives. They sit in their wheeled chairs or

port & General Press

KILKENNY'S HISTORIC CASTLE LOOKS DOWN AT THE PROCESSION OF THE GREAT IRISH PILGRIMAGE TO LOURDES

The Roman Catholic Church has ever been famed for the stately magnificence of its pageantry, and this is seen to very great advantage in some of the processions that are organized in connexion with the pilgrimages to Lourdes. The effectiveness of such a procession depends to a large extent on the surroundings in which it takes place, and when the locale of the pageant is such a city as Kilkenny the effect is impressive in the extreme. One would have to go a very long way to find a more fitting setting for a great religious procession than the tree-lined open space flanked on one side by the cathedral buildings and on the other by the bold hill crowned by the majestic thirteenth-century castle, the seat of the Ormonde family.

Sport & General Press

BLESSING THE SICK BEFORE THEY SET OUT ON THEIR GREAT ADVENTURE

The pilgrimage to Lourdes is very popular among Irish Roman Catholics, large numbers of whom leave the Free State every year to visit Our Lady of Lourdes. Everything is done to ensure repose of mind and body for the invalids who are seeking cure, and they are usually blessed before they start their journey. Sick persons taking part in one of these Irish pilgrimages to Lourdes are here seen lined up in their invalid chairs at Kilkenny, while the bishop of Ossory, carrying the Host under the canopy, passes along their ranks, blessing them.

lie on their stretchers, waiting hopefully to be blessed by the local bishop and sprinkled with the miracle-working water from the grotto. A regular service of helpers is maintained for the benefit of the halt, the lame and the blind. The helpers are volunteers, some of them priests, some young men of noble families ; they wear badges and leather harness, and give their assistance with kindly, sympathetic grace.

Most of the visitors come in large parties, accompanied by priests. Most Catholic churches throughout Europe display posters setting forth the advantages of going to Lourdes and the cost of the journey. Hotel expenses need not be incurred. A great many of the pilgrims arrive in special trains at an early hour of the morning and leave again at night. They walk in long processions to the grotto and basilica, often singing hymns or litanies as they go. All day long and into the evening one sees and hears them. Often one notices people among them who look very poor and very weary. Often one is saddened by the ghastly appearance of men, women or children in the last stages of disease. They lie, packed close together, in the Grotto (where the vision appeared), on to which one can look down from the terrace of the upper church—there is another church below—and then, going down the broad stairway, get a closer view. It is an amphitheatre cut in the rock, with the water from the spring flowing out on one side of it—not flowing freely, but under control, out of taps. Here are filled the cans and jugs and bottles that pilgrims have brought with them. Here they can drink the ice-cold water in cups supplied by the management. Hundreds of crutches hang in the Grotto, placed there by grateful folk who need them no longer, having been miraculously cured. That there are cures at Lourdes cannot be doubted ; though some of them may not last long, the triumph of mind over matter occurs frequently. Emile Zola, who devoted a novel to Lourdes, described vividly the atmosphere of fervent belief which causes these triumphs :

> Suddenly a paralytic rises, walking towards the Grotto, holding his crutch aloft, and that crutch above the sea of heads so close together, waved like a flag, sets the faithful cheering loudly. They are sure that miracles are going to

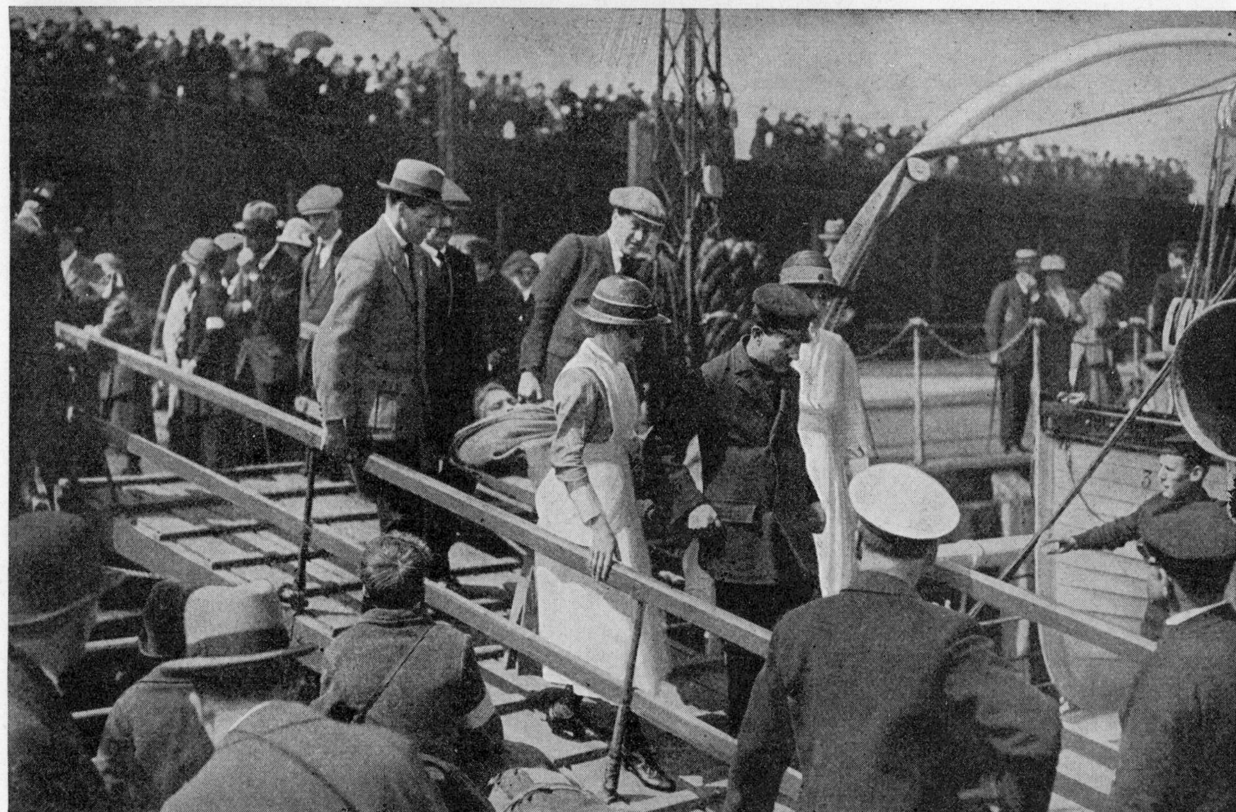

Keystone

STAGES IN THE PILGRIMS' PROGRESS TO THE WONDER-WORKING WATERS OF LOURDES

Summer is the season of the year specially favoured for organized tours to Lourdes. In a single day as many as a thousand pilgrims may leave London or other large centres on their way to its far-famed shrine. Not a few of the travellers are on crutches or in wheeled chairs; some even have to be carried on stretchers. Special trains are run at a low speed, to eliminate jolting as far as possible. The upper photograph shows a service being held at Victoria Station, London, before the train starts. Below pilgrims are seen embarking at Folkestone.

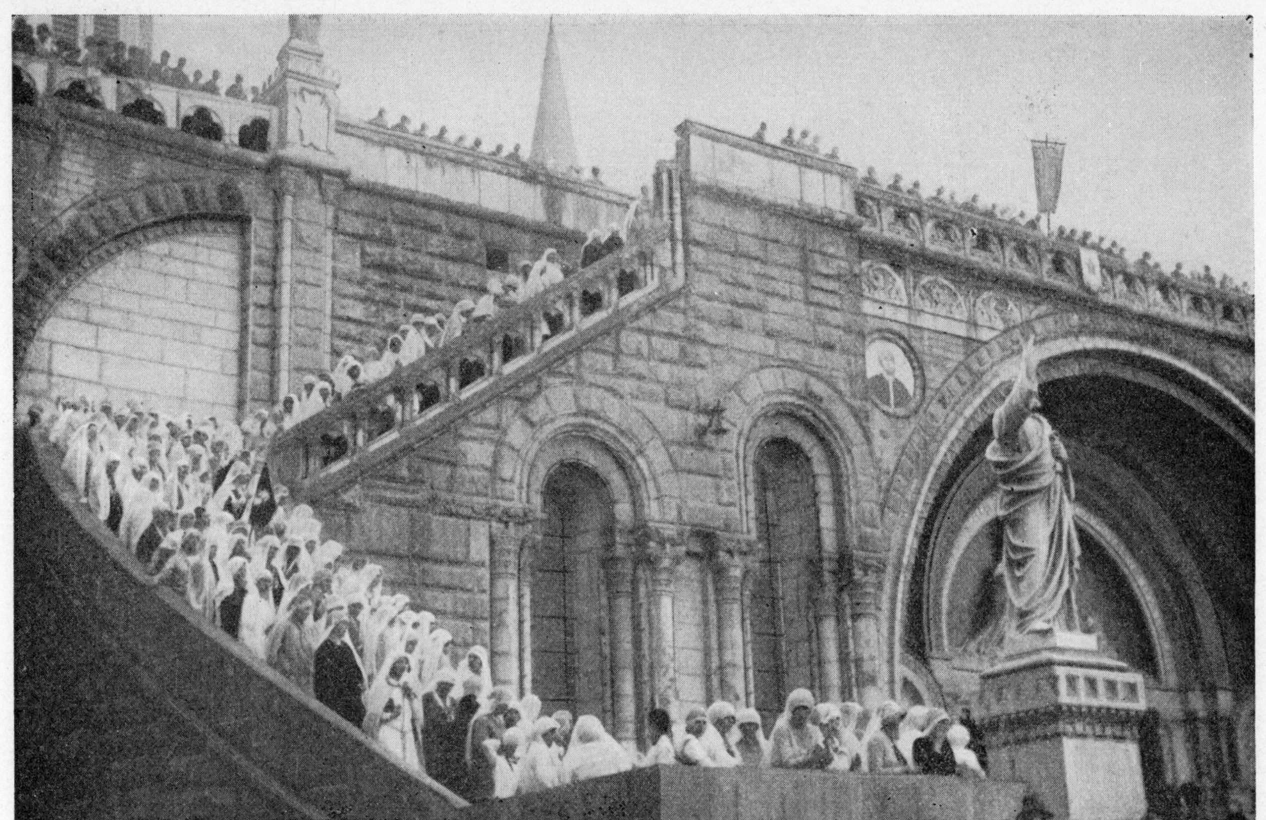

Wide World Photos

WHITE VEILS OF PILGRIMAGE AT A RALLYING POINT OF THE CATHOLIC FAITH

There are two sacred buildings by the Grotto at Lourdes. The upper church, known as the Basilica, was completed in 1876, while the lower, the Church of the Rosary, dates from 1889. From each of these a view of the Grotto can be obtained. The upper picture shows a band of devoted pilgrims crowded together on the great winding stairway that leads up to the main chapel. Below, a picturesque concourse of white-veiled maidens is seen looking down from the heights of the Basilica upon the Grotto beneath, waiting for the bishop to make his arrival.

E.N.A

PROCESSION OF PILGRIMS MARCHING THROUGH BETHLEHEM IN HOLY WEEK

As the birthplace of Christ, Bethlehem is a much frequented pilgrim resort, and one of the most important industries of the town is the carving of crucifixes and other mementos to meet the demands of the pilgrims. The traditional scene of the Nativity is a grotto on the eastern part of the limestone ridge upon which the town stands. Over this grotto was built the Church of the Nativity. It was erected by order of the Emperor Constantine in 330, and is perhaps the oldest church in the world. Besides the Grotto of the Nativity the church contains such traditional sites as the Altar of the Magi and the cave in which S. Jerome made his translation of the Bible. The church is surrounded by conventos and chapels belonging to various Christian communities.

occur, they are waiting for them, many and marvellous. Eyes are convinced they can be seen, feverish voices hail them. There is another cured, and another, and another! A deaf woman who can hear, a dumb woman who can talk, a consumptive restored to health. A consumptive? Why not? It is an everyday occurrence! Nothing causes surprise, you might speak of an amputated leg growing again, and no one would turn a hair. The miraculous becomes natural, usual, commonplace because it is so ordinary. To these overheated imaginations the incredible is easily believed, it is what they expect of the Blessed Virgin. When a sick person or a cripple cries 'I am cured,' the story goes round, no one throws doubt on it, it is related with quiet assurance. There's another, there's another! Sometimes, however, a despairing voice is heard to murmur 'She's cured, all right. Some people have all the luck.'

But not all the pilgrims are concerned about physical cures. Here are women who pray for the salvation of the soul of a child, for the conversion of a husband, for the success of a business. Here are men who seek forgiveness for crimes, prosperity for their farms, the promise of a son and heir. Many go merely out of curiosity, and these are seldom disappointed. Here is Zola's account of the night scene:

There must have been thirty thousand people already, and others were arriving every minute. All held candles, wrapped in white paper with a picture of Our Lady of Lourdes printed on it in blue. The candles were not lit yet. One could see over the heads of the crowd the illuminated Grotto; it threw out a glow like a blacksmith's fire. A vast murmur of talk and breathing made you feel that there were thousands of people jammed together, finding it hard to breathe, lost in the shadows. . . . . Then, here and there, candles were lit: one might have thought they were stars suddenly piercing the dusk. Now they were growing in number, little islets of stars were formed, elsewhere thick groups and milky ways appeared among the constellations. The thirty thousand candles were being lit one by one, one from another, paling the ineffectual fires of the forge, sending from one end of the great open space to the other the little yellow flickers of an immense brazier fire.

Of all the cure-pilgrimages those of Lourdes are the most famous. Now let us see how pilgrims fare who go to Jerusalem, not in comfortable trains and luxurious liners, but in pilgrim ships which carry poor Christians from the Balkans, from the Levant, from Syria, and used to carry a great many Russians. The passengers are crowded into the holds of trading steamers. Their voyage may last a few days, it may last a fortnight or more. They carry their food with them, sometimes only bread, which becomes mouldy before they land; they make it into soup with a little oil, black olives and perhaps an onion or some cabbage leaves. Storms throw them into a state of panic that is almost frenzy. They live in indescribable squalor and filth. On calm days when the sun shines they are fairly happy. They sit about on deck, sing, read aloud, chatter, look at the islands and squabble about their names. When the hurricane blows and they have to stay below, they are seasick and terrified and miserable. But they soon recover when the storm is over, and as they approach port all are careful to put on their best clothes and, if they have them, new boots, for they feel it is unfitting

American Colony

PILGRIMS IN A STREET OF HALLOWED MEMORY

The city of Jerusalem has been destroyed and rebuilt again and again, and in the course of its history one city has risen upon the ruins of another. The places associated with the life of Christ have been largely localised by tradition. Pilgrims are here seen carrying a great cross along the Via Dolorosa, the street regarded as that through which Christ bore the cross.

Ewing Galloway

CARAVAN OF SPANISH PILGRIMS ON THEIR WAY TO A MIRACLE-WORKING SHRINE

Of the many pilgrimage places of modern Spain none has any very wide appeal. The most famous of all is Santiago de Compostela, which owed its attraction to its reputed possession of the body of James the son of Zebedee, the patron saint of Spain. In the early middle ages the saint, who was put to death by Herod Agrippa, was believed to lie buried in the Holy Land, but according to a later account his relics were removed to Spain, and as early as the twelfth century the pilgrimage to Santiago took equal rank with those to Rome and Jerusalem.

and almost impious to tread the soil of Palestine in old ones.

From Jaffa, where they land, those who can afford it take the train ; the rest tramp, after spending a night in a monastery, where the monks lay thin straw mattresses on the stone floors and provide hot water for tea. In Jerusalem they are put up in hostels, where in the height of the pilgrim season they sleep on shelves 'like those of an exaggerated railway station cloak-room,' said Stephen Graham, who himself made this pilgrimage with Russian peasants. 'There were no beds,' he added, 'no bedding. Over the unvarnished painted wood was spread a rather muddy straw pallet, one for each pilgrim. It certainly was a dirty place. On the floors was a considerable amount of refuse, orange peel and locust nut ends. But the great amount of light in it rather gave the idea that it was not so bad as it looked.' This great amount of light was due to the place being walled and roofed almost entirely with glass.

The pilgrims go, of course, to Nazareth and Bethlehem and the Lake of Galilee and the Dead Sea. They plunge into the Jordan, some in white garments provided by a monastery, some with nothing on. Crowds of them are in the water, standing, shivering, saying prayers, crossing themselves. Crowds are climbing up the steep banks and then getting dry again in the air and the sun, no towels being provided. They see the well at Nazareth where the Blessed Virgin drew water. They climb the mountain where Jesus was tempted by the Devil and that other one where He fed five thousand people with miraculous food. They go into the house where water became wine. They stand on the spot where Jesus talked with the woman of Samaria. They visit Bethany, where Lazarus was raised from the dead. In Jerusalem itself they attend innumerable long services, spend all the time they can at the Holy Places, and go home again exalted and refreshed.

In Russia many pilgrims used to visit the Lavra at Kiev, filing with shuffling step through the underground passages and pausing at the shrines cut in the rock to abase themselves before holy relics of martyrs and saints. The strongest impression which a foreign visitor brought away after making this unsavoury round was that of the rattling kept up incessantly by the money boxes of the priests. The one anxiety seemed to be to extract as much as possible from the pockets of the pilgrims. The monastery in whose charge the Lavra was had vast possessions. In precious metals and stones alone it was enormously rich. Its ambition was to be richer still. All this has been changed in Russia under the dictatorship which succeeded the Tsardom. In Italy, however, the dictator is inclined to encourage superstition, and the number of pilgrims to the shrine of S. Januarius at Naples shows no diminution. The congealed blood of this martyr, kept in an ancient phial, is supposed to melt and bubble on certain occasions, as if it had just flowed from his wounds. No intelligent Catholic believes in this 'miracle' or in any of the other like marvels which rival Neapolitan churches offer to the credulous. But it attracts large numbers of these and is a rich source of income to the church of S. Januarius, as the Lavra relics were to the monks at Kiev.

Very different is the spirit of Rocamadour in south-western France, not far from Cahors. Hither in May and September come pilgrimages from far and near, and at all times wayfarers are welcomed and kindly treated. No one quite knows who Amadour was. Tradition calls him a saint and represents him as having come to this spot to see Zacchaeus, the publican (tax-collector) who is mentioned in the Gospels and who (also according to tradition) journeyed this way from Palestine and became a hermit here. He removed before he died, but the tomb of Amadour is among the places visited by all pilgrims and most of them throw him money. Often after a busy day his statue, lying behind a grille, is covered with small copper coins. The churches, and indeed the whole town, are built up the rocky side of a hill which rises from a narrow green valley with a stream running gently through it. As you approach it from the higher land you do not see it until you are almost on the top of it. But the pilgrims mostly enter from below and climb the rocky steps which lead up to the sacred buildings. The proper thing to do is to make the ascent on your knees. Not a few still do this, and reckon to be repaid in Heaven for their bruised shins and damaged garments.

E.N.A.

PROCESSION OF S. JANUARIUS IN NAPLES

The shrine of S. Januarius in Naples attracts a large number of pilgrims. The martyr is said to have been a native of Naples, and is regarded as the protector of the city. Some of his blood is preserved in the church, and on certain days this is said to turn liquid again.

American Colony

PILGRIMS' WAY UP MOUNT SINAI

As a seat of the Deity and the scene of the Hebrew law-giving, Mount Sinai has long been a resort of pilgrims. It is not known for certain which group contains the Mountain of Moses, and pilgrim steps are found on Mount Serbal as well as on Gebel Musa.

Rocamadour is a fascinating little town, with a real atmosphere of the Middle Ages about it and a delicious natural freshness. Santiago de Compostela, the most famous pilgrimage place in Spain, has little to recommend it save an attractive cathedral and quaint arcaded streets. Once it was visited by vast numbers of pilgrims from all parts of Europe, for here is the tomb of Saint James, one of the disciples of Jesus and the patron saint of Spain. Now it is rare for a foreign party to arrive, or even people from other provinces of Spain. But the Galician peasants still keep up the ancient ceremony of censing the cathedral congregation from an incense-holder which is swung up to the roof. There is first a march to the cathedral through the principal square, which has coloured hangings on its balconies by way of decoration. A band leads, then come the men and then the women. Each band of parishioners has its priest walking alongside like an officer. Guns are fired and the beautiful mellow bells of the cathedral are set rocking. Wide open are the great west doors, and inside waits the chief verger in a robe of crimson velvet, carrying a

Ewing Galloway

PROCESSION OF THE ICON AT THE LOURDES OF THE ORTHODOX CHURCH

On March 23 of every year the little island of Tenos, in the Cyclades group, is the scene of a strange ceremony, which, like the Roman Catholic pilgrimages to Lourdes, is attended by great numbers of invalids in every stage of sickness and infirmity. In the cathedral is kept a miracle-working icon of the Virgin, which was discovered in the fifteenth century. This is taken from its resting-place and borne in procession by the priests, who for a distance of a quarter of a mile or so tread upon the prostrate bodies of those seeking to be cured (see following page).

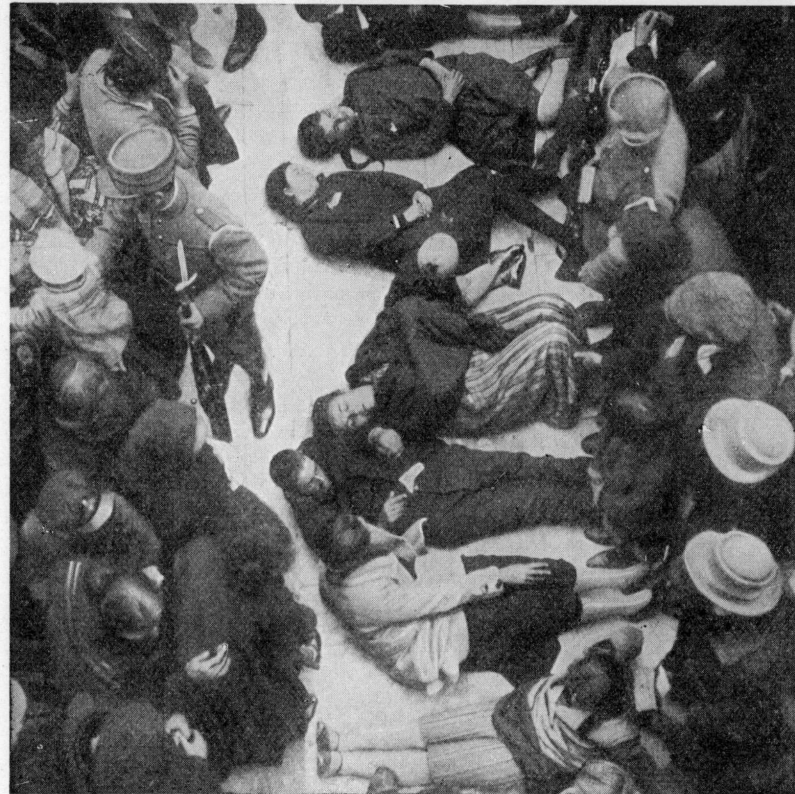

Ewing Galloway

ACT OF HUMILITY TO THE PILGRIMS AT TENOS

The afflicted who look to be cured in the icon procession of the Greek island of Tenos present a touching spectacle. Lying on the ground along the route, they anxiously await the coming of the priests, who tread upon them as they pass. The priests wear soft shoes, and part of their weight is taken off by soldiers who march on each side of them.

A journey to Echternach and participation in the 'jumping procession' through the town is supposed to guarantee the jumpers against attacks of his disease. From the parish church the procession starts. Musicians with all kinds of instruments, from violins to penny whistles, go with it, playing an old tune called 'Adam's Seven Sons.' The pilgrims take three steps forward and two back, so their progress is slow. Through the streets they skip their way, and finish up at the church from which they started, still dancing up the nave and finishing before the High Altar.

On the American continent the pilgrimage habit has never become popular, probably because Christianity reached there late in the day. There are no real 'holy places' in the United States, but French Canadian Catholics have a popular shrine of pilgrimage in the province of Quebec. This is the shrine of S. Anne de Beaupré. The clergy do all they can to induce their parishioners to visit it, and have managed to revive in the New World a good deal of the fervour which was attached to pilgrimages in the Old.

silver-topped staff of office. Men on one side, women on the other, the pilgrims hear mass, and then the great event of the day takes place. Seven men haul on a rope and the big silver censer moves upwards. Up to the roof, down again with a thick puff of incense, up again, down again, many times repeated while a hymn of exultation is sung. At last it reaches the ground and stays there ; the yearly ceremony is over. Now every pilgrim must secure a 'compostela,' a medal with on one side S. James (Saint Iago) destroying the Moors and a view of the cathedral on the other ; or else a souvenir in the shape of a scallop shell. Once the wearing of these shells was proof that the wearer had been a pilgrim.

When little boys and girls in London streets put up a few shells at a corner on S. James's Day (August 5) and ask you to 'remember the grotto,' they are unconsciously keeping up a very old custom that grew out of the pilgrimage habit.

Another of its very strange outgrowths is the Whit Tuesday assemblage of ten to fifteen thousand pious Catholics and curious tourists at Echternach in Luxembourg. Here is the shrine of S. Willibrod, who was an Englishman and founded an abbey in 868. But the pilgrimage is less connected with him, it would seem, than with S. Vitus, who gave his name to that painful affliction known as S. Vitus's Dance.

Topical Press

'PLEASE REMEMBER THE GROTTO'

The wearing of a scallop shell was formerly the mark of a pilgrim. On S. James's day shell grottos were set up, and at these people who could not make the pilgrimage presented offerings. The grottos made by children on this day are a relic of the custom.

H. von Perckhammer

OUTER COURT OF THE GREAT NATIONAL TEMPLE OF THE ANCESTORS IN PEKING.

The Temple of Heaven, or the Temple of Ten Thousand Generations, stands on the right as one enters the southern gate of the Outer City of Peking. It was built in 1420, and is surrounded by walls over three miles in circumference. Between the inner and the outer walls is a park planted with cypresses, pines and acacias. It was in this temple that the emperors of China offered prayer in person to Shang Ti, the Supreme God, on certain stated occasions, notably at the winter solstice, and also in times of drought or famine. The temple contains the spirit tablet of Shang Ti, and the ancestral tablets of the Five Emperors.

ANCESTOR WORSHIP AND THE CULT OF THE DEAD

THE mode of disposal of the dead has usually a more or less direct bearing on the attitude entertained as to the life after death, though not always involving a cult of the dead. Separate chapters deal with such topics as European Death and Burial Customs and Red Indian Burials. The festival of All Souls is discussed in the chapter on All Souls' and All Saints' Days

ANCESTOR worship, the reverent service and veneration accorded dead members of the social group, has been termed one of the greatest of the religions of mankind. It is found, though only in a rudimentary form, among the most backward of peoples, the Australians : for thousands of years it has been the guiding principle of the daily life of so great a civilization as that of the Chinese Empire. Some authorities, indeed, would go so far as to make it the basis of all religion. This may perhaps carry us too far ; but there can be little doubt that it has served to breathe into the belief in spirits that warmth and intimacy which have done much to mitigate the fear which is the dominant note in the cruder forms of early belief ; and it has helped to build up the conception of a Supreme Being as an all-beneficent Father.

It must not be inferred, however, that the cult of the dead, and more particularly ancestor worship, entirely eliminates the fear with which primitive man looks upon the mysterious change from life to death. This would be untrue even of modern civilization ; for fear of the dead has not entirely vanished among ourselves, though we may not always be fully conscious of this element in the complex feelings with which we contemplate death. Yet we still close the eyes of the corpse and carry the body from the house feet first, perpetuating the memory of a former belief that the spirit of the dead man might otherwise find its way back. In former days a special door was sometimes made which was built up when the coffin had passed through so that a returning spirit would fail to find the entrance. Similar precautions are taken among most primitive peoples. The Ibos of Nigeria place food, the native of India a thorn bush, on the paths leading to the village so that the spirits of the dead may be diverted.

SUCH precautions are still more necessary when death is untimely or the result of violence ; for then the envy of those still in this world, felt in some degree by every departed spirit, is aggravated by a desire for vengeance or an intensified longing to return to this world. In China it is believed that if a murdered man can steal away the soul of some living person, he may return to earth. It is for this reason that warriors after a raid, or head-hunters such as those of Assam and Timur, have to undergo a special purification before it is safe for them to resume daily life in their village. These are the rites of fear.

But there is another side of the picture. Even among the crudest of barbarians who may value human life lightly the intimacy of human relations does not pass away entirely with death. To employ a phrase common among ourselves, they do not ' realize ' that the beloved one is dead ; and so the body is kept for a period in the house before burial, or it may lie in a temporary grave, perhaps for as long as a year. Among some peoples it is then buried

Ewing Galloway

IN HONOUR OF THE FAMOUS DEAD

Dotted over China, a country which has throughout the ages made ancestor worship its guiding principle, are monuments to eminent persons such as this pailou, or memorial archway, seen on Hangchow Bay. They usually consist of wooden pillars with a tiled roof.

Francis Birtles

ALTAR WITH PRAYING TABLETS IN A CHINESE JOSS-HOUSE

Chinese manners are changing, though very slowly, through contact with Western civilization and also as a result of the alteration in the constitution, but the age-old customs are kept up in many parts of the republic. In some old houses in the interior of China it is still possible to see an altar loaded with ancestral tablets, to which members of the household offer prayers. The tablet is made of wood, somewhat in the form of the headstone of a grave, and is inscribed with the name of the ancestor, together with other particulars.

in its permanent resting place ; among others it is broken up. Some parts may be kept, as the Andaman Islanders do, wearing a bone as a personal ornament or charm—a pendant—thus securing intimate relation with, and the protection of, the dead. Or the body may be cremated in order that the soul may be released from the restraint of the body to rejoin its friends.

But the good offices of the living for the dead do not stop here. Provision is made for their after-life in customs familiar to us from burials which go back so far as palaeolithic times. There red pigment is laid by the body or smeared over the limbs, it may be presumed to give it the vital principle of blood in the next world. On the breast is the magic charm of a necklace of shells and by its side the joints of meat, of which the bones survive to serve as provender on the journey the soul must take to reach the land of the blessed. Later on, as material wealth increases, pottery, personal ornaments and valued weapons are deposited in the grave, and by a refinement of thought evidenced in many parts of the world the pots, weapons and other offerings have been broken ceremonially, or even made with a ceremonial defect such as a hole in the base of a vessel, so that their 'souls' may accompany the owner. Hence, also, the sacrifice of human slaves, of the wife of the dead man, and even of the queen and her attendants at the graveside, as has been revealed recently by the excavations of Mr. Woolley in the royal tombs at the Sumerian city of Ur in Mesopotamia ; or in the models of slaves engaged in the daily occupations of the household, found in the tombs of ancient Egypt, which have taken the place of the human victims.

In ancient Egypt in fact the cult of the dead reached its most highly developed form in the tomb as the dwelling-place of the soul with an aperture in the wall through which the offerings of food for its nurture were passed ; and with large estates hypothecated in order that their revenues might provide for ever for the support of the attendants to whom the care of the soul had been assigned. If less elaborate, even more intimate is the custom of the Bantu peoples of Africa, some of whom bury the dead chief at the entrance to his kraal, and others lay him beneath the floor of the hut which once belonged to him and in which his successor lives. The latter custom, repugnant and insanitary as it seems to us, is common and widespread.

Ancestor Worship and the Cult of the Dead

It may seem that as we must all die and some means must be found to get rid of our body, the mere fact of burial has little significance in relation to the cult of the dead. But this is not so, for not all peoples are at any pains to dispose reverently and in seemly manner of the mortal remains of their fellows. Among the pagan tribes of the Malay peninsula the body is merely cast into the bush. Many other peoples, however, look upon any haphazard method of disposal of the body as the last indignity, only to be inflicted on the lowest criminal or outcast. It may be taken that the mode of disposal of the dead, in the vast majority of cases, implies some specific theory of the life after death, as it undoubtedly did among the ancient Egyptians, who showed it in their practice of embalming. When to this is added the meticulous care with which the mourners provide and arrange the grave furniture — implements, weapons, utensils, food, etc.—to meet the needs and preferences of the individual as known to them in his lifetime, we are justified in assuming, even if we did not know it from other sources, that the life of the soul after death is envisaged as differing very little from that on earth. The chief continues to be a chief and to act as the head of his tribesmen, and the tribesman obeys.

On the other hand, the dead are not divorced from interest in the living. Neither the chief of a tribe nor the head of the family ceases to be interested in its affairs. At the same time, each seeks the reverence and respect accorded to him in his lifetime. Worship must be paid, not so much by prayer and invocation, but, as is usual among primitive peoples, by invitation to share in communal festivals and sacrifices, such as the great seasonal feasts held among certain of the people of New Guinea, and, in the case of the family, periodical celebrations as well as those on special occasions, such as a marriage and so forth. Thus the clansman seeks to keep in touch with his fellow-clansmen who have passed away, and the head of a family with the ancestors who have preceded him in that office. Failure to pay due respect to the ancestors will lead to disaster—disease or tempest which will bring misfortune or death to the members of the group. Then the ancestors must be appeased.

It is not proposed to follow here in detail the various forms which may be taken by the cult of the dead, but enough has already been said to indicate the general attitude of mind towards the dead which is precedent to any specific manifestation of ancestor worship. It must be evident that the cult of the dead, except on the great occasions of communal festival when the whole group is concerned, will proceed rather through the smaller group of the family. This is what happens virtually in the last of the great pagan festivals of the dead to be recognized officially in Europe, the Feast of All Souls, a universal festival of the Church, but one in which the family rite of mourning is carried out privately at the graveside. The part of the family is still more

Underwood

CHINESE SACRED TABLET DEDICATED TO THE KING OF HEAVEN

At the time of the Imperial Sacrifice this tablet occupied the highest platform of the Altar of Heaven, with the ancestral tablets of five of the Imperial Fathers. Mounted on a marble pedestal, within a carved throne-screen, the golden characters, Wang Tien Sh'an Ti (God, the King of Heaven), stand out boldly against the blue of the ancient tablet, which is enclosed in a chest of black mahogany.

Ewing Galloway

marked in the traditional custom still observed in certain parts of Scandinavia in which the dead members of the family are expected to be present and to share in the Christmas meal.

Those authorities who have attributed the origin of religion as in great measure due to ancestor worship have not gone very far beyond the warrant of the facts. It is evident that any distinguished member of a tribe or family to whom worship is paid will tend to live long in the memory of his former group. Among the Chinese, founders of the imperial dynasties are singled out from among the others of the emperor's ancestors. Still more will this be the case if any distinguished ancestor should prove peculiarly trustworthy in the delivery of oracles, one of the purposes for which worship is given with some regularity to the ancestral spirits. Among certain of the Siberian tribes the period during which funerary honours are paid by the family to a deceased member rests with the shaman, and sometimes may be as long as three years. Should the spirit of the deceased prove to be particularly successful in his delivery of oracles, the shrine is not unnaturally visited more frequently than custom demands, the period of mourning is prolonged, and the offerings may become of such magnitude that the cult becomes of greater consequence than that of the spirits of the gods

E.N.A.

WHERE RICH AND POOR ALIKE REVERE THE SPIRITS OF THEIR ANCESTORS

Among the upper classes in Japan the keeping of an ancestral closet is usual. Inside this closet, which by reason of its contents makes a sacred corner in the house, is a little cupboard or shelf, and here are housed relics of ancestors and family records. The upper photograph shows a Japanese lady of quality opening the sliding door of the shelf. Below, a peasant is seen in an attitude of devotion before the graves of his ancestors. He believes that their spirits will protect him and his possessions, and will advise him in all emergencies.

Sport & General Press

THE MOTHER OF A DEAD EMPEROR OF JAPAN PAYS HOMAGE TO HIS MEMORY

Shintoism, the national religion of Japan, lays great stress upon reverence for ancestors and loyalty to the state. From the sun goddess, Amaterasu, the chief deity, the emperors claim descent. Among other deities are the powers of nature and the deified spirits of ancestors descended from the gods and exalted by great deeds. The dead are held to have power to bring joy or sorrow into the lives of their survivors The Lady Yanagiwara, mother of the emperor Taisho, is here seen praying to his spirit at the Meiji shrine on the anniversary of his death

themselves. From this to the permanently recognized hero cult, such as played so important a part in ancient Greece, is obviously no more than a step.

An even more important aspect of religious belief upon which ancestor worship has had great influence —perhaps even has been its origin—is the doctrine of reincarnation and transmigration of souls. Family likeness has led to the belief that the spirits of the ancestors regularly become reincarnated in their descendants. This belief is firmly held among Bantu tribes of South Africa, who name the children after the ancestor whose spirit has taken up its new existence in the person of its descendant.

Ancestor worship has a wide distribution. It is firmly rooted in Melanesia and Polynesia, it is the prevailing cult over a wide part of Africa. It is of the greatest moment in both India and China, where it is the integrating force of the family and of society. It may not be without interest to describe the form it takes in China a little more fully in detail.

In China, then, ancestor worship has attained its highest manifestation, and in combination with Confucianism has established its claim to be considered one of the great spiritual forces of the world. This

G.P.A.

HOW A SUMATRAN CHIEF GUARDS THE BONES OF HIS ANCESTORS

The Karo Batak, a people of Indonesian stock who dwell in the uplands of north-central Sumatra, hold their ancestors in the highest regard and devote much care to cherishing their remains. They are an artistic race; besides being skilful potters and weavers, they adorn their buildings with elaborately carved and coloured designs. The highly decorative boat-shaped coffin here seen contains the bones of a chief's ancestors. At its head is a representation of a rhinoceros bird, while at either end is a guardian figure—a man and a woman.

is not merely on the ground of the vast number of its adherents among the millions of China's teeming population, but in virtue of its ethical and social significance. The doctrines of Confucius, an all-pervading philosophy of life rather than a systematic body of theology, made filial piety the head and front of the duty of man. Unquestioning obedience and absolute devotion were demanded of the son towards the father. So far was this carried that neither personal interest nor bodily safety, even to the limit of life itself, was allowed to weigh against the claims of the parent. Many sons have suffered imprisonment, torture, and even death without complaint for their father's crimes. An English traveller in China in the middle of the last century records the case of a young girl of fifteen who cut off two joints of her fingers to be used as ingredients in a medicine for her mother, who lay ill of a mortal disease. The recipe, a typical Chinese formula, required that the flesh should be taken from the thigh; but when the girl began to cut the flesh her courage failed her and she cut off the finger joints instead.

The duty toward the family ancestors was no less exacting, and in practice was carried out with no less readiness and assiduity; but it involved something more than merely a punctilious regard for their requirements in the family and religious ceremonial. For, although the man at his death at once takes up in the after-life a position relatively identical with that which he filled in his former life, his future depends upon the conduct of his descendants. Should any attain honour and civil advancement his position is advanced with theirs; but, on the other hand, he suffers equally for their degradation. Thus the obligation of filial piety and respect for the ancestors which Confucius laid upon the individual requires

G.P.A.

ARMED WATCHER IN WOOD ON AN ANCESTRAL COFFIN IN SUMATRA

This grotesque figure with turbaned head, body enveloped in a blanket, and gun on knee, is guarding the relics of a Karo Batak chief's ancestors. It is the male watcher on the coffin shown in the preceding page, the one resting against the rhinoceros bird figurehead. Although in the arabesque embellishments of their buildings and in other directions the Karo Batak display considerable artistic taste and ability, they cannot be said to excel in representing the human form. Crude, however, though this figure may be, it succeeds in conveying a distinct impression of alertness, and thus achieves a part of its purpose.

a high ethical standard in private and public life. In the face of common criticism of Chinese morality, public and private, it must be remembered that such criticism is usually based on our standards, which differ radically from those of the Chinese, and much that we should consider detrimental to public and private morals is accepted by them as a matter of course.

It was the double bond of duty toward the parent and toward the ancestor that held together the whole structure of Chinese society under the Empire and up to the formation of the Republic. Its loosening under the new constitution is at the root of the present disintegration of the Chinese people. For as son stood to the parent, so the parent stood to the magistrate and the magistrate to the emperor, who in his sacred person was at once in the relation of a parent to his people and the divine representative of divine ancestors and ultimately of the Supreme Being himself. The state religion and loyalty and patriotism were thus one, just as worship of the divine emperor and his divine ancestors is the root of patriotism in the related civilization of the Japanese, the most loyal and patriotic people in the whole world, and just as the cult of the royal ancestors is the state religion of the African kingdom of Dahomey to-day.

The founders of the imperial dynasties of China, as is the way with monarchs elsewhere, claimed divine descent. The Shan dynasty (1766 B.C.) originated from a 'black bird,' i.e. a swallow, which came from heaven; Kian Yuin (2345 B.C.) stepped on the footprint of the god, whence she conceived and bore a son, How tsi, the associate of the gods, from whom were descended the Chou dynasty. Such divine founders of dynasties always appeared in the national ancestral cult.

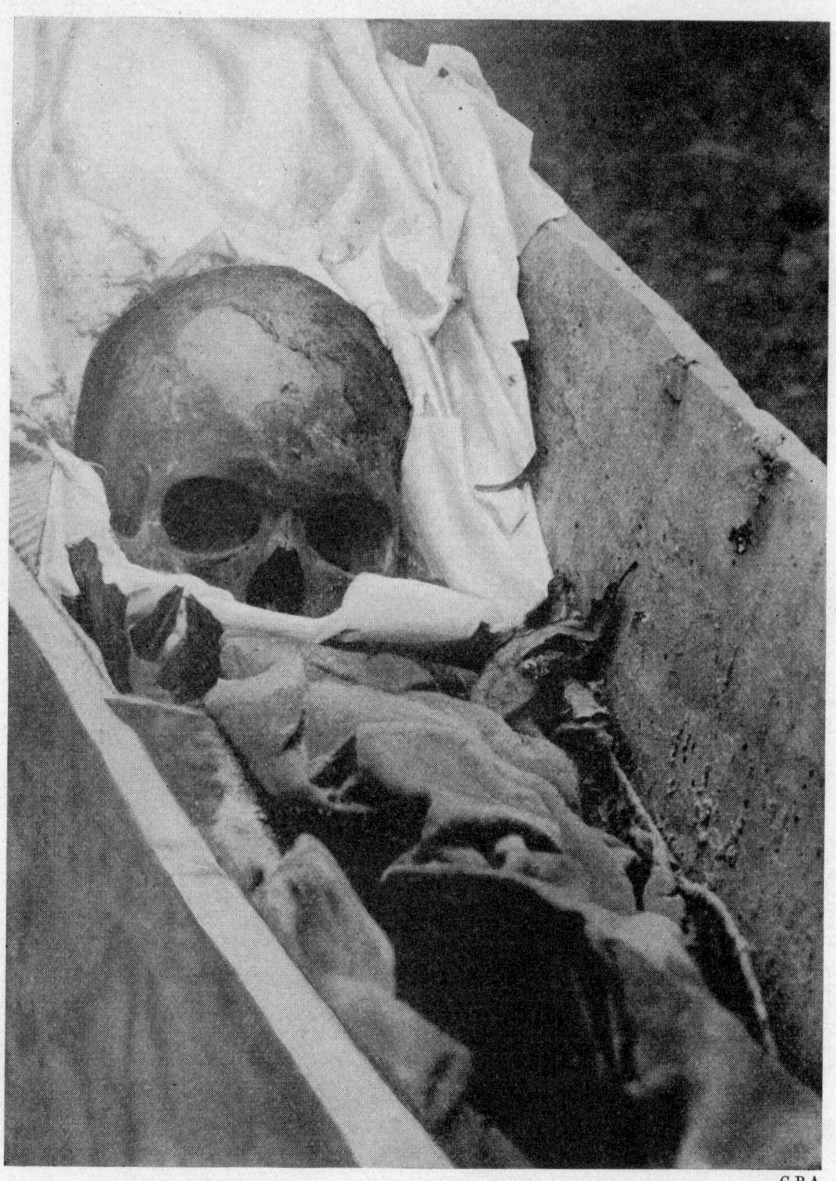

G.P.A.

HONOURING THE HEAD OF A DEPARTED CHIEF

The attention which the Karo Batak people of Sumatra give to the relics of their ancestors extends far beyond the provision of an elaborate coffin, placed high on a pillar-supported platform. Only superfine textiles are used for swathing the remains of the deceased. The skull of a chief here seen is wrapped in cloth of the finest quality obtainable in the island.

THE Chinese conception of life after death always depicts the departed as guests on high, serving God and acting as mediators between Him and the members of their family, in the affairs of which they continue to take interest. Though their home is in heaven they come and go as they will, and no one knows where they may be at any moment. Hence it is possible that they may not be present when sacrifice is offered to the ancestral spirits, but the worshippers must conduct themsel es as if they were. Those who have failed to perform their duty towards their ancestors during their lifetime have no place in heaven.

Not all ancestors are held in equal honour. The practical Chinese mind, confronted with the difficulty of an ever-growing list of ancestral spirits, has solved it by confining the chief honours to three generations. In the Imperial line the number recognized is five generations, together with the founders of dynasties, as already mentioned, and notable or honourably conspicuous individuals. These have a common place of worship in the great national Temple of the Ancestors. Exception is made in the case of the great emperor Yu, to whom a temple was dedicated exclusively on the supposed site of his birthplace, and Confucius, who has a temple in each district town. All ancestors above the third generation are held in veneration, and are assumed to be present at the family festivals, but not as chief guests. This is in accordance with Chinese convention at a banquet, where only one person is the guest, others present bearing him company. A special feast is held on the fifteenth day of the seventh moon, the 'Feast of the Hungry Ghosts,' for those ancestral spirits who have no descendants to do them honour.

The worship of the ancestors takes place on certain fixed dates in certain moons of the year and also on special occasions—in a private family such occasions as a wedding, a betrothal or the assumption of the cap of puberty by a son. The Imperial Ancestor worship was associated particularly with the great festival of the year at the winter solstice, when the tablet of Sh'an ti was placed on the Altar of Heaven and the tablets of the Five Emperors were ranged on each side of it. One of the offerings was a piece of blue jade, symbolising the royal authority. The emperor also made a special offering in the Temple of the Ancestors on his accession.

Among the people sacrifices in the spring and autumn are offered to the family ancestors at the grave. At other times the sacrifices are offered in the ancestral hall.

The ritual of the ancestral sacrifice is that of a banquet in which the ancestors are the invited guests. The sacrifice takes place before the ancestral tablet. This tablet consists of two pieces of wood standing upright on a wooden base and bearing the names, titles, dates, etc., relating to the ancestor. On the base is an inscription consisting of two characters which are incomplete until a completing dot has been added by a high official, a ceremony which has been compared to canonisation. This tablet is kept in the house until after the period of mourning is over. It is probable that originally it was a miniature replica of the monument at the head of the grave. The spirit of the dead is supposed to enter into the tablet at the time of the sacrifice, but it is not its permanent abode, as has sometimes been supposed. An interesting feature of the ceremonial in former days was the 'Impersonator of the Dead,' a relative, sometimes a grandson, but never a son, of the deceased, who entered the hall suitably dressed when the 'perfume' of the burning fat of the victim summoned the spirits to attend. He sat in the hall during the ceremony and retired when the master of the ceremonies announced its close by saying that the spirits were 'fed to repletion.' He was then escorted from the hall with bells and drums. His place has now been taken by a portrait of the ancestor, which is hung up in the hall, but only for certain sacrifices.

E.N.A.

ANCESTRAL EFFIGY OF A MAORI WARRIOR

Such admirably carved wooden figures as this of a tattooed warrior were often set up in New Zealand along the outer palisade of a fortified place. They usually represent celebrated ancestors of the tribe—chieftains whose names and deeds have been handed down from generation to generation.

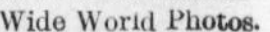

Wide World Photos.

Mondiale

ANCIENT WISDOM OF THE SIMPLE THAT IS FOLLY TO THE MODERN WISE

Belief that the gods may give man intimations of future happenings is rooted in the beginnings of human life and naturally leads to search for such omens before undertaking any act of importance. Almost any natural object may serve the modern professional diviner's purpose. Here, for example, a Liberian soothsayer is examining coloured shells in a calabash to decide whether the native carriers may prudently accompany the white man into the forest. Throughout history Europeans have shown themselves as credulous as Africans. The lower photograph shows a village fortune-teller in Southern Moravia forecasting the future by dropping sand into a mug of water

OMENS SIGNS AND PORTENTS

MASCOTS or luck-bringers have provided the matter for an earlier chapter, and elsewhere, also, various aspects of the general subject of superstition are dealt with. Here we are concerned chiefly with things that are regarded as 'ominous' in the common acceptation of that word—as portents of ill—and, to a less extent, with some of the methods in use for divination of the future.

PERHAPS the still most lively limb in the slowly dying body of superstition is that which symbolises the ominous or portentous. We may laugh at people who refuse to walk under a ladder or cross the road after a funeral, but we are liable to an involuntary shudder at the nightly howling of a dog or the breaking of a mirror. For omens, signs and portents, things which appear to prophesy, have for the human mind an even more deep-seated significance than the most dreaded taboo, as partaking more of the spiritual and the uncanny.

Let us give a moment's attention to the subject of death warnings. In some parts of Wales and Scotland it is still thought of as most ominous to see ghostly 'corpse-candles.' If the visionary candle be large, the death of an adult is portended, if small and blue in colour, that of a child. An almost universal superstition in Great Britain is that the ticking noises of the small insect popularly known as the 'death-watch' are ominous of a coming fatality in the family. The noise is caused by the scarabaeus galeatus pulsator trying to worm its way through wood.

In some parts of Lancashire it is almost instinctively believed that the building or rebuilding of a house is always fatal to one member of the family—a relic of the notion that in order to bring luck to a building it was necessary to sacrifice a life. Some of the oddest signs and portents still current are also associated with domestic utensils. When even the cheapest looking-glass is cracked or broken it is very generally believed that seven years' sorrow will follow. Formerly, to break a mirror was to destroy the human image or 'soul' of the person it reflected, for the reflection was thought of as part of the man. For this reason many savages refuse to have their photographs taken, believing that the process 'steals their souls away.' An analogous notion is that which holds that the falling of a picture is ominous of the death of the person it represents. His image, a part of himself, has fallen, therefore he will 'fall.' Here a process of sympathetic magic is certainly implied.

MANY consider it most ominous to see the new moon reflected in a mirror or through a window-pane, for the moon was formerly regarded as a source of life and spirit, and to see it 'weirdly,' or at second hand, was a sinister portent. To break certain objects of glass, especially drinking-glasses, was in some cases regarded as peculiarly prophetic of evil. The celebrated example of the Luck of Edenhall, in Cumberland, a chalice the breaking of which would terminate the good fortune of the house and family, will be familiar to everyone.

It is also regarded as a bad omen if, when a person leaves a house, he replaces against the wall the chair on which he has been sitting, the assumption being that he will never visit the place again. It was thought an unlucky omen to get out of bed with the left foot first, or to place a pair of boots or a pair of bellows on the table. To place a pair of boots on the table portends, in Scotland, the death of the wearer, and a similar action with the bellows a possible cessation of the breath of the person who places it there.

CERTAIN omens are associated with rings. To lose a ring which has been given as a pledge of affection is unlucky, as also is the breaking of a ring on the finger. A pin lying on the floor is an omen of good luck if it is picked up. Sneezing is a sign which in various countries is regarded as lucky or the reverse. To sneeze three times before breakfast is a pledge that one will soon receive a present of some kind. As sneezing is usually considered of unlucky prognostication, it is the custom in some British counties to salute the sneezer to avert any evil likely to arise. Scottish women on hearing a child sneeze almost invariably cry 'Bless the bairn!' and in the Midlands grandmothers still exclaim: 'God help you!' In other countries good luck resided in the sneeze because it was frequently brought about by the heat of the sun, the beneficent god. Greek tradition said that as the heavenly fire of the sun permeated the clay figure made by Prometheus the Titan, it sneezed, and its creator invoked blessings upon it.

In Scotland and the north of England it is thought to be a warning that bad luck will follow if a button or hook be placed in the wrong hole while one is dressing. To put on a garment inside out is lucky if it is retained in that position. Formerly clothes were regarded as part of the man himself, and the reversing of any article had a magical significance, sometimes even a sinister meaning. In Northamptonshire it is said that servants who go to their places clothed in black will never stay the year out. A Dorsetshire superstition is that if a man accidentally burns the tail of his coat or a lady the hem of her skirt during a visit at a friend's house, it is a sign that they will never return.

In Yorkshire, when a married woman's apron falls off, it is a sign that something will vex her. Many auguries are gathered from shoes and the position they are left in. Girls in Germany are in the habit of placing their shoes at right angles to each other, hoping by this means to bring about a visit from their sweethearts.

F. Kingdon Ward

WARY OF WHAT MIGHT STEAL THEIR SOULS AWAY

Many primitive peoples have a nervous terror of the camera. Some of them regard it as a sinister receptacle out of which a devil may spring, others have a quasi-religious idea that some part of their own soul or personality will be abstracted by the image of themselves secured by its means. In Tibet—to which country these two women belong—this prejudice against being photographed is dying hard.

If the Cromarty Firth fisherman meets a woman with splayed feet, he will not go to the fishing. If anyone cries to a Firth of Forth fisherman 'Brounger's in your headsheets he resents it, and some thirty years ago would have turned his vessel three times round in the water to avert the omen, Brounger being the god of the storm. If the nose itches, say people in the north of England, it is a sign that the person affected will be 'crossed, vexed or kissed by a fool.' One drop of blood falling from the nose foretells death in some parts of Scotland, three drops are even more ominous. In some parts one drop falling from the left nostril is a sign of good luck and vice versa. The itching of the right eye is a lucky omen.

Marks on the finger-nails are sometimes regarded as prognostications of death, at others as indicative of the number of children a person will have. To cut the nails on a Sunday or hair on a Friday is generally still regarded as unlucky. Sunday was a day of sacred influences, and to pare the nails was an invitation to evil spirits, always on the outlook for man's rejections with which to compass a magical act against him.

To spill salt is also still considered unfortunate. Indeed no superstition appears more widespread. Harm is generally averted by casting the spilt salt over the left shoulder. Salt was formerly regarded as a propitiation to the infernal gods. To spill it was to attract their attention, and to throw it behind one to distract them and prevent their creating an influence.

To dream about teeth is widely held to signify that sorrow of some kind is at hand. The sudden loss of hair is unlucky, being said to prognosticate the loss of children, health or money. To stumble upstairs is a prognostic of good hap, but to do so on firm ground is ominous of evil, for if the man staggers, so will his fortunes.

Quite a number of interesting omens are connected with household work. Thus in Suffolk it is said that if, after sweeping a room the broom is accidentally left in a corner, strangers will visit the house in the course of the day. In some parts of Scotland it is thought that if a spider be killed in the act of sweeping, the sweeper will certainly break a piece of crockery in the course of the day. To see a spider cross the wall is a sure sign of luck, just as the fact of meeting three black cats in succession is of good augury. If a servant break two pieces of crockery she will, it is held, break a third.

Omens and portents associated with fire and the domestic hearth abound. If it blazes up in the Midlands it is thought that a stranger is near. If a cinder leap from the flames it is regarded as a coffin if it is long, and a money-box if it be round. Many weather omens are presaged by the conduct of the domestic fire; thus, if it make a buzzing noise tempest is near, and the leaping of ashes forebodes rain. If a person suddenly shivers, it is a sign that someone is walking over his future grave. In Sweden, if one turns round when going on business it will turn out ill. To meet a left-handed person on a Tuesday morning in Holland or Germany is a bad omen. It is considered of evil augury to find money, and one should turn it in his pocket on seeing the new moon. If two people pronounce the same words or phrase simultaneously, they 'shake little fingers to keep the witches away.' The meaning of this custom is obscure.

The idea underlying the superstitions regarding omens, signs and portents is derived from the ancient notion that the gods sent more or less direct intimations to man regarding future happenings. The correct reading of these signs was usually in the hands of soothsayers, but a certain degree of this knowledge became popular property, and the remains of this still exist in no small measure in folklore, the wisdom of the people. Portents, as seen in flaming comets or falling stars, are not commonly regarded even by semi-civilized peoples to-day as of an ominous nature, although savages and some partly cultivated peoples still pay extraordinary attention to eclipses, the Chinese endeavouring to drive away the dragon which they think devours the sun on these occasions by the din of gongs and bugles.

The East, that mother ot superstition, is naturally greatly addicted to the belief in omens, only in many instances Oriental peoples, instead of waiting for portents to appear, force their appearance. In Burma the direction in which the blood of a sacrificed animal flows, the knots in torn leaves, the length of a split bamboo pole, and the whiteness or otherwise of a hard-boiled egg serve, among others, as methods of augury. But by far the most important mode of divination in use in Burma is that by means of the bones of fowls. It is, indeed, universal as deciding all the difficulties of Burmese existence. Those wing or thigh bones in which the holes exhibit regularity are chosen. Pieces of bamboo are inserted into these holes, and the resulting slant of the stick defines the augury. If the stick slants outward it decides in favour of the measure under test. If it slants inwards the omen is unfavourable. Other methods of divination are by the entrails of animals and by the contents of blown eggs, the shapes of these picturing events to come.

It is not surprising that in Cambodia, where good and evil powers are ascribed so lavishly, much attention should be paid to omens and much time spent in rites to avert misfortune. The wind, the fog, the trees, are objects of fear and awe, and must

THANK-OFFERINGS FOR GLADDENING LIGHT RESTORED

It is no matter for surprise that eclipses of the sun should arouse great excitement among peoples in a low stage of culture, for they are awe-inspiring phenomena In May, 1929, a total eclipse was visible in Siam, and after it was over vast celebrations were held by the natives, who brought in thank-offerings to their gods for the return of the light.

Keystone

LIGHT-HEARTED DEFIANCE OF ALL EVIL PORTENTS AND BAD OMENS

While enlightened common sense ridicules all lingering superstitions, the members of the Thirteen Club are certainly exceptional in their open defiance of all the generally accepted portents of bad luck. Their numbers are limited to thirteen, and once a year they meet at luncheon to proclaim their sturdy faith. The luncheon is held on the thirteenth of the month, at 1 p.m., that is thirteen o'clock. On entering the room each member passes under a ladder and an opened umbrella and, among other ritual acts, makes a point of spilling salt.

be approached with circumspection, lest they send disease and misfortune or withhold some good. For instance, trees whose roots grow under a house bring ill luck to it. The bamboo and cotton plant are also dangerous when planted near a house, for should they grow higher than the house they would wish, out of a perverted sense of gratitude, to provide a funeral cushion and matting for the occupants.

When omens or portents are noticeably absent the savage is often compelled to seek direct oracular utterance from his gods or spirits. Nowhere is this practice so rife as among the American Indians. The piages or priests of the Uapes, of Brazil, have a contrivance known to them as the paxiuba, which consists of a tree-stem about the height of a man, on which the branches and leaves have been left. Holes are bored in the trunk beneath the foliage, and by speaking through these the leaves are made to tremble, and the sound so caused is interpreted as a message from Jurupari, a principal deity.

But all over the American continent, from the Eskimo to the Patagonians, the methods of oracular divination or omen-getting are practically identical. The shaman or medicine man raises a tent or hut, which he enters carefully, closing the aperture after him. He then proceeds to make his incantations, and in a little while the entire lodge trembles and rocks, the poles bend to breaking point, and the most violent noise comes from within, seemingly emanating now from the depths of the earth, now from the air above, and now from the vicinity of the hut itself. The reason for this disturbance has never been properly accounted for, and medicine men who have been converted to Christianity have assured scientific workers amongst Indian tribes that they have not the least idea of what occurred during the time they occupied these enchanted lodges, for the simple reason that they were plunged in a deep sleep. After the supernatural sounds have to some extent faded away the medicine man proceeds to question the spirit he had evoked, the answers of whom, for sheer ambiguity, are equal to those of the Pythonesses of ancient Greece. There is little doubt that the shamans who practise this method of oracular utterance are the victims of hallucination, and many cases are on record in which they have excited themselves into a condition of permanent lunacy.

ANCIENT CUSTOMS OF ENGLISH SCHOOLS

MOST communities whose members live at very close quarters, as do those of public schools, or trace their origins far back, develop various rigid customs. So, too, do such services as the Army and Navy, and such corporate bodies as the Law and Parliament, and their etiquette is dealt with in chapters on Naval and Military Customs, The Lawyers, and Customs of Parliament.

THE public schools of England have all developed peculiar customs to which they hold tenaciously. The treatment of new boys has called forth a good many of these. At Winchester, where there are no boys but only 'men,' a new boy must, at once, and also on the first day of every succeeding term, choose a socius (partner or associate) with whom for the rest of the term he walks either into 'Books' or about the precincts of the school. Winchester men may not go alone or in threes. The origin of the custom is probably derived from the habits of the monks of the fourteenth century, when William de Wykeham founded the school. Monks had to go about in pairs. There is one other conventual custom at Winchester. The Foundation Scholars, who live in College, do not work in private studies, but in recesses, called 'toyes,' one side of which is open to the hall, so that a Wykehamist Scholar is always under the eye of his fellows.

At Westminster a new boy is placed under the governance of another small boy, slightly senior to himself, for about a fortnight. The new boy is called 'Shadow' and his mentor 'Substance,' and Substance is under the duty to instruct Shadow in all the rules and customs. If Shadow breaks any of these, Substance must bear the blame, including the beatings, which no doubt he passes on. The idea of this is exactly the same as the old Saxon frankpledge, by which all the men of a neighbourhood were made responsible for the lawful behaviour of each other; and there is little doubt that the early monitors of Westminster had some such idea. At Rugby, on the other hand, another Elizabethan foundation, a new boy is left severely alone for a fortnight, during which period he may break all rules and customs with impunity; and this lasts until after Lamb Singing, of which more hereafter.

A GOOD many schools have singing customs, which may possibly have been invented in order to try to discover new material for the choir. Some, however, think that they were invented as a test of nerve. The common basis of the custom is that every new boy shall be made to sing before either the whole school or his House. At Harrow he is simply put on a table in the dining-hall of the House one night after supper and told to sing a verse of 'Men of Harlech,' which, if he does it successfully, brings him great applause. Similar methods prevail at Shrewsbury and other places. But at Rugby, in the School House (Head Master's House), there is a much more picturesque affair. About ten days after the beginning of term, one night after supper, the Head of the House calls out 'Lamb Singing,' and thereupon all the boys troop off into the large dormitory, where the 'bucks' sit or loll on beds and the proletariat squat anywhere they can. One bed is left vacant, and upon it are perched the new boys in succession. Each is commanded to sing a song of his own choice, and if he manages to do this well he is loudly cheered. If he makes but a botch of it, yet struggles through the ditty and refuses to break down, he is 'ruled'—that is, the company sings 'Rule Britannia.' But if he stands mute, or breaks down and refuses to continue, he is booed off the stage. Until a comparatively short time ago the custom was to administer to the stickit singer a large dose of salt and water, because salt is notoriously good for the vocal chords.

THE question of holidays touches the heart of every schoolboy; and there are quite a number of traditions connected with extra holidays. In ancient days such an event was called a 'remedy'; and when Dean Colet founded St. Paul's School in 1585 he ordained that if the High Master should grant any remedies to the boys he should forfeit the sum of forty shillings, except for a bishop or archbishop. This provision has given rise to the custom that when a bishop or archbishop visits the school he is expected to ask for a remedy, and one is granted. If his lordship be an Old Pauline, he asks for and is granted two remedies; because, nobody knows how many years ago, an ingenious Head of the School propounded the theory that an Old Pauline bishop was equal to two bishops from any other school, and so worth two remedies. At Winchester, also, there are certain occasions when a remedy may be asked for, e.g. when the Judge of Assize at Winchester is an old Wykehamist. When the request is granted the Head Master hands to the Captain of the School a gold ring inscribed with the words 'commendat rarior usus,' which may be freely translated 'don't ask too often.' At the end of the day the ring, which is called the Remedy Ring, is handed back to the Head Master.

One of the sacred customs of Winchester is the keeping ever white and plain Domum Cross. The story is that in the fifteenth century a boy was left behind during the holidays and had to remain at school alone. He occupied himself first in writing some verses which have now become the celebrated Winchester song, 'Dulce Domum'; and, next, in carving out of the turf on St. Katherine's Hill (Hills) a large cross. Readers will know that the soil of the Hampshire downs is chalk, so that the cross shows up

Planet News

TOPPERS V. BOATERS IN THE PLAYING FIELD

Every secondary and public school has its own proper head-gear. At Westminster the silk top-hat is the prescribed wear. At Aldenham, a school with which Westminster has an annual athletic contest, straw hats are compulsory.

white. Every new boy must run up St. Katherine's Hill, round a certain deep trench, find his way blindfold through some trees, and lastly climb up Chalk Pit, take out a bit of chalk, and carry it to the Cross, on which he lays it. Thus Domum Cross is kept ever renewed.

ANYONE who goes to Westminster School at the hour of Latin prayers (Westminster, like St. Paul's, keeps up the custom of praying in Latin, as everybody used to do before the Reformation) will see standing outside the school door a monitor clad in cap and gown, a costume which denotes him a King's Scholar. Inside the door he will find standing another similarly attired. The one inside is called Mon. Stat., short for ' monitor stationis,' and the one outside is called Mon. Os.—' monitor ostii.' It is interesting to trace the history of these two functionaries. When the boys of Westminster School in the late sixteenth and seventeenth centuries used to go to play, their playground was Tuttle Fields, where Vincent Square now is, and they had to traverse some rather unsafe country between ; wherefore one of the biggest of the monitors was appointed to take charge of them out and home, and as the Westminster word for a game is ' station ' he was called the monitor of the station ; while another and generally smaller monitor was left to guard the gate, and he was the monitor of the gate. The functions of Mon. Stat. and Mon. Os. have now been reduced to keeping the door at Latin prayers.

There are some customary inhibitions with regard to places in many schools, and these frequently take the form of the seniors asserting their right to exclusive use of some place. Thus, at Rugby nobody except a colour may walk across Big Side, the football ground. At Shrewsbury, unless on Speech Day, only praeposters, school monitors, scholars, and double firsts may walk on grass. At Winchester for the first three years no ' man ' may walk across Flint

Court. At Rugby, again, only the Sixth Form may walk straight in at the gate to the hall door through the Big Arch. All others have their own arches, which vary according to their seniority.

The Christmas term at Winchester is called ' Short Half,' and on the last day thereof occurs a celebration, hallowed by centuries of usage, called ' Illumina,' which no doubt obtains from monkish times, when it was customary to light a candle as an act of devotion. Round the great field known as Meads is a flint wall, and in this wall there are small niches. On the last night of Short Half the boys place candles in these niches and light them so as to illuminate the field, round which they then parade in a sort of informal procession. It is extremely probable, though traces of it are no longer to be found, that at one time these niches contained altars dedicated to various saints, and that the scholars of Winchester, who at that time consisted only of sixty Foundation Scholars, were accustomed to offer their devotions to their favourite saint before making the perilous journey home for the vacation.

Eton, though not so old as Winchester, is of respectable antiquity, and it has one curious survival known as ' Threepenny.' It should be said that this custom only applies to Collegers or King's Scholars, who number seventy. The other Eton boys, to the number of 1,100 or so, are called Oppidans, because they formerly were town boys, i.e. from the neighbouring town. A very early Provost of Eton, one Bost, who died in 1504, left a sum of money to provide twopence a year for each Colleger, to be given to the fortunate donee on each February 27. As consideration for the money, the boy had to say a prayer for the soul of Bost. It is supposed that the twopence was intended to enable the Colleger to buy half a sheep, and colour is lent to this explanation by the fact that from the days of Henry VI to the middle of the nineteenth century Collegers were never fed on any other meat except mutton. Provost Lupton, who succeeded Provost Bost, thought twopence not quite enough, so he left another penny all round; and to this day, on every February 27, each of the seventy Collegers receives a threepenny bit.

In all communities there is a tendency to create an aristocracy; and although the English public school is in one sense very democratic, in that the boys govern themselves quite as much as they are governed by the masters, yet within the democracy there is an aristocracy, which not only exercises functions of government, but which takes care to assert for itself privileges of various kinds. An instance of this is found at Marlborough, where prefects, members of the first and second cricket XI's, of the first XV, or the Fourty (second XV), or Sixty (third XV); and a few others of athletic distinction are called ' Bloods.' Nobody but a Blood is allowed to wear grey flannel

Topical Press Agency

CHRIST'S HOSPITAL'S UNIQUE DISTINCTION: THE BLUECOAT UNIFORM

Save that a hat has been discarded the Bluecoat boys' uniform is exactly as prescribed by a statute of 1553. It comprises a long blue coat with pleated skirt reaching to the ankle, moleskin breeches buttoned at the knee, yellow worsted stockings and square-toed shoes. A leather belt encircles the waist, and under this the boys tuck up the skirts of their coats when at play. The dress, once a familiar sight in London, is seldom seen there now except on S. Matthew's day, when the boys come up from Horsham to attend service at Christ Church, Newgate.

Central Press

CALLING BILL ON FOUNDER'S DAY AT HARROW ON THE HILL

John Lyon was granted a charter for a school in 1571, and in 1611 it was opened at Harrow, in Middlesex, originally as a school for the poor children there. As time passed the property left by Lyon increased enormously in value and the status of the school rose steadily, until towards the end of the eighteenth century Harrow had become a leading public school, the chief rival of Eton and Winchester. The memory of the philanthropic yeoman John Lyon is honoured on Founder's Day, in October, when Old Harrovians gather from all parts of the world. The photograph shows the ceremony known as Calling Bill, with the boys filing past the master to answer to their names as he calls the roll.

Central Press

SPEECH DAY AT HARROW SCHOOL: GREETING DISTINGUISHED OLD HARROVIANS

Speech Day is the second of Harrow's two great annual ceremonial occasions. It falls in the summer term, and, like Founder's Day, draws Old Harrovians from all parts of the world, the more distinguished among them being received with an uproarious welcome from the assembled boys, who now number about six hundred. Speeches in the handsome modern Speech Room and the performance of a Greek or Latin play are among the events provided for their entertainment. In the photograph in the opposite page the salient feature is the distinctive Harrow straw hat. This photograph emphasises the importance of Speech Day at Harrow as a Society function comparable with Eton's Speech Day on the fourth of June.

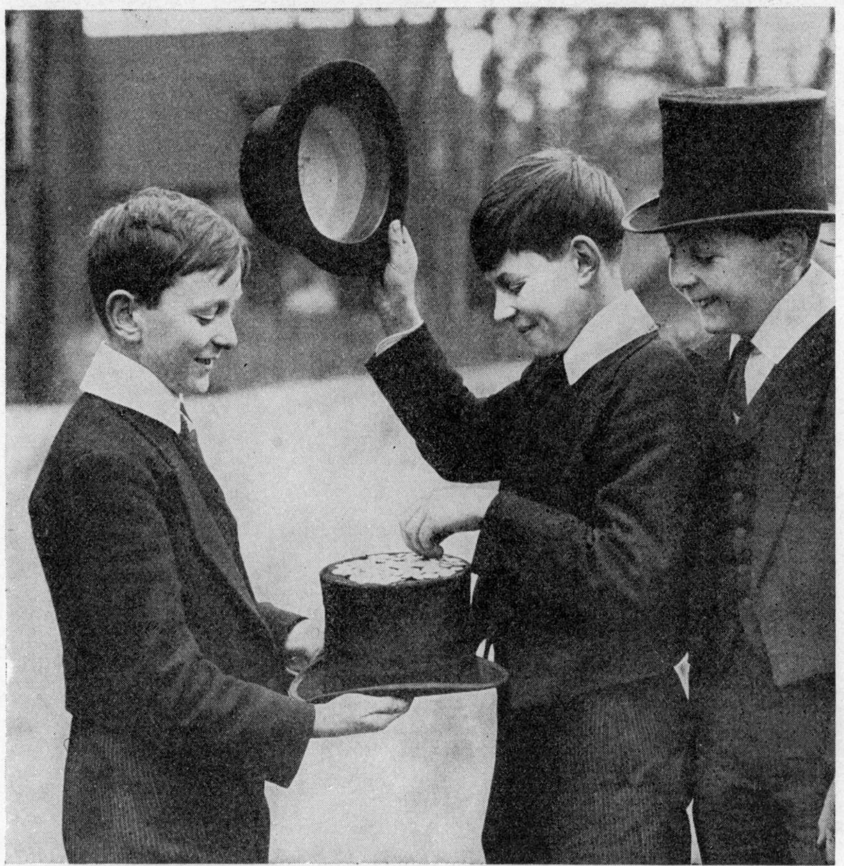

Keystone

THREEPENNY DAY: ONE OF ETON'S OLDEST CUSTOMS

Provost Bost, dying in 1504, left a sum of money sufficient to provide twopence a year for each of the seventy King's Scholars on the foundation of Eton College. His successor, Provost Lupton, raised the sum to threepence, and every year, on February 27, the Collegers attend in College Hall where each of them picks up a threepenny bit from the top of a silk hat.

buttoned at the knee, a long blue coat with pleated skirt reaching to the ankles, and bands, worn not like a barrister's, but one on top of the other. A Bluecoat boy wears no collar. This dress, which was prescribed by an original statute of the school about 1553, originally included a hat, but this has been discarded for about two centuries, and the boys go bareheaded. Round the waist of the coat a leather girdle is worn, and under this the boy tucks up the skirts of his coat when he is playing. Similar costumes were worn at many charity schools until the middle of last century.

There is at Harrow an athletic aristocracy called the Philathletic Club, composed of the leading sportsmen of the school; while Eton rejoices in a peculiar institution known as 'Pop,' which plays a great part in the government of the school. In 1811 a boy named Townshend collected about nineteen other senior boys and founded the Eton Society, which used to meet at Mother Hatton's Sock (Tuck) Shop every week for debate. The Latin for eating-house is 'popina,' hence the society

trousers or to go about bareheaded. At Harrow the odd custom prevails that no boy except a Fez is allowed to play football in brown boots. A Fez is one who has his House colours at football and wears a very small fez perched on the back of his head. The ordinary hat at Harrow is a stiff straw hat, very low in the crown (it has to be kept on by the wearing of a piece of elastic) and very wide in the brim. At one time Harrovians developed the fashion of wearing hats with highly exaggerated brims, which became ridiculous, so a regulation was promulgated cutting them down to the present uniform width. At Harrow, winged collars must be worn by juniors only; while at Westminster and Eton only certain seniors may wear them. All Etonians unbutton the bottom button of the waistcoat, but only senior Harrovians. The origin of this custom has been entirely lost. Eton goes so far in the matter of distinctive dress as to prohibit the wearing of white flannels by any except members of the first XI. All other cricketers wear light grey flannels.

The only school that has retained its original costume is Christ's Hospital. This costume consists of elastic-sided, square-toed, thick-soled shoes, yellow worsted stockings, a sort of moleskin breeches

became known as 'Pop.' It has always been a most exclusive institution. The Captain of the School, the Captains of the Oppidans, of Cricket and of the Boats, and the Keeper of the Field belong to it ex officio, but the rest of the society are co-opted, and it is to an Etonian a much greater honour to be elected to Pop than to be made a duke. This self-chosen body of about thirty boys has for a hundred years almost ruled Eton, and its members arrogate to themselves certain privileges and distinctions

ETON was founded by King Henry VI under the shadow of his castle, and has always enjoyed the smiles of royalty; and the great day of the Eton year is a Royal birthday—not that of the founder, but of George III which falls on June 4. This is always kept as Speech Day. Until 1844 parents and guests driving down from London to the celebrations used to be waylaid on Salt Hill, just before arriving at the school, and there the waylayer used to demand 'salt,' in other words alms, for the collection of which they presented silken bags. In this way they gathered substantial sums of money, to be given to the Head Colleger or Captain of the School to defray his expenses at the University. There is still,

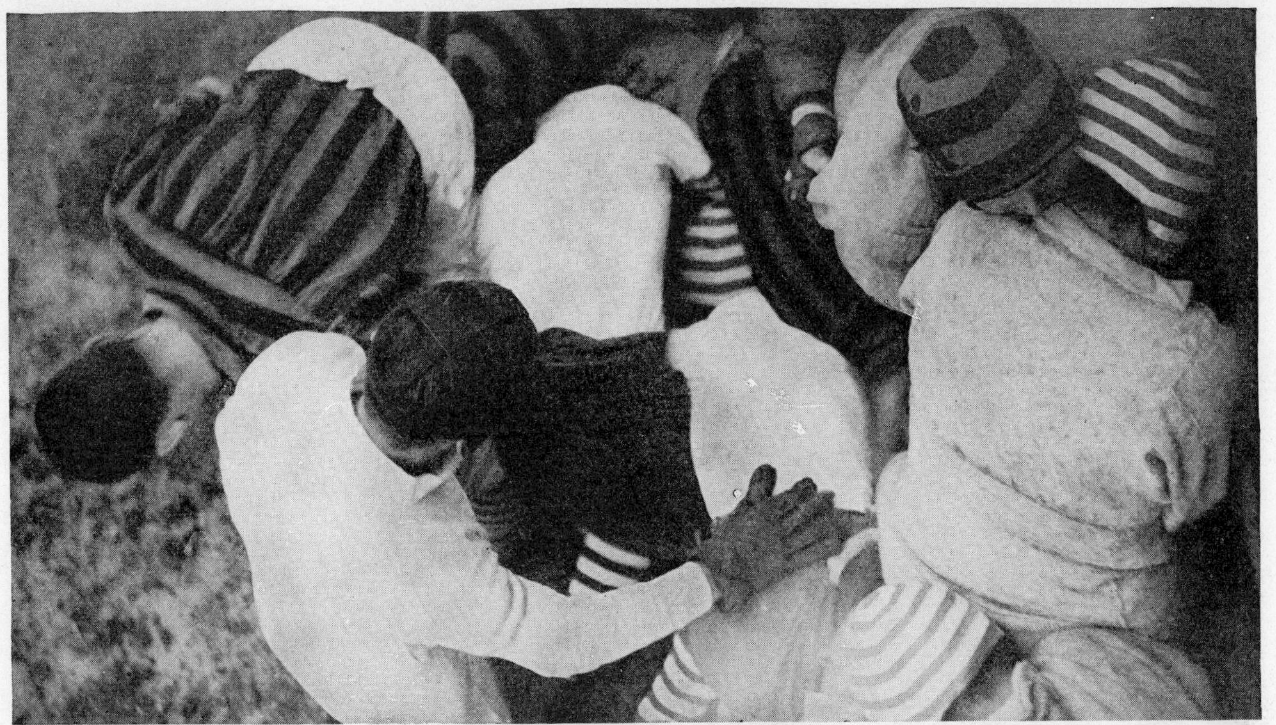

Central Press

ROUGH PLAY IN THE ETON WALL GAME ON S. ANDREW'S DAY

Several schools, notably Eton, Harrow and Rugby, have their own peculiar game of football, but the most completely original variant, unlike any game of football seen elsewhere, is the Wall Game played between Collegers and Oppidans at Eton on S. Andrew's Day. The teams, eleven a side, line up at the centre point of a wall along the top of which small boys sit. The game starts with a scrimmage, and, as explained in the text, the players try to push the ball behind a chalk mark at either end. The game is one fierce maul from beginning to end.

Calling absence is the first item on the agenda list on Speech Day at Eton. The roll is called in Weston's Yard by masters attired in cap and gown, the boys answering to their names by raising their hats. At this assembly the curious have opportunity to observe some of Eton's peculiar ordinances concerning dress, such as the general turning up of the trousers and leaving the bottom button of the waistcoat unfastened.

SPECTACULAR MOMENTS IN ETON'S FOURTH OF JUNE CELEBRATIONS——

The culminating moment in the Fourth of June festivities is the Procession of the Boats, here seen moving off for their first course up stream. Ten boats are engaged in the procession, one—named Monarch—manned by a crew of ten, the others by eight oarsmen. Four courses in all are rowed by the boats, the termination of the final one down stream being timed to coincide with the display of fireworks on the river bank. On a fine evening the scene, with Windsor Castle dominating the background, is indescribably beautiful.

Speeches follow the calling of absence, and then, with the termination of the more strictly academic part of the proceedings, relatives and friends are free to enjoy what is by common consent a social and fashionable function of the first importance. Cricket provides old 'dry bobs' with material for pleasant reminiscence; old 'wet bobs' take personal interest in the impending procession of the boats.

Sport and General Press

—FROM 'ABSENCE' TO THE RIVER PAGEANT THAT ENDS A GLORIOUS DAY

An especially picturesque appearance is given to the Procession of Boats by the fact that all the crews are dressed like sailors of the time of George III, whose birthday is observed at Eton as Speech Day. The coxswain of each of the ten boats is attired as an Admiral of the Fleet, and the details of the other costumes are correct in every particular except that the socks worn are of pink silk; while a further non-nautical touch is supplied by the flowers carried as bouquets and worn as posies.

L.N.A.

OLD-FASHIONED CUSTOMS OF A MODERN SCHOOL

Although only founded about 1853, Hurstpierpoint College has established some picturesque customs. One is the annual bringing in of the boar's head with choir and torch-bearers to the Great Hall, where the boys of the Upper School participate in the feast. Another custom, known as Lowe's Dole, is observed on Ascension Day, when the choir sing a Latin hymn on the top of Walstonbury Beacon, being rewarded with half a crown apiece.

however, left one very picturesque event on the Fourth of June called the Procession of the Boats. There are ten boats altogether, one of them, called Monarch, manned by a crew of ten, and the others by eight oarsmen. The crews are all dressed in the costumes of sailors of the time of George III, except that their socks are of pink silk. The coxswain of each boat is attired as an Admiral of the Fleet, complete with cocked hat. The boats, in order of seniority, row up and down and up the river again, and finally down once more, timing their arrival to coincide with a display of fireworks which is taking place on the bank. This magnificent display was originally given about 150 years ago, to please George III on his birthday; and has been continued ever since until it has become almost a part of the Eton religion.

Another annual event at Eton is the Wall Game between Collegers and Oppidans, played from immemorial antiquity every St. Andrew's Day. There are 11 a side and the game is unlike any game of football seen elsewhere. The players line up at the middle point of a wall upon the whole length of which small boys sit. At a certain distance on each side of the centre is a chalk mark, called at one end Good Calx and at the other Bad Calx (chalk). The game starts with a bully, or scrummage, and the players endeavour to push the ball behind the opponents' calx and there touch it on the wall with the hand. If this be done, the attacking side is allowed a shy at goal, which is at one end the door of a garden and at the other a marked space on a large elm. The game is one fierce maul from beginning to end, and is generally decided on a majority of shies obtained, for a goal is scored with such rarity that it is equal to 10 shies.

Founder's Day at Harrow, in honour of John Lyon, the Harrow yeoman who founded the school, is held every October. The occasion is one for meeting old Harrovians. Speech Day at Harrow is in the Summer Term and is the occasion of speeches in the school and a Latin or Greek play, a custom at least 200 years old.

Fagging customs vary somewhat in schools, though the more strenuous of these are declining. At Rugby

Keystone

'HILLS': WINCHESTER 'MEN' UPWARD BOUND FOR DOMUM CROSS

S. Katherine's Hill rises 500 feet above the water meads at Winchester, and in the early days of William of Wykeham's foundation was the scholars' only playground. Out of the turf, legend says, a homesick lad left alone at school during the holidays carved a cross, and this is still religiously kept renewed by Wykehamists with chalk taken from the chalk pit on the hill top and laid upon the cross. Twice a year now all the boys climb the hill; a short service is held at the top, followed by roll call; and so back to school.

Central Press

ETIQUETTE OF THE HAT IN ENGLAND'S OLDEST PUBLIC SCHOOL

The room in which the 'collegers,' or scholars, of Winchester College do their lessons is called Seventh Chamber. The little cubicles (known as 'toyes') arranged along the walls of Seventh Chamber serve most of the purposes that studies do in other schools. Winchester College, founded in 1382, is the oldest of the great public schools, and many of the quaint customs that are observed there date back several centuries. Among them is the unwritten rule concerning the 'collegers'' hats. These must be hung up on the partitions of the 'toyes.'

a person entitled to the services of a fag puts his head out of his study door and shouts 'Fag!' whereupon all the fags in the building run to the place, and the last one is taken. Marlborough has a similar institution. At Shrewsbury the master shouts 'Doul!' and selects any one of those who run to the call. At Eton a Colleger shouts 'Here!' if he wants a fag, while an Oppidan calls 'Boy!' Fags are in some schools the small boys of the lowest forms, and in others only boys in their first year, and the duties of the fag are to fetch and carry for his master, to make his toast, clean his boots, and generally to make himself useful.

To conclude with a school custom the most singular of all—the Westminster Pancake Grease. Annually, on Shrove Tuesday, the whole school assembles in the great hall, with a number of privileged spectators, at about midday. A row of boys, clad in their oldest rags, may be seen standing almost underneath a beam which separates the upper from the lower school, and at the right moment enters the school cook, bearing a frying-pan which contains a pancake. The ragged champions, each of whom has been selected by his own form as its most redoubtable gladiator, brace themselves up for a rush. The cook tosses the pancake over the bar, and as it begins to descend the champions rush forward and hurl themselves upon it as soon as it touches the floor. For a period of two minutes there is a maul, compared with which the fiercest battle between two sets of Welsh football players is mere child's play (see illustration in page 22).

At the end of the two minutes a whistle is blown, the combatants unravel themselves, and each one who has secured a piece of the pancake exhibits it, and he who has the largest piece is entitled to receive one guinea from the Dean of Westminster. The origin of this custom, which has proceeded certainly for 200 years at least, dates from the time when a certain humorous Dean of Westminster offered a guinea as a prize for the boy who should secure the largest piece of a pancake tossed in the air by the cook. At first the whole school used to scramble, but now only a chosen few take part in the 'grease,' as it is called.

MIDSUMMER BELIEFS AND PRACTICES

THE summer solstice has been celebrated from time immemorial, and, as with other widespread seasonal customs, many of the Midsummer observances now associated with S. John are ultimately of pagan origin. Further aspects of love-divination and magic directed against evil, which figure so largely in Midsummer customs, are treated in the chapters on magic in Love and War and Outwitting the Forces of Evil.

THERE are throughout the country certain hills and groups of megaliths where little companies of people assemble to watch the sun rising on the longest day of the year. Rural folk explain the custom as one supposed to be productive of good luck, especially in the form of good health. In these motoring days, however, the increasing numbers of people who assemble at the famous Stonehenge circle are moved mainly by feelings of curiosity, for at the summer solstice, when the apparent movement of the sun towards the north reaches its farthest limit, the 'avenue' points approximately to the spot on the horizon where the sun appears. Those who stand at the 'altar' experience a thrill of wonder when they see its rays striking the outlying stone known as the 'Friar's Heel.' Evidently, to the ancient builders, Stonehenge was a 'clock of the seasons.' Its 'observation line,' at the summer solstice, apparently gave indication that the time for observing an important annual festival was at hand.

Midsummer day falls a few days later, on June 24, when the sun appears to be definitely in retreat. The pagan celebrations connected with it were formerly so deep-rooted and widespread that the early Church found it necessary to impart to them a Christian significance. Midsummer day consequently became known as S. John the Baptist's day—his birthday—and as the birth of Christ had taken place at the winter solstice, when the days begin to lengthen, a new emphasis was imparted to the text: 'He (Christ) must increase and I must decrease.' Thus Christ's precursor is found 'bearing witness to the light' (John i, 7).

In conservative Brittany Midsummer or S. John's eve customs are still widely observed. The peasants assemble on an eminence, or at cross-roads, or on an open green space near a church consecrated to S. John, carrying faggots, logs and bundles of gorse, which are heaped up to make bonfires. The opening proceedings are of solemn character and conducted with much decorum. When vespers are over bonfires are lit with ceremony, either by a priest or some old man, and, as the flames leap up, heads are bared, prayers are repeated and appropriate hymns sung. The worshippers then march solemnly by the right three times round each fire. Thereafter there is much merrymaking. Lively airs are struck up by the musicians and dancing begins. Lads and girls dart to and fro amidst the smoke and, as the fires die down, leap over the embers. The more daring make attempts to pass through the flames. If anyone should get burned, or should stumble and fall amidst the embers, he or she is hooted and expected to retire from the company. In some parts of Brittany domesticated animals are driven through the bonfire smoke and over the smouldering embers in the belief that they will thus secure protection against evil eye, witchcraft and disease. Charred sticks and charcoal taken from the bonfires are used to purify wells and to provide charms to protect houses against ill luck in its various forms. There is thus a curious mixture of pagan and Christian practices.

F. Caird Inglis

MIDSUMMER FIRE AT THE CALTON BRAE, EDINBURGH

In Scotland Midsummer fires are rare. One of the most notable instances of the custom survives in the parish of Durris, Kincardineshire, where a bonfire is still kindled annually on Midsummer Day on the hill of Cairnshee. The Tarbolton fire is lit on the first Monday after June 11. In Edinburgh the date for lighting Midsummer fires has been changed to Victoria Day.

Country folk in Provence still light Midsummer fires, the fuel for which is collected by children who beg from door to door. Householders, as a rule, consider it is lucky to give, and do so freely. Although the Midsummer celebration is nowadays mainly an affair of youngsters, who dance around and leap through the flames as do the Bretons, the priest, mayor and aldermen were formerly wont to head the procession to the bonfire and take part in the march around it. Country people in the Poitou area likewise have their Midsummer fires. The belief is not yet extinct that the drifting smoke, in some mysterious way, is good for the crops. In the Vosges, Midsummer bonfires may still be seen blazing on the hills. The merrymakers throw garlands of flowers through the flames, and some keep up the old custom of marching round their fields with lighted torches. Boys twist straw round old wheels and, setting them on fire, let them roll down inclines. Similar customs still linger in Picardy and Normandy. Until about the middle of last century all France blazed with bonfires on Midsummer eve.

A remarkable survival in Britain of the ancient Midsummer bonfire custom is found in the north-eastern Scottish county of Kincardine. Each year

George Long

DRUID SERVICE AT STONEHENGE AT THE SUMMER SOLSTICE

Midsummer morning, according to old tradition, was the occasion of a great sun-worship festival at Stonehenge, and it has long been the custom for people to watch the sun rise over the famous stone monument on the morning of June 21. For many years, too, the religious body known as the Druid Church of the Universal Bond has held a summer solstice service here, originally on June 21, but latterly on the day following, to avoid the crowds. Their rites closely resemble those of the Christian Church, the sacrament (top) consisting of bread and wine.

Photopress

ANCIENT RITES OF MIDSUMMER PERFORMED BY THE DRUIDS OF TODAY

The service held every year by the Druid Universal Brotherhood at Stonehenge at the summer solstice is a very picturesque and moving ceremony. The Druids who officiate at the rite are attired in purple and flowing white surplices, and all wear scarlet hoods except the Chief Druid, whose hood is white. The sacramental wine is contained in a magnificent ewer, from which it is poured into small glasses for the Brethren and for the Chief Druid into a silver cup. Bells are sounded at intervals and incense is burnt.

on the evening of June 24 a bonfire is lit upon the hill of Cairnshee ('hill of the fairies') in the parish of Durris. Alexander Hogg, a native of the parish, who died about 1790, bequeathed a sum of money for the maintenance of the bonfire custom on Cairnshee, because as a boy he had herded cattle in the neighbourhood and taken part in the Midsummer ceremonies. According to the terms of the trust, the sum of ten shillings is paid to the local herdsmen, and money is also provided to procure for the merry-makers bread, cheese and ale. It is provided in this Hogg trust that the bonfire must be lit as the sun sinks below the horizon. As the hill is the highest in the district, the bonfire is seen far afield.

In Edinburgh the Midsummer fire custom has been transferred to the evening of Victoria day, and the authorities permit of bonfires being lit in various streets. As in France, the old custom of collecting the fuel is still observed; for some days before bonfire evening Edinburgh youngsters beg for wood, etc., from door to door, and the supply is always sufficiently abundant. Until about the beginning of the seventeenth century London had similarly its street bonfires 'on the Vigil of S. John the Baptist, commonly called Midsummer Eve.' Indeed, all over England Midsummer bonfires were exceedingly common, and the ceremonial customs associated with them survived in not a few areas well into the nineteenth century. Nowadays the bonfires are prepared and lit in some rural districts by boys, who, however, run the risk of being charged with 'malicious mischief.' The Penzance custom of erecting bonfires and burning tar-barrels in the streets is now only a memory. In Wales the rolling of fiery wheels down inclines, a magical custom perhaps intended to stimulate the retreat of the sun, as well as the lighting of bonfires round which people danced and leaped, were formerly common. S. John's day is still remembered in County Leitrim, Ireland, as 'Bonfire day,' and one may still see Midsummer fires on the hills. Nor have the young folk of Kerry forgotten the immemorial custom. Girls who succeed in leaping over smouldering bonfires backward and forward three times are supposed to be assured of a speedy marriage and much good luck. Cattle driven through the smoke and over the ashes are supposed to prosper by securing protection against various ills. These inherited ideas are, however, nowadays not too seriously entertained.

Throughout Spain, the Scandinavian countries and in Germany, Midsummer fires were formerly lit

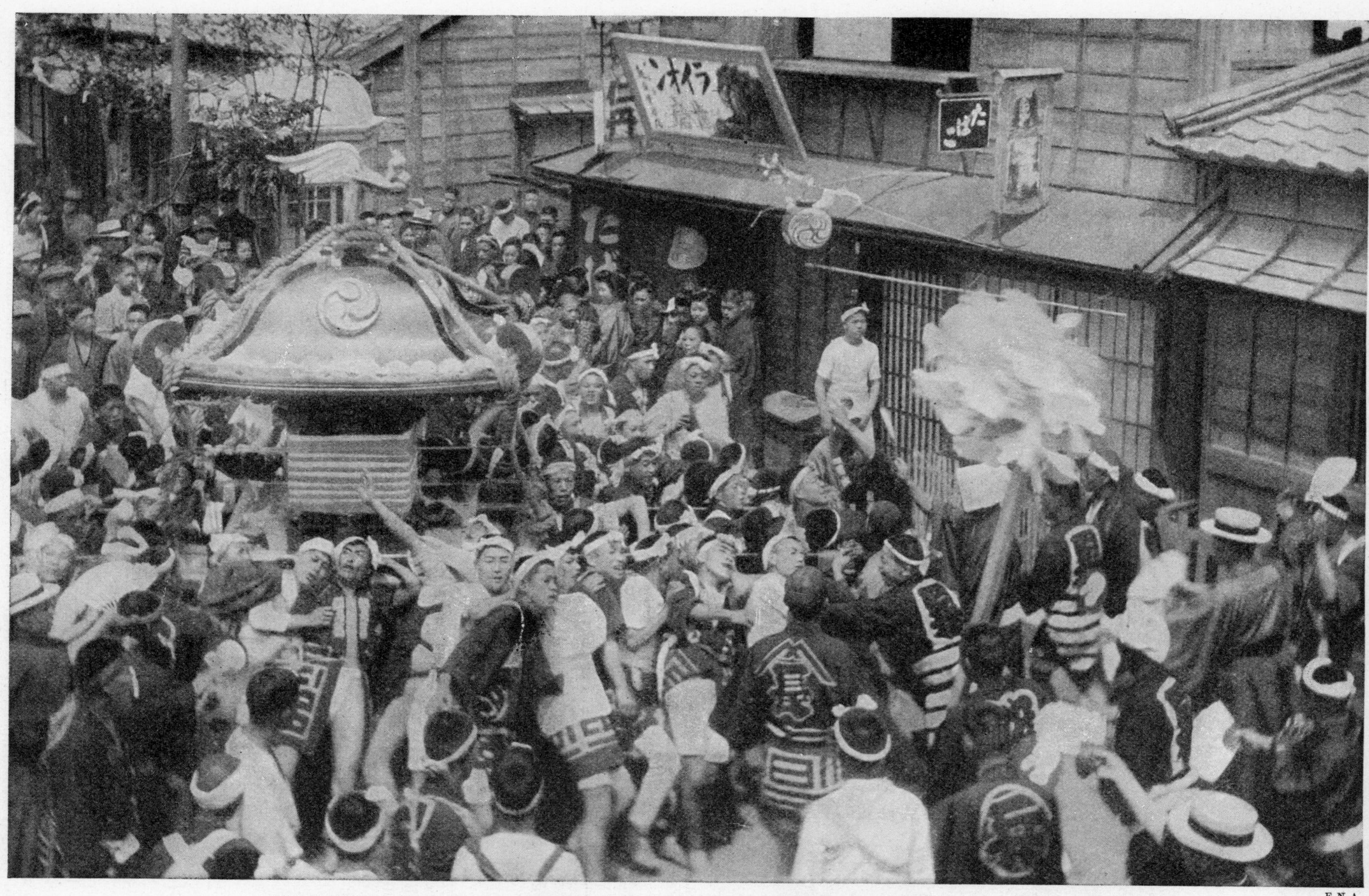

E.N.A.

MIDSUMMER FESTIVAL IN JAPAN: PROCESSION IN HONOUR OF THE GOD OF WAR

Through the length and breadth of Japan festivals are held thrice yearly—in spring, summer and autumn—in honour of the god Hachiman. This deity, the god of war, is the deified form of the fifteenth Mikado, Ojen Tenno, son of the warlike empress Jingo, conqueror of Korea. At festival time the image of the god is brought before the public eye. It is taken from its temple resting-place, placed in the shrine, and carried through the streets amid a tumultuous throng of worshippers. All the shops are closed for the occasion, except those in which food and drink are sold. Very often a miniature representation of the god is borne in procession by the children of the town at the same time.

E.N.A.

PROCESSION OF THE CARS IN ROME ON THE FESTIVAL OF S. JOHN

To safeguard the fertility of the soil, the ancient Druids at their quinquennial festivals were accustomed to burn great wicker images filled with live men and animals. Similar festivals on a smaller scale were observed annually, and from these are perhaps descended the yearly Midsummer fire festivals and processions, in which artificial giants figure, that still linger in some parts of Europe. The cars here seen moving through the streets of Rome during the fête of San Giovanni—the giant tortoise, the old-fashioned omnibus, the pasteboard tower—all convey the fantastic spirit of rejoicing so long associated with Midsummer.

with unfailing regularity, and the custom still lingers here and there. Greek and Macedonian peasants continue to perpetuate the fire ceremony. Of especial interest is the fact that the Midsummer bonfire custom prevails among the Moslems of Morocco and Algeria. The natives light their charm-fires on hills and at cross-roads and like European peoples dance, make merry and leap through the flames and smoke. The ashes of bonfires are credited with magical properties, as in Brittany. Animals are driven through the smoke because it 'makes them thrive.' The usual view is that the Moslems of North Africa, like the Christians of Europe, in performing Midsummer fire ceremonies perpetuate an old calendar festival which dates back to that remote period when agriculture was first introduced. Behind the widespread fire-lighting customs appear to lie ancestral fears that nature might fail to provide the necessary food supply unless the sun were magically stimulated and directed to proceed in its proper course.

Surviving customs, even in those areas where bonfires are no longer lit, reveal other curious and antique Midsummer folk-beliefs. One is that on S. John's eve it is possible to peer into the future and ascertain something of one's destiny by performing some divination ceremony. Another is that at the summer solstice evil, as well as good, influences are let loose, and houses and individuals must be magically protected against them. Certain birds are supposed to behave in a certain manner. It is, for instance, unlucky to hear the voice of the cuckoo after June 24, because that fairy bird was anciently connected with the Otherworld, to which it migrated after the summer solstice.

Love divinations are still practised in rural areas on Midsummer eve, especially by young women. One custom is to bake a cake with ceremony and then break it into several portions. When these are given to the young women who are concerned about their future, silence is maintained by each of them. They go to bed, placing the portions of cake under their pillows. During the night the future husband is expected to appear in a dream. Another custom requires that a girl should walk backward into a garden and pluck a dewy moss-rose. She wears this flower on Midsummer day, and the young man who asks her to give it to him is sure to become her husband if she so desires. In some rural areas a request by a young man for a girl's Midsummer rose is still regarded as equivalent to a proposal of marriage. The refusal of the request for the rose is a plain hint that the suitor is rejected. Stalks of orpine are still known to villagers as the 'Midsummer men,' and are used in a divination ceremony. The stalks are put into a flower-vase and placed in a bedroom, and in the morning a girl takes note of them. If they lean towards one another her lover and she are sure to enjoy happiness after marriage; if, however, the stalk representing the young man leans away from the other representing the girl

E.N.A.

LEAVES AND FLOWERS AND TOYS TO WELCOME MIDSUMMER IN LATVIA

S. John's Day (June 24) is the most joyful festival of the year in Latvia. The people deck themselves and their houses with foliage and flowers, strew boughs of fir about the rooms, and hold high carnival with dancing and singing. When night comes bonfires gleam on the hills. Farmers fix little barrels filled with wood or tar on poles and set them alight. The upper photograph shows peasants in the market square of Riga on the eve of S. John's Day, their heads adorned with oak leaves, selling garlands for the festival. Below is a stall for carnival toys.

E.N.A.

STRANGE MASKED MIDSUMMER DANCE OF THE YAQUI INDIANS

The Yaqui, a warlike Indian tribe, formerly lived on both banks of the Yaqui River in the state of Sonora, Mexico, but the Mexican government deported many to distant states. They have ceremonial societies not unlike those of the Pueblo Indians, whose ritual dances are connected with the fertility of the crops. The upper photograph shows Yaqui dancers on their way to take part in the annual Midsummer festival while below are four arrayed for the dance; clearly a fertility rite. The masks are made of wood and the beards of horsehair.

it is evident he is fickle and unfaithful. S. John's wort is another plant still used for love divination. The custom is not yet extinct of sowing hemp-seed in the darkness, although it may nowadays be perpetuated mainly as an amusement. A girl who has sowed the seed is supposed, on glancing over her shoulder, to catch a glimpse of her future husband. The eager rural admirer on such an occasion sees to it that he is not far away.

A curious Midsummer eve custom, still practised in some rural areas, is to attempt the collection of fern-seed so as to acquire the power of finding treasure or prospering in business. A young man, holding a plate in his right hand, goes towards a fern in the darkness. He must not touch the plant, but by holding the plate below it attempt to catch the magical seed supposed to fall upon that magic night. There are old literary references to this belief in 'the wond'rous one-night-seeding fern.' One of Ben Jonson's characters says:

> I had
> No medicine sir, to go invisible,
> No fern-seed in my pocket.

Beaumont and Fletcher refer to 'the herb that gives invisibility,' while the sage Shakespeare ridicules the belief.

This custom of gathering, or attempting to gather, the seeds of fern on Midsummer eve is still known in parts of France, Germany and Austria, as well as in Italy and in Russia. It is only in Russia, however, that we hear of a belief about the fern-seeds causing an explosion like thunder in the middle of the night. In Bohemia they are supposed to sparkle like fire just before they fall. Elsewhere the belief is that the invisible elves await their falling and immediately carry them away.

Another old custom, still observed, is to sit up late on Midsummer eve. Rural Midsummer eve parties are still fairly common, and in some areas there are 'watch-night services.' It used to be thought that at midnight souls left the bodies of sleepers and proceeded to the point on land or sea where death was destined to take place. It was formerly customary for the more daring to keep watch during the night in a church porch to see the souls of those who were destined to die during the ensuing twelve months walking up to the church door and knocking for admission. This belief in the temporary liberation of the soul of a person doomed to die before long is still very prevalent in the Scottish Highlands, where it is intimately associated with the persisting ideas regarding 'second sight,' or, as it is called in Gaelic, 'double vision.' 'Night watching' was formerly a common custom in London. Large numbers of men and women, adorned with garlands of flowers and carrying torches, staves, branches with green leaves, etc., marched through the streets until dawn. Henry VIII suppressed this custom during the latter years of his reign, but it was revived after his death. Some think 'the watch' was supposed to be considered necessary so that the soul might not wander and, by so doing, cause life to be shortened, while others connect the custom with the scaring away of evil spirits that on Midsummer eve were supposed to threaten human dwellings.

Midsummer processions, in which artificial giants figured prominently, were formerly common in England and on the Continent. Belgian giants are preserved in a hall in Antwerp and the last of the English giants survived in the hall of the Tailors' Company at Salisbury until 1844.

The custom, not yet extinct in Britain, of gathering on Midsummer eve for house decoration white lilies, sprigs of S. John's wort, long fennel, various wild flowers and branches of birch appears to be a relic of the belief that houses had to be charmed against the spells of witches and the visits of evil beings. On the Continent, too, this practice is still well known. It is emphasised, however, that those particular qualities imparted on S. John's eve are not permanent, but pass to other plants and flowers at other seasons. 'S. John's herb' is popular in France and it is usually tied up in bouquets with white lilies and other flowers for Midsummer house decoration. In Tirol garlands are made of wild flowers and suspended from windows, or fixed upon the roofs of houses, so that all evil may be kept at a distance. According to folk-belief in some parts of Germany, Midsummer eve is the best time for the plucking of curative herbs. S. John's wort is in great favour, and is said never to be lacking in any collection made by rural folk who keep alive ancient customs and beliefs. Love divination by means of Midsummer flowers and herbs is practised in Estonia. Garlands are also hung inside houses 'to scare away evil spirits.' Swedish girls place herbs and flowers under their pillows so as to dream of their future husbands.

Almost everywhere in Europe it is believed that very special virtues are possessed by mugwort (Artemisia vulgaris) gathered on Midsummer eve. It is supposed to cure a great variety of diseases, and not only to protect an individual against disease, but to prevent him or her from growing weary at a task or during a journey. Houses in which the mugwort is suspended are supposed to be charmed against ill luck. The widespread fame acquired by this plant is emphasised when we find that the Chinese still perpetuate their ancient recorded custom of making dolls of mugwort and suspending them over house entrances 'to expel poisonous airs or influences,' that is, 'bad luck.'

According to folk-belief, the magical qualities credited to various forms of vegetation collected on Midsummer eve, or on Midsummer morning just as day breaks, are supposed to come from the sun, which as it retreats immediately after the summer solstice, is believed to shed like honey-dew certain virtues beneficial to mankind.

TATTOOING AND ITS SIGNIFICANCE

Apart from the purely ornamental aspect of body-marking, concerning which further information is contained in the chapter on Strange Ideals of Personal Beauty, the motives underlying the practice touch many sides of primitive thought. Some of these are referred to in such chapters as Initiation and other Ceremonies of Puberty, Totems and Totemism, and Distinctions of Rank.

NOWADAYS, when the schoolboy, the sailor and sometimes the man of fashion has symbols or pictures punctured on his skin, he usually regards the process as an ornamental one. If you are romantically inclined you may have your coat of arms tattooed between your shoulders, or the mark of membership in 'the Black Bandits of Balham' on your forearm if you happen to be in your first decade, or perhaps you prick your sweetheart's initials over your heart. But this is not to say that you do so for ornamental reasons. You want to identify yourself with something, with your family fame, with your 'band,' with a sweetheart, a friend, or an ideal.

That is, roughly, the reason why the savage tattoos. The ornament involved is, with him, only a secondary affair. He thinks the operation makes him into an individual, and that it guards him from evil. The odd thing is that until quite recently the great mass of educated people looked upon tattooing as the doubtful and meaningless privilege either of the barbarian, the vagabond or the man with low-caste ideas—as a thing most well-brought-up and decent citizens eschewed.

But primitive man's main reason for tattooing himself is capable of being subdivided into quite a number of intentions. For him it has a very real significance beyond making him a mere perambulating picture gallery which may attract attention and gain him fame as a local beau, although that is certainly a part of his desire. The real and underlying meanings of tattooing are either religious, magical, or social. The Naga of Assam believe that tattoo marks are useful as an identification in the spirit world, a means by which not only will the gods know their chosen people, but husband and wife will recognize each other in the hereafter. Some Polynesians used to have the figures of their patron gods tattooed on their bodies, and Ainu women still mark themselves to look like the goddess Aioina. The Indian Brahman paints the marks of Vishnu or Siva on his forehead, and dark-skinned Mahomedans, on whom a tattoo mark would scarcely be seen, gash themselves on the cheek in imitation of the Prophet, who first did so.

These are, of course, strictly religious 'signatures,' but similar designs are employed for magical purposes. Some people have talismans or charms tattooed on various parts of the body to keep away pain, the Malays paint themselves black, white and red to avert cholera, and body-marking to bring good luck is fairly common, children often being painted with symbols of happy omen soon after birth. Again, body-markings for tribal or social purposes are widely spread: they identify the person as a member of the community, and without them he would be an outcast and of no account in the clan, either in this world or the next.

BEFORE pursuing this part of the subject farther, let us glance at the technique and method of the art itself. That it developed from face or body painting we can hardly doubt. Prehistoric man, judging from his remains, painted the bones of his dead a brilliant red to give them the colour of life and induce the vitality needed for a future existence. That he painted his face and body in a similar way is probable, and the habits of primitive people to-day support this view. The North American Indian, for example, even though he tattoos freely, among certain tribes, has never lost the art of face-painting, which may therefore be tentatively regarded as the basis of tattooing, a more permanent form of body-marking.

Patterns evidently of an elementary character are to be found among the Andaman Islanders, a people long separated from others. But, gradually, a symmetrical system appears to have been developed among more advanced communities. These pass from a mere haphazard collection of dots and lines, as found among the Australian blacks, to the more intricate patterns of the African Bushongo, which reveal spirals and swastika shapes, the quite elaborate markings

D. A. Mackenzie

MAORI TATTOO FACE DESIGN

The Maoris of New Zealand brought the art of tattooing to a very high pitch of excellence. The face was the part most decorated, the designs being largely built up on the basis of the spiral.

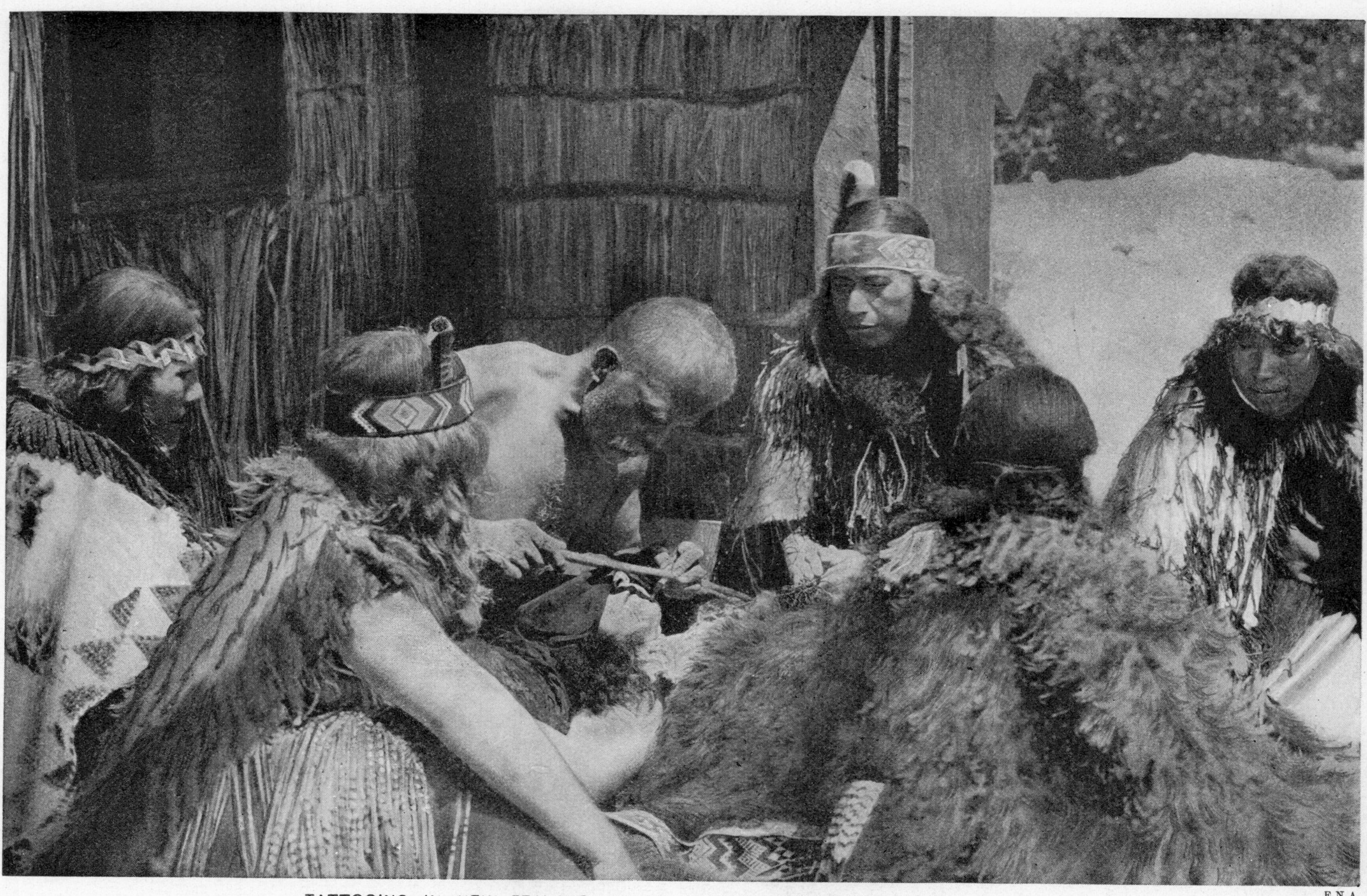

E.N.A.

TATTOOING IN NEW ZEALAND: MAORI WOMAN SUFFERS FOR BEAUTY'S SAKE

Few races of mankind have practised tattooing in so thorough a fashion as the Maoris. The faces and bodies of their warriors were positively trenched with grooves made by the tattooing needle, and nearly every man in former days submitted to the operation. Nowadays it is the women only that are so decorated, and that only in certain districts, more particularly the Bay of Plenty coast, the Arawa-Taupo country, and the Urewera country. The young Arawa woman here seen is having her chin and lips tattooed. She rests her head on the operator's knee, and is blindfolded so that she may not flinch. The tattooer first draws the pattern, and then follows the design with his needle. The result of such an operation is shown in the opposite page.

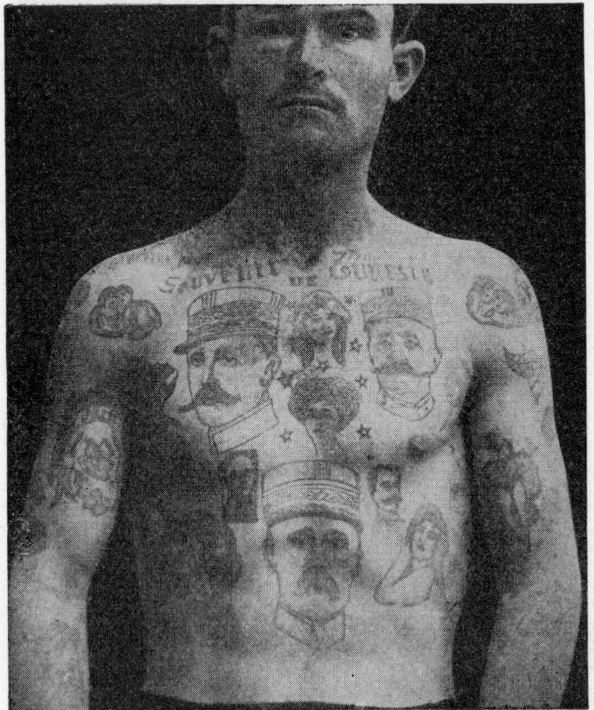

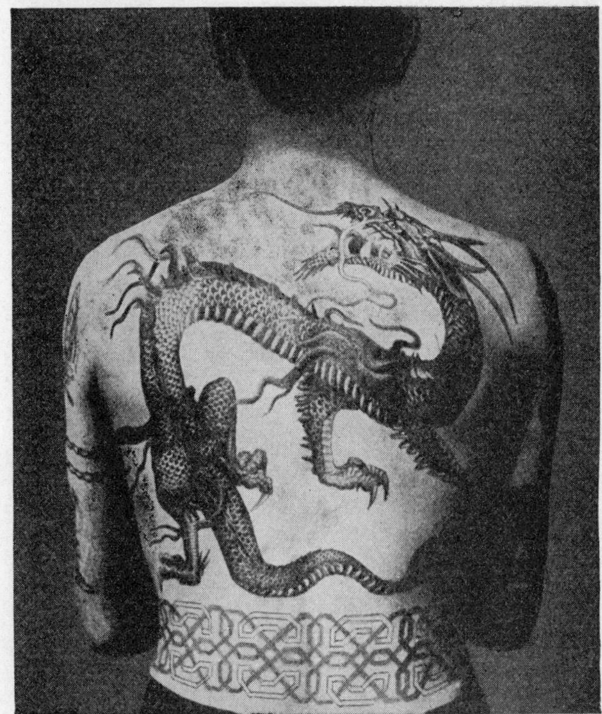

S. & G. and Ashton Wolfe

HUMAN CANVASES DECORATED WITH WARRIORS, WOMEN AND A DRAGON

The Japanese are the supreme masters of the art of tattooing. They execute most intricate patterns in blue, red and yellow on a background of varying shades of blue, conveying values, perspective, and the idea of motion with consummate skill. Their high imaginative power finds expression in the production of fabulous monsters, such as the dragon (right), which is a stereotyped design. The extraordinary tattooing on a member of the Foreign Legion (left) shows his ruling passions. Many of his fellows are similarly decorated.

of the people of Borneo, and lastly the very involved designs of the Maoris of New Zealand and the delicate and artistic coloured tattooing of Japan, in which the art reached its height.

With the Borneans we reach a phase in which a beautiful symmetrical arrangement of scroll-work, intermingled with straight lines, reveals the actual beginnings of artistic impulse. The Polynesians and Maoris exhibit a further proficiency in dealing with geometrical figures and a finer balance in the designs with which the cheeks are marked, especially in the wonderful 'Moko' system of the latter, in which the spiral is employed as a basis on which to build up complex ornament. The Maori tattooer first traces the designs in black, and then goes over them with a small adze-shaped needle dipped in red ochre. Some of the patterns employed would have been difficult to attain even with perfect mathematical instruments, and the 'Moko' system frequently results in giving the Maori women the appearance of wearing a close-fitting chintz dress, so fine and involved is its intricate tracery.

The Samoan tattooing, still extensively practised, is a symmetrical arrangement of lines, dots, arrow-heads and stars, the combinations of which are almost inexhaustible. It is usually effected on the inner side of the thigh, but often follows the curves of the whole body, and may be regarded as the development of an independent school of the art. A common pattern is like the crown of a palm tree,

Wide World Photos

GILDING THE LILY WITH TATTOOING

The tattooing on the face of this high-born Maori lady is effective by its very simplicity. Such complicated designs as that shown in page 437 demand great skill, particularly in view of the fact that no preliminary sketches were used, the pattern being traced freehand.

springing from the centre of the back and curving round both sides.

Natural objects are frequently shown in tattooing—animals, birds and fishes—and perhaps the plainest examples of such a system are those current among the Haida Indians of the Queen Charlotte Islands, off the coast of north-west Canada. Often these are highly conventionalised, but bears, frogs and the squid are the favourite designs, doubtless the emblems of tribal totems or patrons. The people of the Torres Straits and the Tamils of Ceylon also employ naturalistic body-markings.

Burma and Japan have produced types of tattooing so superior to all others that they rise quite out of the aboriginal class of art. In Burma the artist uses an implement a couple of feet long, weighted at the top with an image of Buddha, and with its point divided into four fine needles, so made as to retain coloured stains. Opium is first administered to the subject, and the work is accomplished with marvellous celerity, a dozen figures often being laid on within an hour.

The Japanese tattooer outlines his designs with a camel's hair brush and then pricks them in with an instrument ending in a number of needles, which vary in length and shape with the nature of the picture to be made. For blue, Indian ink is used, and ordinary vermilion, yellow and madder are employed. Like his Burmese colleague, the Japanese tattooer works at an extraordinary rate, and seldom draws blood. In Japan the process is nowadays almost entirely ornamental, although it may have some lingering magical meaning, as the favourite designs, dragons and other fabulous animals, seem to indicate.

R. Dykes, F.R.P.S.

ARTISTIC SCARRING ON A CONGO CHIEF'S FACE

Apart from its purely ornamental aspect, tattooing may have social, religious, or magical significance, according to the country in which it is practised and the age at which it is performed. The Congo provides examples of cicatrisation carried to a fine art, as is here seen on the face of Chief Ebaka of the Bapoto, a Bantu tribe dwelling along the middle Congo.

As face-painting, an important type of body-marking, is chiefly in use among the American Indians, a short account of it as employed by them must suffice as generally descriptive of the art. They take little account of the natural divisions of the face, and surround the eyes with regular coloured circles, while from the mouth yellow or black stripes seem to issue. The cheeks are often covered with a semicircle of green dots, and the forehead is covered with parallel lines. Frequently they divide the face into two halves, one being painted black or blue and the other a light colour, yellow, red or white. One side will be crossed with thick lines, daubed on by hand, while the other is painted in arabesque with the aid of a brush. At other times the face is divided into upper and lower sections, the former being dark-coloured and the remainder light. That the significance of these symbols has been long lost is proved by the statement made frequently that it is 'a mere matter of taste,' like the designs in wampum work on moccasins or pouches. Formerly, however, the system was certainly ceremonial and significant.

Mondiale

SCARS TO INDICATE HER TRIBE

One of the functions of cicatrisation is to show tribal and clan distinctions, as in Africa and Australia. The marks used may have been adapted from the shape or markings of animals found in the districts. The photograph shows an Azarde woman of Yambio, in the Sudan, with tribal marks.

Quite as interesting as the art itself are the ideas which underlie it. We have already seen that tattooing has not only a religious but a magical and social significance. The North American Indian believed that after death he would be halted on the way by guardian spirits and searched for his tattoo marks to discover if he were in communion with his tribal or patron deity. Some women in the south of India think that their tutelary god will beat them should they die without his symbol on their bodies, and the Ainu woman fears the process will be carried out in the Otherworld should she neglect it here.

Among the Red Men of North America the ceremonial use of body paint was taught by gods and culture-heroes, and Pawnee babies are still dedicated to the sky god by painting their little bodies. The Polynesians and Samoans preserve legends of the divine origin of tattooing, and in Formosa, and formerly among the Maoris, it was a necessary adjunct to priesthood. That many aspects of body-marking were and are totemic, that is, associated with the tribal sacred animal, there is plenty of proof, especially in North America and Australia.

Very important is the significance of tattooing with reference to the puberty, marriage and fertility of women. Among the hill tribes of Fiji a girl was compelled to fast for twelve hours, to search all night for prawns (perhaps symbolical of the sharp spines used in the process), and to secure three lemon thorns for the tattooing instrument employed by the wise women. Among some South American tribes the ritual is most elaborate. In most African tribes

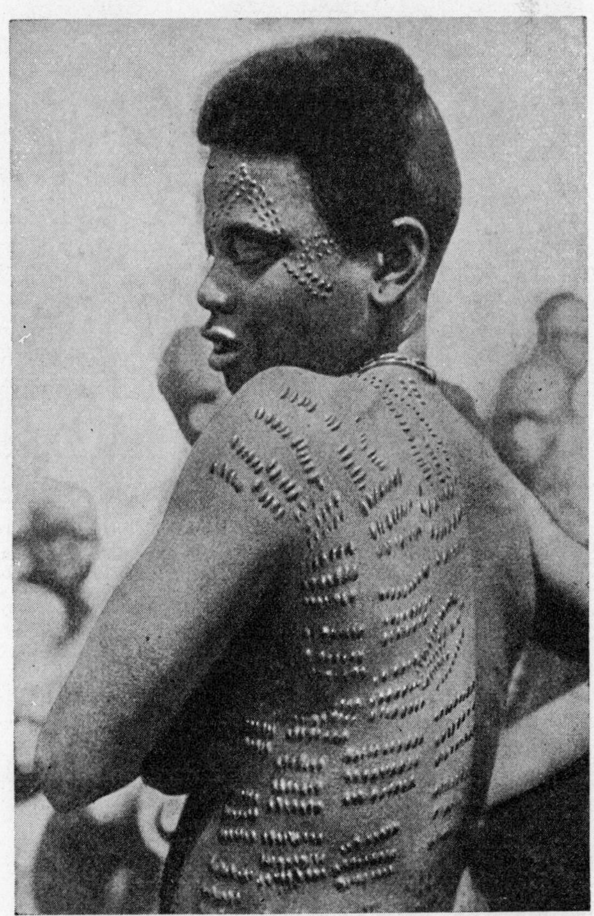

Domville Fyfe

ADORNMENT FOR YOUTHFUL VANITY

Among the Nuer, a Nilotic negro tribe of marsh-dwellers of the Bahr-el-Ghazal province of the Sudan, dwelling between the Shilluk and the Dinka, tribal marks are tattooed on the forehead. The elaborate arrangement of scars on the back and shoulders of this Nuer boy are for ornament.

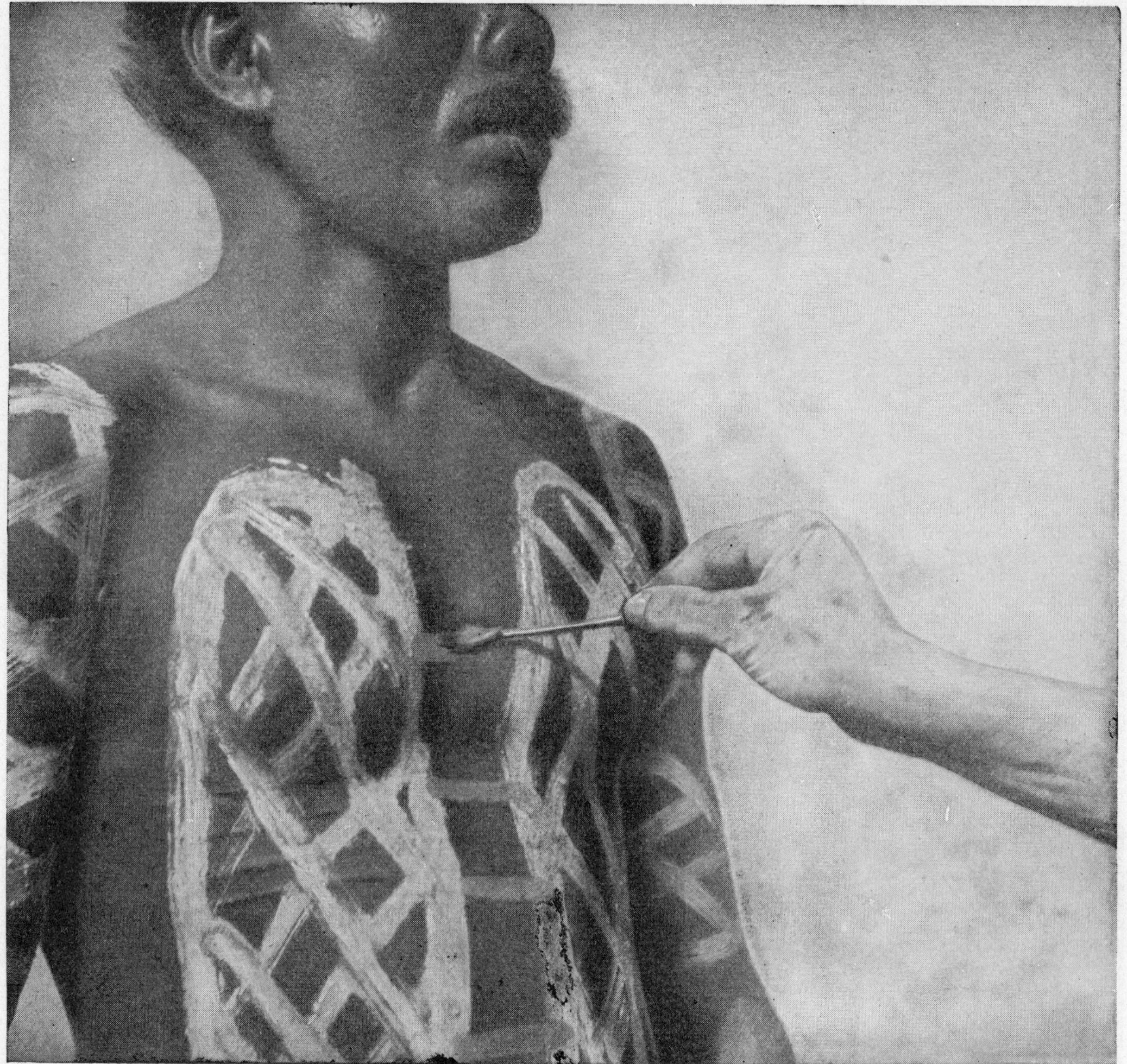

E. O. Hoppé

AGE-OLD FORM OF BODY DECORATION ON AUSTRALIAN NATIVE OF TODAY

The practice of painting the body and face has come down from very early times. In caves in western Europe have been found hollowed-out stones, which were not improbably used by prehistoric man for grinding coloured clays for body-painting. Nowadays this kind of decoration is employed for a variety of purposes—religious, magical, social, tribal, totemic. Tattooing, a more lasting form of marking, probably developed from body-painting. The Australian aborigines afford ample illustration of body-painting as practised by primitive peoples.

girls must be scarified or cicatrised on the back and loins before marriage. The chin tattooing of women has a very wide range, and probably has a sex significance.

From the social point of view, tattooing is employed as a distinctive tribal or clan mark. The theory has been advanced that man, seeing certain animals marked alike by stripes or spots, adopted similar stigmata. Whether the hypothesis be correct or otherwise, the fact remains that among many tribes to-day a man is not considered a member of the community unless he be marked with its particular symbols or tokens, and with certain primitive peoples it is even a 'class affair,' the rank or caste of an individual being indicated by his or her body-markings. Savage man also tattoos, gashes, and paints himself as a sign of mourning, or to placate the angry spirits of the dead.

But tattooing has also a curative or medical and protective significance for primitive peoples. It is used as a charm against the evil eye, as a cure for defective eyesight and for rheumatism, and as a defence against the weapons of enemies. Many semi-civilized and low-caste whites also use it to express crude emotions, such as sentimental love-affairs, or old friendships. The picture of a sweetheart or of 'my dear old pal so-and-so' is no uncommon device adopted by sailors and navvies today. After all, the desire to possess a readily portable and ineffaceable picture of a person one loves is a very human

E. O. Hoppé

ABORIGINAL DANCERS GETTING THEMSELVES READY FOR A CORROBBOREE

Among the aborigines of Australia body-painting is used in connexion with totemic ceremonies, rain making, and other ritual practices. At the yearly ceremony for producing fecundity among kangaroos men of the kangaroo totem paint their bodies with alternate red and yellow stripes, in imitation of the shape of the animal. At their corrobborees Australian blackfellows depict scenes of tribal history, war or the chase with their skins painted with stripes arranged in awe-inspiring patterns.

Domville Fyfe

GOSSAMER OF TATTOOING HER ONLY GARMENT

In the Amazon region tattooing, painting and cicatrisation of the body and face are common. The Indians here seen belong to the Putumayo river district. Note the elaborate tattooing on the girl's body and also the bandages on her leg, to develop the calf.

aspiration and scarcely to be ridiculed, as it indicates true warmth of feeling. Whether the sentiment be a passing one, or the permanent results are found to be inconvenient in later circumstances, is altogether another matter.

The therapeutic or health-protecting nature of some tattooing or body-painting processes, the application of these to avoid or lessen pain, has been widely observed. When the Andaman Islander has taken a too full meal of turtle he paints himself with olive-coloured clay in order to lessen the bilious effects of the surfeit, the spirits of evil being prevented from smelling the savour of the turtle by the earthy application. The Sarawaks of Borneo formerly bound a palm leaf round the wrist 'to keep the soul in the body,' but as this was apt to fall off, they now tattoo the semblance of a leaf round the wrist, and this practice may explain the adoption of many such symbols in tattooing. The Ainu of Sakhalin tattoo smallpox marks on their bodies so that the smallpox demon will conclude they have already had the disease. Tattooing and scarification appear to have some association with therapeutic blood-letting, but precisely what the connexion may be is obscure. But scarification was probably practised for the purpose of 'letting out' disease.

We see, therefore, that the practice of marking the body by means of paint, tattooing or scarification had its origin in ideas of life, fertility and preservation after death, that it was associated with fertility cults and puberty initiation and thus with the notion of human reproduction. The main idea was to protect or insure life, either by marking the body with the protective symbol of a patron deity or with the symbols of life and fertility. The more definite and conventional these markings were, the more assured of existence and fortune was their wearer, and this gave him a certain social prestige—or perhaps persons of social position were the favoured wearers of these symbols.

As regards the origin of the practice, that is undoubtedly very ancient, figurines bearing tattoo-marks having been discovered in Egypt and Sumeria. Nay, tattooing is almost certainly to be recognized in the weird conventionalised engraving on ivory of a woman, found at Predmost, in Bavaria, and of late Palaeolithic (Solutrean) age. In Europe the Pictish tribes of Gaul and Britain were known to the Romans as ardent practitioners of tattooing, and in one Roman poem the symbolical figure of Britannia is described as wearing a wolf-skin and with face tattooed. The Maya of Central America and the ancient Mexicans tattooed and painted their faces and bodies, as did the Incas of Peru.

The probability is, so far as the evidence goes, that the custom had its origin in a North African fertility cult in prehistoric times, and that it spread to Egypt, India, and thence to Polynesia on the east in the course of ages, and thence to America, and on the west to Gaul and Britain, which had trading and racial connexions with North Africa and Spain at an early period, at least 2000 B.C. Indeed, the practice in Europe may well have originated among the prehistoric Aurignacians of the Biscay region in Spain, who were probably immigrants from North Africa, and whose beliefs and culture-complex show them to have conceived at a very remote time an entire system of ceremonial burial and preservation of human bones in view of a future existence.

THE MEANING OF THE COUVADE

THE subject of this chapter is one of the most curious in the history of sex psychology. To the primitive mind it is important that the father should pretend to play the maternal part at childbirth, since he is better fitted than the mother to combat the influences of evil spirits at such a critical time. Other avoidances and prohibitions are dealt with in the chapter on the Mysteries of Taboo.

PERHAPS no custom known to man, whether savage or semi-civilized, holds so much of the spirit of ancient magic or appears so fantastic to enlightened eyes as that which anthropologists have labelled ' the couvade,' in which men actually mimic motherhood for a season. The word is derived from the French ' couver,' ' to hatch,' but the custom has perhaps never existed under this or any other name in France.

It had been known for generations that among primitive peoples in many parts of the world it was usual for a father to take to his bed at the birth of a child and submit to certain restrictions of food and treatment. In its perfect form the husband behaves as if he had been confined and was ' lying in,' while the wife goes about her usual duties as soon as possible after delivery. The practice, in one form or another, is to be found in South America, among the Californian Indians, in Southern India, in Malabar, the Nicobars, in Celebes, and among the Dyaks of Borneo, while it also prevailed, according to Diodorus Siculus, among the ancient Corsicans, and, we are assured by Apollonius Rhodius, among the Iberians of northern Spain. The frequently quoted statement that it was practised by the Basque population in the south of France appears to have no very trustworthy authority behind it.

The belief prevails among primitive peoples that the conduct of the parents both before and after birth affects the child. Should either the father or mother partake of the flesh of certain animals, the characteristics of these animals, it is thought, will be transmitted to the infant. For example, the Hottentots believe that if a pregnant woman eat lion's or leopard's flesh the child will acquire the courage and ferocity of these animals.

MOREOVER, a spiritual bond is assumed between the child and its parents, and this idea is strengthened by the doctrine of contact which plays so large a part in savage philosophy. Among the Andaman Islanders a pregnant woman must abstain from eating pork, turtle and the iguana, as their flesh is esteemed unsuitable to children for divers reasons. In some cases, among the Malays, for example, the woman is regarded as ' unclean ' after parturition for forty-four days (perhaps two ' moons '), and this taboo is also placed upon the husband, who may not shave his head or engage in the chase during the prescribed period.

The most elaborate example of the couvade known is perhaps that to be encountered among the Indians of Guiana. The woman pursues her tasks as usual until within a few hours of delivery, when she goes to the forest, accompanied by other women, and there the child is born. Little the worse for her ordeal, she rises in an hour or two, and carries on with her household tasks. But the father takes to his hammock, and is refused his ordinary nourishment, being allowed only a little cassava gruel, nor may he smoke or wash himself. He is nursed ceremoniously by the women of the tribe for days or even weeks. Among the Panes of Brazil he paints himself black and remains fasting in his hammock until the umbilical cord of the child has fallen off. In Celebes and among the Indians of California he is actually attended to by his wife from the moment after her recovery.

IN Southern India when the woman knows herself to be on the point of delivery she tells her husband, who dresses himself in some of her clothes, paints the sex-mark of the woman on his forehead, and retires to a darkened room, where he takes to his bed. As soon as the infant is born it is washed and laid beside the father, who is dosed with drugs appropriate to female recovery. While the period of ceremonial uncleanness lasts the man is treated according to the code laid down for the treatment of women on such occasions.

Those who study the habits of primitive peoples have divided couvade customs into two classes, which sometimes fuse or combine, but which are nevertheless essentially distinct. The first is of widespread acceptance, and has already been alluded to as associated with the idea that the parents must avoid certain foods and acts for fear of injuring the child before or after birth. For instance, a prospective Carib father must not eat the flesh of the dugong or sea-cow lest his child should be born with little round eyes like it. But, even so, this is by no means the full explanation of the couvade, but merely of that part of it which is founded on the notion that what is or has been in contact with a person retains that connexion in a material form, and that sympathetic influence is thus maintained between them. Sometimes this influence is carried so far that, as among the Chiriguanos, not only the father, but the other children lie in and fast at the time of birth.

The other side of couvade custom is that associated with the actual substitution of the man for the woman. The simulation by the father of the mother's part is really the essence of the custom The period of birth is one of peril, especially from evil spirits, which lie in wait to harm both mother and child, and as savage man is the natural protector of his womenkind and children, he takes upon himself the duty

E.N.A.

INDIANS OF BRAZIL WHO OBSERVE THE COUVADE

The curious custom of the couvade, in which at childbirth the father simulates the maternal condition, is found among the Indians of South America, the Californian Indians, on the Malabar coast, in Celebes and elsewhere. Among the Panes of Brazil, a group of whom is seen here, the father paints himself black and takes to his hammock.

of guarding them against the unseen agencies of evil. He defends both mother and infant by pretending to be the mother. If he acts as the woman of the house, and if his wife refrains from drawing attention to herself, but proceeds with her ordinary duties, he thinks, evil spirits or forces will be deceived, and concentrate upon himself. But instead of a weak woman, prone to magical influences, they will have to deal with a hale and healthy man, a veritable 'changeling,' who succeeds in bringing their devilries to naught, affording an opportunity for natural recovery to the woman and for normal and unhindered thriving to the infant.

PARALLEL customs are not unknown. Thus in certain East Central African tribes another woman pretends to be the expectant mother, dressing up for the part, in order that the spirits may be deceived. In the Watubella Islands when the wife's delivery is retarded some of her husband's garments are placed beneath her to render the process more easy, the idea being that the man's vigour is transmitted to the woman from the clothes he wears. In Central Australia, in similar circumstances, the husband's girdle is tied round the woman's breasts, and the husband parades past the woman's camp to induce the child to follow him! In ancient Mexico wristlets of ocelot skin were tied round the wrists of a woman in labour in order to give her the courage of the animal, and in China the father's trousers are hung up in the birth chamber in order to deflect any evil agency to them instead of to the child.

Evil spirits are regarded by primitive people as easily tricked and befooled. Sometimes, as with the Babar Islanders, the parents change their names at the birth of their first child, and in some tribes the parents are actually called after the first child in order to deceive the demons.

Long spells of food taboo must be undergone by some peoples before the birth of their children, and among the Dyaks this is gradually increased during the last month. Nor may either parent go near a fire, lest the child be born spotted. They may not eat fruit lest the infant have colic, may not bore holes in wood for fear that it be born blind, nor bathe in deep water in case it be suffocated before it is born. In New Guinea the father must abstain from eating any animal with protruding teeth, or the babe will certainly grow such teeth later on. In short, there is no end to the fantastic notions of correspondence entertained by the savage mind in this connexion. These may be partially illustrated by the modern proverb: 'Show me what a man eats and I will tell you what he is.'

That some primitive superstitions connected with childbirth have persisted to our own time is proved by the widespread belief that certain days are regarded as lucky or the reverse as birthdays, a subject that is pursued further in our chapter on Lucky and Unlucky Days. Sunday is thought to be peculiarly fortunate, as being a day on which evil spirits might not prevail against the infant. The belief, prevalent in Germany, that a child born in leap year is fated to die soon, and that its mother is not exempt from a like chance, is associated with the notion that evil agencies have peculiar and heightened power in such a year, and especially on February 29, a 'saintless' or unprotected day. Extraordinary precautions were formerly taken against the evil eye. In the Highlands of Scotland the child was 'sained' or charmed against evil by being sprinkled with water in which a gold and a silver coin had been placed, and ash sap was given it as a preventive against the powers of darkness. The common belief, too, frequently entertained by pregnant women, often by no means ignorant, that their children may be born with certain blemishes or in the likeness of some monstrosity they have seen or dreamed of, is an obvious folk-memory of the ancient superstitions induced by the practices associated with couvade.

WEDDINGS AMONG EASTERN PEOPLES

MARRIAGE in general is discussed in the chapter on the Various Forms of Marriage, while specific aspects are treated under Polygamy and Polyandry, Customs Connected with Divorce and others. Wedding ceremonies are considered in groups, as in the present chapter dealing with Asiatic peoples. Other chapters cover Africa and Oceania, and a series of chapters is devoted to Europe.

MARRIAGES in Eastern lands are not, as is generally the case among ourselves, the unions of couples inspired by mutual love, but rather family alliances which have been arranged by parents. Nor is sex equality similarly recognized. Eastern marriage customs emphasise that the male sex is superior to the female, and that a wife must be subordinate to a husband. In some cases the law may be said to be almost neutral, recognizing the right of a couple to terminate a union with the freedom that they have effected it. The part played by religion is likewise different. An Eastern wedding ceremony is not necessarily one of religious character. It may dispense with the assistance of the clergy, or simply permit their co-operation in a formal way before and after the union. Domestic religious rites may be performed instead by the individuals immediately concerned.

At the same time, marriage in the East generally is regarded as a religious as well as a social necessity. In southern India, for instance, much concern is felt among a people like the Tangalān Paraiyans if a young man should die unmarried. Before his body is buried or cremated a mimic marriage takes place to remove the disability of bachelorhood. This ceremony is performed in a 'marriage booth,' the corpse, with a garland of flowers round its neck, being united to an image or symbol of a bride. The importance of marriage is equally recognized in Korea, where a young man has no social standing until he is married. As long as he remains single he is a nondescript and the inferior of a wedded male of his own age or even one younger. He has no social position; he wears the garb of a juvenile, and his long hair is parted in the middle and pleated at the back, even although he should reach the age of twenty. When, however, he marries he assumes the black hat and long coat of manhood and has his hair cropped and arranged in the characteristic 'top knot,' while the equivalent of our 'Mr.' is added to his name. The Korean marriage is thus an initiation into manhood.

Sport & General

HINDU BRIDAL PAIR BY SACRED FIRE

When a Hindu bridegroom takes his bride from her father's house to his own, the sacred fire that has figured in the marriage ceremony goes with the couple, to serve as the domestic fire. Should it ever be allowed to go out, an act of expiation must be performed.

GIRLS in Korea who belong to the higher classes live secluded lives after reaching the age of seven. It is regarded as a scandal if one is not married before twenty. The girl has no say in the choice of a husband. One may be selected for her when she is yet of tender years, and the only right she can exercise is to decline to marry before she is sixteen. There is no betrothal ceremony, no dowry, and no bride-purchase payment. When a marriage is arranged by a go-between, who acts as a 'match-maker,' the formal consent of the bridegroom's father is signified by his sending a present of silk to the prospective bride. This, the first part of the wedding ceremony, is reminiscent of the ancient custom of marriage by capture. The present of silk is conveyed by a party of men armed with staves and carrying lanterns. Near the house of the girl's father they are met by another armed party, representing the bride, and a scuffle ensues which is sometimes so realistic that injuries are sustained on both sides.

On the night before the wedding religious ceremonies are performed at the ancestral tablets in the houses of both bridegroom and bride, the aim being to inform the ancestors regarding the impending union. Next morning the bridegroom and his attendants, including one attired in red and carrying a goose and another with a white

umbrella, proceed to the house of the bride's father. There the goose is formally presented as a symbol of conjugal fidelity on the part of the bride. It is on this visit that the young man sees his future wife for the first time and is married to her. She is carried out to the veranda in her elaborate wedding attire, but no conversation takes place, or is, indeed, possible. A taboo of silence must be observed by the bride, and she must not even see her ' lover.' Her eyelids are kept closed with an adhesive mixture and her face covered over with white powder and spotted with rouge.

The marriage ceremony itself is of brief and simple character ; the bridegroom bows four times and the bride, as prompted, bows twice. Then a cup

Ewing Galloway

WEDDING DAYS IN INDIA: HINDU BRIDEGROOM AND MOSLEM BRIDE

When the wedding morning arrives the Hindu bridegroom is carried (top) to the house of his bride, whence, after the performance of various ceremonies and the presentation of gifts to the parents, he takes her to their future home. The degree of pomp attending this journey depends upon the social status of the groom. If he is of high rank the litter and its bearers will be correspondingly magnificent. The trappings of the wedding horse in a Moslem ceremony (below) are as gorgeous as the silks and velvets in which this bride is swathed

of wine is presented to the bridegroom, who moistens his lips, after which the bride takes a sip from the same cup. A feast of sweetmeats follows, the bridegroom partaking of a little in a room along with the male wedding guests. Meanwhile, the bride has been taken to one of the female apartments. Next day the bride, with her eyelids again gummed together, is conveyed to the house of the bridegroom's father, to be formally presented in her wedding attire to her father-in-law and mother-in-law. Thereafter, she is taken back to her father's house, where her eyelids are opened and her face cleansed of powder and rouge. In the evening her young husband arrives, but he returns to his father's house next morning.

This coming and going continues for three days, after which the bride is carried to her future home and across its threshold. The taboo of silence is still maintained and may not be broken for some weeks. For a still longer period the young wife does not speak to her father-in-law, or even lift her eyes in his presence. A cloud of inferiority hangs over her until the end of her days. Among the poorer classes the wife begins to work, not only as housewife, but perhaps as the 'bread-earner,' soon after marriage.

Ewing Galloway

QUEER HOBBY HORSES FOR AN INDIAN PROCESSION

A wedding procession in India is a striking spectacle. If the parties are wealthy, richly caparisoned elephants, horses, and even camels may further contribute to the gorgeousness of the scene. As in most Oriental pageantry, however, there may be an element of tawdriness, such gaudy 'hobby horses' as those seen here often figuring in Indian wedding processions.

ONE of the results of the adoption of European customs in Japan is the introduction of the temple wedding. The contracting parties and their guests assemble in the sacred house of Amaterāsu, the sun-goddess, where the Shinto priests in their white robes invoke not only the solar deity, but Izanagi and Izanami, the creator deities, who at the beginning, according to Shinto mythology, descended from the sky-world to the first island and, having there set up a central house-pillar, walked round it in opposite directions to meet face to face and take one another as man and wife. The old-fashioned house wedding is still, however, observed, the temple ceremony being really an elaboration of it, preserving its essential ritual.

As in Korea, a 'match-maker' arranges a union by visiting the parents on both sides. Then an interview, called mi-ai ('seeing') takes place, the young couple being introduced in a house, a theatre, or flower garden, or at a picnic. In theory the young man accepts or rejects the prospective bride, but she herself has no choice. The parents subsequently discuss the business aspect of the proposed union, and then there is a formal betrothal called yuinō and an exchange of presents. A fortune-teller is consulted, and he fixes a 'lucky day' for the wedding ceremony. Three days before the marriage the bride's party convey to her future home those household articles a wife is expected to provide, including linen, silk, bedding material, her wardrobe, cabinets, writing tables, kitchen utensils, and so on.

Wide World Photos

SEQUENCE OF CEREMONIES IN A MARRIAGE IN THE PHILIPPINE ISLANDS

The Moros of the Philippine Islands, once notorious head-hunters and slave traders, are Mahomedans. They live in the island of Mindanao and in the Sulu archipelago, chiefly in villages built on piles, and are the most distinctively Malay people in the Philippines. Moro men are here seen (top) going to fetch a bridegroom, who has to be brought by them to the bride's house. Women are bringing a bridesmaid (centre) into the bride's home. On the nuptial bed (bottom) are seen a bridesmaid and her family. The bed is decorated with the dowry—coins and paper money.

Wide World Photos

MORO BRAVE AND HIS BRIDE AFTER THE WEDDING CEREMONY

At a Moro wedding the ceremonial costume of the bridegroom is put on over his ordinary clothes. It includes a gauze shirt and trousers and a silk skirt. Two ribbons, one embroidered with gold and the other with silver, cross his breast and back and encircle his waist. The priest puts five large rings on the fingers and thumb of the groom's right hand. The bride has her face painted white. On entering she turns her back on the groom and sits down, the groom sitting down behind her. She then rises, turns towards the groom, and sits down again.

American Field Museum, Washington

MARRIAGE CEREMONIES, SIMPLE AND COMPLICATED IN THE DUTCH EAST INDIES

In the middle of Java are two autonomous states, Soerakarta and Jokjokarta, in which a medieval etiquette is still kept up. The rulers of these old-world kingdoms exert their sway under Dutch Residents. The upper photograph shows a prince of the blood royal of Soerakarta on his way to the court, where the marriage rite is performed by the high priest in all its elaboration of traditional ceremonial. Below is seen a simpler marriage ceremony in Dutch Borneo, in which the central fact is that the bridal couple should squat side by side.

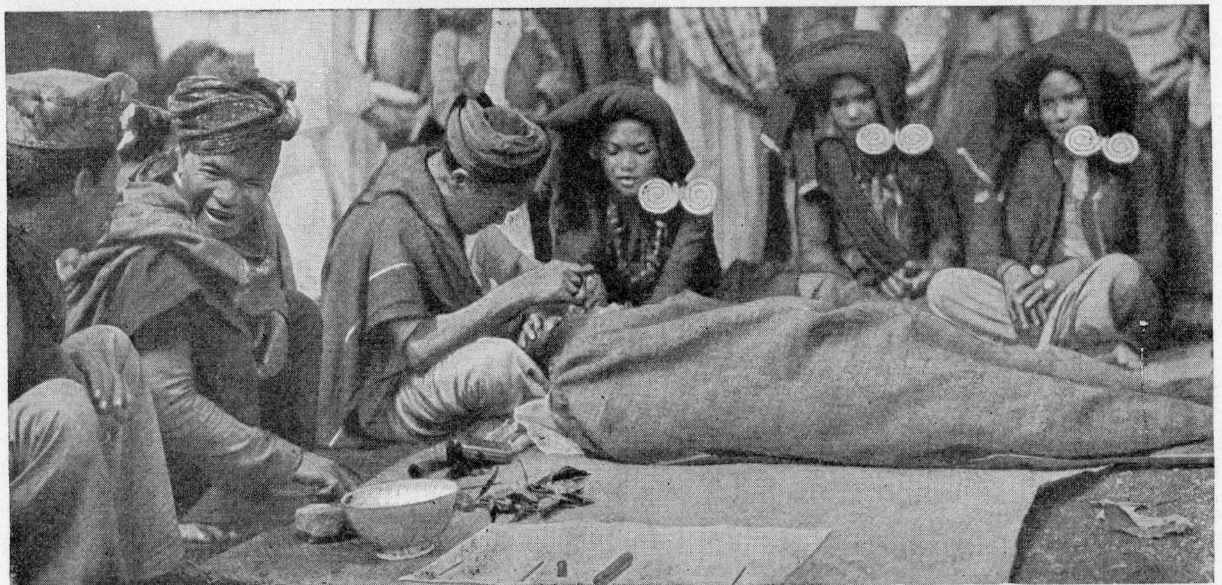

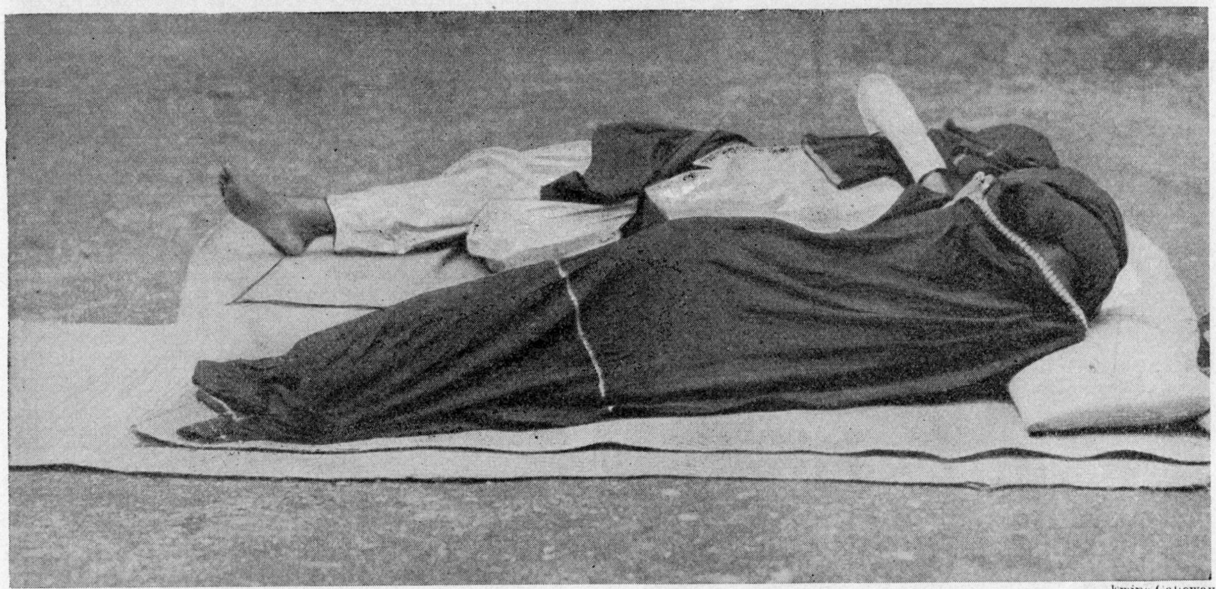

Ewing Galloway

STRANGE PRELIMINARIES TO MARRIAGE IN THE ISLANDS OF SUMATRA AND BALI

Among the mountain peoples of the island of Sumatra many peculiar marriage customs survive. The Minangkabau, for instance, conduct most of their wedding ceremonies in the absence of the bride (see page 37). Part of the marriage rites of the Bataks of north-central Sumatra consists in the bridal couple lying down together in the middle of the village square (bottom), a sort of public siesta to show that they are man and wife. In another of the Dutch East India Islands, Bali, young men have their teeth filed (top) before they can marry.

A touching ceremony on the wedding morning is the bride's formal farewell to her parents. Attired in white, with her hair arranged in virgin fashion, she bows before them, shedding tears. White is the Japanese mourning colour, and symbolises the final departure of the girl from her parents' home. Her father presents to her a short sword for her defence, and when she leaves the house is ceremonially swept and sometimes a bonfire is lit outside. This is a ceremony of purification similar to that which takes place after a corpse is carried out.

The bride is borne to the house of the parents of the bridegroom or, according to the modern fashion, to the Shinto temple where the simple wedding ceremony is performed. In an old-fashioned house wedding there are no bridesmaids. The house is artistically and symbolically decorated. All the flowers have their meanings, those of red being male and those of white female. There must be no purple flowers at a wedding, or branches of willow or other drooping plants. If the bride is being adopted into the bridegroom's family, white is the central line in floral design, and if the bridegroom is adopted into the bride's family, red is the central design. Blossoms or fruits symbolise good wishes and invoke good influences.

The actual wedding ceremony in house or temple is the act of drinking sake, or wine. From three cups

WEDDING COMPLETED BY SHARING A CHAIR
In some rich families of Malaya the nuptial ceremonies last several days. They include and end with the anointing of bride and bridegroom with flower-scented water, the bridal pair, in ceremonial robes, sitting on the same chair on a decorated dais (top).

of different sizes the bride and bridegroom each take three sips in turn, making nine in all. The bride sips first at this preliminary drinking. Thereafter she retires and puts on a coloured dress. The bridegroom also changes, unless he has adopted the European evening dress suit. Then comes the wedding feast, after which the ' match-maker ' and his wife conduct the young couple to the bridal chamber, where the second wine-sipping ceremony takes place. On this occasion, however, the husband drinks first to signify that he has become the lord and master. A formal visit is paid by the young people to the house of the bride's parents either on the day after the wedding or, as the fashion now is, after the honeymoon. If it happens that the bride's parents have no heir, the young husband may be adopted as their son, and reside as such with them.

The terms of a marriage are also arranged by the parents in China, where there is a formal betrothal. If it should chance, however, that one of the contracting parties dies before the day fixed for the wedding a mimic ceremony, similar to that known in southern India, invariably takes place. Should the young man die, the girl is formally married to his ghost, which is represented by the tablet bearing his name in the house-shrine. Thereafter she is regarded as a widow and, as such, becomes a member of the household of her husband. This means that she is little more than the slave of her mother-in-law, a household drudge. Suicides of girls in this sad position are said to be not uncommon.

When, however, in ordinary circumstances, the betrothal is followed by marriage the ceremonial proceedings are somewhat similar to those in Korea and Japan. The young bride is attired in wedding costume of picturesque character with an elaborate head-dress from which dangle strings of gems and jewels, while she wears a long bridal veil and carries a symbolic bouquet of luck-flowers. There is no bridesmaid, but an elderly woman acts as an attendant and guide. If the bride is of high rank she is carried to the house of the bridegroom's parents in a magnificently decorated sedan chair, in which she is completely concealed so that she may be protected from the influence of ' evil eye ' and magical spells. This chair is sent for her by the bridegroom and accompanied by a number of the guests as it is borne shoulder-high by carriers attired in appropriate costumes.

When she arrives at the house in which the wedding ceremony is to take place her first act is to pay ceremonial reverence to the father and mother of the bridegroom, who remain seated. The grandfather and grandmother, if they chance to be alive, are similarly honoured, but if they should be dead, the bride kneels before their memorial tablets. As in Japan and Korea, the actual marriage ceremony consists in drinking liquor from vessels, the bride taking the first sip and then handing the vessel to the bridegroom. The religious aspect of the marriage is, however, emphasised, for the drinking ceremony

E. O. Hoppe

DRUGGED BRIDE OF CELEBES WHOSE FEET MAY NOT TOUCH THE EARTH

The marriage of a daughter is an important event among the Bugis, a semi-civilized Moslem tribe of Celebes. The nuptial ceremony lasts three days, and often the savings of a lifetime are spent on it. Custom ordains that the bride may not raise her eyes or look upon a man until after her marriage, and to ensure observance of this rule she is drugged. In this condition she is carried about, balanced on one shoulder of the head of the family, for another rule is that the bride's feet must not touch the ground during the wedding ceremony.

Ewing Galloway

PROCESSION OF BEARERS OF GIFTS FOR THE BRIDE AT A JAPANESE WEDDING

For centuries the women of Japan, and especially those of the upper classes, were regarded as little more than the servants of their husbands, but of late years Japanese women have been gaining more freedom. Formerly it was not unusual for the bride to see her future husband at the wedding ceremony for the first time. Nowadays, although the marriage negotiations are in theory left in the hands of the parents, the young people have a decided say in the matter. The actual marriage contract is sealed by the ceremonial drinking of nine cups of saké. When the parties are people of quality the bride's presents may include quite large pieces of furniture. These, as well as the smaller gifts, are carried through the streets by long lines of bearers

Topical Press

CHAIR IN WHICH A CHINESE BRIDE IS BORNE UNSEEN TO HER LORD AND MASTER

The widespread custom of concealing the bride from the bridegroom is observed in China. The young man and his parents arrange the marriage with the parents of the bride-to-be, and very often the young couple do not meet until the wedding ceremony. When the bride is conveyed to her future husband's house her face is veiled, and the sedan chair in which she travels is heavily curtained, so that no one can see her. Red is the marriage colour of the Chinese. The veil the bride wears is of red silk, and the wedding chair also is red.

takes place while the young couple adore the tablets of the bridegroom's ancestors and the jade symbols of the sky and the earth. In the marriage ceremony the very amulets and colours worn have a religious significance. Jade is reputed to be composed of yang matter, the source of life and the essence of the sky. The marriage also symbolises the union of the male heaven and the female earth—of yang, the male principle, and yin, the female.

A VARIETY of marriage customs is found in the Philippine Islands. Among the Bagobos the wedding ceremony is performed by the young couple eating rice out of the same dish after offerings have been made to the spirits. The bridegroom's parents, who have arranged the union, make a generous purchase gift to those of the bride, and for some time after the marriage the young husband has to serve his father-in-law without compensation and as a duty. Other Philippine peoples likewise observe the ancient but modified bride-purchase custom and then have a brief marriage ceremony of mutual eating and drinking. Wedding costumes are of simple but picturesque character, the wearing of amulets in the form of necklaces and ear-rings being indispensable.

Moslem influence has elaborated the original marriage ceremony in Java so that there is a mixture of rites. The parents arrange the union, and the principle of bride-purchase survives in the custom of giving special presents to the young girl's parents as well as to herself. On the eve before the wedding the young couple squat side by side, observing a religious vigil to which much importance is attached. Next day the bridegroom, who is ceremonially attired and has his face painted, proceeds to the mosque for the preliminary wedding ceremony, but the bride does not attend, being represented by her father.

Thereafter the bridegroom goes to the home of the bride, and there his young spouse performs the significant ceremony of washing his feet. The young couple are then conveyed to the house of the bridegroom's parents, where a feast is held. Next day they proceed to the house of the bride's parents, and there are entertained to another feast. The young couple go to their new home on the third day. In Formosa, where marriages are arranged by a match-maker and the actual wedding ceremony is one of mutual eating and drinking, the young wife remains in the house of her parents until a child is born, after which she goes to live with her husband.

Keystone

WHERE THE GOOSE IS THE EMBLEM OF FAITHFULNESS IN MARRIAGE

On the morning of his wedding day a bridegroom of Korea sets out for the home of the bride's parents. Here he will see his bride for the first time, and here the marriage ceremony will be carried out. On this journey the bridegroom is mounted, and the men composing his retinue travel on foot. One member of his suite holds a white umbrella, but the most striking object in the little company is a live goose, which is carried by a red-clad attendant. The bird symbolises conjugal fidelity, and is formally handed over when the destination is reached.

If no birth takes place, the union automatically comes to an end.

A Siamese marriage is likewise of very simple character. The wedding guests collect in the house of the bride's parents, and during their eating and drinking the young couple enter. As they kneel together a Buddhist monk formally unites them by making ceremonial use of a sacred cord. Then the guests throw rice over them and sprinkle holy water from shells. The young bride is thereafter conveyed to her room, but her husband is expected to pass the night in the company of serenading musicians, who play selections and sing ditties outside. A feast is held next day, and when darkness comes on the young couple are ceremonially escorted to the bridal chamber. They live together in the house of the bride's parents until a child is born, after which they proceed to their own home.

The marriage of a member of a ruling family in India is accompanied by elaborate ceremony and in accordance with the religious rites of his sect. The Hindu marriage is arranged by the parents, and before the ceremony takes place the near relatives on both sides pay visits to each other's homes to perform acts

Keystone

BRIDE OF KOREA WITH FACE WHITENED AND SPOTTED WITH ROUGE

In Korea a girl is not allowed to choose her future husband. He is always selected for her, sometimes through the medium of a go-between. The bride is not only under a taboo of silence, but in addition she may not look upon the bridegroom. To this end her eyelids are gummed together, both on the day of the marriage ceremony and on the day following. On both days white powder is dusted all over her face, which is further adorned with dabs of rouge. In the photograph the bride's ceremonial head-dress is being held over her head as she proceeds in the marriage litter.

Press Cliché

WEDDING SCENES AMONG THE MAHOMEDAN PEOPLES OF CENTRAL ASIA

In the lower photograph, depicting a marriage by the registrar in Tashkent, the veil worn by the Mahomedan bride is the 'parandja.' It is made of black horsehair, and is the form affected in Turkistan. Although the veil is being gradually discarded, most women in the remoter strongholds of Islam retain it. The Waziris, a tribe of the North-West Frontier Province, are nominally Mahomedans. Their country is a labyrinth of hill ranges and valleys, and camels are the chief means of transport. The upper photograph shows a Waziri wedding party on camels.

E.N.A

HEAD-DRESS OF A DRUSE BRIDE OF LEBANON

This curious head-horn was formerly worn by Druse women night and day. It is placed in position by the bridegroom on the wedding day. The mode of wearing is subject to endless variation, and indicates the district to which the wearer's husband belongs.

of symbolic and religious character. On the wedding morning the bridegroom is ceremonially purified by bathing. If he is of high rank he is conveyed to the residence of the bride in a gorgeous palanquin, wearing his marriage crown and robes and veiled so that he may not be injured by 'evil eye.' A stately procession is formed, in which richly decorated elephants and horses take part as well as armed and uniformed attendants. The processions of lesser men may not be so dignified, but are invariably headed by a band of trumpeters and drummers, mingled with other instrumentalists, who may be more noisy than musical.

When the bridegroom arrives at the bride's home he is sprinkled with rice. A bracelet of mango leaves enclosing rice is placed on the right wrist of the bridegroom and the left of the bride. The latter is seated between her mother's knees when she receives the bridegroom, who kneels and bows before her. Then follows the ceremony of paring the nails of the young couple. The marriage is celebrated in the 'wedding booth' and a Brahman officiates, reciting religious texts and performing various rites. The bride is seated on her father's knees for a time. When the Brahman has tied together portions of the clothing of the young couple, they are ceremonially united. Then they walk 'by the right' around the sacred fire in adoration of the god Agni, sprinkling rice, while the Brahman burns incense. A significant symbolic act is the applying of a spot of red substance on the bride's forehead. This must be done by the bridegroom. Acts of worship follow, and thereafter the bridegroom returns home. The young couple remain apart for a few days, after which they are ceremonially bathed and the wedding bracelets taken off. If the bride is of age, she is thereafter conveyed in a palanquin to the bridegroom's home, where she is received with ceremony.

IN connexion with Moslem marriages a vigil is held, as in Java, and there is a mosque ceremony. Among the customs of mixed character, it is of interest to find, as in Korea, the observance of the silence and sightless taboo. When the bride is shown to the bridegroom her eyes are kept shut either by will or by being gummed, and as it is also taboo that her feet should touch the ground, she is carried on the shoulders of her father or another relative. Thus blinded, and perhaps drugged, she is borne after a brief marriage ceremony to the house of the husband and not set down until after she crosses the threshold. Some days later she returns with her husband to her parents' house, where the couple remain for a time, and by doing so complete the marriage ceremony.

The Sinhalese of Ceylon have a simple wedding ceremony in which the young couple feed one another with rice and then have their little fingers tied together with a sacred cord by a male member of the bride's family. In Burma a young couple on their wedding day are guided by an astrologer, who informs them when to begin the ceremony. First they clasp each other's hands, then they feed each other with rice taken from a single vessel; thereafter their hands are tied together with strings of cotton and they kneel to be sprinkled with holy water. The reciting of Buddhist texts before and after the ceremony gives it a religious character, but the symbolic acts performed in the presence of witnesses are considered to be those which are really vital and binding.

MASKS AND MUMMERS

THE use of the mask and of pantomime covers a wide field. Elaborate posture-dancing forms a large part of the subject matter of the chapter on the Golden Ballet of the East, while masks figure prominently in some of the dances described in the chapter on Devil and other Spirit Dances and in the savage secret societies dealt with under Mystical Societies.

'EVERYWHERE I have been, in every country I have visited,' Sir Francis Younghusband has recorded, 'I found two forces of universal appeal—religion and the drama.'

From the earliest days of primitive man to the world of to-day, whether of western civilization or of untutored native races, these two forces have ever been closely allied. And the connecting link which, in one form or another, has ever been the strongest is the mask, or conventional disguise. For the mask implies mystery, and mystery is the essence both of primitive superstition and of all the great religions of history. In the same way, mystery, or the appeal to the imagination, is the essence of every art work and in particular of the drama. The more primitive that drama, the more closely it is allied to the fundamentals of human nature or of race, the more the mask, or its equivalent, plays a leading part. The other part is pantomime, which is mumming.

No better example of the combination of mask and mummer could be offered than that of Charles Chaplin, the most famous mummer in the world to-day. Chaplin's conventional mask of bowler hat, moustache, cane, baggy trousers and queer boots is known to millions of all races. Without that mask Chaplin would be unrecognized. His art would fail. The mask is an integral part of the mumming. So was the mask the essential of the characters of the Italian Commedia dell' Arte, or of Punch of our street-corner show. Similarly we have the conventional masks and livery of the cinema 'Felix,' 'Mickey Mouse,' cow-boys, detectives, 'strong, silent men,' Chinese villains, and others. Without these masks they would not be recognized. They are formal types to which popular audiences have grown accustomed. No variations are permissible. In all these characters we witness expressions of fundamentals in human nature.

BUT there is another and a more subtle link between the mask and the mummer which must be emphasised, for it provides the key to the whole matter, whether primitive or present-day. And that is the psychological effect produced both upon the masked mummer and upon the audience. It is attested by Mr. W. T. Brenda, the greatest living authority on the mask, that so soon as a man dons a mask and starts to interpret the character his face unconsciously imitates the expression of the mask. Further, the expression of the mask is reflected in the faces of the spectators and so back again to the wearer. All this implies close mental reaction.

If this be so—and the experiment may readily be made by anyone—we shall at once appreciate how and why masks and mummers have held so firm a grip upon peoples of all ages and races, and notably in the practice of superstitious or religious rites, wherein pantomime, expression in dumb show, is so strongly in evidence.

THUS among native races where primitive beliefs still survive—certain North American Indian tribes, for example—the folk do not pray or sacrifice to graven images of the god or spirit, but it is the chief or medicine man himself who assumes the mask and livery of the god and, with that mask, the 'breath' or living spirit of the god. He himself, by auto-suggestion, for the time becomes the god, and the mutual mental reaction between folk and priest is achieved.

Among the Pueblo natives of Mexico, with whom the Catholic faith widely obtains, masked ceremonies are still observed, grafted on to Christian conditions and festal days. The masks are of hide or leather heavily ornamented with buckskin, corncobs, arrows, rainbow designs and the like, all in a large variety of colours. The mask itself is regarded as sacred. The wearer believes himself transformed into the being represented. Both before and after the ceremony he performs an elaborate ritual of purification.

Here it should be remarked that the brilliant colouring, the linear or circular designs upon masks or upon painted faces, such as are found in every land where primitive rites are practised, are all carefully wrought to specific meanings. The Chinese actor paints or masks to special and distinctive colours and lines no less than the natives of Mexico or New Guinea. And it is a noteworthy

Mondiale

DANCER'S MASK

This mask, with its elaborate trimmings, consisting of tow, human hair and feathers, is a type used in New Caledonia.

Maurice Beck

DOLL ACTORS OF JAVA: A STIRRING EPISODE IN THE WAJANG GOLEK

Of the various forms of the Wajang (see pages 43, 463 and 355), the national drama of Java, the most primitive and one of the most popular is the Wajang Purva, which is enacted with puppets whose shadows are cast upon a screen. The figures here seen are used in the form of the drama known as the Wajang Golek. They are carved in the round, and are displayed direct on the stage, not through the medium of the shadow-screen. These puppet shows deal with mythological history, and throughout the performances appropriate comments are recited by the owner to the accompaniment of an orchestra of gongs and xylophones. The dolls are modelled with considerable skill, and in this respect do not compare unfavourably with the Italian marionettes

fact that these designs and colours have an apparent world-wide universality of motif, not only in masks but in buildings, pictures and other art forms. 'A mere line,' Mrs. Emerson has said in comment, 'becomes a vehicle for the expression of the profoundest aspirations of humanity—preservation and resurrection.' Thus a native medicine man will heal the sick by drawing ceremonial lines in the earth from the prone body.

In Tibet no entertainments are more popular than the sacred masked dramas which depict the several births of Buddha ; and also the mystery plays which centre around gods and demons, in particular the Dance of the Red-Tiger Devil (see pages 47 and 263). Here the masks are truly awe-inspiring. They are made of papier-mâché, of gilded copper, of hardwood and of cloth. Wigs of coloured yak-tail hair are worn.

Mr. L. Austine Waddell has broadly classified these masks and mummers into five groups : (1) the King of the Ogres, supreme in bulk and hideous of aspect, with three eyes ; (2) the Ten Awful Ogres and the Ten Ogresses, with their attendant animals; (3) the Ghouls, with their skull masks and skeleton bodies ; (4) the Earth-Master-Demons, huge and hideous ; (5) the Teachers, the first Buddhist missionaries, who are the jesters of the plays.

Planet News

ZULU WARRIOR WEARING GOATSKIN MASK OF CEREMONY

In Africa the use of masks is largely restricted to the forested region of the Congo watershed and the west coast. The masks are chiefly of wood, with decorations of fur, feathers, beads, or shells. Usually they represent a guardian spirit or famous folklore figure. They serve a variety of purposes—to express totemistic ideas, to terrify enemies, to ward off demons.

Other mumming dances closely bound up with religious observance are the Lion Dance of Buddhism, known in variants throughout the East (see page 47), the Fish Dance of the Tierra del Fuego natives (with masks of seal hide), and the masquerades of certain powerful secret societies of Melanesia and of West African natives, whose fibre-fringed, wooden masks have, as Mr. Brenda affirms, 'in their expression an artistic distinction above those of any living people.'

The mumming plays of Java afford us a stepping-stone from religious ceremonial to the secular entertainment, for the origin of the Java drama lies in ancestor worship, and while the process of evolution through the centuries is clearly marked, we have the very interesting fact that each stage of that evolution is represented today by actual performances.

Within a few days' tour the visitor may witness : (1) the primitive Wajang Purva, or shadow-screen puppets, of animal hide, cut very angular and controlled by sticks ; (2) the Wajang Klitik, or flat puppets carved from soft wood and displayed direct to the spectator. At this stage the dramas become secular ; (3) the Wajang Golek, with puppets carved in the round and approximating to human forms ; (4) the Wajang Topeng, with actors masked like puppets. The mask, of skin or wood, is held to the face by a strap gripped between the teeth. Birds and animals are also represented. The period of this stage of evolution is circa A.D. 1000 ; (5) the Wajang Wong, described in detail in the chapter on Animal Dances of the East, in which the mask is discarded for make-

Dorien Leigh

INSIPIDITY IN LACQUER ON DANCE MASKS OF SUMATRA

Masks are made of very diverse materials. Those worn in savage Africa are mostly of wood, though sometimes of bark, ivory or goat-skin. The Pueblo Indians use deer-skin masks in their ritual dances. The theatrical masks of the Japanese are of carved and lacquered wood. The Sumatran women here seen are wearing lacquer masks. With their brightly coloured and richly decorated sarongs, their intricate bead embroideries, and their queer masks and head-dresses, they are equipped for enacting leading parts in one of the mask dances of Sumatra.

Dr. S. M. Manton

WOODEN MASKS AND WOODEN HANDS IN A BATAK CANNIBAL DANCE

Not so very long ago the Batak people of Sumatra were addicted to cannibalism, but the practice is now more or less suppressed, at least in those areas that are near the road and accessible to Dutch influence. Mask dances used to accompany the cannibal feasts and other village ceremonies. With the dying out of cannibalism the mask dance is disappearing, and the masks here seen, which have been acquired by the Amsterdam Museum, are probably one of the last sets extant. The dance is being performed outside a Batak village not far from Lake Toba.

up; (6) similar dramas, but with the minimum of make-up. Of the six stages of evolution it is the first or most primitive which today makes the strongest popular appeal.

The motto of the Chinese drama would seem to be 'leave everything to the imagination.' Thus the masks, the make-up and the properties are all upon the most conventional lines. A red mask or make-up signifies the god of war or a famous soldier, a black mask signifies an honest man, or else invisibility (a subtly humorous touch, this !), a white mask denotes cunning, a golden one means a god, and so forth. A single oar may represent a ship or a fleet, a banner may indicate an army of 10,000 men. Thus, the audience always knows precisely what to expect and is very content. Women are not allowed to perform with men, but the masks of the female impersonators are so perfect that they have at times actually set the standard of feminine beauty and deportment. Mai Lan-fang, the most famous actor of the modern Chinese stage, is a female impersonator, and his favourite rôle is that of a demi-mondaine.

The dramatic art of Japan falls, broadly, into three classes, and each one is mainly pantomime, with the mask or conventional make-up strongly in evidence. There is, first, the Doll Theatre, with its life-size puppets manipulated by a performer in full view of the audience. This puppet theatre has inspired much of the best of Japanese dramatic literature, and also the invention of much important stage scenery and accessories. It is, for example, to the Doll Theatre of Japan that we owe the revolving stage.

There is, second, the 'Kabuki,' which more perfectly than any other form expresses Japanese national ideals and tastes. Every Kabuki actor is a dancer and a born pantomimist, and 'at his best he is the master pantomimist of the world.' He will hold his audience breathless for fifteen minutes

Van Damm

THE MASK MAKES A LEADING LADY IN CHINA: MAI LAN-FANG IN A FEMALE ROLE

Of all dramas that of the Chinese is perhaps the most highly conventionalised. Masks, properties, make-up—all are meticulously formal. A single banner will indicate an army, and whips in the hands of fighting warriors that the combat takes place on horseback. Men and women do not act together. When impersonating women, the men wear masks of singular beauty. The famous Chinese actor, Mai Lan-fang, plays only women's parts. In grace of movement he has been compared to Pavlova.

without uttering a word or moving from one spot. Nor must we forget the famous conventional horse of the 'Kabuki.' Played, as usual, by two men, he is the most delightful pantomime animal ever invented. To see him rearing magnificently in battle, drooping with pathos under the hand of his defeated master, trotting happily home after victory, or playing the maddest pranks in a comic scene is to witness the perfection of the mummer's art.

The third is the famous 'No' drama, so often described. Originally, in the fifteenth century, the chief entertainment of the nobles and feudal lords, and acted by them, with the public occasionally admitted to the performances, the No drama still remains something of an exotic, even for Japan. Or, to quote the summary of Professor Jiro Harada, 'On the whole the No performance may well be compared to a masterful oriental picture in black monochrome, both being guided by highly idealistic aims and artistic aspirations and possessing great impelling qualities that thrill the devotee and weary the uninitiated.'

There are 250 plays in the No drama, divided, roughly, into five classes: (1) the 'waki-no,' dealing

SACRED PUPPETS OF BALI: MASKED GIANTS WHO WALK WITH THE LEGS OF OTHERS

The inhabitants of the island of Bali are Hindus, but their Hinduism is deeply tinged with animism. Dotted all over the island are little temples roofed with thatch, and at almost every hour of the day men and women may be seen praying at these shrines and carrying offerings to them, for life flows easily in the island, and the Balinese devote much of their ample leisure to religion. The strange figures here seen in front of a group of temples play a part in the religious rites of Bali. The images, which are used in processions, are more than life-size. The effect of height is obtained by the puppets being mounted on men, who are almost entirely concealed by the voluminous skirts. A variety of masks and head-dresses are used.

with the Buddhist deities; (2) the 'shara-nono,' dealing with the ghosts of departed warriors; (3) the 'kazura-nono,' with noble ladies portraying the principal parts; (4) the 'genzai-nono,' or modern drama of human appeal; (5) drama of demons and goblins. A prologue is always given, with Okina, the radiant sun-goddess, as principal. The whole is accompanied by music and chorus. Masks are worn only by the principal and secondary characters.

With the Japanese such masters in the art of mumming we must not omit reference to the admirable work which they are performing in cinematography. This art industry in Japan is a very large one. In 1929 no fewer than 1,000 'feature' films were produced, through 20 studios, and there are over 1,000 cinema theatres in the country. The pictures, however, are rarely, if ever, presented outside Japan, for their appeal is purely native.

Thus far we have considered mumming drama performed for the people, or as religious ceremony. We turn now to mumming performed by the people. Of this perhaps the most noteworthy example is the mumming play of England, still performed, though rarely, together with its European variants. The original impulse to create this drama may be summarised very briefly. With the downfall of the Roman Empire, and under the interdict of the Christian Church, both the classical drama of Greece and the 'ludi' of Rome disappeared. The folk had to depend either upon the troupes of itinerant

Mauritius

SPRING DANCE BY MEMBERS OF A JAPANESE KABUKI COMPANY

Of the various forms of drama in Japan the Kabuki dates back to the late sixteenth century, when a certain ex-priestess, taking up dancing as a profession, brought out a troupe of girl dancers. These female comedians came to be superseded by boys, who in their turn were replaced by men, and it was from this company of comedians that the Kabuki arose. The new form of drama was sponsored by the commercial classes, who had grown tired of having no theatre of their own. Between the acts of the Kabuki posture dances are performed.

H. von Perckhammer

TRAGIC MASK OF THE JAPANESE 'NO' DRAMA

When the great aristocrats of Japan began to patronise the classic 'No' drama some of them even condescended to take part in the plays. Splendid costumes were made for these noble amateurs, and artists of renown vied with each other in chiselling the masks

players or they had to create for themselves. Their drama was built upon pagan rites and adapted to Christian ceremonies.

The Pace Egg play (Pace=Pasque=Easter), still performed by young folk in many parts of England, Scotland, Ireland and Wales, usually at Christmas, is essentially a springtime celebration. As observed in the chapter on Surviving Customs of Springtide, its origin may be traced back through interpolations of Tudor times and of the conflict between Cross and Crescent to the primitive tree-worship and the resultant myths. The central theme of the play, in its purity of traditional text or oral transmission, is the violent death of the hero at the hands of an adversary, and his speedy and miraculous resurrection. Upon this slender plot innumerable variants have been built in the manner of variants upon a folk-song or folk tune.

Thus a typical variant, to be witnessed in certain Yorkshire centres, runs in this manner: S. George, the hero, enters and announces himself. Slasher enters. They fight. Slasher is mortally wounded. A comic Doctor is summoned. Slasher is healed. There follows a succession of other adversaries, including a King of Egypt or some other Eastern native. Each one is defeated in turn, and cured. Beelzebub enters. He summons his attendant sprite, Little Devil Dout, who speaks the epilogue, collects money from the audience and, with his broom, sweeps the actors off the stage.

S. George is invariably the hero. But S. George is really George-(or Jack-) in-the-Green of the May Day festival. In South of England variants it is, very properly, the hero who is killed and revived. Very often, also, the legendary dragon and princess are introduced. A blackamoor and the Doctor always appear in one form or another. One form of tradition is that the 'Nine Worthies of Christendom' should appear as successive adversaries. Then the 'Nine Worthies' are amended to include topical heroes of the moment—Nelson, Wolfe, Napoleon, Kitchener or Charlie Chaplin. The Christmas performances, which may still be seen in various villages of

H. von Perckhammer

WRINKLES OF MIRTH ON A 'NO' MASK

The plays of the Japanese 'No' drama deal mainly with sombre themes, such as the transitory nature of life and the grim pranks of Nemesis. But not all the characters in it are gloomy, and some of the masks worn are fashioned in the true comic spirit.

Tokyo Asahi Photos

VIVID PANTOMIME ON THE BOARDS OF THE STAGE OF JAPAN

As with the ' No ' and the puppet dramas of Japan, the ' Kabuki ' (farce) consists mainly of pantomime, and the make-up employed is to a great extent conventional. Formerly this class of play was tabooed by the aristocracy, but since the introduction of Western civilization it has been patronised by persons of all ranks. The upper photograph shows a Samurai chief taking part in a fight in a bathroom, while the lower depicts an episode at a rest-house on Mount Hakone, taken from ' The Humorous Journey of Yaji and Kida on the Tokaido Highway.'

Courtesy of Rochdale Observer

ENGLAND'S PATRON SAINT AS HERO OF OLD ENGLISH MUMMING DRAMA

A form of folk play that survives in several parts of the British Isles is that known as the Pace Egg play, which is usually performed by the mummers at Christmas. Its hero, according to the general rule, is S. George, and many variants of the play are found. The episodes seen here are from the version played at Easter in the Lancashire borough of Rochdale. S. George slays the dragon (top), and, with the other Christian knights, S. Andrew S. Patrick and S. David (bottom) does obeisance to Queen Sabra, who is accompanied by her attendants

Hampshire, Warwickshire and Oxfordshire, naturally serve to introduce Old Father Christmas:

> Here comes I, Father Christmas, welcome or welcome not,
> I hope Old Father Christmas will never be forgot

a doggerel which may be compared with the traditional masked mumming of Guy Fawkes Day. So has Devil Dout (or 'Do Out'), with his broom, his counterpart in Puck's epilogue to Shakespeare's 'A Midsummer Night's Dream.'

The conventional mask is usually little more than a shoulder sash of distinguishing colour for each character with a ribbon or ribbons of similar colour for the cap or wide-brimmed hat, and for the trousers.

The mumming troupe, then, is given the bare bones of the primitive plot and proceeds to dress it with every ingenuity of invention at command. It is essentially the concern of the 'rude mechanicals' of the folk. The moment the local vicar or schoolmaster takes the play in hand it is ruined. In Peebles (Scotland) S. George becomes Galatian, who fights a Black Knight, and Beelzebub becomes Judas, with money-bag. At Steyning (Sussex) the Dragon is very active, and the whole troupe fight him at once in a gorgeous mêlée, ending in a Morris dance. In

George Long

THE DOCTOR IN A COUNTRY MUMMING PLAY ADMINISTERS A DOSE

The central motive of the English mumming play is the fights between the hero and various antagonists, who are slain by him and restored to life by the doctor. The cast includes King George (originally S. George), the Quack Doctor, Rumour, and the leader, Father Christmas. The play is usually performed by working men, and the words have been handed down orally. The costumes are made of strips of wall paper or thin coloured fabric. The mummers here seen belong to two Hampshire villages, the Longparish troupe (top) and the Overton (bottom).

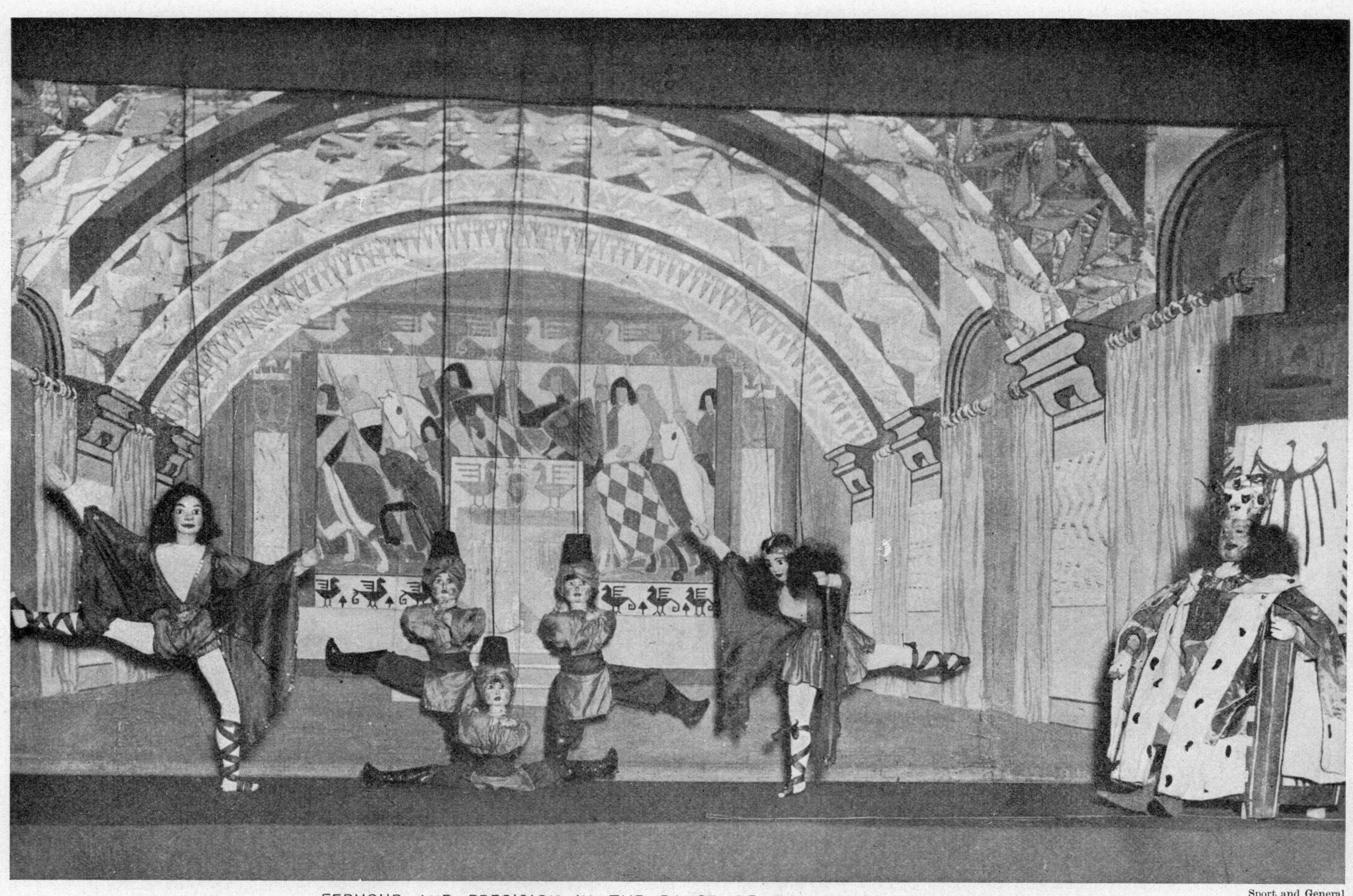

Sport and General

FERVOUR AND PRECISION IN THE DANCE OF THE ITALIAN MARIONETTES

Marionettes are of great antiquity. They were used by the ancient Egyptians at the festivals of Osiris, and were popular with the Greeks and the Romans. For several centuries they have maintained their position as a form of entertainment in most European countries, and particularly in Italy. Goethe, Le Sage and Maeterlinck are among the famous authors who have written plays for puppets, and such composers as Mozart and Haydn have produced music for marionette plays. The Doll Theatre is a very important form of dramatic art in Japan, while it is on the Javanese principle that Professor Richard Teschner works his exquisite puppets in Vienna. Italian marionettes are here seen in the palace scene in 'Puss in Boots' at the Scala Theatre, London.

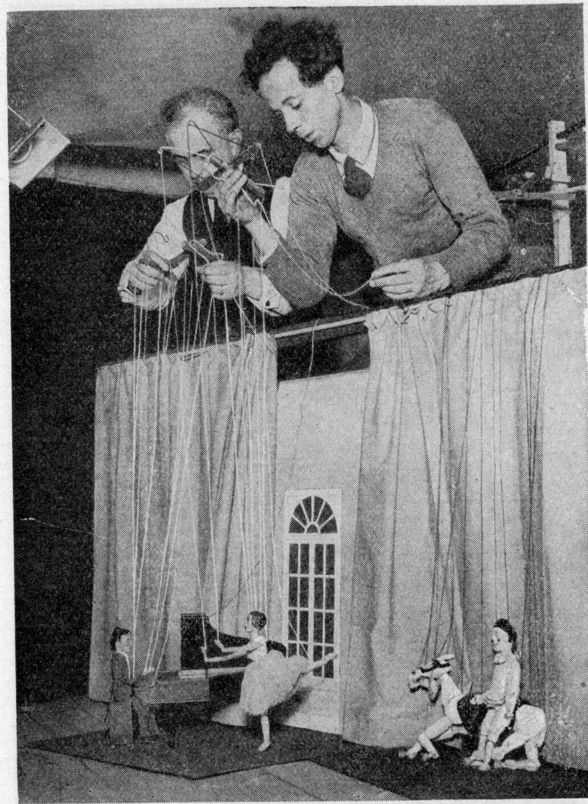

Planet News

PULLING THE WIRES FOR THE MARIONETTES

Marionettes are usually worked by strings or wires from above the stage. In Vienna sticks are used from below. The life-size puppets of the Doll Theatre of Japan, however, are manipulated in full view of the audience, but as a general rule the operators are unseen.

Berkshire, Molly or Queen Mary, a woman, takes the prologue and sweeps a space for the troupe. In a Dorset variant Father Christmas has a wife, Dame Dorothy. The two quarrel and fight over the cooking of a hare. Dame Dorothy is killed, and the Doctor revives her.

FROM Dorset to Thessaly, in Greece, is a far cry. Yet in Thessaly, upon Epiphany Eve, a very similar variant is played by four characters—a bridegroom, his bride, the Doctor and a blackamoor in Arab dress. But always, everywhere, we encounter at least a suggestion of the central motif—the revival or resurrection of the spirit in a new, young form before the year-old one becomes too enfeebled for effective transfusion. And always we find the conventional masks which unify the drama and make the popular appeal.

We now turn back to the most primitive form of the mumming drama, and of which we witness so remarkable and widespread a revival in the modern world ; and that is the puppet or marionette drama.

Some examples, those of Java and Japan, we have already noted, together with their influence upon the modern revival. Indeed, it is the puppet drama of Java which is primarily responsible for this, and distinguished artists like Mr. E. Gordon Craig and Professor Richard Teschner, of Vienna, pay warm tribute to it by their careful development of the primitive models.

Once again we find the twofold division of superstitious ritual and purely secular entertainment. Thus amongst the Hopi Indians of the south-west American States the puppets are used for sympathetic magic. The favourite characters are the Great Serpent and the Corn Maidens. The Maidens enact their play of grinding or winnowing corn so as to secure a bountiful harvest. The Serpent is the great protective Spirit which encircles the world. The ritual is usually observed in the semi-darkness of the hut or tent in order that, to the spectators, the puppets may seem to move of their own volition.

Similar ritual performances, with appropriate local characters, are found among the primitive tribes of New Guinea, Southern Nigeria, the Congo—indeed, among almost every primitive people where the ancient superstitions still hold ground before the advance of Islam or the Christian missionaries. Readers of the African romances of Sir H. Rider Haggard will recall the many examples given of sympathetic magic by puppets, either for the destruction of an enemy or the propitiation of spirits.

Of secular performances the puppet shows of China, presented by wandering showmen, hold a

A. R. Slater, F.R.G.S.

READY FOR A PUPPET SHOW IN INDIA

In every continent puppet shows are found, for the art of the manipulation of marionettes is as widespread as it is ancient One of the favourite amusements of the villagers of India is watching the entrancing antics of the marionettes.

Sport and General

PUPPETS OF THE OUT-OF-DOORS THAT FASCINATE THE CHILDREN OF THE EAST AND WEST

Punch and Judy is the only outdoor puppet show that survives in England. It is more than probable that it was introduced from France at the time of the Restoration. Though less frequently seen than formerly, the hook-nosed, shrill-voiced, cowardly braggart, ever at war with his wife Judy, with the police, and indeed with everyone he meets, is still a firm favourite wherever he is found. The Chinese counterpart of Punch and Judy (right) is a very popular form of entertainment. In China the plots cover a much wider field than in England.

very strong appeal to the folk of that vast land, where the drama is the prime form of national entertainment. The craft is a secret one, jealously guarded from father to son, and the repertoire of folk tales and legends, episodes from heroic drama and modern comedy, is very extensive. For a few cash your showman will gladly fix his stage—just like that of our own Punch and Judy—and present four or five plays of some ten minutes each. A great favourite is that of the widow whose only son was eaten by a tiger. The tiger is haled before the magistrate and sentenced to support the widow for the rest of his life by providing food and raiment.

Among the English folk the old puppet showman is virtually extinct. Only Punch and Judy remains. There is, for example, a 'pitch' near Lime Street station, Liverpool, which has been held continuously for over eighty years, to the delight of young and old of several generations. But, in private ownership, the puppet theatre is being swiftly developed. Mention may be made of the London Marionette Theatre, created by Mr. Waldo E. Lanchester with a remarkably fine repertoire.

In the United States the puppet drama movement is so extensive that a national Fellowship was formed in 1930. There is a subsidised puppet theatre in New York, and the plays performed by puppets, both in the cities and on tour, are truly astonishing in their character and audacity of theme. Recent examples are 'Rumpelstiltskin,' 'The Miracle of the Cherry Tree' (with décor after Fra Angelico), 'The Emperor Jones' and Shakespeare's 'Romeo and Juliet.' It is significant, too, that puppet drama is often used in American schools for purposes of health enlightenment.

And now the wheel of religion and drama has come full circle in the mumming mystery plays which today are being increasingly performed within the churches and cathedrals themselves, and to great and deeply attentive audiences.

MAGIC AND THE MEANS OF LIFE

MAINTENANCE of the food supply is the first necessity of all communities, and in the measures taken by primitive peoples to secure this, sympathetic magic plays a large part. Some of these practices are studied in the following pages, and other aspects of the subject are considered in the chapters on Strange Sacrificial Rites, Rain-makers and Rain-making Ceremonies, and others.

TO be uncertain about the whence and the when of the next meal is an uneviable state of mind, more especially if circumstances tend to make it a permanent condition. Yet this is precisely the preoccupation that haunts the daily and nightly thoughts of the savage who remains at what is known as the food-gathering stage. He must take up his spear and go after game that shows no desire to be caught, while his wife, basket or wooden trough in hand, must scratch the soil for roots or scour the bushes for berries or even grubs, both in season and out of season. It is by no mean unknown that whole families should starve to death.

For it is not as if the human race had clung to the warm and plentiful zone that must have furnished its original habitat. On the contrary, it is found making the best of things in all the most inhospitable environments, even though still dependent on the scraps that chance throws in its way. Indeed, the animal world presents no other example of so widely ranging a creature ; and nothing but the confidence proceeding from a high brain charged with immense if chiefly latent powers could have justified this reckless dispersion, extending through long periods of time and from the equator to the utmost verge of the Polar seas.

Now faith is but another word for confidence, and it needs faith to conceive a deity and pray to him for help. Such an attitude would always be classed as religious. But when the hunting savage puts his trust in rites that, however sacred in his eyes, do not clearly imply relations with any kind of personal power at the back of nature, we are apt to set them down as magical. Yet so rigid a distinction cannot but obscure the fact that, alike in motive and method, the two procedures have a great deal in common.

MAN'S object being in either case to move the assumed friendly influence to work wonders on his behalf, he tries to do so by using some means, whether word or gesture, of suggesting exactly what he wants. How precisely the meaning is conveyed or how it makes itself felt is a question on which the primitive mind is quite unable to frame a clear opinion. But that it somehow helps in practice to relieve the situation in times of crisis is known and appreciated as a matter of direct experience.

Nor is the efficacy of spell or prayer tested simply or even mainly by the extent to which the behaviour of the external world is actually observed to be swayed. It is rather the inward effect—the conviction acquired of succour at hand—that heartens the hungry folk so that they are fed on the very hope of food, and a little miraculously stands for plenty. What, then, is popularly described as magic is really religion in the making, if instead of stressing the difference between savagery and civilization one insists rather on the continuity of the process of development. Passing on, therefore, from what, after all, is largely a question of words, let us study in the concrete some examples of rites of the economic type, taken both from the food-gatherers, who, though of prehistoric origin, can be found in existence in various parts of the world today, and from their more advanced brethren the food-producers.

ANYONE who has had the luck to visit one of the painted caves of France or Spain will have noticed the javelins affixed to the flanks of the game animals there depicted, together with numerous other signs showing that this was no mere art for art's sake, but served some symbolic purpose. Not the faintest whisper has reached us, however, of what the prehistoric European believed when he held his mysteries in these dark and silent places. On the other hand, the Stone-Age man who survives in Australia still carries out ceremonies that in spirit, if not in detail must be similar enough to afford an instructive analogy.

In the barren centre of the continent the leading interest from a mystic point of view consists in encouraging the animals and plants to multiply, and incidentally in encouraging mankind to look forward to this consummation. Thus the witchetty grub is ceremonially stimulated by the witchetty-grub men, who bear that name and deem themselves one in kin with the insect in question. Their headman, in order to induce it to lay eggs, makes solemn bows over a shield decorated on one side with wavy lines to show how former grubs walked about in ancient times, and on the other side with circles, the larger ones representing the bushes on which they fed, the smaller ones being their eggs. This is done once a year just a little before their breeding time. When the animal has obligingly increased in numbers, then the grub man, who must otherwise religiously abstain from eating his namesake, has to partake of a small portion in order to retain his power of persuading it to be fertile ; after which the rest of the tribe on whose behalf he has exercised his magic powers are free to take their fill of the delicacy.

Again, the emu men for like reasons make a sacred design, but this time it is on the ground, a plot being cleared and levelled, then drenched with their own blood to form a hard surface, and finally decorated with black, white, yellow and red paint. The drawing is not realistic in the style of the cave art of Europe, but, on the contrary, is highly conventionalised, so that, for instance, two large yellow patches stand for lumps of emu fat, of which the natives are very fond, other smaller patches in yellow are the eggs in the ovary, and so on. Once more, the kangaroo men trust to the symbolism of a painting, which in this case has a rock face for its ground.

This, too, is very far from imitating nature, consisting as it does in little more than rows of vertical lines, some white to represent bones and the rest red to indicate the fur. The performers of the rite solemnly open their veins and allow the blood to spurt over the ceremonial stone. Being 'all-one-flesh,' as the native phrase puts it, with the sacred animal, they renew their communion with it through this sacrificial act. Those who choose to speak of magic in such a connexion should at least be ready to recognize here the first beginnings of religious practices and beliefs of the most profound significance.

Dr. W. D. Walker

SUCCULENT LARVAE AND THEIR BUSH ABODE

Grubs of various species supply an important proportion of the food of the Australian aborigines, the large butter-yellow witchetty grub being esteemed a particular delicacy. These larvae—two specimens of which this man is carrying strapped to his arm—are found among the roots of a shrub known as the witchetty bush (top). Much magic is employed in securing their proper abundance.

PASSING from Australia to north-eastern Asia we find nature-fed tribes, evidently long established there and in many respects reminiscent of the ancient hunters of the far past, who indulge in like observances with intent to conciliate the game, having devised this method of keeping up the live stock before ever the art of domestication had brought the problem down from the spiritual to the material plane. Thus bear meat appeals to the Ainu, who must therefore see to it that the bear does his part to maintain the supply—a thing that he is not likely to do if he is not kindly disposed towards the Ainu. So a baby bear is secured and for a time nurtured with the greatest solicitude, the women actually giving the infant animal the breast as if it were one of their own children.

At last, however, comes the day—the cub having become fat and succulent in the meantime—when it must die, or, rather, must go back to be reborn ; and this is obviously a good opportunity of asking it to take a message to the bears and generally to the gods assuring them of the love—a cynic might call it the cupboard-love—of the Ainu. 'The Ainu who will kill you,' they explain, 'is the best shot among us. There he is, he weeps and asks your forgiveness; you will feel almost nothing, it will be done so quickly. We cannot feed you always, as you will understand. We have done enough for you; it is now your turn to sacrifice yourself for us. You will ask God to send us, for the winter, plenty of otters and sables, and, for the summer, seals and fish in abundance. Do not forget our messages; we love you much, and our children will never forget you.'

Or, again, among the Otawas of Canada, the Bear clan—who, after all, were bears, and so might well enter into the animal's private feelings—made him a feast of his own flesh, addressing him thus: 'Cherish us no grudge because we have killed you. You have sense; you see that our children are hungry. They love you and wish to take you into their bodies. Is it not glorious to be eaten by the children of a chief?' Surely no reasonable bear ought to mind when treated so handsomely, more especially if, as often among the American Indians, the bear was no sooner slain than a pipe was lit and put into his mouth, while after he had been eaten his head was hung on a post and complimentary orations were lavished upon it. And so it may have happened ages ago in prehistoric Europe; for in the cave of Tuc d'Audoubert the head of a grizzly bear had been set high upon a pillar of shining stalagmite, while numerous foot marks in the clay floor testify to the presence of congregations long departed.

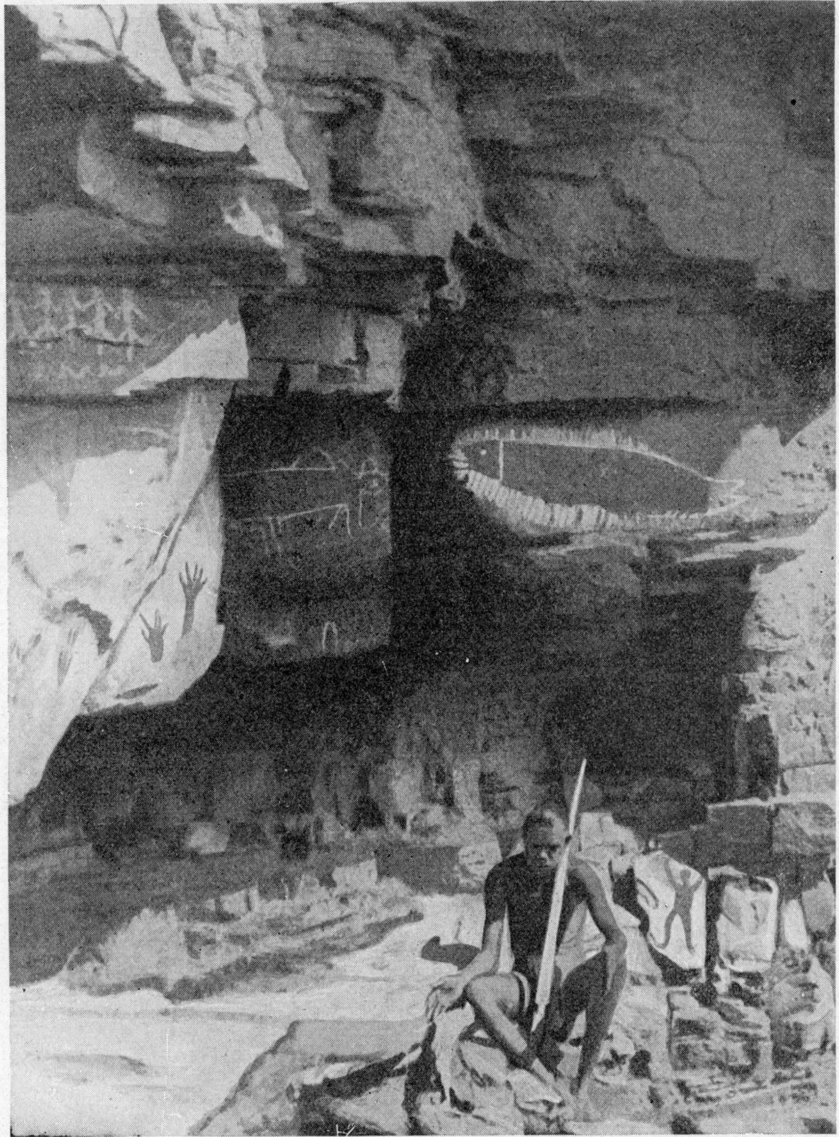

Francis Birtles

IMITATIVE MAGIC OF THE WITCHETTY TOTEM

European symbolic cave paintings of Neolithic times are parallelled in this cave at Kurringi Chase, New South Wales, where among other crude drawings a large number of witchetty grubs appear. Grub men, emu men, kangaroo men, all utilise conventional designs of the food-supplying creatures to which they are akin in rites intended to stimulate their productivity.

Again, America can provide other hunting rites that possibly throw light on the very remote history of our race. It was no less an authority than Boucher de Perthes, who was the first to prove palaeoliths to be the genuine handiwork of man, that brought forward certain figure-stones, as they are termed, from the same layers that contained the flint implements that he had just vindicated; and these, too, he claimed to be of human workmanship. Indeed controversy rages to this day over the question whether these animal-like forms roughly shadowed forth in battered stone are merely freaks of nature or the symbols of some vanished faith. Be this as it may, the making of figure-stones not unlike in appearance is something that appeals to the primitive mind today.

Thus among the Pueblo Indians of Zuñi in New Mexico six kinds of hunting animal, the eagle, the wolf and so on, are held to preside over the six regions of the world, and all the medicine powers contained therein. Hence it is extremely lucky to find a stone shaped like one of these, or one which by artificial means can be made to resemble it. For the beast of prey through its image can control the game

Mondiale

CEREMONIAL SLAUGHTER OF THE SACRED ANIMAL AT AN AINU BEAR FESTIVAL

In every community of the Ainu of Japan the men each spring capture a young bear cub, which they bring home to be brought up by their women, who actually suckle it. When it is too old to be nursed in this way it is kept and fed in a special cage until the autumn of the following year, when the grand bear festival is held. The bear is then brought out, fastened to a post in the centre of the village, and after being treated to a harangue of apology and entreaty that the supply of bear meat may be increased, is despatched by the most expert archer in the community. The carcass is cut in pieces and distributed among the families of the community. Much saké drinking accompanies this rough and exciting scene.

which it is wont to hunt, thus enabling the hunter who carries the charm to do the same. Now, though the rest of the animal has become stone, the heart is alive within. So the hunter puts it to his mouth, draws a deep breath, and presently emits the hunting cry of the powerful beast, which so daunts the game that a kill is ensured. The hunter, however, must be careful to dip the stone in the blood, bidding it 'drink, that it may enlarge its heart.' The act undoubtedly enlarges his own heart.

It might be thought that the domestication of animals would once for all rob them of their

E. O. Hoppé

SACRED KINE SUPPORTED BY VOLUNTARY CONTRIBUTIONS

Cows are regarded as sacred by all Hindus, and their upkeep and care are matters of public concern. Throughout Central India sheet metal collecting boxes are set up in conspicuous places with placards appealing for donations for this purpose. The lower photograph shows two natives attending to the facial make-up of one of these sacred animals at Madura.

sacred and quasi-divine character; for, if a wild boar excites respect and even awe in one who sets about its capture, the same feelings can scarcely be entertained towards the pig in its sty; though the uncleanness so often imputed to it is really a mark of holiness. But old notions die hard, and to this day there is as much sentiment as business in the keeping of cattle, as the primitive pastoralist views the matter.

Just as in Homeric times the women must utter formal lamentations when the ox was slain, though it was but for a feast, so now in the Nile valley the Dinka indulge on similar occasions in weeping that is not entirely conventional, seeing that the man who has actually reared the beast can never bring himself to eat its flesh. Partly, no doubt, this is sheer policy on the part of the wily savage, who does not want to annoy his animal friends more than may be necessary. It is, for instance, taboo to seethe the kid in the mother's milk, for the obvious reason that, if this happens, the mother will go off her milk, and small blame to her! But there is more in the respect displayed towards the sacred animal—for example, towards the cow in India—than a calculated

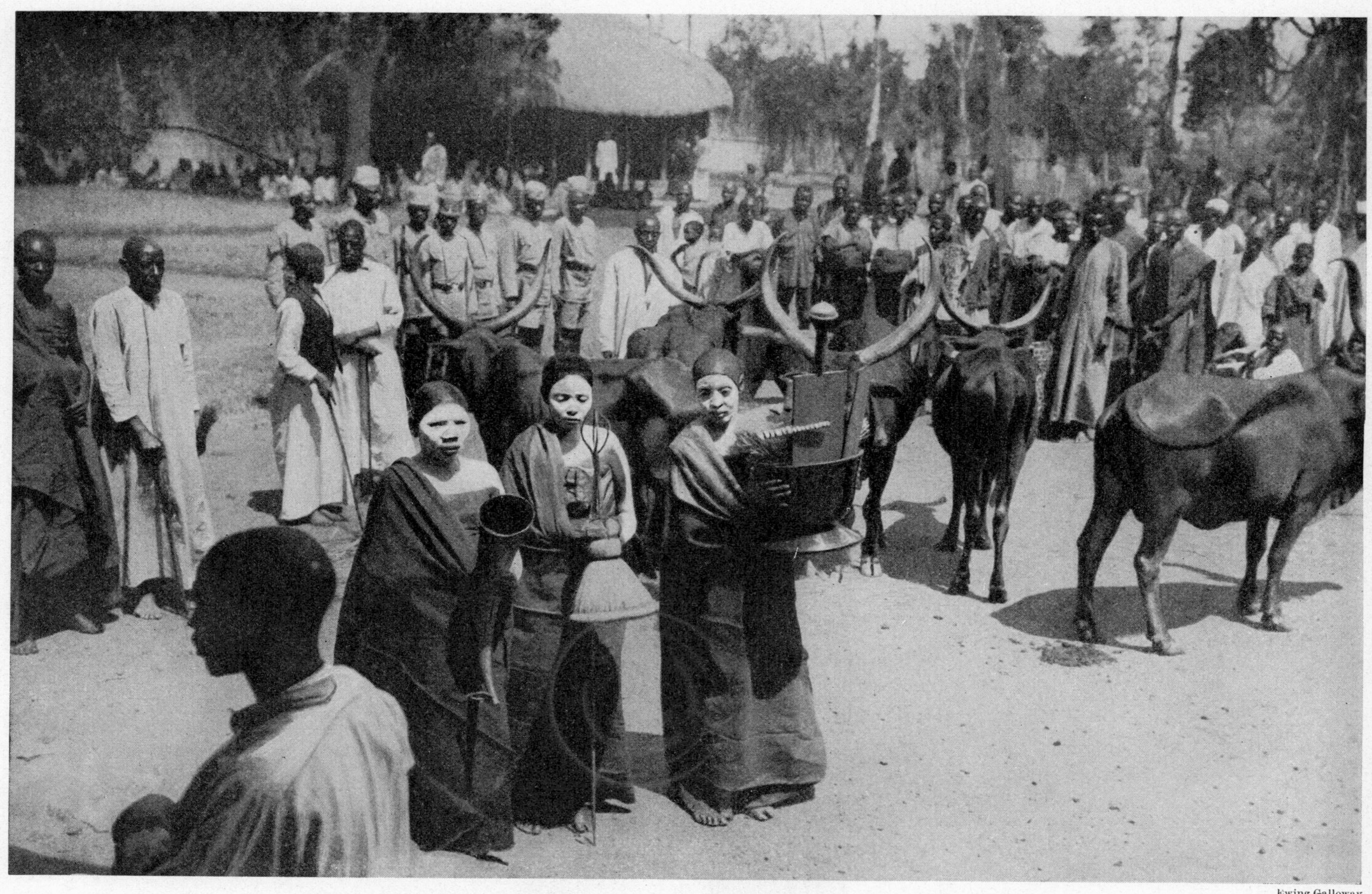

Ewing Galloway

WHERE MILKMAIDS RANK AS PRIESTESSES AND THE DAIRY IS A SHRINE

Like the Todas of the Nilgiri Hills in India mentioned in the text, the Bunyoro of Uganda treat their sacred cows with quite extraordinary reverence. Three dairymaids are dedicated exclusively to their service, virgins vowed to perpetual chastity and to abstinence from all worldly pleasures and temporal occupation other than the charge of the sacred dairy, the milking of the sacred cows, the making of the sacred butter, and the serving of these to the king and his two wives, who alone may partake of them. For the purposes of this photograph the king commanded the royal milkmaids to pose with the animals in their care. They are distinguishable by their whitened faces and by the vessels they are holding, which none but themselves may touch.

Ewing Galloway

MASTER AND MAIDS FAST BOUND BY RITUAL REGULATIONS

Two of the royal dairymaids in the service of the king of Bunyoro are seen here seated at the feet of their master in his palace. These women occupy a position of great authority in the royal household, where, indeed, their word is law. The dietary of the king is restricted to beef and milk, never, however, partaken of at the same meal. Three times a day he proceeds to the royal dairy and drinks milk drawn there from the sacred herd. Vegetables and mutton are forbidden to him.

cajolery. The source of so many benefits to mankind is regarded with truly devout feelings of wonder and gratitude.

Nevertheless, primitive worship is apt to express itself in a curiously negative way by means of taboos that in themselves simply remove the sacred object from the category of common things. Thus for the Todas of the Nilgiri Hills the milk of their sacred cattle is itself too sacred for ordinary use. Turned into buttermilk, however, it has been desanctified and can therefore be drunk with impunity. Thus the dairy where this process is carried out becomes a sort of temple, with the dairyman as the priest—an office exacting strict chastity and all manner of other abstinences from worldly joys and pursuits. The dairy is made with a partition, on one side of which are ranged the sacred vessels containing the unconverted milk, while on the other are the profane vessels ready to receive the product from which the taboo has been lifted. Especially sacred is the pot, kept buried in that holy of holies, the cattle-pen, in which is stored the ferment in the form of some sour milk kept over from the last brew that is needed to start the process of coagulation. No doubt hygienic considerations support religious in providing a more wholesome nutriment in a climate in which milk does not keep. At the same time, no biochemical view of the transaction would yield the accompanying emotions of reverence and thankfulness which by treating it as a beneficent mystery these simple souls are able to experience.

In similar vein one might discourse at length on the mystic devices associated with fowling, or again with fishing. Among the Malays, for instance, whose acquaintance with the higher religions is often but skin-deep, the pigeon-wizard invites the birds to his noose by requesting them in King Solomon's name, that name of power, to enter the king's audience hall and don his breast ornaments and armlets. This is quite in the style of the spider inviting the fly into his parlour. Or there is the story of another wizard who, when his comrades had long toiled at the nets and caught nothing, flung leaves into the water and by singing over them turned them into fishes, so that

Topical Press

HONOURING THE CORN SPIRIT AT HARVEST TIDE

One of the few old harvest customs that still survive in England is concerned with the last sheaf cut, which in many districts is left in the field when the rest has been carried home. In some few places, as here in Cheshire, the last sheaves are tied up with coloured ribbons to represent a human figure, known as the Kirn Doll, and are carried home by two maidens.

a miraculous haul forthwith resulted. Negative means will likewise lead to the same ends, as, for instance, the use of a taboo language so that the game may not understand what is on foot, as doubtless they would do if their ordinary names were mentioned. Moreover, for a Malay to speak of a Buddhist monk—though he may refer to him darkly as a 'yellow robe'—would be as unlucky as it would be for a Scotch fisherman to talk of the minister under like conditions.

It remains to notice all too briefly the attempts of man to bring persuasion to bear on the plant life so necessary to his existence. So much, indeed, has been written on vegetation rites that Andrew Lang once protested at the undue prominence given to the subject by what he called 'the Covent Garden school of mythology.' The rice in India, the maize in Mexico, the wheat among ourselves are literally 'mothers' to those whom they feed, and are honoured and besought accordingly. Right back to the beginnings of agriculture in Europe and perhaps beyond can be traced the cult of a great female divinity, with large breasts and swelling hips, whose fecundity enriches the earth and all that therein is. Now, the various ceremonies connected with the stimulation of the soil have their darker side, and much blood, not only animal but human, has been shed as a spiritual fertiliser. Here, however, it will suffice to glance at some of the more familiar and kindly aspects of these age-long and world-wide practices as they survive along our own countryside to-day.

Thus in the Midlands Plough Monday, the first Monday in January after Twelfth Day, was within living memory, and perhaps is still, celebrated by carrying round a gaily decorated plough from house to house, those who drew it along being called the Plough Bullocks and wearing bunches of corn in their hats. Skipping alongside and rattling a money-box for contributions was Bessy, a man dressed up as an old woman and formerly furnished with a bullock's tail that hung down behind. All the party must jump about, the higher the better, no doubt because the corn would be sympathetically induced to grow tall in like proportion. Bessy in particular must exert himself, or rather herself; for this may well have been the corn maiden in person.

All over the British Isles, however, the most typical representative of the corn spirit was the 'maiden,' or 'queen,' or 'baby,' that is, doll, consisting in the last sheaf to be cut, which was thereupon dressed up as a human figure and placed over the kitchen door or the chimney hob to ward off witches and bring good luck the winter through. When the last stalks of the standing crop had to be severed, the reapers would slash at it in turn blindfolded, or else would throw their sickles at it from a distance; the reason perhaps being that thus they distributed and concealed the responsibility for dealing the fatal blow.

In the Highlands they make up for it later in the day by drinking each their glass of whisky to the sheaf, crying, 'Here's to the Maiden.' We hear, too, of local taboos, such as that in one place the sheaf must not be allowed to touch the ground, and that in another no girl of questionable virtue must lay a finger on it. The like need of chastity in dealing with a holy thing is probably to be discerned in the not uncommon requirement that the cutting of the last sheaf should be left to some innocent child.

Thus side by side with the harvest festival celebrated in church linger pagan customs instinct with a natural religion that is the common heritage of man from days when his material resources were slender and his greatest asset was an unconquerable hope.

Ewing Galloway

FAITH AND WORK GO HAND IN HAND IN BALI

Throughout Indonesia, where rice is the staple food, the belief prevails that the rice is animated by a soul like that possessed by mankind, a vital yet separable principle which must be treated with deference and consideration if the crop is to thrive. All the processes of rice cultivation are attended by rites connected with the so-called spirit of the rice crops. In Bali much of the labour in the rice-fields is done by the women, four of whom are here seen before a shrine of the earth goddess praying for an abundant crop.

Ewing Galloway

FUNERAL PYRE OF A KING OF SIAM IN THE PALACE GROUNDS AT BANGKOK

The cremations of the kings of Siam and members of their families are marked by public festivities lasting several days, during which processions, firework displays, and dramatic entertainments take place. The body is embalmed, and a feature of the obsequies, as indeed of most Siamese funerals, is the length of time that elapses before the corpse is burnt. The dead king lies in state on a splendid catafalque, and the funeral pyre is an even more imposing structure, decked with sumptuous hangings. King Rama VI, whose pyre is here seen, lay in state in a copper shell within a gilded wood coffin for four months, during which period priests offered up prayers to the departed while holding in their hands a cord connected to his head.

WHERE THE DEAD ARE BURNED

THE disposal of the dead by burning, now a growing practice, mainly for hygienic reasons, in European countries, particularly Germany, is a very ancient custom. In its original forms it is chiefly found in the equatorial regions of Asia, where fuel is abundant. Related customs are discussed in the chapters on Ceremonial Use of Effigies, Tree and Platform Burial, and Exposing the Dead.

THE disposal of the bodies of the dead has given rise to a vast amount of superstition, ritual and ceremonial. With the exception of the observances connected with the sexual act, in other words, the rite of marriage in its endless ramifications, there is no other field of human custom better worth studying as a means of eliciting origins and comparisons in regard to the human race than this.

Earth, air, fire and water—the ' elements ' of the ancients, for the word is used in a very different significance now—are all enlisted in the disposal of the flesh of man, that is, if we count as ' air ' the various methods of exposure of corpses that they may be consumed by the carrion feeders of the air. The Parsees, who expose their dead on their strange Towers of Silence for the delectation of the vultures and crows, would not agree to this definition, for their creed forbids the pollution of these elements by the consignment to them of the bodies of the dead.

Earth burial has always been predominant among these methods, but the disposal of the body by fire, what we, in this latter day, call cremation, is gaining ground rapidly, particularly in Germany, which is showing remarkable energy in the adoption of modern ideas all round. Burning the dead is a very ancient custom, but it does not appear that it was the regular practice in any country or with any particular race. Excavations have proved it was practised in Britain before the coming of the Romans, and sporadic instances crop up all through history, as, for example, the burning of the bodies of Saul and his two sons: ' they came to Jabesh and burnt them there.'

Sir Thomas Browne, author of the ' Religio Medici,' has written of cinerary urns and urn burial in the tenth century, but he is more concerned with alchemy, astrology and witchcraft than with actual cremation. A scene that captivates the imagination is that of the Viking ship which bore the body of the dead chieftain in its flames, and went out westward to the sinking sun, a vivid and moving funeral pyre over the darkening waters. Matthew Arnold has described this strikingly in his poem ' Balder the Beautiful.'

Ancient instances might be multiplied indefinitely, showing that cremation and earth burial were practised side by side, but we are not now so much concerned with these urn burials as with those strange spectacles still to be seen among Eastern races, which are suggestive of a vast amount of lore, much of which has still to be unravelled.

FOR large sections of the human race such a method would be not only impracticable but impossible. Human flesh is not easily ignited or reduced to ashes; the bones particularly require careful treatment and intense heat. Now fuel is one of the necessaries of life, ranking next to water and food, and the procuring of fuel is, with many races, the greatest difficulty of existence. Those of mankind who live in the Arctic regions, and do their cooking and heating by seal blubber and oil, could not possibly use this method, though they are equally debarred from earth burial while the frost holds the land and water in its grip. Nevertheless, Dr. Uno Holmber says that cremation occurs among certain peoples in the north-east corner of Siberia (Chuckchee and Koriaks) and also among

STONE FOLLOWS THE FLAMES TO KEEP HIM IN MEMORY

No honour was felt to be too great to pay to the chieftain of Lampang, in Northern Siam, whose cremation took place in the year 1927. In addition to the particularly gorgeous cremation ceremonies a beautiful monument was set up to his memory, and this stone of remembrance is tended with loving care by the priests of his ancient creed.

the Buriats, but cannot have been among the earlier methods of the disposal of the dead, which was probably exposure.

At the other end of the scale are those who inhabit the great desert spaces of Africa and Arabia, and who treasure, as their sole fuel for cooking, the droppings of camels ; they certainly could not get enough heat or spare enough material for burning the dead. It is obvious that the method of burning was in its origin adopted by races who live in jungly country where wood is plentiful, and it is in such countries nowadays that we find the rite in its fullest manifestation. In that group of countries in Asia near the Equator, comprising India, Further India, Siam and Cambodia with the East Indies, constant burnings still take place.

It is among the Hindus that the practice is most widespread. We get the clue to this from Marco Polo, who says of the Brahmans that they burn the dead because if they were not burned worms would be bred which would eat the body, and when the body was all consumed they would die, and the soul belonging to that body would bear the sin and punishment for their death. He speaks (see page 61) of the burning of the dead in China, where the people were for the most part idolaters, i.e. Buddhists. As a matter of fact, among Buddhists at the present time the burning is confined to priests and sometimes royalties. Though abbots of long sanctity are regularly burnt in Burma, the kings of the royal house (when Burma had a royal house) were not burnt. The ceremony attending the burning of a Buddhist member of the hierarchy is described in the chapter on The Ceremonial Use of Effigies.

In Cambodia, where a king still reigns, though under French authority, it is the king himself who is the subject of these obsequies. The body, as with the Buddhist priests, is kept a long time, but whereas

THRONED ON HIS SUBJECTS' SHOULDERS FOR HIS JOURNEY TO THE CONSUMING FIRE

The death of a distinguished personage in Siam is attended by ceremonies almost as impressive as those observed for royalty. At the obsequies of the chieftain of Lampang, in Northern Siam, in 1927, the catafalque and bier were of the utmost magnificence. For four and a half years the body of the great ruler had lain in state in his palace, and when the time arrived for the cremation the bier was carried on the shoulders of a picked company of his devoted subjects, followed by representatives of royal families of the Far East.

the Buddhist is placed in a coffin and seethed in honey, the Cambodian kings are embalmed. At the ceremonial in Burma, when the coffin is finally opened, and this may be two or three years after death, before the final disposal of the body by fire the populace crowd and crush inward in the hope of dipping their fingers in the honey and sucking them and thereby gaining sanctity for themselves.

At the ceremony in Cambodia the king's body is deposited in a silver urn, and when taken out, some time within the year, it is set up in state on a throne for seven days that all may see. Not until the body is reduced to ashes may the new king really feel himself to be in authority; this ensures that there is no undue delay. It is the new king who sets a light to the huge pyathat decorated with gold tissue and costly hangings. The up-to-date method is to light a train or long fuse which burns slowly in a line of living fire towards the pyre, this being more decorous than the noisy rocket-snapping of Burma. When the whole has been reduced to ashes these are placed in a golden urn and eventually scattered over the river. The body of the Siamese king is also disposed of in much the same way.

The neighbouring people of Annam vary the custom and bury their emperors in a fine mausoleum, burning only a quantity of objects made of paper to represent the rooms and furniture amid which they lived. We have seen that the Chinese also do this, and in it we

FIRST STAGES OF A CAMBODIAN KING'S OBSEQUIES

Before cremation the body of a king of Cambodia is placed in a silver urn containing mercury, where it remains for a considerable time. It is then taken out and exposed to view. The lower photograph shows the funerary urn of King Sisowath (died 1927), the upper the dead monarch on his funeral couch.

THE KING OF CAMBODIA LIGHTS HIS FATHER'S FUNERAL PYRE

In the course of its passage to the funeral pyre the body of King Sisowath of Cambodia, contained in a silver-gilt urn, was conveyed in procession on a motor car made like a throne (top). After the lapse of an interval of eight days the cremation took place. A long fuse of inflammable cord led up to the funeral pyre, and after bowing with his ministers in prayer for the last time King Monivong, the dead ruler's son and successor, proceeded to set fire to the cord (bottom) which ignited the pyre.

E. O. Hoppé

STATUESQUE WOMEN OF BALI CARRY GIFTS TO THE BURNING PLACE

On the occasion of a cremation in the island of Bali, off the east coast of Sumatra, the principal part played by the women is the conveying of offerings of fruit and flowers to the place where the body is to be burned. These gifts are invariably carried on the head, and are frequently piled to a height of several feet. The vessels that contain them are sometimes very beautiful, nor would it be easy to find physique more magnificent and grace of bearing more superb than are possessed by these Balinese portresses.

E. O. Hoppé

FUNERAL PROCESSION IN BALI: HOW THE BEARERS TRY TO OUTWIT THE SPIRIT OF THE DEAD

In Bali the bodies of the dead are conveyed to the cremation ground in a towerlike structure, which varies in size and elaborateness of decoration according to the means of the departed. The journey to the burning place is no orderly procession, but a rude scramble. The tower with its precious burden is swayed from side to side and hurried to and fro, this way and that, by a noisy rabble of bearers. On no account, so the Balinese believe, must the deceased be allowed to revisit the old home; and all this jolting and zigzagging and side-tracking is done to confuse the spirit of the dead, to make sure that, once gone, it cannot possibly find its way back to trouble the living.

find some connexion with the ideas of the Egyptians, where objects of every sort that might be useful to the deceased in his new life were walled in with his embalmed body in the rock-hewn sepulchre. But whereas the Egyptians wished in every possible way to preserve the body, these ardent cremationists of the East would destroy it utterly. One would say that the burning of only the semblance of objects, without destroying the things themselves, shows a purer belief and grasp of the spirit world and its conditions than the Egyptian practice.

It is in the island of Bali, in the Dutch East Indies, that the ceremony is seen in its most elaborate aspect. Though there are some Buddhists and Mahomedans here, the great majority of the native races are Hindus, and their beliefs are mixed with animism, as are those of the hill tribes of Burma, and many another half-wild and highly superstitious people. It has been said of the Balians that religion is their chief occupation. Here, not only the great and wealthy, but every poor cultivator, aspires to a funeral pyre, and the relatives are as much concerned to secure it as the poor in England to have a showy funeral. But burning is not a cheap process, and often entails a considerable time of waiting before it can be achieved.

INDEED, as in Burma, where the interval becomes a regular gold-mine to the attendant Pôngyis, who harvest loudly ticking clocks and oil lamps by the score, until the lying-in-state looks like a bazaar, so here contributions are expected and received, in order that the great act may be carried out handsomely. Sometimes, however, it is to the bounty of royalty that the poor owe their satisfaction. For there are still royalties of a sort in Bali, who, though without a shadow of power, are recognized by the common folk as being different from themselves. When a royalty dies, those who have been keeping bodies hasten to take advantage of the chance; and not the poor only, even the well-off may come forward, too, on such an honourable occasion, which will bring folk from all the islands, far and near.

The rich preserve the bodies in the interval of waiting by placing them in a hollow tree trunk, and the poor make a shallow grave in the compound or kampong which is common to a group of thatched huts. If a member of the royal family does not die within a reasonable time, there is always the chance that sufficient neighbours, in possession of corpses, may come forward so as to spread the overhead charges. It is perhaps as well that the white ants and other scavengers do their work quickly in tropic climates, for when the time comes for exhumation what remains is harmless to the living, and may in fact be only a few bones. That so long a time has elapsed since the actual death relieves the tension of sorrow, allowing the people, even the relatives, to enjoy what is really their greatest festival.

Nothing spoils the day for the Bali crowd set out to enjoy themselves. The people put aside all care and business and, donning their gayest garments, gather eagerly at the news of a burning. But first

E. O. Hoppé

GRAVELY PERFORMING HIS SAD OFFICE

Mounted on the shoulders of his sturdy human steed, this little boy is the chief mourner at a Balinese cremation. His rich costume and adornments show that he comes of a cultured race. Even the lightly clad umbrella-bearer wears a floral head-dress.

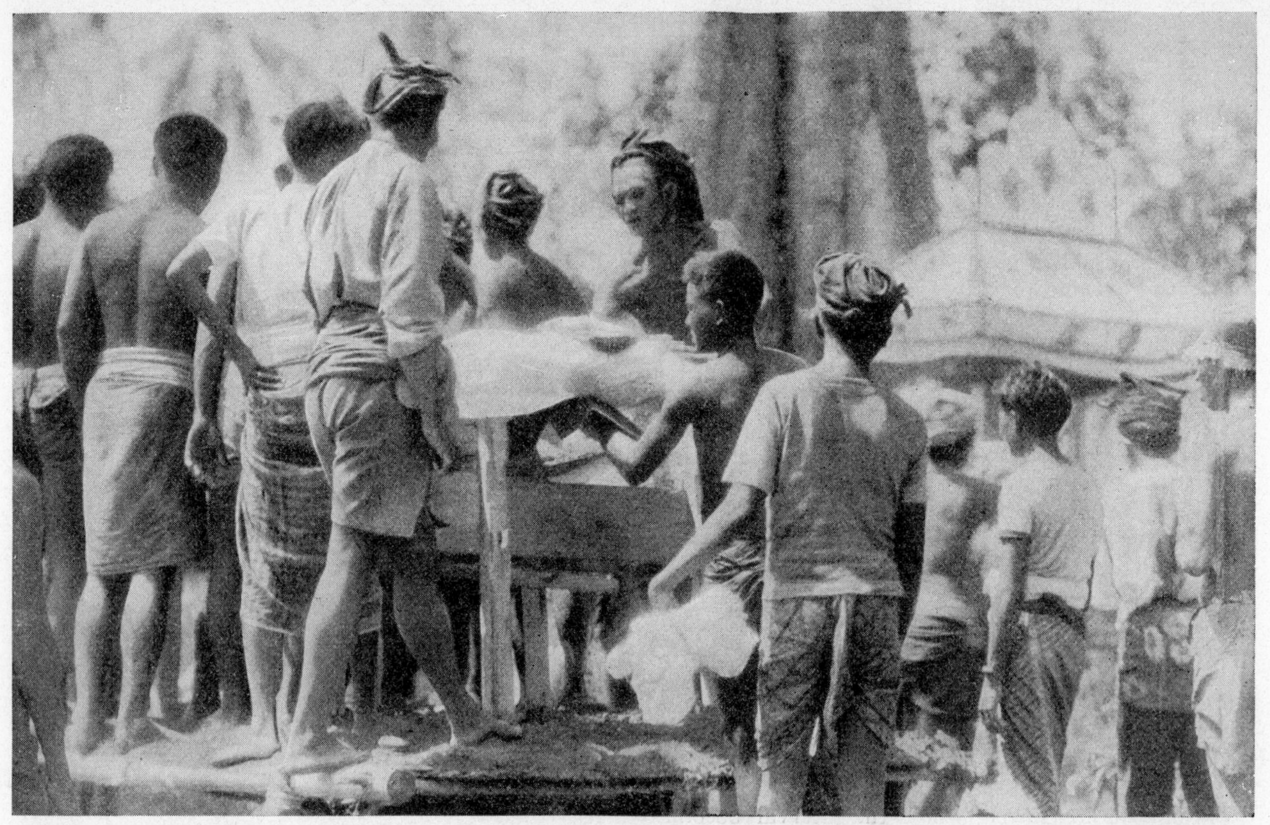

E. O. Hoppé

ATTENTIONS FOR THE BODY AND THE FIRE BEFORE THE CREMATION

It is the ambition of every Balinese, however poor, to be cremated, but cremation in Bali is an expensive process, and frequently it is a considerable time before sufficient contributions have been made. Where several years have elapsed between death and the time fixed for the burning all that remains of the corpse is fragments of bone. In such cases an effigy of wood is painted to represent the departed. The upper photograph shows the bodies or effigies being placed in the coffin, and the lower the fires being built under the coffins.

the corpse has to be collected and placed in the funeral pyre. It is considered unlucky for a dead body to go through the gate of the living in the compound, and so it is either lifted over the wall or some of the loosely built structure is knocked out to allow it egress. We say the corpse, but the ceremony seldom follows so hard on the death as to admit of that. If there are only bones, an effigy, which may be but a wooden board with a rough drawing of a man or woman on it, is substituted, and treated in every way as if it were the real thing. In the case of lepers, indeed, only effigies are permitted.

The tower or pyathat varies enormously, from the many-tiered and costly building, decorated with rich silks and tinsel hangings, to the humble, undraped framework of bamboo and paper, which, indeed, forms the basis of them all.

But before the corpse is placed in its tower many strange scenes take place. Ceremonial washing is carried out with water fetched from a holy well. Of all the odd customs connected with this ceremony, some of the oddest follow on this. The priest puts a ruby and gold ring on the tongue of the deceased; this is not burned, the same ring doing duty in any number of cases. A little piece of iron is placed between the incisors, and a melati flower between the eye-teeth. The bud of a lily is put into the nostrils, a little wax into the ears, a piece of plate-glass placed on the eyes, and a leaf of the intaran plant on the brow. This means that the deceased will be endowed at the reincarnation with a gifted tongue, strong yet dainty teeth, splendid nose, a sharp ear and lustrous eyes. The body is rubbed with a mixture made of yolk of egg, flowers and holy water.

When the corpse or its effigy is to be transferred from its temporary resting place to the tower, a wild scene takes place. The men of Bali, with their long hair flying and their bodies almost naked, attack the coffin and try to wrench it from the relatives, swaying backwards and forwards and even swinging it high above their heads. The effect is that of a huge football scrum. All this is done to signify the reluctance of the relatives to part with their dead. It may be likened to the artificial and hired keening which goes on at an Irish wake.

The women of Bali take no part in this rough-and-tumble scene, but content themselves with bringing offerings of flowers and fruit to the burning place. Amazing some of these are. They are piled as high as the tower of baskets a Covent Garden porter carries on his head. They are interwoven cunningly and balanced with supreme dignity.

When the body nears the niche, high up in the tower, intended for it, the relatives, with pointing forefingers, shout out their wishes to the departing one, who, if he were good, may carry their prayers with him upwards.

E. O. Hoppé

RITE OF WATER PRECEDES FINAL RITE OF FIRE

When the tumultuous funeral journey of a Balinese has been completed one rite alone remains before the body is given over to the flames. It is sprinkled with holy water. In order to accomplish this the corpse is removed from the tower, the ceremony being performed beneath a canopy of white cloth, which is held high over the body by attendants

Ewing Galloway

DEATH CUSTOM AMONG THE BATAKS: WIVES AND RELATIVES DANCE AND FEAST ROUND THE FUNERAL PYRE

Among the Bataks, who cremate their dead, there is as much celebration on the occasion of a funeral as there is for a wedding. The Bataks are a people of Indonesian stock, dwelling in the north-central uplands of Sumatra. Though possessing a fair measure of culture and a written language, they have long been notorious for particularly revolting forms of cannibalism. When a Batak dies he is laid in state upon his bier within a funeral pyre. All day long the wives and relatives of the departed dance around the pyre and feast. The number of wives will be in proportion to the deceased's wealth. At the moment when the sun sinks below the rim of the horizon the pyre is lighted, and the flames rapidly consume the corpse.

Ewing Galloway

WHERE THE FIRES OF THE DEAD SMOKE AND FLAME BY INDIA'S HOLY RIVER

From Hardwar to Calcutta a feature of the Ganges, the holiest river of India, is the ghats, or flights of steps on the banks. These are designed primarily to facilitate bathing, drinking, and other ritual acts of Hinduism ; the burning ghats have cremation grounds. Of the burning ghats those of the sacred city of Benares are in most request, but the Calcutta burning ghat here seen is very popular. The body to be burnt is anointed with ghee, and after suitable prayers have been said the next of kin sets fire to the pyre.

Hundreds of carriers are willing to convey the tower to the burning. No one who has seen an ordinary Hindu funeral coming along a street is likely to forget the running and singing, and swaying of the bier this way and that, so different from the funereal walk of the mutes at an English funeral. It is the same with the tower. The men run and sway and sing ; they halt and retrace their steps ; where the ground permits they return in a circle and they zigzag here and there. All this is to cover up their tracks and make it hard for the spirit of the deceased to find its way back home. This is a dread shared by many of the hill tribes of Burma, who will do anything to ensure that the dead, however beloved in life, will not return to disturb them ; and not only by them, but, as we have seen in other chapters, all over the savage world.

The commonest form of bier for the wealthy is a huge animal (see page 67) that stands four-square in his niche. This adds to the weird scene. A long white rope is attached to the top of the tower, and with this the movements of the carriers are directed. When a prince is burned this is decorated with gold leaf ; it represents a snake, the head of which is carried by the priests, and before the burning the snake is 'killed' by having four arrows from the four quarters of the compass shot into its head.

Before burning the body is taken from the animal receptacle or from the simple wooden bier, whichever it may be, and sprinkled with holy water. The boys now make haste to secure the treasures of tinsel and bits of decoration, swarming up the bamboo scaffolding and stripping it as if it were a Christmas tree. Then the replaced body is burnt with the tower, which makes fuel for it, with the sacrificial gifts thrown in, and with, lastly, a few wretched chickens tied to the top to teach the soul to soar !

In Batak, Sumatra, the wives and relations dance around the pyre, which is lighted at the sinking of the sun.

With cremation ceremonies as performed in India most people have been made familiar by descriptions of the burning ghats beside the holy river Ganges.

E.N.A.

TOWERING SPIRE SOON TO FALL BY THE FLAMES

The Laos, a people of Tai stock found in parts of Siam and French Indo-China, practise both burial and cremation; the latter they reserve for rulers and monks. Their funeral pyres are similar to those of the other parts of Siam. The photograph shows a cremation ceremony at Chieng-mai, the capital of the Laos state of that name

ascend the heavenly regions.'

The nearest relative sets fire to the pile.

In European countries the rapid development of sanitary science has given a great impetus to cremation. Even in early times it was recognized as the only measure that could be taken, for instance, after a battle, when large numbers of corpses were left on the field, or in case of plague or famine; though in the first instance it may have been as much the fear of mutilation by the returning enemy as the more prosaic desire for sanitary precaution that instigated the act.

The first case of cremation in modern times in Europe seems to have been in Italy about the middle of the nineteenth century. The Cremation Society of England was founded in 1875, but had to meet and overcome harassing opposition. The then Home Secretary declared it illegal when it desired to open the first crematorium. It was not, indeed, until ten years after the founding of the society that the rites of cremation were legally recognized. Since then the society has grown apace, and is now dropping the qualifying words 'of England' in its title. It began with one crematorium and three cremations in the first year of active work; in 1930 there were twenty-one crematoria in the United Kingdom and between four and five thousand cremations. But the results in Germany are much more startling, for the figures there are fifty-three thousand cremations in

That at Calcutta is widely used. It is maintained at the expense of the Calcutta municipality. Nobody belonging to an inferior caste is allowed to touch the corpse. The dead body is anointed with ghee (clarified butter) and prayers are said: 'Let the holy waters of the sacred rivers and holy places sanctify the deceased.' 'Oh, thou departed spirit,' runs the invocation, 'I am burning every part of this your earthly body, which, being full of passions and ignorance, did pious as well as impious acts. May the Supreme Lord pardon all sinful acts committed by you, either knowingly or unknowingly, and mayst thou

the one year, or a thousand more than all that have taken place in the United Kingdom since the foundation.

There is no need to describe the details of the process as carried out among us, for these are sufficiently familiar to most people. A noteworthy fact, however, is that the modern Briton is inclining to dispense with the cinerary urn and to prefer free disposal of the ashes, scattering these in the Gardens of Rest provided at the crematoria for that purpose or elsewhere in fulfilment of some expressed desire.

RITUAL PRACTICES OF BAPTISM

In what follows Baptism is considered only in its aspect of initiation into a duly organized society and without regard to its acceptance by Christians as one of the sacraments 'necessary to salvation.' Divergences in its practice alone are surveyed here. Reference may also be made to the chapter on Ceremonies of Dedication and Consecration

Around one of the most beautiful rites of Christianity there has gathered a tangle of custom, tradition and, inevitably, controversy —for each man sees the road to salvation with different eyes, and sometimes, so certain chapters in the history of Christianity would seem to suggest, pauses so long to debate and wrangle about which is the right road that he forgets to travel at all. When Jesus was baptized by John in the river Jordan, He was held to have sanctified the water to the mystical washing away of sin. This is the one point upon which a majority of Christian sects (not all, however) are agreed, though there would appear to be nothing in Holy Scripture to warrant the doctrine. Among nearly all those who profess the name of Christ (the Quakers are an exception) the rite is practised. Divergences in method, arising partly out of the theological theories involved and partly from different interpretations of the Scriptures, have, however, taken place during the passing of the years. There arose the nice point as to the meaning of the Greek origin of the word Baptism. Was it 'dipping' or 'washing'? Our Lord, seeing that John the Baptist performed the rite in the Jordan, was probably immersed, and S. John in his Gospel places it on record that when he himself desired to perform the ceremony he went to Aenon, near Salim, because there was much water there.

The advocates of 'affusion,' as opposed to total immersion, support their view by bringing forward the action of S. Paul, when he was in prison, in baptizing the jailer and his family. It is distinctly stated that the ceremony was performed at night, and it is argued that it is inconceivable that conveniences could have existed in such circumstances for total immersion. And then there was another difficulty. If baptism is in itself an actual cleansing from all sin, wouldn't it be better to defer submitting to the rite until near the close of our pilgrimage, so that the guilt of a whole life might thus be washed away? On the other side it is claimed that at baptism the gift of the Holy Ghost is imparted, and that no one has a right to deprive a human being for the major portion of his existence upon earth of this priceless virtue, and that therefore the newborn infant should be baptized. But how—so runs the controversy—can an infant have been guilty of any sins which require washing away by baptism? To this it is answered that by the invocation of the Trinity and the sprinkling of water the infant's participation in the guilt of Adam is sacramentally washed away. Some attribute to christening what is called an 'immortalising efficacy,' so that by baptism alone a person becomes entitled to that immortality which Jesus of Nazareth revealed. And yet others look upon baptism and regeneration as co-relative.

This necessarily incomplete exposition of the controversial points involved explains to some extent the divergences in practice, which it is our main business here to touch upon. What is the effect of baptism? In the old days the theory of the infant's participation in Adam's guilt was carried so far that the child, it was held, was possessed by an evil spirit, and in the first Prayer Book there occurred a variation of the ancient Prayer of Exorcism in which the priest commanded the unclean spirit 'that thou come out and depart from these infants.'

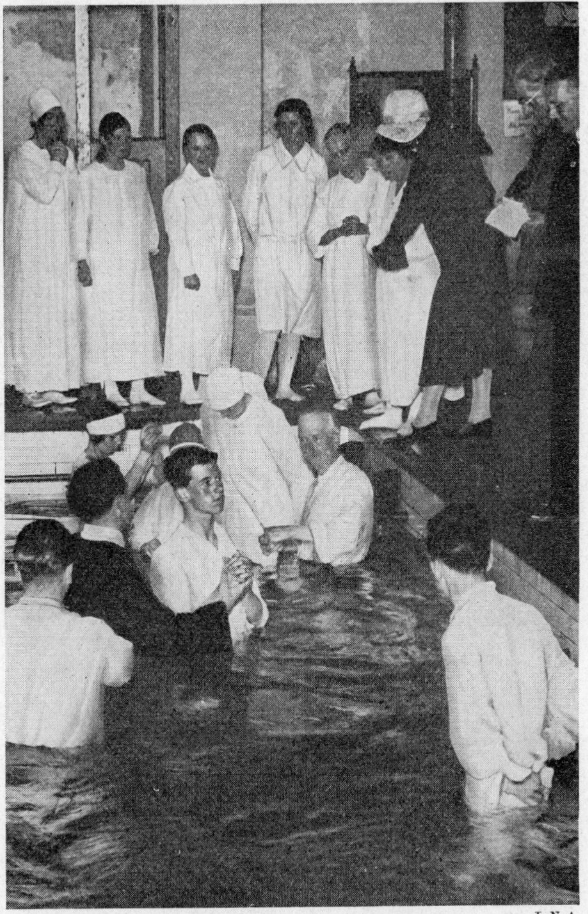

L.N.A.

BAPTISMAL SERVICE IN A SWIMMING BATH

A most unusual event occurred at Worthing in the summer of 1929, when a pastor of the Elim Four Square Gospel Alliance baptized a number of converts in the Corporation swimming bath. The candidates, male and female, were totally immersed by the pastor.

Topical Press

ASTONISHING SCENE IN A LONDON GARDEN—A PUBLIC BAPTISM AT CLAPHAM

What may not improperly be described as mass baptism is a ceremony not infrequently performed by the Elim Four Square Gospel Alliance in Britain, a sect that has no connexion with the American religious society of the same name, although its teaching is similar. This photograph shows the remarkable scene in the grounds of the Institution's college near Clapham Common in the summer of 1929, when the Principal publicly baptized three hundred converts, by total immersion in a large tank provided for that special purpose, in the presence of some three thousand spectators. This community holds the belief that curative properties attach to the rite of baptism, and demonstrations of faith healing often accompany its celebration

The cursed spirit was also asked to remember 'Thy sentence, remember thy judgement, remember the day to be at hand wherein thou shalt burn in fire everlasting prepared for thee and thy angels, and presume not hereafter to exercise any tyranny towards these infants whom Christ has bought with His Precious Blood, and by His Holy Baptism calleth to be of His flock.'

In the Roman Catholic service not only is a Prayer of Exorcism employed, but the rite is elaborated by the blessing of the Salt of Wisdom, which is placed in the child's mouth, the touching with spittle in the form of a cross of the ears and nostrils of the child, and the anointing of its breast and shoulders with the oil of catechumens. This belief in an evil spirit present in the infant until baptism is preserved in a very ancient tradition, still extant, that it is unlucky for the child not to cry when touched by the holy water—the cry being regarded as the passing out of the demon. Anxious mothers, or conscientious godmothers, of today have been known to give the baby a sly pinch before handing him over to the minister to ensure the lucky wail.

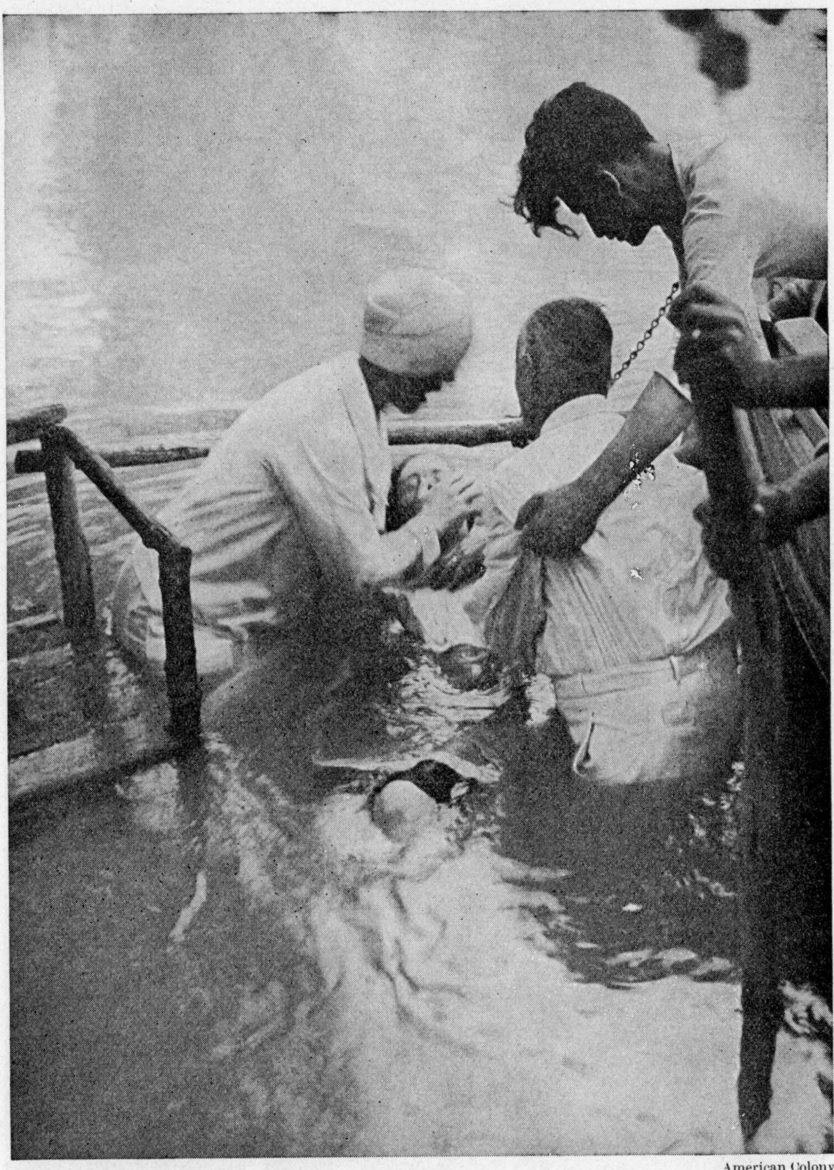

American Colony

WOMAN EVANGELIST BAPTIZING IN A SACRED STREAM

Controversy has raged round the personality of Aimee McPherson, leader of the Elim Four Square Gospel Alliance in America, but there can be no question of her energy in evangelistic work. She lays especial stress upon the baptismal rite in her ceremonies, and has herself conducted tours of pilgrims to the Holy Land and baptized converts in the river Jordan.

The huge fonts in some of our churches point to the practice of total immersion right up to the time of the Reformation and probably beyond. The child was dipped three times, at first on the right side, at the second on the left, and at the third face downwards. The Baptist community practise immersion, and on the grounds that the apostles were commanded first to go and teach all nations and then baptize them only administer the rite to adults. Tertullian, who lived towards the second century A.D., declared that there is no difference whether a man is baptized in the sea, a pool, in a lake, in a river, or in a fountain, adding that 'all waters from the ancient privilege of their origin obtain, after prayer to God, the sacrament of sanctification.' Many baptisms, following this view, are performed in the open air. Tertullian also mentions a curious elaboration of the ceremony which has apparently disappeared—the giving of milk and honey to the baptized person immediately after immersion. According to the same authority it was the rule that the person having received this sacred washing should never wash himself again!

Special importance attached to the water in which the child or adult was to be baptized. Nowadays every priest of the Anglican Church is careful to see that it is safely disposed of after a private christening. In the olden times special days were set aside for the benediction of the water, the favourite ones being Easter Eve and Whitsun Eve. Considerations of health would appear to have ultimately brought about an alteration in this procedure, and the water is now sanctified as required. In the Anglican ritual a prayer for this purpose is included. Originally, too, the blessing of the water was performed only by a bishop.

This last statement brings to mind one of those many disputes which have arisen in this country between the law of the land and the custom of the Established Church. According to strict ecclesiastical tradition, baptism, which is one of the two sacraments formally retained by the English Church 'as generally necessary to salvation,' can only be performed by a priest. The law, however, says otherwise. A clash came in a famous case in 1809. The Rubric in the Prayer Book at the commencement of the order for the burial of the dead lays it down that 'the Office ensuing is not to be used for any that die unbaptized or excommunicate or have laid violent hands upon themselves.' A man called Kemp desired his child to be buried. The clergyman refused to perform the service on the ground that the deceased had not been baptized. The father objected that the child had been baptized, the ceremony having been performed by a layman. The clergyman still refusing, the case was brought into court, and judgement was ultimately delivered to the effect that the baptism was sufficient, and that the clergyman had acted contrary to the law.

American Colony

EPIPHANY PILGRIMS ON THE BANKS OF THE JORDAN

In the Greek Orthodox Church Epiphany is a day set aside for baptism. It is the ambition of every member of that church to be baptized in the Jordan, and at that season of the year the banks of the holy river are lined with pilgrims. The lower photograph shows pilgrims waiting for the service, and above, a party is seen having tea while baptismal robes dry upon the bushes

The naming of the child is another interesting part of the ceremony of baptism, which seems to have derived its origin directly from the example of the Jews, who assigned a name when the ceremony of circumcision was performed. This becomes the Christian name of the child, though in England the only legal name is that entered by the registrar of births. The Roman Catholic Church allots another name at the time of confirmation. The employment of godfathers or godmothers as sponsors—never less than three—is an interesting survival of the days of Christian persecution.

American Colony

WHITE ROBES OF BAPTISM GLEAM BY THE HOLY RIVER

The Greek Orthodox pilgrims who flock to the river Jordan to be baptized at the Epiphany service wear a special kind of white robe for the occasion, and these they keep, to be used eventually as their burial shrouds. The scene by the river is very striking. First of all the priests, wearing gorgeous vestments, bless the water, and then the candidates, having put on their baptismal robes, plunge into the stream. Crowds of interested spectators watch the ceremonies, and tents are set up for the shelter and refreshment of the travellers.

Seeing that the parents of the little Christian, or the adult convert, might very soon be hurried away to death, these friends of the family were called in as sponsors to see that the child or person lately received into the Church should not miss any opportunities of a proper knowledge of the Christian faith.

From very primitive times there would seem to have existed a belief in the curative virtues of baptism. Quite recently extraordinary scenes arising out of this belief have taken place in London under the auspices of the Elim Four Square Gospel Alliance. In the summer of 1929 this religious society carried out wholesale baptisms of converts in their grounds at Clapham Park, and even at the corporation swimming bath at Worthing. Men and women of all ages were totally immersed, amid scenes of extraordinary religious fervour. In the spring of 1930 and 1931 Principal George Jeffreys, the head of the sect in England, carried out monster demonstrations at the Albert Hall. He himself performed the baptismal ceremony by total immersion on one of these occasions for two hundred persons.

The ceremony was clearly used as a confirmation of faith, and the faith so engendered, not only in the baptized person but in the audience, was directed towards the cure of bodily infirmities. After the singing of many hymns and an address, and the singing of another hymn, by which time the fervour of the congregation had become electric, the Principal called upon those who had been healed to testify to their cures. There followed scenes not unlike those which can be witnessed at Lourdes. People waved their hands to signify that they had been cured of such diseases as cancer or tumours; no fewer than twenty-six persons claimed that they had been crippled and were now whole; and finally fourteen publicly confessed that they had been blind, in one or both eyes, and now could see.

Underwood & Underwood

BAPTIZING A NEGRO OF GEORGIA IN THE OPEN STREAM

Outdoor baptism, in streams, lakes or ponds, is a very widespread practice. Negroes in the southern states of America are rarely christened inside a church. They usually line up outside the building and then walk in procession to the waterside, where prayers are said and chants sung. The photograph shows a convert on the point of being immersed in the Savannah river.

Though the Elim Four Square Gospel Alliance in Britain disclaims any connexion with the American sect and its notorious leader, Aimee McPherson, of whom Mr. Sinclair Lewis gave a rather unkind picture in 'Elmer Gantry,' their teaching is similar. Aimee McPherson, indeed, features the baptismal rite very strongly in her ceremonies. She has even arranged personally conducted tours to the Holy Land, and has carried out wholesale baptisms in the sacred waters of the Jordan itself.

But Aimee McPherson and her converts are not the only people to make use of the Jordan for baptismal purposes. For generations that stream has figured to the Greek Church very much as Mecca does to the Mahomedans. From wherever the Eastern version of the Faith is held pilgrims flock at the time of Epiphany to the banks of the Jordan. After the waters

West India Committee

CHRISTENING PROCESSION OF NEGROES IN THE WEST INDIES

Among the negroes of the West Indies open-air baptism is common, and a christening is generally made the occasion of a procession. These functions are picturesque in the extreme. As a rule the candidates for baptism wear white clothes, while many of the others indulge the taste for bright colours which is innate in their race. Through the enchanting landscape of the islands wind long lines of negroes, some carrying gay banners bearing elaborate devices and texts. A service is held beside the stream before the actual ceremony of immersion.

have been blessed by the priests in attendance the pilgrims don special garments of white, which are afterwards carefully put away to be used as their burial shrouds. They then descend into the water to receive the sacrament of baptism. Subsequently they take tea on the banks, where the scene is made picturesque by the variety of costumes and the streets of tents erected for accommodation of the pilgrims.

How man's mind clings naturally to the magical virtues, superimposed upon a very simple and a very beautiful piece of ritual, is demonstrated by the special sanctity supposed to attach to the waters of Jordan. The fact that the Forerunner carried out his ministrations there, and that Christ himself was baptized in the river, not unnaturally aroused a feeling of special reverence. And from this sentiment springs the whole belief that there is something extraordinarily potent for good in the muddy and, it must be confessed, rather insanitary waters of Jordan. To this day flasks of the fluid are imported from Palestine for christenings, in spite of Tertullian's ruling, already quoted, that all waters obtain, after prayer to God, the sacrament of sanctification.

Ordinary rivers and ponds are, indeed, used for christenings not only in this country but in every part of the world. In the southern states of America baptism among the negroes in these conditions is still practised. A procession is formed in the church and from there it marches to the river or stream. One of our illustrations shows a convert just previous to immersion in the Savannah river. Processions with banners also form part of the ceremonies which were performed in the West Indies, where pools or streams are employed. Usually the priest and the person to be baptized are dressed in white robes, but sometimes the negro minister clings to the black garments of his profession even in the water—a severe tax, one would imagine, on the ministerial wardrobe.

In the British Isles the carrying out of baptisms in the open air, with some river or stream as a font, is most common today in Wales. They have become there, indeed, a recognized custom. Annually now

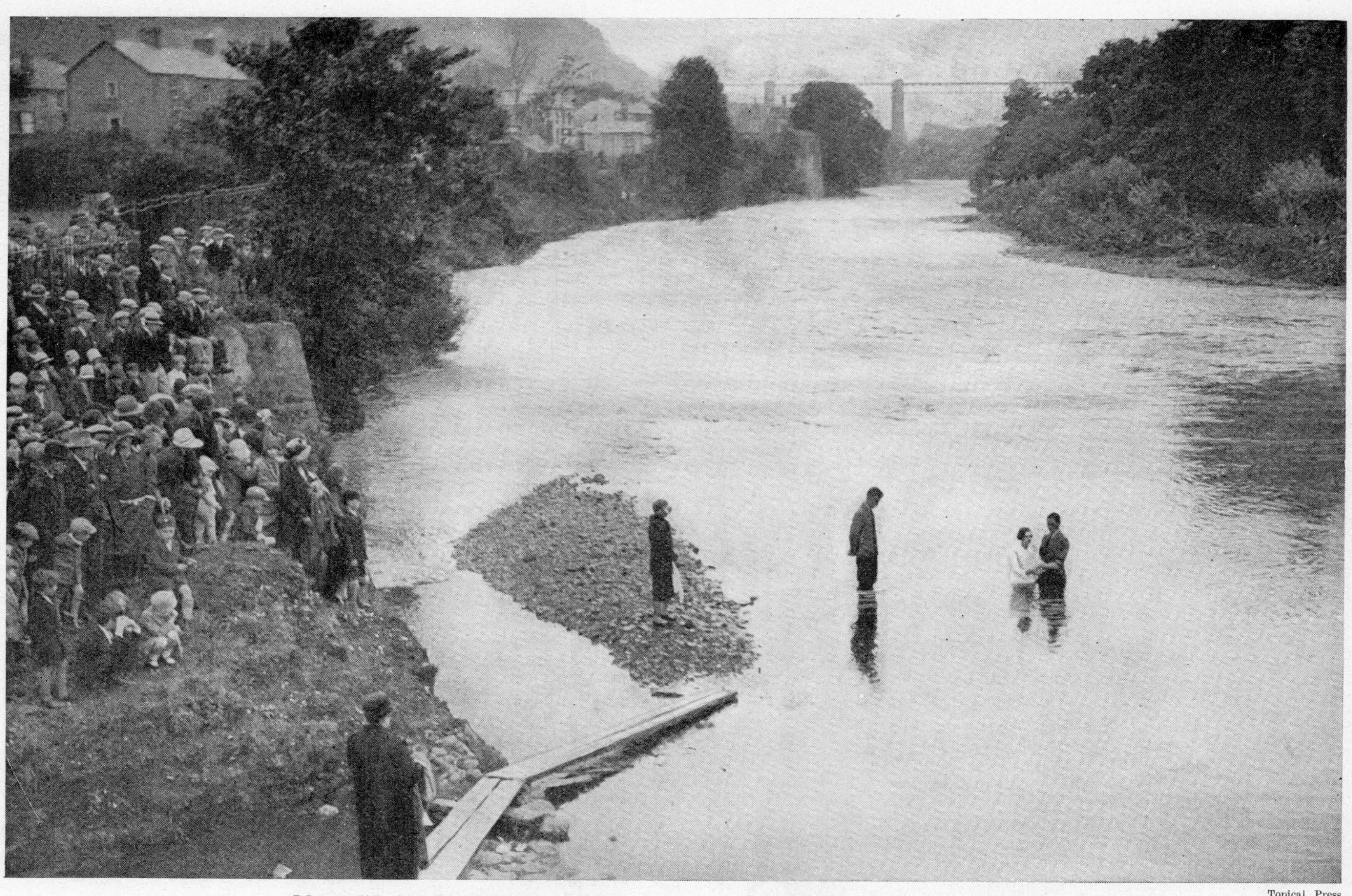

Topical Press

DRAMATIC PROFESSION OF CHRISTIANITY ON THE BANKS OF A WELSH RIVER

Public baptism by immersion in some river or stream is a recognized custom in Wales, and deeply impressive scenes are witnessed at the performance of these ceremonies. Welsh people are notorious for their religious emotionalism, and this is excited to a high pitch of exaltation by the dramatic profession of faith made by those submitting to the sacramental rite. The river Howey near Llandrindod Wells is frequently selected for the ceremony; so, too, is the river Taff, on the banks of which at Taff's Wells, a mining village near Cardiff, the baptismal service shown in this photograph was held in the presence of a considerable congregation in September 1930.

Keystone

'AND THE PARENTS BROUGHT IN THE CHILD'

A pretty ceremony that dates back to the thirteenth century has been revived at Blidworth, near Mansfield, Nottinghamshire. The baby boy last baptized in the village is laid in a cradle before the altar in the church and gently rocked by the officiating priest, the act symbolising the presentation of the infant Jesus in the Temple. The ceremony is known as the Blidworth Rocking.

photo-journalism makes the public familiar with scenes that would otherwise appear to the majority of people somewhat bizarre and out of the ordinary. The superior person may still smile when he sees the picture of a black-coated minister apparently teaching some girl fully clothed to swim on her back. But those who have actually witnessed the ceremony, both in the river Howey near Llandrindod Wells or in the river Taff, speak of the deep impressiveness of the scene. Faith and sincerity can, indeed, rob any such ceremony of the suggestion of the grotesque. It should be remembered that the Baptists, who most frequently perform these open air rites, regard the act as a profession of faith in Jesus Christ by the participant. It is his act rather than the act of the Church. As someone has said : ' It is with the Baptists essentially " Believers' Baptism "—an act in which a particular individual experience is dramatised ; ' and the blue sky and the running waters and the tree-covered banks — the sense of God's presence everywhere--must make the performance of the rite for the participant very memorable and produce a lasting effect.

There are some curious variations of christening ceremonies—some purely religious, some, on the other hand, which seem to merge with paganism. Of the former is the quaint ceremony known as the ' Blidworth Rocking,' which dates back to the thirteenth century. The latest baptized baby in the village is placed in the cradle before the altar and rocked gently several times, the ceremony symbolising the presentation of the child Jesus in the Temple. The cradle used for the ceremony, which has lately been revived, was given to the church by a woman whose family had owned it for many hundreds of years.

Of the semi-pagan rites the christening of battleships and the like can be ignored, but the same does not apply to bells. According to the doctrine of the Church of Rome bells ' have much virtue,' and pray God for the living and the dead. They also produce devotion in the hearts of believers, and finally, drive away storms, tempests and devils. In the old days—and the practice still exists—the baptism of a bell followed exactly that of the baptism of a child. The bell was anointed with water, oil and spittle, was sprinkled with holy water, named and crossed. The concluding prayer asked for a special blessing upon the bell so ' that when it sounds in people's ears they may adore Thee—and the devil be afraid and tremble and fly at the sound of it . . . that it may deliver from danger of wind and thunder.' The practice of naming bells, presumably after some form of christening service, long survived—as the curious may see if they care to climb the steeple of one of the ancient parish churches in the country.

Finally, the sacrament of baptism, or the ordinance of christening, has this distinguishing feature : it can only be received once. This principle has always been acknowledged in the Church as following directly from the object of the Sacrament—incorporation into the body of the Church—and its violation is to be avoided as sacrilegious. Hence the question with which the order for the administration of public baptism in the Church of England opens : ' Hath this child been already baptized, or no ? '

Wide World Photos

VICTIM WHOSE BLOOD MUST BE SHED ON A HOLY BUILDING IN AFRICA

The ritual immolation of animals is a common and old-established practice A widespread form is the sacrifice of goats and other creatures at the foundation or opening of a new building In Greece today an animal is usually killed and its blood allowed to flow over a foundation stone. The photograph shows a priest of the Habbe tribe, a race inhabiting Mount Bandiagara, in Nigeria, dragging a sacrificial goat to the door of a mystery house. The animal will be slaughtered on the roof and its blood poured over the façade of the building.

STRANGE SACRIFICIAL RITES

ALTHOUGH human sacrifice is very rarely met with nowadays, the sacrifice of animals is a common feature of many primitive cults. The curious bear festival of the Ainu is dealt with in the chapter on Magic and the Means of Life, and forms of propitiation of spirit forces are touched upon in the chapters on Medicine Men and their Magic, and Driving Out the Devils of Disease.

SINCE man first became man he has offered up sacrifices to his gods, whether it be to propitiate them for his misdeeds, to enlist their support in his enterprises, or to unite with them in a kind of mystical communion.

On the principle that the gods love best that which costs their worshippers most, human sacrifices were originally much in vogue; but for ages past the divinities have had to content themselves as a rule with offerings of birds and beasts, cereals and fruits. Old customs die hard, however, especially when they are concerned with religion; and as recently as April, 1931, a case of human sacrifice in India was reported in The Times.

A village woman, it appears, lay ill with smallpox, and her husband had resort to one Godwen, who was reputed to be able to cure sickness by singing songs in honour of the goddess Mariamman. For two days after he was called in Godwen roamed around in a state of extreme excitement. Then he went to the sick woman's house, snatched up her five-months-old baby, and after swinging it round the rude granite image worshipped by the villagers when their cattle are stricken with murrain, strangled it and threw its body into a prickly pear bush. Godwen was arrested and tried for murder; and although in his defence he pleaded that he was led astray by an evil spirit, the judge ruled that he had fully intended to make a human sacrifice, and sentenced him to death.

It would be difficult to find a parallel in other lands of so extraordinary an episode, but still the sacrificial rites practised by primitive peoples are sufficiently remarkable. One of the strangest, both in conception and in execution, is the bear festival of the Ainu, described in the chapter on Magic and the Means of Life. The bear, it must be borne in mind, plays a great part in the life of all the peoples inhabiting the region of the Amur and Siberia as far as Kamchatka, both as the most formidable beast of prey and as providing a specially palatable food. The animal, indeed, is regarded as a being of a higher order than man, some portion of whose powers, particularly its courage and strength, may be acquired by those who partake of its flesh

E.N.A.

PROPITIATING THE GODDESS KALI

Siva's consort is worshipped under many names, among them being Kali, the bloodthirsty goddess of death. Sacrifices innumerable are made to appease her. The Indians here seen have already slain seven goats, and the eighth is on the point of being decapitated.

THE Gilyaks and several other Siberian peoples also hold annual bear festivals. In the main the procedure follows that adopted among the Ainu, but there are, of course, local variations. Among the Gilyaks, for instance, the bear to be sacrificed is led first to the river bank to ensure a plentiful supply of fish, and then from house to house, being offered fish and brandy en route. After it has been killed a number of dogs are slain in couples, male and female, apparently in the expectation that 'the lord of the highest mountain' will change their skins and allow them to return next year as bears.

Among the Altaians on the Siberian-Mongolian frontier—the Oirots and Buriats, in particular—animal sacrifices are very common, being made the occasion for great assemblies, at which marksmen and riders, wrestlers and leapers, display their skill; and one and all unite in the ritualistic drinking of buttermilk. As a rule the meat of the victims is devoured forthwith, but the head, legs, tail, lungs, larynx and heart are left attached to the

Kurt Lubinski

BOLSHEVIST PROPAGANDA AGAINST HORSE SACRIFICE

The Soviet government opposes the horse sacrifices of Shamanism. The lower of these two posters shows a sacrificial feast, and bears the legend, ' There are no gods ! No sacrifice of horses will deliver you from your need . . .' The comment on the idyllic scene depicting the horse as the friend of man runs, ' . . . but the Soviet government guarantees you wealth and progress.'

skin ; and this, stuffed with straw or twigs, with birch branches stuck in its nostrils and a piece of bark affixed to its forehead, is then suspended on a consecrated birch tree. With the Buriats the sacrifice is preceded by the strange little ceremony of planting in the ground a number of birch rods, the tops of which are then tied together with a rope of hair, intertwined with black and white ribbons. Next the shaman reads a prayer, and then, at his command, all present empty the contents of their drinking vessels on to the ground. After this has been twice repeated the cups are thrown away, and he whose cup falls on its bottom is believed to be exceedingly lucky. Then after the victim has been slain and flayed, and its hide exposed, the shaman goes on his hands and knees and butts at the worshippers with imaginary horns, and does his best to dislodge the birch rods from their positions.

In the case of a horse sacrifice the ceremonial requires three days, or rather, evenings, for its completion. The first evening is devoted to a preparatory ritual. In the midst of a thicket of birch trees the shaman, attired in all his magical toggery, plentifully beribboned and loaded with bells, erects a kind of leafy bower, called the ' yurta.' In this is set a young tree, covered with a flag, with its lower branches lopped off and a number of notches cut in its trunk—each notch representing one of the numerous heavens of shamanistic mythology. The yurta is surrounded with a fence, and by the entrance is set a birch stick with a noose of horsehair attached.

The proceedings commence with the shaman flourishing a birch twig over the head of the horse that is to be sacrificed, to indicate that its soul is being driven to the abode of Bai-Yulgen. He then ' collects spirits ' in his tambourine with a sweep of his arm,

Kurt Lubinski

NOMADS OF THE ALTAI OF TODAY USE THE SACRIFICE OF THE SCYTHIANS OF OLD

Sacrifices of animals, especially horses, are common among the Shamanists of the Siberian-Mongol region. A kind of altar (bottom), known as a 'yurta,' is erected of leafy birch boughs, and over this is set a young birch tree on a V-shaped support. In the ground are thrust birch rods, between whose tops is hung hair rope decked with black and white ribbons. After the horse is killed the skull and hide are displayed on the birch tree over the yurta. The ancient Scythians surrounded the burial places of their chiefs with slaughtered horses impaled on stakes.

F. Kingdon Ward

ALL THAT IS LEFT OF BULLOCKS AND BUFFALOES SACRIFICED TO THE GODS

The Dinka are a Nilotic negro people who devote themselves to cattle breeding. Dependent on rain for their subsistence, they worship a rain god, Dengdit, shrines to whose honour are scattered over the Dinka country. At these bullocks are sacrificed in order to move the heavenly rain-maker to send down rain on the parched land. The horns of the animals are fastened to the post in front of the rain god's shrine (top). The lower photograph shows a Maru hut, in north-east Burma, with skulls of sacrificial buffaloes nailed to the main support.

calling each spirit by name and answering for each as he is supposed to arrive: 'I also am here, kam.' When the full complement of spirits is present, the shaman, or kam, leaves the yurta and mounts a scarecrow made to resemble a goose, and, flapping his arms to simulate the movement of wings, chants loudly and slowly:

Beneath the white sky,
  Above the white cloud;
Beneath the blue sky,
  Above the blue cloud,
Skyward ascend, O bird!

The goose replies (through the shaman, of course) with a series of quack-quacks; and the kam, still mounted on the scarecrow's back, acts as if he is pursuing the soul of the sacrificial horse, neighing like a horse and flapping his arms like a goose, until, with the help of the spectators, he is supposed to drive the horse into the enclosure to where is the horsehair noose. After violent efforts the horse is supposed to break away, and again the shaman neighs and flaps and pursues. At last, after much effort, it is finally 'captured,' and the shaman dismounts from his scarecrow steed.

Now the real sacrificial horse is brought forward by the 'holder of the head,' blessed by the kam, and then killed by a thrust through the aorta. The flesh is consumed by those present, and it need hardly be said that the choicest morsels are reserved for the shaman. Then the skull and hide are affixed to the young birch tree placed in readiness in the yurta. The next day after sunset the shaman performs a kind of religious drama, illustrating a kam's pilgrimage to the abode of Bai-Yulgen; and the third day is taken up with feasting and libations to the gods. Of late years the Bolshevist government has waged a strenuous campaign against shamanism in general and horse sacrifices in particular; but it is yet too early to evaluate its results.

SACRIFICIAL GOAT OF VOODOO IN HAITI

The goat standing in front of this Voodoo priestess is to be sacrificed to one of the old African nature gods. It has been dressed up in a red robe, and its horns have been decorated with ribbons and tinsel. The animal's throat will be cut, and its blood drunk and sprinkled over the worshippers.

Animal sacrifices play a great part in Voodoo—that extraordinary conglomeration of pagan rites and Christian concepts that constitutes the religion of the Haitian negroes. On the occasion of the 'Petro' ceremony, says Mr. W. B. Seabrook in his remarkable book, The Magic Island, hundreds of natives assemble in a clearing in the forest, in the centre of which is erected a 'tunnelle'—a kind of leafy passage-way. Before its entrance stands a papaloi or priest—an old man, clad in a surplice, blue overall, and a turban; and a mamaloi (priestess) dances for a while, and then falls prostrate.

Now from the 'mystery house' is led a small black bull, adorned for the sacrifice, robed and garlanded and with lighted candles affixed to its horns. It is placed on a platform beneath the leafy canopy, and all the company kneel before it; while the women chant 'O Lord, forgive our sins.' Next, the other sacrificial beasts—goats, kids and sheep—are dragged into the 'tunnelle'; and while some of the devotees are engaged in supplicating 'Maîtresse Eziliée (the Virgin Mary) to intercede with the old gods of Africa and persuade them to rest content with animal sacrifices instead of the human that had been theirs in the old days before the negro was carried overseas, preparations are made for the actual sacrifice.

A long wooden trough, made out of a hollowed tree trunk, is placed in front of the bull; and beside it are set wooden bowls, china cups and a sharp-edged machete. Now the killing begins. One by one the

E.N.A.

OLD VOODOO MEETING-HOUSE AT PORT AU PRINCE

Not only the secret places of the jungle are the rendezvous of the votaries of Voodoo, that strange medley of African nature worship and Christianity whose stronghold is Haiti. Buildings of quite substantial make, of brick and wood and iron, have witnessed its mysterious and bloodthirsty rites, of which the sacrificial killing of goats and cocks constitutes a prominent feature

sacrificial victims are seized by the horns or head, their throats slit with the machete and their blood let flow into the trough. Then their bodies are tossed carelessly aside into the undergrowth. At last it is the bull's turn. Held upright by four men, it is dispatched with a thrust from the papaloi's sword. The mamaloi, kneeling down, transfers some of its blood into the trough. Now she and the papaloi drink ceremonially of the holy blood, after which all present eagerly press forward to be sprinkled and to drink.

A little later Mr. Seabrook describes for us another extraordinary scene, enacted in a mamaloi's private mystery-temple, in which after the mamaloi has executed a number of furious gyrations, wringing the necks of cocks as she goes, a young girl and a goat face each other with hypnotised gaze before the altar; and, so we are told, after a while the child began to bleat like a goat, while the goat whimpered like a child.

Voodooism has many supporters in the United States—among the negro population, of course—and it is said that in days gone by girl-sacrifices were offered up at the midsummer and mid-winter festivals. No child has been sacrificed for at least seventy years, however; and the American Voodooists, like their fellow-believers in Haiti, content themselves with the blood of slaughtered goats and cocks. On the two occasions mentioned the papaloi summons his flock to meet him in some lonely field or ravine; and there leads them in what is called 'the fire dance of the Old Master' (i.e the devil) about a huge bonfire of wood and tar. After the religious fervour has been raised sufficiently high a 'goat without horns,' previously stupefied with drugs, is sacrificed on the altar. Its flesh is divided among the worshippers, and as each receives his portion he whirls and howls and leaps with frantic enthusiasm, until daylight puts an end to the orgy.

The age-old practice of slaughtering an animal or animals on the occasion of laying the foundations of a new building is very widespread. The Sea Dyaks of Borneo, when removing a village to a new site, take care to smear the blood of a newly killed fowl on the timbers in order to pacify the earth deity for opening up its bosom. In the Malay Peninsula the blood of fowls, goats, or buffaloes is spilt in the foundation holes; and beneath the posts are placed little offerings of ebony and scrap iron. Instances of similar customs have been reported from Belgium and Brittany; and in parts of France, until quite recently, it was the custom to bury in the foundations some small animal, such as a frog. It is possible, too, that the mummied cats found occasionally walled up in old houses were the victims of superstition. In Greece, even to-day, there is a saying that 'there must be blood in the foundations'; and hence it is customary to kill a cock, ram or lamb when a building is about to be erected, and to allow its blood to flow on to the foundation stone, beneath which it is subsequently interred.

Readers of Isadora Duncan's colourful autobiography will remember that the custom was strictly observed when the foundations were marked out of the house at Kopanos, across the valley from the Acropolis. The old priest, she says, dressed in black robes with a black hat and a black veil, demanded a black cock as a sacrifice. When this had been provided he asked that the exact lines of the foundations should be shown him—a request that was answered by Isadora's dancing feet. He then found the cornerstone nearest the house, and 'just as the great red sun was setting, he cut the throat of the black cock, and its crimson blood squirted upon the stone.' Then, holding the knife in one hand and the slaughtered bird in the other, he solemnly promenaded three times around the foundations; and followed up his perambulation with prayers and incantations, blessing the house and all that should dwell therein. This done, musicians performed on their primitive instruments; great barrels of wine were broached; and in the light of a huge bonfire the Duncans and the mystified peasantry danced and drank and made merry throughout the night.

THE LAWYERS: THEIR COSTUMES AND CUSTOMS

As with most ancient institutions, the Law has gathered round it many customs with regard to procedure and costume which are very jealously guarded. Other aspects of the Law, in native as well as in more civilized communities, are dealt with in the chapter headed At the Seat of Justice.

LAWYERS in all ages have had their customs, and the Bench and Bar of England are particularly tenacious of theirs. Advocates have been known for centuries in all European countries as men of the long robe. The gown worn by English barristers may be descended from the Roman toga or from the priestly robes worn by the clerics who in the earliest days of the Courts were the only advocates; and it is quite certain that the robes of the Common Law judges (King's Bench) descend from the robes of the prelates who were formerly the judges. Indeed, a Common Law judge is obliged to have a whole assortment of robes and stoles; for by custom he must make certain changes on certain ecclesiastical festivals. Judges whose office has been created in more modern times, namely, the Lords Justices of the Court of Appeal and the Judges of the Chancery Division, have no such costumes as the scarlet and ermine of the judges of the Common Law. A plain black silk gown is their proper dress, though for state occasions the Lords Justices of Appeal have a rich black gown trimmed with gold lace.

King's Counsel, who are frequently called 'silks,' because they wear silk gowns—which have a small square cape at the back—also put on a special coat and waistcoat of fine broadcloth, curiously cut. The full costume of a King's Counsel, only worn by him on state occasions, namely when he is taking his seat within the Bar on his admission to his new rank, and when he goes to the king's levée or to Court, consists of the dress that used to be worn by a soberly garbed gentleman of fashion in the eighteenth century. The aforesaid coat and waistcoat, black, rather tight-fitting silk knee breeches, silk stockings and court shoes of patent leather with paste buckles, fine lace ruffles at the wrist, and round his neck folds of fine lawn, the ends of which are gathered together in the front and tipped with lace, which falls over his chest (called a jabot), complete the costume save for a full-bottomed wig, the long ends of which hang down over the shoulders in front. This wig is never worn as part of the working dress, except when the K.C. is appearing before the House of Lords. On ordinary occasions he simply wears a barrister's wig with little curls at the back, and instead of the jabot, a collar with two strips of lawn or fine linen made into 'bands' which hang down in front instead of a neck-tie. A curious change is made when the Court is in mourning. The King's Counsel must then discard his silken gown and appear in one made of bombazine; and round the cuffs on his coat must be placed deep pieces of white linen commonly called 'weepers.'

Sport & General

MASTER OF THE ROLLS IN HIS ROBES

This legal functionary presides over the Court of Appeal, and ranks after the Lord Chief Justice. He has charge of the public records, and is chairman of the Historical Manuscripts Commission. Ordinarily he wears a plain black silk gown, but on state occcasions his gown is of rich black trimmed with gold lace.

Photopress

POMP AND CEREMONY ASSOCIATED WITH THE REOPENING OF THE LAW COURTS: THE JUDGES LEAVE WESTMINSTER ABBEY

The opening of the Law Courts provides opportunity for what is perhaps the most picturesque legal custom. A service is held in Westminster Abbey, attended by the judges, after which they walk in procession in order of precedence to the House of Lords, where by invitation they take breakfast—that is, take wine—with the Lord Chancellor. This display of the dignity and splendour investing the representatives of English justice provides a spectacle that always attracts large crowds. From the House of Lords they proceed to the Law Courts in the Strand, and another procession is formed in the great hall, their lordships being followed by the King's Counsel and a certain number of the junior Bar; after which they disperse to their several courts.

Planet News

PICTURESQUE PAGEANTRY AT THE REOPENING OF THE LAW COURTS

When the Law Courts open for Michaelmas term the first part of the proceedings consists of a service at Westminster Abbey and a Red Mass at Westminster Cathedral. At these are present the Lords Justices, the High Court Judges, County Court Judges, K.C.'s, as well as members of the junior Bar. A breakfast is then given by the Lord Chancellor in the House of Lords, and when this is over the courts are formally opened with a procession. The Lord Chancellor is here seen, preceded by the mace-bearer.

Recorders are also entitled to, and sometimes must, wear the same costume as a King's Counsel.

The robes of the outer or junior Bar are very simple and are the same for all occasions: a gown of stuff—hence a junior barrister is sometimes called a 'stuff gownsman'—and a wig of the kind called a 'tie wig.' There is this, moreover, to be said, that although the junior barrister is not bound to wear a coat of any particular cut, he must appear in a black coat and waistcoat and with trousers of grey stripes or some other sober pattern. Should any man have the temerity to don his robes on top of a tweed suit or wear a light coat or waistcoat and stand up in court and address the judge, his Lordship will say 'I cannot see you, Mr. Jones.' In vain Mr. Jones may protest that he has lost the rest of his wardrobe in a fire. Inexorably comes the answer, 'I cannot see you, Mr. Jones.' The result is the same if the luckless counsel forgets to put on his bands or his wig.

Wigs have not always been worn by barristers and judges. In the earliest days they wore either coifs, which were close-fitting caps of linen, or bonnets of black velvet edged with fur. Wigs came in with Charles II, and were adopted by barristers and judges, who are the last members of society to retain them. The robe now worn by the junior barrister has a curious origin. Just as the Yorkshire Light Infantry still wear mourning for General Wolfe, so the junior Bar is still in mourning for William and Mary; for the present gown is a mourning gown adopted on the occasion of the demise of these sovereigns and never since discarded. Prior to that, the junior barrister used to wear a long gown which fell down straight and was trimmed with velvet.

Judges wear full-bottomed wigs on occasions of high state, but only then. They sit in court in wigs slightly different from those worn by barristers, more close-fitting to the head and without rows of curls dangling at the back. When a judge is trying criminals, as well as on certain Saints' days and festivals of the Church, he wears scarlet and ermine, but when he is trying civil cases on other days he puts on a black silk gown like that of a King's Counsel.

'Yes, sir, and who are you?'

'I am the high sheriff of Gloucestershire.'

'And do you think I am a rabbit? You are fined five hundred pounds! Go home and return suitably attired!'

Not only must the high sheriff furnish carriage and equipment but also a chaplain, who sits in the criminal court all day, attired in a black Geneva gown, and whose duty it is to say 'Amen' when the judge pronounces sentence of death. It is the invariable custom for a judge to place on the top of his wig a square piece of silk called the 'black cap when he goes through this dread ceremony, and to remove it immediately the chaplain has said 'Amen.' The black cap is merely part of a judge's full dress, donned on occasions of especial solemnity.

The custom of the sheriff meeting the judge at the train and giving him constant attendance dates from those lawless times when his lordship used to ride circuit. The sheriff would meet him with an armed escort at the border of the county as he rode in, remain with him to protect him against bandits

Sport & General

DRESS OF MEMBERS OF THE INNER AND OUTER BAR

The King's Counsel here seen (top) are in full state costume—full-bottomed wig, silk knee breeches and stockings, and patent leather buckled shoes. The caped silk gown in always worn, but ordinarily the full-bottomed wig is replaced by a barrister's wig with curls at the back. The dress of barristers (bottom)—stuff, not silk, gown and tie-wig—never varies.

A judge is a great man at all times; but when he goes on circuit to hold assizes he becomes a still greater personage. He sits by virtue of a special commission under the great seal and is the king's alter ego; so much so that to kill a judge of assize is high treason and not plain murder or manslaughter. While he is holding assizes in any county he takes precedence of all persons whomsoever, and this is carried to such an extent that if he invites people to dine with him at his lodging, as he very often does, he is served first at his own table, just as the king would be. All the time he is in the county the high sheriff must attend him in person, unless specially excused, must provide him with a carriage and an escort, and trumpeters to announce his arrival at and departure from the assize court. Moreover, the sheriff must be properly attired in the fullest dress he is entitled to wear. There is a story of the late Mr. Justice Hawkins going down to Gloucestershire to hold assizes. When he descended from the railway carriage he was met by a country gentleman dressed in cord breeches and gaiters and the ordinary costume of such a man when he is at home on his estate. The following dialogue ensued:

'Mr. Justice Hawkins, I believe.'

and lawless nobles all the time he was there, and on his departure escort him to the far boundary and hand him over to the sheriff of the next county on the circuit.

The leader of the Bar is the Attorney General, with the Solicitor General next, and after these two come King's Counsel in order of seniority, and then the junior barristers in order of their date of call. It is customary when a King's Counsel is briefed in a case for a member of the junior Bar to be briefed with him, but that rule is relaxed in criminal cases, when a silk can, though he rarely does, appear without a stuff gownsman in support. The Attorney General and the Solicitor General have a few special privileges. One is that by custom if either of these two is appearing in a case he can apply to the court to have it fixed for a particular day, even out of its turn in the list; and the other is that in a criminal case a Law Officer of the Crown, who must be for the prosecution, always has the right of reply; that is, to speak after counsel for the defence. Except this, the custom is that where no witnesses are called for the prisoner, the prisoner's counsel has the last word before the judge's summing-up.

L.N.A.

'TWELVE LAWFUL MEN OF THE VICINAGE'

Jurors are drawn from the residents of each county, the list of their names being drawn up by the rating authorities. Their function in a trial is to hear the evidence and to give a true verdict in accordance with the facts, on points of law accepting the instructions given to them by the judge in his summing up, as shown in this actual photograph.

Legal custom in England is very good to prisoners accused of crime. A prisoner who is put in the dock has a right by custom to choose any barrister who is sitting in court and to hand him down the sum of one guinea to act as his counsel; and unless the barrister is on the other side or has a peremptory engagement in another court, he must accept the brief, which is known as a 'dock brief.' Apart from this custom, a barrister is not supposed to appear in any case except on the instructions of a solicitor. He may give advice in a non-contentious matter without a solicitor's intervention, but very few barristers would do it.

COMMENT has often been made on the fact that counsel will sometimes accept a brief and then not appear. Such a thing very rarely happens; but that it can happen is due to the fact that a barrister's fees are not a payment or debt but an honorarium for which he cannot sue his client. In one instance, however, a member of the Bar will be well advised if, after accepting a brief, he appears promptly in court and stays there; and that is when the case is an appeal to the House of Lords. By custom, anyone who is briefed in the House of Lords must be there all the time, and must not leave to attend to other business unless he obtains permission from their lordships. A breach of this customary regulation is likely to bring upon the offender a public rebuke.

Anyone who wishes to obtain the services of a particular counsel for a particular case may do so by handing to that counsel's clerk a retainer, which is a sheet of paper bearing the name of the case, the name of instructing solicitors, the word 'retainer,' and counsel's name, together with the sum of one guinea. It is also possible for a man or a firm who anticipate litigation to give a general retainer to some counsel; and on this being accepted the barrister must not accept any brief against the client during their joint lives without giving the client the opportunity to brief him and pay him a suitable fee on his brief whenever he has a case either as plaintiff or defendant. The fee on a general retainer is five guineas.

The custom is for a barrister to consider himself in a sense a public servant, so that he must not pick and choose his clients, and is bound to accept a retainer or a brief if offered to him, provided that the brief is marked with a fee in accordance with the barrister's standing in the profession. He may not refuse to appear for a client whom he considers unmeritorious; though he may not do anything personally dishonourable; and if, in the course of a case or when he reads his brief, it becomes plain to him that he is being used as a medium for, let us say, a blackmailing action, he ought to throw up his brief; but as every litigant and every prisoner or prosecutor is entitled to have his case put for what it is worth to the

Planet News

TEMPORAL AND SPIRITUAL POWERS HONOUR THE FOUNTAIN OF JUSTICE

Prior to the opening of the proceedings in the Assize Court a judge when on circuit is escorted in state by the High Sheriff to a service where a special assize sermon is preached by the Chaplain appointed to attend his lordship. In 1930 the Surrey assizes were held in Kingston, for the first time after an interval of fifty years, and this photograph shows the judge's procession leaving the parish church for the assize court in the Parish Hall, and passing through a guard of honour provided by the mayor and the corporation.

court, the throwing up of a brief ought to be of rare occurrence.

A solicitor is 'admitted' to the profession and is placed on the Roll of Solicitors of the Supreme Court, when he can be removed only by the Court after a report of the discipline committee of the Law Society for misconduct. A barrister is 'called to the Bar' by the Benchers of his Inn of Court, and can only be disrobed by his own Inn, acting through the Benchers, who are the governing body. There is an appeal from the Benchers to the Lord Chancellor and the whole body of judges, who, however, do not sit as a court but like the visitors of a college.

Benchers of the Inn or Court are co-opted, not appointed or elected by the body of members. A meeting of Benchers at Lincoln's Inn is called a 'Council,' at Gray's Inn a 'Pension,' and at the Middle and Inner Temples a 'Parliament.'

One of the curious customs of the Inns of Court is in the way of keeping terms. There are four terms in the year; and before being entitled to be called, a student must keep twelve terms. He does this by dining in the Hall of the Inn three times a term if he is a graduate or undergraduate of a university, and six times if not. This custom probably began because if a student was dining in the Hall it showed that he was on the spot and might be, at any rate, attending to his studies. In the Middle Temple the hour of dinner is announced by one of the porters blowing a horn in the various courts within the precincts of the Inn.

His examinations safely passed, the student is proposed for call, and on his proposal being accepted, he goes through a ceremony which varies in the different Inns. In Gray's Inn, students for call assemble in Hall just before dinner and line up. Precisely at seven o'clock the Treasurer (President) of the Inn, accompanied by several of his brother Benchers, enters the Hall and stands on the dais. An officer of the Society reads out the names in order, and as each name is called out the student advances to the dais, and the Treasurer repeats the words 'I call you to the Bar and publish you barrister' and shakes him by the hand. At Lincoln's Inn the proceedings are

Topical Press

SWEARING IN THE LORD CHIEF JUSTICE BEFORE THE LORD CHANCELLOR

The Lord Chief Justice of England is the head of the permanent judiciary, in judicial rank second only to the Lord High Chancellor, who is the head of the legal system in Great Britain. Before the Lord Chancellor, therefore, the Lord Chief Justice is sworn in on appointment, in the presence of many of His Majesty's Judges and learned Counsel, all in full robes. This picture is especially interesting because this ceremony provides the sole occasion when the taking of a photograph in the High Courts is not a misdemeanour entailing serious penalties.

similar, except that the formula used by the Treasurer is 'By the authority and on behalf of the Masters of the Bench I publish you a Barrister of this Society.'

The Middle Temple also calls its members in Hall; but the aspirants follow the Benchers into the hall in procession. The Treasurer shakes each man by the hand and says, 'I have pleasure in calling you to the Bar, Mr. Jones.' The Inner Temple differs from the other three in that the call does not take place in Hall nor before dinner. After dinner, while the Benchers are at dessert in their Parliament chamber, the candidates are summoned in a body to attend them. The Treasurer, seated, delivers a short address, containing much good advice; and finishes by saying, 'I call you to the Bar, and drink your health.' The senior student called makes a suitably modest reply, and, having been furnished with a glass of port for the purpose, proposes and drinks the health of the Treasurer and Masters of the Bench. The other new barristers join in the libation; and then all file out.

The Old Bailey or Central Criminal Court has its customs. It is supposed to be the court of the Lord Mayor and Aldermen of London, and the bench is not properly constituted and no prisoner can be tried unless the Lord Mayor or one of the aldermen is present on the bench. In fact, these dignitaries take no part in the proceedings, which are conducted entirely by the Recorder, Common Serjeant, assistant judge, or a judge of the King's Bench Division, who comes down to try capital offences and a few other serious cases. There is invariably placed on the bench in front of the judge a posy of sweet-smelling flowers, and his lordship always carries another posy. A few sprigs of scented herbs are also scattered on the floor. This pleasant custom dates from the time when gaol fever was very prevalent in Newgate Prison, and to prevent the infection reaching their lordships a sort of floral barrier was interposed between the dock and the bench. At the Old Bailey, too, the entrance of the judge into court is always announced by a loud knock with a mallet on the door.

Barratt's

PROGRESS O'ERLEAPS THE OBSTACLE OF SEX

Admission of women to the English Bar was legalised by the Sex Disqualification (Removal) Act of 1919, and a woman was first called to the Bar in 1922. Women barristers wear the same attire as their legal brothers and enjoy the same privileges.

At assizes, when the judge is about to try criminals, custom demands that a proclamation shall be made in these terms: 'If anyone can inform my Lords the King's Justices of any treasons, felonies or misdemeanours done or committed by the prisoners at the bar let him now step forth and he shall be heard.' This proclamation dates from those days before there were any regular police whose duty it was to arrest criminals; and when the procedure was for the people of the neighbourhood to lay hands upon an offender and hale him to the Grand Jury, a body of county magistrates and gentlemen of position. If the Grand Jury thought there was a case of reasonable suspicion, they then 'presented' him to the judge for trial. To these primitive methods of procedure succeeded written accusations which were taken to the Grand Jury; and these were called 'indictments.' The Grand Jury wrote, and if they find there is a prima facie case made out, still write on the back of the bill of indictment the words 'true bill,' but if they think there is not sufficient evidence to warrant the prisoner being put in peril they write 'Ignoramus' (we do not know), and this is called 'ignoring' the bill.

The number of jurors is probably twelve because that was the number of the Apostles. They are always sworn to find a true verdict according to the evidence; but there are differences according to whether the offence charged is a felony or a misdemeanour. In the case of a misdemeanour the jury are all sworn together. In felonies each juryman is sworn separately On trials for felony the jury may not separate until after verdict, and may not hold any communication with the outside world. In cases of misdemeanour they may separate. Yet another difference: in misdemeanour the accused or the prosecutor is not allowed to object to any juror as unfit to sit upon the jury except for cause, which must be stated and if necessary the truth of it investigated. In felony a prisoner has a right to challenge twenty nominated jurors without assigning any reason, and this is called the right of peremptory challenge. These differences between felony and misdemeanour, and the rights of challenge also, are all customary and nobody knows their origin; but the customs are so inveterate that they have become part of the Common Law. Indeed, the Common Law of England is very largely composed of customs, and that part of it known as the Law Merchant is all custom.

Photopress

STATE COSTUME OF A KING'S BENCH MASTER

Both picturesque and dignified is the appearance presented by a King's Counsel when in the full costume worn on state occasions. The K.C. shown here thus arrayed is one of the Masters of the King's Bench division of the High Court.

MODERN HOLIDAY HABITS

THE subject of holidays is treated here from the point of view of those seeking rest and recreation. The secular side of incidental holidays is dealt with in such chapters as that on Customs of Christmastide, while several chapters, including Feast Days of the Christian Church, and The Celebration of the Nativity, are devoted to the religious aspects of holidays, or holy days.

HOLIDAYS are a recent habit. So far as the mass of people are concerned, they may be called a twentieth-century habit. They are made necessary by the increased strain of toil, the intensified monotony, the nerve exhaustion, which accompany industrialisation and life in great cities, where noise and grime and crowding have reached a pitch of discomfort never experienced by humanity before. Before the revolution in industry, when people worked in their homes or small workshops, when shopkeepers lived over their shops, when bankers had residences and business premises in one, when work was unhurried and fresh air plentiful, when the fields and woods were within easy reach of all, there was no thought of a yearly break, no desire for any periods of leisure other than Sundays and such times as the Church appointed for rejoicing and repose.

When a man worked at a loom in his own cottage, he had time to look after his garden as well. The cobbler was interested in his cabbages as well as his boots and shoes. Work was not wearisome, it offered scope for some artistic endeavour, and therefore rewarded the worker with something of the artist's joy in creation. That joy is entirely absent from the lives of factory workers who are engaged on some small process repeated over and over again all through their hours of labour, some purely mechanical process which does not occupy their minds or stir their imaginations. Nor does it allow them to derive satisfaction from their skill and craftsmanship, since neither is required. They are, in truth, no more than parts of a machine. Proof of that lies in the constant invention of contrivances which take the place of human fingers. Such mechanical occupation is actually more fatiguing than work which calls for a large output of energy, mental or bodily, or both. As the famous German, Walther Rathenau, put it in his book on The New Society, a man or a woman, after eight hours spent in this way, is not capable of taking normal reasonable recreation. They cannot go for a quiet walk or take a book and read, they cannot play with their children and find happiness in the pleasures of home. They need some violent stimulus to brace up their jangled, tired nerves—a murder story in the newspaper, some wildly improbable or sensational film at the cinema. They need, also, more frequent intervals of rest than those who work at something which interests them, and these intervals must be filled with activity of one kind or another. The energy which is repressed by the smallness of effort called for in their working hours must find some outlet. The effect of this upon seaside resorts has been very striking. To that we shall come later.

UNTIL the nineteenth century had well advanced 'holidays' meant 'holy days,' that is to say, days which were traditionally consecrated to rest or play. Holidays in the sense which signifies a period—a week or longer—of release from the daily round and of absence from home were not heard of until about 1850, except in connexion with schools. Of course, many people who could afford to travel moved about for change of air and scene. Many went to take the waters at some celebrated spa. Then, early in the nineteenth century, the doctors began to discover the value of sea air. Weymouth became fashionable because George the Third went there, and Brighton because it was the favourite residence of his son, who became George the Fourth. But it was not until the latter part of the century that the middle class formed the habit of going to the seaside every summer or early autumn to get colour into the cheeks of

Sport & General

PAMPERING THE HOLIDAY MAKER ON THE NORMANDY COAST

There is no end to the comforts and luxuries that are provided for visitors at Deauville, the well-known watering place opposite Trouville. Bathers are particularly well catered for. Instead of having to walk from their tents to the sea the caterpillar tractor here seen calls for them and deposits them at the water's edge, besides taking them for short trips along the beach.

Keystone

MEDICINE BALLS PROVIDE HEALTHFUL EXERCISE ON THE SHORE AT CANNES

Ever since Lord Brougham brought it to the notice of English people, the Riviera resort of Cannes has been a favourite with holiday makers. As at other places on the Riviera, the season lasts from November to May. Every year a regatta and carnival are held. In front of Cannes are the Iles de Lérins, of which S. Marguérite, with its fort, was the place of imprisonment of the Man with the Iron Mask. The fine stretch of sands affords an excellent field not only for bathing, but for all manner of beach sports and games.

Keystone

HOLIDAY SEASON IN FULL SWING AT HOLLAND'S PRINCIPAL BATHING RESORT

Scheveningen affords an example of a modern manner of holiday making developed on the shores of the Low Countries. Below a stone wall which prevents encroachment by the sea the sands extend for miles, making an extremely popular gathering place for bathers in sun and water. The very practical kind of chair used on the beach affords protection from the wind on a low-lying shore. Such chairs are also found at some Belgian coast resorts. The long row of tall poles seen on the left of the photograph is a temporary erection, used for illuminations

children made pale by city air and to enjoy relaxation from the daily round of business or social life. They took lodgings or apartments in well-conducted houses on the parade. They sat about on the beach in the morning, bathed, read books or newspapers, played with the children. After mid-day dinner they slept, went for a walk, visited the 'sights' of the district, had picnic teas. In the evening, after supper they read a little, yawned a good deal, and went early to bed. Back at home they felt all the better for their quiet, healthful holiday.

French families still go to the seaside and enjoy themselves there very much in this fashion. At the smaller 'plages' along the Norman coast they are to be seen in large numbers during July and August, taking their pleasure in a quiet, sensible way. Perhaps there will be a small casino, to which they go in the evenings for dancing or to read the newspapers, or to indulge in a little flutter at 'boule,' a mild gambling game not unlike roulette which has taken the place of 'little horses' in the life of the French holiday resort. Deauville is the place for the rich who seek the hectic delights of the night club and the baccarat table. Trouville is for the wealthy who have more respectable tastes But the small places are the more truly typical.

As the English middle class went up in the world, they continued to send their families to the seaside while they themselves, with their wives, and perhaps their eldest daughters, went abroad to a French plage or a German 'kur-ort.' As soon as a seaside place ceased to be quiet and 'select' it ceased to attract this class of holiday makers. 'Trippers' made them shudder. Yet the towns like Margate and Yarmouth and Blackpool, which laid themselves out to cater for people who arrived in excursion trains for the day trips (these were for a good many years all the holiday they could compass) grew in size and prosperity, thanks to increasing patronage by visitors who stayed a week or a fortnight.

The early part of this century saw the middle class go farther afield in their search for rest and change. They were to be seen in Antwerp and Amsterdam, in Brussels and The Hague. They

Keystone

A QUIET CORNER AWAY FROM THE CROWD AT A HOLIDAY HAUNT OF THANET

One of the most popular seaside resorts on the Kent coast, Ramsgate was for many years a member of the Cinque Port of Sandwich. It has a splendid beach of firm sand. It was while spending the summer at Ramsgate that the artist W. P. Frith began the sketch for his picture 'Life at the Seaside,' better known as 'Ramsgate Sands,' the success of which led him to produce other paintings of crowds. Even at Ramsgate, however, it is possible to find secluded spots for those whose habit it is to avoid holiday crowds.

invaded Switzerland, made every mountain ring with their voices and every lake reflect their cheerful faces. Crossing the Alps, they gazed respectfully at Milan cathedral, lolled in gondolas at Venice, dutifully paced the picture galleries of Florence.

The next development was the winter holiday. Some went to the Riviera, enjoying both the blue sea and sunshine and the feeling that they were in close contact with fashionable life. Some got as far as Egypt . others went to Biarritz, or to Switzerland for winter sports Swiss hotels that had remained shuttered and silent from September till July were now filled with gay parties of guests from Christmas until April The thrills of tobogganing and ski-ing became familiar to thousands who before had never even heard of them. The delight of snow sparkling under warm sunshine and shining coldly on the summits against blue sky made winter seem the best time for a holiday. Soon there were a great many middle-class people who managed to snatch a few weeks both in summer and in winter. They went abroad—to Brittany or Normandy, to the Black Forest or Tirol, to the Riviera, now visited by as many holiday-makers in August and September as in February and March, on shipboard to the Mediterranean, the fiords of Norway, the Baltic or the Adriatic.

During the last few years extended cruises have been largely patronised. Voyages to South Africa or to South America and back are highly popular. Trips round the world, costing several hundred pounds are taken by a great many of the wealthier orders who feel they require a long holiday. Directors of companies, heads of businesses, captains of industry, appear to suffer in the same way as the workers in their factories or the clerks who add up the figures in their books. They are warned not to neglect brain-fag or nerve strain. Their work wearies them ; it no longer gives them the same exultant pride, the same glow of content, that were got out of the building up of businesses by individuals when conditions were easier and life less complicated.

What, in the meantime, had happened to the seaside ? It had altered its character to suit the demands of its new patrons. It ceased to be the abode of peace and quiet, it became a centre of amusement and gaiety Naturally enough, the workers in offices, shops or factories who now thronged seaside places wanted something different from the simple life which had satisfied their predecessors. The middle-class visitor sought escape from his usual recreations, as well as his usual labours. He was content to find his own pleasures. His life at home had in it plenty of variety, plenty of entertainment. Nature sufficed him when he took his holiday. The new seaside public wants to be entertained all the time. That is why all popular resorts have orchestras discoursing excellent music morning, noon and night, why they entertain in varied and original ways. The Americans were the first to establish such holiday resorts as Coney Island, which resound with the cries of the

Wide World Photos

BANK HOLIDAY CROWD ENJOYING THE SUNSHINE ON BRIGHTON BEACH

The fishing village of Brighthelmstone, as Brighton was formerly called, was brought into notice in the middle of the eighteenth century by Dr. Richard Russell, a physician who recommended sea-bathing there. Thus the place was by way of being a seaside resort before royalty smiled upon it. In 1782 George, Prince of Wales, afterwards George IV, took it up, and it was through his patronage that the town acquired popularity. With the coming of cheap railway fares Brighton became a paradise for trippers, and on bank holidays it is filled to overflowing.

Sport & General Press

WINTER SPORTS IN SWITZERLAND: ROPED SKI RACE AT A PLEASURE RESORT

Holiday makers began going to Switzerland for winter sports towards the close of the nineteenth century, after that country's summer charms had become known. The sports include skating, tobogganing and ski-ing, and among favourite centres are St. Moritz, Davos and Mürren. Long used for travelling over snow, skis were first adopted purely for sport in Norway in 1860. For good ski-ing the snow should be well frozen and quite six inches deep. The poles, fitted with disks to prevent them from sinking too deep, are used for brakes in going down steep slopes.

'barkers' standing outside the shows and bellowing their attractions, which offer every kind of excitement and thrill, in addition to beach bathing and the consumption of 'hot dogs' (sausages) and ice cream. There is something in the American nature which demands that holidays shall be packed tight with whatever pleasures happen to be on hand. Those who travel in Europe are just as vigorous in walking through picture galleries, museums and churches as those who go to Coney Island are in trying all the contrivances for 'treating the body rough' and seeing all the shows. This demand is a consequence of tired nerves; it has made its appearance almost everywhere. Consequently all English popular seaside towns have orchestras, lay out gardens and lengthen their esplanades, provide tennis courts, putting greens, lawns for bowling, ponds for children to paddle and sail boats in. Some make magnificent swimming pools where, independent of the tide, bathers can take their pleasure at any hour. Most of them have Fun Fairs where all sorts of violent delights can be indulged in without fear of violent ends. The cause of all this has been the enormous increase in the number of visitors to the seaside. Workers in the mills of Lancashire and Yorkshire formed the habit long ago of saving up for 'the wakes,' the annual closing of their work-places, and going to Blackpool or Scarborough, Bridlington or Skegness. Now the wish for an annual holiday has spread to all classes of workers. Trade unions seek to secure it for their members without cessation of pay.

As Thomas Cook & Sons made foreign travel easy for the middle class, so other agencies, such as the Workers' Travel Association, are rendering the same service to the new holiday-makers. The number of wage earners who are eager to see something of other countries increases every year. Those who have all arrangements planned for them and who travel with conducted parties cannot, of course, make acquaintance with foreign lands and peoples as intimately as those who blaze their own trail. Still, they have enlarged their experience, have added to their stock of ideas.

L.N.A.

ENGLISH HOLIDAY MAKERS WHO SPEND THEIR CHRISTMAS AMONG THE SNOWS

John Addington Symonds is regarded as the founder of winter sports in Switzerland. So much did his health benefit from a winter spent at Davos in 1878 that he decided to settle in that then little-known resort, at the same time making known the health-giving properties of Swiss air and the opportunities the country offered for winter sports. English colonies began to spring up in the Engadine, and before long holidaying in Switzerland for winter sports became a recognized custom. Many resorts have an English church served by an English chaplain.

Wide World Photos

NEW YORK CROWDS GATHER YET CLOSER ON HOLIDAY: THE FOURTH OF JULY ON CONEY ISLAND BEACH

Of the many sand spits that fringe the southern shores of Long Island, Coney Island has pride of place by reason of the enormous mass of people that visit it and the astonishing number of pleasure devices used to attract them. In no other spot in the world is there gathered together such an array of roundabouts, switchbacks, swings, chutes, and other ingenious devices for amusing the populace. The whole place is given over to noisy recreation. Besides the wealth of sideshows there are three magnificent beaches, of which West Brighton is the most popular. The island is five miles long and at its widest three-quarters of a mile broad, and forms part of New York City, being included in the borough of Brooklyn.

Dorien Leigh

MOTORISTS COME TO ENJOY AND DESTROY THE SOLITUDE OF THE MOUNTAINS

The national parks of the United States afford wonderful opportunities for an enjoyable camping-out holiday. In all of them the tourist may wander at will, so long as he respects the regulations for the protection of the forests, wild animals and natural curiosities. Mount Rainier National Park, in the state of Washington, with an area of some 207,000 acres, contains the superb volcanic peak, Mount Rainier, and is noted for its marvellous fields of wild flowers, which stretch to the very margin of the ice fields.

have deepened and widened their sympathies. Also they have helped to circulate money. Tourism (as the French say) is among the largest branches of international commerce. From all parts of the United States tourists come to Europe; some with 'dollars to burn,' others obliged to observe careful economy. Wealthy South Americans spend profusely. Germans, Dutch and Scandinavians travel a great deal; the French and the Italians not much. In fifty years the amount of money spent on travelling throughout the world must have increased at least fifty-fold.

Whether this increase will continue depends partly upon the general condition of world industry and world trade, partly upon the growth of the movement towards cheaper travel which began in Germany during the years following the War. It started among boys and girls who called themselves the 'Wandervögel' (wandering birds). With scarcely any hindrance in the way of luggage, carrying what they needed in ruck-sacks, sleeping and eating wherever they could, they made their way about their own country in large parties, often walking to the music of guitars, which some of their number had slung on their backs. At first there were protests, there was uneasiness as to their behaviour; but very soon it was seen that this new holiday habit was all to the good. Throughout Germany there are now hostels where for very small sums the 'hikers' (to adopt an American word) can get meals and beds. Some of these are old castles, some old rows of huts left over from war-time, some are barrack-like buildings: all are clean, and in a purposely rough manner comfortable. They can be used, at slightly higher rates, by walkers who are not members of the society which runs them, but who accompany members. Many British young men have joined in their tours and come back enthusiastic about them.

Now an effort is being made in England to imitate the provision of hostels, and to make it easier than it has been for Britons, especially young people, to see their own country. Already the habit of walking in parties has caught on in many parts of England. It is a revolt, perhaps unconscious, against the

G.P.A.

THE DELIGHTS OF THE OPEN ROAD ON FOOT

In England walking, or 'hiking,' is coming increasingly into favour as a means of spending a week-end or a longer holiday. Parties of lightly clad walkers may be seen tramping the lanes and fields, enjoying to the full the freedom of the countryside. In some parts of the country meals and sleeping accommodation are provided for walking parties at a specially low cost.

mechanisation of existence, against the torment of the city, against the tyranny of the motor on the high roads. Every Sunday morning at the railway stations of great cities groups of young men and women meet and start. They carry out their programmes even in bad weather. Their lunch they carry with them and eat it on a hill-side or by a stream. In the evening they return with pleasantly tired limbs and agreeable memories and nerves under better control, pitying the folk who have spent the day sitting in cars or, worse still, sitting at home, trying in vain to digest a midday meal too heavy and too large. Naturally many of these 'hikers,' when their holidays come in view, arrange to make more extended tours on foot together. It is thus that a movement similar to the one in Germany has grown up in England, though as yet on a much smaller scale. If in all countries there were facilities for touring in this fashion, and a constant interchange of tourists, the result would be to strengthen greatly that international sense of comradeship on which world peace depends.

THE motor age has substituted the holiday of movement for the holiday spent in one spot. Many who went to Baden-Baden or Homburg saw nothing else of Germany. Many who wintered at Nice or passed the early spring in Monte Carlo made no acquaintance with other parts of France. Now the number of people who stay in any place for any length of time is small. The range of holiday travel has widened. Fashion in holiday resorts is more fickle than it used to be. Few sights are more melancholy than that of such a place in decline. Once it was filled with visitors, its hotels packed, its casino crowded. Now it is empty, silent, dead. At Homburg in August not so very many years ago there was a brilliant throng of water-drinkers drawn from all Europe. Monarchs, prime ministers, ambassadors, men famous in art and literature, women of social charm and political influence, walked in its meadows and its woods. The writer was there a few years ago and found it a desert. Even before the War Marienbad in Austria had become more fashionable. Now that also has lost its power to attract.

And Monte Carlo as well seems to be going the way of those gambling places which once made rich harvest out of the folly of people with 'more brass than brains.' It has had a long period of popularity, this town in beautiful surroundings which, like Marathon, is looked on by the mountains and itself looks on the sea: mountains more romantic and a sea more blue and sparkling than those of Greece. Seventy years ago the Prince of Monaco sold the fifty-year concession which enabled a gambling palace to be built in his tiny dominion. How much was then paid is not known, but when he granted an extension in 1898 he received a million pounds down

Keystone

Wide World Photos

MOTOR COACH TRAVELLING FOR PLEASURE AND FOR MAKING PATRIOTS

To preserve the national sentiment unimpaired, Italian children whose parents have emigrated spend the summer in their native country at the expense of the Fascist state. Motor coach-loads of the children are here seen (bottom) at Rome, ready to start for a trip to the sea. In England long-distance holiday travelling by motor coach has become a very popular institution. Stations have been established at various centres, from which bookings can be made to most of the popular resorts. The upper photograph shows a large motor coach station in London.

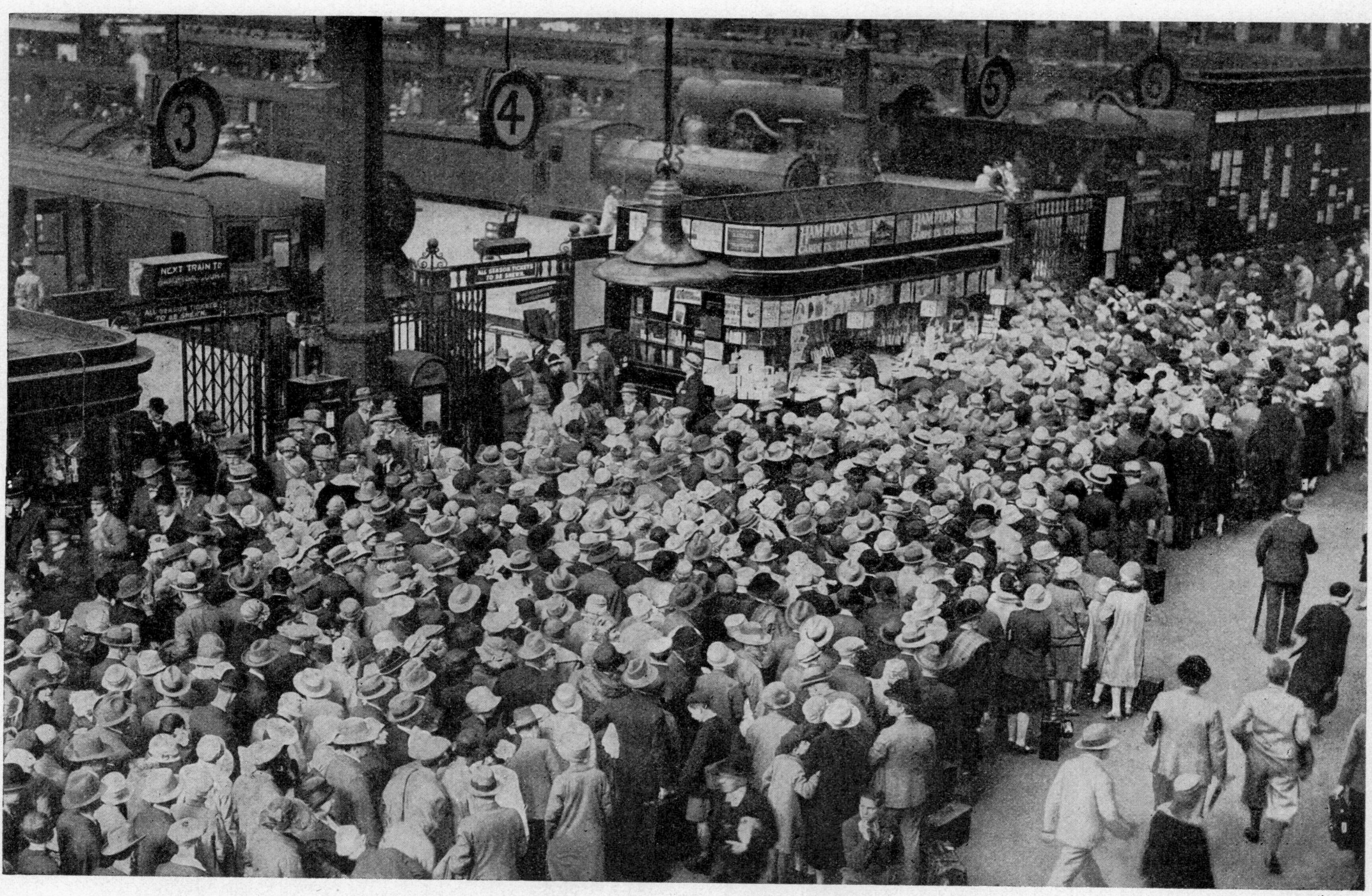

Keystone

UPHOLDERS OF RAILWAY TRAVEL: HOLIDAY MAKERS PACKED CLOSE AT WATERLOO STATION

Despite the enormous multiplication of motor cars and motor coaches in recent years, and the attractiveness and comparative cheapness of foreign travel, there are a great many people who content themselves with spending their holidays in one spot on their own coast and travelling to their destination by train. Throughout the holiday season such an important London railway terminus as Waterloo station is packed with eager crowds of holiday makers. Since the reorganization of the railways of Great Britain Waterloo has been not only the terminus, but also the headquarters of the Southern Railway system. The magnificent modern station, opened in 1922, covers 24½ acres, and has room and to spare for dealing with the heaviest holiday traffic.

Wide World Photos

WHERE FORTUNES ARE WON AND LOST: THE CASINO AT MONTE CARLO

Those who spend their holiday, or part of it, at Monte Carlo are attracted not so much by the beauty of its setting or its delightful climate as by the opportunity for a flutter at the famous gaming tables. The casino, in which play takes place, is a palatial structure, adorned with fine statuary and paintings and standing in well-kept gardens. At night, when the building is illuminated, the play of light on the casino and on the flowers and trees and sward of the gardens creates a scene of enchanting loveliness.

and a tribute of £50,000 a year, which was to be increased every ten years until it reached double that sum. The present prince receives £90,000 a year, and in 1937 will have this increased to £100,000. Not nearly all this is for himself. Monaco has to be kept going with it, since there are no taxes or rates. All the expenses of government come out of the stakes of visitors which the croupiers sweep away.

THE tables exercise a curious fascination, and by no means all of those who sit at them are holiday-makers. Many people live in the neighbourhood and spend most of their time in the Casino. They have their 'systems,' and sit hour after hour ticking off the numbers which come up on the roulette table, putting on small stakes and possibly making a meagre living out of their assiduity. One wonders sometimes why the management allows them to take up space day after day and night after night at the tables. They are certainly not the sort of visitors for whom the casino exists, or the splendour of Monte Carlo's hotel and restaurant life. It must be that they 'dress' the rooms, create the impression that the tables are always crowded, and so help to induce casual visitors to lose their money and keep going the old-fashioned magnificence of the place.

For a complete contrast to the beauty and luxury of Monte Carlo, the holiday resort of fashion, we might go to such a place as Cleethorpes, near Grimsby, on the Lincolnshire coast. Here, instead of mountains sparkling against a blue heaven, there is a flat landscape under usually grey skies. The sea is grey too; it looks muddy. Rows and rows of cheap lodging-houses offer accommodation to the thousands who arrive with their holiday savings. On a ramshackle pier a band plays and concerts are given in a bare hall which make one think of Monte Carlo's music, operatic and orchestral, with the most famous of world performers taking part. As for the cheapness and crudity of the 'amusement park,' it is pathetic. Yet if you had to decide which set of holiday-makers enjoyed themselves the more, you would probably say the clerks and shop assistants, the mill workers and factory employees on the shore of the North Sea rather than the jaded pleasure-seekers by the side of the Mediterranean.

G.P.A.

BATH CLUBS IN A LAND WHERE CLEANLINESS IS A PARAMOUNT AND PUBLIC VIRTUE

Of all the living races of mankind the Japanese are probably the most fastidious about their bodily cleanliness. Men and women, rich and poor alike, all have a hot bath daily. Until quite recent times the streets were lined—and in remote villages are still so lined—with rows of troughs in which both sexes took their baths in public together, making them an occasion for evening gossip. These are now being replaced in the towns by public bath houses with separate divisions for the sexes, some of them free, others as expensive as Turkish baths in England. In the women's bath shown here the hot water basins on the left are of marble. On the right, women are enjoying hot mud baths; head-rests are provided to protect the elaborate coiffure

CONFLICTING STANDARDS OF DECENCY AND DECORUM

OTHER chapters have dealt with the widely divergent standards of decorum set by different peoples in regard to such matters as Customs of Courtesy and Table Manners. Here some of the conventions governing behaviour in ordinary social life are reviewed; exposure of the body, mixed bathing in public, and joint participation of the sexes in the dance.

THERE is no subject which has provoked so much controversy between savage and civilized races as the standards of propriety in dress and conduct. The facts fall under two main headings: Social practices, including clothing or the lack of it; and the behaviour of the sexes to one another in public.

Under the former must be classified the very startling practice of eating deceased parents. It is true that this is no longer permitted, but the Bataks of Sumatra, among whom it has been the custom for generations, do not regard it with reprobation, and there are those still living among them who remember its being done. They say that the old people were partly cooked, and eaten with a dash of lime juice. Junghuhn speaks of the practice, and though he does not say so in so many words, he implies that when the parents died they were hoisted into tall trees, which were shaken, as though they said, ' the fruit is ripe, come let us eat it.'

These old people were not murdered, or brought to death by exposure as among the American Indians, but died a natural death. The eating was looked upon as a far more decorous method of disposing of their dead bodies than earth burial, which leads to decay and the breeding of base and unclean creatures. It suggests, however, that other strange custom of eating the heart and liver of enemies, especially of notable warriors, which was supposed to impart the qualities of the deceased to the devourer and was not due to revenge or to a carnal appetite.

What, again, are we to say of the Sura tribe of Bauchi, where the proper thing was for the chief to eat women convicted of adultery? However the custom is to be explained—whether as the penalty to be paid by the offender, or as an exceptional privilege accorded to the chief—it was a violation of all British ideas of decency and was suppressed, but to the Suras themselves it still seems justifiable and right.

The covering or leaving uncovered certain portions of the human body has been a sure source of misunderstanding among almost all the nations of the earth. The best-known and most widespread instance of this, the veiling of the face by Mahomedan women, is dealt with in the chapter on The Veil and its Significance. To the races who practise it, it is essentially decorous, to others simply ridiculous. The fact that the faces of the white women were unveiled caused consternation and reprobation among the peoples of India who first saw them, and not less did their unseemly conduct in regard to men. To ride, to dance, to talk freely with unmarried men, was considered by most of the races of India the mark of a certain class of women only. Baring the neck and shoulders and arms was to them simply shameless, and still worse appeared the round dances, the waltz and so forth, in which women were actually hugged by men.

IT all depends on the point of view. Native servants of all races now estimate these customs more fairly. Various forms of dancing are a source of constant misunderstanding between race and race. To the European mind the dances of almost all the dark-

T. Butler

INNOCENCE THAT THINKETH NO EVIL

' Propriety ' is a matter of convention, and that has to be learned. Thus it would never occur to a child that there was anything to be ashamed of in nudity, and even in such sophisticated parts of the world as Tao-ling, in China, a small boy considers it only natural and sensible to take off his clothes if he happens to find them too hot.

W F Taylor

AN ORNAMENT BUT NO GARMENT

Decoration, not use, is the purpose for which the Kagoro women of Nigeria wear dorsal appendages like this, for they are regarded as much too precious to be sat upon. The disks are made of plaited grass, and except with these the women cover no part of their bodies.

skinned peoples are not only indecent but revolting The dances of most African tribes, in particular, are simply sex invitation, and the posturing and shaking of the body are highly indecorous to us, but to the African the sight of white men and women embracing and twirling round and round together is no less so.

The question of dress is so various that it can only be lightly touched upon in some of its widest manifestations Notions of decency in regard to the covering of the human body are not inherent in men and women, but must be inculcated One has only to see the simple unashamedness of a small child to understand that in this matter it represents the earlier stages of civilization. Probably the first attempts to conceal the more obvious parts of the person arose rather from considerations of safety from injury than from any idea of decency It is common knowledge that the aborigines of Australia, who are one of the most primitive peoples remaining on the globe, taking rank with the Veddas of Ceylon and the Bhils of India, think nothing of exposing the whole person, and though their totem dresses, with gigantic feather erections and much beadwork, are marvellous works of art, they are designed as ceremonial vestments to symbolise religious ideas, not as clothes to cover the body, and reveal rather than conceal those parts of the human frame which civilized man hides as parts without honour.

EVEN among peoples much more civilized than these, such as the Akha women in the hills of Burma, though quite a complicated dress is worn, comprising skirt, short coat and head-dress, yet there is always left a bare triangle of flesh over the abdomen at the very place a European considers most needs covering. It is all a question of habit.

The apron, or 'ridi,' of the South Seas, made of innumerable hanging strips of pandanus leaves, is giving way to cotton skirts or whole-piece costumes. But among the almost innumerable Nigerian tribes of Africa the dress of the greater part of the women still consists of a bunch of leaves, sometimes long enough to sit down upon. Sometimes the girls wear a bunch of leaves behind, and only after they are married do they add one in front. In the Kadara tribe the men are clothed ; the women believe clothes to be prejudicial to childbirth and go naked, except—in the case of virgins—for a tail-like tassel of string hung with cowries But among the Kukuruku the opposite idea prevails, for the unmarried girls go naked, and only when marriage is arranged does the bridegroom present his bride with a small piece of locally woven loin cloth. This agrees with the practice of the Solomon Islanders, where only after marriage is an apron worn. Koro women of Nigeria and their children wear nothing, though the men are clothed to some extent. Even nowadays there are some inland tribes, far from civilizing influences, where both sexes go naked, but many of the tribes who formerly wore only a bunch of leaves or a string, with a bag of plaited palm fibre in front, have now adopted the robe of the Arabs.

This question of decorum in dress is inexhaustible, for it is determined not only by the habits of the different tribes and races of man, but by the influence or necessities of climate Moreover, the passage of time introduces a varying factor, for what is decorous in one period is abhorrent to another, so that it may be said to be three-dimensional There is the recent home instance of shortened skirts. Miss Edgeworth wrote in 'Moral Tales' of a little girl of twelve or so who, when she had sprained her foot, 'decently covered her ankle with her skirt' when her brother or cousin came to help her. But nowadays running girls in shorts and shirts are to be seen around London on any holiday ground, though this sight still shocks some old-fashioned people.

The Eskimo, suffering from their climate, pile all the skin clothes they can get upon themselves, but not for the sake of decency, for within their domed and snow-built winter houses, with every breath of air excluded, the temperature rises fast, and they strip themselves altogether, and think nothing of it.

At the Russian watering places along the shores of the Caspian it has long been the custom to bathe stark naked, and anyone who dares to don a bathing suit is a subject of malicious inquiry, as it is supposed he or she must suffer from some disfiguring skin complaint. A goodly number of the people undress on the open beach, and others lie out on the verandas on deck chairs in the sun.

R. St. Barbe Baker

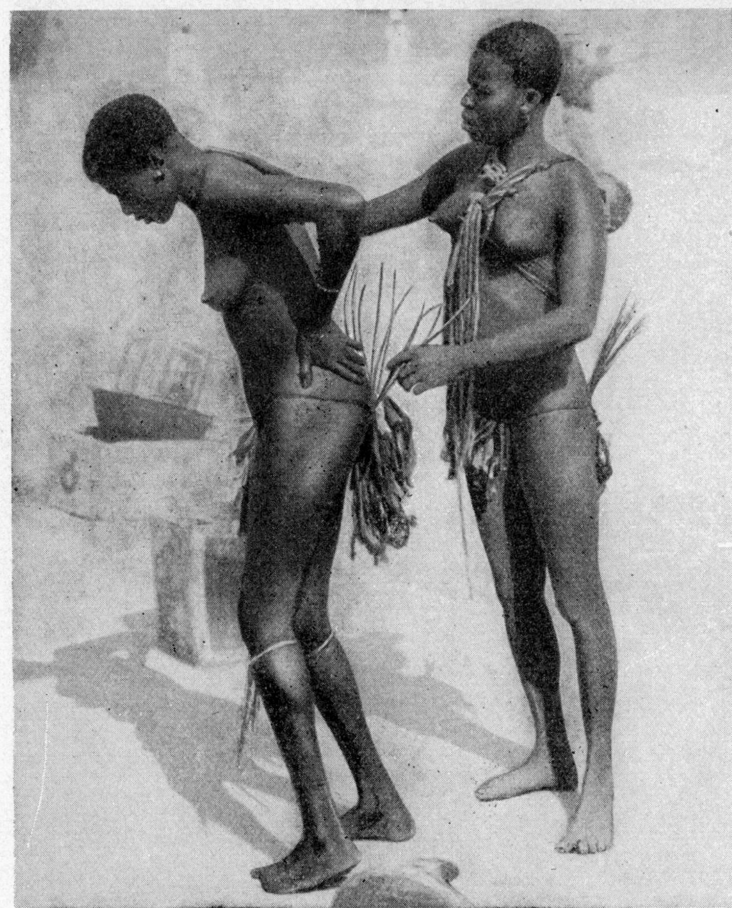

Reginald Silk

WHERE ART, NOT MODESTY, DICTATES THE FASHION

Among many African tribes the women go naked except for skirts made of leaves (top). In other tribes only a bunch of leaves is worn, either in front or behind as local custom prescribes. Some native women, on the Bauchi plateau, for example, smear their skin with a red paste made from juice extracted from the bark of a tree.

As we have seen, the women of the hill country in Farther India do not huddle themselves up with veils and draperies, or wear sarees, that long shawl-like scarf of the Parsees which falls over the head and figure. They display, on the contrary, quite a good deal of undraped body. Thus the women of the Lao country, well up in the north of Siam, wear nothing above the waist, and are so noticeable that a blunt-spoken traveller described Chiengmai as 'half a mile of nudity.' There are so many offensive white men about nowadays that the Chiengmai ladies have learnt to throw scarves over their shoulders in the town, but farther east, in Muang Nan and right over to the Mekhong, there is nothing worn above the waistline, which is here drawn close above the hips, and nobody thinks it indecorous. All the world over this fashion for women is found, especially among the African tribes where the women are carriers. On the other hand in entering Hindu temples a woman must cover the upper part of her person, in the same way that the Christian

Underwood & Underwood

SOCKS AND SLEEVES AND LITTLE ELSE BESIDES

All kinds of materials are used for human wear in various parts of the world. Metal, one may suppose, is the most uncomfortable ; yet many African women load their arms and legs with rings of brass or copper. These are often so numerous as to serve the purpose of sleeves and stockings with us, completely covering the bare flesh. For the rest, the clothing here is restricted to a combination of petticoat and drawers contrived from a single piece of cloth. In Borneo the Dyak women cover the entire torso with corsets made of brass rings

Photopress

Wide World Photos

VESTMENTS AND CLOTHES SERVE DIFFERENT PURPOSES

Ceremonial vestments are designed to symbolise religious ideas—here, for example, men of the Nigerian Habbe tribe are representing their ancient crocodile god. Normally they would go almost entirely naked, and the festal coverings are not intended for body cover. Clothes, on the other hand, are intended to cover the body, and this purpose is most completely achieved among Mahomedan peoples who require their women to go veiled and among those Hindus who maintain purdah. The upper photograph shows conventionally decorous women of Tangier.

Sport & General Press

TERPSICHOREAN FRENZY THAT WOULD OFFEND THE SAVAGE MIND

It is unusual for native men and women to dance together in Africa, and many a so-called savage would be horrified by such complete abandonment to the intoxication of the dance as is displayed in the Argentine tango. Even in England such an exhibition as this, given by professional dancers in London in 1930, would have been regarded as scandalous in late Victorian days.

church enjoins hats on women in church, following the dictum of S. Paul. This rule as to the covering of the female body in temples is widespread.

Within the last fifty years the long tameins or skirts of the Burmese ladies were not stitched up at the side, but showed the whole expanse of the thigh as they walked but this led to comment, and it was decreed a woman's bare leg should not be revealed so indiscreetly. The women's tamein, or best frock is a simple square of silk or cotton, wound tightly over the bosom under the armpits, and hitched with a simple twist. Though now stitched up the whole length, it is wide enough to be folded over in front, and the symmetry of the thigh is shown in walking, but a peculiar outward jerk of the heels, which is acquired by the girls, prevents any suggestion of immodesty.

To go back to Africa for a moment, we find among the Muhima tribe, a fairly widespread race scattered in Buganda and southward, that the girls run freely among the kraals and drink quantities of milk in order to get fat. They think of nothing, hear nothing, talk of nothing but milk and cattle. How terribly this would shock a tribe on the western side of Africa, where the women are never allowed to go into the cattle kraals or even near them.

Among the Kaffirs also it would be a gross breach of decorum for women to handle cattle. This differentiation of labour is dealt with in the chapter on the Separation of the Sexes.

Betrothal customs are touched upon in most of the chapters dealing with marriage, but we may remark that for many years past companies of young men and maidens have been allowed to go on walking tours extending over many days, in Norway and Sweden, without a hint of chaperonage, and in Germany cheap guest-houses for these young people are springing up all over the country. Engaged couples in England are allowed a vast amount of freedom, but have hardly got generally so far as this. In Burma courtship facilities are strictly defined; about nine at night the lover makes his appearance at the girl's house. He is allowed to go up and to see her alone, but her parents are all the time on the other side of the palm-thatch mat that defines a room. A meeting in the woods or lanes would horrify the Burmans and ruin the girl's character.

A MOST curious difference in ideas is manifested in the habit of kissing, which is confined almost entirely to the white races. To the Chinese, Japanese and almost all Orientals the practice is not only indecent, but disgusting. Among more savage races what is called the 'Malay kiss' predominates; it is partly a sniff, partly a touching of noses. This is found among the Polynesians, Malays, Eskimo and certain negro tribes. While both sexes among the Finns bathe together in a state of complete nudity, the kiss is regarded as something indecent. Kisses and embraces are almost unknown in Japan as tokens of affection; mothers fondle their babies, but except in the case of infants, do not kiss their children. Among certain people the kiss has only a religious significance, which may be traced in the Roman Catholic practice of kissing the images of saints.

WITH us, as with most white races, it is considered insulting for a man to retain his hat in the presence of ladies, and irreverent to do so in holy places, but it is altogether the reverse in the East, where for a man to remove his turban or to be seen without it, save in privacy, is highly indecorous. With us the head-gear, with them the shoes! For an inferior to come into the 'presence' wearing shoes is considered outrageous. In the cold weather up-country where a Madrassee dons shoes, he will leave them behind every time he comes up to the sahib's veranda, even though he is preparing dinner over a few sticks in the compound, has his hands full of dishes, and has to shuffle up and down between every course.

Closely connected with the hat question is that of hair, as to which there are many and various conventions. Perhaps the oddest is that a Chinaman must

H. A. Bernatzik

GRACE UNPLEASING TO WESTERN NOTIONS

Sex invitation as the motive of a dance finds its most notorious exemplification in the so-called 'danse du ventre.' Actually this is not so much a dance as an exhibition of posturing and movement of the body muscles, and many of the Sudanese dancing girls display astonishing suppleness and grace.

SHAMELESS BY EASTERN STANDARDS

In comparison with the tango shown in the opposite page and the 'danse du ventre' above, English ball-room dancing such as this would seem free from anything to which the most prudish could take exception. Yet by many an Oriental a woman thus engaged would be stigmatised as shameless.

not come into the presence of a superior with his pig-tail curled round his head, as he would wear it for convenience in his own garden. If he is a clerk in an office he must let it down before he enters. To pull a Mahomedan's beard is a deadly insult, and even to touch the head of a man in Fiji is equally so. Heads and hair are closely associated, and the Polynesians regard the hair as sacrosanct. After cutting the hair of a Maori chief his wife's hands were tabooed for a week. The most truculent prisoners in Fiji would collapse when their hair was cut for a long sentence. The Burmans detest their hair being touched, and this applies also to their children. If a well-meaning bishop or padre, coming along, pats the children's heads, he causes black looks and gnashing of teeth in their parents.

The Chinese are the most formal and polite people on earth, and what shocks a Chinaman as much as anything is the indecorous way Europeans behave on social occasions. Visitors to a private house usually sit at small tables in groups of four, and in front of each is a bowl of tea with a porcelain cover like an inverted saucer. The drinking of this 'guest' tea should be the last act before leaving—in fact it is the intimation that the visitor is preparing to leave, but, unless specially coached beforehand, the white man commonly seizes his cup and gulps down its contents at any gap in the conversation, thereby outraging the Chinaman, who, in any case, would sip the beverage elegantly.

Divergencies in the standard of decorum in regard to eating and drinking are studied in the chapter on Table Manners, Primitive and Polished. As noted there, among most eastern peoples it is considered highly indecorous for the women to eat with the men; they should wait upon their lords, and then, in privacy, content themselves with what is left. To see white men waiting upon their wives and helping them first appears, to Orientals unused to it, to be most unseemly.

Questions of polygamy and polyandry, again, are treated in a special chapter, but we may in passing refer to the tribes of Dera and Jera, where the chief may have 500 wives, and many men have thirty or forty without anyone being shocked. These people are worth studying, for they are a very moral race, despite the fact that they are habitually drunk by 10 a.m., and they are very polite. Should one man fail to salute another, he is fined the equivalent of ten shillings.

P. & A.

Henri Manuel

COSTUME AND CUSTOM

The exposure of bare flesh by English ladies wearing evening dress is regarded as indecent by many Eastern races, who also think it most unseemly for women to eat at the same table as men, and for husbands to wait upon their wives and serve them first.

THERE is a wide divergence as to what is seemly in the way of ablutions among different races and different peoples. The Burmese wash, not only themselves, but their clothes, every day, and enjoy it; the Japanese think us savages in this respect because we do not each have a bath every day with water so hot that it is almost boiling. In this respect also we might note that the Japanese have no objection to taking such baths in public, and that not so very long ago both sexes did so in troughs provided for the purpose in the streets, and it was no uncommon sight to see a Japanese man, without a rag of clothing, going home through the snow from some hot bath which he had thus enjoyed.

Many savage races are clean, but a great many are not. The wild Wa know of no uses for water at all, preferring their own home-brewed spirits as a drink. The dirt their persons accommodate is only limited by the amount that will adhere to their flesh before dropping off. Most savage races are more or less afflicted with parasites, but not a hundred years ago this also was very common in Europe, especially in regard to the head-dress of ladies. Now a girl of any class would be deeply ashamed to be so accused. But other races see no shame in it. A couple of women sit in a public place, maybe on a convenient railway wagon in a siding, in the East, and pick the insects from each other's hair alternately, as monkeys hunt in their neighbour's fur. This can be seen in every street in Hanoi or Haiphong, with the additional loathsome detail that the spoil is devoured.

WOMAN'S STATUS IN PRIMITIVE SOCIETY

ALTHOUGH among many primitive people women are in a state of subjection, the position held by the women is not an infallible test of the cultural condition of a community Further reference may be made to the chapter on The Matriarch, and other aspects of the subject are touched upon in the chapters on The Separation of the Sexes, and The Family among Savages.

IT has long been the custom to use ' the position of woman ' as a measuring-rod by which to compare the cultures of various peoples. Such questions as: Have women the vote? Are they allowed to become doctors or lawyers? May they hold property in their own right?—have been asked; and then, when the answers returned have been in the negative, the people under discussion have been assigned a lowly place in the human scale. Of late years, however, with the growth of our anthropological knowledge, there have been increasing signs of doubt not only as to the validity of the test, but also as to the alleged subjection of women among the races that may still be styled primitive. To resolve the doubts it is necessary to eschew sweeping, and usually flimsily based, generalisations, and examine the facts that have been accumulated by patient and arduous 'field work.'

The Australian aborigines, by almost universal consent, are regarded as being among the lowest of the human race, and in support of this view it is asserted that the 'lubra' is a beast of burden, despised, ill-treated and over-worked. The black-fellow — a misnomer, by the way, for he is by no means black— to quote a member of the Kurnai tribe, 'hunts, spears fish, fights and sits about'; while the woman is the agriculturist and builder, potter and weaver, tanner and basket-maker, as well as being what she is in all cultures, house-wife and nurse. The extent and variety of her occupations may be gauged from the contents of the basket which most Australian women carry strapped to their foreheads or shoulders. A typical basket will contain some or all of the following: a flat stone for pounding roots; quartz to make spears and knives; stones for hatchets; cakes of gum for making and mending weapons; kangaroo sinews for sewing and for binding spears; needles made from kangaroo shin-bones; opossum hair for belts; pieces of kangaroo skin to serve as polishers; mussel shells for cutting hair; a knife or two; an axe; pipe-clay; red and yellow ochre for painting the body; paper-bark for carrying water; waist-bands and other ornaments; pieces of fungus and dry wood to act as tinder; whale grease; and, finally, roots collected during the day's wanderings. Then, in addition to the basket with its motley collection of oddments, the 'lubra' is often loaded with her husband's spare weapons, a skin or two, and, more often than not, a baby.

Dr. Walker

HOW THE ABORIGINAL WOMAN AGES

So hard is the lot of the aboriginal Australian woman that she is old at forty and usually dies about fifty. The body flesh falls away, the lips thicken and protrude, the brow grows heavy. Old women often carry their dogs under their arms, to keep themselves warm.

The case for the subjection of the Australian woman seems conclusive, yet we have it on the authority of Sir Baldwin Spencer, who speaks from a long and intimate acquaintance with the aborigines, that the life and treatment of the black lubra are far preferable to those of hundreds and thousands of women in the British slums. The women, he asserts, are not treated with excessive harshness; and if (as is, of course, the fact) their lot is hard, so, too, is that of the men. In times of plenty both sexes are kept busy; and in those of dearth the men are equal sufferers with the women. Unlike her civilized sister, the 'lubra' is not required to spend long hours in making dresses or darning socks, for the Australian male is generally nude; and when he wears anything at all he is quite content with a waist-belt and a tassel about the size of a five-shilling piece. As for the 'lubra' herself, her dress is composed of a belt of bark, supplemented in some tribes by an apron of opossum fur. In an aborigine encampment housework is reduced to a minimum, and it may be supposed that children are hardly the problem they are with us.

It is true that love in our sense of the word is rarely, if ever, encountered, and that wives who have offended against the marital laws of the tribe are liable to a severe castigation with a fire-stick; but the terrible gashes to be seen on women's bodies—Sir Baldwin Spencer once counted as many as forty great weals between the navel and just above the breasts—are not the result of cruel treatment by irate husbands. More often than not they are self-inflicted wounds, made by pieces of flint or glass, enlarged and rendered permanent by being rubbed with ashes, with a view to demonstrating to all the world the extent and sincerity of the grief felt at the death of a husband. Besides, the men maltreat themselves in the same fashion, although with them it is probably with a view to ornament.

Sport & General

Dr. W. D. Walker

IN A LAND WHERE WOMEN BEAR THE BRUNT

Among the Australian aborigines almost the only job a woman can get done for her is hair-cutting. The upper photograph shows a North Australian blackfellow cutting his wife's hair to supply material for weaving his waistband. The body scars on the Central Australians (bottom) may be mourning or initiation marks, or for ornament.

Then, too, child-bearing, often a dangerous process for the civilized woman, is for the native Australian a matter of small moment, causing her merely a temporary inconvenience. 'An Australian tribe on the march,' says one writer, 'scarcely take the trouble to halt for so slight a performance as a childbirth. The newly-born infant is wrapped in skins, the march is resumed, and the mother trudges on with the rest.'

Nevertheless it must not be imagined that, even when every allowance has been made for the advantages of living in a 'state of nature,' the lot of the 'lubra' is an enviable one. She shares her husband's dangers and privations—and they are many; she carries his burdens; hers are the menial tasks, the jobs that are monotonous and require long-sustained and arduous labour. She is married at the dawn of puberty, and rarely is permitted any choice of mate. She may be lent by her husband without so much as a 'by your leave': and at his death, after performing what is, in effect, a long period of penitential mourning, she becomes willy-nilly the wife of her dead husband's brother.

Small wonder, then, that the Australian women, although as girls their carriage is erect and graceful and their bodies plump and firm, become with increasing years bent and shrivelled, their flesh hanging in ugly folds. At twenty or twenty-five they have lost all their youthful looks and charm; and at thirty, or at most forty, they are veritable old hags. And such is the toll of labour and privation that probably few live beyond the age of fifty.

In tribal Africa, where primitive concepts and practices still manage to withstand the corroding contact of western ideas and influence, the position of woman is very similar to that of the 'lubra.' 'The militant side of primitive culture belongs to men,' says Havelock Ellis; 'the industrial belongs to women'; and in Africa, as in Australia, the woman busies herself with the care of the children and with the tasks that radiate from the hearth, while the man engages in those which demand a powerful development of muscle and bone and the capacity for intermittent spurts of energy.

'The life of the average Congo woman,' writes Mr. G. C. Claridge, 'vacillates, pendulum-like, between farms and babies, which form the two principal interests of her existence.' From sunrise to sunset she digs and plants, hoes and waters and reaps, oftentimes carrying a child on her back. Twice each day she goes to the river or spring with the water-pots, and brings them back, filled, poised on her head. (Incidentally it is to this that is ascribed the erect, even stately, carriage of the native women.) She grows the bulk of the food, and cooks it; it is mostly her labour that builds the hut in the first place, and which remedies the damage caused by rain and wind. So capable and useful is she that throughout tribal Africa a wife is a gilt-edged investment, returning a rich dividend in the shape of children and services; and one, moreover, whose value and attractiveness are enhanced by the fact that if the woman dies, her spouse has the right to demand from her father, without further payment, one of her unmarried sisters as a substitute.

N. I. Sholto Douglas

ZULU WOMEN MAKE MUSIC AFTER WORK IS OVER

Apart from the tending of the cattle, which is the men's province, the whole of the work of a Zulu community is performed by the women. Over and above their housewifely duties in the kraal, the women have entire charge of the cultivation of the crops, and often the shadows are lengthening fast before they are able to relax from their labours.

Yet just as we have seen that the lot of the 'lubra' has some compensations, so that of the African woman is not one of unrelieved gloom and servitude. Some travellers assure us that the picture representing her as a beast of burden, the slave of man's lust and the victim of his laziness, is hardly in accordance with the facts. In East Africa, for instance, there is little evidence of women killing themselves with hard work, and a woman is never seen to hurry. Up country, of course, far from the bazaars and the

au Hoefler (Columbia

Topical Press Agency

WHERE COMELY WOMEN WERE MADE UGLY TO SAVE THEM FROM PERSECUTION

The Ubangi of French Equatorial Africa cherish their women, who are very good-looking and in former times were constantly being carried off by slave-traders. The chiefs of those days conceived the idea of the lip-ring (top, from 'Africa Speaks') to disfigure the women, but its use is now forbidden by the French authorities. Among the African forest pygmies the status of woman is low. The tribes are constantly on the move in search of game, and it is the woman's duty to build the dwellings (bottom), which are made of branches covered with leaves.

G.P.A.

CHIEF OF A TRIBE OF CENTRAL AFRICA BEING DRESSED BY HIS WIVES

The life of a woman of Central Africa consists for the most part of an endless round of more or less fatiguing duties. In addition to looking after the babies she does the whole of the housework. Not only does she build the hut, but she is expected to repair it whenever necessary. From early morning until sunset she is busy in the fields, for she does all the work required for raising and gathering the crops; and every drop of water that is needed in the hut she carries from the stream. Always she is required to attend upon her lord and master.

shops of the Indian traders, women are kept busy with the mortar, winnowing-basket and grinding-stones; but even there, according to one observer, a German, the women do not work so hard or for so long as many a hausfrau in the Fatherland.

Elsewhere, among the Yorubas, for instance, women are subjected to a number of pettifogging and even humiliating restrictions, yet enjoy at the same time a considerable measure of freedom in other directions. The Yoruba women must not whistle, unless they are prepared to face a charge of witchcraft. They must not ply canoes on the lagoon, nor may they climb into the roof of their huts, for there, beneath the thatch, are kept the garments used by the men-folk in the rites of their secret societies—holy vestments that the eye of woman would pollute. Then, too, a woman may be pawned by her husband for debt, or by her father; and in the latter case she may, if she be young and comely, have to submit to incorporation in the creditor's harem. (It may be noted, by the way, that sometimes a sick woman, unable to find the doctor's fee, arranges with one of the medical fraternity that she shall be his slave for life if he is successful in curing her complaint.) Yet, side by side with these marks of subordination, Yoruba women frequently have their own little businesses, out of the proceeds of which they support themselves and their children; and as a rule it is the husband who finds the small preliminary capital that is necessary.

If anywhere, it is among the pygmies of the tropical forests and the bushfolk of the Kalahari desert that the condition of woman approaches most nearly to the popular conception. Though, as nomads, there is little housework or agriculture to be done, life for the women is one long round of privation and child-bearing, broken all too seldom by bouts of gluttony, followed by the consequent slumber of stupefaction. Yet it should be noted that their hard fate is not the result of male dominance, but of a malign environment.

The Todas, that racial fragment—they number only some six or seven hundred souls—who have their home in the Nilgiri Hills in South India, provide us with an illustration of a people among whom women are regarded not so much as convenient drones, but as beings inferior to men in their very nature. Contact with them is supposed to impart a degree of uncleanness, and hence we find that they are forbidden any part in the tending or milking of

Dr. Wirz

WOMEN RETURNING FROM WORK ON THE PLANTATIONS IN DUTCH NEW GUINEA

In primitive societies it is usually the men's part to hunt and fight, while the domestic and industrial sides of life are in the hands of the women. Among the tribes living about Lake Sentani, in Dutch New Guinea, near Humboldt Bay, the men spend most of their time in hunting ; any leisure they may have they idle away. The women have no time for recreation. They do the work on the plantations, which goes on without intermission. Every day they paddle themselves in their canoes to and from the scene of their labours.

either the ordinary or the sacred buffaloes—the care of which constitutes for the Toda men almost their only occupation. They are even debarred from the churning process, or from attending the buffaloes in calving time. Special paths to the sacred dairies are provided for them to use when fetching butter-milk ; and when the buffaloes go in procession from village to village the women are bound to leave their houses and betake themselves to the wood until the holy animals have passed, taking with them the feminine emblems of pounder, sieve and broom. The only exception to the ban is made in favour of the girl—always one who has not yet reached the age of puberty—who is given food in the dairy of the village the buffaloes are leaving and who sweeps the front of the dairy of that to which they are proceeding.

The inferiority of women is evidenced still more unmistakably by the fact that the dairymen of various grades, during their term of office in the sacred dairy, are allowed practically unlimited sexual relations with the women of the village, only provided that the emblems of womanhood above-mentioned are carefully removed from the hut while a dairyman is present. In a word, women are regarded as 'impure,' and this conception is carried to such a length that in child-bed a woman is carried to a special seclusion-hut in which she lives for two or three days after the child has been born. Nevertheless we are assured that the Toda women, unlike their Hindu sisters, enjoy a considerable degree of freedom and opportunities for social intercourse. They are not treated harshly or contemptuously, and the polyandrous system in vogue among the Todas—when a woman marries a man she automatically becomes the wife of all his brothers, including those as yet to be born—at least preserves her from an indigent widowhood.

The sexual taboo encountered among the Todas has many parallels in other lands. In Cambodia a wife must never use the pillow or mattress of her husband, and in Siam she uses a lower pillow than his as a sign of her inferiority. With some peoples it is considered indecent, that is, dangerous, for women to mention their husbands' names, and in many places the sexes are segregated at night, the women and girls generally sleeping at home, but the men-folk in their equivalent of a club-house.

The Dusuns of North Borneo, on the other hand, provide an illustration of quite the opposite conception.

Press Cliche

WHERE A WOMAN IS WORTH NO MORE THAN A DOG OR A BOAT

The **Gilyaks of the** island of **Sakhalien are a very** primitive race of fishers, hunters and trappers. Among their most **treasured** possessions are **their boats and** their dogs. Their women they look upon as mere chattels, and if a man hankers after a particularly desirable boat or dog. he does not hesitate to offer a **woman in exchange for it.** The northern part of Sakhalien belongs to Russia, and a Soviet representative is **here** seen expostulating with a party of Gilyaks on their attitude towards women, explaining that such exchanges cannot be tolerated.

E.N.A.

MATRIARCHS AMONG THE NORTH AMERICAN INDIANS

A woman among the Hopi Indians enjoys many privileges. She is regarded as the head of the household, and, although she does all the domestic work, her warrior husband acts as nursemaid to the children. When she marries, her husband takes her name. The wife owns everything, and should she feel inclined to get rid of her husband all she has to do it to place his saddle outside the door ; he will then understand on his return that he is no longer wanted. Married Hopi women wear their hair as here seen.

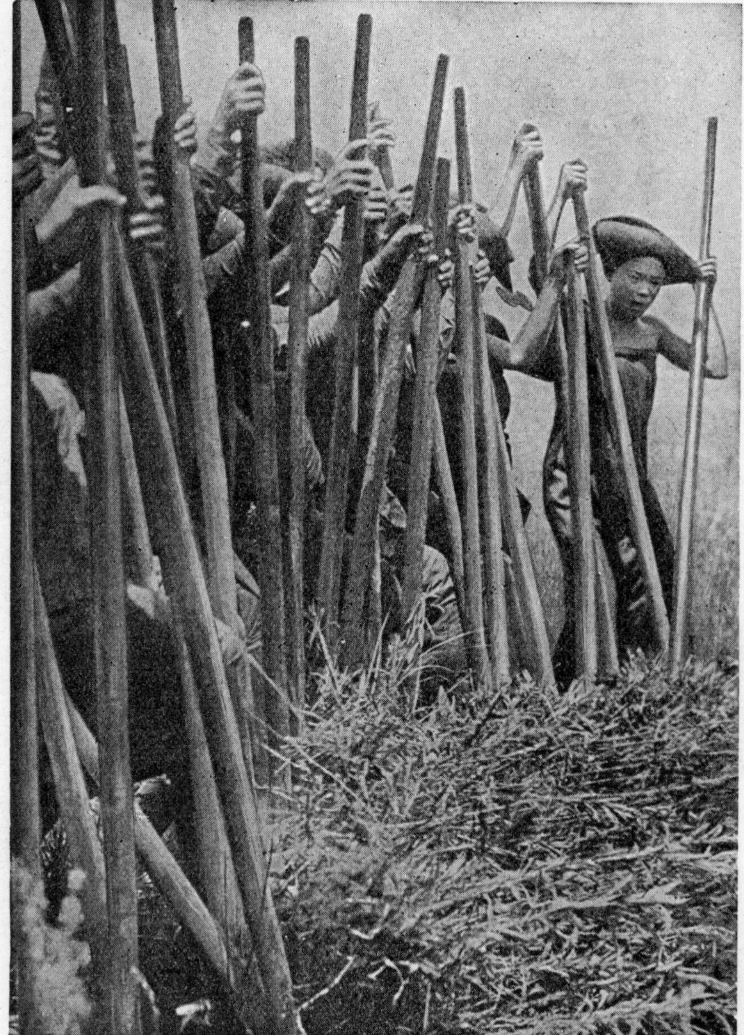

Underwood & Underwood

PLOUGHING WITH WOMEN INSTEAD OF OXEN

Among the Bataks of Sumatra the women do all the work, both in the fields and at home, while the men bask in the sun and gamble away their wives. The agricultural methods are very crude. Instead of ploughing with oxen or other beasts, gangs of women loosen the soil by means of long poles sharpened at one end

So far from women being debarred by their sex from participating in the sacred mysteries, the chief performers in all the religious ceremonies are females, the men contenting themselves with the lowly position of beaters of gongs and drums. Women constitute the priesthood and it is said that they perform the rites in a language not understood by the men. The annual expulsion of evil spirits from the village is the work of the women initiates, who proceed from house to house in slow but noisy procession, stopping every now and again to dance and posture. And when the procession arrives at the river bank where the boat is moored, loaded with such things as are best calculated to please bad spirits—food, little models of men and women, of buffaloes and deer, and so on—it is the priestess who gives the order for the cutting adrift of the bark in order that it, with the spirits who are supposed to have taken refuge upon it, may drift down stream to some other village.

The cave-dwelling Veddas of Ceylon, like the Todas, are a primitive and diminishing remnant. Descended, it is believed, from the original inhabitants of the island, they are to-day outcasts and not far removed in their way of life from the wild animals of the forests in which they have their homes. Yet they are not only strictly monogamous, but marital infidelity is practically unknown among them; and in every respect women are the equal of men.

Among a third aboriginal people, the Ainu of Japan, the position of the women compares very favourably with that accorded to the women of many another race generally considered as being far higher in the human scale. Despite the westernisation of their supplanters, their manners are still patriarchal; women are treated with consideration, have a voice in all domestic matters, and are, in effect, rulers of their households. It is interesting to note, however, that age-old custom forbids them to offer up prayers to the ancestral deities, because it is thought that, with feminine perverseness, they might use their prayers against the men-folk, and more particularly against their husbands. In the South Seas women, as a rule, enjoy a considerable measure of independence, and even in the field of sexual relationships are accorded a degree of licence almost unknown elsewhere. According to Professor Malinowski, women in the Trobriands may attain a high position in the councils of the tribe, and the same holds good, doubtless, of other islands.

From the examples given above it will be seen that the position of women among primitive peoples is not so simple a question as might at first appear. Their social status, freedom and privileges depend largely on the preponderance of males or females within the tribe, while matrilocal or patrilocal conditions are likely to determine the rigidity of tribal law and punishments which apply to the female sex. The oft-made assertion that in the lower cultures woman is a beast of burden is seen on examination to be applicable to certain races only; while in many others just as primitive in their social and economic arrangements women are treated with a high degree of honour.

The old idea that among primitive peoples womanhood is synonymous with slavery and subjection is, obviously, no longer tenable. It must be abandoned; and its abandonment will be accompanied, of necessity, by the realization of the inadequacy of 'the position of women' as a test of cultural position and achievement.

NORTH AFRICAN MARRIAGE CEREMONIES

WEDDINGS and the customs which precede them are necessarily described under wide territorial headings. The manners of African marriage easily separate into the entirely distinctive set here discussed and those which are grouped in the chapter Marriage Customs of Savage Africa. Reference may also be made to The Various Forms of Marriage.

MARRIAGES in North Africa are at once the joy of the womenfolk, whose almost only recreation they are, and the bane of the men, who celebrate them with such lavish profusion that they are often ruined in the process.

The first step in the long-drawn-out proceedings is, of course, the choosing of the bride. The wishes of the young people concerned are rarely heeded; indeed, the consent of the girl is neither required nor asked, with the result that she oftentimes finds herself married, willy-nilly, to a man who, very probably, is thirty or forty years older than herself and whom she has never seen before. Among the Kabyles in the mountainous north along the Mediterranean littoral the mother selects the bride for her son, and only when she has made her choice does her husband proceed to negotiate with the girl's father. In Egypt a youth has his bride found for him by his relations or by the professional matchmaker; and unless she happens to belong to the lowest classes he does not see her before the wedding-day.

Similarly in Fez a young man of Moorish race is denied a choice, and it is his parents who decide when the time has arrived for him to marry, and who commission a trusted servant, neighbour, or business acquaintance—often the second-hand dealer, owing to his extensive knowledge of the families in the district—to make diplomatic and non-committal inquiries concerning all the eligible girls. Then, when one has been found who seems to answer requirements, the lad's mother arranges to have a 'private view' of the girl from the vantage point of a convenient balcony, from which she can see without being seen. Two qualities she looks for. The first, youth, is an absolute essential; the second, plumpness, though eminently desirable (for, as they say there, if an illness befalls a plump wife, at least something is left of her afterwards; whereas in the case of one already lean——), may be waived if there are compensatory advantages. Having seen all that can be seen, the lady reports the result to her husband; and then (providing, of course, that the report be favourable) the negotiations concerning the 'dot' are begun.

IN western lands the 'dot' or dowry is received by the husband from his bride's family; but in North Africa and many other countries the transaction is reversed, the bridegroom's father paying it to the father of the bride. In effect, therefore, the process is hardly to be distinguished, if at all, from an ordinary mercantile transaction. The nomenclature of the payment is, however, of comparatively small importance; what interests us more is the fact that the settlement of the amount to be paid, whether as 'dot' or as bride-price, entails delicate and protracted negotiations, affording abundant scope for the exercise of the Easterner's love for haggling. Sometimes the figure is determined by the local notabilities; but more usually the respective fathers confer direct and, with the utmost politeness, engage in a duel of words and gestures that bids fair to continue interminably. A time does arrive, however, when the supply and demand prices coincide, and preparations for the actual wedding are begun.

DESPITE the fact that Mahomedan law does not prescribe any particular procedure to be adopted at the marriages of Moslems, they are in fact celebrated with a considerable degree of pomp and ritual. The actual procedure differs, of course, from place to place and tribe to tribe, but among the peoples of the Barbary coast, at least, the customs and ceremonies are essentially similar.

Turning, then, to Morocco we find what is called 'the cleaning of the wheat' or 'the bridegroom's day of cleaning.' Four flags having been hoisted on the house-top, the grain—barley, wheat and durra—that is to be used during the wedding is heaped up in the courtyard of the bridegroom's house, and there cleaned by the unmarried girls of the family or neighbourhood; not, however, before they and the heaps of grain have been carefully sprinkled by the bridegroom's father with water as a safeguard against the machinations of evil spirits. A dagger is thrust into one of the heaps, and a bowl containing a mixture of raw egg and salt is placed on its summit: the dagger and salt being directed against evil spirits, and the egg to ensure a happy wedded life. Eventually the bowl and its contents are buried beneath the threshold by the bridegroom's mother in order that they shall be stepped upon by the young couple as they enter the house for the first time; while as for the salt, the groom purloins this himself and puts it in the roof above the bed which he is to share with his bride.

Next in order comes 'the bridegroom's night,' passed by him and his boon companions in a round of feasting and perambulation about the town. Henceforth until the end of the wedding proceedings the bridegroom is regarded and addressed as 'sultan,' his bachelor companions become his 'ministers,' while his 'best man' is promoted to being his 'vizier.'

EXCITEMENT SWAYS THE POPULACE WHEN A BRIDEGROOM TOURS THE TOWN

Marriage customs in Morocco include one festive occasion for the bridegroom, comparable perhaps to the 'stag' dinner often given in England by a bridegroom to his men friends on the eve of his settling down as a staid married man. In Morocco the 'bridegroom's night,' as it is called, is spent by the bridegroom and his boon companions in feasting and perambulation of the town, the hero of the occasion being styled the 'sultan,' his bachelor friends his 'ministers,' and his best man his 'vizier.' In some parts of Morocco—for the customs vary a good deal—the bridegroom passes in procession round the town riding in a palanquin borne on an ass, followed by all his friends and acclaimed by the entire populace.

Now comes the quaint custom of painting the bridegroom with henna. Seated in the courtyard of his home, with his head and face muffled in his robe, he is greeted by his mother, who carries in one hand a bowl containing henna, an egg, and four candles, and in the other a bottle of water. 'May Allah be gracious unto you,' she says, and deposits the bottle and bowl on the ground. Then the 'vizier' steps forward, picks up the bowl, and taking therefrom the candles, lights them and hands them to four of the attendant 'ministers.'

This done, he theatrically breaks the egg on the bowl and allows its contents to trickle down on to the henna, after which he gently stirs the mixture with the little finger of his right hand, while one of the 'ministers' tilts water over it from the bottle. At length, when the sticky mass is of the right consistency, he approaches the 'sultan' and in a curious sing-song conjures him to 'Stretch out your hand, my lord; stretch out your hand from your sleeve.' One after the other the hands are protruded, and each is smeared with henna by the 'vizier.'

E.N.A.

THE BRIDE SETS OUT UPON LIFE'S GREAT ADVENTURE

In North Africa, when a bride leaves her father's house for her new home, every precaution is taken to shield her from the evil eye. She is muffled up in blankets and borne off on the back of a camel in what is known as the bridal box, a structure rather suggestive of a large meat safe, consisting as it does of a wooden framework covered with thick draperies.

The latter then takes the four lighted candles from their bearers, places them upright in the bowl, and, perching this somewhat precariously on his head, begins to dance before the 'sultan.' After a while he stops and hands the bowl, still with its cargo of candles, to one of the 'ministers.' He, too, dances, slowly and solemnly, and then hands his burden to another of the 'ministers.' So one after the other the whole of the courtiers perform their dance, until the last deliberately lets the bowl fall to the ground, where, of course, it is smashed to fragments. It must be presumed that the henna is regarded as being rapid in its working, for only a few hours later all traces of its application are carefully removed at the nearest spring.

Having dried his hands, the bridegroom then proceeds to the mosque, where he is undressed by the 'vizier' and has his head shaved by the barber. The shaved-off hair is collected, put inside a bundle of the bridegroom's old clothes, and taken to his mother, who promptly places the bundle on her back. 'I was told,' says Professor Westermarck, who has spent many years in Morocco studying the marriage and other customs of the people, and to whom we are indebted for the present details, 'I was told that all such customs must be carefully observed, since otherwise Yiblis, the devil, would make husband and wife fight, being displeased with people getting married.' Apparently the practices associated with henna are due to the belief that it possesses a kind of 'virtue,' and that, therefore, those to whom it is applied are not only purified from earthly taint but rendered immune from the attacks of evil spirits.

The bride, too, has her henna-painting. In Fez, for instance, three days before that appointed for the actual wedding, she is taken to the bath by a crowd of young girls and rigorously cleaned by a sturdy washer-woman. Then holding a wax taper in her hand she leans over a basin (after taking care that her eyes are shut to avoid offending the spirit of the water) while those about her pour over her bucketful after bucketful. Then, still with her eyes tightly shut, she is garbed in her wedding finery and seated on a cushion placed on the floor of her home. There, like a trussed-up doll, she sits mute and unseeing while the 'hennaria' adorns her feet and hands with stars and crosses and other lucky emblems. It is interesting to note that among one Moroccan tribe not only are the bride's feet and hands smeared with henna, but two lines resembling whiskers are drawn with saffron on her cheeks, being met by a third line drawn along the bridge of the nose. In some districts, too, henna is applied to the bride's legs, arms and hair.

We now come to what is perhaps the most important of the marriage ceremonies: the fetching of the bride from her father's house to that which she is henceforth to occupy. Rarely, if ever, is she fetched by the bridegroom; as a rule the task falls to one of his relatives, or, in a few instances, to the unmarried men of his village. The bride awaits her escort in her chamber, scantily attired and, of course, in tears —actual or feigned. Then when their arrival is announced she is closely muffled in blankets and, mounted on the back of a female relative, carried into the courtyard. There she is placed on a mule, mare or camel, in the 'bridal box'—a curious structure consisting of a wooden framework draped in a large sheet and which has been described as being like 'a huge meat safe, with a conical roof.' Safely seated in the bridal box, and well shielded from the 'evil eye, the bride is conveyed in procession to her new home. Every precaution is taken to avoid meeting another wedding procession on the way (if, however, one is encountered, the women in each party throw stones at each other to drive away the evil); and generally a little boy rides in front of the bride on her mount, in order that she may be helped to bring forth male offspring.

In Morocco the procession on arrival at its destination is usually met by the bridegroom's mother, who hands her new daughter-in-law food and drink. In Andjra the mother throws some handfuls of dried fruit over the bridal box in order that the young couple shall never want food to eat, and also breaks an egg on the forehead of the mule or mare to ensure that the bride shall bring nothing but good fortune to her husband. Then the bride, still closely muffled, is lifted out of the box and carried over the threshold into the house on the back of a lusty woman.

Among the Kabyles, in some tribes at least, the bridegroom awaits the coming of his wife, and gives her a blow with his fist as soon as she enters the house—partly to demonstrate his mastery, partly to counteract in advance the force of the amulet, generally a piece of paper, given to the bride by her mother with the intention that it should be slipped adroitly beneath the nuptial bed. Elsewhere the girl is expected to kiss the lintel of the door to express her affection for her new home; and sometimes she breaks an egg against it to induce fertility, knowing full well that if she fails to give her husband a son, her residence under his roof will be of short duration. Another Kabyle peculiarity that may be noted is the flight of the bride on the morning of the wedding, and her pursuit from house to house by the musicians who have been engaged for the event, and who, we may readily believe, are in no hurry to overtake their quarry so long as the fun lasts.

Up country, among the foothills of the Atlas, the bride is conveyed on a camel to her husband's encampment, where she is received by her brother-in-law and carried by him to the bed. After a while the bridegroom, who has been sitting some distance away, having a meal, gets up and walks towards the tent, accompanied on either side by a man dressed like himself so that the onlookers—and, it is hoped, the bride—will be unable to recognize him. Arrived near the tent, the three men rush towards it. Their onset is the signal for the men and boys of the bride's village to beat them with sticks; and within the tent they are assailed by women who are in attendance upon the bride. She, too, strikes out with her slipper, and if she is successful in hitting the bridegroom it is supposed to imply that she will 'wear the trousers.' Among another hill tribe the wedding procession marches three times round the mosque and then three times round the marriage tent—a tent specially erected for the occasion. As it begins its circumambulation the men standing by snatch at the women's headgear, and do their best to deprive the bride of her slippers. When the threefold circuit has been completed the bride rides to the bridal tent and beats it with a small cane with the purpose of expelling any evil spirits who may have found entrance there.

Such customs, still practised despite the ever-growing influence of western ideas, seem to bear witness to the 'unchanging East'; but in some districts, particularly in Egypt, the influence of modernism is very noticeable. The old-time wedding processions are still to be seen in the streets of Cairo, with their bands and clowns and dancers, the bride in her quaint and gaily decorated carriage; but more and more often she is encountered proceeding to her husband's house seated in the more prosaic but far more comfortable motor car.

To return to Morocco. The bride having arrived at her new home and been conducted to her apartments, the bridegroom prepares to follow. Still ceremony dogs his footsteps. Having said his evening prayers he slowly proceeds to the door of the bedroom, accompanied by attendants bearing flags and candles. On the way he stops to kiss the heads of his parents, and it is now that his mother puts down the bundle of old clothes which, as we have seen, she has been carrying on her back, and

Wide World

PRETTY SYMBOLISM IN THE RITUAL AT AN ALGERIAN BETROTHAL

Procedure at Mahomedan betrothals varies greatly but contains many picturesque details. On the occasion illustrated here, dinner in oriental style was served in the mosque (bottom), the actual rites being performed afterwards. The bridegroom's father applied to the bride's forehead a gold coin, symbolising prosperity, and then two little girls presented her with a basket containing henna, sugar plums and slippers, these last symbolising her entry into the nuptial home. On the hands of each person present some brown paste was placed, supposed to ensure them good luck throughout the year.

Keystone

ARAB BRIDAL CARRIAGE COMPLETE WITH WEDDING BELLS

European ideas and methods are inevitably having their effect on native life in Egypt, robbing it of much of its distinctive colour and pageantry. Even in Cairo, however, where the influence of modernism is most felt, we may still encounter an old-time Arab marriage procession, with the bride travelling in a quaint wedding carriage borne by two camels gay with embroidered and tasselled trappings, and musical with bells tinkling in the belfry swaying high upon their backs.

asks her son to step over it three times, so as to prevent him being harmed by the magic of anyone who has been successful in obtaining one of his hairs. The best man then opens the door or pulls back the curtain of the nuptial chamber, and throws into the room the flags, a carpet and a cushion. Within the bride is seated, still closely veiled; and after the bridegroom has partaken of the food that is laid out in readiness, he lifts the girl's veil and puts some of the choicest morsels between her lips. In many cases this is the first time the bride sees her husband. The marriage is then consummated, although in Fez the act is deferred to the next night, the actual wedding night being passed in the expression on the part of the bridegroom of what may be described as 'sweet nothings,' received by the bride with an air of supreme indifference (to display any signs of interest would be regarded as proof positive of a most immodest disposition).

In conclusion, a few words may be said on the subject of wedding presents. The bride-price, as we have seen, is paid by the bridegroom or his father to the bride's family; and often it is stipulated that a portion of the price shall be handed to the bride. In well-to-do households the girl's father generally gives her presents to the full value of the price that he has received for her from her husband. Among the Kabyles the bridegroom provides the trousseau, and in Egypt the bridegroom, soon after the betrothal, sends his prospective bride cart-loads of farm produce, fruit, sweets and dress lengths. Among the Gallas of Abyssinia the wedding presents are selected by the girl's father as soon as she attains marriageable age—thirteen or fourteen—and before a suitor has put in an appearance. Going the round of the village, he indicates that such and such an article will be required as a 'present' when his daughter marries. Then when the marriage has been actually arranged he dispatches one of his servants, who collects from each house the various 'presents.' Strange though it may appear to us, the practice is not abused, for the father in making his selection is restrained by the reflection that sooner or later he, in his turn, will be visited by other parents on the same errand. Even so, it is easy to see that girl babies are at a discount in Abyssinia; so much so, in fact, that it is said that even today female infants are sometimes taken to the woods and there abandoned.

THE DANCE IN THE EAST

APART from the various symbolic and mystical dances peculiar to the East and here described, some of the dances founded on the legends of the great Oriental culture-heroes are dealt with in the chapters on The Golden Ballet of the East, and Animal Dances of the East. Other varieties of Eastern dances are treated in the chapter on Devil and Other Spirit Dances.

THE conception of dancing in the East is rarely if ever associated with the idea that it is merely an expression of happiness manifested in the rhythm of music. It is taken to convey more philosophical, almost ritualistic atmosphere. The whole phenomenon is viewed with symbolism ; so that if we see the mystic dances of the Dervishes for the sake of 'purifying' of their soul, we see ancestor worship connote the temple dances of the Siamese ; even amongst the warlike Afghans the dance stands for definite ideas ; hero worship, religious wars, and even spirit worship are depicted by the dances of the Eastern people. For the most part men dance alone, and where women are employed they are considered as a class by themselves.

The dance of the Dervishes of the Naqshbundi Order in the agricultural province of Konieh in Asiatic Turkey is a unique example of ancient practice of mystic dances of Islam. The shrine of Moulana Tallaluddin (Ala-ed-din), the Great Sufi, at Konieh is still regarded as a most sanctified mystic temple in the Near East. At one time the religious importance of the Sufi was so great that no coronation of the Turkish Sultans was acceptable till the Spiritual Guide of the Order of the Dancing Dervishes fastened the Imperial Osmanli sword to the girdle of the new monarch of Turkey.

The dance takes place within the Moulavi Khana, or the House of Dervishes, near the grave of the Great Sufi. A low door covered by a vine admits one into the precincts of the quadrangle. There are cloisters here for the disciples, and on the left-hand side a door leads to the apartments of the Sheikh Chalabi, the descendant of the saint. Adjoining this is the room where the Great Sufi Tallaluddin is buried, and through this one passes to a large hall of Sama, or the hall of the mystic dance, where passages of the Masnavi poem have been recited at the mystic dances for over seven hundred years.

ABOUT half-past two in the afternoon of Thursdays the faithful gather in the hall. They wear long trailing coats tied at the waist and high conical hats made of grey or black felt. Everyone sits along the three sides of the carpeted hall, whilst the singers with their flutes and small drums occupy the fourth side. The performance is strictly confined to the men of the Order.

Presently their Spiritual Guide, clad in a long white coat, which is tied at the waist by a broad red sash, arrives and sits in the centre of the room ; then the music begins, big hands are thumped on small drums, the man with the flute is also blowing mightily through his reed instrument, the slow chant of the poems of the Great Sufi is taken up by the disciples. Rising from their seats, they join hands with each other, whirling and going round and round at growing speed. Frenzied with intense religious feeling, the whole company of some hundred men strain their throats to the utmost, they toss their heads to and fro, twirl their bodies and sing in low, sonorous rhythm the Chant of the Mystic Song of the Moulana. Again and again the shrill notes of the flute rise above the general din, the drums are beaten faster and faster, and the whole is a scene of an extraordinary ecstasy, in which, for well over a quarter of an hour, one sees nothing but swiftly moving bodies.

P. & A.

WOMAN STREET DANCER OF MADRAS

Although dancing and singing constitute a phase of life which is rapidly dying out in India under stress of modern conditions, at Madras there is a school for both subjects. The turning back of the right hand here seen is a characteristically Indian pose.

The following is one of the tunes heard on the specific occasion described above which has been set to Western music as closely as it can be done, and gives a good interpretation of the mystic dances of the Dervishes :

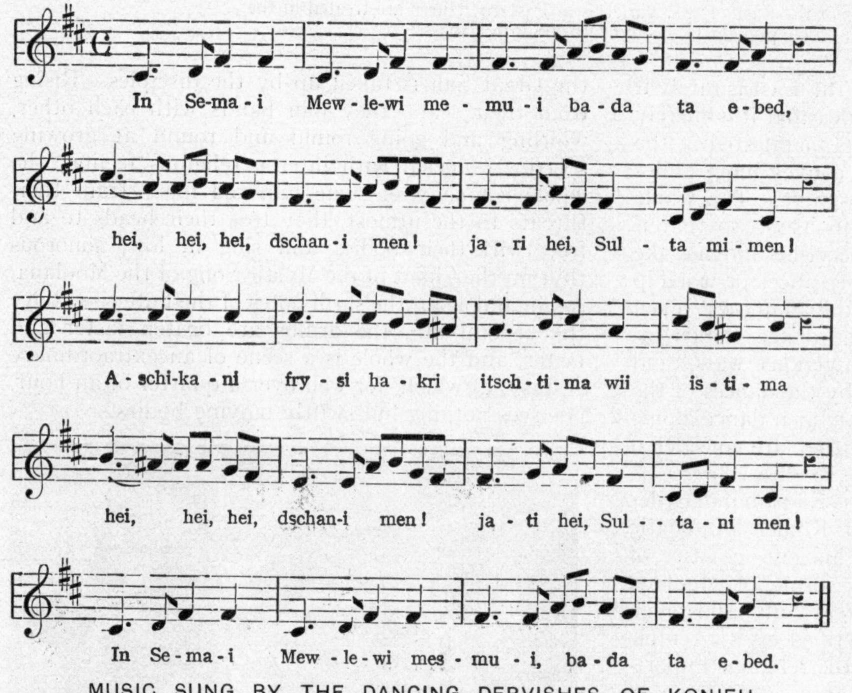
In Se-ma-i Mew-le-wi me-mu-i ba-da ta e-bed,
hei, hei, hei, dschan-i men! ja-ri hei, Sul-ta mi-men!
A-schi-ka-ni fry-si ha-kri itsch-ti-ma wii is-ti-ma
hei, hei, hei, dschan-i men! ja-ti hei, Sul--ta-ni men!
In Se-ma-i Mew-le-wi mes-mu-i, ba-da ta e-bed.

MUSIC SUNG BY THE DANCING DERVISHES OF KONIEH

Music as an art was deprecated by strict Mahomedans, but gradually developed from intonation upon two or three notes of the verses of the Koran, which word itself means chanting. With regard to this version of the Dervishes' chant, taken down by the writer of this chapter, t must be remembered that it is sung unharmonised, harmony being replaced by the conflicting rhythms of the drum accompaniment

But whereas the occult science of Moslem Sufism found its greatest expression in Anatolia amongst the Dervishes, the cradle of the cult remains in Bokhara in the Central Asian Khanates to this day, where as well as at Nishapur, in the province of Khorassan, in the north-east of Persia, at the shrine of Omar Khayyam, who was born here, such religious dances of the Sufis take place.

The meaning of these dances can only be comprehended by some brief knowledge of the Sufi cult, in which not only the origin but the continuance of this extraordinary dance is to be found ; for although the Sufi idea exhibits a close connexion with the Neo-Platonism of Alexandria, it nevertheless is somewhat different in its conception of the origin of man and the purpose of life, and also regarding the ultimate destination of man's existence.

The soul of man is considered by the Sufis as being in exile from its Creator, who is not only the author of its being, but also its spiritual home. The man's inner self is regarded as a spark of the ' Divine Light ' into which after death a Sufi's soul should be ' absorbed.' But if that absorption is to be effected, the disciple must undergo a rigorous programme of mental discipline both when in prayer and during his daily worldly task.

Day by day the Sufi must offer prayer, recite formulae of mystic meaning, and engage in occult dance, where it is enjoined upon him so as to get ' purified ' and be ultimately ' absorbed ' into Divine Light, whence he came. The Moulana Rum has thus included the whole Sufi lore in his Masnavi, which is often recited and sung at the occult dances. Two of its stanzas ran thus :

Oh ! hear the flute's sad tale again :
Of separation I complain :
E'er since it was my fate to be
Thus cut off from my parent tree,
Sweet moan I've made with pensive sigh,
While men and women join my cry.

Man's life is like this hollow rod ;
One end is in the lips of God,
And from the other sweet notes fall
That to the mind and spirit call,
And join us with All in All.

The same call is taken up by the Sufi practitioners at the shrine of Omar Khayyam, where in place of the Turanian Sufism of the Masnavi, the Persian mysticism of Omar gives an impetus to the Middle Eastern peoples. At the shrine of this master Persian singer twice a week poems are recited, and the whole company of disciples dance a slow step dance, clinging on to one another. No instrumental music is employed in this case, but a mellow-voiced youth sings, whose chant is taken up by the devotees. As in the Anatolian practice, none but the Sufis are admitted to this prayer-dance.

Nor is this method peculiar to these shrines, for at the shrines of local saints amongst the Moslems of India the Urs, or the religious gatherings at Delhi, Ajmare and Kulyar, are well known. The same chanting and dancing take place, but certain conditions are modified · for instance, the number of the singers is larger than at Konieh or Nishapur, and these singers almost always are professional men, and not infrequently even women. The general company, too, does not dance, but a devotee or two may, as often as not, be so affected by the atmosphere that ' the Spirit enters his body,' and flinging off his turban and behaving like one possessed, he dances in the middle of the room till he is carried away apparently unconscious. The action is considered to be of great spiritual merit and happens at least three or four times during the afternoon's performance. The real difference, however, lies in the fact that in such mystic dance gatherings everybody can join in, whether he belongs to the Order or not ; but the character of the song and the dance does not greatly differ from what is practised in Persia or Turkey.

E.N.A.

Sirdar Ikbal Ali Shah

SKILLED EXPONENTS OF THE SWORD DANCES OF THEIR RACE

Among the many dances of the Middle East perhaps the most stirring are the sword dances of the Arabs, such as are performed at some of the great Moslem festivals. During the Bairam festival at Aleppo, for instance, a fair is held, and to this flock Arabs from miles around to take part in the sword dances, which are a very prominent feature of the proceedings. Each tribe furnishes picked champions, who execute astonishing feats of swordsmanship before admiring crowds. The photographs show sword dancers of Arabia (bottom) and of the Lebanon.

Underwood & Underwood

Sirdar Ikbal Ali Shah

DANCES, FRENZIED AND STATELY, OF SYRIA AND PERSIA

In Persia dancing is for the most part looked upon as an undignified and even degrading proceeding, and is left almost entirely to professionals, except among the remoter tribes, who often celebrate weddings with dancing. In the serpentine dance (top), performed by villagers of the Mukri district, in the province of Azerbeijan, the men and women hold each other's hands and move their bodies and feet in a fantastic manner to the music of pipe and drum. Dancing is popular with the Arabs, a party of whom are seen (bottom) at a festival celebration at Aleppo.

In direct contrast to these philosophical dances amongst the Moslems are dances associated with national or semi-religious ceremonies. The Arabs of Syria, for instance, hold a great gala fair during the Bairam festival in the great square facing the citadel of Aleppo, where thousands gather during the afternoon to see the various sword and fencing dances, at which, of course, the inevitable drum and flute are very much in evidence. They are celebrated at the conclusion of the Day of Sacrifice, when the yearly Moslem pilgrimage takes place in Mecca.

Sirdar Ikbal Ali Shah

WHEN THE DANCING FLOOR IS A CAMEL'S BACK

A curious feature of the celebrations of the Bairam festival at Aleppo is a dance executed on the back of a camel by a man dressed as a bride. At times kneeling, at other stages standing, first veiled, then unveiled, the dancer postures on the costly rugs spread over the camel's back. The dance symbolises in turn youth, married life and old age.

Thousands of Beduins trek to the city for the sword dance contest, when experts from each tribe jump out in the arena and contest their skill in swordmanship. They whirl themselves about and raise war whoops, slashing the empty air with their Damascus blades. The real skill is comprised in defending oneself by the sword, as no shields are used.

When this is over, small groups of men dance round and round a camel, holding their arms aloft, whilst others keep time by clapping their hands. The same kind of dance is seen during an Arab procession which goes to Nabi Musa to celebrate the birth of Moses in Jerusalem. But the crowd becomes greatly enlarged towards the late afternoon, when a short dance is given for the edification of women.

Veiled women sit concealed behind latticed balconies of the houses that surround the square in front of the citadel. A small procession of boys ranging from eight to twelve in age approaches the gathering and takes up its stand in the centre of the ring. Big drums are beaten mightily, and a chant is taken up by the crowd as a veiled performer, riding a camel, is seen emerging from the arcaded bazaars. With slow and measured tread the camel, on which heavy and expensive rugs are thrown, wends its way through the crowd. The rider, though really a man, is dressed in woman's clothes, the dress being the dress of a bride.

When the camel has reached the centre of the space, the boys form a ring round it; the music swells to very high notes, every throat is working overtime. Then the performer balances herself on her knees, her face still veiled, throws her arms up, then twists and bends her form to the tune of the music. Then she stands up on the back of the camel and dances with more dignity. This is considered to be the 'spirit of youth' expressed by the newly wed. Presently a slower chant is heard, the performer unveils herself and repeats the previous dance, sitting on her knees on the back of the camel. The unveiling expresses her wedded life; and finally a much slower music is struck, symbolising the on-coming of a woman's old age, with which the performance terminates. In the real sense of the word, these may be called the folk-dances of the northern races of Arabia.

The Dance in the East

It is in the countries farther eastwards that we find the evidence of early war dances, which during the progress of Aryan civilization in Central Asia are now the true national dances, as, for instance, the Attan dance of the Afghans and the Afridis of the Khyber Pass. In Afghanistan during the celebrations of the melting of snow—which may be at any time during April—large numbers of clansmen hold gala fairs all over the country to rejoice over the end of the bleak winter days and the sprouting of the green shoots on the fruit trees. The larger Afghan towns, like Herat, Kabul or Kandahar, are generally the centre of great tribal gatherings for such festivities. Each clan marches to the town with its village team of sword dancers. With banners flying, and playing of flute and thud-thudding of drums, they arrive at the place of contest on the night previous to the day of the contest. The gatherings often collect more than thirty thousand men. The field of sport is so chosen that one of the snow-clad mountain peaks is visible from it.

With the arrival of the Afghan king or local governor, as the case may be, the Maidan or the arena of some three hundred yards square is at once turned into a miniature battleground, where first of all the contesting parties range themselves against each other in friendly array. Then large drums are beaten or a cannon is fired as a signal for the contest to begin. The whole mass of humanity is dancing and singing, youths attacking and defending themselves against one another. They yell, shriek, jump, while a thousand drums beat, and the players on flutes can scarcely be heard.

Keystone

NAUTCH GIRLS IN FULL REGALIA AT TANJORE

The dancing of the Nautch girls of India consists of slow steps and elaborate posturing, by which they can convey to their audience the most delicate shades of meaning. The costumes worn by the girls are very rich, being often studded with jewels. The dancers are selected for their beauty at an early age to be priestesses of the god Rondzu.

For more than an hour human energy in sword dancing is manifested in supreme intensity, and then groups of men form themselves into little rings, when, joining hands, they dance, reminding one of the old English village dances, with the exception that at the end of each round one of them, detaching himself from the rest, leaps in the centre of the ring and plays with his sword perilously near the heads of his fellows, and so it ends at dusk.

No account of the dance of Moslem Asia will be complete without a reference to the Patta as seen during the procession of Moslems carrying the effigies of the mausoleums of Hasan and Hussein; for, although this dance is only a small item in the whole period of mourning in which the Islamic East is plunged during their Moharram festival, the festival details of which are described in the chapter on the Passion Plays of the East, mention of the Patta may be made here. The procession of the abovementioned effigies is always escorted by a group of men who are called Patta Baz, or those who perform the war dance with the aid of sticks or staves where swords are not much in use.

Every hundred yards or so during the progress of this procession a group of men

SYMBOLIC DANCE IN THE ORIENT: SPRING DANCE IN PROGRESS IN AN OSAKA THEATRE

In Japan the dance has long had a very intimate connexion with the drama as well as with primitive folklore. Indeed, according to an old tradition the Japanese drama had its origin in the Kagura ('The Seat of the Gods'), which was a religious dance of a pantomimic character. The Kagura is still performed at one of the two great harvest festivals that are celebrated in Japan. Dances similar in character, such as that seen here, are associated with the beginning of the agricultural year. The farce theatre, or Kabuki, of Japan was inaugurated by a woman dancer, and from the time of its origin pantomimic posture dances, known as Shosagoto, have been used as interludes. The Kabuki actors are, to a man, accomplished dancers. Make-up is as important in the dances of the Japanese as it is in their drama.

PROCESSION OF ELEPHANTS PRECEDES THE DANCE OF THE SACRED TOOTH AT KANDY

Not until the long line of temple elephants has made the circuit of the town does the sacred dance begin. The most gorgeously caparisoned of the elephants, here seen, the one in whose silver howdah is carried the Tooth of Buddha, is halted near the shrine, beside which the dance takes place before the august assembly of splendidly arrayed Kandyan chiefs. The young men who take part in the dance form into lines and wheel round and face each other; they then go through a series of whirlings, crouchings, and other complicated evolutions.

Ewing Galloway

BURMESE DANCING GIRL IN A TEST OF ENDURANCE

In Burma professional dancing girls figure in the ritual dances, but, apart from the religious side of their activities, they can always find employment as private entertainers. One of the most popular dances in Burma is the graceful but trying pwe dance, which taxes the powers of the performers to breaking-point. A person of wealth will give a party, and hire dancers to entertain his guests. These latter eat, drink, and watch the dance until the performers collapse, and then the party breaks up. The pwe is danced by men as well as women.

Ewing Galloway

DANCES OF THE INDONESIANS, FUNEREAL AND FESTIVE

There is much interesting dancing in the East Indies. The Dyaks of the Tandjoeng tribe have a very curious skipping dance (bottom). It is performed not with a rope but between two ironwood poles, which are moved in time with the music of gongs and tomtoms. The upper photograph shows a funeral dance round the coffin in the public square of a Batak village in Sumatra. The dance is executed by women, who wear a special dress for the occasion. It is characterised by a strange movements and postures of the hands and arms.

TWO OF THE PRINCIPAL PERFORMERS IN A STILT DANCE OF CHINA

The performance of plays by actors dancing on stilts is one of the oldest forms of Chinese entertainments. In recent times these plays were most commonly seen up-country at fairs and festivals. As a rule the actors were not paid by the onlookers, but by the innkeepers and merchants, since they attracted large audiences and so brought business to the locality. All the female rôles were taken by men. The public performance of the stilt dances has been suppressed by the Nationalist government, and the actors have mostly taken to farming.

display, singly or in pairs, their skill in sword dancing; some take up heavy iron chains and swing them round; others lift heavy leaden balls as they dance round the circle of their admirers. All these exhibitions purport to portray the physical strength of the warriors who took part in the battle of Kufah in Irak, now more than a thousand years ago. It is an effort to keep alive the historic battle of the celebrated grandsons of the Prophet Mahomet.

Beyond the usual Hindu festival dances, Ceylon has the advantage of celebrating other cults when dancing takes place; one such is during the festival of carrying the 'Sacred Tooth.' It takes place at Kandy, where it lies as a sacred emblem of kingship. This is carried on a highly caparisoned elephant led by priests and worshippers, followed by the chiefs of the town. Dressed in their beautiful native costume of flat and bejewelled hats ornamented by a golden spike, tight-fitting trousers and twenty yards or more of brocaded silk tied round their waists, these venerable-looking chieftains of Kandy stride along under huge silk umbrellas.

When the procession has done the round of the town and the shrine is reached, the elders watch the sacred dance from where stands the elephant bearing the emblem of the Tooth. Young men range themselves in rows, and with cymbal playing and drum beating the dance begins. Each dancer takes a step forward, another, and he is past the one facing him. Then they turn and face each other. Then they stretch their hands and almost touch each other, they whirl round and stoop with the musical tune; and finally the whole gathering burst into a long-drawn religious song, and thus ends the festival of the year.

Unlike the Moslem faith, where even in symbolism the representation of saints is not permitted, the Hindus of India have more than one dance wherein both the minor and major saints are presented by dancers. The dramatic performances of Ramayan and Mahabharata are a case in point. The exploits of Rama, the great hero of the epic, whose wife Sita was kidnapped by the king of Ceylon, and who was rescued ultimately by Rama with the help of

Hanuman, the monkey-general, are celebrated at Ram Lila throughout India. Young boys dress as Rama and Sita at the play, and at the procession hundreds of other boys dance in as a token of rejoicing at the rescue of Princess Sita from the evil-minded Ravana, the king of Lunka or Ceylon.

To those who are not quite clear about the historic background of this great Hindu epic poem, it is often baffling to know whether the dancing boys in the procession are enacting the part of the warriors of Rama or merely of civilians making merry at their hero's conquest, because the dance consists in gracefully jumping upon one foot first, when garlands are exchanged between the rows of other boys, and the next step is that they strike their gaily-coloured bantoms upon each other. The latter procedure seems to recall the practice of Moslem dancers at the Moharram in India and those of the Arabs in Syria, where such practices are definitely meant to represent the soldiers of a conquering army.

This, however, is soon explained, for when the procession escorting Rama and his spouse through a town reaches the field where the effigy of Ravana, the king of Ceylon, is erected to be burnt, the Chata-Batta boys, as dancers are called, form in a ring and strike upon each other's bantoms more frequently, keeping time with no musical instrument, thus

Sport and General Press

DANCERS WHO ACT THE CHINESE CLASSICS PERCHED ON STILTS

The plays acted by the stilt dancers of China were taken from the ancient classic drama. The costumes, as well as the songs, mostly dated back to the Ming dynasty, but many of the jokes introduced were of a topical or political character. In spite of the extreme difficulty of movement the actors contrived to give an extraordinarily natural presentation of the plays. The lower photograph shows a private performance of a stilt dance in progress. Above is seen a dancer representing a court official sitting down to adjust his stilts.

Photopress

SUMMER FOLK-DANCE IN FULL SWING BY THE RIVERSIDE IN TOKYO

The preservation of their folk-dances and folk-songs is a task to which the Japanese give much attention. Societies have been formed with this express object in many parts of Japan, and from time to time these organizations hold festivals at which exhibition performances are given. The folk-dance and song society of the famous religious centre, Nikko, for instance, produces some very interesting examples, among which may be mentioned the Nikko-no-Kasdodori, or parasol dance. Tokyo, too, does much to foster these traditional dances and songs.

proving conclusively that they represent the ancient army of the Hindu King.

At the other two Hindu festivals of Divvali and Hooli professional singers are employed to entertain the people. Women dancers, generally called Nautch girls, here come upon the scene; but, although as a class they are more or less of outcast in Indian society, yet the dances which they perform have very definite artistic meaning. When a woman dances striking her feet on the floor, and makes the little bells on her feet jingle and keep time with the music, keeping her body erect and her arms thrown back, she presents a very delicate picture of "youth in blossom' as it is termed in Hindi. The symbolism of the growing corn and the breeze rustling in a wheat field is depicted with equally delicate grace by the dancer rising slowly upon her feet in keeping with the music, and gradually gaining her full height with arms stretched so as to depict the growing of corn. When she has attained her full height, she moves her hands with palms up and then down with extraordinary rapidity, to give an effect of the wind passing through the crop.

It is on the fringe of the Far East that quite a different element is introduced into Eastern dancing. In Siam, for instance, during the Kathi Kashem festival, which takes place for about ten days at the end of January each year, rituals by dancers are performed in honour of the dead. The deceased is represented by one of his relations at the ceremonies, and there is much feasting and wine bibbing. On arrival of such 'dead' person in front of his house, he performs a dance, consisting chiefly of high jumping in the air and waving a bundle of twigs to capture the hovering spirit.

In Burma, where nat worship, or the worship of representatives of the true animistic spirit of the heathen deity is still carried on, the cult is peculiar in that it is a pure and simple ghost worship (see also page 58). These nats are represented by their devotees year by year; on a festival day a large field of worship is cleared in the jungle. The spirit-nats, merely men dressed up, enter the field, wearing highly ornamented loin cloths, short coats with very broad sleeves, with white shawls upon their shoulders; and holding shells in their right hands and branches of a holy tree in their left; and thus nat-inspired they dance for hours together. Similar though more refined spirit dances are to be seen both in China and Japan, where almost always some local celebrity is installed as a saint and dances are more in the nature of ancestor worship.

SCHOOLS AND SCHOOLMASTERS OF MANY COUNTRIES

MANY of the most interesting of the traditional customs and rules of etiquette that exist in the great public schools are dealt with in a separate chapter under the heading Customs of Famous Schools. Here we are concerned with the educational systems obtaining in various parts of the world. There are separate chapters on The Care of the Young, and Childhood Games of Savages

ALTHOUGH W. E. Forster's first Education Act became the law of the land so long ago as 1870, the question whether book learning is really beneficial to the human race is still debated with acrimony. One of the favourite arguments against it was submitted on a certain occasion by Boswell to Dr. Johnson. 'Wouldn't it,' the famous Scotch biographer inquired—and it is reasonable to suspect that he was merely trying to lure the doctor into a general discussion which would fill some more pages of his note-book—'tend to make people less industrious?'

'No, sir,' replied Johnson; 'while learning to read and write is a distinction the few who have that distinction may be the less inclined to work; but when everybody learns to read and write it is no longer a distinction. A man who has a laced waistcoat is too fine a man to work; but if everybody had laced waistcoats we should have people working in laced waistcoats. . . . Sir, you must not neglect doing a thing immediately good from fear of remote evil; from fear of its being abused. A man who has candles may sit up too late, which he would not do if he had not candles; but nobody will deny that the art of making candles, by which light is continued to us beyond the time that the sun gives us light, is a valuable art and ought to be preserved.'

But to debate the value of education is now a waste of time. The schoolmaster is abroad in the land, and not only in this land but in nearly every land. The business of 'opening the windows of the soul,' as somebody has aptly described education, goes on in nearly every place under the sun; even in the Tonga Islands the native boys study geography, and in Siam the girls now go to school.

The competition of religions is largely responsible for what may be called the universality of education. When the Jesuits first coupled education with their admirable missionary activities—when, too, they set about getting possession of the child's mind—they taught a valuable lesson which the other organized religious bodies were quick to learn. When the states commenced competing with the Churches, controversies which still exist inevitably arose, but over a great part of the world religion and education go hand in hand. And this is as true of the non-Christian religions as it is of the Christian.

One of the most astonishing schools in the world

STUDYING THE KORAN ON THE ROOF OF A MOSQUE

At Sidi Okba, in Algeria, not far from Biskra, is one of the best known Mahomedan schools in north-west Africa. It is housed in the mosque which contains the tomb of the Alexander of the Arabs, Sidi Okba, who conquered Africa for Islam in the first century of the Hegira. Most of the lectures are given on the roof.

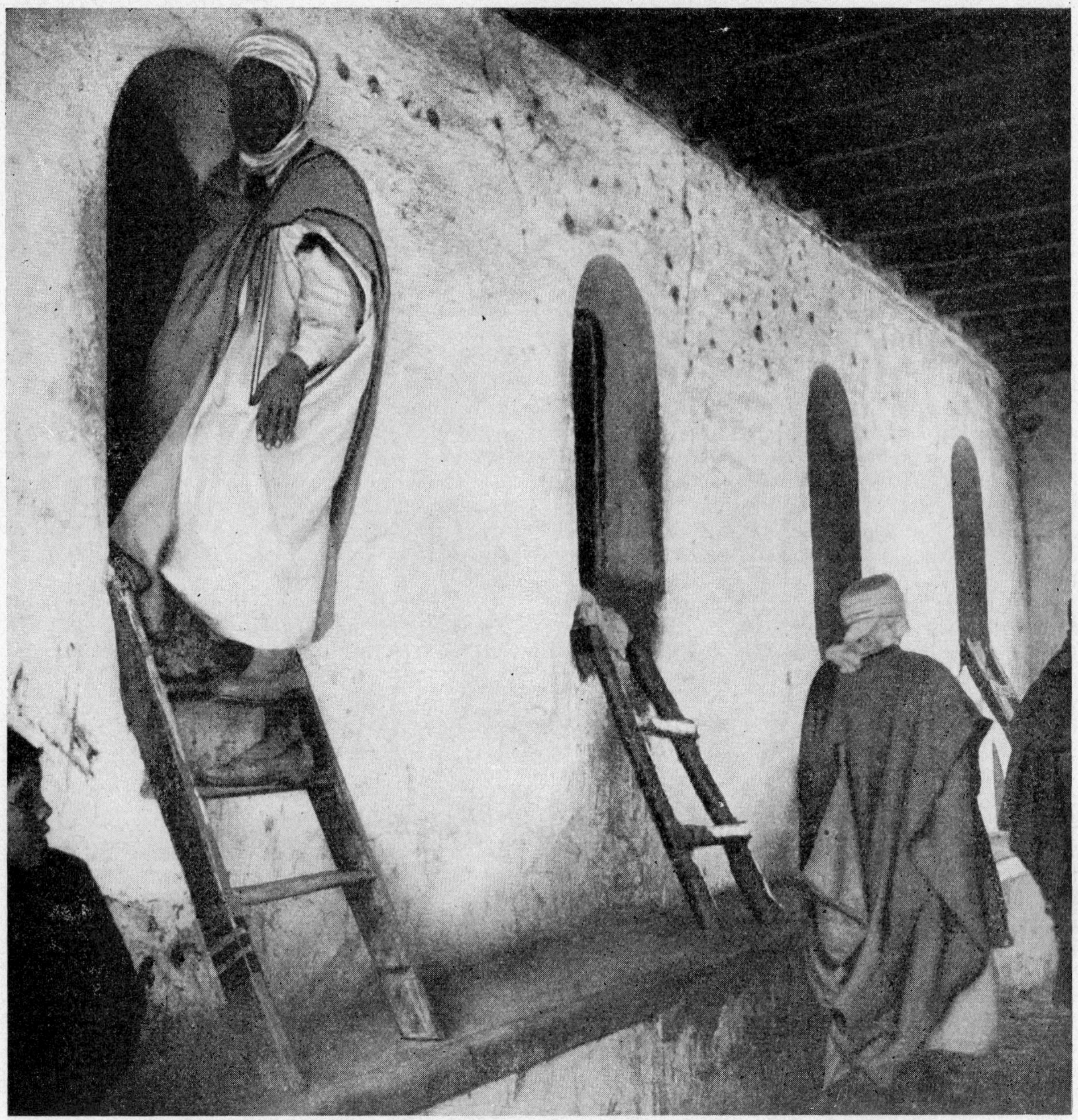

HOW THE STUDENTS GO TO ROOST AT THE MOSLEM SCHOOL OF SIDI OKBA

The sleeping arrangements at the Mahomedan school of Sidi Okba are peculiar. The bedrooms have no windows and are destitute of furniture, the students sleeping on the floor. In front of each little cell is a short ladder, at the top of which is a low doorway, through which the student enters his dark chamber. The school and the students' quarters, including the kitchen, are all under one roof. The subjects of the lectures at the school consist for the most part of interpretations of the Mahomedan scriptures and ancient history.

is Sidi Okba, called after the famous Mahomedan conqueror of northern Africa. It is situated about twelve miles south-west of Biskra in Algeria, and forms part of the mosque in which the Arabian hero lies buried. Here from all parts of the Mahomedan world come students to learn the sacred texts and ancient history and to pass examinations. During their course they are not only boarded but lodged. Their sleeping apartments are cells, which somebody has aptly described as being exactly like a hen-roost. To reach these cells the student has to climb up a ladder very similar to that placed at the door of a chicken-house. When inside, he lies down to rest on the bare floor—not that this is regarded as a hardship, for the true son of the desert, if he should by chance be compelled to stay in an hotel, usually lies down by the side of the bed instead of in it. The lecture room is the roof of the mosque, but if the heat of the sun should be unbearable, or the classes be interrupted by the arrival of sightseers, the study of the sacred writings is continued in the shaded courtyard. These Mahomedan students excel in hardiness even those famous Scotch undergraduates who while they were working for their degrees used to live on a sack of oatmeal brought from home, for they bring with them to Sidi Okba literally nothing more than what they stand up in. The rector of this desert high school is reputed to be a man of great learning and a skilful teacher.

In these sun-scorched areas the desire to learn is not limited to the students who enter the high school at Sidi Okba. Quite recently there was published an autobiography of an American cowboy in which the author related how an old French-Canadian trapper who had adopted him taught him his letters from the labels on meat tins and preserved fruits. The shepherds of South Tunisia on the very edge of the Sahara employ an even more primitive device during their long watches with the flocks. So that they may gratify their hunger for knowledge, some of their number secure boards on which there are inscribed extracts from the Koran or passages from the traditional history of the race. These boards, which are lent them by the marabouts, serve as books and lectures, and some of them, with their cracks roughly mended, are very reminiscent of the dog-eared volumes that may be found in any elementary school.

In another part of the world peopled by the Mahomedan race there has been of late years a great educational ' push,' synchronising with an attempt to modernise national life. This is in Turkey, which after the disasters of the Great War has not only miraculously survived, but has taken a big step along the road of progress. Besides effecting the emancipation of women, the government of the country has taken education largely out of the hands of the Mahomedan priesthood, and in order to emphasise its passion for modernity and to bring the country into line with the rest of Europe has adopted the Roman alphabet. This revolution of a basic method of learning presented immense difficulties, but the government faced it with courage and ingenuity. In order to familiarise the public with the new ' Alafabe ' they have fixed letter placards to the walls of houses and other public places. This alphabet differs in some respects from the one we use, following as it does very closely the classical Roman alphabet revived at the beginning of the sixteenth century. The letters C, G, I, O, S, U are duplicated and the letters Q, W, X are omitted altogether. One of the common sights of Turkey in late years has been the picture of ordinary men in the street pausing with their donkeys or mules or in the midst of their labours to memorise the alphabet from one of the posters.

In medieval times the link between religion and education—the Church and learning—was so strong that a clerk might claim exemption from the civil laws of the state. In our own ' rough island story ' many chapters are devoted to the inevitable struggle between the Church and state which arose in consequence. Perhaps the shadow of that link is retained

Ufa

LOWLY WORKER'S THIRST FOR KNOWLEDGE

Boards inscribed with passages from the Koran and from ancient history are supplied by the marabouts to the shepherds of south Tunisia. These primitive ' books ' the shepherds hang round their necks, and study whenever opportunity offers.

L.N.A.

ALFRESCO EDUCATION IN BASUTOLAND: STUDIES IN BLACK AND WHITE

The Basutos of South Africa are a tribe possessing very marked intelligence; indeed, they are among the ablest of the Bantus. They take a keen interest in education. Not only do a large proportion of them send their children to the mission schools, but many Basutos have themselves qualified as teachers. At the various open-air classes taught by the native teachers the equipment used is characterised by extreme simplicity; it consists of a blackboard, chalk, the alphabet, and the multiplication tables, and the pupils squat on the ground. Note the albino boy in the foreground. The birth of a white baby in Basutoland creates a great stir. The witch doctors are sent for, and they decide whether the prodigy is for good or for evil.

Reginald Silk

NIGHT SCHOOL BY THE LIGHT OF A FIRE IN THE HEART OF WEST AFRICA

Of the various religions whose missionaries are working for the spread of education in Africa, Islam is very much to the fore, and there is hardly a locality which Mahomedan teaching has not reached. Even in the very heart of the West African jungle Moslem schools are found. The photograph shows such a bush school at Mada, in the Bauchi province of Nigeria. Here the teaching is carried on at night, as most of the children are out in the bush during the day gathering wood or tilling the land.

today at Oxford and Cambridge, where the ceremony of conferring a degree includes an invocation of the Trinity, though the recipient may have no intention of taking Holy Orders. In Tibet this old medieval practice still survives and, though there are many schools, the pupils are regarded as candidates for the priesthood, and the lamas do not demean their high sacerdotal office by instructing the mere laity.

In India, with its three hundred and fifteen million population, split up by religions, castes and racial differences, the devising of any general system of education has always presented immense difficulties—how difficult is demonstrated by the fact that out of every thousand persons only 139 males and 21 females can be classified as literate, in the sense of being able to write a letter and read the reply. The Imperial government, aided by the missionaries, has generally adopted a system of elementary education based, so far as possible, on an adaptation of indigenous institutions and traditions. Many of these elementary classes are held in the open air, and are attended not only by children but by adults seized with ambition to learn. In the state schools education is secular, and costs something like twenty millions a year. Of the 254,700 institutions which supply education for some nine million males and two million females, half are maintained by the state or aided by grants, the rest being private and unaided. The custom of child marriage presents obvious difficulties to the educationist, and this has been partly met by providing schools for those children who have been so unfortunate—or so fortunate—as to become widows.

While there has always been some system of elementary education in India, higher education, which has become very popular, is purely an imported product. By some people the present state of unrest in India has been ascribed to the influence of this higher education, which appeals particularly to a people naturally intellectual. There are at present fifteeen universities in India, that at Benares being devoted to Hindus and that at Aligarh to Mahomedans. Ambitious students from these universities proceed

Nils Thomasson

Donald McLeish

CRUDENESS AND POLISH IN SCHOOLS OF TWO COUNTRIES OF EUROPE

In Lapland the problem of how to keep warm in school has been ingeniously solved. The teaching takes place in a low shed (top), and both teacher and pupils sit on the litter with which the floor is liberally strewn. The lower photograph shows the village school of Staphorst, in Holland. The girls wear a cap of astrakhan up to the age of six, after which they adopt the local head-dress of the women of the village—a close-fitting black cap ornamented with a carved band of silver or plated metal.

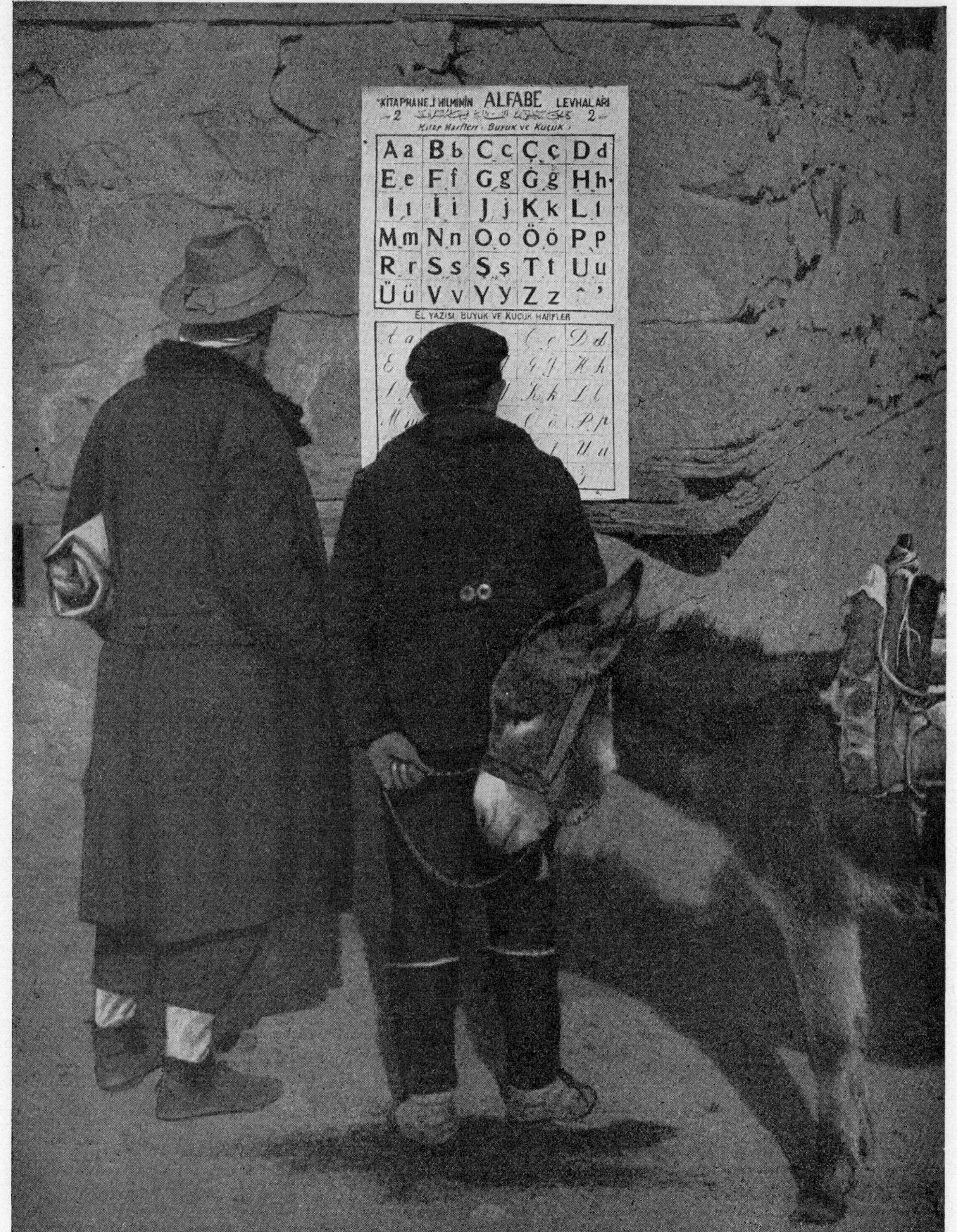

Martin Munkacsy

EDUCATIONAL REFORM IN TURKEY: A STREET SCHOOL FOR THE NEW ABC

The reforming zeal of Turkey knows no bounds, and this is particularly true of education. From being the province of the Moslem priests, teaching has now passed largely into the hands of the government. Among the many revolutionary changes that have been made one of the most drastic is the adoption of the Roman alphabet. To help on the difficult task of teaching a whole people a new alphabet, posters of the letters have been put up in prominent positions, so that the unfamiliar signs may be studied and memorised at odd times by passers-by.

Sport & General Press

to Oxford or Cambridge, where they usually gain distinction in their examinations.

In China, which centuries ago set the example of advancing its servants in the service of the state by a system of examinations, there are some 134,000 schools absorbing four and a half million pupils—something like a hundredth part of the population. Among the upper classes education is a tradition and every child passes as long a time at school as his European counterpart. There is, however, only one university in the whole of China—that of Peking. The fact, however, that there are twelve hundred and fifty Chinese newspapers suggests that there is a greater number of literates among the population than the number of pupils at the schools might lead one to suppose.

JAPAN, in her extraordinary efforts to modernise herself, pays great attention to education. The system in vogue, indeed, is very similar to that practised in most European countries, elementary education being provided by the state and being compulsory. High schools are also state-aided and prepare for a three years' course at the university, of which there are six, excluding five specially devoted to medicine. There are also high schools for girls and technical and special schools, all of which are well attended. The use made of the 'abacus' is one of the features of elementary school life in Japan. The pictures of Japanese children trying to learn the Japanese script suggest that the path to knowledge

SCHOOLS FOR CHILDREN AND ADULTS IN THE UNION OF SOVIET REPUBLICS

There is no central educational authority in the Soviet Union. Each republic has a separate autonomous commissariat for education. The first standard comprises children from the age of eight to twelve, and the second children from the age of twelve to seventeen. Above that come the higher educational institutions. There are several kinds of schools for the adult population. The upper photograph shows students of the newly organized cooperative courses in Turkmenistan, and the lower a united labour school in Tiflis for the Kurds.

W F Taylor

TIBETAN SCHOOLBOYS AT THEIR MONKISH STUDIES

The link between education and religion is specially marked in Tibet. In that land of monks such teaching as the children receive is entirely in the hands of the lamas, who fill the minds of their young charges with a fog of demonology and superstition. The children are not taught in the monasteries, but in schools which are staffed by monks.

is beset with many more difficulties than it is in the western world. Examinations are held at various institutions in the complicated caligraphy of the country, and the candidates, instead of using pen or pencil, come armed with paint brushes.

How the old and the new blend together in Japan is admirably illustrated by the fact that at the women's university classes are held in court traditions and social life. For employment in the state Civil Service educational qualifications are now considered necessary, and all aspirants have to satisfy an examination test. How strenuous is the competition is shown by the fact that to fill thirty-three positions at banks no fewer than 500 girls recently presented themselves for examination.

Among the teeming population of Africa the problem of education is as difficult as it is in India. Out of an estimated total of 143 millions calculated on a religious census—the figure, of course, is inaccurate—there are claimed to be some eight million Christians, some forty-four million Mahomedans, half a million Jews, and some ninety and a half millions who are classified as Animists. The education of the Christians, Mahomedans and Jews is more or less provided for on a religious basis. It is the animists who remain the problem for the schoolmaster, even in areas brought definitely under white rule. In the Union of South Africa, for example, the native population is to the European population as five is to one, and yet the number of non-European scholars is returned as being almost the same as that of the European. There are many native teachers who have qualified, but among the animists the great work of education is carried on under formidable difficulties almost entirely by missionaries.

The missionary zeal of the Mahomedans especially is spreading the light of learning in dark places, and there are some 'Africans' who profess to detect in this propagation of the Moslem faith, which during the last fifty years has penetrated to nearly all parts of the continent, a serious threat to European rule. Even in the dense bush of central West Africa their teachers have their schools—some of them night schools, held around a camp fire. The children use flat wooden boards cut from trees, and write with short pieces of cane or elephant grass shaped like a quill pen. For ink they use a mixture made from the bark of a native tree. In the Province of Oyo the chiefs and their families are given a special education

C. Carthrew

HOW SCHOOLBOYS IN KASHMIR DRILL

In so vast and heterogeneous a country as India the problem of evolving a workable educational system has been a very difficult one. Although there is still a great deal of illiteracy, the provision of state scholarships enables a boy, however poor, to pass from the village school to a university. Proper attention is paid in the schools to physical development.

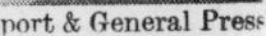

Sport & General Press

G.P.A.

METHODS OLD AND NEW IN THE SCHOOLS OF THE FAR EAST

In the past only the children of the well-to-do in Japan and China were educated at all. The Japanese were the first among the nations of the East to adopt up-to-date teaching methods, and under the Chinese republic the modern idea of education is gradually spreading. The Japanese still retain the abacus in their schools, an abacus counting contest at a primary school in Tokyo being shown in the upper photograph. Below is seen a class at a very exclusive Chinese school near **Canton.**

Wide World Photos

Fox Films

SCHOOLS IN SOPHISTICATED SURROUNDINGS AND AT THE BACK OF BEYOND

The children who astonish us by their cleverness on the films do not suffer educationally by starting their stage career so early, for there are excellent schools provided for them. The lower photograph shows a class at one of the film studio schools at Hollywood. In the remote parts of Australia education is a far from easy problem, for often very long distances have to be travelled by the children and the teachers. In the upper photograph pupils are seen outside a tiny outback school in Victoria, Australia.

Central Press

THE FIRST CLASS AT THE CANAL BARGE SCHOOL

The education of the children of canal folk has presented great difficulties. That they should attend the school nearest the mooring spot proved impracticable, but a solution may have been found in the proposal for floating schools. Such a barge school has been endowed by the Union Canal Company for the children of its employees who live afloat

to enable them to administer their districts more or less in accordance with modern views. Already the system has shown promising results.

AMONG the Indian population of South America again the schoolmaster is also faced with very great difficulties. In the backwoods of Brazil, about the upper reaches of the Amazon, some of the native races are as wild as any of the Indians of the old story books. To bring them to school is a problem which has been partly solved by the erection of educational posts, but to get them to come other than in a state of nature would tax the resources of a quartermaster's store. Some of the schools are very primitive buildings. In Venezuela they are often built of red mud, and thatched so roughly that they look for all the world like a broken-down stable. This reminds one that some of the most curious school buildings in the world are to be found in Lapland where in low-ceilinged wooden huts the children sit cosily on litter-covered floors to learn their lessons.

Wherever the confines of ordinary civilization are passed, the business of teaching and of learning alike is fraught with obstacles—most of which, however, are got over. On the prairies in Canada and in the remotest districts of Australia the long distances the children have to come are obviated by their travelling to the schools on horseback instead of on foot. Some of these frontier schools are very small, but the pupils get there, and the work of learning goes on.

But not only the backwoods produce hard nuts for the schoolmaster to crack. There are some at home in the very centres of civilization. For years our own authorities were at their wits' end how to deal with the children of the canal folk. Theoretically these were supposed to attend the school nearest to the point where the barge was tied up on any given day. This meant in practice that they never went to school at all. Attendance officers could do nothing with them. A special effort was made to establish an educational centre at Brentford, but this was never wholly successful. Lately the Grand Union Canal Company launched a special barge, designed and fitted to act as a floating school, and all canal workers are now urged to co-operate with the authorities in an effort to give their children a regular education.

In America, where children are employed in the big film studios schools are established, and classes are held in which some of the foremost figures in the Hollywood hierarchy take a part. Another aspect of education which faces America is that of the immigrants who come over from Europe with standards of education and hygiene quite foreign to the community in which they are to be absorbed. In the great industrial centres such as Pittsburgh these new arrivals are given lessons in English and inculcated with the doctrines of cleanliness.

The schoolmaster has already performed miracles, but his most remarkable achievement is the educational system applied to the Royal Air Force. Recruits for the Air Force are drawn from the public and secondary schools. Having qualified by a somewhat stiff entrance examination, they are enlisted at the Halton School of Technical Training, where for three years they are given a comprehensive education more than equal to that obtainable at any public school. Their passing-out examination—if they pass high enough they may qualify for a commission—is of a highly advanced type. This state experiment in specialised education is one of the most extraordinary in the world.

MODERN SURVIVALS OF WITCHCRAFT

THE openly and regularly practised witchcraft that plays so large a part in the life of savage peoples, and contains more than a tinge of genuine religion, is dealt with in the chapters on Medicine Men and Their Magic, Magic in Love and War, Magic and the Means of Life, and elsewhere. Here we are chiefly concerned with certain forms of witchcraft that still hold their ground in civilized countries.

NOTWITHSTANDING the great advances made in science and in education generally, superstition exists among all classes of society in all parts of the world and belief in witchcraft still has remarkable vitality. The root conception of the belief is that certain individuals have the power of casting spells or curses and producing some malignant effect on any object, animate or inanimate, upon which their eye may rest, when exercised upon the victims of their displeasure. The iniquity of witchcraft lies in the supposition that possession of the necessary supernatural powers is acquired as a result of express compact made with the devil and sealed with the witch's own blood. From the fact that the chief agents and possessors of these powers were mostly women we have the prevalence of the female name of witch and its synonym in other languages.

In the sixteenth century superstition permeated human life, concentrating around birth, marriage and death, and belief in planetary influence, omens and the power of the witch became general. It was to the village wise woman, usually some old withered dame with hairy chin and palsied fingers, that the power of evil was attributed when a child fell sick with a mysterious ailment or the cattle did not thrive. With this reputation she was soon dubbed a witch and credited with casting the 'evil eye,' or 'wishing ill' by fashioning figures in wax and pricking them with needles or thorns, in order that those on whom she wished to wreak her vengeance should become afflicted.

Her 'familiar,' which was constantly with her, was supposed to take the shape of a black cat, dog or great toad, and in this way the first-named animal became associated with witchcraft. Of this type were the witches who were tortured, burnt or otherwise executed in thousands down to the end of the seventeenth century.

One of the chief survivals of witchcraft at the present day is the widespread belief in the 'evil eye,' which in many countries is still as common as it was in early times. Evidence of the belief is to be found upon the most ancient monuments of Babylonia, the cradle of civilization, as well as in Egypt. Among the Jews, Moslems, Hindus and Oriental races the supposed terrible effects of the evil eye are still dreaded by all classes, and 'Eat thou not the bread of him that hath an evil eye' is an old Eastern maxim that holds good today In Palestine the belief still persists that the evil eye can 'throw down a horse, break a plough, cause sickness, and even destroy a person, animal or plant.'

DOMESTIC animals have always been believed to be specially susceptible to the dreaded fascination, and, as a protection, both the Turks and Arabs festoon their horses and camels with amulets in the form of crescent-shaped brasses or blue glass beads, some of which are fashioned to represent an eye. The eye as a defence against the effects of the 'evil eye' is a survival of sympathetic magic, and protective charms of this kind, made of metal or faïence, are used all over the world. Even in England the brass horse-charms still frequently seen decorating the martingale and other parts of the harness of our cart horses are but the unconscious survival of the same idea.

Examples of the persistence in England of belief in witchcraft, spells and the evil eye are numerous. Only a few months ago a County Council health

Courtesy of Royal College of Surgeons

SKULL JU-JU OF A NIGERIAN WITCH DOCTOR

The objects stuck in the central part of the fetish include four human thigh bones, a hand carved in wood, a knife, a dagger and an iron skewer. Under one of the eight human skulls were found pieces of paper, some apparently torn from government documents, intended to work an evil magic against a European official.

visitor in Herefordshire, calling at a house on a mountain side, found a woman who had been held a prisoner in one room for twenty years because 'she had been looked upon with the evil eye.' On her second visit to the homestead one of the brothers who had kept the woman a prisoner actually accused the visitor of having the evil eye, threatened her with a gun, and chased her down the mountain side 'uttering terrible cries.'

In Essex and Dorsetshire there is often a wise woman in a village who is believed by some to be capable of casting spells or taking them off, and in a Suffolk village as lately as 1930 the death of a man was attributed to his being overlooked by the evil eye of a woman who was unpopular with her neighbours and had acquired the reputation of being a witch The prevalence of elder bushes and bay trees in the gardens of many cottages in Gloucestershire is said to be due to the belief that they will keep away witches and evil influences. This tradition is mentioned by Culpeper in the seventeenth century He declares that 'neither witch nor devil, thunder or lightning will hurt a man where there is a bay tree.'

Many of the Norfolk peasantry still have equal belief in the power of the evil eye. The rector of Merton recently stated that some of the country folk in that district had an ingrained faith in good and evil spirits He also related how he was once called to lift a curse locally known as the 'Curse of Sturston,' which had lain on the district from the time of Queen Elizabeth. According to tradition, the rector of the parish in those days was an accommodating priest who held a Protestant service in the church on Sunday mornings and recited Mass in his parlour for the Popish gentry afterwards In consequence, an old woman in the village who was a staunch Protestant, as she lay dying, laid a 'curse' on the parson, the church and the great folks' Hall, and the 'curse' seemed to become effective. 'When I came,' continued the rector, who told the story, 'I was asked to lift the curse, for the old Hall had become a farmhouse surrounded by cottages, and the people feared that the curse might still be working I held a public service, using an old altar tomb in the ruined churchyard as a lectern. People flocked to the service from miles around. Nothing further dreadful happened I had laid the curse.'

FROM the early part of the Middle Ages the Romany tribes that have wandered over Europe have had a reputation for dealing in magic and witchcraft, and their modern descendants, the gypsies, are still believed by country folk to possess certain occult powers. As recently as 1928 one of these gypsy practitioners, named Mary Hearn, was sent to prison for six months for obtaining money by false pretences from a gardener called Paddy, who lived at St. Mawes, Cornwall. She was charged with exercising 'witchcraft, sorcery or enchantment.' It transpired that the gypsy obtained such an influence over Paddy that he had given her about £500. She convinced him that an illness from which he was suffering was due to him being 'over-looked' by the evil eye, and that as she was a 'white witch' she could cure the 'black

W. F. Taylor

TREES THAT WARD OFF BALEFUL INFLUENCES FROM THE HOME

Of the many beliefs that have gathered round the elder and the bay tree, one was that witches and other evil influences could not come near them. This may account for the elders and bay trees common near cottages in Gloucestershire. The ancients had the greatest reverence for the bay tree They thought that lightning could not strike it, and during a thunderstorm the Emperor Tiberius always put on a wreath of bay. The photograph shows an elder growing by a cottage at Duntesbourne.

H. Tillema

Wellcome Historical Medical Museum

MAGIC DOLLS THAT WITCHES USE TO BRING BACK HEALTH

The employment of dolls in the curing of disease is a form of witchcraft that is found in many parts of the world. Among the Dyaks of Borneo a little puppet fashioned out of boiled rice (left) is often fastened by the magician outside the house of the sufferer. It is believed that the illness dwells within the doll, and that if the doll is taken away the malady also will be removed. The dolls on the right are from Italy, and are used for the same purpose. Similar uses of puppets are found the world over, as in the examples from Ashanti illustrated below.

magic.' She performed various incantations over him, talked about the planets and Venus, and waved a compass over his head, but Paddy got no better. He declared in court that for twenty-five years she had been telling him that he was 'ill-wished' and constantly asked him for money to take the ill-wish off. This so upset the old man that his heart became affected and he began to look wasted and weak, which the gypsy attributed to the evil eye. Paddy's misfortunes were ended by the police, who arrested the gypsy witch and put an end to her activities.

Another instance of the kind came to light at Higham Ferrars, Northamptonshire, in 1926, when a gypsy of the historic name of Smith was charged with obtaining money from a widow and selling her 'charms to burn, to wear and put under her pillow.' She told her victim that if the charms burnt brightly it indicated that £400 was coming to her, but if the fire was dull, some enemy was holding the money back. Smith received a month's hard labour from an unsympathetic bench, and the police superintendent in charge of the case remarked that the widow was only one of many simple folk in the district who were constantly being gulled by gypsy magic.

THE use of stones called 'holey stones,' which are usually flints with a natural perforation, as a protection against witchcraft is very widely distributed; they are commonly employed, both in England and in Ireland. In Lancashire and Yorkshire they are sometimes hung up inside the house door as a safeguard against witches, while in Devonshire and Somersetshire they are suspended on the fruit trees in the orchards to protect the fruit from the pixies. In some parts of Ireland such stones are tied to the horns of the cows with the idea of preventing the

Clarendon Press

HELPERS OF THE WITCHES OF ASHANTI

Ashanti witches work in league with the red or mischievous fairies and a demon called Sasabonsam. This latter takes the form of a hairy forest monster with long legs, bloodshot eyes, and feet pointing both ways. The photograph (from Captain R. S. Rattray's 'Religion and Art in Ashanti') shows figures of Sasabonsam and two fairies.

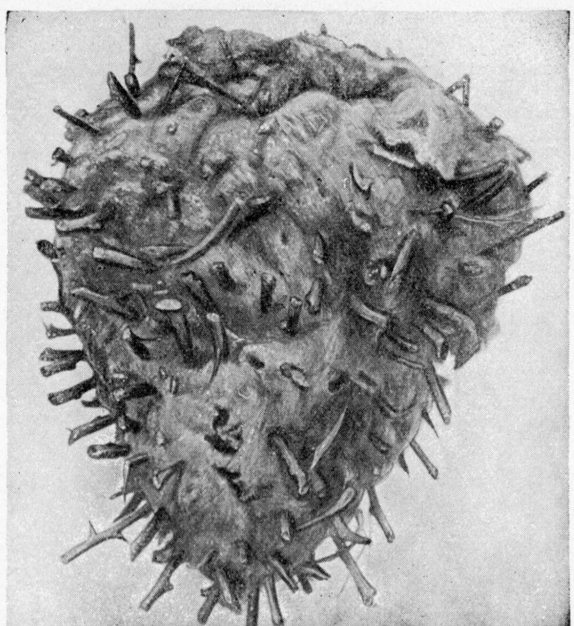

Courtesy of Royal College of Surgeons

TWENTIETH CENTURY DORSETSHIRE WITCHCRAFT

This calf's heart, studded with pins, thorns and twigs of witch-hazel, was found in a cottage chimney near Bridport in 1902. Such piercing of the heart was believed to produce a like effect on the person against whom the operation was directed.

fairies from stealing the milk, and, hung round the neck they are believed to ward off the murrain.

It is not often that a man is charged with witchcraft, but in 1926 an application was made to the Glastonbury magistrates for a summons on this ground. The applicant stated that his neighbour had 'bewitched his clock, and in consequence 'it would tick three times as loud as usual and then stop every night, although it was wound up. He further declared that the man he accused 'came to him as a witch at night when he sat by the fire, but only his head and beard appeared. He spat at him twice, and he disappeared as a ball of smoke. In spite of these allegations the magistrates decided not to grant a summons, and the victim of these witcheries left the court disconsolate.

SUPERSTITION has been general in Ireland from early times. Lucretius mentions that the Irish in his time believed 'that their cattle were often injured by a kind of witches whom they called Eye-biters,' and the power of the 'evil eye' is regarded with dread today. An illustration was brought to light in a case that was tried at the Quarter Sessions at Dungannon, Co Tyrone, in 1927 in which a lady sued two farmers for spreading rumours that she had power to bewitch cattle. The plaintiff stated that in this district a large number of people believed that their cattle could be 'blinked' (bewitched), and that her reputation had spread for miles around so that no one in the neighbourhood would speak to her. One of the defendants pleaded that the statements were true, for 'the thatch of his house had cured the cattle. He added that burning thatch was one of the recognized cures for 'blinked' cattle, and he had burned it under the cow's nose and the cow had jumped to her feet and got better.

It was stated that after the cows had been cured the farmers protected their animals by tying a red rag on their tails. This custom is another interesting survival, for red everywhere is inimical to witchcraft of all kinds. Red was the witches' colour, symbolic of the blood with which they had sealed their compacts, and is used in connexion with witch charms throughout the world. In Italy and Sicily, charms against the evil eye are often made of red coral and are usually tied with red woollen braid, or they are painted red.

THERE is perhaps no country in Europe where belief in the power of the evil eye is more general than in Italy. South of Rome and in Sicily superstition is as strong as it was a couple of centuries ago, and the peasant will cross his thumb with his forefinger if he meets a hunchback or 'gobbo' or a person who happens to squint. In Naples, where charms, usually of red coral, are commonly to be seen in the shop windows, even the mention of the word 'fascino' or 'jettatura' is sufficient to give rise to suspicion. In certain streets in the old quarter of the city the writer observed that a large red hand was sometimes to be seen hanging from a balcony to protect those who lived in the house from the evil eye. Curiously enough, although the 'gobbo' is usually credited with having the power of casting the 'evil eye,' when his influence has been counteracted he is considered to be a protection against its effects, and hunchbacks are not infrequently to be found officiating as waiters in Italian restaurants.

Both witchcraft and black magic are still practised in some parts of France, and according to a leading French barrister, who has made these survivals a special study, scarcely a week passes but such a case comes before the courts in some part of the country. It is a common occurrence for a peasant to accuse some old woman, who is supposed to possess the power of the evil eye, of making his milk turn, his pigs ill, or his children bad-tempered. These beliefs are not confined to the remote mountain and country districts, and as recently as 1930 a pastry-cook at Fontenay-sous-Bois, a suburb of Paris, prosecuted a neighbour for turning his cream sour in mid-winter.

Maître Garcon states that in 1930 he actually witnessed a novice making a pact with the devil in the woods near Fontainebleau. Knowing the exact rendezvous where the rite was going to be performed, he and a friend crawled up under some bushes where they could watch the proceedings. It was a moonless night, and they waited at the crossroads until they saw a man suddenly appear from a path in the wood. He first traced a magic circle on the ground around him, and drew the monogram of Christ behind, so that the devil should be unable to creep up and catch him unawares. In front he then lighted two candles and burnt incense in a bowl. Opening a book, he began to curse God and invoke blessings on Satan, from whom he asked riches and the fulfilment of his various desires. Finally, standing on tiptoes, the man held up the contract he had written with his own blood and adjured the devil to give him power and fortune, promising to find the Evil One a human soul for every blessing conferred upon him. 'The scene,' says Maître Garcon, 'at first grotesque became tragic, for he worked himself up to a paroxysm approaching dementia and began to call on Satan to appear. But nothing happened, and eventually the would-be wizard slunk off into the woods.'

Belief in witchcraft still persists in many parts of Germany, and a recent case reported from Berlin shows that even in the capital the superstition yet survives. The complainant, a shopkeeper, suspected his wife of practising witchcraft, and told the court that his suspicions were aroused one night when he heard her apparently talking to herself in her bedroom. Listening at the door, he heard her repeating the words, 'He will be true, he will be true,' several times. On entering the room, to his astonishment he found his wife feeding the flames of the stove with one of his waistcoats. Upon expostulating with her, she confessed she was carrying out the instructions of a witch whom she had consulted, who had assured her that she could secure her husband's fidelity if she burnt one of his garments while repeating an incantation. The husband, after remonstrating with her, let the matter pass until, a few weeks later, he caught her burning his trousers, when he decided it was time he put a stop to the proceedings by haling the witch before the magistrates.

ANOTHER form of witchcraft which has continued throughout the world for thousands of years, among both civilized and barbaric races, consists in the use of a figure in human shape, modelled in wax, in order to injure or destroy an enemy. Such manikins were used in ancient Egypt and employed in the liturgy of the god Amen Ra, whose great temple was at Thebes. From Egypt the practice passed to Greece, and thence to Rome, and so in early times was introduced into western Europe. The same idea can be traced in the Far East, and in Vedic magic the wax or clay figure is used in various operations. Thus, to destroy an enemy, a figure of clay is modelled and the spot over the heart is pierced with an arrow, or death may be compassed by the Hindu wizard by causing an image of wax to be made and melting it slowly before a fire.

In England, after the figure had been moulded in human form it was customary to pierce it with pins on all sides. The Lord's Prayer was then repeated backwards, and supplications made to the devil that he would inflict the person whom the figure was supposed to represent in like manner as it had been pierced with the pins. Another method of using the wax figure in order to injure an enemy was to place it near a fire and as it slowly melted so it was

Clarendon Press

STOOPING POSTURES AND SHUFFLING GAIT IN THE DANCE OF THE WITCH-FINDERS

Fetishes are frequently used for the purpose of discovering witches. In the dance here seen (from Captain R. S. Rattray's 'Religion and Art in Ashanti') the attendants of a very famous Ashanti fetish named Fwemso are taking part. The women, who for the occasion were thickly smeared with white powdered clay and dressed in voluminous white skirts scalloped round the edges, shuffled about inside a space marked off by a white line and an egg, while the onlookers swayed backwards and forwards and sang. The line was regarded as forming a symbolical fence to ward off evil from the dancers.

INDIAN WOMEN SPINNING MAGIC YARN TO BRING GOOD LUCK IN MARRIAGE

Faith in magic and witchcraft has survived, below the surface of Christianity, among the ignorant people of Europe, and much the same is true of the East. From early times the religion of the common folk in India seems to have been little more than belief in many spirits ready to work mischief. In some Indian villages women soak cotton in goat's milk under a certain kind of tree for a whole moonless night and then spin it into yarn. This, they believe, will ward off demons and ensure successful marriage.

believed the person whom it was supposed to represent would waste away by some lingering disease.

The use of a heart, or something in the shape of a heart, is of wide distribution, and exists in many forms. The heart was regarded as the source of life, and anything affecting it was vital; therefore it came to be believed by practitioners of witchcraft that if a heart was stuck with sharp thorns or pins, with suitable incantations, the person whom it was desired to injure would suffer in a like manner. The heart of a cow or sheep was generally used for this purpose. Only a few years ago an old woman living in a village in Dorsetshire was seen sticking nails and pins into a sheep's heart, which procedure she accompanied by muttered imprecations. This object was afterwards found secreted in the chimney of her cottage, and when asked why she did it, she admitted that she wished to work ill on a neighbour against whom she had some grievance.

The heart was also used in a similar way to put a spell on cattle, and when a real heart could not be obtained a piece of leather cut into the shape of one was sometimes employed. In certain seaport towns it is still customary to give a sailor when starting on a voyage a heart-shaped pincushion, stuck full of beaded pins in fancy designs, to keep as a charm against storms and tempests, which in early times were supposed to be caused by demons.

Certain forms of witchcraft still persist in London, and in the East End, shortly before All Hallow E'en, there is usually a brisk demand in the chemists' shops for the gum-resin called dragon's blood (Pterocarpus indicus), which has from time immemorial been used by women as a charm on Walpurgis night. To attract a lover or to cause a fickle husband to return it is necessary to mix the dragon's blood with quicksilver, sulphur and saltpetre and throw the mixture on a clear fire at midnight, repeating at the same time a certain incantation. The root of the herb tormentilla is sometimes used for the same purpose, but it must be burnt on a Friday, when, it is believed, it will so terribly torment the recalcitrant lover that he will quickly return to the disconsolate damsel.

WITHIN the writer's knowledge, in recent years, tiny glass tubes filled with quicksilver were sold in a chemist's shop in the City, chiefly to business men, who firmly believed that carrying one in the pocket would prevent rheumatism. Belief in a knotted cord of red silk as a preventive of headache and nose-bleeding still survives, while in some districts in London glass necklaces composed of amber-coloured beads are placed round the necks of babies to ward off croup and bronchitis. Many of these superstitious practices can be traced to a very early origin, and the use of the knotted cord goes back to a period of at least two thousand years.

It is apparent that the tenacity of some of these survivals is due to mental influences and psychology, while in others the superstitious mind, which is quite independent of education and training, aids in their perpetuation. Mainly through these causes and the power of contagious fears of the unknown, superstition still survives throughout the world.

WAYSIDE ENTERTAINERS OF THE EAST

WHEREAS Europeans incline to find their amusement in games and sports in which they themselves participate the adult Asiatic prefers to be a spectator, and a host of professional itinerant entertainers have come into existence for his delectation. Other aspects of this subject of popular amusement are dealt with in chapters on Childhood Games of Savages and, for civilized peoples, in that on Circus Folk.

THE people of Asia are inclined to hold feasts or gala fairs at the slightest excuse, and call off work in consequence for not only one but for several days.

On the frequency of such occasions the wayside entertainers thrive, for when going to the great gala fair at Idd, or any of the Hindu celebrations here and there, you will see groups of men watching a man performing baffling feats of juggling, others showing the so-called rope trick or sword-swallowing, or, farther on, snake-charmers gathering enormous crowds.

Whatever view a Western observer may take of such performances, to the oriental mind practically all these stand as more magical in atmosphere than mere manifestations of no importance calculated to while away an idle hour. The Asiatic considers these entertainments as inseparable from his daily life. He regards them as supernatural, and yet paradoxically as quite normal, because he has come to think of them as something within the sphere of human operation within the world in which he has his being.

Take, for example, the rope trick. That hundreds of Anglo-Indians have recorded having heard of it and yet no one has actually seen a boy climb a rope suspended in mid-air, or the severed parts of his body fall from the sky, goes to prove that the trick has never been performed that way. But the facts must be stated. A large crowd gathers to see the various tricks, the fame of the master magician has already spread in the neighbourhood, the mental attitude of the spectators is not sceptic, they have not come to examine the truth, they have come to see the trick and hope that it will not fail. Amongst much drum beating an atmosphere is created, a rope is thrown up in mid air; that it does not keep suspended there is beside the question, for no one is paying attention to it. There is a smoky fire in the centre to which the magician fixes your attention; he announces that his son is now climbing the rope to fight the demons in the air. A boy does undress and approach the smoke, drums are beaten, women wail, the master magician tears his hair, bemoaning his fate for having allowed his son to fight the evil spirits, for the dismembered parts of his body are shown in the distance; then the boy emerges from behind the smoke. The trick is complete.

NOW this has actually happened, but how to explain it? The truth lies in the fact that it is a case of the ability of the performer to induce collective hallucination in his audience; that is, he has probably the power of hypnotising the onlookers and making them believe that they see such and such a thing. There is no doubt, of course, that the acquiring of such a strong influence is a rarity, and so is the chance of witnessing a rope trick. That there are still such men in the East is undeniable, and the history of the Near East is replete with instances to show that again and again men have acquired such powers of producing mass hallucination.

Of the lesser craft are the sword-swallowing, which is only a trick, and also the great bamboo trick, by which a bamboo tree is made to grow before the eyes of astonished beholders. A pot full of earth is placed on the ground and the performer waves a thin carpet over it. In this carpet are concealed portions of bamboo rod articulated like the parts of a fishing-rod, which fit into each other. These are withdrawn one by one and attached to each other by skilful sleight of hand, so that the tree actually seems to grow and eventually is crowned by a tuft of leaves

A. R. Slate

MASTERY OF UNSTABLE EQUILIBRIUM

Peripatetic acrobats make a good living in any part of India, carrying their scanty apparatus with them and setting it up wherever the prospects seem hopeful. In the balancing feat shown here the acrobat swings round at the top of a swaying pole

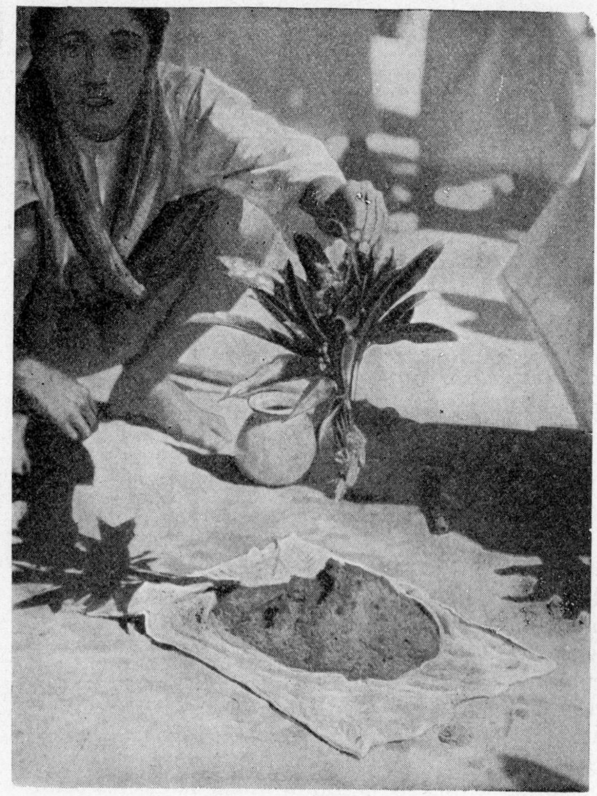

E. O. Hoppé

WHERE THE QUICKNESS OF THE HAND DECEIVES THE EYE

Indian jugglers excel particularly in legerdemain—tricks of deception performed, in the narrower sense of the term, by sleight of hand only. The mango trick, in which the juggler places a mango seed in a pot of earth, and covering it with a cloth thereafter discloses it in various stages of its growth to maturity, comes into this category of jugglery, in which success depends more upon the juggler's power of diverting the onlookers' attention at crucial moments than upon his own celerity of movement.

Then there are men who perform feats of which catalepsy is the essence: such are well founded. They are carried out by real students of the cult, and often with the aid of drugs. Some cases were authenticated in which several performers were buried in earth at one festival and were dug up alive at another after several weeks. The drugs that chiefly enter into these cases are fairly well known. The chewing of opium can keep away the sense of hunger for days, and anyone who has been in Africa knows that the mixture which the Berber tribesmen prepare from honey and roasted and bruised corn is so nourishing that a handful of it eaten in the morning suffices a man for the whole day. Again charus, the resin which is exuded by the hemp plant in Nepal, is being extensively used to produce a delirium in which the performer's disciple is supposed to prophesy.

But perhaps the greatest of all the side-shows at a wayside is the play of the cobra snake. Thousands will gather round the Saparah, as the serpent charmers are called, to see enormous snakes taken out of big baskets and played about by these performers. The cult is associated with serpent worship, but before describing it, a few details about the training in the art are pertinent here.

The people who charm the snakes initiate their sons from the age of ten into the craft The boy is not allowed to cut his hair ; he is required to recite certain Muntara, or formulae in the nature of incantation, for forty days, usually standing waist-deep in running water at night. Year by year his course of instruction increases from mystery to mystery, from the first stages of merely physical exercises of how to swing from the bough of a sacred pepal tree—the longer and higher the approach of the swing of his rope the better ; for thus, it is contended, the Monkey-General of Rama deposited his troops in Ceylon from the Indian mainland—to catching the snake by its tail with sufficient smartness before the reptile can turn upon itself, and finally to extracting the fangs, if need be. Besides being mere performers, these men are often employed by Mahomedans to charm a snake away from their homes, which is done by their playing upon their special flute before the hole of the snake, and to lead him out of the house.

But essentially their skill is due to their allegiance to the cult of serpent worship which alone is said to give them the power over the deadliest cobra as it plays and sways when the charmer puffs and blows before it, and Hindu worshippers of the snake-god stand aghast and bewitched, watching the performance. As often as not the king cobra must be

E. O. Hoppé

MUSIC THAT CHARMS MAN'S REPTILE ENEMY

Snake charmers rank among the most popular wayside entertainers in India. The snake used is the king cobra, to be struck by which means death, and the performance consists in the Saparah, or charmers, playing upon their special wind instruments fashioned from a gourd until the formidable reptile raises its head from the basket in which it is carried about, spreads its hood, and sways in obedience to the piping. The Saparah undergo years of training in their art and are faithful adherents to the cult of serpent worship.

'JUST AN ORDINARY BASKET, GENTLEMEN'

Best known of the 'vanishing lady' forms of mystery is the Indian basket trick. The basket is rectangular, larger at the base than at the top, and the conjurer begins by showing that it is a perfectly simple construction, without any trick device.

played to for at least an hour, or he will strike from which all the remedies and incantations of the charmer cannot save him.

Amongst the roadside entertainments nothing surpasses the ram fights staged in the open air at Bokharan markets where the peasants come to perform their Friday prayer and to do the weekly shopping to boot. Young and old are shaking the dust off their slippers as they enter the mosque, the high mullah is already leading the prayer, the babble of tongues in the public square dies down to a mere hush, for they are now bending low in response to their mullah's sermon. Presently a thousand palms are lifted skyward, the faithful are seeking Allah's blessings at the close of the prayer.

Then the village youths mix with the Begs in watching the ram fight For many months the ram keeper performer has tended his animal in far-off mulberry avenues of golden Samarkand, and his rival announces with greater force the skill and pedigree of his ram, which he has bought, so he avers, from the Amir's own grandson. 'It is a fine animal, aye, praise be to Him!' say the spectators as they are being pushed aside by the combatants' owners to form a ring in the centre of Ragistan Square, overlooked as it is by the Turret of Mercy from where the ruler himself is expected to watch the contest.

The rams have twisted horns, their tails hang heavily with pounds of fat Their skins shorn almost to a shave, they are being borne by two men towards the arena. 'Make way, make way for the lion of the desert!' calls the trainer. 'Make way and see how my warrior will devour the miserable goat of my adversary!' The other jeers and shouts back praises of his ram—a ram which, he says, could fight an elephant if there were any in barren Turkistan.

The people press forward to have a closer look at the first round. The rams, with fire in their eyes, are butting at each other. One runs round the circle and charges at the enemy. Again and again they rise on their hind legs, thudding once, twice, thrice, and then their horns get entangled. Separated by their respective trainers, they run backward and then hurl themselves against each other with renewed force. Drums are being beaten, spectators have formed themselves into rival camps, the trainers are shouting themselves hoarse. The little drums are keeping different time.

For the third time the smaller of the two rams is seen beating his larger adversary towards the edge of

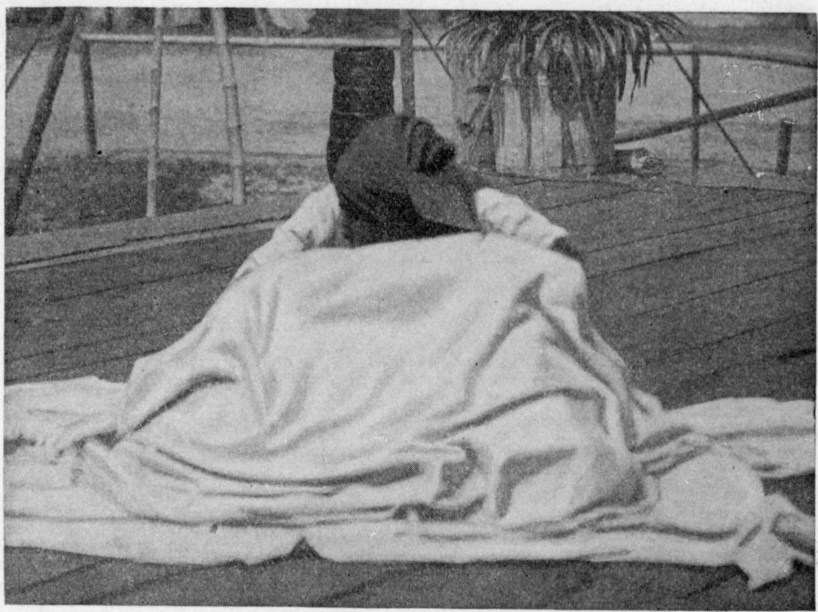

Helmers-Arfo

WEAVING MAGIC TO MAKE A MORTAL VANISH

The conjurer proceeds to press his female assistant down into the basket, which is seemingly too small to hold a human being, first binding her hands; then, covering the basket with a cloth, he proceeds to 'magic' her invisibly into thin air, rapidly muttering his patter until she has had time to disappear, when he himself jumps into the basket to show that it is empty.

the circle. Its trainer has wagered a hundred gold Tillah coins with the governor's son; till, panting and foaming, the larger animal, maddened with the pain of his broken horn, charges like a wounded demon at the little ram from Samarkand. The latter, avoiding the thud, gives him a broadside and brings him to his knees; he rises, and receives another thud; another, and the last one sends him pelting and defeated, not only to the edge of the circle, but past the spectators to the near-by stall where the water-melon sellers ply their humble trade.

The gathering is now in an uproar. The rival bands of village youths are vociferously discussing the fight. Some have thrown wet melon seeds at the party of the defeated ram; who, taking up the challenge, plunge into the ranks of the victor's supporters. Words are forgotten; the ram contest is forgotten; blows are now being freely exchanged, the arms of trailing coats are rising in the air and descending on dismantled turbans, headgears are being trampled upon, horse-whips are cracking, till the grey-beards of the town come upon the scene, nodding their heads in disapproval. They disperse the crowd, and thus ends one of the most eventful wayside entertainments in the most ancient part of the East.

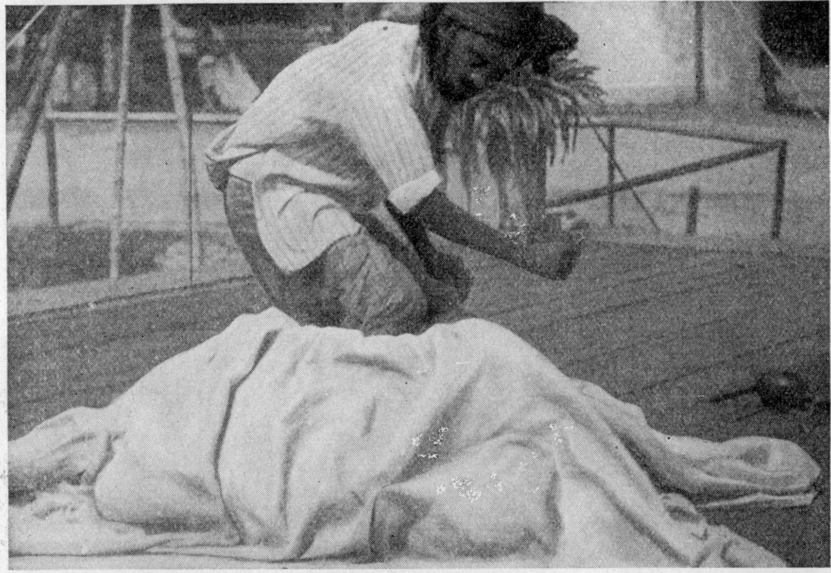

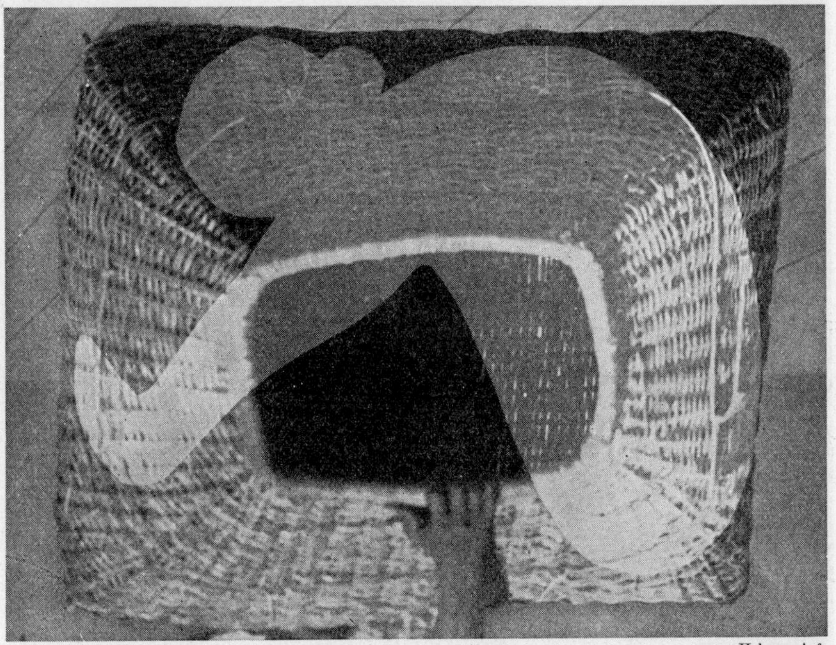

Helmers-Arfo

THE CAMERA REVEALS WHAT THE EYE CANNOT SEE

Photography has revealed the secret of the basket trick, and anyone can now perform it who can find a sufficiently supple assistant. All that happens is that she curves her body and presses it against the walls of the basket, as shown in this photographic diagram, leaving a space in the centre into which the conjurer jumps, and through which he can thrust his sword.

In comparison with these somewhat warlike games of entertainment, where the meeting generally ends with a free fight, and the real reason of the show is to attract prospective ram owners to have their pets trained by the man who had reared the winner of the day, the wayside entertainers of the Middle East variety styled as Jadugar, or makers of magic, are known to perform very marvellous tricks. There are, for instance, those who gather a crowd in the Asiatic bazaars, where such remarkable performances as the 'transporting of matter' are shown.

Undeniable proof is at hand to show that this transportation is possible and is beyond the reach of ordinary magic-men, as they are called. At such entertainments, for example, it has time and again been shown that the performer borrows a ring or even a watch from one of the spectators. This he places inside a melon, and then has the melon thrown in a well. Shortly afterwards, another man is asked to salvage the sunken melon from the well, which, when brought before the audience, shows no cut whatever, and, on being cut, the ring or the watch is found inside it. In like manner the producing of such fruit as are quite out of season has been reported on quite unimpeachable authority.

It is, however, not without interest to note that some of these wayside entertainments have actually

H. von Perckhammer

CHEERFUL CHARLATANS WHO WAX FAT ON THE CREDULITY OF THE IGNORANT

Superstition and credulity are dominant characteristics of the Chinese, with the result that astrologers and fortune-tellers abound and prosper among them. The people will hardly take any step in daily life without first applying to an astrologer to determine a happy day for it, and calendars are published indicating the red-letter happy days for such more important events as weddings, funerals, and so forth. Itinerant fortune-tellers of rather lower status than the consultant astrologers do a thriving business in the public thoroughfares, setting up the exiguous properties required for their hocus-pocus in any convenient corner and encouraging possible patrons by reminding them that Confucius ordained consultation of the gods on every occasion.

C. P. Skrine

'COME, MY SWEET ONES, TO THE OUTER COURTYARD: COME TO THE STORY RECITATION'

From time immemorial the professional story-teller has flourished all over the East, and nowhere does he enjoy greater popularity than in the bazaars of Chinese Turkistan. This photograph, taken in Khotan, shows a scene which could be matched in many an **Asiatic market town**—a crowd of townsmen and villagers from the neighbourhood who, their day's business finished, have hurried to listen to a story recitation. Fluent of speech, dramatic in action, the story-teller holds the audience pressing round him spellbound, playing upon their emotions with consummate skill and working them up to a pitch of breathless excitement, when he stops abruptly, leaving them all agog to hear the next instalment of the story the next day.

W. Bosshard

MAKING MUSIC IN THE PLEASANT OASIS OF YARKAND

There are only five notes in the Chinese musical scale, and one consequence of this is that to a Western ear even the simplest melody soon becomes monotonous, while the further fact that Chinese music is utterly devoid of harmony as Europeans understand that term speedily reduces it to the level of intolerable noise in their opinion. Yet to the Chinese it gives great pleasure, and itinerant musicians wander from oasis to oasis of Chinese Turkistan, giving pleasant open-air concerts with their zithers, lutes and tambourines.

been exalted to almost religious devotions amongst the Hindus. One such is the walking upon sharp swords, and another walking through a flame of fire. Both of these are performed at the religious feasts on the banks of the holy Ganges at Benares. The priest mutters certain formulae, his disciples throw oil upon the faggots, and after a few moments the old sadha walks through the flames and emerges on the other side apparently unharmed. One by one his disciples do the same. Then the old man walks barefooted upon the naked blades of swords, and the disciples do likewise.

This has been seen scores of times by those who can have an entrée into that area where only the Hindus can enter during the festival; and for its religious significance as well as its origin one is referred to the test of fire and sword to which Princess Sita was subjected upon her rescue from the hands of the 'Bad King' of Ceylon, who, finding Rama and his brother in exile, accosted Rama's wife and kidnapped her. The story is contained in the Ramayana, the most popular Oriental epic and, as related and depicted in the chapter on Animal Dances of the East, the favourite drama of the Javanese Wajang Wong. The Hindu princess, so the ancient Brahminic tradition has it, walked through the flame and then on the edge of the sword to prove that her chastity had not been violated, and proved it by being unhurt. This performance, although centuries old, has not been allowed to dwindle down in significance, for none but the high-caste Brahmins are allowed to perform it; and, what is more, those who are privileged to witness it are believed to reap much spiritual reward by being present at the performance. It is, therefore, not uncommon to see a gathering of thousands when a sadha is preparing to walk through the flames.

DESCENDING from these 'higher' entertainers of more or less occult appeal, one comes across a host of lesser performers, such as the one who sets his monkey to do his bidding, and others who make bears dance or wrestle with them; or, again, the man who does tricks showing no more skill than the ordinary sleight of hand. As often as not an acrobat performs with them whose chief trick, at least amongst the usual sort, is walking on a tight rope. And, curious to relate, portable peep shows are getting quite a rage in the East. In the streets of Damascus in Syria any day one can see a man carrying his show on his shoulder from one bazaar corner to another.

H. von Perckhammer

INVOCATION TO CHARITY BY A CHINESE LUTANIST

Music has a definite place among the arts in China and is used on all such occasions as birthdays, weddings and funerals, but its performance is almost exclusively by professional musicians ; amateur performers are seldom met with. The instruments in most common use are guitars or lutes, of four and of three strings, violins of two and of four strings, clarinets and flutes, and drums, gongs and castanets. Street musicians—many of whom are blind—for the most part use the three-stringed lute, sometimes singing nasally while they play.

H. von Perckhammer

Keystone

ALL THE FUN OF THE FAIR IN CHINESE THOROUGHFARES

In almost every Chinese street an alfresco entertainment of some kind may be seen in progress. Jugglers and acrobats always draw a large audience, for the Chinese have a natural aptitude for acrobatics, and make expert performers and keen critics. A common sight is an acrobat doing a tight-rope turn, perhaps with a trained monkey for partner (top). Portable peep-shows are now becoming common in the East, and the lower photograph, taken at Dairen in China, shows a row of Chinese with their eyes glued to the little peep-holes of one of these magic machines.

Wayside Entertainers of the East

Dorien Leigh

A. R. Slater

STEP-DANCES AND SHAM FIGHTS BY BEARS SHAM AND REAL

Among the lesser wayside entertainments met with in the East, performing bears are to be included. Plenty of these animals are captured in the Himalayas, big shaggy brutes, and these are trained to dance, to wrestle with their master, and to have sham fights with one another. When a real plantigrade is not available an itinerant showman will present as an amusing turn a dancing bear represented by a human actor good at pantomime and made up crudely to look as much like a bear as the property wardrobe will permit.

The most distinguished amongst this class of entertainment is the recitation of the wayside story-tellers. Nowhere can it be seen to better advantage than in the bazaars of Chinese Turkistan. When the village men have feasted after bartering their sheeps' wool for salt or other provisions the town crier goes round the Sara: 'To the outer courtyard, to the wide corner of the bazaar!' he shouts to the men as he places his right hand over his right ear. 'To the story recitation. Come, my sweet ones!' he calls on in his sonorous chant.

HUDDLED they sit, in silence, when the story-teller stands at one side of the shed. He has a story to relate, he says, 'that will freeze your blood at one part, and at another your eyes will be like lotus flowers filled with dew.' A long preface has his story. It is a tale of long ago, when the Amir's sons came to that land to hunt. Then he builds up his suspense. One could hear his listeners breathe heavily, the hero of his story is being chased by the guards of the princess. He is heaping anti-crisis after anti-crisis of the story. Now he sways his hands, depicting the wrath of the father of the beautiful princess; now he crouches to show how the youthful prince hid under the heap of freshly plucked apricots. He holds his audience spellbound. His language is rapid, or slow, now rising into a high-pitched tone, now hushed to a whisper in the garden of the princess. Sentence by sentence he is weaving pathos, romance and adventure into his story. 'Does the princess love him?' he asks his audience. A peasant boy wakes from his reverie to answer 'Surely, yes! by the grace of the Holy Priest'; others look at the boy, and look away. The story-teller scans the silent throng. 'Well, it is like this,' he begins, then takes another pinch of the snuff, coughs, sneezes, and tells them no more The next instalment of the story will be related the next day, provided they leave sufficient silver coins for him for this entertainment—which they generally do, in anticipation of pleasure to come, for if the Eastern people are born story-tellers, they are also very keen story-hearers, so keen indeed that they will walk miles to hear a story; and that form of entertainment will live in the East for ever

E.N.A.

CELEBRATING THE FESTIVAL OF CORPUS CHRISTI: PROCESSION OUTSIDE THE CATHEDRAL AT VILNA

The festival of the Roman Catholic Church known as Corpus Christi was instituted in 1264 in honour of the Holy Eucharist, but was not generally observed throughout the west of Europe until the fourteenth century. It was struck out of the English calendar by Henry VIII. The festival is celebrated on the Thursday after Trinity Sunday. A notable feature is the outdoor procession of the Blessed Sacrament, which usually takes place on the following Sunday. On this occasion the Host is carried under a canopy inside the church and also through the streets. Banners and images of saints frequently figure in the procession, and sometimes the streets through which it passes are decorated with boughs and flowers.

FEAST DAYS AND FAST DAYS OF THE CHRISTIAN CHURCH

THE more important general Christian festivals, such as Corpus Christi and Candlemas, the interest of which is mainly religious, are dealt with here. Christmas, Easter, All Souls', All Saints', and other festivals, which have gathered additional interest from the seasonal secular customs associated with them, are treated in separate chapters which discuss both religious and lay aspects.

WHEN the Reformation split the already divided Christian Church, many traditional customs were retained in their existing form, or survived because the habits and aspirations of man cannot be successfully put aside by a mere fiat of king or parliament. Still in the Book of Common Prayer there is a table of all the Feasts—they can be more easily remembered by the fact that there is for each a special collect, epistle and gospel—and also a table of vigils, fasts and days of abstinence—all of which are common alike to the Roman and Greek Churches. For every saint's day there is an 'Even,' including Sundays, but only some have vigils, eight of these being dedicated to Apostles, and one to that day which commemorates S. John the Baptist. The festivals that fall during the seasons of Christmas, Easter and Whitsuntide have no vigils, and S. Luke's Day is also excluded from the table, either because he died in peace without martyrdom or because October 17 celebrates the minor festival of S. Etheldreda. The other days of fasting, according to the Anglican Code, are the forty days of Lent, the Ember days at the four seasons—these are the Wednesday, Friday and Saturday after respectively the first Sunday in Lent, the Feast of Pentecost, September 14 and December 3—the three Rogation Days, which are the Monday, Tuesday and Wednesday before Ascension Day, and all the Fridays in the year except Christmas Day.

An exponent of the theology of the Church of England once declared rather despondently that 'the proportion of professing members of the Church of England who carry out these rules is probably small, but the obligation remains none the less.' In the days of the Reformation the strict observance of the vigil—a night spent in watching and prayer—had already fallen into desuetude. Cranmer himself remarked in his answer to the Devonshire rebels 'now these many years those vigils remained in vain in the books, for no man did watch.' There were scandals, too, connected with the vigils, and eventually fast days were substituted 'to chastise the flesh that it be not too wanton, but tamed and brought in subjection to the spirit,' that 'the spirit may be more fervent and earnest in prayer,' and that 'our fast be a testimony and witness with us before God of our humble submission to His high Majesty.' There are, of course, many devout churchmen and churchwomen who carry out to this day these practices of self-discipline, but throughout the great body of the Anglican Church the rules are honoured more in the breach than in the observance. Whether the Holy Communion should be received fasting, as S. Augustine lays it down, or not is still a matter of controversy among members of the Church.

Planet News

ORANGES AND LEMONS AT S. CLEMENTS

Every year at the church of S. Clement Danes, London, oranges and lemons are presented to London school children. The custom is derived from the old nursery rhyme about the London belfries. There was once a Danish colony in the parish, and Danish children are here seen taking part in the distribution.

Bitten deep into the habits of our people are many pre-Reformation customs connected with the feasts and fasts of the old order. The most famous is Corpus Christi Day, which, probably

Mondiale

HIGH FESTIVAL IN A CATHOLIC STRONGHOLD

Of all the states of Germany Bavaria regards itself as the special champion of Roman Catholicism, and in Bavaria the great Roman Catholic Festival of Corpus Christi is observed with much ceremony. The photograph shows a Corpus Christi procession passing through the streets of Eichstätt, a picturesque old Bavarian town, whose bishops were princes of the Empire.

because it was instituted by Pope Urban IV in 1264, has no place in the Anglican Calendar. Still in London on this Thursday after Trinity Sunday the Worshipful Company of Skinners—they used to be attended by boys from Christ's Hospital School strewing herbs before them—walk in procession to church, and throughout the country we still meet here and there with relics of the celebrations in honour of that doctrine of transubstantiation which colleges at both Oxford and Cambridge perpetuate in defiance of strict Protestant doctrine. Oddly enough, we probably owe the great dramatic literature of this country to the Roman Catholic celebrations of Corpus Christi Day, for part of the proceedings were Mystery or Miracle plays, to which the evolution of our drama owes so much. Long after the Reformation these annual performances were continued, 'the Protestant clergy,' as somebody remarked, 'vainly endeavouring to extinguish what was not merely religion but amusement.'

To this day abroad, in all countries professing the Roman Catholic faith, Corpus Christi Day is celebrated with great pomp and rejoicing. The main feature of the festival is the procession in which the Pyx containing the consecrated bread is carried, both within the church and throughout the adjacent streets, by one who has a canopy held over him. There are many variations of the order, but, generally speaking, the following details are observed:

Sundry figures follow the canopied Pyx, representing favourite saints in a characteristic manner — Ursula, with her maidens, S. George killing the dragon, Christopher wading the river with the infant Saviour upon his shoulders, Sebastian stuck full of arrows, Catherine with her wheel; these, again, succeeded by priests bearing each a piece of the sacred plate of the church. The streets are decorated with boughs, the pavements strewn with flowers and a venerative multitude accompany the procession. As the Pyx approaches everyone falls prostrate before it.

In Germany in particular this feast is celebrated with many elaborate rites. Sometimes the day is ushered in with the discharge of artillery, and a feature of the proceedings in such a town as Rottenburg on the Neckar, for example, is the altars at the street corners, where the procession pauses to receive the Benediction of the waiting priest.

February 2 is a festival common both to the Anglican Church and to the Roman Catholic Church. It celebrates the Purification of the Virgin Mary, or alternatively the Presentation of Christ in the Temple. From the coincidence of the time with that of the Februation or 'Purification of the People' in Pagan Rome it has been held that this is a Christian festival engrafted upon a heathen one in order to take advantage of the established habits of the people.

E.N.A.

SYMBOLS OF FAITH FASHIONED IN FLOWERS ON THE VERY STREETS

In Roman Catholic countries the decorations on the streets along which the Corpus Christi procession passes are often very elaborate. At Genzano, some fifteen miles south-east of Rome, it has long been the custom to embellish the roadways of the route with marvellous designs made with fresh flowers, baskets of which are brought from miles around. The upper photograph shows citizens of Genzano preparing some the decorations, and below is seen one of the finished designs, representing the Sacred Heart.

FAMILY ALTARS AND CARPETS OF FLOWER PETALS AT A FESTIVAL IN HUNGARY

E.N.A.

Although there is a fairly large Protestant minority in Hungary, the bulk of the population is Roman Catholic, and great attention is paid to the festivals of the Church, and especially to the celebration of Corpus Christi. At the market town of Mezökövesd the people set up private altars (top) in the houses, and at these the procession pauses in its passage. At Budaors, near Budapest, myriads of flower petals are laid upon the road (bottom) in lines of different colours, producing the effect of long strips of carpet.

ENA.

RAINBOW HUES OF THE MAIDENS' ATTIRE IN A FEAST DAY PROCESSION IN POLAND

Every year at Corpus Christi the maidens of the Polish town of Lowicz, dressed in their bright-hued native costumes, walk in solemn procession through the streets, carrying banners and images. The scene is a riot of colour, for Lowicz is famed for its coloured wools, and the girls of Lowicz for their striking dress made from these, of which the striped crinoline skirt is a conspicuous feature. These Polish peasant maidens are not afraid of colour. Rose and orange, chocolate and purple blend in the stripes of the rounded skirts and neat bodices. Some of the bodices worn in the procession are white, like the sleeves, while in others the gay stripes of the skirt are continued, though partly hidden by the flowing ends of the head veil.

E.N.A

PAGEANTRY OF POLISH PEASANTS IN FESTIVAL PROCESSION

Under the **Russian régime** the Orthodox Church would not tolerate Roman Catholicism in Poland, but now the **Polish Catholics** are free to practise **their** religion. Ever Roman Catholic by instinct, Poland since it has attained its independence has become one of the strongholds of that faith. **The** photographs show (top) Polish peasants in long white coats carrying great candles in a Corpus Christi procession, and (bottom) peasants of Polish Silesia bowing as the Host is carried past. **Note** the beautiful **embroidery on the** dresses of the two women in the foreground.

Candlemas Day, which is the popular name of this festival, undoubtedly perpetuates the memory of very ancient custom—the walking in procession with tapers and singing hymns—and even Henry VIII, when engaged in pruning 'dangerous superstitions,' authorised the continuation of the traditional custom.

IN Rome, on Candlemas Day, the Pope officiates in the beautiful Chapel of the Quirinal and with his own hands distributes blessed candles amongst those present. The dignitaries of the Church receive theirs first, in order of precedence, from the Cardinal to the sacristan, and then the candles are distributed to the laity. In Ireland, Candlemas Day is employed to provide the churches with the requisite stock of candles for the year. Each member of the congregation sends a packet of the purest wax candles to the church and one odd one. The packet is retained and the odd candle, having been blessed, is returned to the donor to be preserved. The belief that particular virtue attaches to these candles still remains, and they are said to be protection against storms and evil spirits. The light of the candle represents symbolically the words spoken by Simeon in the Temple when he took the infant Jesus in his arms and declared that here was the Light which would lighten the Gentiles.

Photopress

WHITE ROBES GLEAM STILL WHITER AT A WEST INDIAN FESTIVAL

There is a large Roman Catholic population in Trinidad, and huge crowds attend all the ceremonies of that Church. The Corpus Christi procession is very picturesque, the dark skins of the processionists giving their snowy white garments an added brilliance in the strong sunlight of this tropical island. A view of part of the procession passing through the streets is shown in the lower photograph, while above is seen a detachment of young native girls walking in the procession in all their bravery of white dresses and veils.

In Scotland, Candlemas Day was associated with the old heathen vernal rites such as Brud's Bed, which has been dealt with in another chapter of this work. It used also to be the custom in Scotland for the children to have a holiday on this day after making a present of money to the master of their school. At Jedburgh this religious festival was celebrated by a football match, with the whole town as the playing field and most of the population as the players.

THE day following Candlemas Day, February 3, is another noteworthy feast in Catholic Europe, and, until comparatively recently, used to be associated in this country with some secularised rites. It is known as S. Blaize's Day, and commemorates S. Blasius, who in 316 suffered martyrdom by being torn to pieces with iron combs. He is regarded as the particular patron saint of singers and throats. In Ireland, if anybody gets a bone stuck in his throat, S. Blaize's name is used to charm it away. According to the old formula the worker of the charm addressed the bone in the following words, 'Blaize, the martyr and servant of Jesus Christ, commands thee to pass up or down.' A charming rite is performed in many churches each February 3, when the priest, holding two lighted candles,

Alfieri

I.B

KEEPING THE FESTIVALS OF A MARTYR BISHOP AND A MARTYR KING

From a miracle wrought on a child who was suffering from a throat affection S. Blaize is looked upon as the patron saint of the throat. His feast, which is celebrated on February 3, is marked by a pretty ceremony in which, as seen at S. Etheldreda's, Holborn (top), the celebrant places two lighted candles crosswise on the throat of each worshipper and invokes the aid of the saint in healing any ills of the throat. Below is seen a service of remembrance in progress at the statue of Charles I at Charing Cross on the anniversary of his execution.

E.N.A.

PROCESSION OF THE FEAST OF THE REDEEMER CROSSING THE GRAND CANAL AT VENICE

The Roman Catholic **Church** has always been noted for the splendour of its ceremonial. It is perhaps in Rome that this pomp and pageantry are to be seen in their utmost magnificence on the occasions when the **Church** celebrates some important festival, but for sheer picturesqueness the festival processions of Venice are hard to beat, for in them the setting is uniquely beautiful. To see a Catholic procession moving across a bridge in the city of lagoons, its component figures outlined against a background of stately buildings rising sheer out of the water, is a spectacle that can never be forgotten. In front walk the clergy, mostly in white cottas, with crucifixes, banners and candles, while close on their heels the laity devoutly follow.

with his arms crossed, blesses the throat of each worshipper in turn. Because of the manner of his death, S. Blaize was long regarded as the patron saint of districts dependent upon iron ore for their economic welfare; and in Bradford and other towns occupied with the textile industry there used to be processions and much junketing, S. Blaize being oddly linked up with Jason of the Golden Fleece.

Barratt's

CHOIRBOY BISHOP IN AN ENGLISH VILLAGE

It was long the custom on S. Nicholas's Day (December 6) to elect a bishop from the boys of the church choir or the grammar school, who held office until Holy Innocents' Day (December 28). The practice has been revived in an attenuated form, and the villagers of Berden, in Essex, annually enthrone the boy bishop, who is here seen arriving.

This association of a saint with some particular trade or occupation is carried to extremes in Europe. Even automobilists have been placed under the protection of S. Christopher, whose feast is celebrated on July 25. Hairdressers look to S. Louis (August 25), brewers to S. Arnauld (July 18), pork butchers to S. Antoine (January 17), gardeners to S. Fiacre (August 20), and all 'jeunes filles' to S. Catherine (November 25). In honour of this last saint, to whose miraculous escape from the wheel of torture we owe the well-known firework, the midinettes in Paris still hold elaborate celebrations and processions.

Most countries celebrate in some form or another the day dedicated to their national saint. In Ireland, S. Patrick's Day is still a great festival which cuts across all politics and is celebrated as enthusiastically in Orange Ulster as in the Irish Free State. In England, though S. George has been unkindly identified by some people with a defaulting quartermaster in the Roman Army, the day has now become associated with the heroic British naval feat at Zeebrugge in 1918.

In this connexion mention may be made of our one-time English Blessed Martyr King Charles I, whose name was removed from the Anglican calendar by Royal Proclamation on January 17, 1859, and the special service to commemorate his death deleted from the prayer book. A little band of Legitimists still keep green his memory on January 30, and services are still held in his honour. Two religious festivals particularly associated with children continue to be observed. One is the annual distribution of oranges and lemons at the church of S. Clement in the Strand, and the other is the more elaborate honour paid to S. Nicholas on December 6. At this latter festival in Germany fairs are held and gingerbread images of S. Nicholas are sold.

Throughout Catholic Europe an interesting use is made of the day consecrated by religion to the saints. People do not celebrate their birthdays, but their Saint's Day. Napoleon, not having been given a saint's name, had to have one invented for him, and consequently his birthday, August 15, which became the fête day of his son, the king of Rome, was held to be consecrated to S. Napoleon—though you may look in vain, and quite rightly, for his name in any calendar of any Church.

MAHOMEDAN PILGRIMS AWAITING THE KING'S SON IN THE HARAM OF THE MOSQUE AT MECCA

In the spring of 1930 an event occurred that was absolutely without precedent in the history of the traditional 'hidden' kingdom of Hejaz. To celebrate his ascent to the throne by right of conquest five years earlier the king, Ibn Saud, invited a number of diplomats and Mahomedan representatives of the press to visit Hejaz and see the modern developments of the kingdom under his enlightened rule. The king was represented by his son Feisal, and the programme included a visit to Mecca, when prayers for the king were offered in the Kaaba, in the centre of the Haram of the great Mosque, the holy of holies being afterwards entered by the visitors, including photographers, who for the first time were permitted to take photographs of the interior of the shrine.

PILGRIMAGES OF THE EAST

EARLIER chapters have dealt with the general subject of the Pilgrimage in Christendom and with the more limited subject of the 'Pardons' of Brittany. In what follows our attention is directed to Mecca, the magnet that draws all Islam, to Benares, the holy city of the Hindus, and to some of the less well known shrines in the Far East venerated by adherents of various religions and sects.

OF all the shrines which attract pilgrims throughout the world that of Mecca is the one which has most deeply impressed the imagination of mankind generally. The word Mecca is even used in our language as a synonym for something earnestly desired. 'Applied to a place,' says the New English Dictionary, 'which one regards as supremely sacred or which it is the aspiration of one's life to be able to visit.' One example given is 'Stratford, the Mecca of American pilgrims.' Since the death of Mahomet, the Prophet of God, in the year 632, countless pious Moslems have visited his birthplace, thereby gaining the title of 'Hajji' and the right to wear a green turban as a sign that they have fulfilled his command. From every corner of the world where Moslems are settled in any numbers pilgrims to Mecca set out every year by railway train, by camel caravan, by steamship, on foot. The largest number of them are Indians and Malays, then in order come African negroes, Persians, Turks, Egyptians, Syrians, Tatars, Chinese.

One result of this mixture of people from so many countries and of the absence from Mecca of any regular system of money-changing is that almost any metal currency is accepted there. In the tills of the shopkeepers are found Turkish piastres, Indian annas and rupees, Greek drachmas, Spanish pesetas, Rumanian lei, American dollars, Chinese dollars, Russian roubles and kopecks, Persian coins with holes in the centre, Maria Theresa 'thalers' out of Abyssinia, Dutch florins from the Dutch East Indies.

Sometimes there are as many as 100,000 pilgrims in the city, which lives on this tourist traffic and by making rosaries and other souvenirs for the pilgrims to take home.

Jeddah, on the Red Sea, is the port at which they land from the crowded ships in which they have travelled. This has been described as Arabia's 'skyscraper town.' It has hundreds of tall buildings with from six to nine floors, massively built in solid blocks. They are not arranged in orderly rectangular form, however, like an American city; they have been put up here and there, anyhow.

FROM Jeddah to Mecca is a journey of 40 miles, usually done on donkeys. Beduin bandits haunt the road and often attack pilgrim parties. According to Mahomet's instructions, those who go to Mecca should not wear any clothing, but a towel round the loins is considered to be permissible. Almost naked, the riders on donkeys or camels and those who go on foot have to face the burning sun.

The greatest care is taken to keep infidels out of the Holy City of Islam. It is believed that the troops of ownerless dogs which infest the streets (as they used to infest those of Constantinople) can smell out unbelievers. Very barbarous punishment is inflicted on any who are caught. The first case on record of a European visiting Mecca not in disguise, but openly as a Moslem and a pilgrim, is that of Hedley Churchward, an English theatrical scene-painter, whose experiences are described in a book called 'From Drury Lane to Mecca.' He made the pilgrimage in comfort, even in luxury if we compare the way he travelled and was lodged with the hardships which

E.N.A.

ADVERTISING THE GLAD NEWS

Accomplishment of the pilgrimage to Mecca with consequent right to the title of Hajji is the Moslem's supreme gratification. This decoration of his front door with symbolic designs and texts from the Koran is the intimation of his safe return made to his friends by a devout pilgrim of Jerusalem.

Photopress

H. J. Shepstone

GATHERING OF THE FAITHFUL FROM THE FAR ENDS OF THE EARTH

There is no part of the world so remote from Mecca that devout Moslems will not travel from it to make the pilgrimage enjoined by the Prophet. The upper photograph shows West Africans who have trekked across the Sahara lodging in the 'Deims' outside Khartum, a cantonment where natives congregate from all parts of Africa to rest awhile and earn enough money to carry them farther on their journey. Below is a view of the procession in Cairo of the Mahal or Holy Carpet woven there every year for the re-covering of the Kaaba at Mecca.

the mass of pilgrims must put up with, being poor. But he had special difficulties of his own, for, being English, he was suspected of being a spy and not a genuine believer. An Indian denounced him to the authorities as a fraud. He was able very quickly to convince a 'vali' (magistrate) that the charge was unfounded, but the ruler decided to see the mysterious Englishman himself and find out what he was doing in Mecca. So Churchward was again examined. First, he was taken in hand by a learned 'imam,' who began by asking what were the Five Pillars of Islam. Correctly the convert gave them.

There is one God only and Mohammed is the prophet of God.
Pray five times a day.
Give to the poor.
Keep the feast of Ramadan.
Make a pilgrimage to Mecca, if you can.

FORTUNATELY Churchward had good recommendations from Moslems; these served him better than his theological attainments. The ruler was convinced as easily as the magistrate had been. The unusual pilgrim was free to go and come as he pleased. He stayed for five months, and found his life there quite agreeable. In the alleys, four or five feet wide, which pass for streets there is shade always. Awnings of woven palm leaves are hung overhead. The roadways are deep in dust, which rain turns to mud, so everyone who can afford to ride a donkey does so. The houses, as in Jeddah, are high, with elaborately carved shutters to the windows and balconies to every floor.

Smoking long hookahs or water pipes on the steps of their premises squatted the white-robed merchants. Some rose to cry: 'Good watches, by Allah'; others yelled: 'Pearls, pearls of Paradise'; a third fellow vended lemons—'Lemons for true believers.' Round some corners ran half-naked, muscular water-carriers, who held sewn goatskins of liquid round their hips and carried their wares into various houses.

Few women are seen. Those who do go about wear real 'yashmaks,' wide, stiffly starched linen veils covering their faces all except the eyes and falling to their feet—not the light, transparent veil worn by Moslem women in so many parts. All the domestic service is performed by slaves. Thus two-thirds of the population of 50,000 are in bondage. Churchward did not like this, but he declared that he never saw any bond-servant ill-treated. Most of them seemed to him to have an easy life. The male slaves are almost all Africans —Sudanese and Somalis preponderate among them. In the harems are Circassian, Syrian and other white women.

The visits to the Holy Places at Mecca have to be made according to a strict ritual. A 'vakil' (official) acts as guide. Every one of his movements and utterances must be exactly copied by the pilgrims. Through the Gate of Abraham they follow him, after leaving the courtyard where all boots and shoes must be deposited—or rather all coverings to the sole of the foot. Some well-to-do worshippers can detach the soles of their shoes from the uppers and thus obey the letter of the Prophet's law without losing their

Mondiale

LANDING OF THE PILGRIMS AT JEDDAH

Ships arriving at Jeddah have to anchor a considerable distance out to sea and passengers are taken ashore in row-boats. When the rattle of the anchor chains makes it known that the voyage is over, the scene on a pilgrim ship, crowded with natives from almost every country in the world, is one of indescribable excitement.

Keystone

dignity by going barefooted. The cloisters which lead to the sacred enclosure have several lines of carved columns holding up the arched roof. Their marble magnificence is the result of the piety of sultans, khalifs, shahs and amirs throughout the ages. Vast is the size of the quadrangle itself, where the Kaaba is, the black stone which fell from Heaven (evidently a meteorite) and which was venerated for centuries before the religion of Islam came into being. Over the temple which has this stone let into one of its outer walls is the Sacred Carpet, sent by the Khedive of Egypt. This is cut up eventually into small pieces, which are sold to pilgrims as charms against evil. Every pilgrim kisses the stone, murmuring a prayer as he does so, then walks slowly all round the temple, kisses again, walks again, seven times in all. Anyone who wishes to speak Arabic well can go down a few steps and kiss also the foundation stone of the temple, which is supposed to confer the 'gift of tongues,' like the flame of Pentecost.

NEXT, the Well of Zamzam (Bubbling Water) must be visited. Here Ishmael, the son of Hagar, was saved from death by God, who caused a spring to gush forth here when they were almost overcome by thirst. The story is related in the Old Testament. As Hagar ran with her child towards the spring, so all pilgrims must run, and along the same path, which now leads through the town, up hill and down

C. P. Skrine

FROM THE ROOF OF THE WORLD TO THE HEART OF ISLAM

The resolution and endurance of the West African negroes who, as shown in page 610, will trek across the Sahara to make a pilgrimage to Mecca is matched by the Moslems of Chinese Turkistan, to whom the journey presents perhaps greater physical difficulties and hardships. A company of them are seen here setting foot once more in their arid homeland ringed in by snow-capped mountains on the roof of the world, their life ambition achieved. The upper photograph shows a cosmopolitan group of pilgrims just arrived at Mecca from Jeddah.

hill among the streets. Panting and trying to recite prayers as they trot along, men of all ages make this curious progress until they reach the gateway to this second sacred enclosure. But their exercise is not even then over. The gateway is at the bottom of a stairway. Up and down this they must rush seven times before they are allowed to enter and drink the water of Hagar's Well, which by this time they badly need. Many drink an enormous amount of it. The belief is that no true Moslem can drink too much, but cases of sickness, and sometimes worse ailments, caused by excess are not infrequent. Those who are very enthusiastic can bathe in this water as well.

The birthplace of the Prophet is a small house several feet below the present surface, which has risen so much that you have to go down steps to enter it. In a gloomy room lit by a skylight a slab of stone shows where the baby Mahomet's cradle stood. The custom is to pour perfume on to this stone, which gives the place a sweet and rather sickly odour. Anyone putting his hand to the stone is said to keep the scent about him for thirty days. A little way outside the town are the tombs of the Prophet's relatives, looking like a small village with a number of white domed roofs. Here prayers are said at each tomb and the flat stones are reverently kissed. That is the last of the pilgrim's duties. He now rides back to Jeddah and goes back to his place in the workaday world.

Ewing Galloway

OUTSIDE THE BRONZE DOORS OF CEYLON'S HOLIEST SHRINE

Innumerable Buddhists make pilgrimages to Kandy to worship before the Sacred Tooth of Buddha. Bronze doors lead to the shrine where the tooth lies on a lotus flower of pure gold sheltered by bell-shaped shrines. This tooth is an artificial ivory substitute for the original relic, which was burned by a fanatical Portuguese archbishop in the 16th century.

We may put the number of Mahomedans who hold Mecca sacred at 200 millions. As many as 500 millions venerate Benares with the same devotion. It is sacred both to Hindus and to Buddhists. Even before Sakya Mundi, the Buddha, established his religion there, six hundred years before Christ, it was a centre of religious teaching. To-day it has 1,500 temples and is the favourite place of pilgrimage in all India. From the Ganges, the sacred river, the city looks impressive and beautiful. Yellow palaces are reflected in gold on the stream. Where the ochre-coloured stone has been toned to a reddish purple by sun and rain, the reflections glow like ruby and sunset fires. Domes and minarets, cupolas and towers, and numberless pagoda tops make a fascinating skyline. When you are in the city, it is less attractive. The streets are packed closely together and are very narrow. Everyone wants to live as near the river as possible, so as to die close to its purifying waters. Therefore the steep bank on which Benares lies is thickly covered with dwellings as well as temples. Down to the river lead stairways (ghats), which are, as a rule, crowded all day. One of these is the Burning Ghat, where in the open dead bodies, brought long distances many of them, are consumed by fire so that the ashes may be thrown into the stream, which ensures speedy entrance into Paradise.

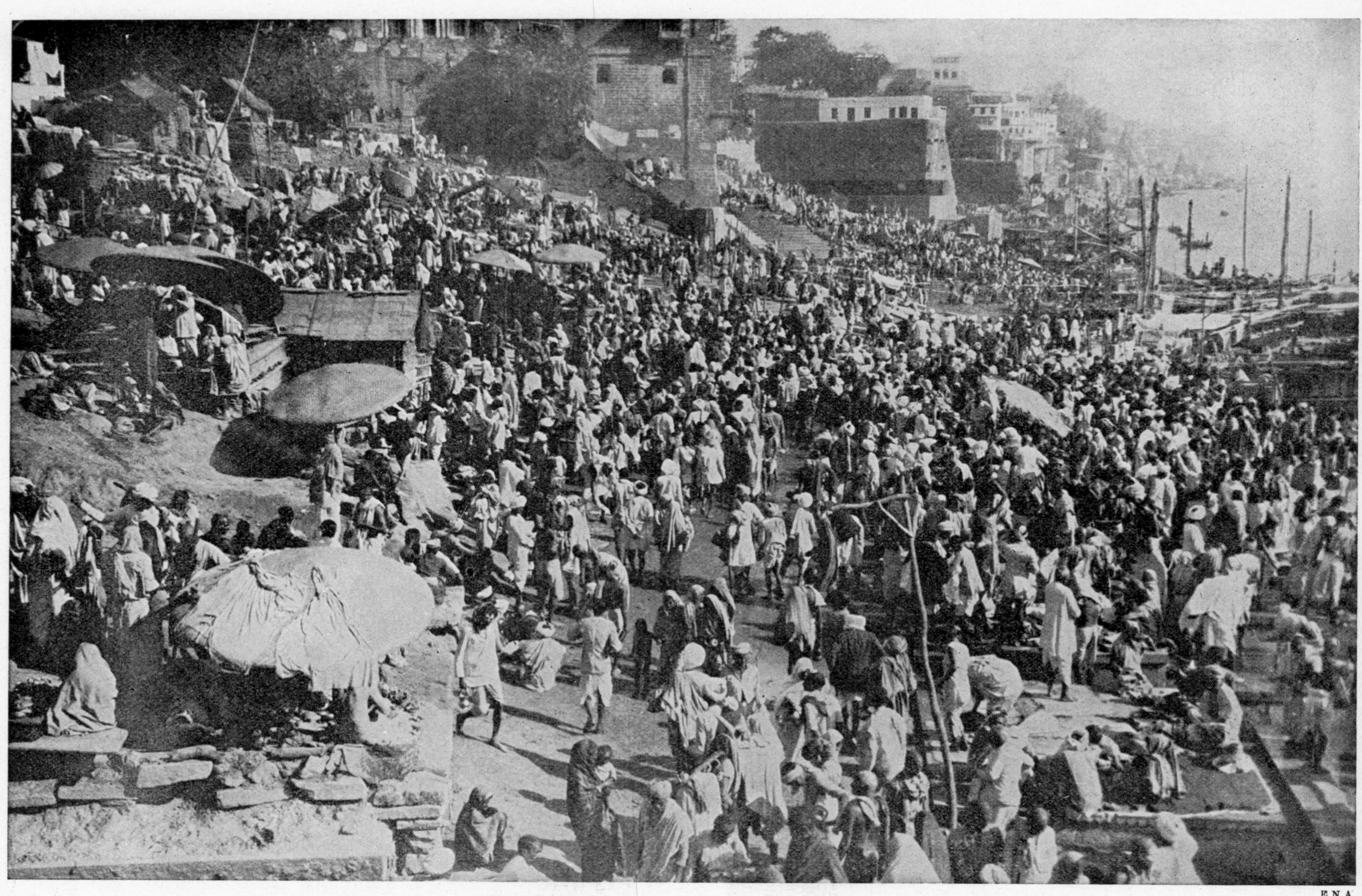

E.N.A.

PILGRIMS AT THE BATHING GHATS OF BENARES, THE HOLY CITY OF THE HINDUS

If Mecca is the place of pilgrimage whose fame has spread most widely over the inhabited world, Benares is the one that is venerated by the largest number of people. All who die within the circuit of the Panch-kos road that forms the boundary of its precincts are sure of admittance into Siva's heaven, be they Brahmin or low caste, Moslem or Christian, and to tread that road once at least is the great ambition of the Hindu's life. At the great festival of the full moon the embankment on the north bank of the Ganges, on which the city stands, is packed along its whole length with a dense crowd of humanity, walking, standing, sitting, praying, bathing in the holy waters and burning corpses in order that their ashes may be borne away upon its sacred stream

E. O. Hoppé

DAILY THRONG OF HINDUS BESIDE THE SACRED GANGES AT BENARES

Even on ordinary occasions the river front at Benares is a scene of surprising animation. The embankment at the foot of the ghats, or landing stages, is always crowded with people of both sexes washing their clothes, their cooking vessels or their babies, or bathing themselves for religious reasons in the purifying waters of the stream. This is the Dasasbansah ghat, at the bottom of one of the more than forty flights of steps that lead down to the water's edge from the city that is set high at the top of the river bank.

An American traveller thus describes the scene :

It is truly a glimpse of hell. Through the greasy smoke the forms of the naked workmen can be seen at their gruesome task among the dead. As they move about, their feet sink deeply into the still warm human dust. Every now and then they pour jars of oil on the flaming piles. . . . In the foreground some bearers have just deposited their burden, which, upon being uncovered from its white wrappings, discloses the delicate form of a sweet-faced girl of about fifteen. The sight of her sad little face is too much for us, and we order the boatman to move off and quickly, and even as he does so the movement of the oars causes the displacement of a little bundle of mortality floating face down—a boy—someone's darling to be eaten by dogs or crocodiles, of which many can be seen on the opposite bank. Horrible ! horrible ! Surely life is not such a joy that our departure from it should be made so gruesome !

That is how Benares struck one visitor. Here is a totally different impression, that of an Englishman (Robert Palmer) :

The city is about three miles long, built all along the top of the high river bank, and from it all along a series of terraces and steps lead down to the river. There are more than forty flights of steps. There is a road connecting them, and this road is lined with booths and beggars on both sides. The water near the embankment is crowded with native boats and barges of all sorts and sizes, and the water opposite each 'ghat,' where the steps lead right down, is full of bathers. Along the top of the bank are the temples, a continuous line of them ; and flanking the broad flights of steps are innumerable shrines and other picturesque buildings. The whole length swarms with humanity like a beehive, and it was a fascinating sight as we rowed slowly along, seeing the crowds walking, standing, sitting, bathing, boating, praying, juggling, dancing, buying, selling, eating, drinking, burning corpses, all in a cinematographic profusion.

'Fascinating' or 'horrible'—which each visitor will call it depends upon temperament. A Slav (Prince Bojidar Karageorgevitch) found the impressions of beauty the strongest that Benares left in his mind :

The atmosphere seemed faintly iridescent like mother-of-pearl, the silence serenely lulled by the distant sound of a flute. The palaces and temples, reflected in the still water, looked in the distance like forts crowned with turrets of gold. The broad stairs of the quays, where the priests' umbrellas glitter, assumed a spacious dignity, the red colour shading off paler towards the bottom, where it was washed off by the lapping Ganges, looking as though a fairy hanging of gauze were spread under the wavelets in honour of the divinities of the river. . . .

A woman on the river-bank was flinging into the water, with devout unction, scraps of paper on which the name of Rama was written, rolled up in a paste made of flour. Not far from her another woman was praying ; she stopped to wash her copper cooking-pots, then prayed again ; gave her baby a bath, and then, squatting on the lowest step, prayed once more and for a long time, after which she picked up her pots and her little one and went her way. . . .

On the bank where there are no more steps, only beaten earth, in a little raised pit a pile of wood was slowly dying out. A man with a cane raked back the sticks as they fell and rolled away. A squatting crowd were waiting until their relation was altogether consumed to cast his ashes on the sacred waters. Then a girl's body was brought out, wrapped in white muslin ; the bier, made of bamboo, was wreathed in marigolds, and on the light shroud there were patches of crimson powder, almost violet. A little way off an old man was wrapping the naked body of a poor woman in a white

A. R. Slater

FLOCKING TO THE RIVER FOR A RELIGIOUS FESTIVAL

More perhaps than any other people in the world do the people of India reverence water. They regard most of their great rivers as sacred, either as being the dwelling places of powerful deities or as possessing in some way a life of their own of peculiar sanctity. At certain festivals, then, and especially at the full moon, many of the rivers in India are crowded with Hindus seeking purification and washing away of their sins by immersion in the holy water.

cloth ; then he fastened it to two poles to dip it in the river . finally, with help, he laid the corpse on a meagre funeral pile and went off to fetch some live charcoal from the sacred fire which the Brahmins perpetually keep alive on a stone terrace overlooking the Ganges.

MANY pilgrims bring with them the ashes of relatives whose bodies have been burned near their homes. Some send them by parcel post to be thrown into the river. But the great majority of those who make the pilgrimage to Benares go for their own sake, to be purified by the water. Another place visited for this same purpose by very large numbers is Hardwar, also on the Ganges. There are many others of less note. All over India troops of pilgrims are to be seen frequently, making their way to some shrine or holy stream or celebrated temple. Among them are many Buddhist seekers after sanctity They do not show the same superstitious credulity as the Hindus, though they come near it when they pour oil and perfume at the foot of the Bo-tree, descended from the one under which Buddha taught, and stick pieces of gold-leaf on its trunk or on the stone steps around it. Burmese Buddhists make many pilgrimages also, but more in a social spirit and for the enjoyment of a holiday.

This is true also of the Japanese pilgrims who are to be met in large numbers all over the two islands. The Japanese love moving about and seeing nature and new places, they like companionship and doing things in common, they like taking exercise because they know it induces health. Therefore they take part in organized pilgrimage tours, visiting so many famous temples or reproductions of famous temples and acquiring merit, not only for themselves, but for their households as well.

Exactly what merit is acquired the pilgrims do not ask. Some may feel that an act of self-denial and devotion is pleasing to Buddha ; some may hope that a sick child or parent will be restored to health as a reward for such an act ; some go because they need a change, or because they think their business may be improved by extending their circle of acquaintances, or simply because they feel like going.

THERE are scores of pilgrim societies in the city of Tokyo alone, and in the quarters of the manual working population one frequently sees over doors the wooden labels which are used as tokens of membership. There are excursions (if one may use the word) two or three times a month. The excursionists meet in the courtyard of a temple, all in the best of humour. They choose a leader, and he collects from each a small sum to pay for refreshments and temple 'tips.' As this takes quite a while, and as there are always some late-comers, the start is usually made an hour or so after the advertised time. Then the pilgrims set off, each bearing on his or her back a miniature straw mat and sandals and carrying

Herbert G. Ponting, F.R.G.S.

JAPANESE PILGRIMS ON THE TOP OF THEIR SACRED MOUNTAIN FUJIYAMA

In Japan pilgrimage tours are organized very much as excursion trips are organized among ourselves, but on a truly national scale. All over the islands there are pilgrim societies, with their own banners and badges of membership, and several times a month pilgrimages, conducted by a chosen leader and a priest, are made to a selected number of temples, in each of which the pilgrim secures a rubber-stamped certificate from the temple scribe as proof that the visit has been paid. Light-hearted gaiety is the note of these ostensibly religious excursions.

W. Bosshard

A. L. Strong

LIVELY FAITH IN ASIA'S SANDY WASTES

These unattractive figures are pilgrim lamas begging their way to one of the Buddhist shrines found about the Gobi desert. The upper photograph, taken at night, shows a group of the numerous pilgrims who in the summer go from Yarkand to the mosque in the Sultan Kara Sukal Mazar to pray for a good harvest.

(1) a number of visiting cards in a satchel, (2) a little notebook, (3) a small pot of paste, (4) a book of hymns. In the notebooks the temple scribes write down or print with rubber stamps proof that the visit has been paid. With the paste the pilgrim sticks his card on to the temple gate or wall. Some of them carry long bamboo sticks with padded end, and fix their cards high up so that they are both conspicuous and difficult to tear down. Any pilgrim who has a business puts this fact on his card, so that it serves for an advertisement too. The pilgrims exchange these cards among themselves, and many have albums into which they are pasted.

The procession is led by a brown-robed priest, then comes the banner of the society; the members straggle after it, trying to keep touch because there are so many temples that one can easily mistake those that are on the list for the day. In the courtyard the stragglers are waited for, the books are filled up, the cards are pasted. When all are gathered the priest chants an invocation and a hymn is sung, then off go the pilgrims to their next stopping-place, some of the older among them slipping away perhaps to take a street-car in defiance of rule. It would be hard to imagine a greater contrast than that between the light-hearted gaiety of these Japanese pilgrims and the stern fanaticism of the Hindus at Benares or the Moslems at Mecca. Some of the Japanese shrines are Buddhist, some Shinto, but no distinction is made between them, all are treated with equal reverence—or lack of it. The Japanese, with their enlightened common sense, have, in fact, nationalised the pilgrimage, made it an end in it itself rather than an act done with a view to some further end.

BELIEFS AND SUPERSTITIONS ABOUT FIRE AND WATER

BOTH fire and water have been associated with the supernatural from very early times. Some of their religious associations are dealt with in the chapters on Where the Dead are Burned, and Baptismal Rites. The lighting of Midsummer fires is discussed in the chapter on Midsummer Beliefs and Practices, and certain beliefs concerning water in that on Well-dressing and Holy Wells.

EARLY human belief clustered round the conceptions of the elements and their forces, and fire and water, like the sky or the wind, came to be personified and regarded as supernatural beings. In some cases this deified notion of fire became confused with that of the sun, while in others it remained apart from solar connexion. Deities of the household hearth arose, for the domestic fireplace was looked upon as an altar to be swept clean daily, and its fuel carefully renewed so that the sacred flame might never fail.

Because of these associations with the supernatural a large body of belief and superstition concerning fire naturally sprang up. The notion that it was either a spirit or was inhabited by a spirit was responsible for such conceptions as that of the salamander, a man-like sprite, who was supposed by the later medieval alchemists to dwell in fire, as did sylphs in the element of air, or undines in that of water. With these, the later representatives of the ancient elemental spirits, magicians were supposed to hold conference, and even unions were thought to have been contracted between human beings and the spirits of flame and flood.

THUS many such beliefs and superstitions as presently survive in all parts of the world in connexion with fire and water may be regarded as having had their origin in an earlier condition of religious faith. In most European countries, however, these ideas are descended from a type of fire worship by no means so advanced as those of the Greek and the Roman. And if fire was regarded as a spirit or the haunt of a spirit, it was, and is, no less believed to be an affrighting and exorcising element where evil agencies are concerned. In Iceland a whole series of superstitions concerning this protective character persists. To cast a live coal after a departing troll-wife or witch-woman is certain to neutralise her spells, and until a child is baptized the fire must never be let out, lest the trolls be able to kidnap the infant.

For precisely similar reasons South American Indians carry torches when they venture into the dark, where demoniac beings swarm. The Malays light a fire near a mother at childbirth, to scare away evil spirits (see page 34), and the Hindu keeps a lamp burning even in broad daylight to keep off spectral foes. Not so very long ago the people of the Hebrides protected mother and child in much the same manner as the Malays, carrying fire round them to ward off Satanic influences.

At certain periods of the year when spirits swarm the agency of fire is frequently employed to frighten them away. In Bulgaria, at the feast of S. Demetrius, lighted candles are placed in the stable and the wood-shed to prevent evil spirits from entering into the domestic animals. Indeed, the Roman Catholic Church in its ritual still evinces its belief in the powers of the holy candle to keep the agencies of evil at bay.

Sirdar Ikbal Ali Shah

DEAD FLAME THAT MAY SPELL HAPPINESS

Some brides of northern India erect this structure, the 'captivator of five hearts,' that is, of the husband, his parents, and his brother and sister. Candles are lit in the globes, and each wedding guest blows one out and wishes the 'capture of the heart.'

Sirdar Ikbal Ali Shah

It is only, of course, by reference to the more elementary ideas of savage peoples that we may glean some notion of the kind of being, good or evil, that is supposed to inhabit living flame. Thus among the Indians of British Columbia and the north and west of North America we find that the fire spirit is supposed to have great influence with the supreme deity, and is approached by the Indians as a mediator with the higher god. In Dahomey again, the fire spirit is looked upon as so mischievous that a pot of fire is placed in a room in order that he may live there as a kind of prisoner, and not go forth to destroy the house. In colder regions the soul of fire is very naturally considered as a more benignant agency, and in Kamchatka is offered game and such tit-bits as the noses of foxes, while among the Ainu of Northern Japan the fire spirit holds a place paramount to all other supernatural beings, and is regarded as the source and origin of all good things.

Among the Mongols fire is personified by Mother Ut, Queen of the Flame, whose father is the steel and whose mother is the flint on which the enlivening spark is struck. She is offered in sacrifice sheep, oil, fat and brandy, and, as in China, is the central figure of worship in marriage ceremonies. In India, under the form of Agni, the god of fire is still worshipped as among the mightiest of the Hindu pantheon. He is, indeed, a personification of the three forms of fire—sun, lightning and sacrificial flame—the ancient,

R. St. Barbe Baker

PRACTICAL APPLICATIONS OF THE SPIRIT OF FIRE IN TWO CONTINENTS

On a site in the Afghan province of Bamyan is an ancient carving of Buddha (top). Every Thursday women from the adjoining villages light little lamps before this colossal image. The oil that is left in the lamps they mix with the hair oil used by their husbands, in order to 'make the head of the bad-tempered man act rightly towards his womenfolk.' Among some tribes of Nigeria, when firing the forest for clearing the ground (bottom), an assembly is held for offering propitiatory incantations to the gods of the flame.

yet ever young, daily born afresh on the altar. He, too, is a moderator betwixt gods and men, and is described as 'the guest of men' and a beneficent god of the household. His fiery chariot is harnessed with ruddy horses, he is seven-tongued and seven-armed, with double face, in this resembling the old Mexican goddess of fire. He is also thought of as the household priest, who personified in himself all the Hindu sacrificial offices, but has nevertheless his appalling side as the devourer and destroyer.

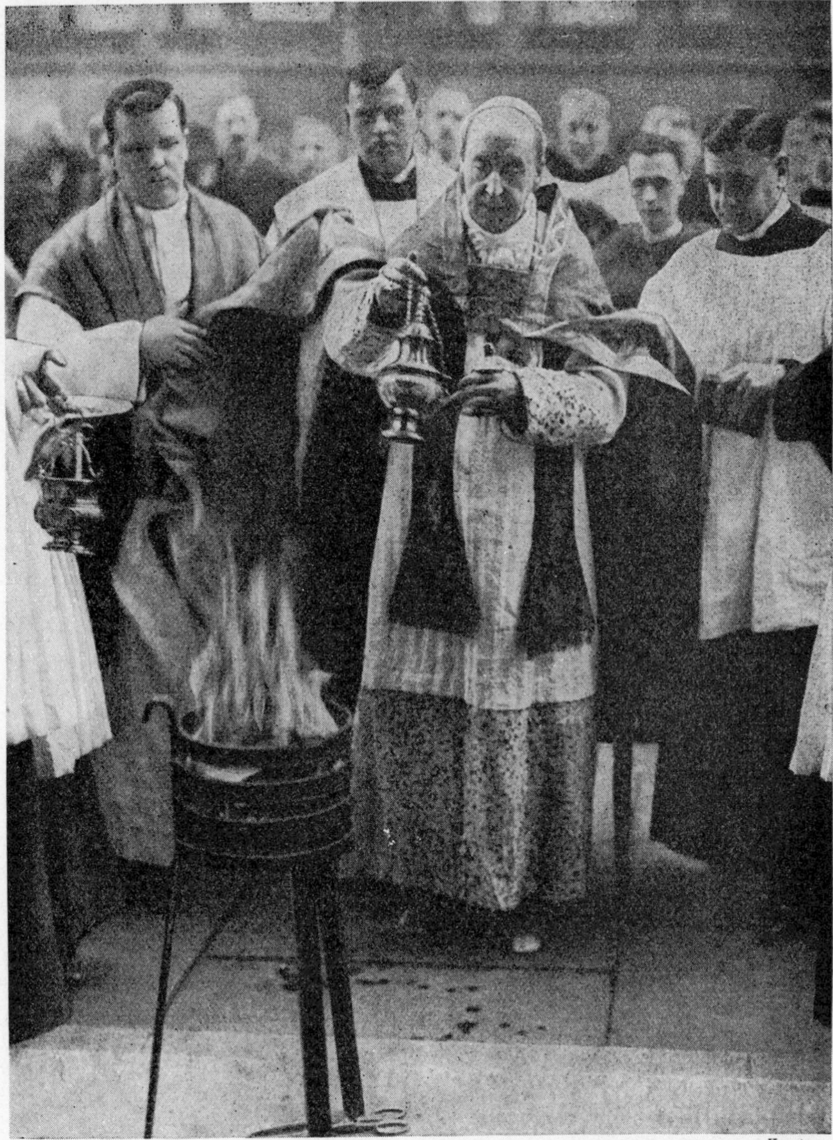

Keystone

BLESSING THE HOLY FIRE AT WESTMINSTER CATHEDRAL

It is customary to extinguish all the lights in Roman Catholic churches on Holy Saturday, and then to make a new fire either with flint and steel or with a burning-glass. At this fire is lit the great Easter candle, which is used to relight the candles and lamps that have been extinguished. The new fire is blessed with due ceremony.

It is a mistake, however, to believe that the present-day Parsees actually worship fire as a supernatural being. That they formerly did so is evident, but today the idea of fire has become so intellectualised among them that in worshipping Ormuzd they merely turn the face to some luminous object, which they regard as an emblem or symbol of their deity and not the deity himself.

Out of similar ideas have developed the few superstitions which still persist in these islands regarding fire. The writer leans to the theory that the fires lit in connexion with Guy Fawkes's day are probably the remnants of a religious rite much more ancient than the reign of James the First, and that a strict examination of these vestigial ceremonies would possibly reveal their extreme antiquity, the conspirator of the Gunpowder Plot having possibly usurped the place of some ancient deity of flame, such as was worshipped when bale-fires were lighted on the occasion of the Beltane festival.

However this may be, certain poor remnants of ideas having a great antiquity have been handed down to us. Yet some of these are assuredly of Christian origin, such as the act of placing a poker across the hearth with the fore part leaning across the top bar of the grate which signifies the sign of the cross, a charm of efficacy to make the fire burn up again, and thus defeat the malice of those sprites who preside over smoking chimneys. If a fire blazes up, they will tell you in the Midland counties that a stranger is near, or that an absent lover, wife or husband is in good spirits. Other beliefs of the kind have already been dealt with in the chapter on Omens, Signs and Portents, along with such weather lore as various changes in the domestic fire are believed to prognosticate.

Another superstition relating to fire which still persists in many parts of Europe is that since light and heat are essential to vegetable growth, by imitating the beneficent glow of the sun in huge bonfires the luminary, by sympathetic magic, will be induced to give out his beams. That the beliefs associated with this idea still linger, although their original provenance and character are generally unsuspected by those who elaborate them, is a tribute to the power of undying superstition in a modern age.

Press Cliché

CAJOLING THE WATERS INTO YIELDING UP THE SECRETS OF THE FUTURE

Innumerable legends exist concerning the supernatural beings that dwell in wells and lakes and rivers, and endless are the devices used to propitiate or consult them. Peasant women of a village in central Russia near Ryazan are here seen using water for purposes of divination. They throw chaplets of flowers into the stream, and from the behaviour of these—from their floating or sinking, or from the direction in which they are driven by the current—they claim to be able to foretell what the future holds in store.

In the study and research of fire customs there has been a good deal of confusion of such rites as those associated with the making of new fire, with others relating to the maintenance of perpetual fire, passing through fire, and so forth. Fire is generally regarded as a good medium for transmitting sacrifices to gods or to the dead, while at the same time it is frequently taken as being symbolic of the sun, and thus any solar connexion should be clearly noted. But certain lingering superstitions are eloquent of pure fire worship. Even now, brides in Estonia cast money on the fire when entering their new homes for the first time, and the spirit of flame, Tule-ema, the fire mother, is specifically evoked by name in this ceremony. The peasants of Carinthia still give offerings of lard or dripping to the household flame, and to the Czechoslovakian it is an infidel act to spit in the fire. Oddly enough, however, he proffers it the crumbs of bread remaining from his meal, while British folklore execrates the burning of bread, and the writer vividly recollects the severe rebuke of an ancient relative when he threw a piece of bread into the nursery fire and was gravely informed that some day he would come to penury because of the act.

Many superstitions regarding water which still obtain among savage peoples are of the most elementary kind. Barbarous man believes the rush and flow of streams to be caused by the presence within them of restless spirits, and that our British ancestors also held this belief is clear from the numerous rhymes and saws concerning our rivers which still survive, and from the legends which actually specify by name their sylphic or demoniac inhabitants.

Among the Australian blackfellows demons are supposed to haunt watering places and pools, and the lurking Bunyip, which carries off native women to his abode beneath the pool, is merely the antipodean version of the Scottish water-kelpie, or river horse, which dwelt in the fall or pool and plunged into the depths with any one foolhardy enough to mount him. The Indians of North America still render offerings to many spirits of the lakes, where, they say, reside those genii who can cure disease, and in Africa practically every spring has its spirit. When a Kaffir crosses a stream he first asks permission of its presiding genius, and in times of drought he sacrifices an ox to the river god to tempt him to return in the full majesty of spate.

The Tatar races of Mongolia and Siberia possess similar superstitions. In the far north the Tatars worship the river Obi, and when fish is scanty will tie a stone to a reindeer's neck and cast the animal

Underwood & Underwood

WATER CEREMONIES FOR THE FLORIDA SPONGE HARVEST

At Tarpon Springs, in Florida, there is a colony of some fifteen hundred Greeks engaged in the sponge fishery, and **every** year, at Epiphany, high dignitaries of the Orthodox Church take part in the blessing of the waters in which the sponges are found. In addition to this ceremony a golden cross is thrown into the bayou, and it is believed that the diver who retrieves the cross from the water will have good luck. The photograph shows a successful diver receiving the blessing of the Metropolitan Patriarch.

into the water as a sacrifice. At the little mountain lake of Ikeougoun the Buriats still carry on their worship of the water spirit in a small wooden temple on the shore, bringing him offerings of milk, butter and fat, which they burn on altars. The people of India, in especial, entertain unbounded reverence for water and regard not only the Ganges but most of their great rivers as the abodes of powerful deities, or as possessed in some way of a life of their own of extraordinary sanctity (see pages 614 to 616).

Respecting the magical potentialities of the element of water, perhaps the most widespread superstition is that which tells how spirits cannot cross a running stream. Robert Burns describes the baffled impotence of the witches to molest Tam o' Shanter once he had crossed Alloway Bridge, people in Burma still stretch threads across a brook to permit of the coming and going of ghosts and supernatural beings, and similar instances abound in the folklore of all lands. Almost equally common is the belief in the protective qualities of water and its power to ward off evil spirits. In Scotland, not so very long ago, children were 'sained' or sanctified in some districts by the application of water into which a gold and a silver piece had been dropped, and which was taken out of the cup or vessel with a small ladle, often kept in some families for the purpose.

INDEED, it is a deeply rooted belief in many countries that a child will not thrive until it is baptized, and in some of the more remote parts of the British Isles an infant who seems unhealthy is frequently baptized before the usual time. In more ancient times it was thought that fairies and witches had more power over a child when unbaptized, and the spirits of such children as died lacking the rite were believed to turn into will-o'-the-wisps. In Sussex until recently it was thought that the water sprinkled on the child's forehead at baptism must not be wiped off, and in many counties peculiar properties were supposed to reside in water which had been used in baptism. It was, for example, a preservation against witchcraft in Scotland, and eyes bathed in it were rendered for life incapable of seeing ghosts.

By many races, particularly the Red Indians, the Chinese, Burmese and Tatars, and indeed the ancient Britons, whirlpools in lakes are looked upon as the sources of all life, as cauldrons boiling and bubbling with the creative faculty, and some writers have advanced the theory that the figure known as the swastika is symbolic of such lacustrine life-centres. 'We are all the children of water,' as an ancient Aztec baptismal ritual phrased it, a statement indeed eloquent of world-wide early belief regarding the origins of the human race.

E. O. Hoppé

INDIAN LITIGANTS OF MADURA WAITING FOR THEIR CASES TO BE TRIED

In India the Presidencies of Madras, Bombay and Bengal, and the provinces of Agra, Bihar and Orissa, the Punjab, and Burma have each a supreme high court, Oudh has a chief court, while some districts have judicial commissioners. The high court of Calcutta is the highest judicial authority for Assam. Below are, for criminal cases, courts of session, and below these, courts of magistrates. The inferior civil courts are determined by special acts or regulations in each province. Nearly all the civil judges and magistrates are Indians.

AT THE SEAT OF JUSTICE

THIS chapter is concerned with the broad question of the administration of justice. Points of legal etiquette as observed in England, as well as the dress worn by the Bench and Bar, are discussed in the chapter on The Lawyers: Their Costumes and Customs, while the penalties inflicted for breaches of the law are touched upon in that on Punishment among Savage and Civilized.

COURTS and legal systems appear to date back to that remote period when a beginning was made in forming organized communities with sedentary habits of life. The rulers were then the judges, and, as experiences were accumulated, laws were framed to control human behaviour in the interests of the welfare of interdependent groups of individuals. Thus we have in the religious systems of early civilizations myths about gods who judged the dead, like Osiris of Egypt and Minos of Crete, and traditions of culture heroes who introduced legal systems, like Oannes of Babylonia, the remote forerunner of the famous Hammurabi, Manu of India, and so on.

In our own day we are afforded glimpses of ancient legal practice and procedure by the study of primitive peoples. The surprising thing, in this connexion, is to discover that even in some otherwise backward communities the laws are wonderfully advanced and the system of administering justice well developed. We find, for instance, Mr. F. H. Melland, a former Rhodesian magistrate, informing us that 'African natives are unique among the primitive races in the richness of their judicial codes.' Trials, among the Bantu peoples especially, are conducted with a wonderful and impressive fairness and solemnity, even although the half-nude, dusky judges may squat in the open air, or in the shade of a kraal, with as little ostentation as if they were engaged in 'a gossiping.' The gravity of the proceedings is, however, reflected in the facial expressions of all concerned and the strict attention to native etiquette.

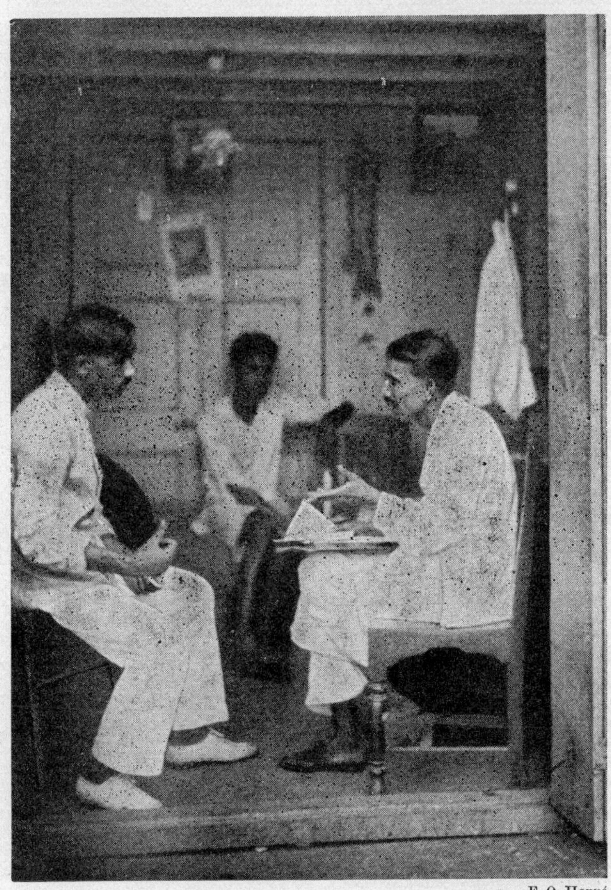

E. O. Hoppé

BOMBAY LAWYER AND HIS CLIENT

The Indian lawyer's consulting chambers are often no more than a shed open to the street. As in Calcutta and Madras, the administration of justice in Bombay is based on the system once in force in England, there being only magistrates' courts and the high court.

When a dispute arises between two individuals involving a question of tribal law, might is not regarded as right, nor is 'spear the king.' The case is first brought before the village headman, and if he is unable to arrange a settlement, it is heard before the local chief. A final appeal may be made to the court of the high chief at some distance from the village, and thither the plaintiff and defendant proceed with all their witnesses. All are accorded on their arrival hospitable entertainment, food and sleeping-huts being provided. The Bantu elders have evidently found from experience that it is as well to 'sleep upon' any trouble before giving it judicial consideration.

NEXT morning an official visits the huts to inform the parties that the court is in session. The high chief is found squatting in some selected place, with his elders and advisers, and attended by an armed bodyguard. As the visitors enter the court area they kneel to honour the high chief, uttering professions of loyalty and respect, which are acknowledged with dignity. A dusky official attends to the procedure. He first calls upon the defendant, who makes a statement in which he invokes his god, or his dead parents, or the spirit of a weapon, or of some dread disease like sleepy sickness or smallpox. The plaintiff is next heard. Then the high chief's legal adviser re-states the case with comments, after which the court hears the representatives of the village headman and the local chief. The witnesses are next brought forward in turn, and when the evidence closes the high chief's legal adviser discusses the whole case, making clear the legal points that have arisen. If the case is a difficult one, the

interrupted by searching questions. The elders do their utmost to extract a confession, and they may judge the accused as much by his behaviour as by his evidence. When blunt accusations are flung at him 'his only chance,' writes an investigator of native customs, 'of influencing his judges lies in laughing at them outright, for no one guilty is supposed to be able to do that.' If the accused survives an examination, witnesses are heard; sometimes they give evidence before the accused is allowed to make his statement.

Trials by ordeal are known among the Melanesians of the

court holds a private discussion, after which the chief pronounces judgement. When the court rises the high chief and the elders are respectfully greeted. There is usually a noisy demonstration after they depart, the successful party rejoicing and the unsuccessful lamenting.

In African witchcraft cases the trial is of somewhat savage character, being one by ordeal. The accused, charged with working evil against an individual or whole village community, has been 'put in log'—that is, secured to a tree trunk. When brought before the court he is seated on a wooden bench with his feet on a block of wood so that they may not touch earth. He may have to pick a pebble out of a pot of boiling water or boiling oil, or drink some poisonous preparation. If his hand and arm are not severely injured, or he vomits the poisonous drink, he is regarded as innocent. Other ordeals include leaping or walking through fires, swallowing pebbles without showing signs of choking, or swimming across a river infested with crocodiles. The mere threat of an ordeal may cause an accused man to confess.

When we pass from Africa to the Pacific area we find similar examples of primitive justice. Native courts in New Guinea are often held at groups of standing stones, called by some 'bolabola' and by others 'gahana,' and used as the ordinary 'squatting and yarning places of the men.' The judges are the elders or 'big men' who rule a community, for chiefs may have little authority except as military leaders. When a court is in session the public remain at some distance lest they should overhear discussions. An accused man is called forward, and when making his statement may be sharply

A. L. Strong

JUSTICE IN SOVIET CENTRAL ASIA

Each of the republics that constitute the Soviet Union has its own autonomous body of laws. The upper photograph shows a judge and scribe of Turkistan in the local court, and the lower a Kirghiz bride and bridegroom awaiting sentence for marrying under age

Ariel L. Varges

HOW MATRIMONIAL DIFFERENCES ARE COMPOSED IN THE ETHIOPIAN CAPITAL

A feature of the legal procedure of Abyssinia is its extreme publicity. In Addis Ababa street courts abound, and debtor and creditor, accuser and accused, chained together to ensure that the defendant does not escape, may be seen mingling freely with the crowd. In the market square is the Court of Domestic Relations (bottom). Here judge and jury carry out their functions on a veranda quite open to the street, though protected from the populace by barbed wire. The upper photograph shows a man and his wife seeking justice before this court.

Ariel L. Varges

WHERE THE OPINION OF AN UNOFFICIAL JUDGE IS ALWAYS ACCEPTED

Impromptu courts of justice are not uncommon in the streets of Addis Ababa. A man may dispute the ownership of beasts, or tax another with some petty theft or with damaging his property. A court is formed then and there, the first likely passer-by is called in as judge, and the case proceeds in the midst of an interested crowd. With much vocal explanation and vivid pantomime witnesses describe the carrying off of a sheep or the stealing of grain, and the decision of the judge is never disputed.

Solomon Islands. One is by lifting heated stones. If the hands of the accused are burned, he is considered to be guilty. Another fire ordeal is to make a man stand upon a log so that his legs may be struck thrice with a burning torch. A substitute may be hired and there is more than a suspicion that he is often in league with the priest who conducts the ordeal. A third ordeal is laying a spear on the head of the accused, who invokes the spirits to prove his innocence. The priest, who lifts the spear, may declare it to be heavier than it should be, and the accused is then declared guilty. The ordeal of swimming in a shark-infested water may be undertaken by a professional substitute, and if he perishes, the hirer must compensate the relatives. The profession of the substitute is an hereditary one, and in certain families protective charms for ordeals are handed down from father to son.

Among people of higher civilizations there are outstanding differences in legal practice and procedure. The Moslems have a system of laws based upon Mahomet's in the Koran. The ruling chiefs try certain cases, and especially those not requiring much knowledge of law. They usually deal with disputes connected with trade and caravans, and those that may arise on bazaar days. Judges, called cadis, or kádees, are drawn from the class of mosque students who have become versed in the legal precepts of the Koran and have acquired a knowledge of Arabic. There is a cadi in each country town in Persia, and one may act for several villages. In an important centre the cadi is assisted by various officials, who, in petty cases, hear and record evidence, which is then submitted to the cadi for decision. An important trial is taken in the cadi's own court, in which a doctor of law may act as assessor and scribes commit everything to writing. An interpreter may also be required. When witnesses testify, it may be necessary to prove by means of other witnesses that they are of good repute and reliable. All swear by the Koran, and an accused man in a criminal case may clear himself by holding the sacred book in his right hand and repeating 'By Allah!' three times. When an intricate point of law arises it is discussed by the cadi and his assessor, and a written judgement signed by the cadi is issued in

G.P.A.

BLACK JUSTICE AND WHITE IN THE HEART OF AFRICA

Among African natives the administration of justice is characterised not only by fairness but also by the dignity of the well-established procedure. The lower photograph shows the chief of the Molungo tribe of Central Africa as he sits each day in state to administer justice and settle disputes. Above is seen the court of justice at Archambault, in the Ubangi-Shari Colony, French Equatorial Africa. In the centre is the white judge and divisional chief: the two assistant judges at either end of the table are indigenous Arabs.

due course. Fees are charged, and it may be, too, that, before the case comes before the cadi, various officials have been bribed. An upright cadi is invariably a just and religious-minded judge who upholds the dignity of the law and acts without fear or favour.

MODERN Japanese legal institutions are a complex in which traditional methods are blended with those adopted from Western Europe, and especially France and Germany. In the old days the accused in a criminal case was not convicted until he made confession, and torture was common. The Japanese legal system remains inquisitorial, but the torture is purely mental. The judge is in full charge of the trial. He examines the accused, and all questions by the prosecuting or defending counsel may have to be addressed to him. A witness makes a sworn asseveration by signing a written document in which he undertakes to tell the truth, and all his statements are recorded. An Oriental calm pervades the proceedings, but they are often tense and dramatic, for the dignified judge is invariably relentless in his examinations and resolute in his quest of truth.

In France a criminal trial is of more demonstrative character, and may often have moments as thrilling as a scene in a melodrama. Before it takes place the accused is examined by a magistrate, who prepares an elaborate 'dossier,' in which he not only records but discusses the evidence, giving his reasons why he considers the accused guilty or not guilty, as the case may be.

When the court of assize assembles in the Palace of Justice in Paris it is presided over by the President and two assistant judges, all clad in red robes and wearing ermine-trimmed caps without brims. They are seated at a long table on a raised bench. The robed members of the bar sit below, and the public prosecutor is accommodated in an elevated desk. On the left are the twelve jurymen, whose seats are also high. Witnesses testify in front of the judges.

WHEN the court has been constituted with due pomp and ceremony the president addresses the jury, telling the story of the crime and summarising the evidence prepared by the examining magistrate. He also states why the prosecution is convinced of the guilt of the accused, and discusses the arguments of the defence. While the witnesses are being heard the president is as active and voluble an examiner as the public prosecutor, and he may quite bluntly accuse the prisoner, during his evidence, of uttering lies to conceal his guilt and deceive the court, or in a low, wheedling voice endeavour to make him confess. Witnesses are allowed a good deal of latitude, and often make general statements and pass opinions which would be regarded as quite irrelevant in an English court. Then suddenly the president may interrupt with a volley of searching questions. There is no summing-up of evidence by the Bench. The president must not comment upon the addresses to the jury of either the public prosecutor or counsel for the defence. The jury retires, therefore, without final guidance from him, to consider their verdict. Meantime the prisoner is removed from the court-room, and he is not taken back until after the jury give their verdict and sentence is pronounced. Then he is led into the court and informed of his fate.

In a German criminal court the proceedings are somewhat similar, the judge being a keen and able inquisitor. Before any witnesses are heard the accused may elect to make a confession of his guilt. The judge permits and encourages him to tell his story in his own words, which may sometimes be that not only of his crime but his whole life, and he may submit explanations of his conduct in relation to his upbringing and the individuals or circumstances which have influenced him by precept or example. The judge may encourage him to go into intimate details of his mental processes that have a bearing on his conduct in various circumstances as well as on the history of his crime. The custom of encouraging or inducing the accused to make confession in open court obtains also in Italy

IN an English criminal court the accused can only plead guilty or not guilty, but before judgement is pronounced either he or his counsel may make a statement regarding any extenuating circumstances in a plea for mercy. An English judge is sparing in his questions put to witnesses, and is invariably concerned merely in making clear some point which may tell for or against the accused after the examination and cross-examination have taken place. He does not admit any evidence which is not strictly relevant or any mention during the case of a prisoner's previous convictions; nor does he allow a police witness to repeat any statement accused may have made after arrest unless a solemn warning had first been given that it would be used against him at the trial.

Legal procedure in English courts is distinguished by decorum and solemnity. The judge and counsel wear wigs and gowns and a strict etiquette is observed. The juries now include women, and they are warned by the Bench to dismiss from their minds anything they may have previously heard regarding the case and to deal only with the evidence heard in the court. When the plea is taken the case against the accused is summarised by counsel for the Crown, and after the evidence has been heard the jury are addressed by counsel on either side. Then the judge sums up with impartiality, bringing out the leading points which tell against the accused or in his favour and, besides giving guidance on points of law, making quite clear to the jury the vital issues regarding which they must make up their minds. The accused must be present in court when the jury return their verdict and the judge solemnly pronounces sentence.

Scottish legal procedure is similarly of solemn and unostentatious character, and judges and counsel are similarly be-wigged and gowned. There is, however, a different system of dealing with individuals arrested on a criminal charge. In England a murder case, for instance, is investigated at a public inquest and again in the police court, where a jury decides whether or not a case must go to a higher court. There is no inquest in Scotland; a criminal case is investigated privately by the procurator fiscal. In the police court the accused is simply charged. No plea is taken, and he is remitted to the sheriff, before whom he is questioned in private, but is not compelled to make any statement. At a later stage the accused attends a Pleading Diet in public in the Sheriff Court. There he simply pleads guilty or not guilty to the charge, no evidence being led. The sheriff then remits him to the High Court of Justiciary, where the evidence is heard in public for the first time. There is no preliminary statement of the case by

P. & A.

P. & A.

JUSTICE IN THE NEW WORLD DEVOID OF THE TRAPPINGS OF THE OLD

In the United States judge and counsel wear everyday dress, and in other respects the procedure is less formal than in the courts of England. When a municipal judge of Los Angeles was dispossessed of his court-room through a misunderstanding he sat himself on the pedestal of a statue in the street and held his court in the open air (top). The lower photograph shows the opening of the trial in the Brooklyn court-house of a murderer shot while resisting arrest. The accused is lying on a stretcher in the body of the court.

Agence Rol

FRENCH SENATE SITTING AS A COURT OF JUSTICE

In addition to sharing with the Chamber of Deputies the honour of being the repository of the legislative power, the French Senate sometimes functions as a court of justice. When constituted as a high court of justice it tries cases of attempt against the safety of the state, or of plotting to change the form of government.

counsel for the crown. The accused having pleaded not guilty, the witnesses are heard in the order arranged. After the evidence has been taken the counsel on either side address the jury, and then the judge sums up. As in England, the accused is present in court when the jury return their verdict and the judge pronounces sentence or acquits him.

Both in England and in Scotland the majesty of the law is upheld by ceremonial proceedings. A fanfare of trumpets heralds the entrance of the judge into the court, and all present rise to their feet until he takes his seat upon the bench. He retires to his room when the jury retire to theirs, but does not again return until after the jury have filed in and seated themselves. Then an official announces his coming by simply calling 'Court.' Again all rise until the chief representative of the law is seated. After judgement is given and sentence passed the case may be carried to the English or Scottish court of appeal, composed of a bench of judges who review the case to ascertain whether or not justice has been done and the procedure has been strictly in accordance with law.

In America the judges and counsel do not wear robes or wigs but ordinary sombre attire. The procedure is traditionally English, but something of the French methods has entered into it. Witnesses are not always as strictly relevant as in an English court, greater latitude being allowed. Withal, a much longer interval may ensue between the arrest of a suspected person and the final disposal of the case. Appeals on various points may delay a trial, or the execution of a verdict, for quite a considerable period. As in France, a case is at every stage discussed in the newspapers with free expressions of opinion, and members of juries cannot help being acquainted with intimate details before a trial takes place. In America the appeals to federal and state courts occupy much time, and may be made during the preliminary stages of a case and again after the trial has taken place. A higher court may order a new trial and, if this happens, there may be fresh appeals after that trial is concluded. The grossest charges of unfairness against a judge are frequently made, and in the courts barristers may display a degree of heat and feeling which would not be tolerated in an English court.

Irish courts are modelled on those of England and the procedure is similar. Counsel are known as barristers, as in England, but in Scotland they are called advocates.

HARVEST CUSTOMS IN EASTERN LANDS

So vital are the grain crops to mankind and so striking is the miracle of their growth, that a vast body of custom has grown up in every land around the harvest. Separate chapters are devoted to the Harvest Home in Europe and **Harvest Time in Savage Life**. The wine harvest is dealt with in the chapter on **the Vintage** and its Celebration.

HARVEST customs among some Eastern peoples are expressions of living faiths, and among others, despite religious changes, folk survivals from the time when they had origin in the innate human sense of the wonder and mystery of growth after decay. The miracle of the harvest has ever made emotional appeal, as it did to the Psalmist who sang: 'He that goeth forth and weepeth, bearing precious seed, shall doubtless come again with rejoicing, bringing his sheaves with him.'

To early man that appeal was profound, because when the discovery of agriculture was made the hunting peoples, who were wont to live on the edge of want, learned how to produce food that could be stored against periods of leanness and dire famine. Natural forces were deified, invoked with tears at the sowing time, and adored with gratitude when rich crops were reaped. In modern Japan the spirit of that early form of agricultural religion still obtains, as it does in a lyric of one of our own modern poets, who sings:

God comes down in the rain,
And the crop grows tall—
This is the country faith,
And the best of all!

The Japanese Shinto faith has a fundamental connexion with the worship of the deities of the sun, growth, grain and the harvest. These include Ama terāsu, the sun-goddess, Uke mochi, the food goddess, Inari, the bearded rice-god, who rides on a white fox, and the three harvest gods, named Oho-toshi no Kami, Mi-toshi no Kami and Waka-toshi no Kami—the 'great harvest god,' the 'august harvest god' and the 'young harvest god' respectively. Of great antiquity is the Japanese rice harvest festival, known as 'Nihi-name'—'new tasting'—when the food-giving and life-giving deities are adored and their worshippers partake with them of the first fruits and give vent to their emotions with ceremony. Little is known regarding the domestic form of the ceremony, because it is observed behind closed doors, no stranger being admitted to witness or take part in the mysteries. It is a time for the performance of archaic rites and for much family rejoicing. The public 'Nihi-name' is accompanied by singing, dancing and feasting. The partakers are attired in holiday dress and presents are exchanged. Before the new rice is eaten a sacred fire is ceremonially kindled at night in the courtyard of a shrine at which offerings are made with due solemnity. Old-fashioned Japanese agriculturists will not partake of the harvest crop until the religious ceremony of offering and blessing has been completed. The merry-making follows.

THE harvest festival in China is celebrated on the 15th day of the Eighth Moon, when the 'harvest moon' is full. It is known as 'the moon's birthday,' and the day before and after are included in the general rejoicing. Moon-cakes of the newly cropped cereals are ceremonially baked and offered to the moon goddess, who is 'Queen of Heaven,' and on the upper part of each is a crescent symbol. According to a Chinese folk-tale, the moon lady was the wife of an ancient worthy, but preserves her youth and beauty because she stole from the goddess of the west the

E.N.A.

HARVEST RITE OF THE BOYS OF JAPAN

Many and picturesque are the ceremonies and beliefs connected with harvest time in Japan, and all have their roots in Shintoism. At harvest time boys carry gaily decorated sacred palanquins such as are here seen through the fields. It is popularly supposed that children who have taken part in dragging these trophies on this occasion are rendered immune from pestilence

E.N.A.

HOW THE GARNERING OF THE RICE IS CELEBRATED IN JAPAN: SHINTO HARVEST FESTIVAL PROCESSION

Shintoism is intimately bound up with agriculture, among the deities worshipped being those of food and growth. Far and away the most important crop of Japan is rice, and the periods of the sowing, transplanting and harvesting of the rice are occasions of great popular interest and rejoicing. Two harvest festivals are held, one to celebrate the presenting of the new rice by the emperor at the shrines of the Imperial Ancestors at Ise, and the other in honour of the offering of the first fruits. Of the two the latter has the stronger and wider appeal, and at every village shrine the best of the rice is offered. All the schools are closed for the occasion so that the children may take part in the festivities.

elixir of life. To mankind she annually gives a portion of this mysterious longevity liquid by means of the crops which she is supposed to ripen. The Chinese, while adoring her, make merry in holiday spirit. Fairs are held, and luck symbols, including highly-coloured clay models of pagodas, are sold, as are also little luck dolls, which are purchased for children born during the year, and on which the little one's names are written. The harvest doll is carefully preserved, and if the child should die, it is placed in her grave.

Another deity worshipped during the harvest festival is the 'Bushel Mother.' She is the goddess of the constellation Ursa Major, the Great Bear, known to us as the Plough and in America as the Dipper. It is formed by seven stars, and in China banners with seven stars are popular during the harvest rejoicings and may be seen fluttering over private houses and tea-houses. The emperor formerly performed symbolic religious rites at sowing time and harvest, but the establishment of the Republic has caused these to be discontinued. Domestic ceremonies are, however, still observed by the agriculturists, to whom the constellation of the 'Bushel' is the 'clock of the seasons,' for its 'pointer'—our 'tail' of the Bear — points eastward in spring, southward in summer, westward in autumn and northward in winter.

Dr. S. M. Manton

WHERE RICE IS HARVESTED WITHOUT THE SICKLE'S AID

In Bali when the time of rice harvest approaches the fields are drained and dry up while the rice ripens. Whole families gather the harvest, picking it by hand as one would bunches of flowers. The rice is tied in bundles, and the straw not bearing ears is left to be trampled. As stated in page 483, rice cultivation in Bali is almost a ritual process throughout.

Although of the Moslem faith, the natives of the Malay peninsula retain the archaic harvest customs of an earlier religion. An aged sorceress ('pawang') is the mistress of ceremony, and the ancient charms she repeats are given a Moslem colouring by the introduction of lines referring to the prophet and the one God. When a rice crop is ripe she comes with her attendants to procure the 'Rice Baby' and the 'Mother Seed' required for the following year. She subsequently superintends the threshing operations. The time to begin cutting having been fixed by an astrologer, the old woman, accompanied by female attendants, walks solemnly towards the rice field, repeating charms and bringing with her the basket cradle for the 'Rice Baby,' in which have been placed various magical articles, including candle-nuts, a hen's egg, a long iron nail, a cockle shell, a strip of white cloth, and a longer and broader strip of red cloth which is used for the purpose of suspending the cradle from the neck of the carrier. There are also several trays of brass, three of them containing rice at various stages of treatment, one with an egg, another with a piece of white quartz, and others containing oil, incense, etc.

Five females are in attendance as assistants, and they are led by the old woman, who chants metrical

E. O. Hoppé

LUSCIOUS FRUITS TO PERSUADE THE GODS TO LOOK KINDLY ON THE RICE HARVEST

The Balinese are very religious, and delight to honour their gods. Among the many beautiful objects to be seen in that isle of beauty are the offerings at the time of rice harvest. These consist of the most wonderful arrangements of fruit and flowers. The fruit is built up in elaborate patterns to a height of several feet, and sometimes the offering is crowned with sacred lotus flowers disposed in the shape of an outstretched peacock's tail.

charms, to the part of the field in which the first sheaf, called ' Mother Sheaf ' is cut with ceremony. It is composed of stalks each having seven joints, an indication that they are ' female.' The sorceress places the magical objects from the basket cradle in the sheaf anoints it with oil, burns incense and, repeating charms cuts off seven ears, which she lays in a white cloth spread out on her lap. Again she applies the incense smoke and then strews old rice over the ears, after which she ties up the ears in the cloth and places it in the basket cradle. The Rice Baby ' having thus been obtained, the Mother Sheaf ' is sprinkled with old rice, the remnant being tossed backward over her head. Proceeding to another part of the field, the sorceress, facing the sun, cuts another seven ears which are placed in baskets, and then leaves two of her assistants to begin the reaping of the field from that point.

The ' Rice Baby ' is carried by a woman who has suspended the basket cradle from her neck by means of the red cloth and holds above her head an umbrella to protect her burden from the hot sun. Led by the sorceress, the carrier walks towards the house of the owner of the crop. There she is awaited by the owner's wife and other women.

' What have you to tell ? ' calls the owner's wife from the threshold.

' All is well,' the sorceress answers.

THE inquirer then sprinkles rice over the old woman and recites a verse in which she expresses the belief that there is a baby of hers in the basket cradle. Verses are recited in reply, first by the sorceress and then by the carrier, which indicate that they are the bringers of good luck. Then the ' Rice Baby ' is borne into the house and placed on a sleeping mat with a soft pillow. Soon afterwards the women reapers come from the field with three baskets of rice, which are also laid upon the sleeping mat. Thereafter the sorceress imposes certain taboos like those connected with a real birth.

Three days later the sorceress superintends the drying and pounding and winnowing of the new rice which has been taken to the house. The straw is pleated to form a wreath and with the chaff deposited in a corner of the rice field under a large stone, while the rice from the 'Baby' is placed in the rice bin.

When the field of rice is being reaped the cutters face the sun lest their shadows should fall upon the crop. The last sheaf is reaped by the farmer's wife, who carries it home. The grains obtained from it are mixed with those from the 'Rice Baby,' and some of the 'Baby' grains are mixed with the rice set apart for seed for the next sowing. There is feasting, singing and dancing when the harvest operations are completed.

The 'Rice Baby,' who is the 'Soul of the Rice,' is met with throughout the East Indies in association with the 'Rice Mother.' In Sumatra the Battas select a virgin to inaugurate the harvest operations. She enters a rice field and makes a little sheaf of plucked ears, and while the reaping proceeds offerings are made to the rice deity. The symbolic sheaf is ceremonially carried to the farmer's house, and when the crop has been threshed and stored it is deposited in the granary with a stone or an egg. As the 'Soul of the Rice' the grains from the first-plucked ears protect the whole crop and ensure that the seed will be fertile. Other peoples in Sumatra call the first sheaf Saning Sari, who is the 'Rice Mother.' It is formed of the first ears plucked by an elderly woman and is borne to the farmer's house by a woman who carries an umbrella. A harvest meal is afterwards ceremonially eaten and the 'Mother' is deposited in the granary. Some of the Sumatra folk connect the 'Rice Mother' with the moon.

A priest plucks the first ears in Java, and ties them with flowers, forming two sheaves, which are anointed with a scented paste. The symbolic couple are known as the 'Rice Bridegroom' and the 'Rice Bride,' and they are carried to a specially prepared chamber in the granary, where they are ceremonially married, the wedding guests being represented by other sheaves. This ceremony takes place at the harvest-home feast, at which there is great rejoicing, everyone making glad holiday and eating, drinking, singing and dancing. The symbolic bridal pair are formally addressed by a priest, who prays for good luck and a life free from want and suffering.

The Tomori of the Celebes regard the last sheaf as the 'Rice Mother,' whose dwelling-place is in the moon, and if she is not duly adored before being placed in the granary, it is feared she will devour much of the crop.

There are various harvest customs in Borneo. The Dyaks have priests who make search for the 'Rice Soul,' which is supposed to have a butterfly form, and ceremonies are performed on the rice field and in the home of the owner. In some areas the 'Rice Soul' is searched for at night in the light of bonfires, while men and women dance slowly and chant metrical charms.

In some parts of Borneo women reap the first ears of the rice crop, and when they reach the farmer's house they must remain in it for a day and a night. The new grain is carried in baskets slung from the

Ewing Galloway

WOMAN OF BALI WITH HARVEST GIFT

This is how the towering erections of fruit which form the harvest offerings of the Balinese are conveyed to the temples. To the practice of carrying heavy burdens on the head are doubtless due the superb figures and carriage of the women.

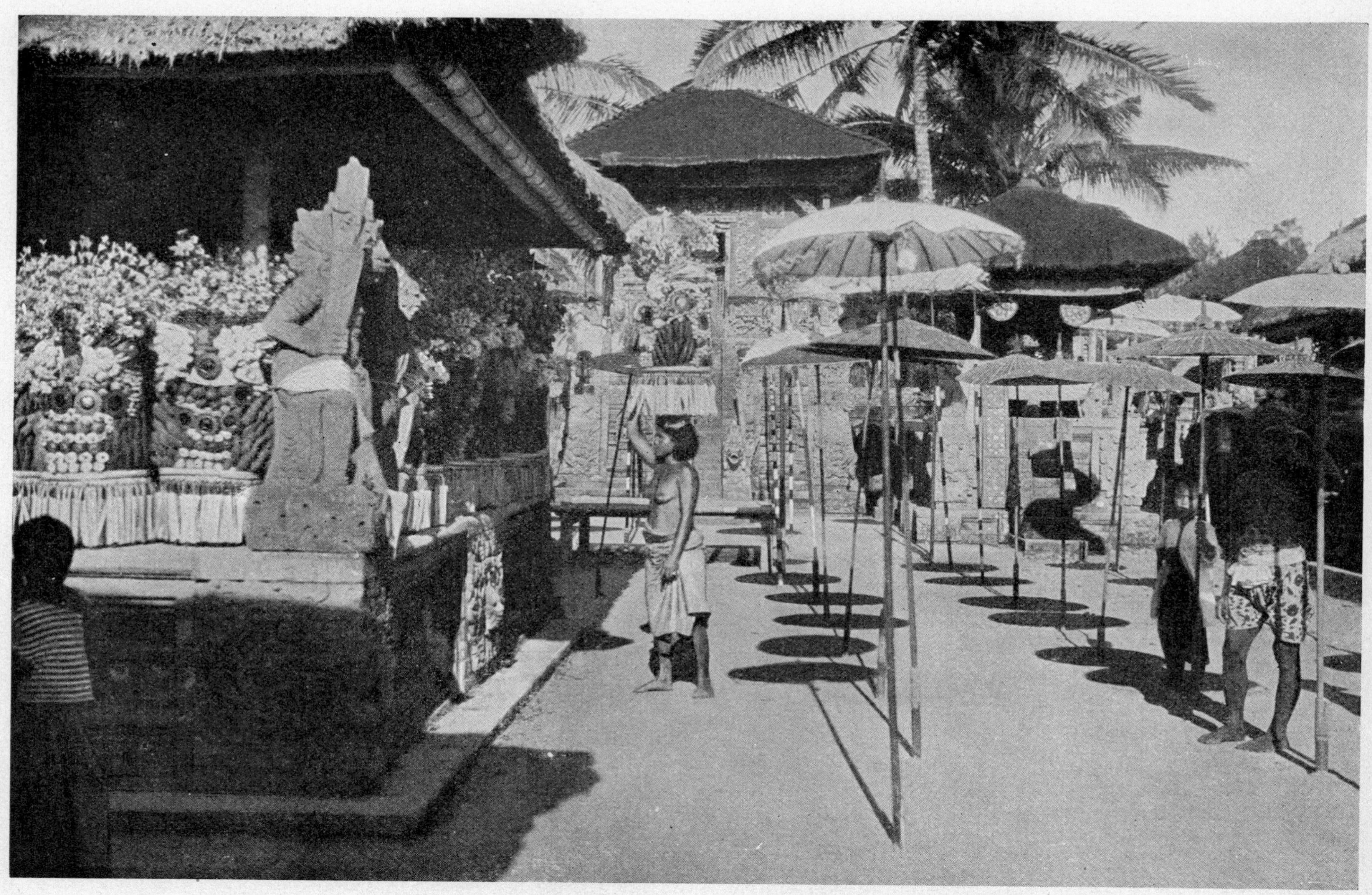

E. O. Hoppé

RITES OF HARVEST IN BALI: READY TO PLACE HER OFFERING ON THE ALTAR OF SACRIFICE

Rice harvest is a busy time in Bali, for, apart from the actual taking of the crop, the gods of the islanders have to be propitiated, to ensure that the harvest be fruitful. To this end the inhabitants make up elaborate baskets of fruit, and soon along the jungle paths of the island may be seen stately women carrying these gorgeous gifts to the temples. The scene in the temple court is very picturesque. A line of brilliantly coloured umbrellas mounted on tall sticks glows in the sun before the sacrificial altar, which is a low stone platform protected by a thatched roof. On the altar are arranged the offerings, row upon row, while the guardian of the shrine, carved in stone, looks down upon the bringer of the gift.

bearers' necks and is spread out on mats on a platform erected in front of the house. When it has been dried, pounded and winnowed, there is much rejoicing.

The festival after the harvest work begins with the ceremony of mixing with the grain reserved for seed some of the seed of the previous years. Each rice grower has a magical basket in which are kept old seeds collected for generations, and these are supposed to preserve the 'Rice Spirit' which ensures fertility. The festival is a boisterous one. In the dances women dress as men, and there is much drinking and eating. For three days the conduct of the young people is loose. Marriages are usually celebrated after the harvest.

In Burma the Karens believe in the 'Rice Soul,' which they invoke with ceremony during the period of growth and adore at the harvest festival. The rice growers of Upper Burma sprinkle unhusked rice from the harvest field to the granary to guide the 'Rice Soul' in butterfly form. A sorcerer is sure to produce a butterfly in connexion with the festival. The Szis of Upper Burma invoke the 'Rice Mother' and 'Rice Father' when the threshing of the crop is in progress. Others dress the last sheaf in female attire, carry it from the field and adore it as the guardian of the rice. This sheaf is known as 'Mother Rice.'

At every stage of rice cultivation in Ceylon the Sinhalese perform ceremonies to ensure fertility and protect the crops against the influences of hordes of evil beings. Astrologers fix the time for each particular operation. As they previously announced the hour for beginning to sow seed, so do they announce the moment when reaping should commence. A crowd of workers and spectators collects at a harvest field and a tom-tom band is in attendance to stimulate the workers and drive away demons. Everyone is in high spirits, with ready smile and laughter, for the harvest time is a period of rejoicing and gladness.

Patiently the assembled crowd awaits a signal from the muttering astrologer. When it is given the male reapers dart forward with their sickles, as do also the women who gather the grain and bind it in sheaves. Meantime, the tom-tom band performs with vigour and vivacity, the reapers keeping time with their sickles.

When a portion of the field has been cut the women carry the sheaves on their heads, marching in Indian file, towards the threshing floor, which is usually situated on an elevated and breezy place near the irrigated land. The floor is circular and about thirty feet in diameter. On it has been traced with wood ashes

British North Borneo Co.

SACRED JAR WHOSE OCCUPANT CONTROLS THE RICE CROP

Some of the coastal Dusuns of North Borneo have a 'gusi' or jar cult. The 'gusi' is held to contain the will of a deity, and it is believed that the rice crop will thrive if the requirements of the 'gusi' are carried out, and will fail if the 'gusi' is flouted. The photograph shows a Tuaran Dusun with a 'gusi.'

Dr. S. M. Manton

GABLED BARN AND BAMBOO TUB TO HOUSE THE SHEAVES AND GRAIN

Among the Bataks of Sumatra the buildings used for storing rice are elaborately carved and painted and supported on pillars; each gable is surmounted by a pair of buffalo horns, supposed to have some religious significance. When harvest comes the Bataks walk up the ladder with the rice sheaves on their heads and tip them into the barn. The bamboo-plaited tub adjoining the barn here seen is for storing the threshed rice grain. The roof is made of interlocked split bamboos, which have all the advantages of corrugated iron

a series of concentric circles intersected by straight lines to mark the cardinal points, the outer circle having symbolic signs ornamenting it. Inside the divisions formed by the straight lines are drawings of religious or magico-religious significance, including a Buddha foot and various implements. In the centre is placed a conch shell stuffed with various charms.

Here again, the astrologer announces the moment when the depositing ceremony is to take place. The farmer lifts the first sheaf, placing it upon his head, and, on receiving a signal from the astrologer, solemnly and slowly walks round the outer circle 'by the right' or sun-wise. Then from a point indicated by the astrologer he advances towards the centre and lays the sheaf upon the conch shell. As he does so, he prostrates himself, holding his hands pressed palm against palm, in front of his face, while he utters mysterious words of magical significance. Three times he rises, to drop down again, adoring the sheaf and conch shell. When he withdraws, three women with sheaves upon their heads walk similarly round the circles and then deposit and adore the sheaves which they have brought from the harvest field in the order in which they were cut and bound.

E. O. Hoppé

PILLARS THAT LEAN BENEATH THE WEIGHT OF HARVEST

The Minangkabau of Sumatra believe that rice is under the special protection of a female spirit, and they perform many rites of sympathetic magic in connexion with the rice crop and harvest. When a rice barn has been built it is customary to hold a feast, and at this a woman who is about to have a child must partake. It is thought that her condition will help the rice to be fruitful. Architecturally, the rice barns of the Minangkabau are much like those of the Bataks.

The rest of the female carriers throw down their sheaves without ceremony until the concentric circles are entirely covered.

Once again the astrologer gets to work. He must discover the auspicious moment for bringing forward the cattle to tread the grain and thus release the rice. The workers collect round the threshing floor. When the signal is given some men guide the animals while others sing harvest ditties. Occasionally a worker springs out from among the others and, shouldering a wooden prong used for pushing the straw under the hoofs of the treading cattle, prances around the threshing floor, singing a magical song which is supposed to drive away evil spirits. When the treading is completed, women pound the grain to unhusk it, and, using wooden trays, toss the rice in the evening breeze to separate it from the chaff. The farmer's house is gaily decorated for the 'harvest home,' at which there is merry-making, drinking and feasting.

N. Bauer

THRESHING CORN IN EGYPT WITH A SLEDGE

The agricultural methods employed to-day by the fellahin of Egypt are very little different from those that were used before the Pyramids were built. The plough remains unaltered; many of the irrigation appliances have come down from remote antiquity; while in order to separate the grain from the ear a sledge, harnessed to bullocks, is driven over the corn.

E.N.A.

BRINGING OUT THE THRESHER IN PERSIA

By means of irrigation, good crops can be produced in Persia on the most unpromising soil. Wheat and barley are important among the cereals. As in Egypt, the implements used in husbandry are very primitive, but at least the Persians employ a machine for threshing.

The July harvest in southern India is inaugurated by householders performing a ceremonial house cleaning to drive away evil spirits during the evening Next day the good spirits, which bring a bountiful harvest, are invoked by women who, having bathed themselves, make offerings of flowers and herbs. A woman is selected to preside over the harvest ceremonies conducted in the home. When, however, the new rice is offered to the mother goddess at the harvest ceremony called 'Nira' a priest comes from the local temple preceded by a man who blows a sacred conch shell. The new ears are deposited in a store-house connected with the temple, while the people chant invocations to the deity to fill their baskets and fill their stomachs. A god called Muni is the protector of food, and he is usually represented by a boulder of granite placed under a tree. Garlands of straw are attached to houses and placed on bushes and trees. A fowl or goat is sacrificed. In some areas the earth goddess is adored, and women dress as men. A stone is set up to represent the goddess, to whom are offered fowls and rice and milk.

Throughout India the harvest festivals are occasions of merry-making as well as the performance of religious rites. The traditional folk religion is, however, everywhere in prominence, indicating the persistence of immemorial customs among communities of different sects.

THE CULT OF THE NUDE IN EUROPE

SOCIAL conventions with regard to the exposure of the person have been surveyed in the chapter on Conflicting Standards of Decency and Decorum. Here the subject is treated in its relation to the recent development of physical culture that has followed upon the discovery of the health-giving properties of sunlight—a development that will inevitably have a modifying effect upon public opinion.

WRITING some two hundred years after the death of Cato the Censor, Plutarch relates of him that he would never bathe in the presence of his son—and that that would appear to have been the common custom of the Romans, so that even ' sons-in-law never bathed with their fathers-in-law, being ashamed to appear naked before them.' He then adds, parenthetically, thinking of his own age, ' It is true, indeed, in process of time the Greeks taught them to bathe naked one with another ; they soon after taught the Greeks to do the same thing before the women, and bathe naked with them.' But though the Greeks, if Plutarch is to be believed, had avoided displaying the human form undraped in what may be called their domestic exercises, they had long pursued the cult of the nude. At the public games competitors of both sexes struggled for the prize clad only as they had appeared first in the world. The Roman extension of this custom is the one which has been revived in our own time—with certain restrictions.

To many people there is still something shocking in the naked form. To track down that mysterious instinct of decency would take us far back into the history of the earth, when primitive man was developing into a social being. Since the eyes of Adam and Eve were opened and they knew that they were naked, mankind, in proportion to the climatic conditions under which he has lived, has tended to pile more and more clothes upon himself, until at last in the present age, under the influence of modern therapeutics, the tide has set in the opposite direction. It is curious to reflect, illustrating as it does the manner in which the human mind swings pendulum-fashion from one extreme to another, that to-day's cult of the nude should follow so hard upon those Victorian times when man padded himself out with waistcoats, and for a woman to undress was almost like dismantling the window of a big drapery establishment.

Not that yesterday's standard of ' decency ' was ever universal. Among savage races the addition of a loin cloth is still only a mark of adolescence. In the name of ' decency ' untold suffering and misery have been caused to many so-called primitive peoples. It has been asserted that British missionaries, apparently wishing to make it quite clear that every human being, like themselves, had fallen from a state of innocency, spread phthisis among the Maoris of New Zealand and depopulated the South Sea Islands with the garments turned out wholesale at English village missionary meetings. In some more civilized countries, too, nudity has never been looked upon askance. The bath woman has long been a feature of life in Finland, and the Japanese do not always segregate the sexes in public bathing. Along the western coast of the Black Sea, men and women still bathe together naked.

THE desire to strip or wander about nude must be an inherited instinct, for all children have it. This freedom from the impediment of clothes of any sort, especially during bathing, was kept alive as an ideal in many of our big public schools when most of our sculpture was draped. But for ordinary purposes the modern cult of the nude may be traced to the 'nineties of last century.

Keystone

DRYADS OF THE WOODS NEAR LONDON

English people have become used to public exposure of the human form at seaside bathing resorts, but moral courage is still required of those sun-bathers who practise their cult in the neighbourhood of inland towns. Yet in the woods near Croydon and Norwood all the year round sun-bathers gather for exercise, and afterwards to enjoy alfresco meals like this.

Into a world which certainly had its dress reformers—though it would be hard to trace any connexion between the ideals of Mrs. Bloomer as represented by the unspeakably ugly garments she recommended and the present ideals—but which still advocated stuffiness, there swept a craze for physical culture. In its first form it pursued strength—merely as strength. Eugene Sandow had come over from the Continent, and in a London music hall had torn the laurels from the brows of Samson, the strong man—breaking iron chains, lifting grand pianos with a selected number of heavyweights sitting on them, and even wrestling with muzzled and

Keyston

Dr Weller. Berlin

GYMNASTIC SKILL AND HARDIHOOD

Scandinavia was the land of origin of the cult of nudism as practised in Europe, and also of ski-ing as a sport. Both may be studied near St. Moritz, where winter sports enthusiasts may be seen ski-ing almost naked over the sun-lit snow. The lower photograph shows a German gymnast giving an exhibition at an athletic meeting.

mittened lions. Sandow, however, was a man of ideas, and instead of being content with the large salary he earned on the music halls, he turned his attention to other matters. He himself as a boy had been weak and sickly, but by careful training of his muscles he had developed that strength and that Hercules beauty of form with which all the world was familiar at one time.

HE founded a school of physical culture which in the first instance propagated the simple ideal of making every man's body strong, healthy and beautiful. The success he won tended rather rapidly to commercialise the movement, but at first the immense advertisement he secured by his feats of strength on the stage concentrated public attention on the real advantages of physical culture. At the same time from Germany and Sweden came teachers of physical training. The English had always played games, but now was the first occasion when what may be called the training of the boxing camp was introduced into the bathrooms and bedrooms of the average home. The complete success of the movement is proved by the establishment of certain papers, some of them still in existence, devoted solely to the subjects of health and body culture.

Side by side with this revived interest in one's own body there naturally grew up a curiosity as to the best method of keeping that body running. The

Keystone

CHORIC DANCES OF DEVOTEES OF HYGIEIA, GODDESS OF HEALTH

Norwood is the home of one of the most prosperous sun-bathing societies yet established in England. It specialises upon the performance of physical exercises in the open, with almost the whole of the body exposed to sunlight and fresh air. Qualified instructors are engaged to conduct classes in calisthenics, and these are attended by large numbers of children (top). The lower photograph shows a class of adolescents and adults of the same society similarly engaged at a less clement season of the year.

Keystone

PHYSICAL FITNESS PROOF AGAINST THE RIGOURS OF CLIMATE

In Germany Nacktkultur, or physical culture in the nude, is officially encouraged, and is doing much to restore the standard of national health that was seriously lowered by privations during the Great War. The women are specially ardent advocates of the movement, and the Women Teachers of Gymnastics of the Physical Culture Institute near Berlin hold their exercises all the year round, practising archery, for example, even in deep snow. In Germany, and in Switzerland, too, there are clubs for dancing naked in the open air.

Keystone

SEMI-NUDE PATRIOTS AT A POLITICAL MEETING IN GERMANY

How thoroughly national the Nacktkultur movement has become in Germany was demonstrated in a remarkable and unprecedented manner in February 1931 on the occasion of the seventh celebration of the institution of the Reichsbanner, the central organization founded to supplement the police in protecting the government against the extreme Hitlerites on the one hand and the Communists on the other. A force of athletes dressed only in running shorts and shoes attended the meeting officially, taking up their position under the Reichsbanner standards.

whole subject of dietetics was discussed Vegetarian restaurants were established in London for the first time A great deal of this physical 'uplift' was probably empirical, but it did establish a natural and proper interest in the human body, then still looked upon as a rather indelicate subject—and so prepared the way for what was to follow

THE discovery of the curative properties of sunlight, especially for rickets and tuberculosis—the doctrine of the ultra-violet ray—gave an instant impetus to the undressing movement. There was no longer any need for the apparatus and exercises of physical culture to be concealed within bedrooms and bathrooms Already a generation had grown up which had begun to regard doctors much as the devout look upon their priests, as in some mysterious way superior beings, whose every word was a glittering truth. Now, fortified by the pontifical authority of the medical councils of the world, men and women rushed to bathe themselves in sunlight, and to do their physical training in the open instead of between four walls. After the war the movement spread enormously, and for long the most popular illustrations in the public press were those of celebrities wearing as little as possible basking themselves in sunshine Mr. G B. Shaw, who had once posed as Rodin's 'Penseur, lent his immense public influence to the movement by becoming one of its most devout followers It is indeed since the Great War that the cult of the nude has made its greatest strides

In this latter evolution Germany has led the way The blockade by the British Navy during hostilities had seriously lowered the standard of health in Germany, especially among children and growing adolescents, and with characteristic national thoroughness the authorities set themselves to remedy this evil. The sun-bathing clubs and societies now firmly established in the country were the result

The German school of 'the bare' is not content merely with lying about in the sunshine The remedial effects of sunlight go hand in hand with physical culture The movement has caught on, particularly among women, and competent observers declare that already the improvement in physique is remarkable A parade of German female athletes is from an aesthetic point of view one of the most beautiful sights in the world.

THE followers of the cult do not limit themselves to the summer, or consider it necessary for the performance of their training to remove during the winter months to warmer climes Their exercises which consist of eurhythmics, archery, javelin throwing and games of ball, are carried on in the most severe weather When all the land is covered in snow the Women Teachers of Gymnastics of the Physical Culture Institute near Berlin 'carry on clad only in the thinnest of bathing costumes Children are encouraged to go naked as often as possible, and this discarding of clothes reached a characteristic climax in a recent huge political demonstration of the defenders of the German Republic, when in addition to the usual uniformed corps there paraded some hundreds of youths clad only in the scantiest of running shorts

Only a comparatively few years ago life models in art classes were regarded as improper Even respectable English artists went discreetly to Paris to study the nude Du Maurier painted this characteristic insular attitude in his description of Little Billee's emotions when he discovered that Trilby was posing for the 'altogether.' Nowadays, in Germany and Switzerland particularly, the pendulum has swung in the opposite direction. In both those countries there are exclusive clubs where the members, devoted to the culture of health and the worship of the sun, dance naked How beautiful some of the poses of the undraped human form can be is shown by one of our illustrations representing a group of three young girls dancing on some rising ground, outlined against the sky. In Germany, it is said, embarrassment arising from meeting a lady with whom one is socially acquainted with practically no clothes on—indeed, on some of the sun-bathing beaches drapery of any sort is exceptional —has long passed Custom indeed can harden human beings to most experiences which at first appear outrageously unusual

IN Austria the cult has been productive of some curious repercussions In the south of France, where the amount of sunshine during the summer is above the normal, places like Mentone close their season on May 15 From then onwards until November, when the season opens again, the famous watering place used to be deserted. In 1926, however, when most of the shops and hotels were closed and the inhabitants of Mentone were living sleepily on their winter earnings, they were roused from their repose by an invasion of Austrians. They came in hundreds, men and women, stayed a fortnight and then went away their places being instantly taken by a fresh batch of visitors The deserted beaches were crowded with men and women lying about almost, or altogether, in a state of nature, being burned and browned by the sun. This was all due to the gospel of the nude and sun worship as preached by an eminent Austrian scientist, who advocated Mentone as the place where the best curative results could be obtained At first the tradesmen in Mentone were alarmed lest these Austrians should usurp the places intended for the moneyed English, but nowadays they welcome their advent, which provides them with a summer season, and keeps them busy throughout the year at the pleasant occupation of making money

In England the cult has already taken firm hold, despite a certain opposition from a people rather more prejudiced and conservative in its views than other nations. In 1930 the sun-bathers who selected a spot at the Welsh Harp at Hendon at which to perform their rites were treated with such hostility that finally the local authority, which had leased

P. & A.

SUN WORSHIPPERS BASKING ON THE ROCKS AT CAP D'ANTIBES

While an ever-increasing number of people are adopting the cult of the nude because they are convinced of the health-giving properties of sunlight, there is also a large class who go in for sun-bathing for less serious reasons. Fashion decreed that deep pigmentation of the skin by sunburn should be the correct mode of the moment, and to acquire it 'society' flocks to various continental seaside resorts, there to lie prostrate and virtually naked upon the sun-baked sands. Cap d'Antibes is one of the places most frequented by these care-free idlers.

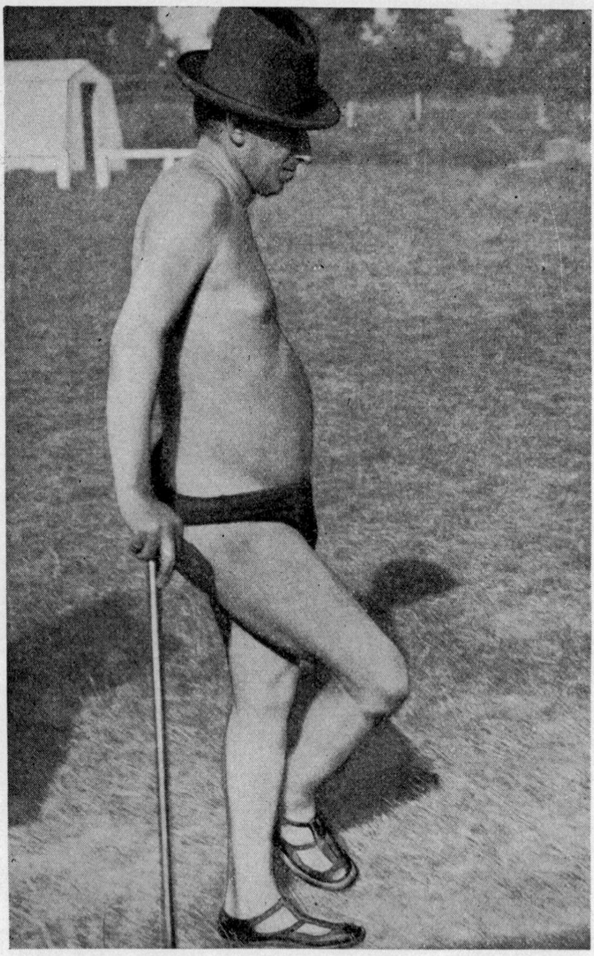

FRENCH PHYSICAL CULTURISTS BEFORE AND DURING TRAINING

In France the official attitude towards nudism is one of rather disapproving reserve and its practice is strictly circumscribed by regulations. Certain islands of the Seine have been given over to its devotees and their camps are under police supervision and are carefully isolated from the outside world by high encircling walls. The unintentionally amusing figure on the left clad in hat and loin cloth is a novice still awaiting training. The efficacy of the system is illustrated by the lady vis-à-vis to him, at exercise with the medicine ball.

them the ground, revoked the contract to prevent a disturbance of the peace. There is, however, a sun-bathing society which reproduces more or less exactly the phases of the movement in Germany Wearing as little clothing as possible, members of the society gather in the woods near Croydon to let their bodies absorb the life-giving rays of the sun They camp there and take their meals in the open. Physical exercise classes are held and dances and sports form part of the routine If the movement continues to spread at its present pace our woods throughout the country—our English climate notwithstanding—will some day be peopled with nymphs!

In the neighbourhood of Norwood there is another temple devoted to the cult A special feature of the sun-bathing here is the number of children who take part. There is no more charming and exhilarating sight than dozens of little ones, clad only in flimsy slips, following the movements of their half-nude instructor as he goes through the poses of physical drill. There are classes, too, for older children, who perform their calisthenics in a similar state of undress. The whole idea is to remove as many clothes as possible, to keep in the fresh air and the sunlight, and so to exercise the body that all the muscles are naturally developed. As in Germany, mere contact of the bare skin with the sun's rays is not considered sufficient, and every possible attention is given to proper physical exercises which add to the charm and fitness of the human body

Of all the habits and customs of mankind this revival of the Greek cult of the body is at the same time one of the most interesting and one of the most useful. In many elementary schools children are encouraged to strip as often as possible, and the clinics that have been established for administering artificial sunlight have been reinforced by increased use of the natural light of the sun itself. Prejudice may object, and the Mrs Grundys who are still with us may hold up their hands in horror at a world filled with so much nudity, but there is little question that this revival of an old cult, that has extended now to every part of the world, will leave its mark in the improved health of the people.

POLYGAMY AND POLYANDRY

THIS is one of many separate chapters devoted to specific aspects of the Life of the Sexes among peoples of differing cultures, for example The Family among Savages, and Woman's Status in Primitive Society. Marriage ceremonies are dealt with in chapters in the section on Courtship and Marriage. Here we are only concerned with two special types of marital relations.

IN our own country there have been not a few who, noting the preponderance of marriageable women over men since the Great War, have considered the feasibility of introducing some sort of secondary marriages for men with minor wives. They use the argument that it is unfair that so many girls should be condemned to celibacy, and that a part-time marriage is better than no marriage at all. Setting aside for the moment objections of religion and moral standards, questions of expense would intervene to prevent any such arrangement becoming widespread in our era and country, where the standard of life, so much higher in England and America than in most other countries, acts amid a singular pressure of financial difficulty.

Even so late as the beginning of the 19th century we have the Elector of Hesse boasting of forty-one natural sons, 'all of whom he has decently provided for.' But however it may have been with kings in times past, that sort of thing is condemned today.

Among Mahomedans it is the fortunate and monied man who is able to afford the four wives permitted, nay enjoined, by the Prophet, as the ideal number. It usually works out that one alone is in sole possession of her lord until his wealth increases, and at the same time, it may be noted, her charms decrease, when, with her full consent, a younger woman is added to the establishment. Among the more intelligent and travelled Mahomedans European habits are being adopted, and in many cases there is now only one legally acknowledged wife, however many of the other sort there may be in the background.

When we consider that there are two hundred and nine million odd Mahomedans out of a world population of, roughly, two thousand millions, we see that a very large proportion of mankind have no ethical qualms about polygamy. But it is not easy to arrive at the real views of such men, as it is considered a gross breach of etiquette so much as to mention their women folk.

MAN is not by nature a polygamous being, as has been too often hastily assumed; by far the greater number of primitive people are in fact monogamous, though it is rather one wife at a time than one wife all the time. In the first instance marriages tended to be periodical, and were, as may be rather crudely stated, like those of the higher anthropoid apes. Polygamy, or polygyny, occurs only among peoples who are comparatively wealthy, or as we should say, comfortably off, and it will be found to run principally among the higher sections of the population, such as chiefs and magic doctors, or those with power in their community.

We hear of no cases of polygamy in these days equal to that of the king of Champa in 1285, who had 326 children, of whom 156 were 'able to bear arms,' in other words, sons, for the whole world is tending, or we should say, reverting, to monogamy. There is, of course, a certain sexual group-communism to be found in widely different parts of the globe, but this is found with polyandry also, and it is not impossible for monogamy to co-exist with it.

In the case of chiefs or petty kings, plurality of wives is found even where there is no Mahomedanism,

E.N.A.

ESKIMO MAN WITH HIS TWO WIVES

Polygamy is not usual among the Eskimos of Greenland, and where it exists it extends to not more than two wives. There are no restrictions to the rights of divorce and re-marriage. The two elder of the seated figures here seen are the wives.

as with the hill tribes of Burma. Within the last fifteen years a noted Sawbwa, or chief, had 29 wives, and after being photographed with each of them in turn, sent the resulting prints to the Political Officer for 'information and record.' But in such cases the first wife, chosen by the parents, or for reasons of state, is the principal wife, and never does any work, which is the duty of the 'little wives,' as the rest are called.

King Mindon of Burma had at least 79 children, and the titular queens were four in number, headed by the Queen of the Middle Palace. This large number of children led to horrible bloodshed, as the succession was more a matter of luck and grasp than of precedence. But plurality of wives does not always lead to multiplicity of children, for in the case of the Sawbwa noted above, one son and one daughter were the total result.

The Mahomedan practice of four legitimate wives is very elastic, for as divorce is merely a matter of repudiation a man may run through ten times that number in his lifetime, and in certain Mahomedan countries, of which Turkistan is an example, the same facilities are allowed to women, so that a woman may equally have a succession of husbands.

Among the unchristianised Eskimo of Greenland, two wives at a time, and not more, is in order, yet here, too, divorce takes place without the least difficulty, so that as much change as desired is easily arranged, and no censure incurred.

Wide World Photos

A FAVOURED TRIO FROM A HOST OF WIVES

The chief home of polygamy is Africa. The custom is in most regions governed by economic conditions, the number of wives being dependent upon the husband's wealth. Chiefs of the Yafouba tribe of the Ivory Coast adorn their favourite wives with the heavy brass anklets here seen, the wearing of which entitles them to a life of comparative leisure (see also page 141).

It is these outstanding examples that catch the imagination of travellers and make them too hastily conclude that a state not far removed from promiscuity is the natural state of man. But men who have made a lifelong study of ethnology have come to very different conclusions. Even if constancy in marriage is not the rule, especially among primitive people, we must still regard the permanent living together of one man and one woman as a state that has always prevailed among human beings, says such an authority as Westermarck. Modern ethnographical research takes a firm stand on this point.

Among the Konde at the northern end of Lake Nyasa women refuse to marry men who have been christianised, as they would be the only wife, and they do not wish to undertake all the work alone. One of the greatest obstacles to Christianity found by the missionaries in divers parts of the world, and amid widely differing races, is this question of polygamy. Men to whom plurality of wives is natural and seemly cannot understand

From Malinowski's 'Sexual Life of Savages'. (Routledge & Sons Ltd,)

WHERE AN ADDED WIFE MEANS AN INCREASE OF INCOME

In the Trobriand Islands, off New Guinea, polygamy is practised only by persons of importance, monogamy being the general rule. To keep up a position, a man must be wealthy. Every chief has a tributary district comprising several villages. From each one of these villages he takes a wife, and each subject community pays him an annual contribution in the form of a dowry. Consequently a chief's income depends solely on his wives' dowries The photograph shows a Trobriand chief with some of his wives and children.

why, if they embrace the new faith, they should be limited to one wife only. The Konde people regard their marriage tie much more seriously than most of the African peoples. Divorce must be properly judged before a court, which supersedes the old fashion of the husband disposing of the erring wife and her lover with the spear, which is still kept hanging on the hut wall to remind her of the fate awaiting her for unfaithfulness.

Such peoples regard the one-wife idea as a disgrace, a sign of poverty and insignificance. It is difficult to reconcile them to it. A man with one wife only is told to hold his tongue in the village assembly and let others better equipped be heard. If the number of wives is reinforced by an exceptional number of children, the man's weight in the village councils is increased. When a chief of one of the Kaffir tribes of South Africa was asked how many children he had, he chortled with joy and, calling to him one of his many children playing in the dust near, he signified by clapping the two hands of the little one together that there were ten at least. He next took another child, and now memory had to be reinforced as he enumerated his family finger by finger, according to the children born of each mother. Thus another ten fingers were disposed of. He then gave way to excessive merriment, but the process was far from being at an end. It did not get near to a conclusion, indeed, until six children had been requisitioned, each with the normal number of fingers; then, and then only, did he revert to his own hands, and after much cogitation showed that he had a total of sixty-seven children, more or less. The oldest of his wives was seventy and the youngest seventeen.

It is mainly chiefs or headmen who run to such establishments. So long as what is called 'cattle marriage' holds among the vast mass of natives in Africa, so long will the actual number of wives be limited by circumstance. In the beginning of the century the old king of Swaziland inhabited a huge kraal filled with hundreds of huts, where lived his many wives, and many, many children, in a sort of collegiate existence. With everyone related to everyone else, with any child cared for by any mother, the social circle ran to the brothers or near relations of the chief, each with his dozen wives, so that in the inner circle, so to speak, there might be a thousand persons.

The outstanding example of plurality of wives among civilized people was among the Mormons, where the practice was instituted by Joseph Smith, whose 'Sacred Law of Marriage' was promulgated in 1852, the Mormon community having then been settled at Salt Lake City for five years. In 1884 the Supreme Court of the U.S.A. decided that polygamy was a crime punishable by law, and five years later the Mormon church was dissolved by Congress. The Mormons bowed to their fate, and their president pronounced against polygamy in 1890. But the 'Beehive' house of Brigham Young, Smith's successor, remained standing as an object of curiosity for tourists. This singular building, circular in shape, had openings on the sides as different entrances for Young's many wives. Seen in section it was like an orange sliced horizontally so that the quarters were laid open. There is no recognized polygamy in the States now; the necessity for it is supplanted by easy divorce.

Polyandry is much rarer than polygamy, and is confined to definite areas, where it has been the custom from time immemorial. It used to be thought that female infanticide was responsible for the scarcity of women in the particular tribes addicted to it, but it is certainly not so always.

The Polynesians inhabiting the Marquesas Islands, now under the mandate of France, are fast vanishing, but whether this is due to their loosely defined system of polyandry is a matter of opinion. A girl of twelve has always been considered of marriageable age among them, and as from that time on she has two or more husbands, it seems small wonder that the race is dying out. In this tribe the men outnumber the women, as usually happens among uncivilized peoples, and the sexual ties might really be regarded rather more as promiscuity slightly veiled than as anything else.

POLYANDRY has always been recognized in Tibet, where among the Ladakhs it is a settled practice. There a woman's head-dress announces the fact that she has husbands in the plural, and her broad smiling face indicates that she considers it a distinction. The cap she wears is not unlike that in favour with our grandmothers, where a tongue projects over the forehead; this is often decorated with turquoise matrix, for turquoises are found in the hilly country. The women fluff out their hair in great woolly tufts over the ears on each side of the decorous cap, and as the hair is never combed or brushed, its state may be better imagined than described.

Polyandry is found also among the Bhotias of the same region. With them it is confined to the brothers of one family. When the eldest brother takes a wife she can have sexual relations with any of her husband's younger brothers, until one of them marries on his own account, when he sets up a separate establishment. Any resulting children are assigned to each

PLURALITY OF HUSBANDS IN THE SOUTH SEA ISLANDS

E.N.A.

A plurality of husbands is a far less common state of affairs than a plurality of wives. Polyandry is generally the marriage of a woman with a family of brothers, although it exists in other forms, and not infrequently verges on communal marriage. It occurs in certain well defined areas, and is most common in Tibet The photograph shows a native woman of the island of Tegua, in the Torres group of the South Sea Islands, with two of her husbands and two of her children.

man in turn, without the least reference to possible paternity. Any women not 'placed' as wives become nuns. Polyandry of this type is also found among certain Sudra castes in the Punjab. Polyandry used to be in common practice among other Punjab and United Province races, but has now died out. Until fairly recently, a woman who married in Ambala took as husbands by that one act not only her husband's brothers, but his first cousins as her secondary husbands as well.

Among the Santals of India there is a further extension of the fraternal type of polyandry. The wife marries her husband's brothers temporarily, and he does the same in regard to her younger sisters. Here we approach the communal type of marriage. This kind of marriage is found as well among the Nairs, a low caste people in Malabar.

In the case where a woman marries an immature boy, as being the right mate for her, she is allowed freedom with his father or any near relation without any strictures on her conduct. This custom obtains among some low Hindu castes, and among such primitive peoples jealousy as we know it does not seem to exist. If a husband of the Tootiyans finds his door barred and the shoe of a relative before it, to signify that the owner is in occupation, he will not seek to enter, nor does he feel any resentment, but such freedom on the part of a man of another caste would arouse him to revenge. This state of affairs is found among the Kudans and Paravans.

While polygamy is the rule among the Todas, one of the primitive peoples of India, known principally as earth-eaters, it is strictly forbidden by the Bhils, who rank with these people in a low scale of humanity, but are monogamous.

As a recognized social institution polyandry is found only among the peoples mentioned above, but there are exceptional and sporadic instances in widely separated parts of the world. For instance, among the Eskimo and Asiatic Polar races it is not uncommon, and in Central Asia it is found among the Bahima and the Baziba with whom brothers too poor to afford to buy wives for themselves club together and have one in common.

The curious custom of 'pirauru' among Australian aborigines has been often described. It had its origin in the custom of giving a young girl to an old man who is able to afford the price her father puts upon her. As it is only the older men of the community who, as a rule, are able to purchase wives, this would bear very hardly on the younger men in the full vigour of their prime, were there not certain tacitly licensed customs which enable each and every young woman to form a sort of secondary union with a man of her own age as she pleases. These unions are recognized, and do not arouse hostility on the part of the husbands. The men of each 'pirauru' group are either nearly related, such as brothers or first cousins, or at any rate belong to the same subdivision of the tribe. The women are also closely related; the children are held in common as far as paternity goes, as is inevitable; and all the mothers would look after any child as if it were her own.

Mondiale

BADGE OF MARITAL PLURALITY

In Tibet, where polyandry has long been an established custom, the woman who has more than one husband wears this form of head-dress, made of wool and cane and decorated with turquoise and coral. Usually the husbands are brothers. The marriage of cousins is illegal

Here we find a connecting line to the community idea of group motherhood, which seems more natural to primitive peoples than it does to us. This is carried out to some degree in the practice of the Nupe people in sending away their own children to relations and receiving those of others. In certain parts of Africa and in Melanesia and elsewhere the bigger children are relegated to special boys' and girls' houses and brought up communally. Interchange of children is common with the Dravidian races.

It has been generally supposed that polyandry led directly to matriarchy, or the dominance of the women in the tribe, but this, like all firmly held theories, is now being questioned. In Briffault's recent work 'The Mothers' it is suggested that religion rather than ignorance of paternity may have been the root cause of matriarchy.

The wide divergence of customs in various parts of the world tends to loom large with people who come across them, but it may be taken as established that monogamy, in spite of these many instances to the contrary, was the original custom of mankind, and that mankind is tending more and more to become once again monogamous.

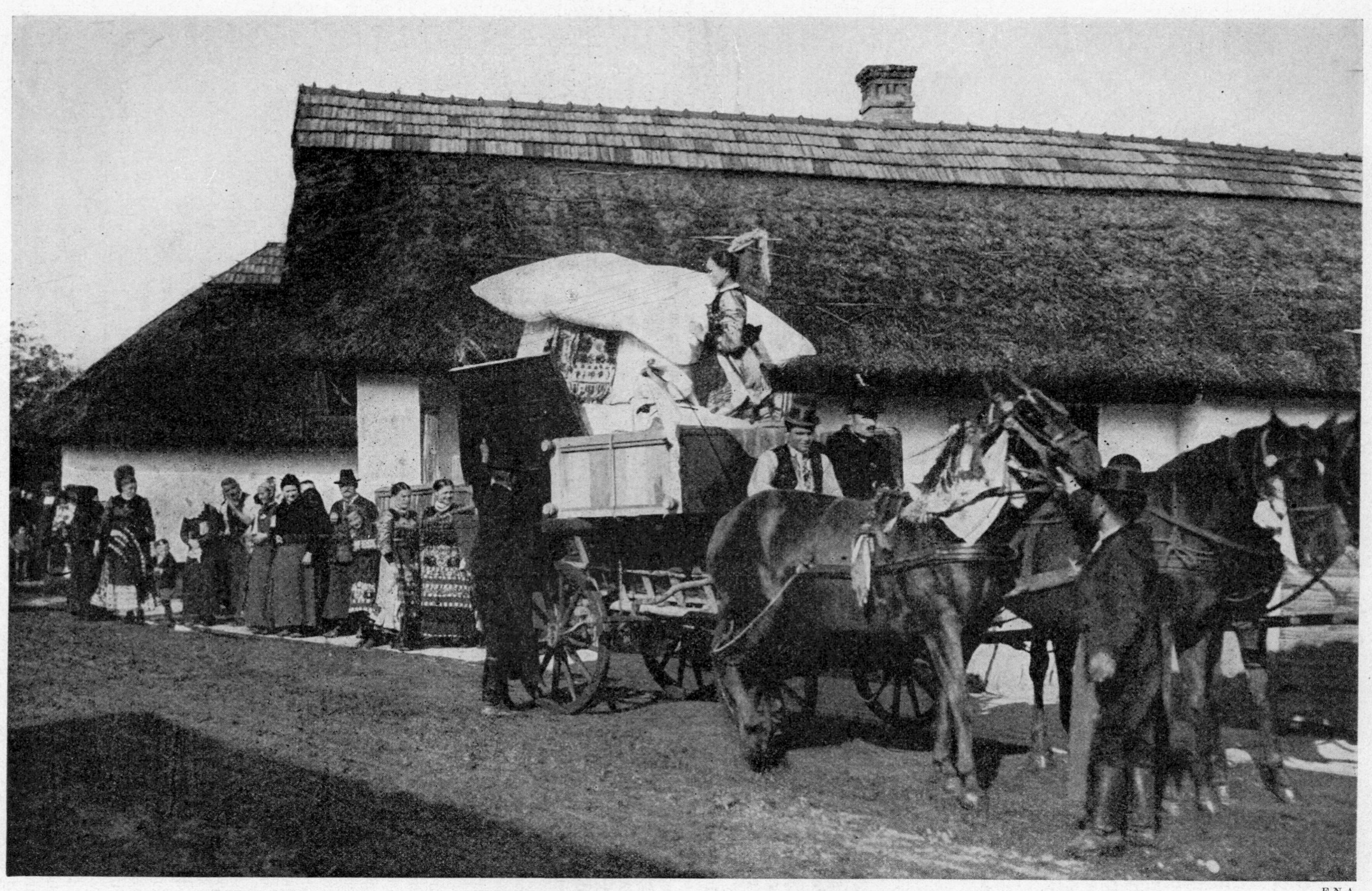

E.N.A.

AFTER THE MARRIAGE IN WESTERN HUNGARY: LOADING THE WAGON WITH THE WEDDING GIFTS

Many quaint wedding customs are observed by the peasants of the Mezökövesd district of Hungary, a region famed for its exquisite embroidery of gorgeous colours and intricate designs, as well as for the sturdy conservatism of its inhabitants. The festivities start in the early morning and finish at sunset. At their close the bridal couple leave the bride's house and proceed to drive to their new home. A wagon is piled high with the wedding presents, for old custom decrees that gifts to the bride and bridegroom must not be delivered at the new home until after the wedding ceremony. When all the presents, including the pillow bed coverings, are safely stowed on the wagon, the happy pair drive off amid the cheers and congratulations of the villagers.

MARRIAGE CUSTOMS OF CENTRAL EUROPE

A SERIES of chapters is devoted to the wedding ceremonies observed in various parts of Europe. Others cover marriage customs obtaining in the East, Africa and Oceania. The subject of marriage in general is discussed in the chapter on The Various Forms of Marriage, while specific aspects are dealt with in the chapters on Polygamy and Polyandry, Strange Marriage Prohibitions, and others.

THE marriage customs of Central and Eastern Europe have a diversity of which the full significance can be appreciated only when it is viewed in relation to the history and development of European culture. In part this variety arises from differences of race ; still more it is due to historical causes. In the west those people who, for linguistic reasons, are grouped as Teutonic came early into the main stream of cultural development : they shared the heritage of the Roman Empire in the western civilization which emerged from the Middle Ages. In the east the Slavs, no less a Nordic people, but geographically remote and submerged under the conquering Turk, the Tatar or the Magyar, made little advance on their tribal or village organization. They retained much of their traditional culture down to modern times. Notwithstanding the levelling effect of a world war and the influence of returning emigrants, parts of Eastern Europe are now only emerging from conditions comparable to those of the early Middle Ages ; and in the Balkans the blood feud flourishes, though cloaked under the veil of political rivalry.

Geographical conditions have played their part. In the great central plains the ebb and flow of racial migration and invasion have obliterated much that was distinctive in racial tradition ; but in the remote valleys of the mountain chains which form the backbone of Europe and in the heavily forested areas customs and beliefs have survived the centuries. Charlemagne's conquering armies were unable to subdue the tribes who withdrew to the mountain fastnesses, and Christian missionaries reported that in the Hartz these people were able to carry on their pagan rites free from hindrance. In modern times Switzerland has successfully maintained her independence and her customs in the face of war and the more insidious dangers of peace.

Consequently it is not surprising to find that in Holland, for instance, in Belgium and in many parts of Germany and Austria there is often little in the marriage customs that can be regarded as racially or culturally distinctive. There are practices and beliefs in plenty connected with marriage which are indicative of a primitive mode of thought ; but they are in the nature of superstitions which have as their object the promotion of the happiness and prosperity of the bridal pair or the averting of ill luck. On the other hand it is equally true that in the remoter districts, which throughout their history have been less accessible to outside cultural influences, such as Switzerland, Tirol, among the Slav population of certain parts of Bohemia and in Transylvania,

E.N.A.

DECORATING THE WEDDING CAKE IN HUNGARY

In Hungary the wedding cake is often of gargantuan proportions and covered with a profusion of elaborate ornaments. In some parts small decorated cakes, made in a variety of complicated shapes—churches, stags, cocks and so forth—are brought by guests to serve as presents for the bride.

traditional ceremonies are observed which can only be interpreted as survivals of some very primitive conceptions of the marriage rite.

In antiquity among Teutons and Slavs alike there were two forms of marriage—marriage by purchase, whereby the bridegroom in virtue of a payment in money or kind secured to himself exclusive rights over the person of his bride, and, secondly, marriage by capture. Both these have left their traces in the marriage customs of the simpler peoples, the peasantry, of the Central Europe of today.

MANY customs point directly to a form of marriage by purchase. Thus in the Upper Palatinate (Bavaria) a young man gives to the lady of his choice an unequal number of coins which he has obtained by exchanging for his own. He must not obtain them from a woman, nor must a woman see them while they are in his possession. Among the Saxons of Transylvania if a girl takes a young man's fancy at a dance he will surreptitiously slip into her hand a coin wrapped in silver paper. A curious form of bidding custom is followed in Tirol. During the period of betrothal the intending bridegroom and bride, accompanied by the personage known as the procurator, take a meal at an inn. A dish of cabbage is placed on the table for which the bridegroom bids a contemptible sum. This the bride rejects with indignation, forcing him to offer more until an amount deemed satisfactory is reached. In this, as in other cases in which money

E.N.A

WHERE THE BEST MAN WALKS IN FRONT OF THE BRIDEGROOM

At weddings of the Bessanyo people, Hungarian folk dwelling south of Lake Balaton, the bridegroom's attendant heads the bridal procession, accompanied by a female companion, who carries a cock, emblematic of the manly qualities of the bridegroom. On his head he wears an evergreen wreath surmounted by a doll, the latter a symbol of the bridegroom's love for the bride. On behalf of the guests he drinks the health of the bride and bridegroom from a wooden flask. In both photographs the bridegroom is seen behind his attendant.

E.N.A.

SOME DUTIES OF THE BRIDE'S AND BRIDEGROOM'S FRIENDS IN HUNGARY

In many parts of Central Europe the bridegroom-to-be takes no personal part in the preliminary negotiations for the marriage ; these are left in the hands of friends or officials. The upper photograph shows a group of young Palocz peasants of the Matra mountain region of Hungary addressing, on behalf of a friend, the mother of a village beauty whose hand in marriage he desires. Below, girl friends of a village bride of Kapuvar, Hungary, are seen about to throw curiously fashioned cakes among the guests.

MAGYAR BRIDE WITH HER TULIP CHEST

A traditional institution among the Magyars is the tulip chest, which answers much the same purpose as the English 'bottom drawer.' The chests vary in size, some being used only for trinkets and other small articles. They are usually made of acacia wood, and are painted with designs, of which the tulip is the commonest motif.

payments are made directly to the bride, it may be concluded that they survive from the time when the bride-price formed part or the whole of the dower of the bride, her marriage settlement, rather than from the earlier form in which payment was made to the bride's family group.

It is, however fully in accordance with the primitive conception of marriage as a concern of the group rather than of the individual that it is exceptional for the principal to appear in or take part in the preliminary negotiations for marriage. These are sometimes assigned to a woman match-maker, especially among the Slav peoples, but more often they form part of the duties of the official known variously as the procurator or the 'wedding announcer,' a personage of great importance whose office is frequently hereditary. He must be a person of great tact and affability. Most generally his duties are to announce the wedding and convey invitations personally to the guests. He himself is the most important of the guests at the wedding feast.

In many places, however, his duties are far wider. In Bohemia he invites the members of the two families to the conference at which the preliminaries are discussed. He takes a prominent part in the discussion and when it is over demands the production of the bride. In Tirol his first visit is paid to the house of the bride and she is the first guest to be invited to the wedding. In some parts he stays in the house for the night. On his calls on other invited guests he is accompanied by the bride's brother, known as the 'hen prigger,' as he improves the occasion by stealing a hen whenever the opportunity arises. In the Thur valley the procurator accompanies the would-be bridegroom to the lady's house, and after breakfast makes a speech to the bride's parents extolling the qualities of the man and asking for their daughter in marriage. He is answered by a rival orator, who praises the virtues of the bride and points out the difficulties which stand in the way of the union.

From these and other customs of a somewhat similar character it is evident that the procurator acts as the representative of the groom's group. Occasionally he is responsible for payments which may represent the marriage payment on their behalf. On the other hand, his function may be connected derivatively with marriage by capture, for at times his place is taken at certain stages of the ceremonial by the groomsman, whose duties in marriage ceremonies are usually interpreted as survivals of the various acts performed by the leader of the groom's friends when they carry

E.N.A.

TIME-HONOURED CEREMONIES OF BRIDAL PROCESSION AND BRIDE CAKE IN MORAVIA

Unlike the Teutonic peoples, the Slavs, in their Eastern home, harassed by the Turks and other alien masters, were little touched by Western culture. And so we find in the Slav countries many of the old traditional customs flourishing today. Especially is this true of wedding ceremonies. In Moravia the route taken by the bride and bridegroom is sometimes decorated with elaborate carpet-like designs in chalk (top). Below is seen a bevy of Moravian girls with floral head-dresses carrying between them a three-tiered wedding cake.

Ewing Galloway

BLENDING OF THE OLD AND THE NEW AT A FASHIONABLE WEDDING IN PRAGUE

In the great centres of Bohemia Western culture holds sway; it is chiefly in the remoter districts that the traditional national customs and costumes are found in all their rich picturesqueness. On such festive occasions as weddings the old and the new are sometimes mingled. In this photograph of a wedding party leaving a Prague church the general note is modern; all wear conventional European attire, the bridegroom being in evening dress. Those waiting outside, however, are arrayed in the traditional costumes. On the steps of the porch a man holds aloft with a striped pole a canopy of leaves and flowers. To this canopy are fastened ribbons, the ends of which are held by women, the whole roughly resembling in shape a vast umbrella.

off the bride on his behalf. In Bohemia before the actual marriage service begins the groomsman places the bride's mantle over the bridegroom so that it covers his whole body. This is said to prevent the 'marriage devil' from slipping in between two hearts which would be united. It is significant, however, that this service should be performed by the groomsman, for it is a very primitive form of the marriage rite.

A curious ceremony takes place in the Bohemian Erzegebirge on the morning after the wedding. Two little girls enter the bride's chamber and put the bride's cap on her head three times. Each time it is crooked and has to be taken off. Then in comes an old frau, who sets it straight. The bride is then escorted downstairs to breakfast, but this is done by the groomsman, who afterwards dances with her while the bridegroom stands by. The dance is stayed, and it is announced that the bride is for sale. The bridegroom offers a few gulden, and she is allotted to him. He then dances with her; but it is a requirement of the ritual that she should dance very clumsily. There are other customs in which the groom has to make a similar payment before the bride's person is ceded to him.

In Switzerland it happens frequently that the bride is stolen either before or after the marriage ceremony. In one case in South Tirol this takes place on the Saturday before the first calling of the banns. The youths who are responsible for the escapade bring her back to the church, when she has to walk three times round the nave. They then carry her off to an inn, where all join in a feast. Not only has the groom to pay for this, but he must make further payment before the girl will be delivered up to him. These customs suggest that the groomsman, and his friends, once had rights such as among savages are often associated with marriage by capture. In East Africa the friends of the groom who bring back the bride exact a recompense which is sometimes commuted for a payment. On the other hand, it may be a dim memory of the time when, as we are told by some of the classical writers, the German women were polyandrous, but were turning to the monogamy which according to later writers was their characteristic form of marriage. Another custom appears to point to the exercise of sexual rights over the bride.

In Bavaria the so-called 'bride's race' takes place before the inn at which the marriage feast is held. The goal is represented by two bundles of straw which the winner carries to the bride. The prize of the race was, in olden times, the key of the bridal chamber. This has now been replaced by a wooden key. In the Upper Palatinate the goal is the best man's hat, and the prize a money present from the bridegroom. The phrase 'key of the bridal chamber' is also used in connexion with a money payment to the bride's

Keystone

BRIDESMAID OF SLOVAKIA IN TRADITIONAL DRESS

Few countries can boast such exquisite peasant needlework as Slovakia, the eastern division of the new republic of Czechoslovakia. With the development of modern commerce the beautiful traditional costume is seldom seen, except on festal occasions. The dress of a bridesmaid of Slovakia comprises a blouse, bodice, skirt and lace cap, all gaily embroidered.

Mondiale

WHERE THE BEST MEN MAY BE AS NUMEROUS AS THE BRIDESMAIDS

In Slovakia the farce of stealing the bride is sometimes enacted, and in other parts of Central Europe the wedding customs provide examples of so-called 'marriage by capture.' In Rumania the bridegroom carries off the bride on his horse; the Magyar groom mounts her on a horse and rides away with her. In Slovakia there is not one best man, but a party of attendants on the bridegroom. The best men and bridesmaids here seen are officiating at a wedding at Piestany, in Slovakia.

family. At Tagerfelden, in Switzerland, when the groom's party come to fetch the bride she hides in her chamber, of which the entrance is guarded by her mother until she receives the 'key' in the shape of a silver coin.

A curious practice is frequently observed in connexion with the custom of fetching or demanding the bride from her family. It occurs among most of the peoples of Central Europe, and as far afield as Rumania. This is the substitution of an old woman for the bride. It may be due to a former reluctance to lose a young member of the family group when raided by outsiders. More probably it arises from a desire to divert to one who is past the age to be harmfully affected all the harmful influences to which a bride is exposed. Thus at the meeting of the families in Bohemia to which reference has been made the bride and bridegroom are present but take no part in the proceedings, the former hiding behind the stove. When the negotiations are complete the procurator demands the bride. A veiled figure is brought forward, but on inspection this proves to be an old woman and not the bride In Tirol the groomsmen call at the bride's house for the bride, demanding 'a maiden whom they bade pick rosemary and darn old linen.' A hideous old woman holding a bunch of nettles and a basketful of torn linen is brought forward, and it is only when she has received a suitable payment that the father brings out the bride, who holds some sprigs of rosemary in one hand and in the other a shirt which she has made for the best man.

It is in favour of the view that this is an attempt to avert evil from the bride that during the period of betrothal, which is usually short—generally not more than a fortnight—the betrothed damsel is peculiarly susceptible to evil influences. In the Upper Palatinate (Bavaria) she must not come into contact with the dead or dying, and may not pick up anything that lies in her path lest evil fortune may follow.

The belief that the bridal pair, or one of them, may be the vehicle of evil influence is illustrated by a number of customs which could only have originated in connexion with the practice of exogamy—marriage with someone of another group, in this case with someone of another village. Frequently the dowry cart which carries the bride's belongings—everywhere an important factor in marriage ceremonial—or the vehicle bringing the bride to her new home, is barred by the youths of the village, who stretch ropes across the highway until a ransom has been paid by the bridegroom. At Aargan (Baden) if the bridegroom refuses to pay he is allowed to pass, but pistols are fired as he moves forward.

E.N.A.

DANCING AND FINE FEATHERS AT WEDDINGS IN POLAND AND TIROL

Both Poland and Tirol are very rich in folklore, and in no direction is this more apparent than in the multiplicity of interesting marriage customs. Some of these, such as the very curious auction ceremony current in Tirol, seem to be survivals from a period when marriage by purchase was the rule. The lower photograph shows a wedding dance in the Lowicz district of Poland; the bride, with her elaborate head-dress, is seen in the background. The upper photograph depicts a Tirolese wedding party.

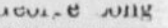

Ewing Galloway

BRIDES AND GROOMS IN REGIONS WHERE OF OLD THE BRIDE WAS PURCHASED

The ancient practice of wife-purchase is traceable in some of the marriage customs of modern Germany. In Hesse, Bavaria and elsewhere a successful suitor presents the girl with a money gift. The costumes of long ago are still everyday wear among the peasantry of Hesse-Nassau, the women sporting a short full skirt, white stockings, buckled shoes, and a curious head-dress. The lower photograph shows a woman friend congratulating a bridegroom, beside whom is the elaborately bedizened bride. Above is seen a wedding party in Bavaria.

The efficacy of gunpowder as a means of scaring spirits is an article of faith in peasant lore in many countries.

How great is the power of the spirits over the married couple is shown by the elaborate precautions taken at the coming of the bride and her possessions to the husband's house in the Upper Palatinate.

G.P.A.

-AVARIAN BRIDE-TO-BE DISCARDS HER HEAD-DRESS

Throughout Germany traditional costume, varying according to the district and the age, station, single or married state of the wearers, is frequently seen in the more sequestered parts. In the Bavarian mountain village of Garmish girls who are not betrothed wear the quaint hats seen in the photograph. As soon as a girl is engaged she ceases to wear the hat.

THE bride follows the dowry cart, weeping as she goes, in order that she may not be forced to shed tears in her married life. Five crosses are sewn on the bed cover so that witches may not cast spells over her. The spinning wheel is placed in the cart with the distaff side toward the horses so that she need not be afraid of dying in childbed ; and in some places the first thing she carries into her new home is a crucifix. On his side the bridegroom is equally anxious to avert misfortune. He marks each article belonging to the bride with consecrated chalk as the cart is unloaded, sprinkling it with holy water. Also as the cart approaches he must pay a fine of a florin to each of the lads who bar its way with poles. The priest blesses all the bride's goods when they have been disposed in the house, and the young pair then go to the churchyard to pray at the graves of their ancestors.

The reluctance to admit an outsider even after marriage is shown in the custom of barring the bride from her future home. For the credit of the peasant it must be said that it is more common for her husband's parents to welcome her at the door. In the Aar Valley of French Switzerland the bridegroom and his parents hurry away from the feast at the inn before the bride and the guests. On reaching home they bar every door and window. When the bride arrives the groomsman knocks at the door and demands admittance, but this is refused until he has answered satisfactorily a catechism as to the qualities and capabilities of the bride In the village of Pergine the mother-in-law used to slam the door in the face of her new daughter-in-law, who demanded admission in words of an unknown tongue of which the meaning had been lost.

In contrast with the exogamy which underlies most of the customs to which reference has already been made is the village endogamy of Switzerland The marriage customs of Switzerland and Tirol embody features which are more primitive than any in the practices of other districts to which reference has been made here. Girls are allowed very great freedom both of election and of action during their courtship. The lover may visit his lady in her chamber at night—a custom known in the north of England and in Scotland as ' bundling,' and at one time followed also in America. Notwithstanding

Wide World Photos

OLD-FASHIONED BONNET OF A BRIDE OF NORTH HOLLAND

Although there is little that is particularly distinctive in the marriage customs of Holland, a wedding in that country is a picturesque affair by reason of the delightful local costumes that are worn on such an occasion. Unfortunately the traditional dress is being largely abandoned by the younger generation; it is most frequently seen in the maritime provinces and on the shores of the Zuider Zee. The photograph shows a bride of Drenthe, North Holland, with her attendants, the bride wearing a bonnet tied with broad ribbons.

this freedom, however, the choice of a husband is usually restricted to a member of the village. In some parts the youths band themselves into a society to keep away wooers from other villages. If a girl is too kind to those from outside her own village she may find that, instead of the young pine decked with ribbons which the lover plants before the door of his beloved on May 1, a straw puppet dangles at her window or her father's wagon lies overturned on the village green.

Many interesting and significant customs must be passed over Such, for instance, as those connected with the making, wearing and taking off of the bridal head-dress. One observance, however, must be mentioned. In Germany the Polterabend is clearly a survival of the consummation as an essential feature in marriage ceremonial which had to be publicly announced. Among the upper classes it is an entertainment given by the bride's family on the eve of the marriage. The party should be as boisterous as possible. All cracked crockery and glass is thrown out of doors, and the greater the quantity the greater the good luck which will be the lot of the married pair. Should a window be broken accidentally assurance is made doubly sure. Among the peasantry it is the custom for the boys of the village to throw crockery against the bride's door, and the greater the pile of sherds the greater the luck.

The marriage customs of the Magyars of Hungary, as distinct from those of the Czech population, are among the most picturesque in Europe. They have adopted certain practices from their Slav neighbours, but the most striking feature is the number of entertainments held at inns and private houses, in which music and singing by Tzigane musicians, dancing and speech-making are never-ending. Equally characteristic is the length of the negotiations, and the caution displayed in delaying final consent and agreement to the match by all concerned, including the principals.

THE BALLET IN MODERN EUROPE

ORIENTAL ballet, sacred and secular, is dealt with in several other chapters in this work. Our subject here is the ballet as presented in the West, mainly as a spectacle and including the forms of highly-trained troupe dancing known as Neo-classical and Eurythmics. National Dances of Europe are described under that heading and also under British Folk Dances.

TO our grandfathers, the ballet meant stage dancing of a formal and rather stiff nature by women in skirts often so short that they could hardly be called skirts at all. These were starched or by other means artificially stiffened and sometimes stuck out almost straight from the waist. They never reached below the knee. To us the ballet means graceful dancing in flowing draperies. Instead of the low-cut tight bodice of the old ballerina the stage dancers of to-day wear, as a rule, Greek tunics. Their feet, instead of being encased in padded shoes, which helped them to walk on their toes, are usually bare. Their steps are not regulated by tradition, but are free, stately, harmonious. This change is due chiefly to the efforts of one person, Isadora Duncan born in 1878.

This remarkable American woman felt that she had been born to give the world a new conception of dancing. She went back to ancient Greece for her inspiration, studied the Greek vases in museums, meditated on the dances of antiquity in Athens 'To dance is to live,' she cried. 'It is to cultivate the soul and the imagination.' If she could have a hundred children to train for five years, she could, she declared, produce beauty and riches beyond imagining Of the impression made on sensitive spirits by her own dancing a famous musical critic (Ernest Newman) wrote:

> What she gives us is a sort of sculpture in transition. Imagine a dozen statues expressive, say, of the cardinal phases of despair—the poses and gestures and facial expressions of the moment in which each of these phases reaches its maximum of intensity. Then imagine some hundreds of statues that represent, in faultless beauty, every one of the moments of slow transition between these cardinal phases and you get the art of Isadora Duncan. . . The muscular control they imply is itself wonderful enough but more wonderful still must be the brain that can conceive and realize all these faultless harmonies of form. She seems to transfer her magic even to the fabrics she works with; no one who has ever seen it can forget the beauty of the slow sinking of her cloak to earth in one of her dances; the ripples in it move the spirit like a series of soft, mysterious undulations in music.

Photopress

DANCE PRACTICE IN A LONDON GARDEN

True dancing demands the service of every particle of the body. In the Margaret Morris School as much attention is paid to the movements of the arms as to those of the legs and feet. How successful the results achieved may be is suggested in this action photograph.

EARLY in the century she gave performances in New York and London, but her revolutionary ideas (' every artist must be a revolutionary to make a mark in the world,' was one of her sayings) made little stir until she went to St. Petersburg in 1905. Russia was the home of the old traditional ballet. At the Imperial Theatres in the capital and in Moscow the short-skirt, tip-toe method of dancing was most carefully and expensively kept up. When Isadora Duncan appeared before a crowd of fashionable spectators she thought: 'How strange these people who are used to sumptuous ballets produced regardless of expense must think the appearance of a young girl in a spider-web tunic dancing to the music of Chopin before a blue curtain!' Yet her performance was enthusiastically applauded, and next day she had a visit of congratulation from the leading dancer at the opera, Kschessinska, followed by one from the equally celebrated Anna Pavlova. True artists, they could see what was beautiful in this new kind of dancing, although it was so totally unlike their own, and although Isadora Duncan considered the old ballet ' false and absurd, not an art at all,' she could not help applauding the fairy-like

Keystone

REALISM AND ANCIENT STYLISM IN THE 'DECOR' OF BALLETS

Although ostensibly a parody of pantomime, the Triumph of Neptune, the final tableau of which is shown below, is really almost early Victorian pantomime itself. The choregrapher was Balanchin, and Sitwell's libretto and Lord Berners' music provide the English atmosphere. The curious décor, by Rieti, has special interest as being taken from the old toy theatre scenery for which Mr. Pollock of Hoxton is famous. The upper photograph shows a particularly successful realistic effect achieved in the Dance of the Gulls as performed by the Eduardowa Ballet in Berlin

J. E. Pryde Hughes

CHORIC JUBILATION WHEN THE FLOWERS ARE IN BLOOM

Somewhat analogous to vintage and harvest festivals, although not of the same antiquity, are the various Continental flower festivals, of which the Fête des Narcisses at Montreux may be considered representative. The lower photograph shows the finale of the ballet Nymphes des Bois as performed at Montreux on one of these occasions by the ballet company of the Théâtre Royale de la Monnaie of Brussels. Similarly, Locarno has its camellia festival in April, and a dance by the school children (top) is a pretty item of the celebrations.

stage appearance of Kschessinska, 'more like a bird or some charming butterfly than a human being.'

The Russian Imperial Ballet was, indeed, an odd mixture of absurdity and charm. While it was impossible for foreigners to appreciate, or even to notice, the technical triumphs which frequently made the whole theatre break out into vigorous applause, it was equally impossible not to be delighted by the exquisite movements of the principal dancers, the grace of their pose, their marvellously agile, yet apparently effortless, jumps and twirls. Whole evenings were devoted to the presentation of ballets based on some old legend or folk-lore tale, and still are, under Soviet rule. 'The Hunchback Horse,' for example, is as much a favourite with popular audiences now as it was with the aristocratic and official frequenters of the ballet. Every scene was regulated by strict adherence to tradition. Pupils attended a special school, which was not easy to get into, and had to go through a very severe training. The old ballet, indeed, always demanded from its exponents long and patient labours. A famous dancer at the Paris Opéra described in a book on theatrical dancing how she had to work as a child.

I began at seven years old, and my mother used to wake me, winter and summer alike, at half-past seven. I had to leave our lodgings at an hour that would enable me to be dressed and in class by nine o'clock. An omnibus was beyond my small means. I had to make the journey on foot. The morning lesson lasted from nine o'clock to half-past ten. After this I changed my dress and returned home for my small lunch at noon. Not that I always got off after my lesson. There were days, frequent enough, on which I had to attend rehearsals at the Opera, where young pupils like myself were employed to 'walk on.' On those days I lunched at the school with my mother off a frugal meal that we brought with us in a basket, after which we went to the rehearsal, which lasted till two o'clock. Then I was at last free. But on the evenings when I had to 'walk on' I had to leave home again at seven o'clock, and often the piece lasted until midnight. On these occasions my poor mother literally dragged me along on her arm, and we would arrive at our lodgings, worn out, at one o'clock.

THE discipline of the Imperial Opera School in Russia was not less severe, yet there was brisk competition to enter it. The rewards of the dancers who reached the highest rank were high, and they enjoyed a brilliant celebrity as well—not only while their vogue lasted, but afterwards as teachers, or perhaps as the wives of high officials—maybe the unofficial wives of Grand Dukes or even Tsars. The ballet was, in fact, part of the Bureaucratic Machine, and might have been expected to offer determined resistance to any 'revolutionary' who attempted to introduce new methods, or, worse still, new ideas. There could be no finer proof of the Russian artist's devotion to the ideals of beauty than the welcome given to Isadora Duncan and her entirely new style of dancing. Sculptors and painters were enchanted by it. In Moscow, where her success was at first in doubt, they turned its tide in her favour. At first there were a good many hisses because she was doing

Keystone

ENERGY AND ELEGANCE TUTORED BY DISCIPLINE

Physical exercises of the most strenuous kind are a necessary part of the training of every ballet dancer. The six girls seen here are members of the Kosloff ballet holding an open-air rehearsal at Los Angeles, California, before appearing in public. The muscular effort required in such leaping as this might tax a powerful male athlete, but long practice, combined with perfect physical fitness, enables these delicately built young women to accomplish it with apparently effortless ease.

Illustrations Bureau

FOUR-AND-TWENTY TILLER GIRLS DANCING IN A RING

If a distinctively English method of dancing may be said to exist, it is that taught at the schools of Mr. John Tiller in Manchester, London and Paris. Tiller girls usually appear in troupes of ten or twelve, occasionally of as many as twenty-four. Buoyancy, freedom from mannerisms, absence of acrobatic extravagance, and easy execution of comparatively simple movements are distinguishing notes of their dancing, with, above all, perfect identity and synchronisation of movement. In their mastery of this last accomplishment English girls are unapproached by the dancers of any other country.

something unusual. But when it was seen that she was warmly applauded not only by stage favourites, but by men famous in other worlds of art and literature, the applause became general and Moscow confirmed the verdict of St. Petersburg. Soon the effect was seen on the Russian stage. Long-skirt dancing was introduced. A ballet called 'Chopiniana' to airs from some of the best-known of the nocturnes and studies, became very popular. The old kind of ballet was not, of course, given up. That would have been fiercely resented; probably it would be if such a step were proposed even now. But the new spirit had made itself felt, and when 'stars' from the Russian State Theatres came to London and Paris and Berlin, their performances were very much in the modern manner. When for the first time a section of the Russian ballet company made a tour in 1909, the arrangements were entrusted to Sergei Diaghileff, a strong supporter of Isadora Duncan, as was also Michael Fokine, the inventor of the Imperial ballets, who gradually put into them what he learned from her, developed and modified by his own genius.

From 1909 on the Russian ballet became an entertainment immensely admired in London. Numbers of famous dancers brought companies of their own and quickly established themselves in public favour. First and always foremost among them was Anna Pavlova, who settled down to live in England permanently. Others of almost equal power to attract were Karsavina, wife of an English diplomatist named Bruce; Lydia Kyasht; and Lopokova, who married the well-known economist, Maynard Keynes. Even the provinces saw the Russian dancers on tour, and companies still go round with a good deal of success, though the novelty of the thing has worn off and it has not taken deep root as it did in Russia.

Meanwhile, in return for the pleasure that the new form of ballet was giving outside that country, the creator of it returned there to start a great school

E. O. Hoppé

occasionally to the Italian short-skirt and tip-toe methods, the new style killed the old. In beauty there could be no comparison between them, and although the new might appear to be very much easier, because it seems easy and natural, it does, in fact, demand as much work and far more thought than the old. Dancing has become to a much greater extent than ever before the interpretation of music. The old ballets had music written to suit them. Many of the new ballets adapt themselves to music by the most famous composers. It can be interpreted in different ways, according to the temperament — and even the political opinions—of the dancer. Cardinal Richelieu is said to have used ballet for purposes of statecraft in the 17th century. Here is a description of Isadora Duncan dancing Tchaikovski's 'Marche Slave,' which is an Imperial Tsarist hymn, and turning it into an idyll of revolution.

She depicted in moving gestures a bent, oppressed, heavy-laden, fettered slave who

of dancing for children—the dream of her life. The Soviet Government asked her to go, but when she had begun with about forty boys and girls, they announced that they could give her no more money. Thus the scheme collapsed and she continued her career as a dancer. For a time she tried to earn enough to keep the school going. She went to America for this purpose, but a foolish speech made from the stage in Boston gave the newspapers the chance to represent her as a 'Red'—a Communist, and when to this charge were added aspersions on her private life and morality, her tour was ruined. She left the United States, declaring that Americans 'knew nothing of Love, Food, Art or Freedom,' She died in 1927, and Yvette Guilbert mourned her as 'a goddess unique, who had made a great dream, a great art, live again, revealing the past, the present and the future; a genius, superhuman.'

Although some of the Russian 'stars' still went back

Sasha

STARS IN THE DIAGHILEFF CONSTELLATION

Choregrapher of many notable productions of the Diaghileff company, Leonide Massine will be remembered also as a dancer of the first rank. He is seen here with Lubov Tchernicheva in the ballet Les Fâcheux. Lydia Lopokova was essentially a dancer of character parts. One rôle in which she was especially successful was that of the doll dancer in Petrouschka (top).

Armand Console

"AND THEY LIVED HAPPILY EVER AFTER": JOYOUS FINALE OF CEPHALUS AND PROCRIS

Proof of the hold that the ballet is securing on the British public is provided by the foundation of the Camargo Society for the production of original and classic ballets in London. In January, 1931, Andre Grétry's Cephalus and Procris was produced under its auspices, an interesting point being that, apart from the music, this was an entirely British performance, choregrapher, costume designer and all the dancers being British. The story tells how Cephalus, resisting Aurora's amorous overtures, is persuaded by the goddess to test the fidelity of his wife Procris by returning to her disguised as a rich merchant. Procris accepts his addresses, but discovering his identity, flees to Diana. Later, Procris tests Cephalus by a similar artifice and, his inconstancy having in turn been established, husband and wife are reconciled.

falls exhausted to his knees. Now see what happens to this slave at the first notes of the accursed 'national anthem.' He lifts his weighed-down head, and his face shows an awful grimace of hate. With all his force he straightens himself and breaks his chains. Then he brings from behind his back his crooked and stiffened arms—forward to a new and joyful life! The allegory was understood by everyone.

She danced also Tchaikovski's 'Pathetic Symphony,' illustrated with her face, her body, the whole of her, flesh and spirit, the joy and sorrow, the birth and death, the descent into the depths and the triumphal uprising, which she found in the music.

Another of the pioneers in this direction was Maud Allan, a Canadian from Toronto, who, beginning as a pianist, decided to study dancing and appeared at the London Coliseum in 1908 (the year before the Russian ballet went to Paris for the first time), arousing immense enthusiasm. At that time the favourite dancer of the capital was Adeline Genée, a Scandinavian of delicious charm and very distinguished ability in the old manner. Without renouncing their allegiance to her, Londoners put Maud Allan on a pedestal equally high. Her method did not derive from the Greek nearly so much as Isadora Duncan's. There was more of the East in it. Her undulating arms (unkind critics said 'writhing'), her swaying body and the ripples of motion which passed over it recalled the dances of India, Japan and Indo-China. Japanese theatre dancers rely less for their effects on legs and feet than on arms and hands. Now these are waved with quiet elegance, now agitated violently yet still with grace, now thrust out in energetic appeal or as a symbol of triumphant force. A fan is often held, and sometimes a scarf in the hand of a dancer is used to suggest various objects or to add to the attractiveness of dramatic movement. Maud Allan's dancing was more akin to this kind than to the classical mode. It captivated quickly a large public, partly because it was beautiful, partly because it was new. At all events, Adeline Genée never recovered her supreme position.

'The Times'

ANNA PAVLOVA IN THE DYING SWAN

Anna Pavlova brought the art of dancing as a medium for the expression of emotion to perfection, being indeed as truly a creative artist as any lyric poet. Her technique, grace and beauty were perhaps most exquisitely displayed in the ballet divertissement Le Cygne, for which Saint Saëns wrote the music.

E. O. Hoppé

LOVERS IN AN IDYLL OF LESBOS

In his choregraphy Michel Fokine ranks as the inventor and the supreme genius of the modern ballet. He is also a graceful and accomplished dancer, as may be judged from this photograph of him with Fokina in his Greek ballet Daphnis and Chloe.

FLOWING RHYTHM AND GRACE OF THE BALLET INDEPENDENT OF COSTUME—

Costume has had a very great deal to do with the evolution of the ballet, and in the history of modern theatrical dancing an epoch-marking event was the re-discovery of the flowing skirt. Kate Vaughan was the first perfect exponent of the skirt dance, and its success with the public was established at the Gaiety Theatre under the management of John Hollingshead from 1870 onwards. Since then no musical comedy has been complete without its chorus of pretty and accomplished skirt dancers, like these charming young women in 'Stand Up and Sing.'

Topical Press

Central Press

—-FULL DRAPERY FOR THE INDOOR DANCE: BARE LIMBS FOR THE OPEN AIR

Miss Margaret Morris founded her well-known school at Chelsea a few years before the Great War, and its influence since then has been widespread, largely owing to the practice of holding summer schools at various places in the country and abroad. The dancing, which is always performed bare-foot, is not 'classical' dancing but is properly described as Margaret Morris dancing based upon Raymond Duncan. Artistic posing is of the essence of the system and many lovely effects are obtained—witness the upper photograph, taken near Harlech.

Armand Console

SPIRIT OF MUSIC INTERPRETED IN THE DANCE OF THE BALLET: KARSAVINA IN LES SYLPHIDES

First produced in 1909, Les Sylphides relies for its success solely upon its musical and choregraphic interests. The music is an adaptation of various compositions of Chopin, and in the choregraphy Fokine's skill is seen at its highest. The piece, it has been said, has no action, no colour, no idea, almost no sentiment. It is one rhythmic flow of faultless gestures, which make a rounded whole of a chaste and immaculate quality like that of the finest sculpture. The dancers wear costumes of pure white, the skirt rather long, and more remarkable than the steps is the purity of the lines of the arms interweaving like the over-arching branches of a forest glade. Madame Karsavina is shown here with the Rambert Dancers in a performance of the ballet at Hammersmith in 1930.

Central Press

FINE CARELESS RAPTURE IN THE SPRINGTIDE OF LIFE

Quite apart from their primary purpose of training dancers for the stage, dancing lessons in the new mode cannot have anything but an extremely beneficial effect upon the health of all who are able to go in for them. For inasmuch as the new mode makes use of the whole body for the expression of emotion, it develops and strengthens all the muscles and all the organs of the frame. The splendid figure posturing here is a pupil at the Northern Heights School of Dancing, Highgate.

Many times had the short-skirt tradition been challenged. There was a whole school of 'skirt-dancers' twenty years before, with Kate Vaughan at their head, and Sylvia Grey, Letty Lind, Mabel Love as lesser lights. That they were called 'skirt-dancers' showed them to be in revolt against the 'regular' ballet, that in which Taglioni had made so great a name during the middle of the 19th century.

At this time ballets were still introduced into operas, sometimes made part of the story, as are the ballets of 'Faust' by Gounod, sometimes having no real connexion with the opera plot at all. Often the ballets excited audiences more than the operas, and until Jenny Lind appeared to entrance everyone with her singing Taglioni was the chief attraction of the operatic stage in London. Of her Thackeray said that 'future ages would never see anything so graceful.' Her method was described as 'floating.' She was light and extremely ethereal in her movements. She did not wear the very short ballet skirt. At that period dancers wore muslin reaching to their knees or below. At one time Taglioni's dress on the stage is said to have touched the ground. But her dancing and that of her contemporaries was toe-dancing. The new mode employed arms as much as legs and made use of the whole body for the expression of the emotions portrayed. It therefore developed and strengthened all the limbs and all parts of the frame, not only the calf and thigh muscles. In many ballet dancers of the old school these were brought to an abnormal size and power. Fanny Ellsler, a rival of Taglioni's, saw a man enter her bedroom one night

Photopress

ECSTATIC DANCE OF VIBRANT YOUTH BY THE SUNLIT SEA

Among English schools which specialise in the teaching of dances based on Greek models the Bagot-Stack Dancing Academy holds high place. These remarkably successful action photographs were taken at an exhibition performance given by some of its pupils at Clacton. Danced by the water's edge, in harmony with the rhythm of the wavelets lapping the sand and with the vibration of the sunlight on sea and shore, every movement was an object lesson in the expression of the strength and health and passionate joyousness of pulsing natural life.

Topical Press

RHYTHM OF MUSIC AND POETRY AS AIDS TO PHYSICAL GRACE

Eurhythmics has been defined as the art of expressing harmony by gesture in which physical movement is made to reflect musical notation. The system was invented by the Swiss composer, Jacques Dalcroze, while professor of harmony at Geneva, and in 1910 he established a school of eurhythmics near Dresden. Others now exist in London, New York and elsewhere. The upper photograph shows a demonstration of the Dalcroze system in London. Below, pupils of the somewhat similar Acton-Bond school of euchorics are seen dancing to a Breton folk song.

Keystone

HANDMAIDENS OF APOLLO CELEBRATING THE FESTIVAL OF DELPHI

In view of the enormous influence that the art of ancient Greece has had upon the ballet in Europe during the present century, it is a little surprising that modern Greece has made no substantive contribution to the development of this lovely art form. Some stirring in her sleep was, however, indicated by the revival in May, 1930, of the great Festival of Delphi—its second celebration in 1,500 years. The revival was largely due to the energy of Madame Eva Sikelianos, American wife of the Greek poet, Angeles Sikelianos.

and search for her jewels, which she kept under her pillow. When he approached the bed she leaped out and gave him one well-aimed kick in the chest. He died on the spot.

Skirt-dancing was at first performed in very voluminous draperies, double and sometimes triple skirts. These were held up in the hands, and a large part of the effect depended on their skilful manipulation. Loie Fuller was a specially clever adept in such performances. Coloured lights were turned on to her in quick succession as she danced. The result was something like the ever-changing combinations of a kaleidoscope ; it was very much to the taste of the variety theatre patrons, though an unfavourable critic called it ' no dance at all, a very monotonous and wearying performance, consisting in the twirling of many yards of some material in the manner of a mill-wheel.

There was some truth in that. The performances of Isadora Duncan and Maud Allan marked a great advance, though the Canadian dancer had neither the technical equipment nor the temperamental force of the American. They both approached nearer to emotional drama than any of their predecessors, and this tendency has been steadily increasing. The latest developments of dancing are really indistinguishable from wordless acting. Examples of this from the Diaghileff repertory are 'The Good-humoured Ladies,' 'The Three-Cornered Hat,' and, greatest favourite of all probably, 'La Boutique Fantasque.'

Scarcely any attempt has been made to construct music drama of this kind in England, but the enterprising German producer Reinhardt made several experiments along this line. He brought to London, just at the time when the new dancing had made a hit, 'The Miracle,' in which Maria Carmi played the Madonna, who takes the place of a nun while she is absent from the convent, making trial of the pleasures and griefs of the world outside its walls. In Germany this way of presenting a story by gesture and movement accompanied by music has gone much farther. It has borrowed something from Dalcroze, the Swiss inventor of eurhythmics (exercises with music), who also influenced Fokine in his reconstruction of the Russian ballet. Dalcroze's scheme is not exactly dancing, but rather callisthenics, designed to discipline both the limbs and the mind and bring them into harmony. As training for dancers in the modern way it is thus very useful, and German producers admit that they owe a good deal to it. They have borrowed a good deal, too, from the dance dramas of India, Indo-China and Malaysia—described in the chapters on Animal Dances of the East and the Golden Ballet of the East.

FOOD TABOOS AND THEIR MEANING

TABOOS concerning food are dictated by various motives. The animal prohibited may be a totem, a form of a deity, or otherwise sacred, or the taboo may hinge on rank or on imitative magic. The subject is touched upon in the chapters on Magic and the Means of Life and Totems and Totemism, and taboo generally is discussed under The Mysteries of Taboo.

DURING the war the Scottish Fresh-water Fisheries Committee issued a pamphlet entitled 'The common eel and its capture, with suggestions applicable to Scotland.' It appeared at a time when the food problem had become rather grave and contained the statement:

> The prejudice which exists against the eel in Scotland is most unfortunate, since it prevents Scotsmen taking advantage of a most nutritious fish which appears to be well distributed throughout our waters. . . . The serpent is a symbol of the devil, and all Highlanders know that the eel, being like the serpent, is like the symbol of the devil, and is associated with the evil influence. People who eat such creatures are, in their opinion, very far from particular in their feeding. The fact that many Continental peoples find the eel a most valuable food only shows that such foreigners will eat anything. The eel remains taboo

Mention was also made of the fact that the eel is eaten in England, and the writer added:

> Many a Scotsman, I have no doubt, has eaten most excellent 'filleted sole' in London and been quite unaware that in reality he was eating eel.

Other Scottish food prejudices are mentioned:

> Some people in the West Highlands will not eat mackerel: in the Solway till quite recently people would not touch skate; all over our country no one thought of eating dog-fish.

IT was added, however, that the war has taught or forced people to think about unfamiliar foods.

As deep-rooted as the eel taboo is the Scottish prejudice against pork, which was formerly widespread but is nowadays confined mainly to Highland areas. Thousands of Highlanders and Hebrideans still refuse to eat the flesh of the pig in any form. Dr. Johnson in his 'A Journey to the Western Islands' wrote:

> The vulgar inhabitants of Skye, I know not whether of the other islands, have not only eels, but pork and bacon in abhorrence; and accordingly I never saw a hog in the Hebrides except one at Dunvegan.

One of the Loyalist songs ridiculing the 'Rump Parliament' in the 17th century refers to

> The Jewish Scots that scorn to eat
> The flesh of swine.

Bishop Leslie, the 16th-century Scottish historian, refers to the pork taboo, and Sir Walter Scott, in a footnote in his 'The Fortunes of Nigel,' says that the Lowlanders 'till within the last generation disliked swine's flesh as an article of food as much as the Highlanders do at present.' Nor were Scottish food prejudices confined to the masses of the people. Ben Jonson, in his 'A Masque of the Metamorphosed Gipsies,' makes a Romany fortune-teller approach King James I and say:

> Here's a gentleman's hand.
> I'll kiss it for luck's sake: you should, by this line,
> Love a horse and a hound, but no part of a swine.

GIFFORD, Jonson's annotator, says this and another reference to pigs was 'a side compliment to the King, who hated pork in all its varieties.' A prejudice against white fish is not yet wholly extinct in the Highlands, nor that against 'white flesh' or 'feathered flesh.' The Sassenachs (Saxons) were formerly sneered at as 'fish eaters' not only in the Highlands but some parts of Ireland. In ancient Ireland the salmon was 'the food of kings,' but, then, its flesh is red. Julius Caesar found existing in ancient England a 'religious scruple' against eating domestic fowl or goose or the hare. Archaeologists have found that in the Swiss lake dwellings there was a superstitious feeling against eating the hare, but Neolithic tribes in Britain used the animal for food. The ancient Irish ate its flesh, and O'Curry says it was one of the prerogatives of the kings of Tara to be fed on 'the hares of Naas.'

It would appear, therefore, that surviving prejudices against eels and pork are not necessarily of Christian origin. If the Scots pork taboo was inspired by the

BIRD STONE AT STRATHPEFFER

The animal figures incised on standing stones in Scotland possibly have a bearing on food taboos. The raven or eagle, here seen with horseshoe symbol and solar rings and fishtails, was perhaps a clan totem, and as such may have been prohibited as food.

Andrew Paterson, Inverness

FOOD TABOO THAT MAY HAVE TRAVELLED FROM ASIA TO SCOTLAND
The pork taboo of Scotland not improbably originated in a porcine form of a deity. The pig was apparently regarded as an embodiment of Attis, whose votaries eschewed it as food, and the Attis cult of the Galatian Celts may have reached Scotland. Figures of boars were used as amulets by some Celtic tribes. The boar stone here seen is near Inverness

Jewish taboo in the Old Testament, there would have been traces of it in England and Ireland, but from the earliest times of which we have knowledge the inhabitants of both countries have eaten pork freely. The Continental Celts were pig-rearers and pork-curers, and Varro tells that they supplied Rome and the rest of Italy with cured pork. But the Galatians, the Celts of Asia Minor, according to Pausanias, became converts to the cult of the god Attis, and refrained from eating pork because that god had been slain by a boar. A view which has been urged in this connexion is that the new religion of the Celts of Galatia reached a section of the Celts in Western Europe who ultimately migrated to Scotland across the North Sea. According to Scottish pig-lore, the eating of pork causes leprosy. A similar superstition has been found by Mr. J. G. Lawson to be prevalent in northern Arcadia, Greece, and he suggests that the pork prejudice there may survive from the cult of Demeter, goddess of the corn-bearing earth and of agriculture, to whom the pig was sacred and to whose honour it was sacrificed at an annual festival similar to a festival in ancient Egypt, where pork was likewise taboo.

Horse flesh is not favoured as food in the British Isles, but is eaten freely on the Continent, especially in Belgium and Germany. The Romany wanderers in Europe eat the hedgehog but invariably taboo the squirrel.

Light is thrown upon the significance of the persisting food prejudices of modern civilized peoples by investigating those of primitive races in various parts of the world. Pig's flesh—see also page 271—is taboo to Zulu girls because of the belief in imitative magic. The pig is regarded as an ugly animal because of its gross snout and repulsive mouth, and it is feared that pork taken as food would tend to disfigure growing girls and, after they are married, impart swinish physical characters to their children. Elephant flesh is similarly avoided by women lest an evil resemblance be transferred to offspring. Young girls must not eat the flesh of a cow which has given birth to a dead calf nor that of a cow which has died when giving birth to a calf, lest they themselves should have stillborn children or should die in childbed. The lower lip of a bullock is taboo to boys because it is always twitching and trembling and there is a danger that when boys grow up such food would cause them to have the trembling mouths of cowards, instead of the firm, stern lips of typical Zulu warriors. Tripe is not eaten by Zulu warriors lest in battle it should attract the weapons of enemies towards their bowels.

In Madagascar the Malagasy warriors must not eat hedgehog, 'as it is feared that this animal from its propensity of coiling up into a ball when alarmed, will impart a timid shrinking disposition to those who partake of it. A warrior who partakes of the flesh from the knee of an ox may, ox-like, become weak in the knees during a long march. Nor must a fighting man eat of any animal that has been speared lest he himself should suffer a like fate, or any animal which has been wounded or killed in conflict with another. In Northern Rhodesia some of the tribes taboo pig, hippo, zebra and mud-fish lest they should contract leprosy or goitre. It is believed that if boys eat a fish called 'jilemba' they will have no families after they grow up and marry.

There are many taboos for women in Southern Nigeria which, as in Zululand, are considered necessary in the interests of their children. When war has been declared the fighting men must not partake of soup, or boiled flesh, or pumpkins, but only roasted meat and roasted plantains and ripe corn, so that they may become hard and vigorous. It is also considered necessary that cooking fires should be of dry branches and not those in which any sap remains. A very widespread belief, not only in Africa but in Asia, is that food cooked by women is bad for fighting men during a time of war. The idea that food exercises a magical influence on men and women is very general in the East. A related survival in the Hebrides appears to be the idea that if the wind changes when a young person is eating flounder, his mouth may be twisted like that of the flat-fish.

Magical food taboos may change as people change their area of residence, but those based upon the belief that an animal, fish or reptile is sacred are found to be binding for long periods and many generations—until, indeed, there is a change in religious beliefs. Some peoples believe they are descended from animals, or even from trees or plants, and therefore avoid eating the flesh of an ancestral animal, or the fruit of an ancestral plant. Among the Melanesians of the Pacific Islands we find one clan which believes in descent from a hawk, a wagtail or a tit. They protect these birds, but their food supply is not restricted by refusing to eat of their flesh. It is otherwise, however, with those who regard the domestic fowl as of the same breed as themselves, for they not only refuse to partake of its flesh but of its eggs. A banana clan taboos bananas as food, but may freely give quantities of ripe bananas in exchange for other fruits collected by non-banana peoples. In the Solomon Islands group Dr. C. E. Fox has found on the Island of Santa Anna a turtle people, who refuse to eat any part of a turtle lest they should immediately suffer death. He was told of a turtle woman who entered a house when very hungry. She saw cooked turtle and, thinking it was pork, ate of it, but she soon sickened and died. In Polynesia the belief was prevalent, as missionaries have found, that certain people had similarly suffered death from eating an ancestral fish or animal. Eel people dared not eat eel, shark people the flesh of the shark, or bird people any bird regarded as sacred to the clan. But a man could eat freely of the sacred animal of another man.

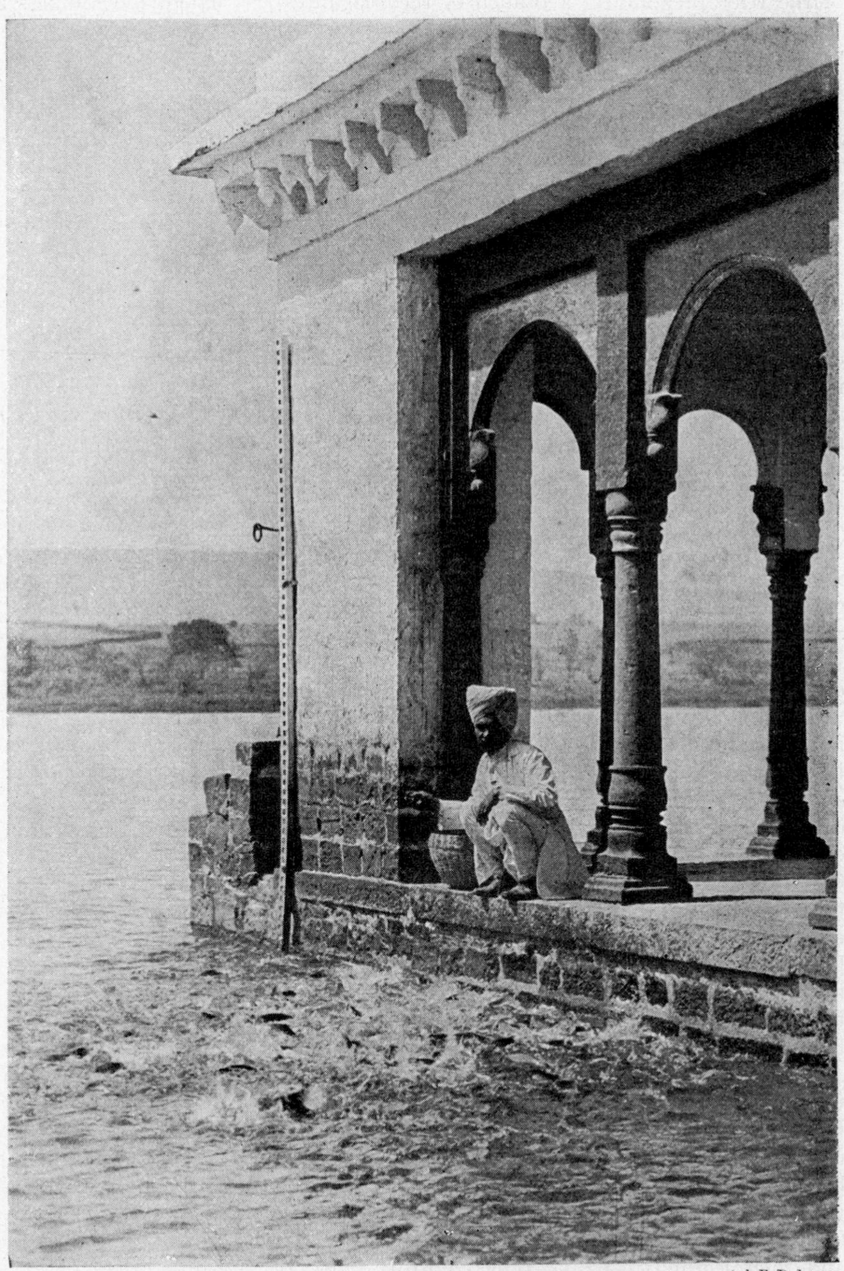

Col. F. D. Fayrer

FEEDING THE SACRED FISH AT GOONDGARH

The lake at Goondgarh, in the Indian state of Rewah, is filled with sacred fish, which may not be eaten by the people. In the lake, too, are sacred crocodiles, which feed upon the fish and keep their numbers down. A special attendant, appointed by the raja, feeds the fish at regular hours, and so tame are they that they know his call.

Traces of similar beliefs and customs are found in various parts of the world. It is, however, not always easy to discover whether the tabooed animal is a clan or family totem or a form of a particular deity. A totem may belong to a tribal group and be shared in by all its members. But an individual may acquire a particular totem when he receives his name. To the latter class belongs the famous Irish hero Cuchulainn (pronounced Koo-hool'in) His name signifies 'Hound (cu) of Culann'—the Celtic Vulcan. As a lad, his name was Setanta (a member of the tribe of Setantii, a branch of the Brigantes), but after he had slain the great watch-hound of Culann he took its place until another dog could be procured. He proved himself an invulnerable hero, but his death was brought about by sorceresses, who placed upon him a spell which involved him in eating the flesh of a dog. The result was that he soon afterwards received his death-wound in battle.

A RELIGIOUS taboo might be extended to things to which a sacred wild creature was partial. Thus a snake clan in Melanesia is found to taboo the milk of the small yellow coconut because snakes partake of it when they have an opportunity so to do. The immediate result of the infringement of this taboo is an attack of some form of skin disease. A most mysterious taboo obtains among the members of a sacred shark cult. It is believed that the shark god may appear as a ray fish, a mullet, or a small fish like a sardine; it may also assume the form of a leaf in the 'arita' tree. The shark worshippers may eat of the fish, but must not partake of the flesh of a white pig or eat bananas. Some birds and fish are taboo because they are messengers of gods or spirits and make appearance to foretell a sudden death in a tribe or family.

Then there are rank taboos. Ordinary people are not permitted to eat of fish or animals reserved for priests or chiefs, while priests or chiefs may not eat of fish or animals which ordinary people may devour with impunity. In Fiji, as late as 1912, the chiefs endeavoured to prevail upon the British Government to make it illegal for common people to catch and eat turtles. These had been formerly reserved for their own tables, and if the taboo was broken by the common folk they were either punished by the chiefs or were stricken with disease. The turtle is the reputed 'King of the Sea' and, according to the native, was the appropriate food for rulers. A similar view obtained in Ancient Ireland, where the salmon, also a 'king,' was referred to as 'the food of kings' and was reserved for the menu of the royal family. In Fiji shark flesh was freely eaten, but the dorsal fin could be eaten only by chiefs, for whom were also reserved the heads of all large fish. Certain 'cuts' of animal flesh were kept for chiefs and their leading men and referred to as 'food of warriors.' The ancient Irish similarly reserved particular portions for their rulers and heroes.

Among the Murrams of Manipur in eastern India, on the border of Burma, a chief must not eat certain foods which his subjects partake of freely. Dog flesh, tomatoes, etc., are taboo to him. The chief of the Red Karens of Burma is denied rice and liquor; his mother, before his birth, had to taboo meat, water from a common well, etc. In Yap, one of the Caroline Islands in the Pacific, priests, who live apart for a period of about three months each year, dare not eat fish or taro. African taboos of like character have been recorded. The heir to the throne of the Loango tribe must not eat pork or 'cola' fruit, nor must he, after entering manhood, eat of fowls unless he has himself killed and cooked them.

A WEST AFRICAN king in Fernando Po must taboo venison and the flesh of the porcupine, while the chief ruler of the Masai tribes can eat of no flesh except the livers of goats and no other food except milk and honey. The person of the king of the Buakitara or Bunyoro of Central Africa is sacred, and the various parts of his body have names not used by common folk. His daily meals are of a ceremonial character and are regarded by the people with religious awe. Of late years, owing to Christian influence, his diet has been varied, although this is not known to all his subjects. According to Roscoe, at one time vegetable food was absolutely taboo to the kings, who lived entirely upon milk and a very small quantity of beef. The milk was taken from sacred cows, chosen because of their colour and reserved for royal use alone. Young bulls were slain to provide flesh, but the king could not eat meat and drink milk at a single meal. Thrice a day he went to the house in which the sacred milk was stored to partake of it in large quantities (see also pages 480-1).

IN Australia the medicine man of the Arunta tribes must abstain from fat or warm meat. Nor must he inhale the smoke from burning bones If he infringes a taboo his medical powers will depart for ever. To wise old men who act as rulers in secular and religious matters is reserved the flesh and fat of a snake called 'Kuljoanju. If a young man should, even by accident or through ignorance, partake of the forbidden food he is sure, according to the tribal lore, to contract a serious illness which may prove fatal.

In Ancient Egypt, according to Diodorus Siculus, the priest-kings (of the Late Empire period) had their flesh diet confined to veal and goose. Herodotus makes a similar statement, and adds that to the priests fish and beans were taboo. To all the Egyptians of the Greek period pork was forbidden, but once a year they sacrificed swine to Osiris and the moon, burning certain parts and eating certain cuts. In Rome the Flamen Dialis could not eat white bread or even touch or make mention of it, nor eat goat's flesh or beans. Lucian tells that in Syria one cult sacrificed bulls and cows alike and goats and sheep, but as pigs were abominated, they were neither sacrificed nor eaten. Another cult,

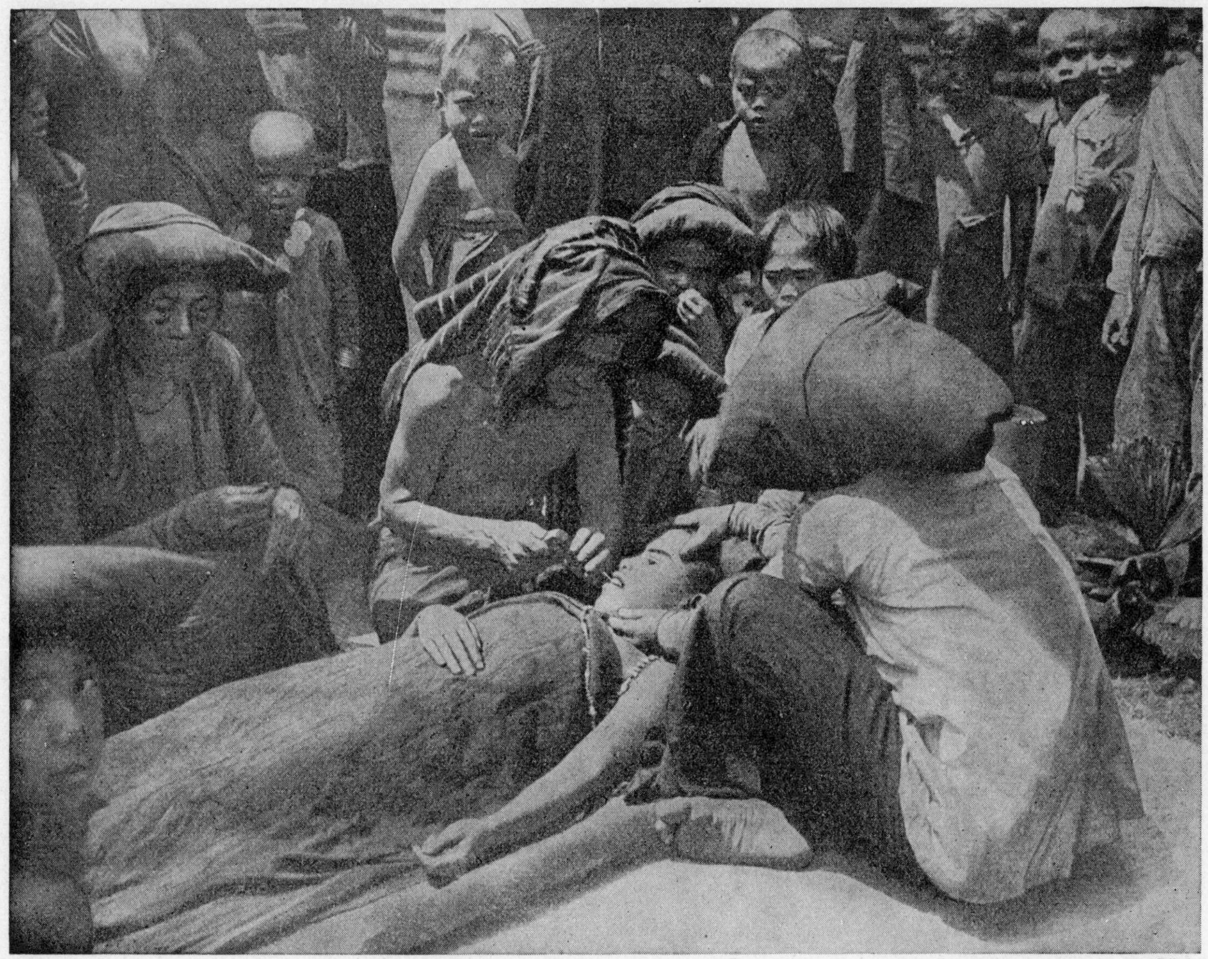

G.P.A.

PAIN ENDURED OUT OF DEFERENCE TO THE SOUL OF RICE

Such store do the Indonesians set by the rice crop that they believe that the rice possesses a soul. Indeed, the Bataks of Sumatra use the same word for the soul of the rice as they do for the soul of human beings. In order that the soul of the rice may not be offended the Karo Bataks of the Toba Lake region file their teeth flat and blacken the stumps. A young girl is here seen having her teeth chiselled in preparation for this operation.

however, regarded swine without disgust, because they were holy animals. The Jews tabooed pork in ancient as in modern times. Moslems and Hindus regard the pig as unclean and refuse to partake of it.

It is obvious in view of the evidence given above that a single theory is not sufficient to account for the existence in ancient England of the taboo of the hare and the goose, of the Irish restriction regarding salmon and the Scottish boycott of pork and eel. It may be that the goose was in England, as in Egypt, a form of a deity and was sacrificed and eaten once a year. We have not yet forgotten that goose-flesh is appropriate at Michaelmas (September 29). An old pagan festival may have been christianised.

The hare was used by Queen Boadicea as a divination animal. She let one loose to ascertain by its movements what lot fate had in store for her and her people. Fishermen and miners in Northumberland used to regard it unlucky if a hare crossed their path. Witches were supposed to appear sometimes as hares. The Scottish pork taboo may, like the English goose taboo, have been due to the fact that the pig was a form of a god. In this connexion it is significant to find Tacitus telling that the amber traders of Celtic speech in the Baltic area regarded the boar as a symbol (or son) of the Mother Goddess and wore boar amulets on their helmets. The Iceni, a Celtic tribe in south-eastern England, had boars on their coins, and they and others used images of boars as mascots. One of the Pictish clans in Scotland was called the 'Orcs' (young boars), and there is a figure of a boar on a standing stone near Inverness. The eel may have also been a form of a deity. In one of the Irish sagas a goddess assumes the form of this fish. A horse-stone in Aberdeenshire may be a relic of the worship of the horse-god. In the 'Life of St. Columba' there is a reference to a convert who became a backslider and was found partaking of horse-flesh, apparently at the annual sacrifice of that animal. Bull sacrifices occurred in the county of Ross and Cromarty as late as the 17th century. Some tabooed animals may have been clan totems and others forms of deities.